# CODE OF FEDERAL REGULATIONS

I0040952

# Title 2

Grants and Agreements

Revised as of January 1, 2018

Containing a codification of documents
of general applicability and future effect

As of January 1, 2018

Published by the Office of the Federal Register
National Archives and Records Administration
as a Special Edition of the Federal Register

# Table of Contents

*Cite this Code:*  CFR

*To cite the regulations in this volume use title, part and section number. Thus, 2 CFR 1.100 refers to title 2, part 1, section 100.*

# Explanation

The Code of Federal Regulations is a codification of the general and permanent rules published in the Federal Register by the Executive departments and agencies of the Federal Government. The Code is divided into 50 titles which represent broad areas subject to Federal regulation. Each title is divided into chapters which usually bear the name of the issuing agency. Each chapter is further subdivided into parts covering specific regulatory areas.

Each volume of the Code is revised at least once each calendar year and issued on a quarterly basis approximately as follows:

Title 1 through Title 16.............................................................as of January 1
Title 17 through Title 27 .................................................................as of April 1
Title 28 through Title 41 ..................................................................as of July 1
Title 42 through Title 50 ...........................................................as of October 1

The appropriate revision date is printed on the cover of each volume.

LEGAL STATUS

The contents of the Federal Register are required to be judicially noticed (44 U.S.C. 1507). The Code of Federal Regulations is prima facie evidence of the text of the original documents (44 U.S.C. 1510).

HOW TO USE THE CODE OF FEDERAL REGULATIONS

The Code of Federal Regulations is kept up to date by the individual issues of the Federal Register. These two publications must be used together to determine the latest version of any given rule.

To determine whether a Code volume has been amended since its revision date (in this case, January 1, 2018), consult the "List of CFR Sections Affected (LSA)," which is issued monthly, and the "Cumulative List of Parts Affected," which appears in the Reader Aids section of the daily Federal Register. These two lists will identify the Federal Register page number of the latest amendment of any given rule.

EFFECTIVE AND EXPIRATION DATES

Each volume of the Code contains amendments published in the Federal Register since the last revision of that volume of the Code. Source citations for the regulations are referred to by volume number and page number of the Federal Register and date of publication. Publication dates and effective dates are usually not the same and care must be exercised by the user in determining the actual effective date. In instances where the effective date is beyond the cut-off date for the Code a note has been inserted to reflect the future effective date. In those instances where a regulation published in the Federal Register states a date certain for expiration, an appropriate note will be inserted following the text.

OMB CONTROL NUMBERS

The Paperwork Reduction Act of 1980 (Pub. L. 96–511) requires Federal agencies to display an OMB control number with their information collection request.

Many agencies have begun publishing numerous OMB control numbers as amendments to existing regulations in the CFR. These OMB numbers are placed as close as possible to the applicable recordkeeping or reporting requirements.

## PAST PROVISIONS OF THE CODE

Provisions of the Code that are no longer in force and effect as of the revision date stated on the cover of each volume are not carried. Code users may find the text of provisions in effect on any given date in the past by using the appropriate List of CFR Sections Affected (LSA). For the convenience of the reader, a "List of CFR Sections Affected" is published at the end of each CFR volume. For changes to the Code prior to the LSA listings at the end of the volume, consult previous annual editions of the LSA. For changes to the Code prior to 2001, consult the List of CFR Sections Affected compilations, published for 1949-1963, 1964-1972, 1973-1985, and 1986-2000.

## "[RESERVED]" TERMINOLOGY

The term "[Reserved]" is used as a place holder within the Code of Federal Regulations. An agency may add regulatory information at a "[Reserved]" location at any time. Occasionally "[Reserved]" is used editorially to indicate that a portion of the CFR was left vacant and not accidentally dropped due to a printing or computer error.

## INCORPORATION BY REFERENCE

*What is incorporation by reference?* Incorporation by reference was established by statute and allows Federal agencies to meet the requirement to publish regulations in the Federal Register by referring to materials already published elsewhere. For an incorporation to be valid, the Director of the Federal Register must approve it. The legal effect of incorporation by reference is that the material is treated as if it were published in full in the Federal Register (5 U.S.C. 552(a)). This material, like any other properly issued regulation, has the force of law.

*What is a proper incorporation by reference?* The Director of the Federal Register will approve an incorporation by reference only when the requirements of 1 CFR part 51 are met. Some of the elements on which approval is based are:

(a) The incorporation will substantially reduce the volume of material published in the Federal Register.

(b) The matter incorporated is in fact available to the extent necessary to afford fairness and uniformity in the administrative process.

(c) The incorporating document is drafted and submitted for publication in accordance with 1 CFR part 51.

*What if the material incorporated by reference cannot be found?* If you have any problem locating or obtaining a copy of material listed as an approved incorporation by reference, please contact the agency that issued the regulation containing that incorporation. If, after contacting the agency, you find the material is not available, please notify the Director of the Federal Register, National Archives and Records Administration, 8601 Adelphi Road, College Park, MD 20740-6001, or call 202-741-6010.

## CFR INDEXES AND TABULAR GUIDES

A subject index to the Code of Federal Regulations is contained in a separate volume, revised annually as of January 1, entitled CFR INDEX AND FINDING AIDS. This volume contains the Parallel Table of Authorities and Rules. A list of CFR titles, chapters, subchapters, and parts and an alphabetical list of agencies publishing in the CFR are also included in this volume.

An index to the text of "Title 3—The President" is carried within that volume.

The Federal Register Index is issued monthly in cumulative form. This index is based on a consolidation of the "Contents" entries in the daily Federal Register.

A List of CFR Sections Affected (LSA) is published monthly, keyed to the revision dates of the 50 CFR titles.

REPUBLICATION OF MATERIAL

There are no restrictions on the republication of material appearing in the Code of Federal Regulations.

INQUIRIES

For a legal interpretation or explanation of any regulation in this volume, contact the issuing agency. The issuing agency's name appears at the top of odd-numbered pages.

For inquiries concerning CFR reference assistance, call 202–741–6000 or write to the Director, Office of the Federal Register, National Archives and Records Administration, 8601 Adelphi Road, College Park, MD 20740-6001 or e-mail *fedreg.info@nara.gov.*

SALES

The Government Publishing Office (GPO) processes all sales and distribution of the CFR. For payment by credit card, call toll-free, 866-512-1800, or DC area, 202-512-1800, M-F 8 a.m. to 4 p.m. e.s.t. or fax your order to 202-512-2104, 24 hours a day. For payment by check, write to: US Government Publishing Office – New Orders, P.O. Box 979050, St. Louis, MO 63197-9000.

ELECTRONIC SERVICES

The full text of the Code of Federal Regulations, the LSA (List of CFR Sections Affected), The United States Government Manual, the Federal Register, Public Laws, Public Papers of the Presidents of the United States, Compilation of Presidential Documents and the Privacy Act Compilation are available in electronic format via *www.ofr.gov.* For more information, contact the GPO Customer Contact Center, U.S. Government Publishing Office. Phone 202-512-1800, or 866-512-1800 (toll-free). E-mail, *ContactCenter@gpo.gov.*

The Office of the Federal Register also offers a free service on the National Archives and Records Administration's (NARA) World Wide Web site for public law numbers, Federal Register finding aids, and related information. Connect to NARA's web site at *www.archives.gov/federal-register.*

The e-CFR is a regularly updated, unofficial editorial compilation of CFR material and Federal Register amendments, produced by the Office of the Federal Register and the Government Publishing Office. It is available at *www.ecfr.gov.*

OLIVER A. POTTS,
*Director,*
*Office of the Federal Register*
*January 1, 2018*

# THIS TITLE

Title 2—GRANTS AND AGREEMENTS is composed of one volume. This volume is comprised of Subtitle A—Office of Management and Budget Guidance for Grants and Agreements and Subtitle B—Federal Agency Regulations for Grants and Agreements. The contents of this volume represent all current regulations codified under this title of the CFR as of January 1, 2018.

For this volume, Susannah C. Hurley was Chief Editor. The Code of Federal Regulations publication program is under the direction of John Hyrum Martinez, assisted by Stephen J. Frattini.

# Title 2—Grants and Agreements

1

# Subtitle A—Office of Management and Budget Guidance for Grants and Agreements

# PART 1—ABOUT TITLE 2 OF THE CODE OF FEDERAL REGULATIONS AND SUBTITLE A

### Subpart A—Introduction to Title 2 of the CFR

### Subpart B—Introduction to Subtitle A

### Subpart C—Responsibilities of OMB and Federal Agencies

AUTHORITY: 31 U.S.C. 503; 31 U.S.C. 1111; 41 U.S.C. 405; Reorganization Plan No. 2 of 1970; E.O. 11541, 35 FR 10737, 3 CFR, 1966–1970, p. 939.

SOURCE: 69 FR 26280, May 11, 2004, unless otherwise noted.

## Subpart A—Introduction to Title 2 of the CFR

### § 1.100   Content of this title.

This title contains—

(a) Office of Management and Budget (OMB) guidance to Federal agencies on government-wide policies and procedures for the award and administration of grants and agreements; and

(b) Federal agency regulations implementing that OMB guidance.

### § 1.105   Organization and subtitle content.

(a) This title is organized into two subtitles.

(b) The OMB guidance described in § 1.100(a) is published in subtitle A. Publication of the OMB guidance in the CFR does not change its nature—it is guidance and not regulation.

(c) Each Federal agency that publishes regulations implementing the OMB guidance has a chapter in subtitle B in which it issues those regulations. The Federal agency regulations in subtitle B differ in nature from the OMB guidance in subtitle A because the OMB guidance is not regulatory (Federal agency regulations in subtitle B may give regulatory effect to the OMB guidance, to the extent that the agency regulations require compliance with all or portions of the guidance).

### § 1.110   Issuing authorities.

OMB issues this subtitle. Each Federal agency that has a chapter in subtitle B of this title issues that chapter.

## Subpart B—Introduction to Subtitle A

### § 1.200   Purpose of chapters I and II.

(a) Chapters I and II of subtitle A provide OMB guidance to Federal agencies that helps ensure consistent and uniform government-wide policies and procedures for management of the agencies' grants and agreements.

(b) There are two chapters for publication of the guidance because portions of it may be revised as a result of ongoing efforts to streamline and simplify requirements for the award and administration of grants and other financial assistance (and thereby implement the Federal Financial Assistance Management Improvement Act of 1999, Pub. L. 106–107).

(c) The OMB guidance in its initial form—before completion of revisions described in paragraph (b) of this section—is published in chapter II of this subtitle. When revisions to a part of the guidance are finalized, that part is published in chapter I and removed from chapter II.

### § 1.205   Applicability to grants and other funding instruments.

The types of instruments that are subject to the guidance in this subtitle vary from one portion of the guidance to another (note that each part identifies the types of instruments to which it applies). All portions of the guidance apply to grants and cooperative agreements, some portions also apply to other types of financial assistance or nonprocurement instruments, and some portions also apply to procurement contracts. For example, the:

(a) Guidance on debarment and suspension in part 180 of this subtitle applies broadly to all financial assistance and other nonprocurement transactions, and not just to grants and cooperative agreements.

(b) Cost principles in parts 220, 225 and 230 of this subtitle apply to procurement contracts, as well as to financial assistance, although those principles are implemented for procurement contracts through the Federal Acquisition Regulation in title 48 of the CFR, rather than through Federal agency regulations on grants and agreements in this title.

[70 FR 51863, Aug. 31, 2005]

## § 1.210 Applicability to Federal agencies and others.

(a) This subtitle contains guidance that directly applies only to Federal agencies.

(b) The guidance in this subtitle may affect others through each Federal agency's implementation of the guidance, portions of which may apply to—

(1) The agency's awarding or administering officials;

(2) Non-Federal entities that receive or apply for the agency's grants or agreements or receive subawards under those grants or agreements; or

(3) Any other entities involved in agency transactions subject to the guidance in this chapter.

## § 1.215 Relationship to previous issuances.

Although some of the guidance was organized differently within OMB circulars or other documents, much of the guidance in this subtitle existed prior to the establishment of title 2 of the CFR. Specifically:

| Guidance in * * * | On * * * | Previously was in * * * |
|---|---|---|
| (a) Chapter I, part 180. | Nonprocurement debarment and suspension. | OMB guidance that conforms with the government-wide common rule (see 60 FR 33036, June 26, 1995). |
| (b) Chapter I, part 182. | Drug-free workplace requirements. | OMB guidance (54 FR 4946, January 31, 1989) and a government-wide common rule (as amended at 68 FR 66534, November 26, 2003). |
| (c) Chapter II, part 200. | Uniform administrative requirements, cost principles, and audit requirements for federal awards. | OMB Circulars A–21, "Cost Principles for Educational Institutions" (Chapter II, part 225); A–87, "Cost Principles for State, Local and Indian Tribal Governments" (Chapter II, part 225); A–89, "Federal Domestic Assistance Program Information"; "; A–102 and a government-wide common rule (53 FR 8034, March 11, 1988); A–110, "Uniform Administrative Requirements for Awards and Other Agreements with Institutions of Higher Education, Hospitals, and Other Nonprofit Organizations" (Chapter II, part 215); A–122, "Cost Principles for Non-Profit Organizations" (Chapter II, part 230); and A–133 "Audits of States, Local Governments and Non-Profit Organizations". |

[79 FR 75878, Dec. 19, 2014]

## § 1.220 Federal agency implementation of this subtitle.

A Federal agency that awards grants and agreements subject to the guidance in this subtitle implements the guidance in agency regulations in subtitle B of this title and/or in policy and procedural issuances, such as internal instructions to the agency's awarding and administering officials. An applicant or recipient would see the effect of that implementation in the organization and content of the agency's announcements of funding opportunities and in its award terms and conditions.

## § 1.230 Maintenance of this subtitle.

OMB issues guidance in this subtitle after publication in the FEDERAL REGISTER. Any portion of the guidance that has a potential impact on the public is published with an opportunity for public comment.

## Subpart C—Responsibilities of OMB and Federal Agencies

### § 1.300  OMB responsibilities.

OMB is responsible for:

(a) Issuing and maintaining the guidance in this subtitle, as described in § 1.230.

(b) Interpreting the policy requirements in this subtitle.

(c) Reviewing Federal agency regulations implementing the requirements of this subtitle, as required by Executive Order 12866.

(d) Conducting broad oversight of government-wide compliance with the guidance in this subtitle.

(e) Performing other OMB functions specified in this subtitle.

### § 1.305  Federal agency responsibilities.

The head of each Federal agency that awards and administers grants and agreements subject to the guidance in this subtitle is responsible for:

(a) Implementing the guidance in this subtitle.

(b) Ensuring that the agency's components and subcomponents comply with the agency's implementation of the guidance.

(c) Performing other functions specified in this subtitle.

7

# CHAPTER I—OFFICE OF MANAGEMENT AND BUDGET GOVERNMENTWIDE GUIDANCE FOR GRANTS AND AGREEMENTS

# PARTS 2–24 [RESERVED]

# PART 25—UNIVERSAL IDENTIFIER AND SYSTEM FOR AWARD MANAGEMENT

## Subpart A—General

AUTHORITY: Pub. L. 109–282; 31 U.S.C. 6102.

SOURCE: 75 FR 55673, Sept. 14, 2010, unless otherwise noted.

EDITORIAL NOTE: Nomenclature changes to part 25 appear at 79 FR 75879, Dec. 19, 2014.

## Subpart A—General

### § 25.100  Purposes of this part.

This part provides guidance to agencies to establish:

(a) The unique entity identifier as a universal identifier for Federal financial assistance applicants, as well as recipients and their direct subrecipients.

(b) The System for Award Management (SAM) as the repository for standard information about applicants and recipients.

[75 FR 55673, Sept. 14, 2010, as amended at 79 FR 75879, Dec. 19, 2014; 80 FR 54407, Sept. 10, 2015]

### § 25.105  Types of awards to which this part applies.

This part applies to an agency's grants, cooperative agreements, loans, and other types of Federal financial assistance included in the definition of "award" in § 25.305. The requirements in this part must be implemented for grants and cooperative agreements by October 1, 2010. The requirements in this part must be implemented for all other award forms listed in § 25.200 requirement at a date to be specified in the future.

### § 25.110  Types of recipient and subrecipient entities to which this part applies.

(a) *General.* Through an agency's implementation of the guidance in this part, this part applies to all entities, other than those exempted in paragraphs (b), (c), and (d) of this section, that—

(1) Apply for or receive agency awards; or

(2) Receive subawards directly from recipients of those agency awards.

(b) *Exemptions for individuals.* None of the requirements in this part apply to an individual who applies for or receives Federal financial assistance as a natural person (*i.e.*, unrelated to any business or non-profit organization he or she may own or operate in his or her name).

(c) *Exemptions for Federal agencies.* The requirement in this part to maintain a current registration in the SAM does not apply to an agency of the Federal Government that receives an award from another agency.

(d) *Other exemptions.* (1) Under a condition identified in paragraph (d)(2) of this section, an agency may exempt an entity from an applicable requirement to obtain a unique entity identifier, register in the SAM, or both.

(i) In that case, the agency must use a generic unique entity identifier in data it reports to USASpending.gov if reporting for a prime award to the entity is required by the Federal Funding Accountability and Transparency Act (Pub. L. 109–282, hereafter cited as "Transparency Act").

(ii) Agency use of a generic unique entity identifier should be used rarely for prime award reporting because it prevents prime awardees from being able to fulfill the subaward or executive compensation reporting required by the Transparency Act.

(2) The conditions under which an agency may exempt an entity are—

(i) For any entity, if the agency determines that it must protect information about the entity from disclosure, to avoid compromising classified information or national security or jeopardizing the personal safety of the entity's clients.

(ii) For a foreign entity applying for or receiving an award or subaward for a project or program performed outside the United States valued at less than $25,000, if the agency deems it to be impractical for the entity to comply with the requirement(s).

(3) Agencies' use of generic unique entity identifier, as described in paragraphs (d)(1) and (2) of this section, should be rare. Having a generic unique entity identifier limits a recipient's ability to use Governmentwide systems that are needed to comply with some reporting requirements.

[75 FR 55673, Sept. 14, 2010, as amended at 79 FR 75879, Dec. 19, 2014]

## § 25.115   Deviations.

Deviations from this part require the prior approval of the Office of Management and Budget (OMB).

## Subpart B—Policy

### § 25.200   Requirements for program announcements, regulations, and application instructions.

(a) Each agency that awards types of Federal financial assistance included in the definition of "award" in § 25.305 must include the requirements described in paragraph (b) of this section in each program announcement, regulation, or other issuance containing instructions for applicants that either:

(1) Is issued on or after the effective date of this part; or

(2) Has application or plan due dates after October 1, 2010.

(b) The program announcement, regulation, or other issuance must require each entity that applies and does not have an exemption under § 25.110 to:

(1) Be registered in the SAM prior to submitting an application or plan;

(2) Maintain an active SAM registration with current information at all times during which it has an active Federal award or an application or plan under consideration by an agency; and

(3) Provide its unique entity identifier in each application or plan it submits to the agency.

(c) For purposes of this policy:

(1) The applicant is the entity that meets the agency's or program's eligibility criteria and has the legal authority to apply and to receive the award. For example, if a consortium applies for an award to be made to the consortium as the recipient, the consortium must have a unique entity identifier. If a consortium is eligible to receive funding under an agency program but the agency's policy is to make the award to a lead entity for the consortium, the unique entity identifier of the lead entity will be used.

(2) A "program announcement" is any paper or electronic issuance that an agency uses to announce a funding opportunity, whether it is called a "program announcement," "notice of funding availability," "broad agency announcement," "research announcement," "solicitation," or some other term.

(3) To remain registered in the SAM database after the initial registration, the applicant is required to review and update on an annual basis from the

date of initial registration or subsequent updates its information in the SAM database to ensure it is current, accurate and complete.

[75 FR 55673, Sept. 14, 2010, as amended at 79 FR 75879, Dec. 19, 2014]

### §25.205 Effect of noncompliance with a requirement to obtain a unique entity identifier or register in the SAM.

(a) An agency may not make an award to an entity until the entity has complied with the requirements described in §25.200 to provide a valid unique entity identifier and maintain an active SAM registration with current information (other than any requirement that is not applicable because the entity is exempted under §25.110).

(b) At the time an agency is ready to make an award, if the intended recipient has not complied with an applicable requirement to provide a unique entity identifier or maintain an active SAM registration with current information, the agency:

(1) May determine that the applicant is not qualified to receive an award; and

(2) May use that determination as a basis for making an award to another applicant.

[75 FR 55673, Sept. 14, 2010, as amended at 79 FR 75879, Dec. 19, 2014]

### §25.210 Authority to modify agency application forms or formats.

To implement the policies in §§25.200 and 25.205, an agency may add a unique entity identifier field to application forms or formats previously approved by OMB, without having to obtain further approval to add the field.

[75 FR 55673, Sept. 14, 2010, as amended at 79 FR 75879, Dec. 19, 2014]

### §25.215 Requirements for agency information systems.

Each agency that makes awards (as defined in §25.325) must ensure that systems processing information related to the awards, and other systems as appropriate, are able to accept and use the unique entity identifier as the uni-

versal identifier for financial assistance applicants and recipients.

[75 FR 55673, Sept. 14, 2010, as amended at 79 FR 75879, Dec. 19, 2014]

### §25.220 Use of award term.

(a) To accomplish the purposes described in §25.100, an agency must include in each award (as defined in §25.305) the award term in appendix A to this part.

(b) An agency may use different letters and numbers than those in appendix A to this part to designate the paragraphs of the award term, if necessary, to conform the system of paragraph designations with the one used in other terms and conditions in the agency's awards.

## Subpart C—Definitions

### §25.300 Agency.

*Agency* means a Federal agency as defined at 5 U.S.C. 551(1) and further clarified by 5 U.S.C. 552(f).

### §25.305 Award.

(a) *Award*, for the purposes of this part, means an award of Federal financial assistance that a non-Federal entity described in §25.110(a) receives or administers in the form of—

(1) A grant;

(2) A cooperative agreement (which does not include a cooperative research and development agreement pursuant to the Federal Technology Transfer Act of 1986, as amended (15 U.S.C. 3710a));

(3) A loan;

(4) A loan guarantee;

(5) A subsidy;

(6) Insurance;

(7) Food commodities;

(8) A direct appropriation;

(9) Assessed or voluntary contributions; or

(10) Any other financial assistance transaction that authorizes the non-Federal entity's expenditure of Federal funds.

(b) An *Award* does not include:

(1) Technical assistance, which provides services in lieu of money; and

(2) A transfer of title to Federally owned property provided in lieu of

money, even if the award is called a grant.

## § 25.310  System of Award Management (SAM).

*System for Award Management* has the meaning given in paragraph C.1 of the award term in appendix A to this part.

[75 FR 55673, Sept. 14, 2010, as amended at 79 FR 75879, Dec. 19, 2014; 80 FR 54407, Sept. 10, 2015]

## § 25.315  Unique entity identifier.

*Unique entity identifier* has the meaning given in paragraph C.2 of the award term in appendix A to this part.

[75 FR 55673, Sept. 14, 2010, as amended at 79 FR 75879, Dec. 19, 2014]

## § 25.320  Entity.

*Entity*, as it is used in this part, has the meaning given in paragraph C.3 of the award term in Appendix A to this part.

## § 25.325  For-profit organization.

*For-profit organization* means a non-Federal entity organized for profit. It includes, but is not limited to:

(a) An "S corporation" incorporated under Subchapter S of the Internal Revenue Code;

(b) A corporation incorporated under another authority;

(c) A partnership;

(d) A limited liability corporation or partnership; and

(e) A sole proprietorship.

## § 25.330  Foreign public entity.

*Foreign public entity* means:

(a) A foreign government or foreign governmental entity;

(b) A public international organization, which is an organization entitled to enjoy privileges, exemptions, and immunities as an international organization under the International Organizations Immunities Act (22 U.S.C. 288–288f);

(c) An entity owned (in whole or in part) or controlled by a foreign government; and

(d) Any other entity consisting wholly or partially of one or more foreign governments or foreign governmental entities.

## § 25.335  Indian Tribe (or "Federally recognized Indian Tribe").

*Indian Tribe* (or *"Federally recognized Indian Tribe"*) means any Indian Tribe, band, nation, or other organized group or community, including any Alaskan Native village or regional or village corporation (as defined in, or established under, the Alaskan Native Claims Settlement Act (43 U.S.C. 1601, *et seq.*)) that is recognized by the United States as eligible for the special programs and services provided by the United States to Indians because of their status as Indians.

## § 25.340  Local government.

*Local government* means a:

(a) County;

(b) Borough;

(c) Municipality;

(d) City;

(e) Town;

(f) Township;

(g) Parish;

(h) Local public authority, including any public housing agency under the United States Housing Act of 1937;

(i) Special district;

(j) School district;

(k) Intrastate district;

(l) Council of governments, whether or not incorporated as a nonprofit corporation under State law; and

(m) Any other instrumentality of a local government.

## § 25.345  Nonprofit organization.

*Nonprofit organization*—

(a) Means any corporation, trust, association, cooperative, or other organization that—

(1) Is operated primarily for scientific, educational, service, charitable, or similar purposes in the public interest;

(2) Is not organized primarily for profit; and

(3) Uses net proceeds to maintain, improve, or expand the operations of the organization.

(b) Includes nonprofit—

(1) Institutions of higher education;

(2) Hospitals; and

(3) Tribal organizations other than those included in the definition of "Indian Tribe."

**§ 25.350    State.**

*State* means—

(a) Any State of the United States;

(b) The District of Columbia;

(c) Any agency or instrumentality of a State other than a local government or State-controlled institution of higher education;

(d) The Commonwealths of Puerto Rico and the Northern Mariana Islands; and

(e) The United States Virgin Islands, Guam, American Samoa, and a territory or possession of the United States.

**§ 25.355    Subaward.**

*Subaward* has the meaning given in paragraph C.4 of the award term in Appendix A to this part.

**§ 25.360    Subrecipient.**

*Subrecipient* has the meaning given in paragraph C.5 of the award term in Appendix A to this part.

APPENDIX A TO PART 25—AWARD TERM

I. SYSTEM FOR AWARD MANAGEMENT AND UNIVERSAL IDENTIFIER REQUIREMENTS

*A. Requirement for System for Award Management*

Unless you are exempted from this requirement under 2 CFR 25.110, you as the recipient must maintain the currency of your information in the SAM until you submit the final financial report required under this award or receive the final payment, whichever is later. This requires that you review and update the information at least annually after the initial registration, and more frequently if required by changes in your information or another award term.

*B. Requirement for unique entity identifier*

If you are authorized to make subawards under this award, you:

1. Must notify potential subrecipients that no entity (*see* definition in paragraph C of this award term) may receive a subaward from you unless the entity has provided its unique entity identifier to you.

2. May not make a subaward to an entity unless the entity has provided its unique entity identifier to you.

*C. Definitions*

For purposes of this award term:

1. *System for Award Management (SAM)* means the Federal repository into which an entity must provide information required for the conduct of business as a recipient. Additional information about registration procedures may be found at the SAM Internet site (currently at *http://www.sam.gov*).

2. *Unique entity identifier* means the identifier required for SAM registration to uniquely identify business entities.

3. *Entity*, as it is used in this award term, means all of the following, as defined at 2 CFR part 25, subpart C:

a. A Governmental organization, which is a State, local government, or Indian Tribe;

b. A foreign public entity;

c. A domestic or foreign nonprofit organization;

d. A domestic or foreign for-profit organization; and

e. A Federal agency, but only as a subrecipient under an award or subaward to a non-Federal entity.

4. *Subaward:*

a. This term means a legal instrument to provide support for the performance of any portion of the substantive project or program for which you received this award and that you as the recipient award to an eligible subrecipient.

b. The term does not include your procurement of property and services needed to carry out the project or program (for further explanation, see 2 CFR 200.330).

c. A subaward may be provided through any legal agreement, including an agreement that you consider a contract.

5. *Subrecipient* means an entity that:

a. Receives a subaward from you under this award; and

b. Is accountable to you for the use of the Federal funds provided by the subaward.

[75 FR 55673, Sept. 14, 2010, as amended at 79 FR 75879, Dec. 19, 2014; 80 FR 54407, Sept. 10, 2015]

# PARTS 26–169 [RESERVED]

# PART 170—REPORTING SUBAWARD AND EXECUTIVE COMPENSATION INFORMATION

## Subpart A—General

Sec.

## Subpart B—Policy

AUTHORITY: Pub. L. 109–282; 31 U.S.C. 6102.

SOURCE: 75 FR 55669, Sept. 14, 2010, unless otherwise noted.

## Subpart A—General

### § 170.100  Purposes of this part.

This part provides guidance to agencies to establish requirements for recipients' reporting of information on subawards and executive total compensation, as required by the Federal Funding Accountability and Transparency Act of 2006 (Pub. L. 109–282), as amended by section 6202 of Public Law 110–252, hereafter referred to as "the Transparency Act".

### § 170.105  Types of awards to which this part applies.

This part applies to an agency's grants, cooperative agreements, loans, and other forms of Federal financial assistance subject to the Transparency Act, as defined in § 170.320.

### § 170.110  Types of entities to which this part applies.

(a) *General.* Through an agency's implementation of the guidance in this part, this part applies to all entities, other than those excepted in paragraph (b) of this section, that—

(1) Apply for or receive agency awards; or

(2) Receive subawards under those awards.

(b) *Exceptions.* (1) None of the requirements in this part apply to an individual who applies for or receives an award as a natural person (*i.e.*, unrelated to any business or non-profit organization he or she may own or operate in his or her name).

(2) None of the requirements regarding reporting names and total compensation of an entity's five most highly compensated executives apply unless in the entity's preceding fiscal year, it received—

(i) 80 percent or more of its annual gross revenue in Federal procurement contracts (and subcontracts) and Federal financial assistance awards subject to the Transparency Act, as defined at § 170.320 (and subawards); and

(ii) $25,000,000 or more in annual gross revenue from Federal procurement contracts (and subcontracts) and Federal financial assistance awards subject to the Transparency Act, as defined at § 170.320; and

(3) The public does not have access to information about the compensation of the senior executives through periodic reports filed under section 13(a) or 15(d) of the Securities Exchange Act of 1934 (15 U.S.C. 78m(a), 78o(d)) or section 6104 of the Internal Revenue Code of 1986.

### § 170.115  Deviations.

Deviations from this part require the prior approval of the Office of Management and Budget (OMB).

## Subpart B—Policy

### § 170.200  Requirements for program announcements, regulations, and application instructions.

(a) Each agency that makes awards of Federal financial assistance subject to the Transparency Act must include the requirements described in paragraph (b) of this section in each program announcement, regulation, or other issuance containing instructions for applicants:

(1) Under which awards may be made that are subject to Transparency Act reporting requirements; and

(2) That either:

(i) Is issued on or after the effective date of this part; or

(ii) Has application or plan due dates after October 1, 2010.

(b) The program announcement, regulation, or other issuance must require each entity that applies and does not have an exception under § 170.110(b) to ensure they have the necessary processes and systems in place to comply with the reporting requirements should they receive funding.

(c) Federal agencies that obtain post-award data on subaward obligations outside of this policy should take the necessary steps to ensure that their recipients are not required, due to the combination of agency-specific and Transparency Act reporting requirements, to submit the same or similar data multiple times during a given reporting period.

### § 170.220  Award term.

(a) To accomplish the purposes described in § 170.100, an agency must include the award term in Appendix A to this part in each award to a non-Federal entity under which the total funding will include $25,000 or more in Federal funding at any time during the project or program period.

(b) An agency—

(1) Consistent with paragraph (a) of this section, is not required to include the award term in Appendix A to this part if it determines that there is no possibility that the total amount of Federal funding under the award will equal or exceed $25,000. However, the agency must subsequently amend the award to add the award term if changes in circumstances increase the total Federal funding under the award to $25,000 or more during the project or program period.

## Subpart C—Definitions

### § 170.300  Agency.

*Agency* means a Federal agency as defined at 5 U.S.C. 551(1) and further clarified by 5 U.S.C. 552(f).

### § 170.305  Award.

*Award*, for the purposes of this part, effective October 1, 2010, means a grant or cooperative agreement. On future dates to be specified by OMB in policy memoranda available at the OMB Web site, award also will include other types of awards of Federal financial assistance subject to the Transparency Act, as defined in § 170.320.

### § 170.310  Entity.

*Entity* has the meaning given in 2 CFR part 25.

### § 170.315  Executive.

*Executive* means officers, managing partners, or any other employees in management positions.

### § 170.320  Federal financial assistance subject to the Transparency Act.

*Federal financial assistance subject to the Transparency Act* means assistance that non-Federal entities described in § 170.105 receive or administer in the form of—

(a) Grants;

(b) Cooperative agreements (which does not include cooperative research and development agreements pursuant to the Federal Technology Transfer Act of 1986, as amended (15 U.S.C. 3710a));

(c) Loans;

(d) Loan guarantees;

(e) Subsidies;

(f) Insurance;

(g) Food commodities;

(h) Direct appropriations;

(i) Assessed and voluntary contributions; and

(j) Other financial assistance transactions that authorize the non-Federal entities' expenditure of Federal funds.

(b) Does not include—

(1) Technical assistance, which provides services in lieu of money;

(2) A transfer of title to Federally owned property provided in lieu of money, even if the award is called a grant;

(3) Any classified award; or

(4) Any award funded in whole or in part with Recovery funds, as defined in section 1512 of the American Recovery and Reinvestment Act of 2009 (Pub. L. 111–5).

EDITORIAL NOTE: At 75 FR 55669, Sept. 14, 2010, § 170.320 was added with two paragraph (b)s.

### § 170.325  Subaward.

*Subaward* has the meaning given in paragraph e.3 of the award term in Appendix A to this part.

### § 170.330  Total compensation.

*Total Compensation* has the meaning given in paragraph e.5 of the award term in Appendix A to this part.

APPENDIX A TO PART 170—AWARD TERM

I. Reporting Subawards and Executive Compensation.

a. *Reporting of first-tier subawards.*

1. *Applicability.* Unless you are exempt as provided in paragraph d. of this award term, you must report each action that obligates

$25,000 or more in Federal funds that does not include Recovery funds (as defined in section 1512(a)(2) of the American Recovery and Reinvestment Act of 2009, Pub. L. 111–5) for a subaward to an entity (see definitions in paragraph e. of this award term).

2. *Where and when to report.*

i. You must report each obligating action described in paragraph a.1. of this award term to *http://www.fsrs.gov.*

ii. For subaward information, report no later than the end of the month following the month in which the obligation was made. (For example, if the obligation was made on November 7, 2010, the obligation must be reported by no later than December 31, 2010.)

3. *What to report.* You must report the information about each obligating action that the submission instructions posted at *http://www.fsrs.gov specify.*

b. *Reporting Total Compensation of Recipient Executives.*

1. *Applicability and what to report.* You must report total compensation for each of your five most highly compensated executives for the preceding completed fiscal year, if—

i. the total Federal funding authorized to date under this award is $25,000 or more;

ii. in the preceding fiscal year, you received—

(A) 80 percent or more of your annual gross revenues from Federal procurement contracts (and subcontracts) and Federal financial assistance subject to the Transparency Act, as defined at 2 CFR 170.320 (and subawards); and

(B) $25,000,000 or more in annual gross revenues from Federal procurement contracts (and subcontracts) and Federal financial assistance subject to the Transparency Act, as defined at 2 CFR 170.320 (and subawards); and

iii. The public does not have access to information about the compensation of the executives through periodic reports filed under section 13(a) or 15(d) of the Securities Exchange Act of 1934 (15 U.S.C. 78m(a), 78o(d)) or section 6104 of the Internal Revenue Code of 1986. (To determine if the public has access to the compensation information, see the U.S. Security and Exchange Commission total compensation filings at *http://www.sec.gov/answers/execomp.htm.*)

2. *Where and when to report.* You must report executive total compensation described in paragraph b.1. of this award term:

i. As part of your registration profile at *https://www.sam.gov.*

ii. By the end of the month following the month in which this award is made, and annually thereafter.

c. *Reporting of Total Compensation of Subrecipient Executives.*

1. *Applicability and what to report.* Unless you are exempt as provided in paragraph d. of this award term, for each first-tier subrecipient under this award, you shall report the names and total compensation of each of the subrecipient's five most highly compensated executives for the subrecipient's preceding completed fiscal year, if—

i. in the subrecipient's preceding fiscal year, the subrecipient received—

(A) 80 percent or more of its annual gross revenues from Federal procurement contracts (and subcontracts) and Federal financial assistance subject to the Transparency Act, as defined at 2 CFR 170.320 (and subawards); and

(B) $25,000,000 or more in annual gross revenues from Federal procurement contracts (and subcontracts), and Federal financial assistance subject to the Transparency Act (and subawards); and

ii. The public does not have access to information about the compensation of the executives through periodic reports filed under section 13(a) or 15(d) of the Securities Exchange Act of 1934 (15 U.S.C. 78m(a), 78o(d)) or section 6104 of the Internal Revenue Code of 1986. (To determine if the public has access to the compensation information, see the U.S. Security and Exchange Commission total compensation filings at *http://www.sec.gov/answers/execomp.htm.*)

2. *Where and when to report.* You must report subrecipient executive total compensation described in paragraph c.1. of this award term:

i. To the recipient.

ii. By the end of the month following the month during which you make the subaward. For example, if a subaward is obligated on any date during the month of October of a given year (*i.e.*, between October 1 and 31), you must report any required compensation information of the subrecipient by November 30 of that year.

d. *Exemptions*

If, in the previous tax year, you had gross income, from all sources, under $300,000, you are exempt from the requirements to report:

i. Subawards,
and

ii. The total compensation of the five most highly compensated executives of any subrecipient.

e. *Definitions.* For purposes of this award term:

1. *Entity* means all of the following, as defined in 2 CFR part 25:

i. A Governmental organization, which is a State, local government, or Indian tribe;

ii. A foreign public entity;

iii. A domestic or foreign nonprofit organization;

iv. A domestic or foreign for-profit organization;

v. A Federal agency, but only as a subrecipient under an award or subaward to a non-Federal entity.

2. *Executive* means officers, managing partners, or any other employees in management positions.

3. *Subaward:*

i. This term means a legal instrument to provide support for the performance of any portion of the substantive project or program for which you received this award and that you as the recipient award to an eligible subrecipient.

ii. The term does not include your procurement of property and services needed to carry out the project or program (for further explanation, see Sec. ___ .210 of the attachment to OMB Circular A–133, "Audits of States, Local Governments, and Non-Profit Organizations").

iii. A subaward may be provided through any legal agreement, including an agreement that you or a subrecipient considers a contract.

4. *Subrecipient* means an entity that:

i. Receives a subaward from you (the recipient) under this award; and

ii. Is accountable to you for the use of the Federal funds provided by the subaward.

5. *Total compensation* means the cash and noncash dollar value earned by the executive during the recipient's or subrecipient's preceding fiscal year and includes the following (for more information see 17 CFR 229.402(c)(2)):

i. *Salary and bonus.*

ii. *Awards of stock, stock options, and stock appreciation rights.* Use the dollar amount recognized for financial statement reporting purposes with respect to the fiscal year in accordance with the Statement of Financial Accounting Standards No. 123 (Revised 2004) (FAS 123R), Shared Based Payments.

iii. *Earnings for services under non-equity incentive plans.* This does not include group life, health, hospitalization or medical reimbursement plans that do not discriminate in favor of executives, and are available generally to all salaried employees.

iv. *Change in pension value.* This is the change in present value of defined benefit and actuarial pension plans.

v. *Above-market earnings on deferred compensation which is not tax-qualified.*

vi. Other compensation, if the aggregate value of all such other compensation (e.g. severance, termination payments, value of life insurance paid on behalf of the employee, perquisites or property) for the executive exceeds $10,000.

[75 FR 55669, Sept. 14, 2010, as amended at 79 FR 75879, Dec. 19, 2014]

# PARTS 171–174 [RESERVED]

# PART 175—AWARD TERM FOR TRAFFICKING IN PERSONS

AUTHORITY: 22 U.S.C. 7104(g); 31 U.S.C. 503; 31 U.S.C. 1111; 41 U.S.C. 405; Reorganization Plan No. 2 of 1970; E.O. 11541, 35 FR 10737, 3 CFR, 1966–1970, p. 939.

SOURCE: 72 FR 63783, Nov. 13, 2007, unless otherwise noted.

## § 175.5  Purpose of this part.

This part establishes a Government-wide award term for grants and cooperative agreements to implement the requirement in paragraph (g) of section 106 of the Trafficking Victims Protection Act of 2000 (TVPA), as amended (22 U.S.C. 7104(g)).

## § 175.10  Statutory requirement.

In each agency award (i.e., grant or cooperative agreement) under which funding is provided to a private entity, section 106(g) of the TVPA, as amended, requires the agency to include a condition that authorizes the agency to terminate the award, without penalty, if the recipient or a sub-recipient—

(a) Engages in severe forms of trafficking in persons during the period of time that the award is in effect;

(b) Procures a commercial sex act during the period of time that the award is in effect; or

(c) Uses forced labor in the performance of the award or subawards under the award.

## § 175.15  Award term.

(a) To implement the trafficking in persons requirement in section 106(g) of the TVPA, as amended, a Federal awarding agency must include the award term in paragraph (b) of this section in—

(1) A grant or cooperative agreement to a private entity, as defined in § 175.25(d); and

(2) A grant or cooperative agreement to a State, local government, Indian tribe or foreign public entity, if funding could be provided under the award to a private entity as a subrecipient.

(b) The award term that an agency must include, as described in paragraph (a) of this section, is:

I. Trafficking in persons.

a. *Provisions applicable to a recipient that is a private entity.*

1. You as the recipient, your employees, subrecipients under this award, and subrecipients' employees may not—

i. Engage in severe forms of trafficking in persons during the period of time that the award is in effect;

ii. Procure a commercial sex act during the period of time that the award is in effect; or

iii. Use forced labor in the performance of the award or subawards under the award.

2. We as the Federal awarding agency may unilaterally terminate this award, without penalty, if you or a subrecipient that is a private entity —

i. Is determined to have violated a prohibition in paragraph a.1 of this award term; or

ii. Has an employee who is determined by the agency official authorized to terminate the award to have violated a prohibition in paragraph a.1 of this award term through conduct that is either—

A. Associated with performance under this award; or

B. Imputed to you or the subrecipient using the standards and due process for imputing the conduct of an individual to an organization that are provided in 2 CFR part 180, "OMB Guidelines to Agencies on Governmentwide Debarment and Suspension (Nonprocurement)," as implemented by our agency at *[agency must insert reference here to its regulatory implementation of the OMB guidelines in 2 CFR part 180 (e.g., "2 CFR part XX")]*.

b. *Provision applicable to a recipient other than a private entity.* We as the Federal awarding agency may unilaterally terminate this award, without penalty, if a subrecipient that is a private entity—

1. Is determined to have violated an applicable prohibition in paragraph a.1 of this award term; or

2. Has an employee who is determined by the agency official authorized to terminate the award to have violated an applicable prohibition in paragraph a.1 of this award term through conduct that is either—

i. Associated with performance under this award; or

ii. Imputed to the subrecipient using the standards and due process for imputing the conduct of an individual to an organization that are provided in 2 CFR part 180, "OMB Guidelines to Agencies on Governmentwide Debarment and Suspension (Nonprocurement)," as implemented by our agency at *[agency must insert reference here to its regulatory implementation of the OMB guidelines in 2 CFR part 180 (e.g., "2 CFR part XX")]*.

c. *Provisions applicable to any recipient.*

1. You must inform us immediately of any information you receive from any source alleging a violation of a prohibition in paragraph a.1 of this award term.

2. Our right to terminate unilaterally that is described in paragraph a.2 or b of this section:

i. Implements section 106(g) of the Trafficking Victims Protection Act of 2000 (TVPA), as amended (22 U.S.C. 7104(g)), and

ii. Is in addition to all other remedies for noncompliance that are available to us under this award.

3. You must include the requirements of paragraph a.1 of this award term in any subaward you make to a private entity.

d. *Definitions.* For purposes of this award term:

1. "Employee" means either:

i. An individual employed by you or a subrecipient who is engaged in the performance of the project or program under this award; or

ii. Another person engaged in the performance of the project or program under this award and not compensated by you including, but not limited to, a volunteer or individual whose services are contributed by a third party as an in-kind contribution toward cost sharing or matching requirements.

2. "Forced labor" means labor obtained by any of the following methods: the recruitment, harboring, transportation, provision, or obtaining of a person for labor or services, through the use of force, fraud, or coercion for the purpose of subjection to involuntary servitude, peonage, debt bondage, or slavery.

3. "Private entity":

i. Means any entity other than a State, local government, Indian tribe, or foreign public entity, as those terms are defined in 2 CFR 175.25.

ii. Includes:

A. A nonprofit organization, including any nonprofit institution of higher education, hospital, or tribal organization other than one included in the definition of Indian tribe at 2 CFR 175.25(b).

B. A for-profit organization.

4. "Severe forms of trafficking in persons," "commercial sex act," and "coercion" have the meanings given at section 103 of the TVPA, as amended (22 U.S.C. 7102).

(c) An agency may use different letters and numbers to designate the paragraphs of the award term in paragraph (b) of this section, if necessary, to conform the system of paragraph designations with the one used in other terms and conditions in the agency's awards.

## § 175.20  Referral.

An agency official should inform the agency's suspending or debarring official if he or she terminates an award based on a violation of a prohibition contained in the award term under § 175.15.

## § 175.25   Definitions.

Terms used in this part are defined as follows:

(a) *Foreign public entity* means:

(1) A foreign government or foreign governmental entity;

(2) A public international organization, which is an organization entitled to enjoy privileges, exemptions, and immunities as an international organization under the International Organizations Immunities Act (22 U.S.C. 288–288f);

(3) An entity owned (in whole or in part) or controlled by a foreign government; and

(4) Any other entity consisting wholly or partially of one or more foreign governments or foreign governmental entities.

(b) *Indian tribe* means any Indian tribe, band, nation, or other organized group or community, including any Alaskan Native village or regional or village corporation (as defined in, or established under, the Alaskan Native Claims Settlement Act (43 U.S.C. 1601, *et seq.*)) that is recognized by the United States as eligible for the special programs and services provided by the United States to Indians because of their status as Indians.

(c) *Local government* means a:

(1) County;

(2) Borough;

(3) Municipality;

(4) City;

(5) Town;

(6) Township;

(7) Parish;

(8) Local public authority, including any public housing agency under the United States Housing Act of 1937;

(9) Special district;

(10) School district;

(11) Intrastate district;

(12) Council of governments, whether or not incorporated as a nonprofit corporation under State law; and

(13) Any other instrumentality of a local government.

(d) *Private entity.* (1) This term means any entity other than a State, local government, Indian tribe, or foreign public entity.

(2) This term includes:

(i) A nonprofit organization, including any nonprofit institution of higher education, hospital, or tribal organiza-tion other than one included in the definition of Indian tribe in paragraph (b) of this section.

(ii) A for-profit organization.

(e) *State*, consistent with the definition in section 103 of the TVPA, as amended (22 U.S.C. 7102), means:

(1) Any State of the United States;

(2) The District of Columbia;

(3) Any agency or instrumentality of a State other than a local government or State-controlled institution of higher education;

(4) The Commonwealths of Puerto Rico and the Northern Mariana Islands; and

(5) The United States Virgin Islands, Guam, American Samoa, and a territory or possession of the United States.

# PART 176—AWARD TERMS FOR AS-SISTANCE AGREEMENTS THAT IN-CLUDE FUNDS UNDER THE AMER-ICAN RECOVERY AND REINVEST-MENT ACT OF 2009, PUBLIC LAW 111–5

**Subpart C—Wage Rate Requirements under Section 1606 of the American Recovery and Reinvestment Act of 2009**

**Subpart D—Single Audit Information for Recipients of Recovery Act Funds**

AUTHORITY: American Recovery and Reinvestment Act of 2009, Public Law 111–5; Federal Funding Accountability and Transparency Act of 2006, (Pub. L. 109–282), as amended.

SOURCE: 74 FR 18450, Apr. 23, 2009, unless otherwise noted.

## § 176.10 Purpose of this part.

This part establishes Federal Governmentwide award terms for financial assistance awards, namely, grants, cooperative agreements, and loans, to implement the cross-cutting requirements of the American Recovery and Reinvestment Act of 2009, Public Law 111–5 (Recovery Act). These requirements are cross-cutting in that they apply to more than one agency's awards.

## § 176.20 Agency responsibilities (general).

(a) In any assistance award funded in whole or in part by the Recovery Act, the award official shall indicate that the award is being made under the Recovery Act, and indicate what projects and/or activities are being funded under the Recovery Act. This requirement applies whenever Recovery Act funds are used, regardless of the assistance type.

(b) To maximize transparency of Recovery Act funds required for reporting by the assistance recipient, the award official shall consider structuring assistance awards to allow for separately tracking Recovery Act funds.

(c) Award officials shall ensure that recipients comply with the Recovery Act requirements of Subpart A. If the recipient fails to comply with the reporting requirements or other award terms, the award official or other authorized agency action official shall take the appropriate enforcement or termination action in accordance with 2 CFR 215.62 or the agency's implementation of the OMB Circular A–102 grants management common rule. OMB Circular A–102 is available at *http://www.whitehouse.gov/omb/circulars/a102/a102.html.*

(d) The award official shall make the recipient's failure to comply with the reporting requirements a part of the recipient's performance record.

## § 176.30 Definitions.

As used in this part—

*Award* means any grant, cooperative agreement or loan made with Recovery Act funds. Award official means a person with the authority to enter into, administer, and/or terminate financial assistance awards and make related determinations and findings.

*Classified* or *"classified information"* means any knowledge that can be communicated or any documentary material, regardless of its physical form or characteristics, that—

(1)(i) Is owned by, is produced by or for, or is under the control of the United States Government; or

(ii) Has been classified by the Department of Energy as privately generated restricted data following the procedures in 10 CFR 1045.21; and

(2) Must be protected against unauthorized disclosure according to Executive Order 12958, Classified National Security Information, April 17, 1995, or

classified in accordance with the Atomic Energy Act of 1954.

*Recipient* means any entity other than an individual that receives Recovery Act funds in the form of a grant, cooperative agreement or loan directly from the Federal Government.

*Recovery funds* or *Recovery Act funds* are funds made available through the appropriations of the American Recovery and Reinvestment Act of 2009, Public Law 111–5.

*Subaward* means—

(1) A legal instrument to provide support for the performance of any portion of the substantive project or program for which the recipient received this award and that the recipient awards to an eligible subrecipient;

(2) The term does not include the recipient's procurement of property and services needed to carry out the project or program (for further explanation, see § ___ .210 of the attachment to OMB Circular A–133, "Audits of States, Local Governments, and Non-Profit Organizations"). OMB Circular A–133 is available at *http://www.whitehouse.gov/omb/circulars/a133/a133.html.*

(3) A subaward may be provided through any legal agreement, including an agreement that the recipient or a subrecipient considers a contract.

*Subcontract* means a legal instrument used by a recipient for procurement of property and services needed to carry out the project or program.

*Subrecipient* or *Subawardee* means a non-Federal entity that expends Federal awards received from a pass-through entity to carry out a Federal program, but does not include an individual that is a beneficiary of such a program. A subrecipient may also be a recipient of other Federal awards directly from a Federal awarding agency. Guidance on distinguishing between a subrecipient and a vendor is provided in § ___ .210 of OMB Circular A–133.

## Subpart A—Reporting and Registration Requirements Under Section 1512 of the American Recovery and Reinvestment Act of 2009

### § 176.40   Procedure.

The award official shall insert the standard award term in this subpart in all awards funded in whole or in part with Recovery Act funds, except for those that are classified, awarded to individuals, or awarded under mandatory and entitlement programs, except as specifically required by OMB, or expressly exempted from the reporting requirement in the Recovery Act.

### § 176.50   Award term—Reporting and registration requirements under section 1512 of the Recovery Act.

Agencies are responsible for ensuring that their recipients report information required under the Recovery Act in a timely manner. The following award term shall be used by agencies to implement the recipient reporting and registration requirements in section 1512:

(a) This award requires the recipient to complete projects or activities which are funded under the American Recovery and Reinvestment Act of 2009 (Recovery Act) and to report on use of Recovery Act funds provided through this award. Information from these reports will be made available to the public.

(b) The reports are due no later than ten calendar days after each calendar quarter in which the recipient receives the assistance award funded in whole or in part by the Recovery Act.

(c) Recipients and their first-tier recipients must maintain current registrations in the System of Award Management (*http://www.ccr.gov*) at all times during which they have active federal awards funded with Recovery Act funds. A Dun and Bradstreet Data Universal Numbering System (DUNS) Number (*http://www.dnb.com*) is one of the requirements for registration in the System of Award Management.

(d) The recipient shall report the information described in section 1512(c) of the Recovery Act using the reporting instructions and data elements that will be provided online at *http://*

*www.FederalReporting.gov* and ensure that any information that is pre-filled is corrected or updated as needed.

## Subpart B—Buy American Requirement Under Section 1605 of the American Recovery and Reinvestment Act of 2009

**§ 176.60  Statutory requirement.**

Section 1605 of the Recovery Act prohibits use of recovery funds for a project for the construction, alteration, maintenance, or repair of a public building or public work unless all of the iron, steel, and manufactured goods used in the project are produced in the United States. The law requires that this prohibition be applied in a manner consistent with U.S. obligations under international agreements, and it provides for waiver under three circumstances:

(a) Iron, steel, or relevant manufactured goods are not produced in the United States in sufficient and reasonably available quantities and of a satisfactory quality;

(b) Inclusion of iron, steel, or manufactured goods produced in the United States will increase the cost of the overall project by more than 25 percent; or

(c) Applying the domestic preference would be inconsistent with the public interest.

**§ 176.70  Policy.**

Except as provided in § 176.80 or § 176.90—

(a) None of the funds appropriated or otherwise made available by the Recovery Act may be used for a project for the construction, alteration, maintenance, or repair of a public building or public work (see definitions at §§ 176.140 and 176.160) unless—

(1) The public building or public work is located in the United States; and

(2) All of the iron, steel, and manufactured goods used in the project are produced or manufactured in the United States.

(i) Production in the United States of the iron or steel used in the project requires that all manufacturing processes must take place in the United States, except metallurgical processes involving refinement of steel additives. These requirements do not apply to iron or steel used as components or subcomponents of manufactured goods used in the project.

(ii) There is no requirement with regard to the origin of components or subcomponents in manufactured goods used in the project, as long as the manufacturing occurs in the United States.

(b) Paragraph (a) of this section shall not apply where the Recovery Act requires the application of alternative Buy American requirements for iron, steel, and manufactured goods.

**§ 176.80  Exceptions.**

(a) When one of the following exceptions applies in a case or category of cases, the award official may allow the recipient to use foreign iron, steel and/or manufactured goods in the project without regard to the restrictions of section 1605 of the Recovery Act:

(1) *Nonavailability.* The head of the Federal department or agency may determine that the iron, steel or relevant manufactured good is not produced or manufactured in the United States in sufficient and reasonably available commercial quantities of a satisfactory quality. The determinations of nonavailability of the articles listed at 48 CFR 25.104(a) and the procedures at 48 CFR 25.103(b)(1) also apply if any of those articles are manufactured goods needed in the project.

(2) *Unreasonable cost.* The head of the Federal department or agency may determine that the cost of domestic iron, steel, or relevant manufactured goods will increase the cost of the overall project by more than 25 percent in accordance with § 176.110.

(3) *Inconsistent with public interest.* The head of the Federal department or agency may determine that application of the restrictions of section 1605 of the Recovery Act would be inconsistent with the public interest.

(b) When a determination is made for any of the reasons stated in this section that certain foreign iron, steel, and/or manufactured goods may be used—

(1) The award official shall list the excepted materials in the award; and

(2) The head of the Federal department or agency shall publish a notice in the FEDERAL REGISTER within two weeks after the determination is made, unless the item has already been determined to be domestically nonavailable. A list of items that are not domestically available is at 48 CFR 25.104(a). The FEDERAL REGISTER notice or information from the notice may be posted by OMB to Recovery.gov. The notice shall include—

(i) The title "Buy American Exception under the American Recovery and Reinvestment Act of 2009";

(ii) The dollar value and brief description of the project; and

(iii) A detailed written justification as to why the restriction is being waived.

§ 176.90 Acquisitions covered under international agreements.

Section 1605(d) of the Recovery Act provides that the Buy American requirement in section 1605 shall be applied in a manner consistent with U.S. obligations under international agreements.

(a) The Buy American requirement set out in §176.70 shall not be applied where the iron, steel, or manufactured goods used in the project are from a Party to an international agreement, listed in paragraph (b) of this section, and the recipient is required under an international agreement, described in the appendix to this subpart, to treat the goods and services of that Party the same as domestic goods and services. As of January 1, 2010, this obligation shall only apply to projects with an estimated value of $7,804,000 or more and projects that are not specifically excluded from the application of those agreements.

(b) The international agreements that obligate recipients that are covered under an international agreement to treat the goods and services of a Party the same as domestic goods and services and the respective Parties to the agreements are:

(1) The World Trade Organization Government Procurement Agreement (Aruba, Austria, Belgium, Bulgaria, Canada, Chinese Taipei (Taiwan), Cyprus, Czech Republic, Denmark, Estonia, Finland, France, Germany, Greece,

Hong Kong, Hungary, Iceland, Ireland, Israel, Italy, Japan, Korea (Republic of), Latvia, Liechtenstein, Lithuania, Luxembourg, Malta, Netherlands, Norway, Poland, Portugal, Romania, Singapore, Slovak Republic, Slovenia, Spain, Sweden, Switzerland, and United Kingdom);

(2) The following Free Trade Agreements:

(i) Dominican Republic-Central America-United States Free Trade Agreement (Costa Rica, Dominican Republic, El Salvador, Guatemala, Honduras, Nicaragua);

(ii) North American Free Trade Agreement (NAFTA) (Canada and Mexico);

(iii) United States-Australia Free Trade Agreement;

(iv) United States-Bahrain Free Trade Agreement;

(v) United States-Chile Free Trade Agreement;

(vi) United States-Israel Free Trade Agreement;

(vii) United States-Morocco Free Trade Agreement;

(viii) United States-Oman Free Trade Agreement;

(ix) United States-Peru Trade Promotion Agreement; and

(x) United States-Singapore Free Trade Agreement.

(3) United States-European Communities Exchange of Letters (May 15, 1995): Austria, Belgium, Bulgaria, Cyprus, Czech Republic, Denmark, Estonia, Finland, France, Germany, Greece, Hungary, Ireland, Italy, Latvia, Lithuania, Luxembourg, Malta, Netherlands, Poland, Portugal, Romania, Slovak Republic, Slovenia, Spain, Sweden, and United Kingdom; and

(4) Agreement between the Government of Canada and the Government of the United States of America on Government Procurement.

[74 FR 18450, Apr. 23, 2009, as amended at 75 FR 14323, Mar. 25, 2010]

§ 176.100 Timely determination concerning the inapplicability of section 1605 of the Recovery Act.

(a) The head of the Federal department or agency involved may make a determination regarding inapplicability of section 1605 to a particular case or to a category of cases.

(b) Before Recovery Act funds are awarded by the Federal agency or obligated by the recipient for a project for the construction, alteration, maintenance, or repair of a public building or public work, an applicant or recipient may request from the award official a determination concerning the inapplicability of section 1605 of the Recovery Act for specifically identified items.

(c) The time for submitting the request and the information and supporting data that must be included in the request are to be specified in the agency's and recipient's request for applications and/or proposals, and as appropriate, in other written communications. The content of those communications should be consistent with the notice in § 176.150 or § 176.170, whichever applies.

(d) The award official must evaluate all requests based on the information provided and may supplement this information with other readily available information.

(e) In making a determination based on the increased cost to the project of using domestic iron, steel, and/or manufactured goods, the award official must compare the total estimated cost of the project using foreign iron, steel and/or relevant manufactured goods to the estimated cost if all domestic iron, steel, and/or relevant manufactured goods were used. If use of domestic iron, steel, and/or relevant manufactured goods would increase the cost of the overall project by more than 25 percent, then the award official shall determine that the cost of the domestic iron, steel, and/or relevant manufactured goods is unreasonable.

§ 176.110 **Evaluating proposals of foreign iron, steel, and/or manufactured goods.**

(a) If the award official receives a request for an exception based on the cost of certain domestic iron, steel, and/or manufactured goods being unreasonable, in accordance with § 176.80, then the award official shall apply evaluation factors to the proposal to use such foreign iron, steel, and/or manufactured goods as follows:

(1) Use an evaluation factor of 25 percent, applied to the total estimated cost of the project, if the foreign iron, steel, and/or manufactured goods are to be used in the project based on an exception for unreasonable cost requested by the applicant.

(2) Total evaluated cost = project cost estimate + (.25 × project cost estimate, if paragraph (a)(1) of this section applies).

(b) Applicants or recipients also may submit alternate proposals based on use of equivalent domestic iron, steel, and/or manufactured goods to avoid possible denial of Recovery Act funding for the proposal if the Federal Government determines that an exception permitting use of the foreign item(s) does not apply.

(c) If the award official makes an award to an applicant that proposed foreign iron, steel, and/or manufactured goods not listed in the applicable notice in the request for applications or proposals, then the award official must add the excepted materials to the list in the award term.

§ 176.120 **Determinations on late requests.**

(a) If a recipient requests a determination regarding the inapplicability of section 1605 of the Recovery Act after obligating Recovery Act funds for a project for construction, alteration, maintenance, or repair (late request), the recipient must explain why it could not request the determination before making the obligation or why the need for such determination otherwise was not reasonably foreseeable. If the award official concludes that the recipient should have made the request before making the obligation, the award official may deny the request.

(b) The award official must base evaluation of any late request for a determination regarding the inapplicability of section 1605 of the Recovery Act on information required by § 176.150(c) and (d) or § 176.170(c) and (d) and/or other readily available information.

(c) If a determination, under § 176.80 is made after Recovery Act funds were obligated for a project for construction, alteration, maintenance, or repair that an exception to section 1605 of the Recovery Act applies, the award official must amend the award to allow use of the foreign iron, steel, and/or relevant manufactured goods. When the basis of the exception is nonavailability or public interest, the amended award shall reflect adjustment of the award amount, redistribution of budgeted funds, and/or other appropriate actions taken to cover costs associated with acquiring or using the foreign iron, steel, and/or manufactured goods. When the basis for the exception is the unreasonable cost of domestic iron, steel, and/or manufactured goods the award official shall adjust the award amount or the budget, as appropriate, by at least the differential established in §176.110(a).

§176.130 Noncompliance.

The award official must—

(a) Review allegations of violations of section 1605 of the Recovery Act;

(b) Unless fraud is suspected, notify the recipient of the apparent unauthorized use of foreign iron, steel, and/or manufactured goods and request a reply, to include proposed corrective action; and

(c) If the review reveals that a recipient or subrecipient has used foreign iron, steel, and/or manufactured goods without authorization, take appropriate action, including one or more of the following:

(1) Process a determination concerning the inapplicability of section 1605 of the Recovery Act in accordance with §176.120.

(2) Consider requiring the removal and replacement of the unauthorized foreign iron, steel, and/or manufactured goods.

(3) If removal and replacement of foreign iron, steel, and/or manufactured goods used in a public building or a public work would be impracticable, cause undue delay, or otherwise be detrimental to the interests of the Federal Government, the award official may determine in writing that the foreign iron, steel, and/or manufactured goods need not be removed and replaced. A determination to retain foreign iron, steel, and/or manufactured goods does not constitute a determination that an exception to section 1605 of the Recovery Act applies, and this should be stated in the determination. Further, a determination to retain foreign iron, steel, and/or manufactured goods does not affect the Federal Government's

right to reduce the amount of the award by the cost of the steel, iron, or manufactured goods that are used in the project or to take enforcement or termination action in accordance with the agency's grants management regulations.

(4) If the noncompliance is sufficiently serious, consider exercising appropriate remedies, such as withholding cash payments pending correction of the deficiency, suspending or terminating the award, and withholding further awards for the project. Also consider preparing and forwarding a report to the agency suspending or debarring official in accordance with the agency's debarment rule implementing 2 CFR part 180. If the noncompliance appears to be fraudulent, refer the matter to other appropriate agency officials, such as the officer responsible for criminal investigation.

§176.140 Award term—Required Use of American Iron, Steel, and Manufactured Goods—Section 1605 of the American Recovery and Reinvestment Act of 2009.

When awarding Recovery Act funds for construction, alteration, maintenance, or repair of a public building or public work that does not involve iron, steel, and/or manufactured goods covered under international agreements, the agency shall use the award term described in the following paragraphs:

(a) *Definitions.* As used in this award term and condition—

(1) *Manufactured good* means a good brought to the construction site for incorporation into the building or work that has been—

(i) Processed into a specific form and shape; or

(ii) Combined with other raw material to create a material that has different properties than the properties of the individual raw materials.

(2) *Public building and public work* means a public building of, and a public work of, a governmental entity (the United States; the District of Columbia; commonwealths, territories, and minor outlying islands of the United States; State and local governments; and multi-State, regional, or interstate entities which have governmental functions). These buildings and works may include, without limitation,

bridges, dams, plants, highways, parkways, streets, subways, tunnels, sewers, mains, power lines, pumping stations, heavy generators, railways, airports, terminals, docks, piers, wharves, ways, lighthouses, buoys, jetties, breakwaters, levees, and canals, and the construction, alteration, maintenance, or repair of such buildings and works.

(3) *Steel* means an alloy that includes at least 50 percent iron, between .02 and 2 percent carbon, and may include other elements.

(b) *Domestic preference.* (1) This award term and condition implements Section 1605 of the American Recovery and Reinvestment Act of 2009 (Recovery Act) (Pub. L. 111–5), by requiring that all iron, steel, and manufactured goods used in the project are produced in the United States except as provided in paragraph (b)(3) and (b)(4) of this section and condition.

(2) This requirement does not apply to the material listed by the Federal Government as follows:

---

[*Award official to list applicable excepted materials or indicate "none"*]

(3) The award official may add other iron, steel, and/or manufactured goods to the list in paragraph (b)(2) of this section and condition if the Federal Government determines that—

(i) The cost of the domestic iron, steel, and/or manufactured goods would be unreasonable. The cost of domestic iron, steel, or manufactured goods used in the project is unreasonable when the cumulative cost of such material will increase the cost of the overall project by more than 25 percent;

(ii) The iron, steel, and/or manufactured good is not produced, or manufactured in the United States in sufficient and reasonably available quantities and of a satisfactory quality; or

(iii) The application of the restriction of section 1605 of the Recovery Act would be inconsistent with the public interest.

(c) *Request for determination of inapplicability of Section 1605 of the Recovery Act.* (1)(i) Any recipient request to use foreign iron, steel, and/or manufactured goods in accordance with paragraph (b)(3) of this section shall include

adequate information for Federal Government evaluation of the request, including—

(A) A description of the foreign and domestic iron, steel, and/or manufactured goods;

(B) Unit of measure;

(C) Quantity;

(D) Cost;

(E) Time of delivery or availability;

(F) Location of the project;

(G) Name and address of the proposed supplier; and

(H) A detailed justification of the reason for use of foreign iron, steel, and/or manufactured goods cited in accordance with paragraph (b)(3) of this section.

(ii) A request based on unreasonable cost shall include a reasonable survey of the market and a completed cost comparison table in the format in paragraph (d) of this section.

(iii) The cost of iron, steel, and/or manufactured goods material shall include all delivery costs to the construction site and any applicable duty.

(iv) Any recipient request for a determination submitted after Recovery Act funds have been obligated for a project for construction, alteration, maintenance, or repair shall explain why the recipient could not reasonably foresee the need for such determination and could not have requested the determination before the funds were obligated. If the recipient does not submit a satisfactory explanation, the award official need not make a determination.

(2) If the Federal Government determines after funds have been obligated for a project for construction, alteration, maintenance, or repair that an exception to section 1605 of the Recovery Act applies, the award official will amend the award to allow use of the foreign iron, steel, and/or relevant manufactured goods. When the basis for the exception is nonavailability or public interest, the amended award shall reflect adjustment of the award amount, redistribution of budgeted funds, and/or other actions taken to cover costs associated with acquiring or using the foreign iron, steel, and/or relevant manufactured goods. When the basis for the exception is the unreasonable cost of the domestic iron,

steel, or manufactured goods, the award official shall adjust the award amount or redistribute budgeted funds by at least the differential established in 2 CFR 176.110(a).

(3) Unless the Federal Government determines that an exception to section 1605 of the Recovery Act applies, use of foreign iron, steel, and/or manufactured goods is noncompliant with section 1605 of the American Recovery and Reinvestment Act.

(d) *Data.* To permit evaluation of requests under paragraph (b) of this section based on unreasonable cost, the Recipient shall include the following information and any applicable supporting data based on the survey of suppliers:

FOREIGN AND DOMESTIC ITEMS COST COMPARISON

| Description | Unit of measure | Quantity | Cost (dollars)* |
|---|---|---|---|
| *Item 1:.* | | | |
|     Foreign steel, iron, or manufactured good ......................................... | | | |
|     Domestic steel, iron, or manufactured good ..................................... | | | |
| *Item 2:.* | | | |
|     Foreign steel, iron, or manufactured good ......................................... | | | |
|     Domestic steel, iron, or manufactured good ..................................... | | | |

[List name, address, telephone number, email address, and contact for suppliers surveyed. Attach copy of response; if oral, attach summary.]
[Include other applicable supporting information.]
[*Include all delivery costs to the construction site.]

## § 176.150 Notice of Required Use of American Iron, Steel, and Manufactured Goods—Section 1605 of the American Recovery and Reinvestment Act of 2009.

When requesting applications or proposals for Recovery Act programs or activities that may involve construction, alteration, maintenance, or repair of a public building or public work, and do not involve iron, steel, and/or manufactured goods covered under international agreements, the agency shall use the notice described in the following paragraphs in their solicitations:

(a) *Definitions.* Manufactured good, public building and public work, and steel, as used in this notice, are defined in the 2 CFR 176.140.

(b) *Requests for determinations of inapplicability.* A prospective applicant requesting a determination regarding the inapplicability of section 1605 of the American Recovery and Reinvestment Act of 2009 (Pub. L. 111–5) (Recovery Act) should submit the request to the award official in time to allow a determination before submission of applications or proposals. The prospective applicant shall include the information and applicable supporting data required by paragraphs at 2 CFR 176.140(c) and (d) in the request. If an applicant has not requested a determination regarding the inapplicability of 1605 of the Recovery Act before submitting its application or proposal, or has not received a response to a previous request, the applicant shall include the information and supporting data in the application or proposal.

(c) *Evaluation of project proposals.* If the Federal Government determines that an exception based on unreasonable cost of domestic iron, steel, and/or manufactured goods applies, the Federal Government will evaluate a project requesting exception to the requirements of section 1605 of the Recovery Act by adding to the estimated total cost of the project 25 percent of the project cost, if foreign iron, steel, or manufactured goods are used in the project based on unreasonable cost of comparable manufactured domestic iron, steel, and/or manufactured goods.

(d) *Alternate project proposals.* (1) When a project proposal includes foreign iron, steel, and/or manufactured goods not listed by the Federal Government at 2 CFR 176.140(b)(2), the applicant also may submit an alternate proposal based on use of equivalent domestic iron, steel, and/or manufactured goods.

(2) If an alternate proposal is submitted, the applicant shall submit a separate cost comparison table prepared in accordance with 2 CFR

176.140(c) and (d) for the proposal that is based on the use of any foreign iron, steel, and/or manufactured goods for which the Federal Government has not yet determined an exception applies.

(3) If the Federal Government determines that a particular exception requested in accordance with 2 CFR 176.140(b) does not apply, the Federal Government will evaluate only those proposals based on use of the equivalent domestic iron, steel, and/or manufactured goods, and the applicant shall be required to furnish such domestic items.

§ 176.160 Award term—Required Use of American Iron, Steel, and Manufactured Goods (covered under International Agreements)—Section 1605 of the American Recovery and Reinvestment Act of 2009.

When awarding Recovery Act funds for construction, alteration, maintenance, or repair of a public building or public work that involves iron, steel, and/or manufactured goods materials covered under international agreements, the agency shall use the award term described in the following paragraphs:

(a) *Definitions.* As used in this award term and condition—

*Designated country*—(1) A World Trade Organization Government Procurement Agreement country (Aruba, Austria, Belgium, Bulgaria, Canada, Chinese Taipei (Taiwan), Cyprus, Czech Republic, Denmark, Estonia, Finland, France, Germany, Greece, Hong Kong, Hungary, Iceland, Ireland, Israel, Italy, Japan, Korea (Republic of), Latvia, Liechtenstein, Lithuania, Luxembourg, Malta, Netherlands, Norway, Poland, Portugal, Romania, Singapore, Slovak Republic, Slovenia, Spain, Sweden, Switzerland, and United Kingdom;

(2) A Free Trade Agreement (FTA) country (Australia, Bahrain, Canada, Chile, Costa Rica, Dominican Republic, El Salvador, Guatemala, Honduras, Israel, Mexico, Morocco, Nicaragua, Oman, Peru, or Singapore);

(3) A United States-European Communities Exchange of Letters (May 15, 1995) country: Austria, Belgium, Bulgaria, Cyprus, Czech Republic, Denmark, Estonia, Finland, France, Germany, Greece, Hungary, Ireland, Italy, Latvia, Lithuania, Luxembourg, Malta, Netherlands, Poland, Portugal, Romania, Slovak Republic, Slovenia, Spain, Sweden, and United Kingdom; or

(4) An Agreement between Canada and the United States of America on Government Procurement country (Canada).

*Designated country iron, steel, and/or manufactured goods*—(1) Is wholly the growth, product, or manufacture of a designated country; or

(2) In the case of a manufactured good that consist in whole or in part of materials from another country, has been substantially transformed in a designated country into a new and different manufactured good distinct from the materials from which it was transformed.

*Domestic iron, steel, and/or manufactured good*—(1) Is wholly the growth, product, or manufacture of the United States; or

(2) In the case of a manufactured good that consists in whole or in part of materials from another country, has been substantially transformed in the United States into a new and different manufactured good distinct from the materials from which it was transformed. There is no requirement with regard to the origin of components or subcomponents in manufactured goods or products, as long as the manufacture of the goods occurs in the United States.

*Foreign iron, steel, and/or manufactured good* means iron, steel and/or manufactured good that is not domestic or designated country iron, steel, and/or manufactured good.

*Manufactured good* means a good brought to the construction site for incorporation into the building or work that has been—

(1) Processed into a specific form and shape; or

(2) Combined with other raw material to create a material that has different properties than the properties of the individual raw materials.

*Public building* and *public work* means a public building of, and a public work of, a governmental entity (the United States; the District of Columbia; commonwealths, territories, and minor outlying islands of the United States; State and local governments; and multi-State, regional, or interstate entities which have governmental functions). These buildings and works may include, without limitation, bridges, dams, plants, highways, parkways, streets, subways, tunnels, sewers, mains, power lines, pumping stations, heavy generators, railways, airports, terminals, docks, piers, wharves, ways, lighthouses, buoys, jetties, breakwaters, levees, and canals, and the construction, alteration, maintenance, or repair of such buildings and works.

*Steel* means an alloy that includes at least 50 percent iron, between .02 and 2 percent carbon, and may include other elements.

(b) *Iron, steel, and manufactured goods.* (1) The award term and condition described in this section implements—

(i) Section 1605(a) of the American Recovery and Reinvestment Act of 2009 (Pub. L. 111–5) (Recovery Act), by requiring that all iron, steel, and manufactured goods used in the project are produced in the United States; and

(ii) Section 1605(d), which requires application of the Buy American requirement in a manner consistent with U.S. obligations under international agreements. The restrictions of section 1605 of the Recovery Act do not apply to designated country iron, steel, and/or manufactured goods. The Buy American requirement in section 1605 shall not be applied where the iron, steel or manufactured goods used in the project are from a Party to an international agreement that obligates the recipient to treat the goods and services of that Party the same as domestic goods and services. As of January 1, 2010, this obligation shall only apply to projects with an estimated value of $7,804,000 or more.

(2) The recipient shall use only domestic or designated country iron, steel, and manufactured goods in performing the work funded in whole or part with this award, except as provided in paragraphs (b)(3) and (b)(4) of this section.

(3) The requirement in paragraph (b)(2) of this section does not apply to the iron, steel, and manufactured goods listed by the Federal Government as follows:

[*Award official to list applicable excepted materials or indicate "none"*]

(4) The award official may add other iron, steel, and manufactured goods to the list in paragraph (b)(3) of this section if the Federal Government determines that—

(i) The cost of domestic iron, steel, and/or manufactured goods would be unreasonable. The cost of domestic iron, steel, and/or manufactured goods used in the project is unreasonable when the cumulative cost of such material will increase the overall cost of the project by more than 25 percent;

(ii) The iron, steel, and/or manufactured good is not produced, or manufactured in the United States in sufficient and reasonably available commercial quantities of a satisfactory quality; or

(iii) The application of the restriction of section 1605 of the Recovery Act would be inconsistent with the public interest.

(c) *Request for determination of inapplicability of section 1605 of the Recovery Act or the Buy American Act.* (1)(i) Any recipient request to use foreign iron, steel, and/or manufactured goods in accordance with paragraph (b)(4) of this section shall include adequate information for Federal Government evaluation of the request, including—

(A) A description of the foreign and domestic iron, steel, and/or manufactured goods;

(B) Unit of measure;

(C) Quantity;

(D) Cost;

(E) Time of delivery or availability;

(F) Location of the project;

(G) Name and address of the proposed supplier; and

(H) A detailed justification of the reason for use of foreign iron, steel, and/or manufactured goods cited in accordance with paragraph (b)(4) of this section.

(ii) A request based on unreasonable cost shall include a reasonable survey of the market and a completed cost comparison table in the format in paragraph (d) of this section.

(iii) The cost of iron, steel, or manufactured goods shall include all delivery costs to the construction site and any applicable duty.

(iv) Any recipient request for a determination submitted after Recovery Act funds have been obligated for a project for construction, alteration, maintenance, or repair shall explain why the recipient could not reasonably foresee the need for such determination and could not have requested the determination before the funds were obligated. If the recipient does not submit a satisfactory explanation, the award official need not make a determination.

(2) If the Federal Government determines after funds have been obligated for a project for construction, alteration, maintenance, or repair that an exception to section 1605 of the Recovery Act applies, the award official will amend the award to allow use of the foreign iron, steel, and/or relevant manufactured goods. When the basis for the exception is nonavailability or public interest, the amended award shall reflect adjustment of the award amount, redistribution of budgeted funds, and/or other appropriate actions

taken to cover costs associated with acquiring or using the foreign iron, steel, and/or relevant manufactured goods.. When the basis for the exception is the unreasonable cost of the domestic iron, steel, or manufactured goods, the award official shall adjust the award amount or redistribute budgeted funds, as appropriate, by at least the differential established in 2 CFR 176.110(a).

(3) Unless the Federal Government determines that an exception to section 1605 of the Recovery Act applies, use of foreign iron, steel, and/or manufactured goods other than designated country iron, steel, and/or manufactured goods is noncompliant with the applicable Act.

(d) *Data.* To permit evaluation of requests under paragraph (b) of this section based on unreasonable cost, the applicant shall include the following information and any applicable supporting data based on the survey of suppliers:

FOREIGN AND DOMESTIC ITEMS COST COMPARISON

| Description | Unit of measure | Quantity | Cost (dollars)* |
|---|---|---|---|
| *Item 1:* | | | |
|     Foreign steel, iron, or manufactured good ..................................... | | | |
|     Domestic steel, iron, or manufactured good ................................. | | | |
| *Item 2:* | | | |
|     Foreign steel, iron, or manufactured good ..................................... | | | |
|     Domestic steel, iron, or manufactured good ................................. | | | |

[List name, address, telephone number, email address, and contact for suppliers surveyed. Attach copy of response; if oral, attach summary.]
[Include other applicable supporting information.]
[*Include all delivery costs to the construction site.]

[74 FR 18450, Apr. 23, 2009, as amended at 75 FR 14323, Mar. 25, 2010]

**§ 176.170 Notice of Required Use of American Iron, Steel, and Manufactured Goods (covered under International Agreements)—Section 1605 of the American Recovery and Reinvestment Act of 2009.**

When requesting applications or proposals for Recovery Act programs or activities that may involve construction, alteration, maintenance, or repair of a public building or public work, and involve iron, steel, and/or manufactured goods covered under international agreements, the agency shall use the notice described in the following paragraphs in the solicitation:

(a) *Definitions. Designated country iron, steel, and/or manufactured goods, foreign iron, steel, and/or manufactured good, manufactured good, public building and public work,* and *steel,* as used in this provision, are defined in 2 CFR 176.160(a).

(b) *Requests for determinations of inapplicability.* A prospective applicant requesting a determination regarding the inapplicability of section 1605 of the American Recovery and Reinvestment Act of 2009 (Pub. L. 111-5) (Recovery Act) should submit the request to the award official in time to allow a determination before submission of applications or proposals. The prospective applicant shall include the information and applicable supporting data required by 2 CFR 176.160 (c) and (d) in the request. If an applicant has not requested a determination regarding the inapplicability of section 1605 of the Recovery Act before submitting its application or proposal, or has not received a response to a previous request, the applicant shall include the information and supporting data in the application or proposal.

(c) *Evaluation of project proposals.* If the Federal Government determines that an exception based on unreasonable cost of domestic iron, steel, and/or manufactured goods applies, the Federal Government will evaluate a project requesting exception to the requirements of section 1605 of the Recovery Act by adding to the estimated total cost of the project 25 percent of the project cost if foreign iron, steel, or manufactured goods are used based on unreasonable cost of comparable domestic iron, steel, or manufactured goods.

(d) *Alternate project proposals.* (1) When a project proposal includes foreign iron, steel, and/or manufactured goods, other than designated country iron, steel, and/or manufactured goods, that are not listed by the Federal Government in this Buy American notice in the request for applications or proposals, the applicant may submit an alternate proposal based on use of equivalent domestic or designated country iron, steel, and/or manufactured goods.

(2) If an alternate proposal is submitted, the applicant shall submit a separate cost comparison table prepared in accordance with paragraphs 2 CFR 176.160(c) and (d) for the proposal that is based on the use of any foreign iron, steel, and/or manufactured goods for which the Federal Government has not yet determined an exception applies.

(3) If the Federal Government determines that a particular exception requested in accordance with 2 CFR 176.160(b) does not apply, the Federal Government will evaluate only those proposals based on use of the equivalent domestic or designated country iron, steel, and/or manufactured goods, and the applicant shall be required to furnish such domestic or designated country items.

APPENDIX TO SUBPART B OF 2 CFR PART 176—U.S. STATES, OTHER SUB-FEDERAL ENTITIES, AND OTHER ENTITIES SUBJECT TO U.S. OBLIGATIONS UNDER INTERNATIONAL AGREEMENTS (AS OF FEBRUARY 16, 2010)

| States | Entities covered | Exclusions | Relevant international agreements |
|---|---|---|---|
| Arizona | Executive branch agencies | | —WTO GPA.<br>—U.S.-Chile FTA.<br>—U.S.-Singapore FTA. |
| Arkansas | Executive branch agencies, including universities but excluding the Office of Fish and Game. | Construction services | —WTO GPA.<br>—DR-CAFTA.<br>—U.S.-Australia FTA.<br>—U.S.-Chile FTA.<br>—U.S.-Morocco FTA.<br>—U.S.-Peru TPA.<br>—U.S.-Singapore FTA. |
| California | Executive branch agencies | | —WTO GPA.<br>—U.S.-Australia FTA.<br>—U.S.-Chile FTA.<br>—U.S.-Singapore FTA. |
| Colorado | Executive branch agencies | | —WTO GPA.<br>—DR-CAFTA.<br>—U.S.-Australia FTA.<br>—U.S.-Chile FTA.<br>—U.S.-Morocco FTA.<br>—U.S.-Peru TPA.<br>—U.S.-Singapore FTA. |

| States | Entities covered | Exclusions | Relevant international agreements |
|---|---|---|---|
| Connecticut | —Department of Administrative Services<br>—Department of Transportation..<br>—Department of Public Works..<br>—Constituent Units of Higher Education. | | —WTO GPA.<br>—DR-CAFTA.<br>—U.S.-Australia FTA.<br>—U.S.-Chile FTA.<br>—U.S.-Morocco FTA.<br>—U.S.-Singapore FTA. |
| Delaware | —Administrative Services (Central Procurement Agency).<br>—State Universities.<br>—State Colleges. | Construction-grade steel (including requirements on subcontracts); motor vehicles; coal. | —WTO GPA.<br>—DR-CAFTA (except Honduras).<br>—U.S.-Australia FTA.<br>—U.S.-Chile FTA.<br>—U.S.-Morocco FTA.<br>—U.S.-Singapore FTA. |
| Florida | Executive branch agencies .... | Construction-grade steel (including requirements on subcontracts); motor vehicles; coal. | —WTO GPA.<br>—DR-CAFTA.<br>—U.S.-Australia FTA.<br>—U.S.-Chile FTA.<br>—U.S.-Morocco FTA.<br>—U.S.-Peru TPA.<br>—U.S.-Singapore FTA. |
| Georgia | —Department of Administrative Services.<br>—Georgia Technology Authority. | Beef; compost; mulch | —U.S.-Australia FTA. |
| Hawaii | Department of Accounting and General Services. | Software developed in the State; construction. | —WTO GPA.<br>—DR-CAFTA (except Honduras).<br>—U.S.-Australia FTA.<br>—U.S.-Chile FTA.<br>—U.S.-Morocco FTA.<br>—U.S.-Singapore FTA. |
| Idaho | Central Procurement Agency (including all colleges and universities subject to central purchasing oversight). | | —WTO GPA.<br>—DR-CAFTA (except Honduras).<br>—U.S.-Australia FTA.<br>—U.S.-Chile FTA.<br>—U.S.-Morocco FTA.<br>—U.S.-Singapore FTA. |
| Illinois | —Department of Central Management Services. | Construction-grade steel (including requirements on subcontracts); motor vehicles; coal. | —WTO GPA.<br>—U.S.-Australia FTA.<br>—U.S.-Chile FTA.<br><br>—U.S.-Peru TPA.<br>—U.S.-Singapore FTA.<br>—U.S.-EC.<br>Exchange of Letters (applies to EC Member States for procurement not covered by WTO GPA and only where the State considers out-of-State suppliers). |
| Iowa | —Department of General Services<br>—Department of Transportation.<br>—Board of Regents' Institutions (universities). | Construction-grade steel (including requirements on subcontracts); motor vehicles; coal. | —WTO GPA.<br>—U.S.-Chile FTA.<br>—U.S.-Singapore FTA. |
| Kansas | Executive branch agencies .... | Construction services; automobiles; aircraft. | —WTO GPA.<br>—U.S.-Australia FTA.<br>—U.S.-Chile FTA.<br>—U.S.-Morocco FTA.<br>—U.S.-Singapore FTA. |
| Kentucky | Division of Purchases, Finance and Administration Cabinet. | Construction projects | —WTO GPA.<br>—DR-CAFTA.<br>—U.S.-Australia FTA.<br>—U.S.-Chile FTA.<br>—U.S.-Morocco FTA.<br>—U.S.-Singapore FTA. |
| Louisiana | Executive branch agencies .... | | —WTO GPA. |

| States | Entities covered | Exclusions | Relevant international agreements |
|---|---|---|---|
| Maine ........................................ | —Department of Administrative and Financial Services<br>—Bureau of General Services (covering State government agencies and school construction).<br>— Department of Transportation.. | Construction-grade steel (including requirements on subcontracts); motor vehicles; coal. | —DR-CAFTA.<br>—U.S.-Australia FTA.<br>—U.S.-Chile FTA.<br>—U.S.-Morocco FTA.<br>—U.S.-Singapore FTA.<br>—WTO GPA.<br>—U.S.-Australia FTA.<br>—U.S.-Chile FTA.<br>—U.S.-Singapore FTA. |
| Maryland ................................. | —Office of the Treasury<br>—Department of the Environment..<br>—Department of General Services..<br>—Department of Housing and Community Development..<br>—Department of Human Resources..<br>—Department of Licensing and Regulation..<br>—Department of Natural Resources..<br>—Department of Public Safety and Correctional Services..<br>—Department of Personnel. ..<br>—Department of Transportation.. | Construction-grade steel (including requirements on subcontracts); motor vehicles; coal. | —WTO GPA.<br>—DR-CAFTA.<br>—U.S.-Australia FTA.<br>—U.S.-Chile FTA.<br>—U.S.-Morocco FTA.<br>—U.S.-Singapore FTA. |
| Massachusetts ......................... | —Executive Office for Administration and Finance.<br>—Executive Office of Communities and Development.<br>—Executive Office of Consumer Affairs.<br>—Executive Office of Economic Affairs.<br>—Executive Office of Education.<br>—Executive Office of Elder Affairs.<br>—Executive Office of Environmental Affairs.<br>—Executive Office of Health and Human Service.<br>—Executive Office of Labor.<br>—Executive Office of Public Safety.<br>—Executive Office of Transportation and Construction. | ................................................ | —WTO GPA.<br>—U.S.-Chile FTA.<br>—U.S.-Singapore FTA. |
| Michigan ................................. | Department of Management and Budget. | Construction-grade steel (including requirements on subcontracts); motor vehicles; coal. | —WTO GPA.<br>—U.S.-Australia FTA.<br>—U.S.-Chile FTA.<br>—U.S.-Singapore FTA. |
| Minnesota ............................... | Executive branch agencies .... | ................................................ | —WTO GPA.<br>—U.S.-Chile FTA.<br>—U.S.-Singapore FTA. |
| Mississippi .............................. | Department of Finance and Administration. | Services ............................... | —WTO GPA.<br>—DR-CAFTA.<br>—U.S.-Australia FTA.<br>—U.S.-Chile FTA.<br>—U.S.-Morocco FTA.<br>—U.S.-Peru TPA.<br>—U.S.-Singapore FTA. |
| Missouri ................................... | —Office of Administration ......<br>—Division of Purchasing and Materials Management. | ................................................ | —WTO GPA.<br>—U.S.-Chile FTA.<br>—U.S.-Singapore FTA. |
| Montana ................................... | Executive branch agencies .... | Goods ................................... | —WTO GPA.<br>—U.S.-Chile FTA.<br>—U.S.-Singapore FTA. |

| States | Entities covered | Exclusions | Relevant international agreements |
|---|---|---|---|
| Nebraska | Central Procurement Agency | | —WTO GPA.<br>—DR-CAFTA.<br>—U.S.-Australia FTA.<br>—U.S.-Chile FTA.<br>—U.S.-Morocco FTA.<br>—U.S.-Singapore FTA. |
| New Hampshire | Central Procurement Agency | Construction-grade steel (including requirements on subcontracts), motor vehicles; coal. | —WTO GPA.<br>—DR-CAFTA.<br>—U.S.-Australia FTA.<br>—U.S.-Chile FTA.<br>—U.S.-Morocco FTA.<br>—U.S.-Singapore FTA. |
| New York | —State agencies<br>—State university system.<br>—Public authorities and public benefit corporations, with the exception of those entities with multi-State mandates. | Construction-grade steel (including requirements on subcontracts); motor vehicles; coal; transit cars, buses and related equipment. | —WTO GPA.<br>—DR-CAFTA.<br>—U.S.-Australia FTA.<br>—U.S.-Chile FTA.<br>—U.S.-Morocco FTA.<br>—U.S.-Peru TPA.<br>—U.S.-Singapore FTA. |
| North Dakota | | | —U.S.-EC Exchange of Letters (applies to EC Member States and only where the State considers out-of-State suppliers). |
| Oklahoma | Department of Central Services and all State agencies and departments subject to the Oklahoma Central Purchasing Act. | Construction services; construction-grade steel (including requirements on subcontracts); motor vehicles; coal. | —WTO GPA.<br>—U.S.-Australia FTA.<br>—U.S.-Chile FTA.<br>—U.S.-Peru TPA.<br>—U.S.-Singapore FTA. |
| Oregon | Department of Administrative Services. | | —WTO GPA.<br>—DR-CAFTA (except Honduras).<br>—U.S.-Australia FTA.<br>—U.S.-Chile FTA.<br>—U.S.-Morocco FTA.<br>—U.S.-Singapore FTA. |
| Pennsylvania | Executive branch agencies, including:<br>—Governor's Office.<br>—Department of the Auditor General..<br>—Treasury Department.<br>—Department of Agriculture.<br>—Department of Banking.<br>—Pennsylvania Securities Commission.<br>—Department of Health.<br>—Department of Transportation.<br>—Insurance Department.<br>—Department of Aging.<br>—Department of Correction.<br>—Department of Labor and Industry.<br>—Department of Military Affairs.<br>—Office of Attorney General.<br>—Department of General Services.<br>—Department of Education.<br>—Public Utility Commission.<br>—Department of Revenue.<br>—Department of State.<br>—Pennsylvania State Police.<br>—Department of Public Welfare.<br>—Fish Commission.<br>—Game Commission.<br>—Department of Commerce.<br>—Board of Probation and Parole.<br>—Liquor Control Board.<br>—Milk Marketing Board. | Construction-grade steel (including requirements on subcontracts); motor vehicles; coal. | —WTO GPA.<br>—U.S.-Australia FTA.<br>—U.S.-Chile FTA.<br>—U.S.-Singapore FTA. |

| States | Entities covered | Exclusions | Relevant international agreements |
|---|---|---|---|
| | —Lieutenant Governor's Office.<br>—Department of Community Affairs.<br>—Pennsylvania Historical and Museum Commission.<br>—Pennsylvania Emergency Management Agency.<br>—State Civil Service Commission.<br>—Pennsylvania Public Television Network.<br>—Department of Environmental Resources.<br>—State Tax Equalization Board.<br>—Department of Public Welfare.<br>—State Employees' Retirement System.<br>—Pennsylvania Municipal Retirement Board.<br>—Public School Employees' Retirement System.<br>—Pennsylvania Crime Commission.<br>—Executive Offices. | | |
| Rhode Island ........................... | Executive branch agencies .... | Boats, automobiles, buses and related equipment. | —WTO GPA.<br>—DR-CAFTA (except Honduras).<br>—U.S.-Australia FTA.<br>—U.S.-Chile FTA.<br>—U.S.-Morocco FTA.<br>—U.S.-Singapore FTA. |
| South Dakota .......................... | Central Procuring Agency (including universities and penal institutions). | Beef ...................................... | —WTO GPA.<br>—DR-CAFTA.<br>—U.S.-Australia FTA.<br>—U.S.-Chile FTA.<br>—U.S.-Morocco FTA.<br>—U.S.-Singapore FTA. |
| Tennessee ............................. | Executive branch agencies .... | Services; construction ........... | —WTO GPA-U.S.-Australia FTA.<br>—U.S.-Chile FTA.<br>—U.S.-Singapore FTA. |
| Texas ..................................... | Texas Building and Procurement Commission. | .............................................. | —WTO GPA.<br>—DR-CAFTA.<br>—U.S.-Australia FTA.<br>—U.S.-Chile FTA.<br>—U.S.-Morocco FTA.<br>—U.S.-Peru TPA.<br>—U.S.-Singapore FTA. |
| Utah ...................................... | Executive branch agencies .... | .............................................. | —WTO GPA.<br>—DR-CAFTA (except Honduras).<br>—U.S.-Australia FTA.<br>—U.S.-Chile FTA.<br>—U.S.-Morocco FTA.<br>—U.S.-Peru TPA.<br>—U.S.-Singapore FTA. |
| Vermont ................................. | Executive branch agencies .... | .............................................. | —WTO GPA.<br>—DR-CAFTA.<br>—U.S.-Australia FTA.<br>—U.S.-Chile FTA.<br>—U.S.-Morocco FTA.<br>—U.S.-Singapore FTA. |
| Washington ............................. | Executive branch agencies, including:<br>—General Administration.<br>—Department of Transportation.<br>—State Universities. | Fuel; paper products; boats; ships; and vessels. | —WTO GPA.<br>—DR-CAFTA.<br>—U.S.-Australia FTA.<br>—U.S.-Chile FTA.<br>—U.S.-Morocco FTA.<br>—U.S.-Singapore FTA. |

| States | Entities covered | Exclusions | Relevant international agreements |
|---|---|---|---|
| West Virginia | | | —U.S.-EC Exchange of Letters (applies to EC Member States and only where the State considers out-of-State suppliers). |
| Wisconsin | Executive branch agencies, including:<br>—Department of Administration.<br>—State Correctional Institutions.<br>—Department of Development.<br>—Educational Communications Board.<br>—Department of Employment Relations.<br>—State Historical Society.<br>—Department of Health and Social Services.<br>—Insurance Commissioner.<br>—Department of Justice.<br>—Lottery Board.<br>—Department of Natural Resources.<br>—Administration for Public Instruction.<br>—Racing Board.<br>—Department of Revenue.<br>—State Fair Park Board.<br>—Department of Transportation.<br>—State University System. | | —WTO GPA.<br>—U.S.-Chile FTA.<br>—U.S.-Singapore FTA. |
| Wyoming | —Procurement Services Division<br>—Wyoming Department of Transportation.<br>—University of Wyoming. | Construction-grade steel (including requirements on subcontracts); motor vehicles; coal. | —WTO GPA.<br>—DR-CAFTA.<br>—U.S.-Australia FTA.<br>—U.S.-Chile FTA.<br>—U.S.-Morocco FTA.<br>—U.S.-Singapore FTA. |

| Other sub-federal entities | Entities covered | Exclusions | Relevant international agreements |
|---|---|---|---|
| Puerto Rico | —Department of State<br>—Department of Justice.<br>—Department of the Treasury.<br><br>—Department of Labor and Human Resources.<br>—Department of Natural and Environmental Resources.<br>—Department of Consumer Affairs.<br>—Department of Sports and Recreation. | Construction services<br><br>—Department of Economic Development and Commerce. | —DR-CAFTA.<br>—U.S.-Peru TPA. |
| Port Authority of New York and New Jersey. | | Restrictions attached to Federal funds for airport projects; maintenance, repair and operating materials and supplies. | —WTO GPA (except Canada).<br>—U.S.-Chile FTA.<br>—U.S.-Singapore FTA. |
| Port of Baltimore | | Restrictions attached to Federal funds for airport projects. | —WTO GPA (except Canada).<br>—U.S.-Chile FTA.<br>—U.S.-Singapore FTA. |
| New York Power Authority | | Restrictions attached to Federal funds for airport projects; conditions specified for the State of New York | —WTO GPA (except Canada).<br>—U.S.-Chile FTA.<br>—U.S.-Singapore FTA. |

| States | Entities covered | Exclusions | Relevant international agreements |
|---|---|---|---|
| Massachusetts Port Authority .. | ............................................. | ............................................. | U.S.-EC Exchange of Letters (applies to EC Member States and only where the Port Authority considers out-of-State suppliers). |
| Boston, Chicago, Dallas, Detroit, Indianapolis, Nashville, and San Antonio. | ............................................. | ............................................. | U.S.-EC Exchange of Letters (only applies to EC Member States and where the city considers out-of-city suppliers). |

| Other entities | Entities covered | Exclusions | Relevant international agreements |
|---|---|---|---|
| Rural Utilities Service (waiver of Buy American restriction on financing for all power generation projects). | Any recipient ........................... | ............................................. | —WTO GPA.<br>—DR-CAFTA.<br>—NAFTA.<br>—U.S.-Australia FTA.<br>—U.S.-Bahrain FTA.<br>—U.S.-Chile FTA.<br>—U.S.-Morocco FTA.<br>—U.S.-Oman FTA.<br>—U.S.-Peru TPA.<br>—U.S.-Singapore FTA. |
| Rural Utilities Service (waiver of Buy American restriction on financing for telecommunications projects). | Any recipient ........................... | ............................................. | —NAFTA.<br>—U.S.-Israel FTA. |
| U.S. Department of Agriculture, Rural Utilities Services, *Water and Waste Disposal Programs* (exclusion of Canadian iron, steel and manufactured products from domestic purchasing restriction in Section 1605 of American Recovery and Reinvestment Act of 2009). | Any recipient ........................... | ............................................. | U.S.-Canada Agreement. |
| U.S. Department of Agriculture, Rural Housing Service, *Community Facilities Program* (exclusion of Canadian iron, steel and manufactured products from domestic purchasing restriction in Section 1605 of American Recovery and Reinvestment Act of 2009). | Any recipient ........................... | ............................................. | U.S.-Canada Agreement. |
| U.S. Department of Energy, Office of Energy Efficiency and Renewable Energy, *Energy Efficiency and Conservation Block Grants* (exclusion of Canadian iron, steel and manufactured products from domestic purchasing restriction in Section 1605 of American Recovery and Reinvestment Act of 2009). | Any recipient ........................... | ............................................. | U.S.-Canada Agreement. |
| U.S. Department of Energy, Office of Energy Efficiency and Renewable Energy, *State Energy Program* (exclusion of Canadian iron, steel and manufactured products from domestic purchasing restriction in Section 1605 of American Recovery and Reinvestment Act of 2009 (ARRA). | Any recipient ........................... | ............................................. | U.S.-Canada Agreement. |

| States | Entities covered | Exclusions | Relevant international agreements |
|---|---|---|---|
| U.S. Department of Housing and Urban Development, Office of Community Planning and Development, *Community Development Block Grants Recovery* (CDBG–R) (exclusion of Canadian iron, steel and manufactured products from domestic purchasing restriction in Section 1605 of American Recovery and Reinvestment Act of 2009). | Any recipient ........................ | ............................................. | U.S.-Canada Agreement. |
| U.S. Department of Housing and Urban Development, Office of Public and Indian Housing, *Public Housing Capital Fund* (exclusion of Canadian iron, steel and manufactured products from domestic purchasing restriction in Section 1605 of American Recovery and Reinvestment Act of 2009). | Any recipient ........................ | ............................................. | U.S.-Canada Agreement. |
| U.S. Environmental Protection *Clean Water and Drinking Water State Revolving Funds* Agency for projects funded by reallocated ARRA funds where the contracts are signed after February 17, 2010 (exclusion of Canadian iron, steel and manufactured products from domestic purchasing restriction in Section 1605 of American Recovery and Reinvestment Act of 2009). | Any recipient ........................ | ............................................. | U.S.-Canada Agreement. |

*General Exceptions:* The following restrictions and exceptions are excluded from U.S. obligations under international agreements:

1. The restrictions attached to Federal funds to States for mass transit and highway projects.

2. Dredging.

*The World Trade Organization Government Procurement Agreement (WTO GPA) Parties:* Aruba, Austria, Belgium, Bulgaria, Canada, Chinese Taipei (Taiwan), Cyprus, Czech Republic, Denmark, Estonia, Finland, France, Germany, Greece, Hong Kong, Hungary, Iceland, Ireland, Israel, Italy, Japan, Korea (Republic of), Latvia, Liechtenstein, Lithuania, Luxembourg, Malta, Netherlands, Norway, Poland, Portugal, Romania, Singapore, Slovak Republic, Slovenia, Spain, Sweden, Switzerland, and United Kingdom.

*The Free Trade Agreements and the respective Parties to the agreements are:*

(1) Dominican Republic-Central America-United States Free Trade Agreement (DR-CAFTA): Costa Rica, Dominican Republic, El Salvador, Guatemala, Honduras, and Nicaragua;

(2) North American Free Trade Agreement (NAFTA): Canada and Mexico;

(3) United States-Australia Free Trade Agreement (U.S.-Australia FTA);

(4) United States-Bahrain Free Trade Agreement (U.S.-Bahrain FTA);

(5) United States-Chile Free Trade Agreement (U.S.-Chile FTA);

(6) United States-Israel Free Trade Agreement (U.S.-Israel FTA);

(7) United States-Morocco Free Trade Agreement (U.S.-Morocco FTA);

(8) United States-Oman Free Trade Agreement (U.S.-Oman FTA);

(9) United States-Peru Trade Promotion Agreement (U.S.-Peru TPA); and

(10) United States-Singapore Free Trade Agreement (U.S.-Singapore FTA).

*United States-European Communities Exchange of Letters (May 30, 1995) (U.S.-EC Exchange of Letters)* applies to EC Member States: Austria, Belgium, Bulgaria, Cyprus, Czech Republic, Denmark, Estonia, Finland, France, Germany, Greece, Hungary, Ireland, Italy, Latvia, Lithuania, Luxembourg, Malta, Netherlands, Poland, Portugal, Romania, Slovak Republic, Slovenia, Spain, Sweden, and United Kingdom.

*Agreement between the Government of Canada and the Government of the United States of*

*America on Government Procurement (Feb. 10, 2010) (U.S.-Canada Agreement):* Applies only to Canada.

[75 FR 14324, Mar. 25, 2010]

## Subpart C—Wage Rate Requirements Under Section 1606 of the American Recovery and Reinvestment Act of 2009

### §176.180 Procedure.

The award official shall insert the standard award term in this subpart in all awards funded in whole or in part with Recovery Act funds.

### §176.190 Award term—Wage rate requirements under Section 1606 of the Recovery Act.

When issuing announcements or requesting applications for Recovery Act programs or activities that may involve construction, alteration, maintenance, or repair the agency shall use the award term described in the following paragraphs:

(a) Section 1606 of the Recovery Act requires that all laborers and mechanics employed by contractors and subcontractors on projects funded directly by or assisted in whole or in part by and through the Federal Government pursuant to the Recovery Act shall be paid wages at rates not less than those prevailing on projects of a character similar in the locality as determined by the Secretary of Labor in accordance with subchapter IV of chapter 31 of title 40, United States Code.

Pursuant to Reorganization Plan No. 14 and the Copeland Act, 40 U.S.C. 3145, the Department of Labor has issued regulations at 29 CFR parts 1, 3, and 5 to implement the Davis-Bacon and related Acts. Regulations in 29 CFR 5.5 instruct agencies concerning application of the standard Davis-Bacon contract clauses set forth in that section. Federal agencies providing grants, cooperative agreements, and loans under the Recovery Act shall ensure that the standard Davis-Bacon contract clauses found in 29 CFR 5.5(a) are incorporated in any resultant covered contracts that are in excess of $2,000 for construction, alteration or repair (including painting and decorating).

(b) For additional guidance on the wage rate requirements of section 1606, contact your awarding agency. Recipients of grants, cooperative agreements and loans should direct their initial inquiries concerning the application of Davis-Bacon requirements to a particular federally assisted project to the Federal agency funding the project. The Secretary of Labor retains final coverage authority under Reorganization Plan Number 14.

## Subpart D—Single Audit Information for Recipients of Recovery Act Funds

### §176.200 Procedure.

The award official shall insert the standard award term in this subpart in all awards funded in whole or in part with Recovery Act funds.

### §176.210 Award term—Recovery Act transactions listed in Schedule of Expenditures of Federal Awards and Recipient Responsibilities for Informing Subrecipients.

The award term described in this section shall be used by agencies to clarify recipient responsibilities regarding tracking and documenting Recovery Act expenditures:

(a) To maximize the transparency and accountability of funds authorized under the American Recovery and Reinvestment Act of 2009 (Pub. L. 111–5) (Recovery Act) as required by Congress and in accordance with 2 CFR 215.21 "Uniform Administrative Requirements for Grants and Agreements" and OMB Circular A–102 Common Rules provisions, recipients agree to maintain records that identify adequately the source and application of Recovery Act funds. OMB Circular A–102 is available at *http://www.whitehouse.gov/omb/circulars/a102/a102.html.*

(b) For recipients covered by the Single Audit Act Amendments of 1996 and OMB Circular A–133, "Audits of States, Local Governments, and Non-Profit Organizations," recipients agree to separately identify the expenditures for Federal awards under the Recovery Act on the Schedule of Expenditures of Federal Awards (SEFA) and the Data Collection Form (SF–SAC) required by OMB Circular A–133. OMB Circular A–133 is available at *http://www.whitehouse.gov/omb/circulars/a133/*

*a133.html.* This shall be accomplished by identifying expenditures for Federal awards made under the Recovery Act separately on the SEFA, and as separate rows under Item 9 of Part III on the SF–SAC by CFDA number, and inclusion of the prefix "ARRA-" in identifying the name of the Federal program on the SEFA and as the first characters in Item 9d of Part III on the SF–SAC.

(c) Recipients agree to separately identify to each subrecipient, and document at the time of subaward and at the time of disbursement of funds, the Federal award number, CFDA number, and amount of Recovery Act funds. When a recipient awards Recovery Act funds for an existing program, the information furnished to subrecipients shall distinguish the subawards of incremental Recovery Act funds from regular subawards under the existing program.

(d) Recipients agree to require their subrecipients to include on their SEFA information to specifically identify Recovery Act funding similar to the requirements for the recipient SEFA described above. This information is needed to allow the recipient to properly monitor subrecipient expenditure of ARRA funds as well as oversight by the Federal awarding agencies, Offices of Inspector General and the Government Accountability Office.

# PARTS 177–179 [RESERVED]

# PART 180—OMB GUIDELINES TO AGENCIES ON GOVERNMENT-WIDE DEBARMENT AND SUSPENSION (NONPROCUREMENT)

## Subpart H—Debarment

## Subpart I—Definitions

APPENDIX TO PART 180—COVERED TRANSACTIONS

AUTHORITY: Sec. 2455, Pub. L. 103–355, 108 Stat. 3327; E.O. 12549, 3 CFR, 1986 Comp., p.189; E.O. 12689, 3 CFR, 1989 Comp., p. 235.

SOURCE: 70 FR 51865, Aug. 31, 2005, unless otherwise noted.

EDITORIAL NOTE: Nomenclature changes to part 180 appear at 79 FR 75879, Dec. 19, 2014.

### § 180.5  What does this part do?

This part provides Office of Management and Budget (OMB) guidance for Federal agencies on the governmentwide debarment and suspension system for nonprocurement programs and activities.

### § 180.10  How is this part organized?

This part is organized in two segments.

(a) Sections 180.5 through 180.45 contain general policy direction for Federal agencies' use of the standards in subparts A through I of this part.

(b) Subparts A through I of this part contain uniform governmentwide standards that Federal agencies are to use to specify—

(1) The types of transactions that are covered by the nonprocurement debarment and suspension system;

(2) The effects of an exclusion under that nonprocurement system, including reciprocal effects with the governmentwide debarment and suspension system for procurement;

(3) The criteria and minimum due process to be used in nonprocurement debarment and suspension actions; and

(4) Related policies and procedures to ensure the effectiveness of those actions.

### § 180.15 To whom does the guidance apply?

The guidance provides OMB guidance only to Federal agencies. Publication of the guidance in the CFR does not change its nature—it is guidance and not regulation. Federal agencies' implementation of the guidance governs the rights and responsibilities of other persons affected by the nonprocurement debarment and suspension system.

### § 180.20 What must a Federal agency do to implement these guidelines?

As required by Section 3 of E.O. 12549, each Federal agency with nonprocurement programs and activities covered by subparts A through I of the guidance must issue regulations consistent with those subparts.

### § 180.25 What must a Federal agency address in its implementation of the guidance?

Each Federal agency implementing regulation:

(a) Must establish policies and procedures for that agency's nonprocurement debarment and suspension programs and activities that are consistent with the guidance. When adopted by a Federal agency, the provisions of the guidance have regulatory effect for that agency's programs and activities.

(b) Must address some matters for which these guidelines give each Federal agency some discretion. Specifically, the regulation must—

(1) Identify either the Federal agency head or the title of the designated official who is authorized to grant exceptions under § 180.135 to let an excluded person participate in a covered transaction.

(2) State whether the agency includes as covered transactions an additional tier of contracts awarded under covered nonprocurement transactions, as permitted under § 180.220(c).

(3) Identify the method(s) an agency official may use, when entering into a covered transaction with a primary tier participant, to communicate to the participant the requirements described in § 180.435. Examples of methods are an award term that requires compliance as a condition of the award; an assurance of compliance obtained at time of application; or a certification.

(4) State whether the Federal agency specifies a particular method that participants must use to communicate compliance requirements to lower-tier participants, as described in § 180.330(a). If there is a specified method, the regulation needs to require agency officials, when entering into covered transactions with primary tier participants, to communicate that requirement.

(c) May also, at the agency's option:

(1) Identify any specific types of transactions that the Federal agency includes as "nonprocurement transactions" in addition to the examples provided in § 180.970.

(2) Identify any types of nonprocurement transactions that the Federal agency exempts from coverage under these guidelines, as authorized under § 180.215(g)(2).

(3) Identify specific examples of types of individuals who would be "principals" under the Federal agency's nonprocurement programs and transactions, in addition to the types of individuals described at § 180.995.

(4) Specify the Federal agency's procedures, if any, by which a respondent may appeal a suspension or debarment decision.

(5) Identify by title the officials designated by the Federal agency head as debarring officials under § 180.930 or suspending officials under § 180.1010.

(6) Include a subpart covering disqualifications, as authorized in § 180.45.

(7) Include any provisions authorized by OMB.

[70 FR 51865, Aug. 31, 2005, as amended at 71 FR 66432, Nov. 15, 2006; 79 FR 75879, Dec. 19, 2014]

### § 180.30 Where does a Federal agency implement these guidelines?

Each Federal agency that participates in the governmentwide nonprocurement debarment and suspension system must issue a regulation implementing these guidelines within its chapter in subtitle B of this title of the Code of Federal Regulations.

## § 180.35  By when must a Federal agency implement these guidelines?

Federal agencies must submit proposed regulations to the OMB for review within nine months of the issuance of these guidelines and issue final regulations within eighteen months of these guidelines.

## § 180.40  How are these guidelines maintained?

The Interagency Committee on Debarment and Suspension established by section 4 of E.O. 12549 recommends to the OMB any needed revisions to the guidelines in this part. The OMB publishes proposed changes to the guidelines in the FEDERAL REGISTER for public comment, considers comments with the help of the Interagency Committee on Debarment and Suspension, and issues the final guidelines.

## § 180.45  Do these guidelines cover persons who are disqualified, as well as those who are excluded from nonprocurement transactions?

A Federal agency may add a subpart covering disqualifications to its regulation implementing these guidelines, but the guidelines in subparts A through I of this part—

(a) Address disqualified persons only to—

(1) Provide for their inclusion in SAM Exclusions; and

(2) State responsibilities of Federal agencies and participants to check for disqualified persons before entering into covered transactions.

(b) Do not specify the—

(1) Transactions for which a disqualified person is ineligible. Those transactions vary on a case-by-case basis, because they depend on the language of the specific statute, Executive order or regulation that caused the disqualification;

(2) Entities to which a disqualification applies; or

(3) Process that a Federal agency uses to disqualify a person. Unlike exclusion under subparts A through I of this part, disqualification is frequently not a discretionary action that a Federal agency takes, and may include special procedures.

# Subpart A—General

## § 180.100  How are subparts A through I organized?

(a) Each subpart contains information related to a broad topic or specific audience with special responsibilities, as shown in the following table:

| In subpart . . . | You will find provisions related to . . . |
|---|---|
| A | general information about Subparts A through I of this part. |
| B | the types of transactions that are covered by the Governmentwide nonprocurement suspension and debarment system. |
| C | the responsibilities of persons who participate in covered transactions. |
| D | the responsibilities of Federal agency officials who are authorized to enter into covered transactions. |
| E | the responsibilities of Federal agencies for entering information into SAM Exclusions |
| F | the general principles governing suspension, debarment, voluntary exclusion and settlement. |
| G | suspension actions. |
| H | debarment actions. |
| I | definitions of terms used in this part. |

(b) The following table shows which subparts may be of special interest to you, depending on who you are:

| If you are . . . | See Subpart(s) . . . |
|---|---|
| (1) a participant or principal in a nonprocurement transaction | A, B, C and I. |
| (2) a respondent in a suspension action | A, B, F, G and I. |
| (3) a respondent in a debarment action | A, B, F, H and I. |
| (4) a suspending official | A, B, E, F, G and I. |
| (5) a debarring official | A, B, D, F, H and I. |
| (6) an Federal agency official authorized to enter into a covered transaction | A, B, D, E and I. |

**§180.105 How is this part written?**

(a) This part uses a "plain language" format to make it easier for the general public and business community to use. The section headings and text, often in the form of questions and answers, must be read together.

(b) Pronouns used within this part, such as "I" and "you," change from subpart to subpart depending on the audience being addressed.

(c) The "Covered Transactions" diagram in the appendix to this part shows the levels or "tiers" at which a Federal agency may enforce an exclusion.

**§180.110 Do terms in this part have special meanings?**

This part uses terms throughout the text that have special meaning. Those terms are defined in subpart I of this part. For example, three important terms are—

(a) *Exclusion or excluded*, which refers only to discretionary actions taken by a suspending or debarring official under Executive Order 12549 and Executive Order 12689 or under the Federal Acquisition Regulation (48 CFR part 9, subpart 9.4);

(b) *Disqualification or disqualified*, which refers to prohibitions under specific statutes, executive orders (other than Executive Order 12549 and Executive Order 12689), or other authorities. Disqualifications frequently are not subject to the discretion of a Federal agency official, may have a different scope than exclusions, or have special conditions that apply to the disqualification; and

(c) *Ineligibility or ineligible*, which generally refers to a person who is either excluded or disqualified.

**§180.115 What do Subparts A through I of this part do?**

Subparts A through I of this part provide for reciprocal exclusion of persons who have been excluded under the Federal Acquisition Regulation, and provide for the consolidated listing of all persons who are excluded, or disqualified by statute, executive order or other legal authority.

**§180.120 Do subparts A through I of this part apply to me?**

Portions of subparts A through I of this part (see table at §180.100(b)) apply to you if you are a—

(a) Person who has been, is, or may reasonably be expected to be, a participant or principal in a covered transaction;

(b) Respondent (a person against whom a Federal agency has initiated a debarment or suspension action);

(c) Federal agency debarring or suspending official; or

(d) Federal agency official who is authorized to enter into covered transactions with non-Federal parties.

**§180.125 What is the purpose of the nonprocurement debarment and suspension system?**

(a) To protect the public interest, the Federal Government ensures the integrity of Federal programs by conducting business only with responsible persons.

(b) A Federal agency uses the nonprocurement debarment and suspension system to exclude from Federal programs persons who are not presently responsible.

(c) An exclusion is a serious action that a Federal agency may take only to protect the public interest. A Federal agency may not exclude a person or commodity for the purposes of punishment.

**§180.130 How does an exclusion restrict a person's involvement in covered transactions?**

With the exceptions stated in §§180.135, 315, and 420, a person who is excluded by any Federal agency may not:

(a) Be a participant in a Federal agency transaction that is a covered transaction; or

(b) Act as a principal of a person participating in one of those covered transactions.

**§180.135 May a Federal agency grant an exception to let an excluded person participate in a covered transaction?**

(a) A Federal agency head or designee may grant an exception permitting an excluded person to participate in a particular covered transaction. If the agency head or designee grants an exception, the exception must be in writing and state the reason(s) for deviating from the governmentwide policy in Executive Order 12549.

(b) An exception granted by one Federal agency for an excluded person does not extend to the covered transactions of another Federal agency.

### § 180.140 Does an exclusion under the nonprocurement system affect a person's eligibility for Federal procurement contracts?

If any Federal agency excludes a person under Executive Order 12549 or Executive Order 12689, on or after August 25, 1995, the excluded person is also ineligible for Federal procurement transactions under the FAR. Therefore, an exclusion under this part has reciprocal effect in Federal procurement transactions.

### § 180.145 Does an exclusion under the Federal procurement system affect a person's eligibility to participate in nonprocurement transactions?

If any Federal agency excludes a person under the FAR on or after August 25, 1995, the excluded person is also ineligible to participate in Federal agencies' nonprocurement covered transactions. Therefore, an exclusion under the FAR has reciprocal effect in Federal nonprocurement transactions.

### § 180.150 Against whom may a Federal agency take an exclusion action?

Given a cause that justifies an exclusion under this part, a Federal agency may exclude any person who has been, is, or may reasonably be expected to be a participant or principal in a covered transaction.

### § 180.155 How do I know if a person is excluded?

Check the Governmentwide System for Award Management Exclusions (SAM Exclusions) to determine whether a person is excluded. The General Services Administration (GSA) maintains the SAM Exclusions and makes it available, as detailed in Subpart E of this part. When a Federal agency takes an action to exclude a person under the nonprocurement or procurement debarment and suspension system, the agency enters the information about the ex-

cluded person into the SAM Exclusions.

[70 FR 51865, Aug. 31, 2005, as amended at 79 FR 75879, Dec. 19, 2014]

## Subpart B—Covered Transactions

### § 180.200 What is a covered transaction?

A covered transaction is a nonprocurement or procurement transaction that is subject to the prohibitions of this part. It may be a transaction at—

(a) The primary tier, between a Federal agency and a person (see appendix to this part); or

(b) A lower tier, between a participant in a covered transaction and another person.

### § 180.205 Why is it important if a particular transaction is a covered transaction?

The importance of whether a transaction is a covered transaction depends upon who you are.

(a) As a participant in the transaction, you have the responsibilities laid out in subpart C of this part. Those include responsibilities to the person or Federal agency at the next higher tier from whom you received the transaction, if any. They also include responsibilities if you subsequently enter into other covered transactions with persons at the next lower tier.

(b) As a Federal official who enters into a primary tier transaction, you have the responsibilities laid out in subpart D of this part.

(c) As an excluded person, you may not be a participant or principal in the transaction unless—

(1) The person who entered into the transaction with you allows you to continue your involvement in a transaction that predates your exclusion, as permitted under § 180.310 or § 180.415; or

(2) A Federal agency official obtains an exception from the agency head or designee to allow you to be involved in the transaction, as permitted under § 180.135.

## §180.210 Which nonprocurement transactions are covered transactions?

All nonprocurement transactions, as defined in §180.970, are covered transactions unless listed in the exemptions under §180.215.

## §180.215 Which nonprocurement transactions are not covered transactions?

The following types of nonprocurement transactions are not covered transactions:

(a) A direct award to—

(1) A foreign government or foreign governmental entity;

(2) A public international organization;

(3) An entity owned (in whole or in part) or controlled by a foreign government; or

(4) Any other entity consisting wholly or partially of one or more foreign governments or foreign governmental entities.

(b) A benefit to an individual as a personal entitlement without regard to the individual's present responsibility (but benefits received in an individual's business capacity are not excepted). For example, if a person receives social security benefits under the Supplemental Security Income provisions of the Social Security Act, 42 U.S.C. 1301 *et seq.*, those benefits are not covered transactions and, therefore, are not affected if the person is excluded.

(c) Federal employment.

(d) A transaction that a Federal agency needs to respond to a national or agency-recognized emergency or disaster.

(e) A permit, license, certificate or similar instrument issued as a means to regulate public health, safety or the environment, unless a Federal agency specifically designates it to be a covered transaction.

(f) An incidental benefit that results from ordinary governmental operations.

(g) Any other transaction if—

(1) The application of an exclusion to the transaction is prohibited by law; or

(2) A Federal agency's regulation exempts it from coverage under this part.

## §180.220 Are any procurement contracts included as covered transactions?

(a) Covered transactions under this part—

(1) Do not include any procurement contracts awarded directly by a Federal agency; but

(2) Do include some procurement contracts awarded by non-Federal participants in nonprocurement covered transactions.

(b) Specifically, a contract for goods or services is a covered transaction if any of the following applies:

(1) The contract is awarded by a participant in a nonprocurement transaction that is covered under §180.210, and the amount of the contract is expected to equal or exceed $25,000.

(2) The contract requires the consent of an official of a Federal agency. In that case, the contract, regardless of the amount, always is a covered transaction, and it does not matter who awarded it. For example, it could be a subcontract awarded by a contractor at a tier below a nonprocurement transaction, as shown in the appendix to this part.

(3) The contract is for Federally-required audit services.

(c) A subcontract also is a covered transaction if,—

(1) It is awarded by a participant in a procurement transaction under a nonprocurement transaction of a Federal agency that extends the coverage of paragraph (b)(1) of this section to additional tiers of contracts (see the diagram in the appendix to this part showing that optional lower tier coverage); and

(2) The value of the subcontract is expected to equal or exceed $25,000.

[70 FR 51865, Aug. 31, 2005, as amended at 71 FR 66432, Nov. 15, 2006]

## §180.225 How do I know if a transaction in which I may participate is a covered transaction?

As a participant in a transaction, you will know that it is a covered transaction because the Federal agency regulations governing the transaction, the appropriate Federal agency official or participant at the next higher tier who enters into the transaction with you, will tell you that you must comply with applicable portions of this part.

# Subpart C—Responsibilities of Participants Regarding Transactions Doing Business With Other Persons

### § 180.300 What must I do before I enter into a covered transaction with another person at the next lower tier?

When you enter into a covered transaction with another person at the next lower tier, you must verify that the person with whom you intend to do business is not excluded or disqualified. You do this by:

(a) Checking SAM Exclusions; or

(b) Collecting a certification from that person; or

(c) Adding a clause or condition to the covered transaction with that person.

[70 FR 51865, Aug. 31, 2005, as amended at 71 FR 66432, Nov. 15, 2006]

### § 180.305 May I enter into a covered transaction with an excluded or disqualified person?

(a) You as a participant may not enter into a covered transaction with an excluded person, unless the Federal agency responsible for the transaction grants an exception under § 180.135.

(b) You may not enter into any transaction with a person who is disqualified from that transaction, unless you have obtained an exception under the disqualifying statute, Executive order, or regulation.

### § 180.310 What must I do if a Federal agency excludes a person with whom I am already doing business in a covered transaction?

(a) You as a participant may continue covered transactions with an excluded person if the transactions were in existence when the agency excluded the person. However, you are not required to continue the transactions, and you may consider termination. You should make a decision about whether to terminate and the type of termination action, if any, only after a thorough review to ensure that the action is proper and appropriate.

(b) You may not renew or extend covered transactions (other than no-cost time extensions) with any excluded person, unless the Federal agency responsible for the transaction grants an exception under § 180.135.

### § 180.315 May I use the services of an excluded person as a principal under a covered transaction?

(a) You as a participant may continue to use the services of an excluded person as a principal under a covered transaction if you were using the services of that person in the transaction before the person was excluded. However, you are not required to continue using that person's services as a principal. You should make a decision about whether to discontinue that person's services only after a thorough review to ensure that the action is proper and appropriate.

(b) You may not begin to use the services of an excluded person as a principal under a covered transaction unless the Federal agency responsible for the transaction grants an exception for the transaction under § 180.135.

### § 180.320 Must I verify that principals of my covered transactions are eligible to participate?

Yes, you as a participant are responsible for determining whether any of your principals of your covered transactions is excluded or disqualified from participating in the transaction.

You may decide the method and frequency by which you do so. You may, but you are not required to, check SAM Exclusions.

### § 180.325 What happens if I do business with an excluded person in a covered transaction?

If as a participant you knowingly do business with an excluded person, the Federal agency responsible for your transaction may disallow costs, annul or terminate the transaction, issue a stop work order, debar or suspend you, or take other remedies as appropriate.

### § 180.330 What requirements must I pass down to persons at lower tiers with whom I intend to do business?

Before entering into a covered transaction with a participant at the next lower tier, you must require that participant to—

(a) Comply with this subpart as a condition of participation in the transaction. You may do so using any method(s), unless the regulation of the Federal agency responsible for the transaction requires you to use specific methods.

(b) Pass the requirement to comply with this subpart to each person with whom the participant enters into a covered transaction at the next lower tier.

DISCLOSING INFORMATION—PRIMARY TIER PARTICIPANTS

**§ 180.335  What information must I provide before entering into a covered transaction with a Federal agency?**

Before you enter into a covered transaction at the primary tier, you as the participant must notify the Federal agency office that is entering into the transaction with you, if you know that you or any of the principals for that covered transaction:

(a) Are presently excluded or disqualified;

(b) Have been convicted within the preceding three years of any of the offenses listed in § 180.800(a) or had a civil judgment rendered against you for one of those offenses within that time period;

(c) Are presently indicted for or otherwise criminally or civilly charged by a governmental entity (Federal, State or local) with commission of any of the offenses listed in § 180.800(a); or

(d) Have had one or more public transactions (Federal, State, or local) terminated within the preceding three years for cause or default.

**§ 180.340  If I disclose unfavorable information required under § 180.335, will I be prevented from participating in the transaction?**

As a primary tier participant, your disclosure of unfavorable information about yourself or a principal under § 180.335 will not necessarily cause a Federal agency to deny your participation in the covered transaction. The agency will consider the information when it determines whether to enter into the covered transaction. The agency will also consider any additional information or explanation that you elect to submit with the disclosed information.

**§ 180.345  What happens if I fail to disclose information required under § 180.335?**

If a Federal agency later determines that you failed to disclose information under § 180.335 that you knew at the time you entered into the covered transaction, the agency may—

(a) Terminate the transaction for material failure to comply with the terms and conditions of the transaction; or

(b) Pursue any other available remedies, including suspension and debarment.

**§ 180.350  What must I do if I learn of information required under § 180.335 after entering into a covered transaction with a Federal agency?**

At any time after you enter into a covered transaction, you must give immediate written notice to the Federal agency office with which you entered into the transaction if you learn either that—

(a) You failed to disclose information earlier, as required by § 180.335; or

(b) Due to changed circumstances, you or any of the principals for the transaction now meet any of the criteria in § 180.335.

DISCLOSING INFORMATION—LOWER TIER PARTICIPANTS

**§ 180.355  What information must I provide to a higher tier participant before entering into a covered transaction with that participant?**

Before you enter into a covered transaction with a person at the next higher tier, you as a lower tier participant must notify that person if you know that you or any of the principals are presently excluded or disqualified.

**§ 180.360  What happens if I fail to disclose information required under § 180.355?**

If a Federal agency later determines that you failed to tell the person at the higher tier that you were excluded or disqualified at the time you entered into the covered transaction with that person, the agency may pursue any available remedies, including suspension and debarment.

**§ 180.365 What must I do if I learn of information required under § 180.355 after entering into a covered transaction with a higher tier participant?**

At any time after you enter into a lower tier covered transaction with a person at a higher tier, you must provide immediate written notice to that person if you learn either that—

(a) You failed to disclose information earlier, as required by § 180.355; or

(b) Due to changed circumstances, you or any of the principals for the transaction now meet any of the criteria in § 180.355.

## Subpart D—Responsibilities of Federal Agency Officials Regarding Transactions

**§ 180.400 May I enter into a transaction with an excluded or disqualified person?**

(a) You as a Federal agency official may not enter into a covered transaction with an excluded person unless you obtain an exception under § 180.135.

(b) You may not enter into any transaction with a person who is disqualified from that transaction, unless you obtain a waiver or exception under the statute, Executive order, or regulation that is the basis for the person's disqualification.

**§ 180.405 May I enter into a covered transaction with a participant if a principal of the transaction is excluded?**

As a Federal agency official, you may not enter into a covered transaction with a participant if you know that a principal of the transaction is excluded, unless you obtain an exception under § 180.135.

**§ 180.410 May I approve a participant's use of the services of an excluded person?**

After entering into a covered transaction with a participant, you as a Federal agency official may not approve a participant's use of an excluded person as a principal under that trans-

action, unless you obtain an exception under § 180.135.

**§ 180.415 What must I do if a Federal agency excludes the participant or a principal after I enter into a covered transaction?**

(a) You as a Federal agency official may continue covered transactions with an excluded person, or under which an excluded person is a principal, if the transactions were in existence when the person was excluded. You are not required to continue the transactions, however, and you may consider termination. You should make a decision about whether to terminate and the type of termination action, if any, only after a thorough review to ensure that the action is proper.

(b) You may not renew or extend covered transactions (other than no-cost time extensions) with any excluded person, or under which an excluded person is a principal, unless you obtain an exception under § 180.135.

**§ 180.420 May I approve a transaction with an excluded or disqualified person at a lower tier?**

If a transaction at a lower tier is subject to your approval, you as a Federal agency official may not approve—

(a) A covered transaction with a person who is currently excluded, unless you obtain an exception under § 180.135; or

(b) A transaction with a person who is disqualified from that transaction, unless you obtain a waiver or exception under the statute, Executive order, or regulation that is the basis for the person's disqualification.

**§ 180.425 When do I check to see if a person is excluded or disqualified?**

As a Federal agency official, you must check to see if a person is excluded or disqualified before you—

(a) Enter into a primary tier covered transaction;

(b) Approve a principal in a primary tier covered transaction;

(c) Approve a lower tier participant if your agency's approval of the lower tier participant is required;

(d) Approve a principal in connection with a lower tier transaction if your agency's approval of the principal is required.

### §180.430 How do I check to see if a person is excluded or disqualified?

You check to see if a person is excluded or disqualified in two ways:

(a) You as a Federal agency official must check SAM Exclusions when you take any action listed in §180.425.

(b) You must review information that a participant gives you, as required by §180.335, about its status or the status of the principals of a transaction.

### §180.435 What must I require of a primary tier participant?

You as a Federal agency official must require each participant in a primary tier covered transaction to—

(a) Comply with subpart C of this part as a condition of participation in the transaction; and

(b) Communicate the requirement to comply with subpart C of this part to persons at the next lower tier with whom the primary tier participant enters into covered transactions.

### §180.440 What action may I take if a primary tier participant knowingly does business with an excluded or disqualified person?

If a participant knowingly does business with an excluded or disqualified person, you as a Federal agency official may refer the matter for suspension and debarment consideration. You may also disallow costs, annul or terminate the transaction, issue a stop work order, or take any other appropriate remedy.

### §180.445 What action may I take if a primary tier participant fails to disclose the information required under §180.335?

If you as a Federal agency official determine that a participant failed to disclose information, as required by §180.335, at the time it entered into a covered transaction with you, you may—

(a) Terminate the transaction for material failure to comply with the terms and conditions of the transaction; or

(b) Pursue any other available remedies, including suspension and debarment.

### §180.450 What action may I take if a lower tier participant fails to disclose the information required under §180.355 to the next higher tier?

If you as a Federal agency official determine that a lower tier participant failed to disclose information, as required by §180.355, at the time it entered into a covered transaction with a participant at the next higher tier, you may pursue any remedies available to you, including the initiation of a suspension or debarment action.

## Subpart E— System for Award Management Exclusions

### §180.500 What is the purpose of the System for Award Management Exclusions (SAM Exclusions)?

SAM Exclusions is a widely available source of the most current information about persons who are excluded or disqualified from covered transactions.

### §180.505 Who uses SAM Exclusions?

(a) Federal agency officials use SAM Exclusions to determine whether to enter into a transaction with a person, as required under §180.430.

(b) Participants also may, but are not required to, use SAM Exclusions to determine if—

(1) Principals of their transactions are excluded or disqualified, as required under §180.320; or

(2) Persons with whom they are entering into covered transactions at the next lower tier are excluded or disqualified.

(c) Sam Exclusions are available to the general public.

[70 FR 51865, Aug. 31, 2005, as amended at 79 FR 75879, Dec. 19, 2014]

### §180.510 Who maintains SAM Exclusions?

The General Services Administration (GSA) maintains SAM Exclusions. When a Federal agency takes an action to exclude a person under the nonprocurement or procurement debarment and suspension system, the agency enters the information about the excluded person into SAM Exclusions.

## § 180.515 What specific information is in SAM Exclusions?

(a) At a minimum, SAM Exclusions indicates—

(1) The full name (where available) and address of each excluded and disqualified person, in alphabetical order, with cross references if more than one name is involved in a single action;

(2) The type of action;

(3) The cause for the action;

(4) The scope of the action;

(5) Any termination date for the action;

(6) The Federal agency and name and telephone number of the agency point of contact for the action; and

(7) The unique entity identifier approved by the GSA, of the excluded or disqualified person, if available.

(b)(1) The database for SAM Exclusions includes a field for the Taxpayer Identification Number (TIN) (the social security number (SSN) for an individual) of an excluded or disqualified person.

(2) Agencies disclose the SSN of an individual to verify the identity of an individual, only if permitted under the Privacy Act of 1974 and, if appropriate, the Computer Matching and Privacy Protection Act of 1988, as codified in 5 U.S.C. 552(a).

[70 FR 51865, Aug. 31, 2005, as amended at 79 FR 75879, Dec. 19, 2014]

## § 180.520 Who places the information into SAM Exclusions?

Federal agency officials who take actions to exclude persons under this part or officials who are responsible for identifying disqualified persons must enter the following information about those persons into SAM Exclusions:

(a) Information required by § 180.515(a);

(b) The Taxpayer Identification Number (TIN) of the excluded or disqualified person, including the social security number (SSN) for an individual, if the number is available and may be disclosed under law;

(c) Information about an excluded or disqualified person, within three business days, after—

(1) Taking an exclusion action;

(2) Modifying or rescinding an exclusion action;

(3) Finding that a person is disqualified; or

(4) Finding that there has been a change in the status of a person who is listed as disqualified.

[70 FR 51865, Aug. 31, 2005, as amended at 80 FR 43308, July 22, 2015]

## § 180.525 Whom do I ask if I have questions about a person in SAM Exclusions?

If you have questions about a listed person in SAM Exclusions, ask the point of contact for the Federal agency that placed the person's name into SAM Exclusions. You may find the agency point of contact from SAM Exclusions.

## § 180.530 Where can I find SAM Exclusions?

You may access SAM Exclusions through the Internet, currently at *https://www.sam.gov.*

[79 FR 75879, Dec. 19, 2014]

# Subpart F—General Principles Relating to Suspension and Debarment Actions

## § 180.600 How do suspension and debarment actions start?

When Federal agency officials receive information from any source concerning a cause for suspension or debarment, they will promptly report it and the agency will investigate. The officials refer the question of whether to suspend or debar you to their suspending or debarring official for consideration, if appropriate.

## § 180.605 How does suspension differ from debarment?

Suspension differs from debarment in that—

| A suspending official . . . | A debarring official . . . |
|---|---|
| (a) Imposes suspension as a temporary status of in eligibility for procurement and nonprocurement transactions, pending completion of an investigation or legal proceedings. | Imposes debarment for a specified period as a final determination that a person is not presently responsible. |
| (b) Must— | |

| A suspending official . . . | A debarring official . . . |
|---|---|
| (1) Have *adequate evidence* that there may be a cause for debarment of a person; and<br>(2) Conclude that *immediate action* is necessary to protect the Federal interest | Must conclude, based on a *preponderance of the evidence,* that the person has engaged in conduct that warrants debarment. |
| (c) Usually imposes the suspension *first,* and then promptly notifies the suspended person, giving the person an opportunity to contest the suspension and have it lifted. | Imposes debarment *after* giving the respondent notice of the action and an opportunity to contest the proposed debarment. |

## § 180.610 What procedures does a Federal agency use in suspension and debarment actions?

In deciding whether to suspend or debar you, a Federal agency handles the actions as informally as practicable, consistent with principles of fundamental fairness.

(a) For suspension actions, a Federal agency uses the procedures in this subpart and subpart G of this part.

(b) For debarment actions, a Federal agency uses the procedures in this subpart and subpart H of this part.

## § 180.615 How does a Federal agency notify a person of a suspension or debarment action?

(a) The suspending or debarring official sends a written notice to the last known street address, facsimile number, or e-mail address of—

(1) You or your identified counsel; or

(2) Your agent for service of process, or any of your partners, officers, directors, owners, or joint venturers.

(b) The notice is effective if sent to any of these persons.

## § 180.620 Do Federal agencies coordinate suspension and debarment actions?

Yes, when more than one Federal agency has an interest in a suspension or debarment, the agencies may consider designating one agency as the lead agency for making the decision. Agencies are encouraged to establish methods and procedures for coordinating their suspension and debarment actions.

## § 180.625 What is the scope of a suspension or debarment?

If you are suspended or debarred, the suspension or debarment is effective as follows:

(a) Your suspension or debarment constitutes suspension or debarment of all of your divisions and other organizational elements from all covered transactions, unless the suspension or debarment decision is limited—

(1) By its terms to one or more specifically identified individuals, divisions, or other organizational elements; or

(2) To specific types of transactions.

(b) Any affiliate of a participant may be included in a suspension or debarment action if the suspending or debarring official—

(1) Officially names the affiliate in the notice; and

(2) Gives the affiliate an opportunity to contest the action.

## § 180.630 May a Federal agency impute the conduct of one person to another?

For purposes of actions taken under this part, a Federal agency may impute conduct as follows:

(a) *Conduct imputed from an individual to an organization.* A Federal agency may impute the fraudulent, criminal, or other improper conduct of any officer, director, shareholder, partner, employee, or other individual associated with an organization, to that organization when the improper conduct occurred in connection with the individual's performance of duties for or on behalf of that organization, or with the organization's knowledge, approval or acquiescence. The organization's acceptance of the benefits derived from the conduct is evidence of knowledge, approval or acquiescence.

(b) *Conduct imputed from an organization to an individual, or between individuals.* A Federal agency may impute the fraudulent, criminal, or other improper conduct of any organization to an individual, or from one individual to another individual, if the individual to whom the improper conduct is imputed either participated in, had knowledge of, or reason to know of the improper conduct.

(c) *Conduct imputed from one organization to another organization.* A Federal agency may impute the fraudulent, criminal, or other improper conduct of one organization to another organization when the improper conduct occurred in connection with a partnership, joint venture, joint application, association or similar arrangement, or when the organization to whom the improper conduct is imputed has the power to direct, manage, control or influence the activities of the organization responsible for the improper conduct. Acceptance of the benefits derived from the conduct is evidence of knowledge, approval or acquiescence.

### § 180.635  May a Federal agency settle a debarment or suspension action?

Yes, a Federal agency may settle a debarment or suspension action at any time if it is in the best interest of the Federal Government.

### § 180.640  May a settlement include a voluntary exclusion?

Yes, if a Federal agency enters into a settlement with you in which you agree to be excluded, it is called a voluntary exclusion and has government-wide effect.

### § 180.645  Do other Federal agencies know if an agency agrees to a voluntary exclusion?

(a) Yes, the Federal agency agreeing to the voluntary exclusion enters information about it into SAM Exclusions.

(b) Also, any agency or person may contact the Federal agency that agreed to the voluntary exclusion to find out the details of the voluntary exclusion.

### § 180.650  May an administrative agreement be the result of a settlement?

Yes, a Federal agency may enter into an administrative agreement with you as part of the settlement of a debarment or suspension action.

[80 FR 43308, July 22, 2015]

### § 180.655  How will other Federal awarding agencies know about an administrative agreement that is the result of a settlement?

The suspending or debarring official who enters into an administrative agreement with you must report information about the agreement to the designated integrity and performance system within three business days after entering into the agreement. This information is required by section 872 of the Duncan Hunter National Defense Authorization Act for Fiscal Year 2009 (41 U.S.C. 2313).

[80 FR 43308, July 22, 2015]

### § 180.660  Will administrative agreement information about me in the designated integrity and performance system accessible through SAM be corrected or updated?

Yes, the suspending or debarring official who entered information into the designated integrity and performance system about an administrative agreement with you:

(a) Must correct the information within three business days if he or she subsequently learns that any of the information is erroneous.

(b) Must correct in the designated integrity and performance system, within three business days, the ending date of the period during which the agreement is in effect, if the agreement is amended to extend that period.

(c) Must report to the designated integrity and performance system, within three business days, any other modification to the administrative agreement.

(d) Is strongly encouraged to amend the information in the designated integrity and performance system in a timely way to incorporate any update that he or she obtains that could be helpful to Federal awarding agencies who must use the system.

[80 FR 43308, July 22, 2015]

## Subpart G—Suspension

### §180.700 When may the suspending official issue a suspension?

Suspension is a serious action. Using the procedures of this subpart and subpart F of this part, the suspending official may impose suspension only when that official determines that—

(a) There exists an indictment for, or other adequate evidence to suspect, an offense listed under §180.800(a), or

(b) There exists adequate evidence to suspect any other cause for debarment listed under §180.800(b) through (d); and

(c) Immediate action is necessary to protect the public interest.

### §180.705 What does the suspending official consider in issuing a suspension?

(a) In determining the adequacy of the evidence to support the suspension, the suspending official considers how much information is available, how credible it is given the circumstances, whether or not important allegations are corroborated, and what inferences can reasonably be drawn as a result. During this assessment, the suspending official may examine the basic documents, including grants, cooperative agreements, loan authorizations, contracts, and other relevant documents.

(b) An indictment, conviction, civil judgment, or other official findings by Federal, State, or local bodies that determine factual and/or legal matters, constitutes adequate evidence for purposes of suspension actions.

(c) In deciding whether immediate action is needed to protect the public interest, the suspending official has wide discretion. For example, the suspending official may infer the necessity for immediate action to protect the public interest either from the nature of the circumstances giving rise to a cause for suspension or from potential business relationships or involvement with a program of the Federal Government.

### §180.710 When does a suspension take effect?

A suspension is effective when the suspending official signs the decision to suspend.

### §180.715 What notice does the suspending official give me if I am suspended?

After deciding to suspend you, the suspending official promptly sends you a Notice of Suspension advising you—

(a) That you have been suspended;

(b) That your suspension is based on—

(1) An indictment;

(2) A conviction;

(3) Other adequate evidence that you have committed irregularities which seriously reflect on the propriety of further Federal Government dealings with you; or

(4) Conduct of another person that has been imputed to you, or your affiliation with a suspended or debarred person;

(c) Of any other irregularities in terms sufficient to put you on notice without disclosing the Federal Government's evidence;

(d) Of the cause(s) upon which the suspending official relied under §180.700 for imposing suspension;

(e) That your suspension is for a temporary period pending the completion of an investigation or resulting legal or debarment proceedings;

(f) Of the applicable provisions of this subpart, subpart F of this part, and any other agency procedures governing suspension decisionmaking; and

(g) Of the governmentwide effect of your suspension from procurement and nonprocurement programs and activities.

### §180.720 How may I contest a suspension?

If you as a respondent wish to contest a suspension, you or your representative must provide the suspending official with information in opposition to the suspension. You may do this orally or in writing, but any information provided orally that you consider important must also be submitted in writing for the official record.

### §180.725 How much time do I have to contest a suspension?

(a) As a respondent you or your representative must either send, or make arrangements to appear and present, the information and argument to the suspending official within 30 days after you receive the Notice of Suspension.

(b) The Federal agency taking the action considers the notice to be received by you—

(1) When delivered, if the agency mails the notice to the last known street address, or five days after the agency sends it if the letter is undeliverable;

(2) When sent, if the agency sends the notice by facsimile or five days after the agency sends it if the facsimile is undeliverable; or

(3) When delivered, if the agency sends the notice by e-mail or five days after the agency sends it if the e-mail is undeliverable.

### § 180.730 What information must I provide to the suspending official if I contest the suspension?

(a) In addition to any information and argument in opposition, as a respondent your submission to the suspending official must identify—

(1) Specific facts that contradict the statements contained in the Notice of Suspension. A general denial is insufficient to raise a genuine dispute over facts material to the suspension;

(2) All existing, proposed, or prior exclusions under regulations implementing Executive Order 12549 and all similar actions taken by Federal, State, or local agencies, including administrative agreements that affect only those agencies;

(3) All criminal and civil proceedings not included in the Notice of Suspension that grew out of facts relevant to the cause(s) stated in the notice; and

(4) All of your affiliates.

(b) If you fail to disclose this information, or provide false information, the Federal agency taking the action may seek further criminal, civil or administrative action against you, as appropriate.

### § 180.735 Under what conditions do I get an additional opportunity to challenge the facts on which the suspension is based?

(a) You as a respondent will not have an additional opportunity to challenge the facts if the suspending official determines that—

(1) Your suspension is based upon an indictment, conviction, civil judgment,

or other finding by a Federal, State, or local body for which an opportunity to contest the facts was provided;

(2) Your presentation in opposition contains only general denials to information contained in the Notice of Suspension;

(3) The issues raised in your presentation in opposition to the suspension are not factual in nature, or are not material to the suspending official's initial decision to suspend, or the official's decision whether to continue the suspension; or

(4) On the basis of advice from the Department of Justice, an office of the United States Attorney, a State attorney general's office, or a State or local prosecutor's office, that substantial interests of the government in pending or contemplated legal proceedings based on the same facts as the suspension would be prejudiced by conducting fact-finding.

(b) You will have an opportunity to challenge the facts if the suspending official determines that—

(1) The conditions in paragraph (a) of this section do not exist; and

(2) Your presentation in opposition raises a genuine dispute over facts material to the suspension.

(c) If you have an opportunity to challenge disputed material facts under this section, the suspending official or designee must conduct additional proceedings to resolve those facts.

### § 180.740 Are suspension proceedings formal?

(a) Suspension proceedings are conducted in a fair and informal manner. The suspending official may use flexible procedures to allow you to present matters in opposition. In so doing, the suspending official is not required to follow formal rules of evidence or procedure in creating an official record upon which the official will base a final suspension decision.

(b) You as a respondent or your representative must submit any documentary evidence you want the suspending official to consider.

### § 180.745 How is fact-finding conducted?

(a) If fact-finding is conducted—

(1) You may present witnesses and other evidence, and confront any witness presented; and

(2) The fact-finder must prepare written findings of fact for the record.

(b) A transcribed record of fact-finding proceedings must be made, unless you as a respondent and the Federal agency agree to waive it in advance. If you want a copy of the transcribed record, you may purchase it.

**§ 180.750 What does the suspending official consider in deciding whether to continue or terminate my suspension?**

(a) The suspending official bases the decision on all information contained in the official record. The record includes—

(1) All information in support of the suspending official's initial decision to suspend you;

(2) Any further information and argument presented in support of, or opposition to, the suspension; and

(3) Any transcribed record of fact-finding proceedings.

(b) The suspending official may refer disputed material facts to another official for findings of fact. The suspending official may reject any resulting findings, in whole or in part, only after specifically determining them to be arbitrary, capricious, or clearly erroneous.

**§ 180.755 When will I know whether the suspension is continued or terminated?**

The suspending official must make a written decision whether to continue, modify, or terminate your suspension within 45 days of closing the official record. The official record closes upon the suspending official's receipt of final submissions, information and findings of fact, if any. The suspending official may extend that period for good cause.

**§ 180.760 How long may my suspension last?**

(a) If legal or debarment proceedings are initiated at the time of, or during your suspension, the suspension may continue until the conclusion of those proceedings. However, if proceedings are not initiated, a suspension may not exceed 12 months.

(b) The suspending official may extend the 12 month limit under paragraph (a) of this section for an additional 6 months if an office of a U.S. Assistant Attorney General, U.S. Attorney, or other responsible prosecuting official requests an extension in writing. In no event may a suspension exceed 18 months without initiating proceedings under paragraph (a) of this section.

(c) The suspending official must notify the appropriate officials under paragraph (b) of this section of an impending termination of a suspension at least 30 days before the 12 month period expires to allow the officials an opportunity to request an extension.

## Subpart H—Debarment

**§ 180.800 What are the causes for debarment?**

A Federal agency may debar a person for—

(a) Conviction of or civil judgment for—

(1) Commission of fraud or a criminal offense in connection with obtaining, attempting to obtain, or performing a public or private agreement or transaction;

(2) Violation of Federal or State antitrust statutes, including those proscribing price fixing between competitors, allocation of customers between competitors, and bid rigging;

(3) Commission of embezzlement, theft, forgery, bribery, falsification or destruction of records, making false statements, tax evasion, receiving stolen property, making false claims, or obstruction of justice; or

(4) Commission of any other offense indicating a lack of business integrity or business honesty that seriously and directly affects your present responsibility;

(b) Violation of the terms of a public agreement or transaction so serious as to affect the integrity of an agency program, such as—

(1) A willful failure to perform in accordance with the terms of one or more public agreements or transactions;

(2) A history of failure to perform or of unsatisfactory performance of one or more public agreements or transactions; or

(3) A willful violation of a statutory or regulatory provision or requirement applicable to a public agreement or transaction;

(c) Any of the following causes:

(1) A nonprocurement debarment by any Federal agency taken before October 1, 1988, or a procurement debarment by any Federal agency taken pursuant to 48 CFR part 9, subpart 9.4, before August 25, 1995;

(2) Knowingly doing business with an ineligible person, except as permitted under § 180.135;

(3) Failure to pay a single substantial debt, or a number of outstanding debts (including disallowed costs and overpayments, but not including sums owed the Federal Government under the Internal Revenue Code) owed to any Federal agency or instrumentality, provided the debt is uncontested by the debtor or, if contested, provided that the debtor's legal and administrative remedies have been exhausted;

(4) Violation of a material provision of a voluntary exclusion agreement entered into under § 180.640 or of any settlement of a debarment or suspension action; or

(5) Violation of the provisions of the Drug-Free Workplace Act of 1988 (41 U.S.C. 701); or

(d) Any other cause of so serious or compelling a nature that it affects your present responsibility.

### § 180.805 What notice does the debarring official give me if I am proposed for debarment?

After consideration of the causes in § 180.800, if the debarring official proposes to debar you, the official sends you a Notice of Proposed Debarment, pursuant to § 180.615, advising you—

(a) That the debarring official is considering debarring you;

(b) Of the reasons for proposing to debar you in terms sufficient to put you on notice of the conduct or transactions upon which the proposed debarment is based;

(c) Of the cause(s) under § 180.800 upon which the debarring official relied for proposing your debarment;

(d) Of the applicable provisions of this subpart, subpart F of this part, and any other agency procedures governing debarment; and

(e) Of the governmentwide effect of a debarment from procurement and nonprocurement programs and activities.

### § 180.810 When does a debarment take effect?

Unlike suspension, a debarment is not effective until the debarring official issues a decision. The debarring official does not issue a decision until the respondent has had an opportunity to contest the proposed debarment.

### § 180.815 How may I contest a proposed debarment?

If you as a respondent wish to contest a proposed debarment, you or your representative must provide the debarring official with information in opposition to the proposed debarment. You may do this orally or in writing, but any information provided orally that you consider important must also be submitted in writing for the official record.

### § 180.820 How much time do I have to contest a proposed debarment?

(a) As a respondent you or your representative must either send, or make arrangements to appear and present, the information and argument to the debarring official within 30 days after you receive the Notice of Proposed Debarment.

(b) The Federal agency taking the action considers the Notice of Proposed Debarment to be received by you—

(1) When delivered, if the agency mails the notice to the last known street address, or five days after the agency sends it if the letter is undeliverable;

(2) When sent, if the agency sends the notice by facsimile or five days after the agency sends it if the facsimile is undeliverable; or

(3) When delivered, if the agency sends the notice by e-mail or five days after the agency sends it if the e-mail is undeliverable.

### § 180.825 What information must I provide to the debarring official if I contest the proposed debarment?

(a) In addition to any information and argument in opposition, as a respondent your submission to the debarring official must identify—

(1) Specific facts that contradict the statements contained in the Notice of Proposed Debarment. Include any information about any of the factors listed in §180.860. A general denial is insufficient to raise a genuine dispute over facts material to the debarment;

(2) All existing, proposed, or prior exclusions under regulations implementing Executive Order 12549 and all similar actions taken by Federal, State, or local agencies, including administrative agreements that affect only those agencies;

(3) All criminal and civil proceedings not included in the Notice of Proposed Debarment that grew out of facts relevant to the cause(s) stated in the notice; and

(4) All of your affiliates.

(b) If you fail to disclose this information, or provide false information, the Federal agency taking the action may seek further criminal, civil or administrative action against you, as appropriate.

**§180.830 Under what conditions do I get an additional opportunity to challenge the facts on which the proposed debarment is based?**

(a) You as a respondent will not have an additional opportunity to challenge the facts if the debarring official determines that—

(1) Your debarment is based upon a conviction or civil judgment;

(2) Your presentation in opposition contains only general denials to information contained in the Notice of Proposed Debarment; or

(3) The issues raised in your presentation in opposition to the proposed debarment are not factual in nature, or are not material to the debarring official's decision whether to debar.

(b) You will have an additional opportunity to challenge the facts if the debarring official determines that—

(1) The conditions in paragraph (a) of this section do not exist; and

(2) Your presentation in opposition raises a genuine dispute over facts material to the proposed debarment.

(c) If you have an opportunity to challenge disputed material facts under this section, the debarring official or designee must conduct additional proceedings to resolve those facts.

**§180.835 Are debarment proceedings formal?**

(a) Debarment proceedings are conducted in a fair and informal manner. The debarring official may use flexible procedures to allow you as a respondent to present matters in opposition. In so doing, the debarring official is not required to follow formal rules of evidence or procedure in creating an official record upon which the official will base the decision whether to debar.

(b) You or your representative must submit any documentary evidence you want the debarring official to consider.

**§180.840 How is fact-finding conducted?**

(a) If fact-finding is conducted—

(1) You may present witnesses and other evidence, and confront any witness presented; and

(2) The fact-finder must prepare written findings of fact for the record.

(b) A transcribed record of fact-finding proceedings must be made, unless you as a respondent and the Federal agency agree to waive it in advance. If you want a copy of the transcribed record, you may purchase it.

**§180.845 What does the debarring official consider in deciding whether to debar me?**

(a) The debarring official may debar you for any of the causes in §180.800. However, the official need not debar you even if a cause for debarment exists. The official may consider the seriousness of your acts or omissions and the mitigating or aggravating factors set forth at §180.860.

(b) The debarring official bases the decision on all information contained in the official record. The record includes—

(1) All information in support of the debarring official's proposed debarment;

(2) Any further information and argument presented in support of, or in opposition to, the proposed debarment; and

(3) Any transcribed record of fact-finding proceedings.

(c) The debarring official may refer disputed material facts to another official for findings of fact. The debarring

61

official may reject any resultant findings, in whole or in part, only after specifically determining them to be arbitrary, capricious, or clearly erroneous.

## § 180.850 What is the standard of proof in a debarment action?

(a) In any debarment action, the Federal agency must establish the cause for debarment by a preponderance of the evidence.

(b) If the proposed debarment is based upon a conviction or civil judgment, the standard of proof is met.

## § 180.855 Who has the burden of proof in a debarment action?

(a) The Federal agency has the burden to prove that a cause for debarment exists.

(b) Once a cause for debarment is established, you as a respondent have the burden of demonstrating to the satisfaction of the debarring official that you are presently responsible and that debarment is not necessary.

## § 180.860 What factors may influence the debarring official's decision?

This section lists the mitigating and aggravating factors that the debarring official may consider in determining whether to debar you and the length of your debarment period. The debarring official may consider other factors if appropriate in light of the circumstances of a particular case. The existence or nonexistence of any factor, such as one of those set forth in this section, is not necessarily determinative of your present responsibility. In making a debarment decision, the debarring official may consider the following factors:

(a) The actual or potential harm or impact that results or may result from the wrongdoing.

(b) The frequency of incidents and/or duration of the wrongdoing.

(c) Whether there is a pattern or prior history of wrongdoing. For example, if you have been found by another Federal agency or a State agency to have engaged in wrongdoing similar to that found in the debarment action, the existence of this fact may be used by the debarring official in determining that you have a pattern or prior history of wrongdoing.

(d) Whether you are or have been excluded or disqualified by an agency of the Federal Government or have not been allowed to participate in State or local contracts or assistance agreements on a basis of conduct similar to one or more of the causes for debarment specified in this part.

(e) Whether you have entered into an administrative agreement with a Federal agency or a State or local government that is not governmentwide but is based on conduct similar to one or more of the causes for debarment specified in this part.

(f) Whether and to what extent you planned, initiated, or carried out the wrongdoing.

(g) Whether you have accepted responsibility for the wrongdoing and recognize the seriousness of the misconduct that led to the cause for debarment.

(h) Whether you have paid or agreed to pay all criminal, civil and administrative liabilities for the improper activity, including any investigative or administrative costs incurred by the government, and have made or agreed to make full restitution.

(i) Whether you have cooperated fully with the government agencies during the investigation and any court or administrative action. In determining the extent of cooperation, the debarring official may consider when the cooperation began and whether you disclosed all pertinent information known to you.

(j) Whether the wrongdoing was pervasive within your organization.

(k) The kind of positions held by the individuals involved in the wrongdoing.

(l) Whether your organization took appropriate corrective action or remedial measures, such as establishing ethics training and implementing programs to prevent recurrence.

(m) Whether your principals tolerated the offense.

(n) Whether you brought the activity cited as a basis for the debarment to the attention of the appropriate government agency in a timely manner.

(o) Whether you have fully investigated the circumstances surrounding the cause for debarment and, if so, made the result of the investigation available to the debarring official.

(p) Whether you had effective standards of conduct and internal control systems in place at the time the questioned conduct occurred.

(q) Whether you have taken appropriate disciplinary action against the individuals responsible for the activity which constitutes the cause for debarment.

(r) Whether you have had adequate time to eliminate the circumstances within your organization that led to the cause for the debarment.

(s) Other factors that are appropriate to the circumstances of a particular case.

## § 180.865  How long may my debarment last?

(a) If the debarring official decides to debar you, your period of debarment will be based on the seriousness of the cause(s) upon which your debarment is based. Generally, debarment should not exceed three years. However, if circumstances warrant, the debarring official may impose a longer period of debarment.

(b) In determining the period of debarment, the debarring official may consider the factors in § 180.860. If a suspension has preceded your debarment, the debarring official must consider the time you were suspended.

(c) If the debarment is for a violation of the provisions of the Drug-Free Workplace Act of 1988, your period of debarment may not exceed five years.

## § 180.870  When do I know if the debarring official debars me?

(a) The debarring official must make a written decision whether to debar within 45 days of closing the official record. The official record closes upon the debarring official's receipt of final submissions, information and findings of fact, if any. The debarring official may extend that period for good cause.

(b) The debarring official sends you written notice, pursuant to § 180.615 that the official decided, either—

(1) Not to debar you; or

(2) To debar you. In this event, the notice:

(i) Refers to the Notice of Proposed Debarment;

(ii) Specifies the reasons for your debarment;

(iii) States the period of your debarment, including the effective dates; and

(iv) Advises you that your debarment is effective for covered transactions and contracts that are subject to the Federal Acquisition Regulation (48 CFR chapter 1), throughout the executive branch of the Federal Government unless an agency head or an authorized designee grants an exception.

## § 180.875  May I ask the debarring official to reconsider a decision to debar me?

Yes, as a debarred person you may ask the debarring official to reconsider the debarment decision or to reduce the time period or scope of the debarment. However, you must put your request in writing and support it with documentation.

## § 180.880  What factors may influence the debarring official during reconsideration?

The debarring official may reduce or terminate your debarment based on—

(a) Newly discovered material evidence;

(b) A reversal of the conviction or civil judgment upon which your debarment was based;

(c) A bona fide change in ownership or management;

(d) Elimination of other causes for which the debarment was imposed; or

(e) Other reasons the debarring official finds appropriate.

## § 180.885  May the debarring official extend a debarment?

(a) Yes, the debarring official may extend a debarment for an additional period, if that official determines that an extension is necessary to protect the public interest.

(b) However, the debarring official may not extend a debarment solely on the basis of the facts and circumstances upon which the initial debarment action was based.

(c) If the debarring official decides that a debarment for an additional period is necessary, the debarring official must follow the applicable procedures in this subpart, and subpart F of this part, to extend the debarment.

## Subpart I—Definitions

### § 180.900  Adequate evidence.

*Adequate evidence* means information sufficient to support the reasonable belief that a particular act or omission has occurred.

### § 180.905  Affiliate.

Persons are *affiliates* of each other if, directly or indirectly, either one controls or has the power to control the other or a third person controls or has the power to control both. The ways a Federal agency may determine control include, but are not limited to—

(a) Interlocking management or ownership;

(b) Identity of interests among family members;

(c) Shared facilities and equipment;

(d) Common use of employees; or

(e) A business entity which has been organized following the exclusion of a person which has the same or similar management, ownership, or principal employees as the excluded person.

### § 180.910  Agent or representative.

*Agent or representative* means any person who acts on behalf of, or who is authorized to commit a participant in a covered transaction.

### § 180.915  Civil judgment.

*Civil judgment* means the disposition of a civil action by any court of competent jurisdiction, whether by verdict, decision, settlement, stipulation, other disposition which creates a civil liability for the complained of wrongful acts, or a final determination of liability under the Program Fraud Civil Remedies Act of 1988 (31 U.S.C. 3801–3812).

### § 180.920  Conviction.

*Conviction* means—

(a) A judgment or any other determination of guilt of a criminal offense by any court of competent jurisdiction, whether entered upon a verdict or plea, including a plea of nolo contendere; or

(b) Any other resolution that is the functional equivalent of a judgment, including probation before judgment and deferred prosecution. A disposition without the participation of the court is the functional equivalent of a judgment only if it includes an admission of guilt.

### § 180.925  Debarment.

*Debarment* means an action taken by a debarring official under Subpart H of this part to exclude a person from participating in covered transactions and transactions covered under the Federal Acquisition Regulation (48 CFR chapter 1). A person so excluded is debarred.

### § 180.930  Debarring official.

*Debarring official* means an agency official who is authorized to impose debarment. A debarring official is either—

(a) The agency head; or

(b) An official designated by the agency head.

### § 180.935  Disqualified.

*Disqualified* means that a person is prohibited from participating in specified Federal procurement or nonprocurement transactions as required under a statute, Executive order (other than Executive Orders 12549 and 12689) or other authority. Examples of disqualifications include persons prohibited under—

(a) The Davis-Bacon Act (40 U.S.C. 276(a));

(b) The equal employment opportunity acts and Executive orders; or

(c) The Clean Air Act (42 U.S.C. 7606), Clean Water Act (33 U.S.C. 1368) and Executive Order 11738 (3 CFR, 1973 Comp., p. 799).

### § 180.940  Excluded or exclusion.

*Excluded or exclusion* means—

(a) That a person or commodity is prohibited from being a participant in covered transactions, whether the person has been suspended; debarred; proposed for debarment under 48 CFR part 9, subpart 9.4; voluntarily excluded; or

(b) The act of excluding a person.

### § 180.945  System for Award Management Exclusions (SAM Exclusions).

*System for Award Management Exclusions (SAM Exclusions)* means the list maintained and disseminated by the General Services Administration (GSA) containing the names and other information about persons who are ineligible.

[79 FR 75880, Dec. 19, 2014]

### §180.950  Federal agency.

*Federal agency* means any United States executive department, military department, defense agency or any other agency of the executive branch. Other agencies of the Federal Government are not considered "agencies" for the purposes of this part unless they issue regulations adopting the governmentwide Debarment and Suspension system under Executive Orders 12549 and 12689.

### §180.955  Indictment.

*Indictment* means an indictment for a criminal offense. A presentment, information, or other filing by a competent authority charging a criminal offense shall be given the same effect as an indictment.

### §180.960  Ineligible or ineligibility.

*Ineligible or ineligibility* means that a person or commodity is prohibited from covered transactions because of an exclusion or disqualification.

### §180.965  Legal proceedings.

*Legal proceedings* means any criminal proceeding or any civil judicial proceeding, including a proceeding under the Program Fraud Civil Remedies Act (31 U.S.C. 3801–3812), to which the Federal Government or a State or local government or quasi-governmental authority is a party. The term also includes appeals from those proceedings.

### §180.970  Nonprocurement transaction.

(a) *Nonprocurement transaction* means any transaction, regardless of type (except procurement contracts), including, but not limited to the following:

(1) Grants.
(2) Cooperative agreements.
(3) Scholarships.
(4) Fellowships.
(5) Contracts of assistance.
(6) Loans.
(7) Loan guarantees.
(8) Subsidies.
(9) Insurances.
(10) Payments for specified uses.

(11) Donation agreements.

(b) A nonprocurement transaction at any tier does not require the transfer of Federal funds.

### §180.975  Notice.

*Notice* means a written communication served in person, sent by certified mail or its equivalent, or sent electronically by e-mail or facsimile. (See §180.615.)

### §180.980  Participant.

*Participant* means any person who submits a proposal for or who enters into a covered transaction, including an agent or representative of a participant.

### §180.985  Person.

*Person* means any individual, corporation, partnership, association, unit of government, or legal entity, however organized.

### §180.990  Preponderance of the evidence.

*Preponderance of the evidence* means proof by information that, compared with information opposing it, leads to the conclusion that the fact at issue is more probably true than not.

### §180.995  Principal.

*Principal* means—

(a) An officer, director, owner, partner, principal investigator, or other person within a participant with management or supervisory responsibilities related to a covered transaction; or

(b) A consultant or other person, whether or not employed by the participant or paid with Federal funds, who—

(1) Is in a position to handle Federal funds;

(2) Is in a position to influence or control the use of those funds; or,

(3) Occupies a technical or professional position capable of substantially influencing the development or outcome of an activity required to perform the covered transaction.

### §180.1000  Respondent.

*Respondent* means a person against whom an agency has initiated a debarment or suspension action.

## § 180.1005   State.

(a) *State* means—

(1) Any of the states of the United States;

(2) The District of Columbia;

(3) The Commonwealth of Puerto Rico;

(4) Any territory or possession of the United States; or

(5) Any agency or instrumentality of a state.

(b) For purposes of this part, *State* does not include institutions of higher education, hospitals, or units of local government.

## § 180.1010   Suspending official.

(a) *Suspending official* means an agency official who is authorized to impose suspension. The suspending official is either:

(1) The agency head; or

(2) An official designated by the agency head.

## § 180.1015   Suspension.

*Suspension* is an action taken by a suspending official under subpart G of this part that immediately prohibits a person from participating in covered transactions and transactions covered under the Federal Acquisition Regulation (48 CFR chapter 1) for a temporary period, pending completion of an agency investigation and any judicial or administrative proceedings that may ensue. A person so excluded is suspended.

## § 180.1020   Voluntary exclusion or voluntarily excluded.

(a) *Voluntary exclusion* means a person's agreement to be excluded under the terms of a settlement between the person and one or more agencies. Voluntary exclusion must have governmentwide effect.

(b) *Voluntarily excluded* means the status of a person who has agreed to a voluntary exclusion.

APPENDIX TO PART 180—COVERED TRANSACTIONS

COVERED TRANSACTIONS

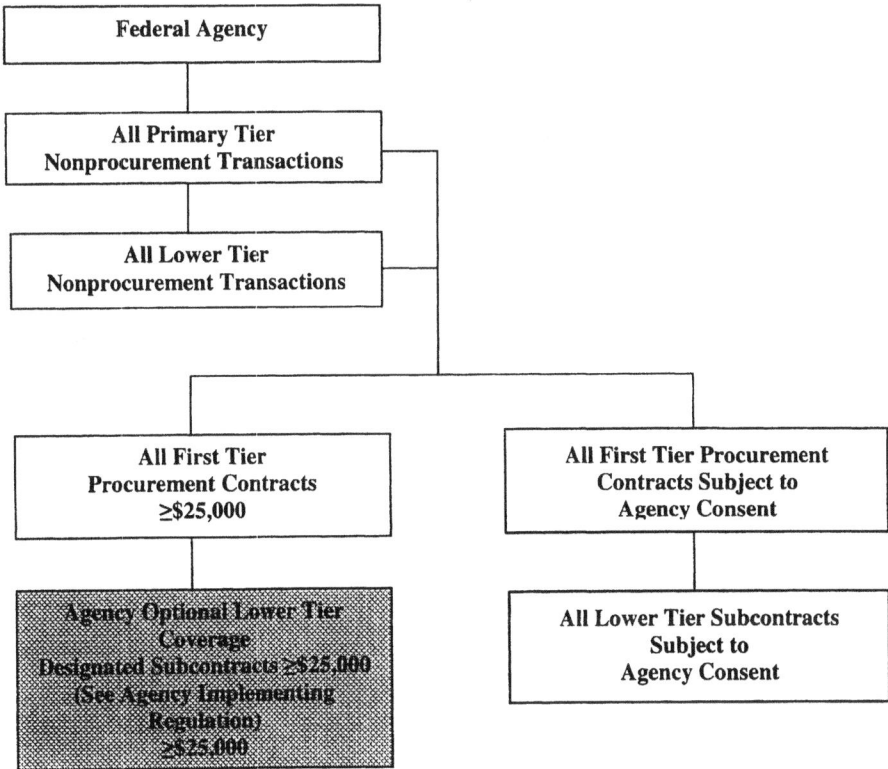

## PART 181 [RESERVED]

## PART 182—GOVERNMENTWIDE RE-QUIREMENTS FOR DRUG-FREE WORKPLACE (FINANCIAL ASSIST-ANCE)

AUTHORITY: 41 U.S.C. 701, *et seq.*

SOURCE: 74 FR 28150, June 15, 2009, unless otherwise noted.

## § 182.5  What does this part do?

This part provides Office of Management and Budget (OMB) guidance for Federal agencies on the portion of the Drug-Free Workplace Act of 1988 (41 U.S.C. 701–707, as amended) that applies to grants. It also applies the provisions of the Act to cooperative agreements and other financial assistance awards, as a matter of Federal Government policy.

## § 182.10  How is this part organized?

This part is organized in two segments.

(a) Sections 182.5 through 182.40 contain general policy direction for Federal agencies' use of the uniform policies and procedures in subparts A through F of this part.

(b) Subparts A through F of this part contain uniform governmentwide policies and procedures for Federal agency use to specify the—

(1) Types of awards that are covered by drug-free workplace requirements;

(2) Drug-free workplace requirements with which a recipient must comply;

(3) Actions required of an agency awarding official; and

(4) Consequences of a violation of drug-free workplace requirements.

## § 182.15  To whom does the guidance apply?

This part provides OMB guidance only to Federal agencies. Publication of this guidance in the Code of Federal Regulations does not change its nature—it is guidance and not regulation. Federal agencies' implementation of the guidance governs the rights and responsibilities of other persons affected by the drug-free workplace requirements.

## § 182.20  What must a Federal agency do to implement the guidance?

To comply with the requirement in Section 41 U.S.C. 705 for Governmentwide regulations, each Federal agency that awards grants or cooperative agreements or makes other financial assistance awards that are subject to the drug-free workplace requirements in subparts A through F of the guidance must issue a regulation consistent with those subparts.

## § 182.25  What must a Federal agency address in its implementation of the guidance?

Each Federal agency's implementing regulation:

(a) Must establish drug-free workplace policies and procedures for that agency's awards that are consistent with the guidance in this part. When adopted by a Federal agency, the provisions of the guidance have regulatory effect for that agency's awards.

(b) Must address some matters for which the guidance in this part gives the agency discretion. Specifically, the regulation must—

(1) State whether the agency:

(i) Has a central point to which a recipient may send the notification of a conviction that is required under § 182.225(a) or § 182.300(b); or

(ii) Requires the recipient to send the notification to the awarding official for each agency award, or to his or her official designee.

(2) Either:

(i) State that the agency head is the official authorized to determine under § 182.500 or § 182.505 that a recipient has violated the drug-free workplace requirements; or

(ii) Provide the title of the official designated to make that determination.

(c) May also, at the agency's option, identify any specific types of financial assistance awards, in addition to grants and cooperative agreements, to which the Federal agency makes this guidance applicable.

### § 182.30 Where does a Federal agency implement the guidance?

Each Federal agency that awards grants or cooperative agreements or makes other financial assistance awards that are subject to the drug-free workplace guidance in this part must issue a regulation implementing the guidance within its chapter in subtitle B of this title of the Code of Federal Regulations.

### § 182.35 By when must a Federal agency implement the guidance?

Federal agencies must submit proposed regulations to the OMB for review within nine months of the issuance of this part and issue final regulations within eighteen months of the guidance.

### § 182.40 How is the guidance maintained?

The OMB publishes proposed changes to the guidance in the FEDERAL REG-

ISTER for public comment, considers comments with the help of appropriate interagency working groups, and then issues any changes to the guidance in final form.

## Subpart A—Purpose and Coverage

### § 182.100 How is this part written?

(a) This part uses a "plain language" format to make it easier for the general public and business community to use and understand. The section headings and text, often in the form of questions and answers, must be read together.

(b) Pronouns used within this part, such as "I" and "you," change from subpart to subpart depending on the audience being addressed.

### § 182.105 Do terms in this part have special meanings?

This part uses terms that have special meanings. Those terms are defined in subpart F of this part.

### § 182.110 What do subparts A through F of this part do?

Subparts A through F of this part specify standard policies and procedures to carry out the Drug-Free Workplace Act of 1988 for financial assistance awards.

### § 182.115 Does this part apply to me?

(a) Portions of this part apply to you if you are either—

(1) A recipient of a Federal assistance award (see definitions of award and recipient in §§ 182.605 and 182.660, respectively); or

(2) A Federal agency awarding official.

(b) The following table shows the subparts that apply to you:

| If you are * * * | See subparts * * * |
| --- | --- |
| (1) a recipient who is not an individual .. | A, B and E. |
| (2) a recipient who is an individual ........ | A, C and E. |
| (3) a Federal agency awarding official ... | A, D and E. |

### § 182.120 Are any of my Federal assistance awards exempt from this part?

This part does not apply to any award to which the agency head, or his or her designee, determines that the application of this part would be inconsistent with the international obligations of the United States or the laws or regulations of a foreign government.

### § 182.125 Does this part affect the Federal contracts that I receive?

This part will affect future contract awards indirectly if you are debarred or suspended for a violation of the requirements of this part, as described in § 182.510(c). However, this part does not apply directly to procurement contracts. The portion of the Drug-Free Workplace Act of 1988 that applies to Federal procurement contracts is carried out through the Federal Acquisition Regulation in chapter 1 of Title 48 of the Code of Federal Regulations (the drug-free workplace coverage currently is in 48 CFR part 23, subpart 23.5).

## Subpart B—Requirements for Recipients Other Than Individuals

### § 182.200 What must I do to comply with this part?

There are two general requirements if you are a recipient other than an individual.

(a) First, you must make a good faith effort, on a continuing basis, to maintain a drug-free workplace. You must agree to do so as a condition for receiving any award covered by this part. The specific measures that you must take in this regard are described in more detail in subsequent sections of this subpart. Briefly, those measures are to—

(1) Publish a drug-free workplace statement and establish a drug-free awareness program for your employees (see §§ 182.205 through 182.220); and

(2) Take actions concerning employees who are convicted of violating drug statutes in the workplace (see § 182.225).

(b) Second, you must identify all known workplaces under your Federal awards (see § 182.230).

### § 182.205 What must I include in my drug-free workplace statement?

You must publish a statement that—

(a) Tells your employees that the unlawful manufacture, distribution, dispensing, possession, or use of a controlled substance is prohibited in your workplace;

(b) Specifies the actions that you will take against employees for violating that prohibition; and

(c) Lets each employee know that, as a condition of employment under any award, he or she:

(1) Will abide by the terms of the statement; and

(2) Must notify you in writing if he or she is convicted for a violation of a criminal drug statute occurring in the workplace and must do so no more than five calendar days after the conviction.

### § 182.210 To whom must I distribute my drug-free workplace statement?

You must require that a copy of the statement described in § 182.205 be given to each employee who will be engaged in the performance of any Federal award.

### § 182.215 What must I include in my drug-free awareness program?

You must establish an ongoing drug-free awareness program to inform employees about—

(a) The dangers of drug abuse in the workplace;

(b) Your policy of maintaining a drug-free workplace;

(c) Any available drug counseling, rehabilitation, and employee assistance programs; and

(d) The penalties that you may impose upon them for drug abuse violations occurring in the workplace.

### § 182.220 By when must I publish my drug-free workplace statement and establish my drug-free awareness program?

If you are a new recipient that does not already have a policy statement as described in § 182.205 and an ongoing awareness program as described in § 182.215, you must publish the statement and establish the program by the time given in the following table:

| If * * * | Then you * * * |
|---|---|
| (a) the performance period of the award is less than 30 days ... | must have the policy statement and program in place as soon as possible, but before the date on which performance is expected to be completed. |
| (b) the performance period of the award is 30 days or more ..... | must have the policy statement and program in place within 30 days after award. |
| (c) you believe there are extraordinary circumstances that will require more than 30 days for you to publish the policy statement and establish the awareness program. | may ask the agency awarding official to give you more time to do so. The amount of additional time, if any, to be given is at the discretion of the awarding official. |

### § 182.225 What actions must I take concerning employees who are convicted of drug violations in the workplace?

There are two actions you must take if an employee is convicted of a drug violation in the workplace:

(a) First, you must notify Federal agencies if an employee who is engaged in the performance of an award informs you about a conviction, as required by § 182.205(c)(2), or you otherwise learn of the conviction. Your notification to the Federal agencies must—

(1) Be in writing;

(2) Include the employee's position title;

(3) Include the identification number(s) of each affected award;

(4) Be sent within ten calendar days after you learn of the conviction; and

(5) Be sent to every Federal agency on whose award the convicted employee was working. It must be sent to every awarding official or his or her official designee, unless the Federal agency has specified a central point for the receipt of the notices.

(b) Second, within 30 calendar days of learning about an employee's conviction, you must either—

(1) Take appropriate personnel action against the employee, up to and including termination, consistent with the requirements of the Rehabilitation Act of 1973 (29 U.S.C. 794), as amended; or

(2) Require the employee to participate satisfactorily in a drug abuse assistance or rehabilitation program approved for these purposes by a Federal, State or local health, law enforcement, or other appropriate agency.

### § 182.230 How and when must I identify workplaces?

(a) You must identify all known workplaces under each agency award. A failure to do so is a violation of your drug-free workplace requirements. You may identify the workplaces—

(1) To the agency official that is making the award, either at the time of application or upon award; or

(2) In documents that you keep on file in your offices during the performance of the award, in which case you must make the information available for inspection upon request by agency officials or their designated representatives.

(b) Your workplace identification for an award must include the actual address of buildings (or parts of buildings) or other sites where work under the award takes place. Categorical descriptions may be used (e.g., all vehicles of a mass transit authority or State highway department while in operation, State employees in each local unemployment office, performers in concert halls or radio studios).

(c) If you identified workplaces to the agency awarding official at the time of application or award, as described in paragraph (a)(1) of this section, and any workplace that you identified changes during the performance of the award, you must inform the agency awarding official.

## Subpart C—Requirements for Recipients Who Are Individuals

### § 182.300 What must I do to comply with this part if I am an individual recipient?

As a condition of receiving a Federal agency award, if you are an individual recipient, you must agree that—

(a) You will not engage in the unlawful manufacture, distribution, dispensing, possession, or use of a controlled substance in conducting any activity related to the award; and

(b) If you are convicted of a criminal drug offense resulting from a violation occurring during the conduct of any award activity, you will report the conviction:

(1) In writing.

(2) Within 10 calendar days of the conviction.

(3) To the Federal agency awarding official or other designee for each award that you currently have, unless the agency designates a central point for the receipt of the notices, either in the award document or its regulation implementing the guidance in this part. When notice is made to a central point, it must include the identification number(s) of each affected award.

## Subpart D—Responsibilities of Agency Awarding Officials

### § 182.400  What are my responsibilities as an agency awarding official?

As a Federal agency awarding official, you must obtain each recipient's agreement, as a condition of the award, to comply with the requirements in—

(a) Subpart B of this part, if the recipient is not an individual; or

(b) Subpart C of this part, if the recipient is an individual.

## Subpart E—Violations of This Part and Consequences

### § 182.500  How are violations of this part determined for recipients other than individuals?

A recipient other than an individual is in violation of the requirements of this part if the agency head or his or her designee determines, in writing, that—

(a) The recipient has violated the requirements of subpart B of this part; or

(b) The number of convictions of the recipient's employees for violating criminal drug statutes in the workplace is large enough to indicate that the recipient has failed to make a good faith effort to provide a drug-free workplace.

### § 182.505  How are violations of this part determined for recipients who are individuals?

An individual recipient is in violation of the requirements of this part if the agency head or his or her designee determines, in writing, that—

(a) The recipient has violated the requirements of subpart C of this part; or

(b) The recipient is convicted of a criminal drug offense resulting from a violation occurring during the conduct of any award activity.

### § 182.510  What actions will the Federal Government take against a recipient determined to have violated this part?

If a recipient is determined to have violated this part, as described in § 182.500 or § 182.505, the agency may take one or more of the following actions—

(a) Suspension of payments under the award;

(b) Suspension or termination of the award; and

(c) Suspension or debarment of the recipient under the agency's regulation implementing the OMB guidance on nonprocurement debarment and suspension (2 CFR part 180), for a period not to exceed five years.

### § 182.515  Are there any exceptions to those actions?

The agency head may waive with respect to a particular award, in writing, a suspension of payments under an award, suspension or termination of an award, or suspension or debarment of a recipient if the agency head determines that such a waiver would be in the public interest. This exception authority cannot be delegated to any other official.

## Subpart F—Definitions

### § 182.605  Award.

Award means an award of financial assistance by a Federal agency directly to a recipient.

(a) The term award includes:

(1) A Federal grant or cooperative agreement, in the form of money or property in lieu of money.

(2) A block grant or a grant in an entitlement program, whether or not the grant is exempted from coverage under the Governmentwide rule that implements OMB Circular A-102 (for availability of OMB circulars, see 5 CFR 1310.3) and specifies uniform administrative requirements.

(b) The term award does not include:

(1) Technical assistance that provides services instead of money.

(2) Loans.

(3) Loan guarantees.

(4) Interest subsidies.

(5) Insurance.

(6) Direct appropriations.

(7) Veterans' benefits to individuals (i.e., any benefit to veterans, their families, or survivors by virtue of the service of a veteran in the Armed Forces of the United States).

### § 182.610  Controlled substance.

Controlled substance means a controlled substance in schedules I through V of the Controlled Substances Act (21 U.S.C. 812), and as further defined by regulation at 21 CFR 1308.11 through 1308.15.

### § 182.615  Conviction.

Conviction means a finding of guilt (including a plea of nolo contendere) or imposition of sentence, or both, by any judicial body charged with the responsibility to determine violations of the Federal or State criminal drug statutes.

### § 182.620  Cooperative agreement.

Cooperative agreement means an award of financial assistance that, consistent with 31 U.S.C. 6305, is used to enter into the same kind of relationship as a grant (see definition of grant in § 182.650), except that substantial involvement is expected between the Federal agency and the recipient when carrying out the activity contemplated by the award. The term does not include cooperative research and development agreements as defined in 15 U.S.C. 3710a.

### § 182.625  Criminal drug statute.

Criminal drug statute means a Federal or non-Federal criminal statute involving the manufacture, distribution, dispensing, use, or possession of any controlled substance.

### § 182.630  Debarment.

Debarment means an action taken by a Federal agency to prohibit a recipient from participating in Federal Government procurement contracts and covered nonprocurement transactions. A recipient so prohibited is debarred,

in accordance with the Federal Acquisition Regulation for procurement contracts (48 CFR part 9, subpart 9.4) and agency regulations implementing the OMB guidance on nonprocurement debarment and suspension (2 CFR part 180, which implements Executive Orders 12549 and 12689).

### § 182.635  Drug-free workplace.

Drug-free workplace means a site for the performance of work done in connection with a specific award at which employees of the recipient are prohibited from engaging in the unlawful manufacture, distribution, dispensing, possession, or use of a controlled substance.

### § 182.640  Employee.

(a) Employee means the employee of a recipient directly engaged in the performance of work under the award, including—

(1) All direct charge employees;

(2) All indirect charge employees, unless their impact or involvement in the performance of work under the award is insignificant to the performance of the award; and

(3) Temporary personnel and consultants who are directly engaged in the performance of work under the award and who are on the recipient's payroll.

(b) This definition does not include workers not on the payroll of the recipient (e.g., volunteers, even if used to meet a matching requirement; consultants or independent contractors not on the payroll; or employees of subrecipients or subcontractors in covered workplaces).

### § 182.645  Federal agency or agency.

Federal agency or agency means any United States executive department, military department, government corporation, government controlled corporation, any other establishment in the executive branch (including the Executive Office of the President), or any independent regulatory agency.

### § 182.650  Grant.

Grant means an award of financial assistance that, consistent with 31 U.S.C. 6304, is used to enter into a relationship—

73

(a) The principal purpose of which is to transfer a thing of value to the recipient to carry out a public purpose of support or stimulation authorized by a law of the United States, rather than to acquire property or services for the Federal Government's direct benefit or use; and

(b) In which substantial involvement is not expected between the Federal agency and the recipient when carrying out the activity contemplated by the award.

### § 182.655 Individual.

Individual means a natural person.

### § 182.660 Recipient.

Recipient means any individual, corporation, partnership, association, unit of government (except a Federal agency) or legal entity, however organized, that receives an award directly from a Federal agency.

### § 182.665 State.

State means any of the States of the United States, the District of Columbia, the Commonwealth of Puerto Rico, or any territory or possession of the United States.

### § 182.670 Suspension.

Suspension means an action taken by a Federal agency that immediately prohibits a recipient from participating in Federal Government procurement contracts and covered nonprocurement transactions for a temporary period, pending completion of an investigation and any judicial or administrative proceedings that may ensue. A recipient so prohibited is suspended, in accordance with the Federal Acquisition Regulation for procurement contracts (48 CFR part 9, subpart 9.4) and agency regulations implementing the OMB guidance on nonprocurement debarment and suspension (2 CFR part 180, which implements Executive Orders 12549 and 12689). Suspension of a recipient is a distinct and separate action from suspension of an award or suspension of payments under an award.

## PARTS 183–199 [RESERVED]

# CHAPTER II—OFFICE OF MANAGEMENT AND BUDGET GUIDANCE

# PART 200—UNIFORM ADMINISTRA-TIVE REQUIREMENTS, COST PRIN-CIPLES, AND AUDIT REQUIRE-MENTS FOR FEDERAL AWARDS

## Subpart A—Acronyms and Definitions

AUTHORITY: 31 U.S.C. 503

SOURCE: 78 FR 78608, Dec. 26, 2013, unless otherwise noted.

## Subpart A—Acronyms and Definitions

ACRONYMS

### § 200.0 Acronyms.

| ACRONYM | TERM |
| --- | --- |
| CAS | Cost Accounting Standards |
| CFDA | Catalog of Federal Domestic Assistance |
| CFR | Code of Federal Regulations |
| CMIA | Cash Management Improvement Act |
| COG | Councils Of Governments |
| COSO | Committee of Sponsoring Organizations of the Treadway Commission |
| EPA | Environmental Protection Agency |
| ERISA | Employee Retirement Income Security Act of 1974 (29 U.S.C. 1301–1461) |
| EUI | Energy Usage Index |
| F&A | Facilities and Administration |
| FAC | Federal Audit Clearinghouse |
| FAIN | Federal Award Identification Number |
| FAPIIS | Federal Awardee Performance and Integrity Information System |
| FAR | Federal Acquisition Regulation |
| FFATA | Federal Funding Accountability and Transparency Act of 2006 or Transparency Act—Public Law 109–282, as amended by section 6202(a) of Public Law 110–252 (31 U.S.C. 6101) |
| FICA | Federal Insurance Contributions Act |
| FOIA | Freedom of Information Act |
| FR | Federal Register |
| FTE | Full-time equivalent |
| GAAP | Generally Accepted Accounting Principles |
| GAGAS | Generally Accepted Government Auditing Standards |
| GAO | Government Accountability Office |
| GOCO | Government owned, contractor operated |
| GSA | General Services Administration |
| IBS | Institutional Base Salary |
| IHE | Institutions of Higher Education |
| IRC | Internal Revenue Code |
| ISDEAA | Indian Self-Determination and Education and Assistance Act |
| MTC | Modified Total Cost |

MTDC   Modified Total Direct Cost
OMB   Office of Management and Budget
PII   Personally Identifiable Information
PMS Payment Management System
PRHP   Post-retirement Health Plans
PTE   Pass-through Entity
REUI   Relative Energy Usage Index
SAM   System for Award Management (accessible at *https://www.sam.gov*)
SFA   Student Financial Aid
SNAP   Supplemental Nutrition Assistance Program
SPOC   Single Point of Contact
TANF   Temporary   Assistance   for Needy Families
TFM   Treasury Financial Manual
U.S.C.   United States Code
VAT   Value Added Tax

[78 FR 78608, Dec. 26, 2013, as amended at 79 FR 75880, Dec. 19, 2014; 80 FR 43308, July 22, 2015]

## §200.1   Definitions.

These are the definitions for terms used in this part. Different definitions may be found in Federal statutes or regulations that apply more specifically to particular programs or activities. These definitions could be supplemented by additional instructional information provided in governmentwide standard information collections.

## §200.2   Acquisition cost.

*Acquisition cost* means the cost of the asset including the cost to ready the asset for its intended use. Acquisition cost for equipment, for example, means the net invoice price of the equipment, including the cost of any modifications, attachments, accessories, or auxiliary apparatus necessary to make it usable for the purpose for which it is acquired. Acquisition costs for software includes those development costs capitalized in accordance with generally accepted accounting principles (GAAP). Ancillary charges, such as taxes, duty, protective in transit insurance, freight, and installation may be included in or excluded from the acquisition cost in accordance with the non-Federal entity's regular accounting practices.

## §200.3   Advance payment.

*Advance payment* means a payment that a Federal awarding agency or pass-through entity makes by any appropriate payment mechanism, including a predetermined payment schedule, before the non-Federal entity disburses the funds for program purposes.

## §200.4   Allocation.

*Allocation* means the process of assigning a cost, or a group of costs, to one or more cost objective(s), in reasonable proportion to the benefit provided or other equitable relationship. The process may entail assigning a cost(s) directly to a final cost objective or through one or more intermediate cost objectives.

## §200.5   Audit finding.

*Audit finding* means deficiencies which the auditor is required by §200.516 Audit findings, paragraph (a) to report in the schedule of findings and questioned costs.

## §200.6   Auditee.

*Auditee* means any non-Federal entity that expends Federal awards which must be audited under Subpart F—Audit Requirements of this part.

## §200.7   Auditor.

*Auditor* means an auditor who is a public accountant or a Federal, state, local government, or Indian tribe audit organization, which meets the general standards specified for external auditors in generally accepted government auditing standards (GAGAS). The term auditor does not include internal auditors of nonprofit organizations.

[79 FR 75880, Dec. 19, 2014]

## §200.8   Budget.

*Budget* means the financial plan for the project or program that the Federal awarding agency or pass-through entity approves during the Federal award process or in subsequent amendments to the Federal award. It may include the Federal and non-Federal share or only the Federal share, as determined by the Federal awarding agency or pass-through entity.

§ 200.9

2 CFR Ch. II (1–1–18 Edition)

## § 200.9  Central service cost allocation plan.

*Central service cost allocation plan* means the documentation identifying, accumulating, and allocating or developing billing rates based on the allowable costs of services provided by a state, local government, or Indian tribe on a centralized basis to its departments and agencies. The costs of these services may be allocated or billed to users.

## § 200.10  Catalog of Federal Domestic Assistance (CFDA) number.

*CFDA number* means the number assigned to a Federal program in the CFDA.

## § 200.11  CFDA program title.

*CFDA program title* means the title of the program under which the Federal award was funded in the CFDA.

## § 200.12  Capital assets.

*Capital assets* means tangible or intangible assets used in operations having a useful life of more than one year which are capitalized in accordance with GAAP. Capital assets include:

(a) Land, buildings (facilities), equipment, and intellectual property (including software) whether acquired by purchase, construction, manufacture, lease-purchase, exchange, or through capital leases; and

(b) Additions, improvements, modifications, replacements, rearrangements, reinstallations, renovations or alterations to capital assets that materially increase their value or useful life (not ordinary repairs and maintenance).

## § 200.13  Capital expenditures.

*Capital expenditures* means expenditures to acquire capital assets or expenditures to make additions, improvements, modifications, replacements, rearrangements, reinstallations, renovations, or alterations to capital assets that materially increase their value or useful life.

## § 200.14  Claim.

*Claim* means, depending on the context, either:

(a) A written demand or written assertion by one of the parties to a Federal award seeking as a matter of right:

(1) The payment of money in a sum certain;

(2) The adjustment or interpretation of the terms and conditions of the Federal award; or

(3) Other relief arising under or relating to a Federal award.

(b) A request for payment that is not in dispute when submitted.

## § 200.15  Class of Federal awards.

*Class of Federal awards* means a group of Federal awards either awarded under a specific program or group of programs or to a specific type of non-Federal entity or group of non-Federal entities to which specific provisions or exceptions may apply.

## § 200.16  Closeout.

*Closeout* means the process by which the Federal awarding agency or pass-through entity determines that all applicable administrative actions and all required work of the Federal award have been completed and takes actions as described in § 200.343 Closeout.

## § 200.17  Cluster of programs.

*Cluster of programs* means a grouping of closely related programs that share common compliance requirements. The types of clusters of programs are research and development (R&D), student financial aid (SFA), and other clusters. "Other clusters" are as defined by OMB in the compliance supplement or as designated by a state for Federal awards the state provides to its subrecipients that meet the definition of a cluster of programs. When designating an "other cluster," a state must identify the Federal awards included in the cluster and advise the subrecipients of compliance requirements applicable to the cluster, consistent with § 200.331 Requirements for pass-through entities, paragraph (a). A cluster of programs must be considered as one program for determining major programs, as described in § 200.518 Major program determination, and, with the exception of R&D as described in § 200.501 Audit requirements, paragraph (c), whether a program-specific audit may be elected.

82

## § 200.18   Cognizant agency for audit.

*Cognizant agency for audit* means the Federal agency designated to carry out the responsibilities described in § 200.513 Responsibilities, paragraph (a). The cognizant agency for audit is not necessarily the same as the cognizant agency for indirect costs. A list of cognizant agencies for audit may be found at the FAC Web site.

## § 200.19   Cognizant agency for indirect costs.

*Cognizant agency for indirect costs* means the Federal agency responsible for reviewing, negotiating, and approving cost allocation plans or indirect cost proposals developed under this part on behalf of all Federal agencies. The cognizant agency for indirect cost is not necessarily the same as the cognizant agency for audit. For assignments of cognizant agencies see the following:

(a) For IHEs: Appendix III to Part 200—Indirect (F&A) Costs Identification and Assignment, and Rate Determination for Institutions of Higher Education (IHEs), paragraph C.11.

(b) For nonprofit organizations: Appendix IV to Part 200—Indirect (F&A) Costs Identification and Assignment, and Rate Determination for Nonprofit Organizations, paragraph C.2.a.

(c) For state and local governments: Appendix V to Part 200—State/Local Governmentwide Central Service Cost Allocation Plans, paragraph F.1.

(d) For Indian tribes: Appendix VII to Part 200—States and Local Government and Indian Tribe Indirect Cost Proposal, paragraph D.1.

[78 FR 78608, Dec. 26, 2013, as amended at 79 FR 75880, Dec. 19, 2014; 80 FR 54407, Sept. 10, 2015]

## § 200.20   Computing devices.

*Computing devices* means machines used to acquire, store, analyze, process, and publish data and other information electronically, including accessories (or "peripherals") for printing, transmitting and receiving, or storing electronic information. See also §§ 200.94 Supplies and 200.58 Information technology systems.

## § 200.21   Compliance supplement.

*Compliance supplement* means Appendix XI to Part 200—Compliance Supplement (previously known as the Circular A–133 Compliance Supplement).

## § 200.22   Contract.

*Contract* means a legal instrument by which a non-Federal entity purchases property or services needed to carry out the project or program under a Federal award. The term as used in this part does not include a legal instrument, even if the non-Federal entity considers it a contract, when the substance of the transaction meets the definition of a Federal award or subaward (see § 200.92 Subaward).

## § 200.23   Contractor.

*Contractor* means an entity that receives a contract as defined in § 200.22 Contract.

## § 200.24   Cooperative agreement.

*Cooperative agreement* means a legal instrument of financial assistance between a Federal awarding agency or pass-through entity and a non-Federal entity that, consistent with 31 U.S.C. 6302–6305:

(a) Is used to enter into a relationship the principal purpose of which is to transfer anything of value from the Federal awarding agency or pass-through entity to the non-Federal entity to carry out a public purpose authorized by a law of the United States (see 31 U.S.C. 6101(3)); and not to acquire property or services for the Federal Government or pass-through entity's direct benefit or use;

(b) Is distinguished from a grant in that it provides for substantial involvement between the Federal awarding agency or pass-through entity and the non-Federal entity in carrying out the activity contemplated by the Federal award.

(c) The term does not include:

(1) A cooperative research and development agreement as defined in 15 U.S.C. 3710a; or

(2) An agreement that provides only:

(i) Direct United States Government cash assistance to an individual;

(ii) A subsidy;

(iii) A loan;

(iv) A loan guarantee; or

(v) Insurance.

## § 200.25   Cooperative audit resolution.

*Cooperative audit resolution* means the use of audit follow-up techniques which promote prompt corrective action by improving communication, fostering collaboration, promoting trust, and developing an understanding between the Federal agency and the non-Federal entity. This approach is based upon:

(a) A strong commitment by Federal agency and non-Federal entity leadership to program integrity;

(b) Federal agencies strengthening partnerships and working cooperatively with non-Federal entities and their auditors; and non-Federal entities and their auditors working cooperatively with Federal agencies;

(c) A focus on current conditions and corrective action going forward;

(d) Federal agencies offering appropriate relief for past noncompliance when audits show prompt corrective action has occurred; and

(e) Federal agency leadership sending a clear message that continued failure to correct conditions identified by audits which are likely to cause improper payments, fraud, waste, or abuse is unacceptable and will result in sanctions.

## § 200.26   Corrective action.

*Corrective action* means action taken by the auditee that:

(a) Corrects identified deficiencies;

(b) Produces recommended improvements; or

(c) Demonstrates that audit findings are either invalid or do not warrant auditee action.

## § 200.27   Cost allocation plan.

*Cost allocation plan* means central service cost allocation plan or public assistance cost allocation plan.

## § 200.28   Cost objective.

*Cost objective* means a program, function, activity, award, organizational subdivision, contract, or work unit for which cost data are desired and for which provision is made to accumulate and measure the cost of processes, products, jobs, capital projects, etc. A cost objective may be a major function of the non-Federal entity, a particular service or project, a Federal award, or an indirect (Facilities & Administrative (F&A)) cost activity, as described in Subpart E—Cost Principles of this Part. See also §§ 200.44 Final cost objective and 200.60 Intermediate cost objective.

## § 200.29   Cost sharing or matching.

*Cost sharing or matching* means the portion of project costs not paid by Federal funds (unless otherwise authorized by Federal statute). See also § 200.306 Cost sharing or matching.

## § 200.30   Cross-cutting audit finding.

*Cross-cutting audit finding* means an audit finding where the same underlying condition or issue affects Federal awards of more than one Federal awarding agency or pass-through entity.

## § 200.31   Disallowed costs.

*Disallowed costs* means those charges to a Federal award that the Federal awarding agency or pass-through entity determines to be unallowable, in accordance with the applicable Federal statutes, regulations, or the terms and conditions of the Federal award.

## § 200.32   [Reserved]

## § 200.33   Equipment.

*Equipment* means tangible personal property (including information technology systems) having a useful life of more than one year and a per-unit acquisition cost which equals or exceeds the lesser of the capitalization level established by the non-Federal entity for financial statement purposes, or $5,000. See also §§ 200.12 Capital assets, 200.20 Computing devices, 200.48 General purpose equipment, 200.58 Information technology systems, 200.89 Special purpose equipment, and 200.94 Supplies.

## § 200.34   Expenditures.

*Expenditures* means charges made by a non-Federal entity to a project or program for which a Federal award was received.

(a) The charges may be reported on a cash or accrual basis, as long as the methodology is disclosed and is consistently applied.

(b) For reports prepared on a cash basis, expenditures are the sum of:

(1) Cash disbursements for direct charges for property and services;

(2) The amount of indirect expense charged;

(3) The value of third-party in-kind contributions applied; and

(4) The amount of cash advance payments and payments made to subrecipients.

(c) For reports prepared on an accrual basis, expenditures are the sum of:

(1) Cash disbursements for direct charges for property and services;

(2) The amount of indirect expense incurred;

(3) The value of third-party in-kind contributions applied; and

(4) The net increase or decrease in the amounts owed by the non-Federal entity for:

(i) Goods and other property received;

(ii) Services performed by employees, contractors, subrecipients, and other payees; and

(iii) Programs for which no current services or performance are required such as annuities, insurance claims, or other benefit payments.

### § 200.35   Federal agency.

*Federal agency* means an "agency" as defined at 5 U.S.C. 551(1) and further clarified by 5 U.S.C. 552(f).

### § 200.36   Federal Audit Clearinghouse (FAC).

*FAC* means the clearinghouse designated by OMB as the repository of record where non-Federal entities are required to transmit the reporting packages required by Subpart F—Audit Requirements of this part. The mailing address of the FAC is Federal Audit Clearinghouse, Bureau of the Census, 1201 E. 10th Street, Jeffersonville, IN 47132 and the web address is: *http://harvester.census.gov/sac/*. Any future updates to the location of the FAC may be found at the OMB Web site.

### § 200.37   Federal awarding agency.

*Federal awarding agency* means the Federal agency that provides a Federal award directly to a non-Federal entity.

### § 200.38   Federal award.

*Federal award* has the meaning, depending on the context, in either paragraph (a) or (b) of this section:

(a)(1) The Federal financial assistance that a non-Federal entity receives directly from a Federal awarding agency or indirectly from a pass-through entity, as described in § 200.101 Applicability; or

(2) The cost-reimbursement contract under the Federal Acquisition Regulations that a non-Federal entity receives directly from a Federal awarding agency or indirectly from a pass-through entity, as described in § 200.101 Applicability.

(b) The instrument setting forth the terms and conditions. The instrument is the grant agreement, cooperative agreement, other agreement for assistance covered in paragraph (b) of § 200.40 Federal financial assistance, or the cost-reimbursement contract awarded under the Federal Acquisition Regulations.

(c) Federal award does not include other contracts that a Federal agency uses to buy goods or services from a contractor or a contract to operate Federal Government owned, contractor operated facilities (GOCOs).

(d) See also definitions of Federal financial assistance, grant agreement, and cooperative agreement.

### § 200.39   Federal award date.

*Federal award date* means the date when the Federal award is signed by the authorized official of the Federal awarding agency.

### § 200.40   Federal financial assistance.

(a) *Federal financial assistance* means assistance that non-Federal entities receive or administer in the form of:

(1) Grants;

(2) Cooperative agreements;

(3) Non-cash contributions or donations of property (including donated surplus property);

(4) Direct appropriations;

(5) Food commodities; and

(6) Other financial assistance (except assistance listed in paragraph (b) of this section).

(b) For § 200.202 Requirement to provide public notice of Federal financial assistance programs and Subpart F—

Audit Requirements of this part, *Federal financial assistance* also includes assistance that non-Federal entities receive or administer in the form of:

(1) Loans;

(2) Loan Guarantees;

(3) Interest subsidies; and

(4) Insurance.

(c) *Federal financial assistance* does not include amounts received as reimbursement for services rendered to individuals as described in § 200.502 Basis for determining Federal awards *expended*, paragraph (h) and (i) of this part.

[78 FR 78608, Dec. 26, 2013, as amended at 80 FR 54407, Sept. 10, 2015]

### § 200.41   Federal interest.

*Federal interest* means, for purposes of § 200.329 Reporting on real property or when used in connection with the acquisition or improvement of real property, equipment, or supplies under a Federal award, the dollar amount that is the product of the:

(a) Federal share of total project costs; and

(b) Current fair market value of the property, improvements, or both, to the extent the costs of acquiring or improving the property were included as project costs.

### § 200.42   Federal program.

*Federal program* means:

(a) All Federal awards which are assigned a single number in the CFDA.

(b) When no CFDA number is assigned, all Federal awards to non-Federal entities from the same agency made for the same purpose must be combined and considered one program.

(c) Notwithstanding paragraphs (a) and (b) of this definition, a cluster of programs. The types of clusters of programs are:

(1) Research and development (R&D);

(2) Student financial aid (SFA); and

(3) "Other clusters," as described in the definition of Cluster of Programs.

[78 FR 78608, Dec. 26, 2013, as amended at 79 FR 75880, Dec. 19, 2014]

### § 200.43   Federal share.

*Federal share* means the portion of the total project costs that are paid by Federal funds.

### § 200.44   Final cost objective.

*Final cost objective* means a cost objective which has allocated to it both direct and indirect costs and, in the non-Federal entity's accumulation system, is one of the final accumulation points, such as a particular award, internal project, or other direct activity of a non-Federal entity. See also §§ 200.28 Cost objective and 200.60 Intermediate cost objective.

### § 200.45   Fixed amount awards.

*Fixed amount awards* means a type of grant agreement under which the Federal awarding agency or pass-through entity provides a specific level of support without regard to actual costs incurred under the Federal award. This type of Federal award reduces some of the administrative burden and record-keeping requirements for both the non-Federal entity and Federal awarding agency or pass-through entity. Accountability is based primarily on performance and results. See §§ 200.201 Use of grant agreements (including fixed amount awards), cooperative agreements, and contracts, paragraph (b) and 200.332 Fixed amount subawards.

### § 200.46   Foreign public entity.

*Foreign public entity* means:

(a) A foreign government or foreign governmental entity;

(b) A public international organization, which is an organization entitled to enjoy privileges, exemptions, and immunities as an international organization under the International Organizations Immunities Act (22 U.S.C. 288–288f);

(c) An entity owned (in whole or in part) or controlled by a foreign government; or

(d) Any other entity consisting wholly or partially of one or more foreign governments or foreign governmental entities.

### § 200.47   Foreign organization.

*Foreign organization* means an entity that is:

(a) A public or private organization located in a country other than the United States and its territories that is subject to the laws of the country in which it is located, irrespective of the citizenship of project staff or place of performance;

(b) A private nongovernmental organization located in a country other than the United States that solicits and receives cash contributions from the general public;

(c) A charitable organization located in a country other than the United States that is nonprofit and tax exempt under the laws of its country of domicile and operation, and is not a university, college, accredited degree-granting institution of education, private foundation, hospital, organization engaged exclusively in research or scientific activities, church, synagogue, mosque or other similar entities organized primarily for religious purposes; or

(d) An organization located in a country other than the United States not recognized as a Foreign Public Entity.

[78 FR 78608, Dec. 26, 2013, as amended at 79 FR 75880, Dec. 19, 2014]

### §200.48 General purpose equipment.

*General purpose equipment* means equipment which is not limited to research, medical, scientific or other technical activities. Examples include office equipment and furnishings, modular offices, telephone networks, information technology equipment and systems, air conditioning equipment, reproduction and printing equipment, and motor vehicles. See also Equipment and Special Purpose Equipment.

### §200.49 Generally Accepted Accounting Principles (GAAP).

*GAAP* has the meaning specified in accounting standards issued by the Government Accounting Standards Board (GASB) and the Financial Accounting Standards Board (FASB).

### §200.50 Generally Accepted Government Auditing Standards (GAGAS).

*GAGAS*, also known as the Yellow Book, means generally accepted government auditing standards issued by the Comptroller General of the United States, which are applicable to financial audits.

[78 FR 78608, Dec. 26, 2013, as amended at 79 FR 75880, Dec. 19, 2014]

### §200.51 Grant agreement.

*Grant agreement* means a legal instrument of financial assistance between a Federal awarding agency or pass-through entity and a non-Federal entity that, consistent with 31 U.S.C. 6302, 6304:

(a) Is used to enter into a relationship the principal purpose of which is to transfer anything of value from the Federal awarding agency or pass-through entity to the non-Federal entity to carry out a public purpose authorized by a law of the United States (see 31 U.S.C. 6101(3)); and not to acquire property or services for the Federal awarding agency or pass-through entity's direct benefit or use;

(b) Is distinguished from a cooperative agreement in that it does not provide for substantial involvement between the Federal awarding agency or pass-through entity and the non-Federal entity in carrying out the activity contemplated by the Federal award.

(c) Does not include an agreement that provides only:

(1) Direct United States Government cash assistance to an individual;

(2) A subsidy;

(3) A loan;

(4) A loan guarantee; or

(5) Insurance.

### §200.52 Hospital.

*Hospital* means a facility licensed as a hospital under the law of any state or a facility operated as a hospital by the United States, a state, or a subdivision of a state.

### §200.53 Improper payment.

(a) *Improper payment* means any payment that should not have been made or that was made in an incorrect amount (including overpayments and underpayments) under statutory, contractual, administrative, or other legally applicable requirements; and

(b) *Improper payment* includes any payment to an ineligible party, any payment for an ineligible good or service, any duplicate payment, any payment for a good or service not received (except for such payments where authorized by law), any payment that does not account for credit for applicable discounts, and any payment where insufficient or lack of documentation prevents a reviewer from discerning whether a payment was proper.

## § 200.54 Indian tribe (or "federally recognized Indian tribe").

*Indian tribe* means any Indian tribe, band, nation, or other organized group or community, including any Alaska Native village or regional or village corporation as defined in or established pursuant to the Alaska Native Claims Settlement Act (43 U.S.C. Chapter 33), which is recognized as eligible for the special programs and services provided by the United States to Indians because of their status as Indians (25 U.S.C. 450b(e)). See annually published Bureau of Indian Affairs list of Indian Entities Recognized and Eligible to Receive Services.

## § 200.55 Institutions of Higher Education (IHEs).

*IHE* is defined at 20 U.S.C. 1001.

## § 200.56 Indirect (facilities & administrative (F&A)) costs.

*Indirect (F&A) costs* means those costs incurred for a common or joint purpose benefitting more than one cost objective, and not readily assignable to the cost objectives specifically benefitted, without effort disproportionate to the results achieved. To facilitate equitable distribution of indirect expenses to the cost objectives served, it may be necessary to establish a number of pools of indirect (F&A) costs. Indirect (F&A) cost pools must be distributed to benefitted cost objectives on bases that will produce an equitable result in consideration of relative benefits derived.

[78 FR 78608, Dec. 26, 2013, as amended at 79 FR 75880, Dec. 19, 2014]

## § 200.57 Indirect cost rate proposal.

*Indirect cost rate proposal* means the documentation prepared by a non-Federal entity to substantiate its request for the establishment of an indirect cost rate as described in Appendix III to Part 200—Indirect (F&A) Costs Identification and Assignment, and Rate Determination for Institutions of Higher Education (IHEs) through Appendix VII to Part 200—States and Local Government and Indian Tribe Indirect Cost

Proposals of this part, and Appendix IX to Part 200—Hospital Cost Principles.

[78 FR 78608, Dec. 26, 2013, as amended at 79 FR 75880, Dec. 19, 2014]

## § 200.58 Information technology systems.

*Information technology systems* means computing devices, ancillary equipment, software, firmware, and similar procedures, services (including support services), and related resources. See also §§ 200.20 Computing devices and 200.33 Equipment.

## § 200.59 Intangible property.

*Intangible property* means property having no physical existence, such as trademarks, copyrights, patents and patent applications and property, such as loans, notes and other debt instruments, lease agreements, stock and other instruments of property ownership (whether the property is tangible or intangible).

## § 200.60 Intermediate cost objective.

*Intermediate cost objective* means a cost objective that is used to accumulate indirect costs or service center costs that are subsequently allocated to one or more indirect cost pools or final cost objectives. See also § 200.28 Cost objective and § 200.44 Final cost objective.

## § 200.61 Internal controls.

*Internal controls* means a process, implemented by a non-Federal entity, designed to provide reasonable assurance regarding the achievement of objectives in the following categories:

(a) Effectiveness and efficiency of operations;

(b) Reliability of reporting for internal and external use; and

(c) Compliance with applicable laws and regulations.

## § 200.62 Internal control over compliance requirements for Federal awards.

*Internal control over compliance requirements for Federal awards* means a process implemented by a non-Federal entity designed to provide reasonable assurance regarding the achievement of the following objectives for Federal awards:

(a) Transactions are properly recorded and accounted for, in order to:

(1) Permit the preparation of reliable financial statements and Federal reports;

(2) Maintain accountability over assets; and

(3) Demonstrate compliance with Federal statutes, regulations, and the terms and conditions of the Federal award;

(b) Transactions are executed in compliance with:

(1) Federal statutes, regulations, and the terms and conditions of the Federal award that could have a direct and material effect on a Federal program; and

(2) Any other Federal statutes and regulations that are identified in the Compliance Supplement; and

(c) Funds, property, and other assets are safeguarded against loss from unauthorized use or disposition.

## § 200.63 Loan.

*Loan* means a Federal loan or loan guarantee received or administered by a non-Federal entity, except as used in the definition of § 200.80 Program income.

(a) The term "direct loan" means a disbursement of funds by the Federal Government to a non-Federal borrower under a contract that requires the repayment of such funds with or without interest. The term includes the purchase of, or participation in, a loan made by another lender and financing arrangements that defer payment for more than 90 days, including the sale of a Federal Government asset on credit terms. The term does not include the acquisition of a federally guaranteed loan in satisfaction of default claims or the price support loans of the Commodity Credit Corporation.

(b) The term "direct loan obligation" means a binding agreement by a Federal awarding agency to make a direct loan when specified conditions are fulfilled by the borrower.

(c) The term "loan guarantee" means any Federal Government guarantee, insurance, or other pledge with respect to the payment of all or a part of the principal or interest on any debt obligation of a non-Federal borrower to a non-Federal lender, but does not include the insurance of deposits, shares, or other withdrawable accounts in financial institutions.

(d) The term "loan guarantee commitment" means a binding agreement by a Federal awarding agency to make a loan guarantee when specified conditions are fulfilled by the borrower, the lender, or any other party to the guarantee agreement.

## § 200.64 Local government.

*Local government* means any unit of government within a state, including a:

(a) County;

(b) Borough;

(c) Municipality;

(d) City;

(e) Town;

(f) Township;

(g) Parish;

(h) Local public authority, including any public housing agency under the United States Housing Act of 1937;

(i) Special district;

(j) School district;

(k) Intrastate district;

(l) Council of governments, whether or not incorporated as a nonprofit corporation under state law; and

(m) Any other agency or instrumentality of a multi-, regional, or intrastate or local government.

## § 200.65 Major program.

*Major program* means a Federal program determined by the auditor to be a major program in accordance with § 200.518 Major program determination or a program identified as a major program by a Federal awarding agency or pass-through entity in accordance with § 200.503 Relation to other audit requirements, paragraph (e).

## § 200.66 Management decision.

*Management decision* means the evaluation by the Federal awarding agency or pass-through entity of the audit findings and corrective action plan and the issuance of a written decision to the auditee as to what corrective action is necessary.

## § 200.67 Micro-purchase.

*Micro-purchase* means a purchase of supplies or services using simplified acquisition procedures, the aggregate amount of which does not exceed the micro-purchase threshold. Micro-purchase procedures comprise a subset of a non-Federal entity's small purchase procedures. The non-Federal entity uses such procedures in order to expedite the completion of its lowest-dollar small purchase transactions and minimize the associated administrative burden and cost. The micro-purchase threshold is set by the Federal Acquisition Regulation at 48 CFR Subpart 2.1 (Definitions). It is $3,000 except as otherwise discussed in Subpart 2.1 of that regulation, but this threshold is periodically adjusted for inflation.

### § 200.68 Modified Total Direct Cost (MTDC).

*MTDC* means all direct salaries and wages, applicable fringe benefits, materials and supplies, services, travel, and up to the first $25,000 of each subaward (regardless of the period of performance of the subawards under the award). MTDC excludes equipment, capital expenditures, charges for patient care, rental costs, tuition remission, scholarships and fellowships, participant support costs and the portion of each subaward in excess of $25,000. Other items may only be excluded when necessary to avoid a serious inequity in the distribution of indirect costs, and with the approval of the cognizant agency for indirect costs.

[79 FR 75880, Dec. 19, 2014]

### § 200.69 Non-Federal entity.

*Non-Federal entity* means a state, local government, Indian tribe, institution of higher education (IHE), or non-profit organization that carries out a Federal award as a recipient or subrecipient.

### § 200.70 Nonprofit organization.

*Nonprofit organization* means any corporation, trust, association, cooperative, or other organization, not including IHEs, that:
(a) Is operated primarily for scientific, educational, service, charitable, or similar purposes in the public interest;
(b) Is not organized primarily for profit; and
(c) Uses net proceeds to maintain, improve, or expand the operations of the organization.

### § 200.71 Obligations.

When used in connection with a non-Federal entity's utilization of funds under a Federal award, *obligations* means orders placed for property and services, contracts and subawards made, and similar transactions during a given period that require payment by the non-Federal entity during the same or a future period.

### § 200.72 Office of Management and Budget (OMB).

*OMB* means the Executive Office of the President, Office of Management and Budget.

### § 200.73 Oversight agency for audit.

*Oversight agency for audit* means the Federal awarding agency that provides the predominant amount of funding directly to a non-Federal entity not assigned a cognizant agency for audit. When there is no direct funding, the Federal awarding agency which is the predominant source of pass-through funding must assume the oversight responsibilities. The duties of the oversight agency for audit and the process for any reassignments are described in § 200.513 Responsibilities, paragraph (b).

### § 200.74 Pass-through entity.

*Pass-through entity* means a non-Federal entity that provides a subaward to a subrecipient to carry out part of a Federal program.

### § 200.75 Participant support costs.

*Participant support costs* means direct costs for items such as stipends or subsistence allowances, travel allowances, and registration fees paid to or on behalf of participants or trainees (but not employees) in connection with conferences, or training projects.

### § 200.76 Performance goal.

*Performance goal* means a target level of performance expressed as a tangible, measurable objective, against which actual achievement can be compared, including a goal expressed as a quantitative standard, value, or rate. In some instances (e.g., discretionary research awards), this may be limited to the requirement to submit technical performance reports (to be evaluated in accordance with agency policy).

### § 200.77  Period of performance.

*Period of performance* means the time during which the non-Federal entity may incur new obligations to carry out the work authorized under the Federal award. The Federal awarding agency or pass-through entity must include start and end dates of the period of performance in the Federal award (see §§ 200.210 Information contained in a Federal award paragraph (a)(5) and 200.331 Requirements for pass-through entities, paragraph (a)(1)(iv)).

### § 200.78  Personal property.

*Personal property* means property other than real property. It may be tangible, having physical existence, or intangible.

### § 200.79  Personally Identifiable Information (PII).

*PII* means information that can be used to distinguish or trace an individual's identity, either alone or when combined with other personal or identifying information that is linked or linkable to a specific individual. Some information that is considered to be PII is available in public sources such as telephone books, public Web sites, and university listings. This type of information is considered to be Public PII and includes, for example, first and last name, address, work telephone number, email address, home telephone number, and general educational credentials. The definition of PII is not anchored to any single category of information or technology. Rather, it requires a case-by-case assessment of the specific risk that an individual can be identified. Non-PII can become PII whenever additional information is made publicly available, in any medium and from any source, that, when combined with other available information, could be used to identify an individual.

### § 200.80  Program income.

*Program income* means gross income earned by the non-Federal entity that is directly generated by a supported activity or earned as a result of the Federal award during the period of performance except as provided in § 200.307 paragraph (f). (See § 200.77 Period of performance.) Program income includes but is not limited to income from fees for services performed, the use or rental or real or personal property acquired under Federal awards, the sale of commodities or items fabricated under a Federal award, license fees and royalties on patents and copyrights, and principal and interest on loans made with Federal award funds. Interest earned on advances of Federal funds is not program income. Except as otherwise provided in Federal statutes, regulations, or the terms and conditions of the Federal award, program income does not include rebates, credits, discounts, and interest earned on any of them. See also § 200.407 Prior written approval (prior approval). See also 35 U.S.C. 200–212 "Disposition of Rights in Educational Awards" applies to inventions made under Federal awards.

[78 FR 78608, Dec. 26, 2013, as amended at 79 FR 75880, Dec. 19, 2014]

### § 200.81  Property.

*Property* means real property or personal property.

### § 200.82  Protected Personally Identifiable Information (Protected PII).

*Protected PII* means an individual's first name or first initial and last name in combination with any one or more of types of information, including, but not limited to, social security number, passport number, credit card numbers, clearances, bank numbers, biometrics, date and place of birth, mother's maiden name, criminal, medical and financial records, educational transcripts. This does not include PII that is required by law to be disclosed. (See also § 200.79 Personally Identifiable Information (PII)).

### § 200.83  Project cost.

*Project cost* means total allowable costs incurred under a Federal award and all required cost sharing and voluntary committed cost sharing, including third-party contributions.

### § 200.84  Questioned cost.

*Questioned cost* means a cost that is questioned by the auditor because of an audit finding:

(a) Which resulted from a violation or possible violation of a statute, regulation, or the terms and conditions of a Federal award, including for funds used to match Federal funds;

(b) Where the costs, at the time of the audit, are not supported by adequate documentation; or

(c) Where the costs incurred appear unreasonable and do not reflect the actions a prudent person would take in the circumstances.

§ 200.85  Real property.

*Real property* means land, including land improvements, structures and appurtenances thereto, but excludes moveable machinery and equipment.

§ 200.86  Recipient.

*Recipient* means a non-Federal entity that receives a Federal award directly from a Federal awarding agency to carry out an activity under a Federal program. The term recipient does not include subrecipients. See also § 200.69 Non-Federal entity.

§ 200.87  Research and Development (R&D).

*R&D* means all research activities, both basic and applied, and all development activities that are performed by non-Federal entities. The term research also includes activities involving the training of individuals in research techniques where such activities utilize the same facilities as other research and development activities and where such activities are not included in the instruction function. "Research" is defined as a systematic study directed toward fuller scientific knowledge or understanding of the subject studied. "Development" is the systematic use of knowledge and understanding gained from research directed toward the production of useful materials, devices, systems, or methods, including design and development of prototypes and processes.

§ 200.88  Simplified acquisition threshold.

*Simplified acquisition threshold* means the dollar amount below which a non-Federal entity may purchase property or services using small purchase methods. Non-Federal entities adopt small purchase procedures in order to expedite the purchase of items costing less than the simplified acquisition threshold. The simplified acquisition threshold is set by the Federal Acquisition Regulation at 48 CFR Subpart 2.1 (Definitions) and in accordance with 41 U.S.C. 1908. As of the publication of this part, the simplified acquisition threshold is $150,000, but this threshold is periodically adjusted for inflation. (Also see definition of § 200.67 Micropurchase.)

§ 200.89  Special purpose equipment.

*Special purpose equipment* means equipment which is used only for research, medical, scientific, or other technical activities. Examples of special purpose equipment include microscopes, x-ray machines, surgical instruments, and spectrometers. See also §§ 200.33 Equipment and 200.48 General purpose equipment.

§ 200.90  State.

*State* means any state of the United States, the District of Columbia, the Commonwealth of Puerto Rico, U.S. Virgin Islands, Guam, American Samoa, the Commonwealth of the Northern Mariana Islands, and any agency or instrumentality thereof exclusive of local governments.

[78 FR 78608, Dec. 26, 2013, as amended at 79 FR 75880, Dec. 19, 2014]

§ 200.91  Student Financial Aid (SFA).

*SFA* means Federal awards under those programs of general student assistance, such as those authorized by Title IV of the Higher Education Act of 1965, as amended, (20 U.S.C. 1070–1099d), which are administered by the U.S. Department of Education, and similar programs provided by other Federal agencies. It does not include Federal awards under programs that provide fellowships or similar Federal awards to students on a competitive basis, or for specified studies or research.

§ 200.92  Subaward.

*Subaward* means an award provided by a pass-through entity to a subrecipient for the subrecipient to carry out part of a Federal award received by the pass-through entity. It does not include payments to a contractor or payments to an individual that is a beneficiary of a Federal program. A subaward may be provided through any form of legal agreement, including an agreement that the pass-through entity considers a contract.

## §200.93 Subrecipient.

*Subrecipient* means a non-Federal entity that receives a subaward from a pass-through entity to carry out part of a Federal program; but does not include an individual that is a beneficiary of such program. A subrecipient may also be a recipient of other Federal awards directly from a Federal awarding agency.

## §200.94 Supplies.

*Supplies* means all tangible personal property other than those described in §200.33 Equipment. A computing device is a supply if the acquisition cost is less than the lesser of the capitalization level established by the non-Federal entity for financial statement purposes or $5,000, regardless of the length of its useful life. See also §§200.20 Computing devices and 200.33 Equipment.

## §200.95 Termination.

*Termination* means the ending of a Federal award, in whole or in part at any time prior to the planned end of period of performance.

## §200.96 Third-party in-kind contributions.

*Third-party in-kind contributions* means the value of non-cash contributions (i.e., property or services) that—
(a) Benefit a federally assisted project or program; and
(b) Are contributed by non-Federal third parties, without charge, to a non-Federal entity under a Federal award.

## §200.97 Unliquidated obligations.

*Unliquidated obligations* means, for financial reports prepared on a cash basis, obligations incurred by the non-Federal entity that have not been paid (liquidated). For reports prepared on an accrual expenditure basis, these are obligations incurred by the non-Federal entity for which an expenditure has not been recorded.

## §200.98 Unobligated balance.

*Unobligated balance* means the amount of funds under a Federal award that the non-Federal entity has not obligated. The amount is computed by subtracting the cumulative amount of the non-Federal entity's unliquidated obligations and expenditures of funds under the Federal award from the cumulative amount of the funds that the Federal awarding agency or pass-through entity authorized the non-Federal entity to obligate.

## §200.99 Voluntary committed cost sharing.

*Voluntary committed cost sharing* means cost sharing specifically pledged on a voluntary basis in the proposal's budget or the Federal award on the part of the non-Federal entity and that becomes a binding requirement of Federal award.

# Subpart B—General Provisions

## §200.100 Purpose.

(a)(1) This part establishes uniform administrative requirements, cost principles, and audit requirements for Federal awards to non-Federal entities, as described in §200.101 Applicability. Federal awarding agencies must not impose additional or inconsistent requirements, except as provided in §§200.102 Exceptions and 200.210 Information contained in a Federal award, or unless specifically required by Federal statute, regulation, or Executive Order.

(2) This part provides the basis for a systematic and periodic collection and uniform submission by Federal agencies of information on all Federal financial assistance programs to the Office of Management and Budget (OMB). It also establishes Federal policies related to the delivery of this information to the public, including through the use of electronic media. It prescribes the manner in which General Services Administration (GSA), OMB, and Federal agencies that administer Federal financial assistance programs are to carry out their statutory responsibilities under the Federal Program Information Act (31 U.S.C. 6101–6106).

(b) *Administrative requirements.* Subparts B through D of this part set forth the uniform administrative requirements for grant and cooperative agreements, including the requirements for Federal awarding agency management of Federal grant programs before the Federal award has been made, and the requirements Federal awarding agencies may impose on non-Federal entities in the Federal award.

(c) *Cost Principles.* Subpart E—Cost Principles of this part establishes principles for determining the allowable costs incurred by non-Federal entities under Federal awards. The principles are for the purpose of cost determination and are not intended to identify the circumstances or dictate the extent of Federal Government participation in the financing of a particular program or project. The principles are designed to provide that Federal awards bear their fair share of cost recognized under these principles except where restricted or prohibited by statute.

(d) *Single Audit Requirements and Audit Follow-up.* Subpart F—Audit Requirements of this part is issued pursuant to the Single Audit Act Amendments of 1996, (31 U.S.C. 7501–7507). It sets forth standards for obtaining consistency and uniformity among Federal agencies for the audit of non-Federal entities expending Federal awards. These provisions also provide the policies and procedures for Federal awarding agencies and pass-through entities when using the results of these audits.

(e) For OMB guidance to Federal awarding agencies on Challenges and Prizes, please see M–10–11 Guidance on the Use of Challenges and Prizes to Promote Open Government, issued March 8, 2010, or its successor.

## § 200.101 Applicability.

(a) *General applicability to Federal agencies.* The requirements established in this part apply to Federal agencies that make Federal awards to non-Federal entities. These requirements are applicable to all costs related to Federal awards.

(b)(1) *Applicability to different types of Federal awards.* The following table describes what portions of this part apply to which types of Federal awards. The terms and conditions of Federal awards (including this part) flow down to subawards to subrecipients unless a particular section of this part or the terms and conditions of the Federal award specifically indicate otherwise. This means that non-Federal entities must comply with requirements in this part regardless of whether the non-Federal entity is a recipient or subrecipient of a Federal award. Pass-through entities must comply with the requirements described in Subpart D—Post Federal Award Requirements of this part, §§ 200.330 Subrecipient and contractor determinations through 200.332 Fixed amount Subawards, but not any requirements in this part directed towards Federal awarding agencies unless the requirements of this part or the terms and conditions of the Federal award indicate otherwise.

| This table must be read along with the other provisions of this section | | |
|---|---|---|
| The following portions of this Part | Are applicable to the following types of Federal Awards and Fixed-Price Contracts and Subcontracts (except as noted in paragraphs (d) and (e) below): | Are NOT applicable to the following types of Federal Awards and Fixed-Price Contracts and Subcontracts: |
| Subpart A—Acronyms and Definitions ............. | —All. | |
| Subpart B—General Provisions, except for §§ 200.111 English Language, 200.112 Conflict of Interest, 200.113 Mandatory Disclosures. | —All. | |
| §§ 200.111 English Language, 200.112 Conflict of Interest, 200.113 Mandatory Disclosures. | —Grant Agreements and cooperative agreements. | —Agreements for loans, loan guarantees, interest subsidies and insurance.<br>—Procurement contracts awarded by Federal Agencies under the Federal Acquisition Regulation and subcontracts under those contracts. |

| The following portions of this Part | Are applicable to the following types of Federal Awards and Fixed-Price Contracts and Subcontracts (except as noted in paragraphs (d) and (e) below): | Are NOT applicable to the following types of Federal Awards and Fixed-Price Contracts and Subcontracts: |
|---|---|---|
| | This table must be read along with the other provisions of this section | |
| Subparts C–D, except for §§ 200.202 Requirement to provide public notice of Federal financial assistance programs, 200.303 Internal controls, 200.330–332 Subrecipient Monitoring and Management. | —Grant Agreements and cooperative agreements. | —Agreements for loans, loan guarantees, interest subsidies and insurance.<br>—Procurement contracts awarded by Federal Agencies under the Federal Acquisition Regulation and subcontracts under those contracts. |
| § 200.202 Requirement to provide public notice of Federal financial assistance programs. | —Grant Agreements and cooperative agreements.<br>—Agreements for loans, loan guarantees, interest subsidies and insurance. | —Procurement contracts awarded by Federal Agencies under the Federal Acquisition Regulation and subcontracts under those contracts. |
| §§ 200.303 Internal controls, 200.330–332 Subrecipient Monitoring and Management. | —All. | |
| Subpart E—Cost Principles | —Grant Agreements and cooperative agreements, except those providing food commodities.<br>—All procurement contracts under the Federal Acquisition Regulations except those that are not negotiated. | —Grant agreements and cooperative agreements providing foods commodities.<br>—Fixed amount awards.<br>—Agreements for loans, loans guarantees, interest subsidies and insurance.<br>—Federal awards to hospitals (see Appendix IX Hospital Cost Principles). |
| Subpart F—Audit Requirements | —Grant Agreements and cooperative agreements.<br>—Contracts and subcontracts, except for fixed price contacts and subcontracts, awarded under the Federal Acquisition Regulation.<br>—Agreements for loans, loans guarantees, interest subsidies and insurance and other forms of Federal Financial Assistance as defined by the Single Audit Act Amendment of 1996. | —Fixed-price contracts and subcontracts awarded under the Federal Acquisition Regulation. |

(2) *Federal award of cost-reimbursement contract under the FAR to a non-Federal entity.* When a non-Federal entity is awarded a cost-reimbursement contract, only Subpart D—Post Federal Award Requirements of this part, §§ 200.330 Subrecipient and contractor determinations through 200.332 Fixed amount Subawards (in addition to any FAR related requirements for subaward monitoring), Subpart E—Cost Principles of this part and Subpart F—Audit Requirements of this part are incorporated by reference into the contract. However, when the Cost Accounting Standards (CAS) are applicable to the contract, they take precedence over the requirements of this part except for Subpart F—Audit Requirements of this part when they are in conflict. In addition, costs that are made unallowable under 10 U.S.C.

2324(e) and 41 U.S.C. 4304(a) as described in the FAR subpart 31.2 and subpart 31.603 are always unallowable. For requirements other than those covered in Subpart D—Post Federal Award Requirements of this part, §§ 200.330 Subrecipient and contractor determinations through 200.332 Fixed amount Subawards, Subpart E—Cost Principles of this part and Subpart F—Audit Requirements of this part, the terms of the contract and the FAR apply.

(3) With the exception of Subpart F—Audit Requirements of this part, which is required by the Single Audit Act, in any circumstances where the provisions of Federal statutes or regulations differ from the provisions of this part, the provision of the Federal statutes or regulations govern. This includes, for

agreements with Indian tribes, the provisions of the Indian Self-Determination and Education and Assistance Act (ISDEAA), as amended, 25 U.S.C 450–458ddd–2.

(c) Federal awarding agencies may apply subparts A through E of this part to for-profit entities, foreign public entities, or foreign organizations, except where the Federal awarding agency determines that the application of these subparts would be inconsistent with the international obligations of the United States or the statutes or regulations of a foreign government.

(d) Except for § 200.202 Requirement to provide public notice of Federal financial assistance programs and §§ 200.330 Subrecipient and contractor determinations through 200.332 Fixed amount Subawards of Subpart D—Post Federal Award Requirements of this part, the requirements in Subpart C—Pre-Federal Award Requirements and Contents of Federal Awards, Subpart D—Post Federal Award Requirements of this part, and Subpart E—Cost Principles of this part do not apply to the following programs:

(1) The block grant awards authorized by the Omnibus Budget Reconciliation Act of 1981 (including Community Services), except to the extent that Subpart E—Cost Principles of this Part apply to subrecipients of Community Services Block Grant funds pursuant to 42 U.S.C. 9916(a)(1)(B);

(2) Federal awards to local education agencies under 20 U.S.C. 7702–7703b, (portions of the Impact Aid program);

(3) Payments under the Department of Veterans Affairs' State Home Per Diem Program (38 U.S.C. 1741); and

(4) Federal awards authorized under the Child Care and Development Block Grant Act of 1990, as amended:

(i) Child Care and Development Block Grant (42 U.S.C. 9858)

(ii) Child Care Mandatory and Matching Funds of the Child Care and Development Fund (42 U.S.C. 9858)

(e) Except for § 200.202 Requirement to provide public notice of Federal financial assistance programs the guidance in Subpart C—Pre-Federal Award Requirements and Contents of Federal Awards of this part does not apply to the following programs:

(1) Entitlement Federal awards to carry out the following programs of the Social Security Act:

(i) Temporary Assistance to Needy Families (title IV–A of the Social Security Act, 42 U.S.C. 601–619);

(ii) Child Support Enforcement and Establishment of Paternity (title IV–D of the Social Security Act, 42 U.S.C. 651–669b);

(iii) Foster Care and Adoption Assistance (title IV–E of the Act, 42 U.S.C. 670–679c);

(iv) Aid to the Aged, Blind, and Disabled (titles I, X, XIV, and XVI–AABD of the Act, as amended);

(v) Medical Assistance (Medicaid) (title XIX of the Act, 42 U.S.C. 1396–1396w–5) not including the State Medicaid Fraud Control program authorized by section 1903(a)(6)(B) of the Social Security Act (42 U.S.C. 1396b(a)(6)(B)); and

(vi) Children's Health Insurance Program (title XXI of the Act, 42 U.S.C. 1397aa–1397mm).

(2) A Federal award for an experimental, pilot, or demonstration project that is also supported by a Federal award listed in paragraph (e)(1) of this section;

(3) Federal awards under subsection 412(e) of the Immigration and Nationality Act and subsection 501(a) of the Refugee Education Assistance Act of 1980 (Pub. L. 96–422, 94 Stat. 1809), for cash assistance, medical assistance, and supplemental security income benefits to refugees and entrants and the administrative costs of providing the assistance and benefits (8 U.S.C. 1522(e));

(4) Entitlement awards under the following programs of The National School Lunch Act:

(i) National School Lunch Program (section 4 of the Act, 42 U.S.C. 1753),

(ii) Commodity Assistance (section 6 of the Act, 42 U.S.C. 1755),

(iii) Special Meal Assistance (section 11 of the Act, 42 U.S.C. 1759a),

(iv) Summer Food Service Program for Children (section 13 of the Act, 42 U.S.C. 1761), and

(v) Child and Adult Care Food Program (section 17 of the Act, 42 U.S.C. 1766).

(5) Entitlement awards under the following programs of The Child Nutrition Act of 1966:

(i) Special Milk Program (section 3 of the Act, 42 U.S.C. 1772),

(ii) School Breakfast Program (section 4 of the Act, 42 U.S.C. 1773), and

(iii) State Administrative Expenses (section 7 of the Act, 42 U.S.C. section 1776).

(6) Entitlement awards for State Administrative Expenses under The Food and Nutrition Act of 2008 (section 16 of the Act, 7 U.S.C. 2025).

(7) Non-discretionary Federal awards under the following non-entitlement programs:

(i) Special Supplemental Nutrition Program for Women, Infants and Children (section 17 of the Child Nutrition Act of 1966) 42 U.S.C. section 1786;

(ii) The Emergency Food Assistance Programs (Emergency Food Assistance Act of 1983) 7 U.S.C. section 7501 note; and

(iii) Commodity Supplemental Food Program (section 5 of the Agriculture and Consumer Protection Act of 1973) 7 U.S.C. section 612c note.

[78 FR 78608, Dec. 26, 2013, as amended at 79 FR 75880, Dec. 19, 2014; 80 FR 54407, Sept. 10, 2015]

### § 200.102 Exceptions.

(a) With the exception of Subpart F—Audit Requirements of this part, OMB may allow exceptions for classes of Federal awards or non-Federal entities subject to the requirements of this part when exceptions are not prohibited by statute. However, in the interest of maximum uniformity, exceptions from the requirements of this part will be permitted only in unusual circumstances. Exceptions for classes of Federal awards or non-Federal entities will be published on the OMB Web site at *www.whitehouse.gov/omb*.

(b) Exceptions on a case-by-case basis for individual non-Federal entities may be authorized by the Federal awarding agency or cognizant agency for indirect costs, except where otherwise required by law or where OMB or other approval is expressly required by this part.

(c) The Federal awarding agency may apply more restrictive requirements to a class of Federal awards or non-Federal entities when approved by OMB, or when, required by Federal statutes or regulations, except for the requirements in Subpart F—Audit Requirements of this part. A Federal awarding agency may apply less restrictive requirements when making fixed amount awards as defined in Subpart A—Acronyms and Definitions of this part, except for those requirements imposed by statute or in Subpart F—Audit Requirements of this part.

(d) On a case-by-case basis, OMB will approve new strategies for Federal awards when proposed by the Federal awarding agency in accordance with OMB guidance (such as M–13–17) to develop additional evidence relevant to addressing important policy challenges or to promote cost-effectiveness in and across Federal programs. Proposals may draw on the innovative program designs discussed in M–13–17 to expand or improve the use of effective practices in delivering Federal financial assistance while also encouraging innovation in service delivery. Proposals submitted to OMB in accordance with M–13–17 may include requests to waive requirements other than those in Subpart F—Audit Requirements of this part.

[78 FR 78608, Dec. 26, 2013, as amended at 79 FR 75881, Dec. 19, 2014]

### § 200.103 Authorities.

This part is issued under the following authorities.

(a) Subpart B—General Provisions of this part through Subpart D—Post Federal Award Requirements of this part are authorized under 31 U.S.C. 503 (the Chief Financial Officers Act, Functions of the Deputy Director for Management), 31 U.S.C. 1111 (Improving Economy and Efficiency of the United States Government), 41 U.S.C. 1101–1131 (the Office of Federal Procurement Policy Act), Reorganization Plan No. 2 of 1970, and Executive Order 11541 ("Prescribing the Duties of the Office of Management and Budget and the Domestic Policy Council in the Executive Office of the President"), the Single Audit Act Amendments of 1996, (31 U.S.C. 7501–7507), as well as The Federal Program Information Act (Public Law 95–220 and Public Law 98–169, as amended, codified at 31 U.S.C. 6101–6106).

(b) Subpart E—Cost Principles of this part is authorized under the Budget and Accounting Act of 1921, as amended; the Budget and Accounting Procedures Act of 1950, as amended (31 U.S.C. 1101–1125); the Chief Financial Officers Act of 1990 (31 U.S.C. 503–504); Reorganization Plan No. 2 of 1970; and Executive Order No. 11541, "Prescribing the Duties of the Office of Management and Budget and the Domestic Policy Council in the Executive Office of the President."

(c) Subpart F—Audit Requirements of this part is authorized under the Single Audit Act Amendments of 1996, (31 U.S.C. 7501–7507).

§ 200.104  Supersession.

As described in § 200.110 Effective/applicability date, this part supersedes the following OMB guidance documents and regulations under Title 2 of the Code of Federal Regulations:

(a) A–21, "Cost Principles for Educational Institutions" (2 CFR part 220);

(b) A–87, "Cost Principles for State, Local and Indian Tribal Governments" (2 CFR part 225) and also FEDERAL REGISTER notice 51 FR 552 (January 6, 1986);

(c) A–89, "Federal Domestic Assistance Program Information";

(d) A–102, "Grant Awards and Cooperative Agreements with State and Local Governments";

(e) A–110, "Uniform Administrative Requirements for Awards and Other Agreements with Institutions of Higher Education, Hospitals, and Other Nonprofit Organizations" (codified at 2 CFR 215);

(f) A–122, "Cost Principles for Non-Profit Organizations" (2 CFR part 230);

(g) A–133, "Audits of States, Local Governments and Non-Profit Organizations "; and

(h) Those sections of A–50 related to audits performed under Subpart F—Audit Requirements of this part.

[78 FR 78608, Dec. 26, 2013, as amended at 79 FR 75882, Dec. 19, 2014]

§ 200.105  Effect on other issuances.

For Federal awards subject to this part, all administrative requirements, program manuals, handbooks and other non-regulatory materials that are inconsistent with the requirements of this part must be superseded upon implementation of this part by the Federal agency, except to the extent they are required by statute or authorized in accordance with the provisions in § 200.102 Exceptions.

§ 200.106  Agency implementation.

The specific requirements and responsibilities of Federal agencies and non-Federal entities are set forth in this part. Federal agencies making Federal awards to non-Federal entities must implement the language in the Subpart C—Pre-Federal Award Requirements and Contents of Federal Awards of this part through Subpart F—Audit Requirements of this part in codified regulations unless different provisions are required by Federal statute or are approved by OMB.

§ 200.107  OMB responsibilities.

OMB will review Federal agency regulations and implementation of this part, and will provide interpretations of policy requirements and assistance to ensure effective and efficient implementation. Any exceptions will be subject to approval by OMB. Exceptions will only be made in particular cases where adequate justification is presented.

§ 200.108  Inquiries.

Inquiries concerning this part may be directed to the Office of Federal Financial Management Office of Management and Budget, in Washington, DC. Non-Federal entities' inquiries should be addressed to the Federal awarding agency, cognizant agency for indirect costs, cognizant or oversight agency for audit, or pass-through entity as appropriate.

§ 200.109  Review date.

OMB will review this part at least every five years after December 26, 2013.

§ 200.110  Effective/applicability date.

(a) The standards set forth in this part that affect the administration of Federal awards issued by Federal awarding agencies become effective once implemented by Federal awarding agencies or when any future amendment to this part becomes final. Federal awarding agencies must implement the policies and procedures applicable to Federal awards by promulgating a regulation to be effective by December 26, 2014, unless different provisions are required by statute or approved by OMB. For the procurement standards in §§ 200.317 through 200.326, non-Federal entities may continue to comply with the procurement standards in previous OMB guidance (as reflected in § 200.104) for a total of three fiscal years after this part goes into effect. As such, the effective date for implementation of the procurement standards for non-Federal entities will start for fiscal years beginning on or after December 26, 2017. If a non-Federal entity chooses to use the previous procurement standards for all or part of these three fiscal years before adopting the procurement standards in this part, the non-Federal entity must document this decision in its internal procurement policies.

(b) The standards set forth in Subpart F—Audit Requirements of this part and any other standards which apply directly to Federal agencies will be effective December 26, 2013 and will apply to audits of fiscal years beginning on or after December 26, 2014.

[78 FR 78608, Dec. 26, 2013, as amended at 79 FR 75882, Dec. 19, 2014; 80 FR 54408, Sept. 10, 2015; 82 FR 22609, May 17, 2017]

### § 200.111 English language.

(a) All Federal financial assistance announcements and Federal award information must be in the English language. Applications must be submitted in the English language and must be in the terms of U.S. dollars. If the Federal awarding agency receives applications in another currency, the Federal awarding agency will evaluate the application by converting the foreign currency to United States currency using the date specified for receipt of the application.

(b) Non-Federal entities may translate the Federal award and other documents into another language. In the event of inconsistency between any terms and conditions of the Federal award and any translation into another language, the English language mean-

ing will control. Where a significant portion of the non-Federal entity's employees who are working on the Federal award are not fluent in English, the non-Federal entity must provide the Federal award in English and the language(s) with which employees are more familiar.

### § 200.112 Conflict of interest.

The Federal awarding agency must establish conflict of interest policies for Federal awards. The non-Federal entity must disclose in writing any potential conflict of interest to the Federal awarding agency or pass-through entity in accordance with applicable Federal awarding agency policy.

### § 200.113 Mandatory disclosures.

The non-Federal entity or applicant for a Federal award must disclose, in a timely manner, in writing to the Federal awarding agency or pass-through entity all violations of Federal criminal law involving fraud, bribery, or gratuity violations potentially affecting the Federal award. Non-Federal entities that have received a Federal award including the term and condition outlined in Appendix XII—Award Term and Condition for Recipient Integrity and Performance Matters are required to report certain civil, criminal, or administrative proceedings to SAM. Failure to make required disclosures can result in any of the remedies described in § 200.338 Remedies for noncompliance, including suspension or debarment. (See also 2 CFR part 180, 31 U.S.C. 3321, and 41 U.S.C. 2313.)

[80 FR 43308, July 22, 2015]

## Subpart C—Pre-Federal Award Requirements and Contents of Federal Awards

### § 200.200 Purpose.

(a) Sections 200.201 Use of grant agreements (including fixed amount awards), cooperative agreements, and contracts through 200.208 Certifications and representations prescribe instructions and other pre-award matters to be used in the announcement and application process.

(b) Use of §§ 200.203 Notices of funding opportunities, 200.204 Federal awarding agency review of merit of proposals, 200.205 Federal awarding agency review of risk posed by applicants, and 200.207 Specific conditions, is required only for competitive Federal awards, but may also be used by the Federal awarding agency for non-competitive awards where appropriate or where required by Federal statute.

[78 FR 78608, Dec. 26, 2013, as amended at 79 FR 75882, Dec. 19, 2014]

**§ 200.201 Use of grant agreements (including fixed amount awards), cooperative agreements, and contracts.**

(a) The Federal awarding agency or pass-through entity must decide on the appropriate instrument for the Federal award (i.e., grant agreement, cooperative agreement, or contract) in accordance with the Federal Grant and Cooperative Agreement Act (31 U.S.C. 6301–08).

(b) Fixed Amount Awards. In addition to the options described in paragraph (a) of this section, Federal awarding agencies, or pass-through entities as permitted in § 200.332 Fixed amount subawards, may use fixed amount awards (see § 200.45 Fixed amount awards) to which the following conditions apply:

(1) The Federal award amount is negotiated using the cost principles (or other pricing information) as a guide. The Federal awarding agency or pass-through entity may use fixed amount awards if the project scope is specific and if adequate cost, historical, or unit pricing data is available to establish a fixed amount award based on a reasonable estimate of actual cost. Payments are based on meeting specific requirements of the Federal award. Accountability is based on performance and results. Except in the case of termination before completion of the Federal award, there is no governmental review of the actual costs incurred by the non-Federal entity in performance of the award. Some of the ways in which the Federal award may be paid include, but are not limited to:

(i) In several partial payments, the amount of each agreed upon in advance, and the "milestone" or event triggering the payment also agreed

upon in advance, and set forth in the Federal award;

(ii) On a unit price basis, for a defined unit or units, at a defined price or prices, agreed to in advance of performance of the Federal award and set forth in the Federal award; or,

(iii) In one payment at Federal award completion.

(2) A fixed amount award cannot be used in programs which require mandatory cost sharing or match.

(3) The non-Federal entity must certify in writing to the Federal awarding agency or pass-through entity at the end of the Federal award that the project or activity was completed or the level of effort was expended. If the required level of activity or effort was not carried out, the amount of the Federal award must be adjusted.

(4) Periodic reports may be established for each Federal award.

(5) Changes in principal investigator, project leader, project partner, or scope of effort must receive the prior written approval of the Federal awarding agency or pass-through entity.

[78 FR 78608, Dec. 26, 2013, as amended at 79 FR 75882, Dec. 19, 2014]

**§ 200.202 Requirement to provide public notice of Federal financial assistance programs.**

(a) The Federal awarding agency must notify the public of Federal programs in the Catalog of Federal Domestic Assistance (CFDA), maintained by the General Services Administration (GSA).

(1) The CFDA, or any OMB-designated replacement, is the single, authoritative, governmentwide comprehensive source of Federal financial assistance program information produced by the executive branch of the Federal Government.

(2) The information that the Federal awarding agency must submit to GSA for approval by OMB is listed in paragraph (b) of this section. GSA must prescribe the format for the submission.

(3) The Federal awarding agency may not award Federal financial assistance without assigning it to a program that has been included in the CFDA as required in this section unless there are

exigent circumstances requiring otherwise, such as timing requirements imposed by statute.

(b) For each program that awards discretionary Federal awards, non-discretionary Federal awards, loans, insurance, or any other type of Federal financial assistance, the Federal awarding agency must submit the following information to GSA:

(1) Program Description, Purpose, Goals and Measurement. A brief summary of the statutory or regulatory requirements of the program and its intended outcome. Where appropriate, the Program Description, Purpose, Goals, and Measurement should align with the strategic goals and objectives within the Federal awarding agency's performance plan and should support the Federal awarding agency's performance measurement, management, and reporting as required by Part 6 of OMB Circular A-11;

(2) Identification of whether the program makes Federal awards on a discretionary basis or the Federal awards are prescribed by Federal statute, such as in the case of formula grants.

(3) Projected total amount of funds available for the program. Estimates based on previous year funding are acceptable if current appropriations are not available at the time of the submission;

(4) Anticipated Source of Available Funds: The statutory authority for funding the program and, to the extent possible, agency, sub-agency, or, if known, the specific program unit that will issue the Federal awards, and associated funding identifier (e.g., Treasury Account Symbol(s));

(5) General Eligibility Requirements: The statutory, regulatory or other eligibility factors or considerations that determine the applicant's qualification for Federal awards under the program (e.g., type of non-Federal entity); and

(6) Applicability of Single Audit Requirements as required by Subpart F—Audit Requirements of this part.

§ 200.203 Notices of funding opportunities.

For competitive grants and cooperative agreements, the Federal awarding agency must announce specific funding opportunities by providing the following information in a public notice:

(a) *Summary Information in Notices of Funding Opportunities.* The Federal awarding agency must display the following information posted on the OMB-designated governmentwide Web site for finding and applying for Federal financial assistance, in a location preceding the full text of the announcement:

(1) Federal Awarding Agency Name;

(2) Funding Opportunity Title;

(3) Announcement Type (whether the funding opportunity is the initial announcement of this funding opportunity or a modification of a previously announced opportunity);

(4) Funding Opportunity Number (required, if applicable). If the Federal awarding agency has assigned or will assign a number to the funding opportunity announcement, this number must be provided;

(5) Catalog of Federal Domestic Assistance (CFDA) Number(s);

(6) Key Dates. Key dates include due dates for applications or Executive Order 12372 submissions, as well as for any letters of intent or pre-applications. For any announcement issued before a program's application materials are available, key dates also include the date on which those materials will be released; and any other additional information, as deemed applicable by the relevant Federal awarding agency.

(b) The Federal awarding agency must generally make all funding opportunities available for application for at least 60 calendar days. The Federal awarding agency may make a determination to have a less than 60 calendar day availability period but no funding opportunity should be available for less than 30 calendar days unless exigent circumstances require as determined by the Federal awarding agency head or delegate.

(c) *Full Text of Funding Opportunities.* The Federal awarding agency must include the following information in the full text of each funding opportunity. For specific instructions on the content required in this section, refer to Appendix I to Part 200—Full Text of Notice of Funding Opportunity to this part.

(1) Full programmatic description of the funding opportunity.

(2) Federal award information, including sufficient information to help an applicant make an informed decision about whether to submit an application. (See also § 200.414 Indirect (F&A) costs, paragraph (c)(4)).

(3) Specific eligibility information, including any factors or priorities that affect an applicant's or its application's eligibility for selection.

(4) Application Preparation and Submission Information, including the applicable submission dates and time.

(5) Application Review Information including the criteria and process to be used to evaluate applications. See also §§ 200.204 Federal awarding agency review of merit proposals and 200.205 Federal awarding agency review of risk posed by applicants.

(6) Federal Award Administration Information. See also § 200.210 Information contained in a Federal award.

[78 FR 78608, Dec. 26, 2013, as amended at 79 FR 75882, Dec. 19, 2014; 80 FR 43308, July 22, 2015; 80 FR 54408, Sept. 10, 2015]

### § 200.204 Federal awarding agency review of merit of proposals.

For competitive grants or cooperative agreements, unless prohibited by Federal statute, the Federal awarding agency must design and execute a merit review process for applications. This process must be described or incorporated by reference in the applicable funding opportunity (see Appendix I to this part, Full text of the Funding Opportunity.) See also § 200.203 Notices of funding opportunities.

### § 200.205 Federal awarding agency review of risk posed by applicants.

(a) *Review of OMB-designated repositories of governmentwide data.* (1) Prior to making a Federal award, the Federal awarding agency is required by 31 U.S.C. 3321 and 41 U.S.C. 2313 note to review information available through any OMB-designated repositories of governmentwide eligibility qualification or financial integrity information as appropriate. See also suspension and debarment requirements at 2 CFR part 180 as well as individual Federal agency suspension and debarment regulations

in title 2 of the Code of Federal Regulations.

(2) In accordance 41 U.S.C. 2313, the Federal awarding agency is required to review the non-public segment of the OMB-designated integrity and performance system accessible through SAM (currently the Federal Awardee Performance and Integrity Information System (FAPIIS)) prior to making a Federal award where the Federal share is expected to exceed the simplified acquisition threshold, defined in 41 U.S.C. 134, over the period of performance. At a minimum, the information in the system for a prior Federal award recipient must demonstrate a satisfactory record of executing programs or activities under Federal grants, cooperative agreements, or procurement awards; and integrity and business ethics. The Federal awarding agency may make a Federal award to a recipient who does not fully meet these standards, if it is determined that the information is not relevant to the current Federal award under consideration or there are specific conditions that can appropriately mitigate the effects of the non-Federal entity's risk in accordance with § 200.207 Specific conditions.

(b) In addition, for competitive grants or cooperative agreements, the Federal awarding agency must have in place a framework for evaluating the risks posed by applicants before they receive Federal awards. This evaluation may incorporate results of the evaluation of the applicant's eligibility or the quality of its application. If the Federal awarding agency determines that a Federal award will be made, special conditions that correspond to the degree of risk assessed may be applied to the Federal award. Criteria to be evaluated must be described in the announcement of funding opportunity described in § 200.203 Notices of funding opportunities.

(c) In evaluating risks posed by applicants, the Federal awarding agency may use a risk-based approach and may consider any items such as the following:

(1) Financial stability;

(2) Quality of management systems and ability to meet the management standards prescribed in this part;

(3) History of performance. The applicant's record in managing Federal awards, if it is a prior recipient of Federal awards, including timeliness of compliance with applicable reporting requirements, conformance to the terms and conditions of previous Federal awards, and if applicable, the extent to which any previously awarded amounts will be expended prior to future awards;

(4) Reports and findings from audits performed under Subpart F—Audit Requirements of this part or the reports and findings of any other available audits; and

(5) The applicant's ability to effectively implement statutory, regulatory, or other requirements imposed on non-Federal entities.

(d) In addition to this review, the Federal awarding agency must comply with the guidelines on governmentwide suspension and debarment in 2 CFR part 180, and must require non-Federal entities to comply with these provisions. These provisions restrict Federal awards, subawards and contracts with certain parties that are debarred, suspended or otherwise excluded from or ineligible for participation in Federal programs or activities.

[78 FR 78608, Dec. 26, 2013, as amended at 79 FR 75882, Dec. 19, 2014; 80 FR 43308, July 22, 2015; 80 FR 69111, Nov. 9, 2015]

## § 200.206 Standard application requirements.

(a) *Paperwork clearances.* The Federal awarding agency may only use application information collections approved by OMB under the Paperwork Reduction Act of 1995 and OMB's implementing regulations in 5 CFR part 1320, Controlling Paperwork Burdens on the Public. Consistent with these requirements, OMB will authorize additional information collections only on a limited basis.

(b) If applicable, the Federal awarding agency may inform applicants and recipients that they do not need to provide certain information otherwise required by the relevant information collection.

## § 200.207 Specific conditions.

(a) The Federal awarding agency or pass-through entity may impose additional specific award conditions as needed, in accordance with paragraphs (b) and (c) of this section, under the following circumstances:

(1) Based on the criteria set forth in § 200.205 Federal awarding agency review of risk posed by applicants;

(2) When an applicant or recipient has a history of failure to comply with the general or specific terms and conditions of a Federal award;

(3) When an applicant or recipient fails to meet expected performance goals as described in § 200.210 Information contained in a Federal award; or

(4) When an applicant or recipient is not otherwise responsible.

(b) These additional Federal award conditions may include items such as the following:

(1) Requiring payments as reimbursements rather than advance payments;

(2) Withholding authority to proceed to the next phase until receipt of evidence of acceptable performance within a given period of performance;

(3) Requiring additional, more detailed financial reports;

(4) Requiring additional project monitoring;

(5) Requiring the non-Federal entity to obtain technical or management assistance; or

(6) Establishing additional prior approvals.

(c) The Federal awarding agency or pass-through entity must notify the applicant or non-Federal entity as to:

(1) The nature of the additional requirements;

(2) The reason why the additional requirements are being imposed;

(3) The nature of the action needed to remove the additional requirement, if applicable;

(4) The time allowed for completing the actions if applicable, and

(5) The method for requesting reconsideration of the additional requirements imposed.

(d) Any specific conditions must be promptly removed once the conditions that prompted them have been corrected.

[79 FR 75882, Dec. 19, 2014]

## § 200.208 Certifications and representations.

Unless prohibited by Federal statutes or regulations, each Federal awarding agency or pass-through entity is authorized to require the non-Federal entity to submit certifications and representations required by Federal statutes, or regulations on an annual basis. Submission may be required more frequently if the non-Federal entity fails to meet a requirement of a Federal award.

## § 200.209 Pre-award costs.

For requirements on costs incurred by the applicant prior to the start date of the period of performance of the Federal award, see § 200.458 Pre-award costs.

## § 200.210 Information contained in a Federal award.

A Federal award must include the following information:

(a) *General Federal Award Information.* The Federal awarding agency must include the following general Federal award information in each Federal award:

(1) Recipient name (which must match the name associated with its unique entity identifier as defined at 2 CFR 25.315);

(2) Recipient's unique entity identifier;

(3) Unique Federal Award Identification Number (FAIN);

(4) Federal Award Date (see § 200.39 Federal award date);

(5) Period of Performance Start and End Date;

(6) Amount of Federal Funds Obligated by this action;

(7) Total Amount of Federal Funds Obligated;

(8) Total Amount of the Federal Award;

(9) Budget Approved by the Federal Awarding Agency;

(10) Total Approved Cost Sharing or Matching, where applicable;

(11) Federal award project description, (to comply with statutory requirements (e.g., FFATA));

(12) Name of Federal awarding agency and contact information for awarding official,

(13) CFDA Number and Name;

(14) Identification of whether the award is R&D; and

(15) Indirect cost rate for the Federal award (including if the de minimis rate is charged per § 200.414 Indirect (F&A) costs).

(b) *General Terms and Conditions* (1) Federal awarding agencies must incorporate the following general terms and conditions either in the Federal award or by reference, as applicable:

(i) Administrative requirements implemented by the Federal awarding agency as specified in this part.

(ii) National policy requirements. These include statutory, executive order, other Presidential directive, or regulatory requirements that apply by specific reference and are not program-specific. See § 200.300 Statutory and national policy requirements.

(iii) Recipient integrity and performance matters. If the total Federal share of the Federal award may include more than $500,000 over the period of performance, the Federal awarding agency must include the term and condition available in Appendix XII—Award Term and Condition for Recipient Integrity and Performance Matters. See also § 200.113 Mandatory disclosures.

(2) The Federal award must include wording to incorporate, by reference, the applicable set of general terms and conditions. The reference must be to the Web site at which the Federal awarding agency maintains the general terms and conditions.

(3) If a non-Federal entity requests a copy of the full text of the general terms and conditions, the Federal awarding agency must provide it.

(4) Wherever the general terms and conditions are publicly available, the Federal awarding agency must maintain an archive of previous versions of the general terms and conditions, with effective dates, for use by the non-Federal entity, auditors, or others.

(c) *Federal Awarding Agency, Program, or Federal Award Specific Terms and Conditions.* The Federal awarding agency may include with each Federal award any terms and conditions necessary to communicate requirements that are in addition to the requirements outlined in the Federal awarding agency's general terms and conditions. Whenever practicable, these specific terms and conditions also should be shared on a public Web site and in notices of funding opportunities (as outlined in § 200.203 Notices of funding opportunities) in addition to being included in a Federal award. See also § 200.206 Standard application requirements.

(d) *Federal Award Performance Goals.* The Federal awarding agency must include in the Federal award an indication of the timing and scope of expected performance by the non-Federal entity as related to the outcomes intended to be achieved by the program. In some instances (e.g., discretionary research awards), this may be limited to the requirement to submit technical performance reports (to be evaluated in accordance with Federal awarding agency policy). Where appropriate, the Federal award may include specific performance goals, indicators, milestones, or expected outcomes (such as outputs, or services performed or public impacts of any of these) with an expected timeline for accomplishment. Reporting requirements must be clearly articulated such that, where appropriate, performance during the execution of the Federal award has a standard against which non-Federal entity performance can be measured. The Federal awarding agency may include program-specific requirements, as applicable. These requirements should be aligned with agency strategic goals, strategic objectives or performance goals that are relevant to the program. See also OMB Circular A–11, Preparation, Submission and Execution of the Budget Part 6 for definitions of strategic objectives and performance goals.

(e) Any other information required by the Federal awarding agency.

[78 FR 78608, Dec. 26, 2013, as amended at 79 FR 75882, Dec. 19, 2014; 80 FR 43308, July 22, 2015]

### § 200.211 Public access to Federal award information.

(a) In accordance with statutory requirements for Federal spending transparency (e.g., FFATA), except as noted in this section, for applicable Federal awards the Federal awarding agency must announce all Federal awards publicly and publish the required information on a publicly available OMB-des-

ignated governmentwide Web site (at time of publication, *www.USAspending.gov*).

(b) All information posted in the designated integrity and performance system accessible through SAM (currently FAPIIS) on or after April 15, 2011 will be publicly available after a waiting period of 14 calendar days, except for:

(1) Past performance reviews required by Federal Government contractors in accordance with the Federal Acquisition Regulation (FAR) 42.15;

(2) Information that was entered prior to April 15, 2011; or

(3) Information that is withdrawn during the 14-calendar day waiting period by the Federal Government official.

(c) Nothing in this section may be construed as requiring the publication of information otherwise exempt under the Freedom of Information Act (5 U.S.C 552), or controlled unclassified information pursuant to Executive Order 13556.

[78 FR 78608, Dec. 26, 2013, as amended at 80 FR 43309, July 22, 2015]

### § 200.212 Reporting a determination that a non-Federal entity is not qualified for a Federal award.

(a) If a Federal awarding agency does not make a Federal award to a non-Federal entity because the official determines that the non-Federal entity does not meet either or both of the minimum qualification standards as described in § 200.205, Federal awarding agency review of risk posed by applicants, paragraph (a)(2), the Federal awarding agency must report that determination to the designated integrity and performance system accessible through SAM (currently FAPIIS), only if all of the following apply:

(1) The only basis for the determination described in paragraph (a) of this section is the non-Federal entity's prior record of executing programs or activities under Federal awards or its record of integrity and business ethics, as described in § 200.205 Federal awarding agency review of risk posed by applicants, paragraph (a)(2) (*i.e.*, the entity was determined to be qualified based on all factors other than those two standards), and

(2) The total Federal share of the Federal award that otherwise would be made to the non-Federal entity is expected to exceed the simplified acquisition threshold over the period of performance.

(b) The Federal awarding agency is not required to report a determination that a non-Federal entity is not qualified for a Federal award if they make the Federal award to the non-Federal entity and includes specific award terms and conditions, as described in § 200.207 Specific conditions.

(c) If a Federal awarding agency reports a determination that a non-Federal entity is not qualified for a Federal award, as described in paragraph (a) of this section, the Federal awarding agency also must notify the non-Federal entity that—

(1) The determination was made and reported to the designated integrity and performance system accessible through SAM, and include with the notification an explanation of the basis for the determination;

(2) The information will be kept in the system for a period of five years from the date of the determination, as required by section 872 of Public Law 110–417, as amended (41 U.S.C. 2313), then archived;

(3) Each Federal awarding agency that considers making a Federal award to the non-Federal entity during that five year period must consider that information in judging whether the non-Federal entity is qualified to receive the Federal award when the total Federal share of the Federal award is expected to include an amount of Federal funding in excess of the simplified acquisition threshold over the period of performance;

(4) The non-Federal entity may go to the awardee integrity and performance portal accessible through SAM (currently the Contractor Performance Assessment Reporting System (CPARS)) and comment on any information the system contains about the non-Federal entity itself; and

(5) Federal awarding agencies will consider that non-Federal entity's comments in determining whether the non-Federal entity is qualified for a future Federal award.

(d) If a Federal awarding agency enters information into the designated integrity and performance system accessible through SAM about a determination that a non-Federal entity is not qualified for a Federal award and subsequently:

(1) Learns that any of that information is erroneous, the Federal awarding agency must correct the information in the system within three business days;

(2) Obtains an update to that information that could be helpful to other Federal awarding agencies, the Federal awarding agency is strongly encouraged to amend the information in the system to incorporate the update in a timely way.

(e) Federal awarding agencies shall not post any information that will be made publicly available in the non-public segment of designated integrity and performance system that is covered by a disclosure exemption under the Freedom of Information Act. If the recipient asserts within seven calendar days to the Federal awarding agency that posted the information that some or all of the information made publicly available is covered by a disclosure exemption under the Freedom of Information Act, the Federal awarding agency that posted the information must remove the posting within seven calendar days of receiving the assertion. Prior to reposting the releasable information, the Federal awarding agency must resolve the issue in accordance with the agency's Freedom of Information Act procedures.

[80 FR 43309, July 22, 2015]

## § 200.213   Suspension and debarment.

Non-federal entities are subject to the non-procurement debarment and suspension regulations implementing Executive Orders 12549 and 12689, 2 CFR part 180. These regulations restrict awards, subawards, and contracts with certain parties that are debarred, suspended, or otherwise excluded from or ineligible for participation in Federal assistance programs or activities.

[80 FR 43309, July 22, 2015]

## Subpart D—Post Federal Award Requirements

STANDARDS FOR FINANCIAL AND
PROGRAM MANAGEMENT

### § 200.300  Statutory and national policy requirements.

(a) The Federal awarding agency must manage and administer the Federal award in a manner so as to ensure that Federal funding is expended and associated programs are implemented in full accordance with U.S. statutory and public policy requirements: including, but not limited to, those protecting public welfare, the environment, and prohibiting discrimination. The Federal awarding agency must communicate to the non-Federal entity all relevant public policy requirements, including those in general appropriations provisions, and incorporate them either directly or by reference in the terms and conditions of the Federal award.

(b) The non-Federal entity is responsible for complying with all requirements of the Federal award. For all Federal awards, this includes the provisions of FFATA, which includes requirements on executive compensation, and also requirements implementing the Act for the non-Federal entity at 2 CFR part 25 Financial Assistance Use of Universal Identifier and System for Award Management and 2 CFR part 170 Reporting Subaward and Executive Compensation Information. See also statutory requirements for whistleblower protections at 10 U.S.C. 2409, 41 U.S.C. 4712, and 10 U.S.C. 2324, 41 U.S.C. 4304 and 4310.

[78 FR 78608, Dec. 26, 2013, as amended at 80 FR 43309, July 22, 2015]

### § 200.301  Performance measurement.

The Federal awarding agency must require the recipient to use OMB-approved standard information collections when providing financial and performance information. As appropriate and in accordance with above mentioned information collections, the Federal awarding agency must require the recipient to relate financial data to performance accomplishments of the Federal award. Also, in accordance with above mentioned standard information collections, and when applicable, recipients must also provide cost information to demonstrate cost effective practices (e.g., through unit cost data). The recipient's performance should be measured in a way that will help the Federal awarding agency and other non-Federal entities to improve program outcomes, share lessons learned, and spread the adoption of promising practices. The Federal awarding agency should provide recipients with clear performance goals, indicators, and milestones as described in § 200.210 Information contained in a Federal award. Performance reporting frequency and content should be established to not only allow the Federal awarding agency to understand the recipient progress but also to facilitate identification of promising practices among recipients and build the evidence upon which the Federal awarding agency's program and performance decisions are made.

[78 FR 78608, Dec. 26, 2013, as amended at 79 FR 75883, Dec. 19, 2014]

### § 200.302  Financial management.

(a) Each state must expend and account for the Federal award in accordance with state laws and procedures for expending and accounting for the state's own funds. In addition, the state's and the other non-Federal entity's financial management systems, including records documenting compliance with Federal statutes, regulations, and the terms and conditions of the Federal award, must be sufficient to permit the preparation of reports required by general and program-specific terms and conditions; and the tracing of funds to a level of expenditures adequate to establish that such funds have been used according to the Federal statutes, regulations, and the terms and conditions of the Federal award. See also § 200.450 Lobbying.

(b) The financial management system of each non-Federal entity must provide for the following (see also §§ 200.333 Retention requirements for records, 200.334 Requests for transfer of records, 200.335 Methods for collection, transmission and storage of information, 200.336 Access to records, and 200.337 Restrictions on public access to records):

(1) Identification, in its accounts, of all Federal awards received and expended and the Federal programs under which they were received. Federal program and Federal award identification must include, as applicable, the CFDA title and number, Federal award identification number and year, name of the Federal agency, and name of the pass-through entity, if any.

(2) Accurate, current, and complete disclosure of the financial results of each Federal award or program in accordance with the reporting requirements set forth in §§ 200.327 Financial reporting and 200.328 Monitoring and reporting program performance. If a Federal awarding agency requires reporting on an accrual basis from a recipient that maintains its records on other than an accrual basis, the recipient must not be required to establish an accrual accounting system. This recipient may develop accrual data for its reports on the basis of an analysis of the documentation on hand. Similarly, a pass-through entity must not require a subrecipient to establish an accrual accounting system and must allow the subrecipient to develop accrual data for its reports on the basis of an analysis of the documentation on hand.

(3) Records that identify adequately the source and application of funds for federally-funded activities. These records must contain information pertaining to Federal awards, authorizations, obligations, unobligated balances, assets, expenditures, income and interest and be supported by source documentation.

(4) Effective control over, and accountability for, all funds, property, and other assets. The non-Federal entity must adequately safeguard all assets and assure that they are used solely for authorized purposes. See § 200.303 Internal controls.

(5) Comparison of expenditures with budget amounts for each Federal award.

(6) Written procedures to implement the requirements of § 200.305 Payment.

(7) Written procedures for determining the allowability of costs in accordance with Subpart E—Cost Principles of this part and the terms and conditions of the Federal award.

## § 200.303　Internal controls.

The non-Federal entity must:

(a) Establish and maintain effective internal control over the Federal award that provides reasonable assurance that the non-Federal entity is managing the Federal award in compliance with Federal statutes, regulations, and the terms and conditions of the Federal award. These internal controls should be in compliance with guidance in "Standards for Internal Control in the Federal Government" issued by the Comptroller General of the United States or the "Internal Control Integrated Framework", issued by the Committee of Sponsoring Organizations of the Treadway Commission (COSO).

(b) Comply with Federal statutes, regulations, and the terms and conditions of the Federal awards.

(c) Evaluate and monitor the non-Federal entity's compliance with statutes, regulations and the terms and conditions of Federal awards.

(d) Take prompt action when instances of noncompliance are identified including noncompliance identified in audit findings.

(e) Take reasonable measures to safeguard protected personally identifiable information and other information the Federal awarding agency or pass-through entity designates as sensitive or the non-Federal entity considers sensitive consistent with applicable Federal, state, local, and tribal laws regarding privacy and obligations of confidentiality.

[78 FR 78608, Dec. 26, 2013, as amended at 79 FR 75883, Dec. 19, 2014]

## § 200.304　Bonds.

The Federal awarding agency may include a provision on bonding, insurance, or both in the following circumstances:

(a) Where the Federal Government guarantees or insures the repayment of money borrowed by the recipient, the Federal awarding agency, at its discretion, may require adequate bonding and insurance if the bonding and insurance requirements of the non-Federal entity are not deemed adequate to protect the interest of the Federal Government.

(b) The Federal awarding agency may require adequate fidelity bond coverage where the non-Federal entity lacks sufficient coverage to protect the Federal Government's interest.

(c) Where bonds are required in the situations described above, the bonds must be obtained from companies holding certificates of authority as acceptable sureties, as prescribed in 31 CFR Part 223, "Surety Companies Doing Business with the United States."

## § 200.305 Payment.

(a) For states, payments are governed by Treasury-State CMIA agreements and default procedures codified at 31 CFR Part 205 "Rules and Procedures for Efficient Federal-State Funds Transfers" and TFM 4A–2000 Overall Disbursing Rules for All Federal Agencies.

(b) For non-Federal entities other than states, payments methods must minimize the time elapsing between the transfer of funds from the United States Treasury or the pass-through entity and the disbursement by the non-Federal entity whether the payment is made by electronic funds transfer, or issuance or redemption of checks, warrants, or payment by other means. See also § 200.302 Financial management paragraph (b)(6). Except as noted elsewhere in this part, Federal agencies must require recipients to use only OMB-approved standard governmentwide information collection requests to request payment.

(1) The non-Federal entity must be paid in advance, provided it maintains or demonstrates the willingness to maintain both written procedures that minimize the time elapsing between the transfer of funds and disbursement by the non-Federal entity, and financial management systems that meet the standards for fund control and accountability as established in this part. Advance payments to a non-Federal entity must be limited to the minimum amounts needed and be timed to be in accordance with the actual, immediate cash requirements of the non-Federal entity in carrying out the purpose of the approved program or project. The timing and amount of advance payments must be as close as is administratively feasible to the actual disbursements by the non-Federal entity for direct program or project costs and the proportionate share of any allowable indirect costs. The non-Federal entity must make timely payment to contractors in accordance with the contract provisions.

(2) Whenever possible, advance payments must be consolidated to cover anticipated cash needs for all Federal awards made by the Federal awarding agency to the recipient.

(i) Advance payment mechanisms include, but are not limited to, Treasury check and electronic funds transfer and must comply with applicable guidance in 31 CFR part 208.

(ii) Non-Federal entities must be authorized to submit requests for advance payments and reimbursements at least monthly when electronic fund transfers are not used, and as often as they like when electronic transfers are used, in accordance with the provisions of the Electronic Fund Transfer Act (15 U.S.C. 1693–1693r).

(3) Reimbursement is the preferred method when the requirements in paragraph (b) cannot be met, when the Federal awarding agency sets a specific condition per § 200.207 Specific conditions, or when the non-Federal entity requests payment by reimbursement. This method may be used on any Federal award for construction, or if the major portion of the construction project is accomplished through private market financing or Federal loans, and the Federal award constitutes a minor portion of the project. When the reimbursement method is used, the Federal awarding agency or pass-through entity must make payment within 30 calendar days after receipt of the billing, unless the Federal awarding agency or pass-through entity reasonably believes the request to be improper.

(4) If the non-Federal entity cannot meet the criteria for advance payments and the Federal awarding agency or pass-through entity has determined that reimbursement is not feasible because the non-Federal entity lacks sufficient working capital, the Federal awarding agency or pass-through entity may provide cash on a working capital advance basis. Under this procedure, the Federal awarding agency or

pass-through entity must advance cash payments to the non-Federal entity to cover its estimated disbursement needs for an initial period generally geared to the non-Federal entity's disbursing cycle. Thereafter, the Federal awarding agency or pass-through entity must reimburse the non-Federal entity for its actual cash disbursements. Use of the working capital advance method of payment requires that the pass-through entity provide timely advance payments to any subrecipients in order to meet the subrecipient's actual cash disbursements. The working capital advance method of payment must not be used by the pass-through entity if the reason for using this method is the unwillingness or inability of the pass-through entity to provide timely advance payments to the subrecipient to meet the subrecipient's actual cash disbursements.

(5) *Use of resources before requesting cash advance payments.* To the extent available, the non-Federal entity must disburse funds available from program income (including repayments to a revolving fund), rebates, refunds, contract settlements, audit recoveries, and interest earned on such funds before requesting additional cash payments.

(6) Unless otherwise required by Federal statutes, payments for allowable costs by non-Federal entities must not be withheld at any time during the period of performance unless the conditions of §§ 200.207 Specific conditions, Subpart D—Post Federal Award Requirements of this part, 200.338 Remedies for Noncompliance, or one or more of the following applies:

(i) The non-Federal entity has failed to comply with the project objectives, Federal statutes, regulations, or the terms and conditions of the Federal award.

(ii) The non-Federal entity is delinquent in a debt to the United States as defined in OMB Guidance A–129, "Policies for Federal Credit Programs and Non-Tax Receivables." Under such conditions, the Federal awarding agency or pass-through entity may, upon reasonable notice, inform the non-Federal entity that payments must not be made for obligations incurred after a specified date until the conditions are corrected or the indebtedness to the Federal Government is liquidated.

(iii) A payment withheld for failure to comply with Federal award conditions, but without suspension of the Federal award, must be released to the non-Federal entity upon subsequent compliance. When a Federal award is suspended, payment adjustments will be made in accordance with § 200.342 Effects of suspension and termination.

(iv) A payment must not be made to a non-Federal entity for amounts that are withheld by the non-Federal entity from payment to contractors to assure satisfactory completion of work. A payment must be made when the non-Federal entity actually disburses the withheld funds to the contractors or to escrow accounts established to assure satisfactory completion of work.

(7) Standards governing the use of banks and other institutions as depositories of advance payments under Federal awards are as follows.

(i) The Federal awarding agency and pass-through entity must not require separate depository accounts for funds provided to a non-Federal entity or establish any eligibility requirements for depositories for funds provided to the non-Federal entity. However, the non-Federal entity must be able to account for the receipt, obligation and expenditure of funds.

(ii) Advance payments of Federal funds must be deposited and maintained in insured accounts whenever possible.

(8) The non-Federal entity must maintain advance payments of Federal awards in interest-bearing accounts, unless the following apply.

(i) The non-Federal entity receives less than $120,000 in Federal awards per year.

(ii) The best reasonably available interest-bearing account would not be expected to earn interest in excess of $500 per year on Federal cash balances.

(iii) The depository would require an average or minimum balance so high that it would not be feasible within the expected Federal and non-Federal cash resources.

(iv) A foreign government or banking system prohibits or precludes interest bearing accounts.

(9) Interest earned amounts up to $500 per year may be retained by the non-Federal entity for administrative expense. Any additional interest earned on Federal advance payments deposited in interest-bearing accounts must be remitted annually to the Department of Health and Human Services Payment Management System (PMS) through an electronic medium using either Automated Clearing House (ACH) network or a Fedwire Funds Service payment. Remittances must include pertinent information of the payee and nature of payment in the memo area (often referred to as "addenda records" by Financial Institutions) as that will assist in the timely posting of interest earned on federal funds. Pertinent details include the Payee Account Number (PAN) if the payment originated from PMS, or Agency information if the payment originated from ASAP, NSF or another federal agency payment system. The remittance must be submitted as follows:

(i) For ACH Returns:

Routing Number: 051036706
Account number: 303000
Bank Name and Location: Credit Gateway— ACH Receiver St. Paul, MN

(ii) For Fedwire Returns*:

Routing Number: 021030004
Account number: 75010501
Bank Name and Location: Federal Reserve Bank Treas NYC/Funds Transfer Division New York, NY
(* Please note organization initiating payment is likely to incur a charge from your Financial Institution for this type of payment)

(iii) For International ACH Returns:

Beneficiary Account: Federal Reserve Bank of New York/ITS (FRBNY/ITS)
Bank: Citibank N.A. (New York)
Swift Code: CITIUS33
Account Number: 36838868
Bank Address: 388 Greenwich Street, New York, NY 10013 USA
Payment Details (Line 70): Agency Name (abbreviated when possible) and ALC
Agency POC: Michelle Haney, (301) 492–5065

(iv) For recipients that do not have electronic remittance capability, please make check** payable to: "The Department of Health and Human Services."

Mail Check to Treasury approved lockbox:

HHS Program Support Center, P.O. Box 530231, Atlanta, GA 30353–0231
(** Please allow 4–6 weeks for processing of a payment by check to be applied to the appropriate PMS account)

(v) Any additional information/instructions may be found on the PMS Web site at *http://www.dpm.psc.gov/*.

[78 FR 78608, Dec. 26, 2013, as amended at 79 FR 75883, Dec. 19, 2014; 80 FR 54408, Sept. 10, 2015]

### § 200.306   Cost sharing or matching.

(a) Under Federal research proposals, voluntary committed cost sharing is not expected. It cannot be used as a factor during the merit review of applications or proposals, but may be considered if it is both in accordance with Federal awarding agency regulations and specified in a notice of funding opportunity. Criteria for considering voluntary committed cost sharing and any other program policy factors that may be used to determine who may receive a Federal award must be explicitly described in the notice of funding opportunity. See also §§ 200.414 Indirect (F&A) costs, 200.203 Notices of funding opportunities, and Appendix I to Part 200—Full Text of Notice of Funding Opportunity.

(b) For all Federal awards, any shared costs or matching funds and all contributions, including cash and third party in-kind contributions, must be accepted as part of the non-Federal entity's cost sharing or matching when such contributions meet all of the following criteria:

(1) Are verifiable from the non-Federal entity's records;

(2) Are not included as contributions for any other Federal award;

(3) Are necessary and reasonable for accomplishment of project or program objectives;

(4) Are allowable under Subpart E— Cost Principles of this part;

(5) Are not paid by the Federal Government under another Federal award, except where the Federal statute authorizing a program specifically provides that Federal funds made available for such program can be applied to matching or cost sharing requirements of other Federal programs;

(6) Are provided for in the approved budget when required by the Federal awarding agency; and

(7) Conform to other provisions of this part, as applicable.

(c) Unrecovered indirect costs, including indirect costs on cost sharing or matching may be included as part of cost sharing or matching only with the prior approval of the Federal awarding agency. Unrecovered indirect cost means the difference between the amount charged to the Federal award and the amount which could have been charged to the Federal award under the non-Federal entity's approved negotiated indirect cost rate.

(d) Values for non-Federal entity contributions of services and property must be established in accordance with the cost principles in Subpart E—Cost Principles. If a Federal awarding agency authorizes the non-Federal entity to donate buildings or land for construction/facilities acquisition projects or long-term use, the value of the donated property for cost sharing or matching must be the lesser of paragraphs (d)(1) or (2) of this section.

(1) The value of the remaining life of the property recorded in the non-Federal entity's accounting records at the time of donation.

(2) The current fair market value. However, when there is sufficient justification, the Federal awarding agency may approve the use of the current fair market value of the donated property, even if it exceeds the value described in (1) above at the time of donation.

(e) Volunteer services furnished by third-party professional and technical personnel, consultants, and other skilled and unskilled labor may be counted as cost sharing or matching if the service is an integral and necessary part of an approved project or program. Rates for third-party volunteer services must be consistent with those paid for similar work by the non-Federal entity. In those instances in which the required skills are not found in the non-Federal entity, rates must be consistent with those paid for similar work in the labor market in which the non-Federal entity competes for the kind of services involved. In either case, paid fringe benefits that are rea-

sonable, necessary, allocable, and otherwise allowable may be included in the valuation.

(f) When a third-party organization furnishes the services of an employee, these services must be valued at the employee's regular rate of pay plus an amount of fringe benefits that is reasonable, necessary, allocable, and otherwise allowable, and indirect costs at either the third-party organization's approved federally negotiated indirect cost rate or, a rate in accordance with § 200.414 Indirect (F&A) costs, paragraph (d), provided these services employ the same skill(s) for which the employee is normally paid. Where donated services are treated as indirect costs, indirect cost rates will separate the value of the donated services so that reimbursement for the donated services will not be made.

(g) Donated property from third parties may include such items as equipment, office supplies, laboratory supplies, or workshop and classroom supplies. Value assessed to donated property included in the cost sharing or matching share must not exceed the fair market value of the property at the time of the donation.

(h) The method used for determining cost sharing or matching for third-party-donated equipment, buildings and land for which title passes to the non-Federal entity may differ according to the purpose of the Federal award, if paragraph (h)(1) or (2) of this section applies.

(1) If the purpose of the Federal award is to assist the non-Federal entity in the acquisition of equipment, buildings or land, the aggregate value of the donated property may be claimed as cost sharing or matching.

(2) If the purpose of the Federal award is to support activities that require the use of equipment, buildings or land, normally only depreciation charges for equipment and buildings may be made. However, the fair market value of equipment or other capital assets and fair rental charges for land may be allowed, provided that the Federal awarding agency has approved the charges. See also § 200.420 Considerations for selected items of cost.

(i) The value of donated property must be determined in accordance with the usual accounting policies of the non-Federal entity, with the following qualifications:

(1) The value of donated land and buildings must not exceed its fair market value at the time of donation to the non-Federal entity as established by an independent appraiser (e.g., certified real property appraiser or General Services Administration representative) and certified by a responsible official of the non-Federal entity as required by the Uniform Relocation Assistance and Real Property Acquisition Policies Act of 1970, as amended, (42 U.S.C. 4601–4655) (Uniform Act) except as provided in the implementing regulations at 49 CFR part 24.

(2) The value of donated equipment must not exceed the fair market value of equipment of the same age and condition at the time of donation.

(3) The value of donated space must not exceed the fair rental value of comparable space as established by an independent appraisal of comparable space and facilities in a privately-owned building in the same locality.

(4) The value of loaned equipment must not exceed its fair rental value.

(j) For third-party in-kind contributions, the fair market value of goods and services must be documented and to the extent feasible supported by the same methods used internally by the non-Federal entity.

(k) For IHEs, see also OMB memorandum M–01–06, dated January 5, 2001, Clarification of OMB A–21 Treatment of Voluntary Uncommitted Cost Sharing and Tuition Remission Costs.

[78 FR 78608, Dec. 26, 2013, as amended at 79 FR 75883, Dec. 19, 2014]

### § 200.307   Program income.

(a) *General.* Non-Federal entities are encouraged to earn income to defray program costs where appropriate.

(b) *Cost of generating program income.* If authorized by Federal regulations or the Federal award, costs incidental to the generation of program income may be deducted from gross income to determine program income, provided these costs have not been charged to the Federal award.

(c) *Governmental revenues.* Taxes, special assessments, levies, fines, and other such revenues raised by a non-Federal entity are not program income unless the revenues are specifically identified in the Federal award or Federal awarding agency regulations as program income.

(d) *Property.* Proceeds from the sale of real property, equipment, or supplies are not program income; such proceeds will be handled in accordance with the requirements of Subpart D—Post Federal Award Requirements of this part, Property Standards §§ 200.311 Real property, 200.313 Equipment, and 200.314 Supplies, or as specifically identified in Federal statutes, regulations, or the terms and conditions of the Federal award.

(e) *Use of program income.* If the Federal awarding agency does not specify in its regulations or the terms and conditions of the Federal award, or give prior approval for how program income is to be used, paragraph (e)(1) of this section must apply. For Federal awards made to IHEs and nonprofit research institutions, if the Federal awarding agency does not specify in its regulations or the terms and conditions of the Federal award how program income is to be used, paragraph (e)(2) of this section must apply. In specifying alternatives to paragraphs (e)(1) and (2) of this section, the Federal awarding agency may distinguish between income earned by the recipient and income earned by subrecipients and between the sources, kinds, or amounts of income. When the Federal awarding agency authorizes the approaches in paragraphs (e)(2) and (3) of this section, program income in excess of any amounts specified must also be deducted from expenditures.

(1) *Deduction.* Ordinarily program income must be deducted from total allowable costs to determine the net allowable costs. Program income must be used for current costs unless the Federal awarding agency authorizes otherwise. Program income that the non-Federal entity did not anticipate at the time of the Federal award must be used to reduce the Federal award and non-Federal entity contributions rather than to increase the funds committed to the project.

(2) *Addition.* With prior approval of the Federal awarding agency (except

113

for IHEs and nonprofit research institutions, as described in paragraph (e) of this section) program income may be added to the Federal award by the Federal agency and the non-Federal entity. The program income must be used for the purposes and under the conditions of the Federal award.

(3) *Cost sharing or matching.* With prior approval of the Federal awarding agency, program income may be used to meet the cost sharing or matching requirement of the Federal award. The amount of the Federal award remains the same.

(f) *Income after the period of performance.* There are no Federal requirements governing the disposition of income earned after the end of the period of performance for the Federal award, unless the Federal awarding agency regulations or the terms and conditions of the Federal award provide otherwise. The Federal awarding agency may negotiate agreements with recipients regarding appropriate uses of income earned after the period of performance as part of the grant closeout process. See also § 200.343 Closeout.

(g) Unless the Federal statute, regulations, or terms and conditions for the Federal award provide otherwise, the non-Federal entity has no obligation to the Federal awarding agency with respect to program income earned from license fees and royalties for copyrighted material, patents, patent applications, trademarks, and inventions made under a Federal award to which 37 CFR part 401,"Rights to Inventions Made by Nonprofit Organizations and Small Business Firms Under Government Awards, Contracts and Cooperative Agreements" is applicable.

[78 FR 78608, Dec. 26, 2013, as amended at 79 FR 75884, Dec. 19, 2014]

### § 200.308  Revision of budget and program plans.

(a) The approved budget for the Federal award summarizes the financial aspects of the project or program as approved during the Federal award process. It may include either the Federal and non-Federal share (see § 200.43 Federal share) or only the Federal share, depending upon Federal awarding agency requirements. It must be related to

performance for program evaluation purposes whenever appropriate.

(b) Recipients are required to report deviations from budget or project scope or objective, and request prior approvals from Federal awarding agencies for budget and program plan revisions, in accordance with this section.

(c)(1) For non-construction Federal awards, recipients must request prior approvals from Federal awarding agencies for one or more of the following program or budget-related reasons:

(i) Change in the scope or the objective of the project or program (even if there is no associated budget revision requiring prior written approval).

(ii) Change in a key person specified in the application or the Federal award.

(iii) The disengagement from the project for more than three months, or a 25 percent reduction in time devoted to the project, by the approved project director or principal investigator.

(iv) The inclusion, unless waived by the Federal awarding agency, of costs that require prior approval in accordance with Subpart E—Cost Principles of this part or 45 CFR part 75 Appendix IX, "Principles for Determining Costs Applicable to Research and Development under Awards and Contracts with Hospitals," or 48 CFR part 31, "Contract Cost Principles and Procedures," as applicable.

(v) The transfer of funds budgeted for participant support costs as defined in § 200.75 Participant support costs to other categories of expense.

(vi) Unless described in the application and funded in the approved Federal awards, the subawarding, transferring or contracting out of any work under a Federal award, including fixed amount subawards as described in § 200.332 Fixed amount subawards. This provision does not apply to the acquisition of supplies, material, equipment or general support services.

(vii) Changes in the approved cost-sharing or matching provided by the non-Federal entity.

(viii) The need arises for additional Federal funds to complete the project.

(2) No other prior approval requirements for specific items may be imposed unless an exception has been approved by OMB. See also §§ 200.102 Exceptions and 200.407 Prior written approval (prior approval).

(d) Except for requirements listed in paragraph (c)(1) of this section, the Federal awarding agency is authorized, at its option, to waive prior written approvals required by paragraph (c) this section. Such waivers may include authorizing recipients to do any one or more of the following:

(1) Incur project costs 90 calendar days before the Federal awarding agency makes the Federal award. Expenses more than 90 calendar days pre-award require prior approval of the Federal awarding agency. All costs incurred before the Federal awarding agency makes the Federal award are at the recipient's risk (i.e., the Federal awarding agency is under no obligation to reimburse such costs if for any reason the recipient does not receive a Federal award or if the Federal award is less than anticipated and inadequate to cover such costs). See also § 200.458 Pre-award costs.

(2) Initiate a one-time extension of the period of performance by up to 12 months unless one or more of the conditions outlined in paragraphs (d)(2)(i) through (iii) of this section apply. For one-time extensions, the recipient must notify the Federal awarding agency in writing with the supporting reasons and revised period of performance at least 10 calendar days before the end of the period of performance specified in the Federal award. This one-time extension may not be exercised merely for the purpose of using unobligated balances. Extensions require explicit prior Federal awarding agency approval when:

(i) The terms and conditions of the Federal award prohibit the extension.

(ii) The extension requires additional Federal funds.

(iii) The extension involves any change in the approved objectives or scope of the project.

(3) Carry forward unobligated balances to subsequent periods of performance.

(4) For Federal awards that support research, unless the Federal awarding agency provides otherwise in the Federal award or in the Federal awarding agency's regulations, the prior approval requirements described in paragraph (d) are automatically waived (i.e., recipients need not obtain such prior approvals) unless one of the conditions included in paragraph (d)(2) applies.

(e) The Federal awarding agency may, at its option, restrict the transfer of funds among direct cost categories or programs, functions and activities for Federal awards in which the Federal share of the project exceeds the Simplified Acquisition Threshold and the cumulative amount of such transfers exceeds or is expected to exceed 10 percent of the total budget as last approved by the Federal awarding agency. The Federal awarding agency cannot permit a transfer that would cause any Federal appropriation to be used for purposes other than those consistent with the appropriation.

(f) All other changes to non-construction budgets, except for the changes described in paragraph (c) of this section, do not require prior approval (see also § 200.407 Prior written approval (prior approval)).

(g) For construction Federal awards, the recipient must request prior written approval promptly from the Federal awarding agency for budget revisions whenever paragraph (g)(1), (2), or (3) of this section applies.

(1) The revision results from changes in the scope or the objective of the project or program.

(2) The need arises for additional Federal funds to complete the project.

(3) A revision is desired which involves specific costs for which prior written approval requirements may be imposed consistent with applicable OMB cost principles listed in Subpart E—Cost Principles of this part.

(4) No other prior approval requirements for budget revisions may be imposed unless an exception has been approved by OMB.

(5) When a Federal awarding agency makes a Federal award that provides support for construction and non-construction work, the Federal awarding agency may require the recipient to obtain prior approval from the Federal awarding agency before making any

fund or budget transfers between the two types of work supported.

(h) When requesting approval for budget revisions, the recipient must use the same format for budget information that was used in the application, unless the Federal awarding agency indicates a letter of request suffices.

(i) Within 30 calendar days from the date of receipt of the request for budget revisions, the Federal awarding agency must review the request and notify the recipient whether the budget revisions have been approved. If the revision is still under consideration at the end of 30 calendar days, the Federal awarding agency must inform the recipient in writing of the date when the recipient may expect the decision.

[78 FR 78608, Dec. 26, 2013, as amended at 79 FR 75884, Dec. 19, 2014; 80 FR 54409, Sept. 10, 2015]

§ 200.309   Period of performance.

A non-Federal entity may charge to the Federal award only allowable costs incurred during the period of performance (except as described in § 200.461 Publication and printing costs) and any costs incurred before the Federal awarding agency or pass-through entity made the Federal award that were authorized by the Federal awarding agency or pass-through entity.

[78 FR 78608, Dec. 26, 2013, as amended at 79 FR 75884, Dec. 19, 2014]

PROPERTY STANDARDS

§ 200.310   Insurance coverage.

The non-Federal entity must, at a minimum, provide the equivalent insurance coverage for real property and equipment acquired or improved with Federal funds as provided to property owned by the non-Federal entity. Federally-owned property need not be insured unless required by the terms and conditions of the Federal award.

§ 200.311   Real property.

(a) *Title.* Subject to the obligations and conditions set forth in this section, title to real property acquired or improved under a Federal award will vest upon acquisition in the non-Federal entity.

(b) *Use.* Except as otherwise provided by Federal statutes or by the Federal awarding agency, real property will be used for the originally authorized purpose as long as needed for that purpose, during which time the non-Federal entity must not dispose of or encumber its title or other interests.

(c) *Disposition.* When real property is no longer needed for the originally authorized purpose, the non-Federal entity must obtain disposition instructions from the Federal awarding agency or pass-through entity. The instructions must provide for one of the following alternatives:

(1) Retain title after compensating the Federal awarding agency. The amount paid to the Federal awarding agency will be computed by applying the Federal awarding agency's percentage of participation in the cost of the original purchase (and costs of any improvements) to the fair market value of the property. However, in those situations where the non-Federal entity is disposing of real property acquired or improved with a Federal award and acquiring replacement real property under the same Federal award, the net proceeds from the disposition may be used as an offset to the cost of the replacement property.

(2) Sell the property and compensate the Federal awarding agency. The amount due to the Federal awarding agency will be calculated by applying the Federal awarding agency's percentage of participation in the cost of the original purchase (and cost of any improvements) to the proceeds of the sale after deduction of any actual and reasonable selling and fixing-up expenses. If the Federal award has not been closed out, the net proceeds from sale may be offset against the original cost of the property. When the non-Federal entity is directed to sell property, sales procedures must be followed that provide for competition to the extent practicable and result in the highest possible return.

(3) Transfer title to the Federal awarding agency or to a third party designated/approved by the Federal awarding agency. The non-Federal entity is entitled to be paid an amount calculated by applying the non-Federal entity's percentage of participation in the purchase of the real property (and

cost of any improvements) to the current fair market value of the property.

[78 FR 78608, Dec. 26, 2013, as amended at 79 FR 75884, Dec. 19, 2014]

## § 200.312   Federally-owned and exempt property.

(a) Title to federally-owned property remains vested in the Federal Government. The non-Federal entity must submit annually an inventory listing of federally-owned property in its custody to the Federal awarding agency. Upon completion of the Federal award or when the property is no longer needed, the non-Federal entity must report the property to the Federal awarding agency for further Federal agency utilization.

(b) If the Federal awarding agency has no further need for the property, it must declare the property excess and report it for disposal to the appropriate Federal disposal authority, unless the Federal awarding agency has statutory authority to dispose of the property by alternative methods (e.g., the authority provided by the Federal Technology Transfer Act (15 U.S.C. 3710 (i)) to donate research equipment to educational and non-profit organizations in accordance with Executive Order 12999, ''Educational Technology: Ensuring Opportunity for All Children in the Next Century.''). The Federal awarding agency must issue appropriate instructions to the non-Federal entity.

(c) Exempt federally-owned property means property acquired under a Federal award where the Federal awarding agency has chosen to vest title to the property to the non-Federal entity without further obligation to the Federal Government, based upon the explicit terms and conditions of the Federal award. The Federal awarding agency may exercise this option when statutory authority exists. Absent statutory authority and specific terms and conditions of the Federal award, title to exempt federally-owned property acquired under the Federal award remains with the Federal Government.

[78 FR 78608, Dec. 26, 2013, as amended at 79 FR 75884, Dec. 19, 2014]

## § 200.313   Equipment.

See also § 200.439 Equipment and other capital expenditures.

(a) *Title.* Subject to the obligations and conditions set forth in this section, title to equipment acquired under a Federal award will vest upon acquisition in the non-Federal entity. Unless a statute specifically authorizes the Federal agency to vest title in the non-Federal entity without further obligation to the Federal Government, and the Federal agency elects to do so, the title must be a conditional title. Title must vest in the non-Federal entity subject to the following conditions:

(1) Use the equipment for the authorized purposes of the project during the period of performance, or until the property is no longer needed for the purposes of the project.

(2) Not encumber the property without approval of the Federal awarding agency or pass-through entity.

(3) Use and dispose of the property in accordance with paragraphs (b), (c) and (e) of this section.

(b) A state must use, manage and dispose of equipment acquired under a Federal award by the state in accordance with state laws and procedures. Other non-Federal entities must follow paragraphs (c) through (e) of this section.

(c) *Use.* (1) Equipment must be used by the non-Federal entity in the program or project for which it was acquired as long as needed, whether or not the project or program continues to be supported by the Federal award, and the non-Federal entity must not encumber the property without prior approval of the Federal awarding agency. When no longer needed for the original program or project, the equipment may be used in other activities supported by the Federal awarding agency, in the following order of priority:

(i) Activities under a Federal award from the Federal awarding agency which funded the original program or project, then

(ii) Activities under Federal awards from other Federal awarding agencies. This includes consolidated equipment for information technology systems.

(2) During the time that equipment is used on the project or program for

117

which it was acquired, the non-Federal entity must also make equipment available for use on other projects or programs currently or previously supported by the Federal Government, provided that such use will not interfere with the work on the projects or program for which it was originally acquired. First preference for other use must be given to other programs or projects supported by Federal awarding agency that financed the equipment and second preference must be given to programs or projects under Federal awards from other Federal awarding agencies. Use for non-federally-funded programs or projects is also permissible. User fees should be considered if appropriate.

(3) Notwithstanding the encouragement in § 200.307 Program income to earn program income, the non-Federal entity must not use equipment acquired with the Federal award to provide services for a fee that is less than private companies charge for equivalent services unless specifically authorized by Federal statute for as long as the Federal Government retains an interest in the equipment.

(4) When acquiring replacement equipment, the non-Federal entity may use the equipment to be replaced as a trade-in or sell the property and use the proceeds to offset the cost of the replacement property.

(d) *Management requirements.* Procedures for managing equipment (including replacement equipment), whether acquired in whole or in part under a Federal award, until disposition takes place will, as a minimum, meet the following requirements:

(1) Property records must be maintained that include a description of the property, a serial number or other identification number, the source of funding for the property (including the FAIN), who holds title, the acquisition date, and cost of the property, percentage of Federal participation in the project costs for the Federal award under which the property was acquired, the location, use and condition of the property, and any ultimate disposition data including the date of disposal and sale price of the property.

(2) A physical inventory of the property must be taken and the results reconciled with the property records at least once every two years.

(3) A control system must be developed to ensure adequate safeguards to prevent loss, damage, or theft of the property. Any loss, damage, or theft must be investigated.

(4) Adequate maintenance procedures must be developed to keep the property in good condition.

(5) If the non-Federal entity is authorized or required to sell the property, proper sales procedures must be established to ensure the highest possible return.

(e) *Disposition.* When original or replacement equipment acquired under a Federal award is no longer needed for the original project or program or for other activities currently or previously supported by a Federal awarding agency, except as otherwise provided in Federal statutes, regulations, or Federal awarding agency disposition instructions, the non-Federal entity must request disposition instructions from the Federal awarding agency if required by the terms and conditions of the Federal award. Disposition of the equipment will be made as follows, in accordance with Federal awarding agency disposition instructions:

(1) Items of equipment with a current per unit fair market value of $5,000 or less may be retained, sold or otherwise disposed of with no further obligation to the Federal awarding agency.

(2) Except as provided in § 200.312 Federally-owned and exempt property, paragraph (b), or if the Federal awarding agency fails to provide requested disposition instructions within 120 days, items of equipment with a current per-unit fair-market value in excess of $5,000 may be retained by the non-Federal entity or sold. The Federal awarding agency is entitled to an amount calculated by multiplying the current market value or proceeds from sale by the Federal awarding agency's percentage of participation in the cost of the original purchase. If the equipment is sold, the Federal awarding agency may permit the non-Federal entity to deduct and retain from the Federal share $500 or ten percent of the proceeds, whichever is less, for its selling and handling expenses.

(3) The non-Federal entity may transfer title to the property to the Federal Government or to an eligible third party provided that, in such cases, the non-Federal entity must be entitled to compensation for its attributable percentage of the current fair market value of the property.

(4) In cases where a non-Federal entity fails to take appropriate disposition actions, the Federal awarding agency may direct the non-Federal entity to take disposition actions.

[78 FR 78608, Dec. 26, 2013, as amended at 79 FR 75884, Dec. 19, 2014]

### § 200.314 Supplies.

See also § 200.453 Materials and supplies costs, including costs of computing devices.

(a) Title to supplies will vest in the non-Federal entity upon acquisition. If there is a residual inventory of unused supplies exceeding $5,000 in total aggregate value upon termination or completion of the project or program and the supplies are not needed for any other Federal award, the non-Federal entity must retain the supplies for use on other activities or sell them, but must, in either case, compensate the Federal Government for its share. The amount of compensation must be computed in the same manner as for equipment. See § 200.313 Equipment, paragraph (e)(2) for the calculation methodology.

(b) As long as the Federal Government retains an interest in the supplies, the non-Federal entity must not use supplies acquired under a Federal award to provide services to other organizations for a fee that is less than private companies charge for equivalent services, unless specifically authorized by Federal statute.

### § 200.315 Intangible property.

(a) Title to intangible property (see § 200.59 Intangible property) acquired under a Federal award vests upon acquisition in the non-Federal entity. The non-Federal entity must use that property for the originally-authorized purpose, and must not encumber the property without approval of the Federal awarding agency. When no longer needed for the originally authorized purpose, disposition of the intangible property must occur in accordance with the provisions in § 200.313 Equipment paragraph (e).

(b) The non-Federal entity may copyright any work that is subject to copyright and was developed, or for which ownership was acquired, under a Federal award. The Federal awarding agency reserves a royalty-free, nonexclusive and irrevocable right to reproduce, publish, or otherwise use the work for Federal purposes, and to authorize others to do so.

(c) The non-Federal entity is subject to applicable regulations governing patents and inventions, including governmentwide regulations issued by the Department of Commerce at 37 CFR Part 401, "Rights to Inventions Made by Nonprofit Organizations and Small Business Firms Under Government Awards, Contracts and Cooperative Agreements."

(d) The Federal Government has the right to:

(1) Obtain, reproduce, publish, or otherwise use the data produced under a Federal award; and

(2) Authorize others to receive, reproduce, publish, or otherwise use such data for Federal purposes.

(e) Freedom of Information Act (FOIA).

(1) In response to a Freedom of Information Act (FOIA) request for research data relating to published research findings produced under a Federal award that were used by the Federal Government in developing an agency action that has the force and effect of law, the Federal awarding agency must request, and the non-Federal entity must provide, within a reasonable time, the research data so that they can be made available to the public through the procedures established under the FOIA. If the Federal awarding agency obtains the research data solely in response to a FOIA request, the Federal awarding agency may charge the requester a reasonable fee equaling the full incremental cost of obtaining the research data. This fee should reflect costs incurred by the Federal agency and the non-Federal entity. This fee is in addition to any fees the Federal awarding agency may assess under the FOIA (5 U.S.C. 552(a)(4)(A)).

(2) *Published research findings* means when:

(i) Research findings are published in a peer-reviewed scientific or technical journal; or

(ii) A Federal agency publicly and officially cites the research findings in support of an agency action that has the force and effect of law. "Used by the Federal Government in developing an agency action that has the force and effect of law" is defined as when an agency publicly and officially cites the research findings in support of an agency action that has the force and effect of law.

(3) *Research data* means the recorded factual material commonly accepted in the scientific community as necessary to validate research findings, but not any of the following: preliminary analyses, drafts of scientific papers, plans for future research, peer reviews, or communications with colleagues. This "recorded" material excludes physical objects (e.g., laboratory samples). Research data also do not include:

(i) Trade secrets, commercial information, materials necessary to be held confidential by a researcher until they are published, or similar information which is protected under law; and

(ii) Personnel and medical information and similar information the disclosure of which would constitute a clearly unwarranted invasion of personal privacy, such as information that could be used to identify a particular person in a research study.

[78 FR 78608, Dec. 26, 2013, as amended at 79 FR 75884, Dec. 19, 2014]

§ 200.316  Property trust relationship.

Real property, equipment, and intangible property, that are acquired or improved with a Federal award must be held in trust by the non-Federal entity as trustee for the beneficiaries of the project or program under which the property was acquired or improved. The Federal awarding agency may require the non-Federal entity to record liens or other appropriate notices of record to indicate that personal or real property has been acquired or improved with a Federal award and that use and disposition conditions apply to the property.

PROCUREMENT STANDARDS

§ 200.317  Procurements by states.

When procuring property and services under a Federal award, a state must follow the same policies and procedures it uses for procurements from its non-Federal funds. The state will comply with § 200.322 Procurement of recovered *materials* and ensure that every purchase order or other contract includes any clauses required by section § 200.326 Contract provisions. All other non-Federal entities, including subrecipients of a state, will follow §§ 200.318 General procurement standards through 200.326 Contract provisions.

§ 200.318  General procurement standards.

(a) The non-Federal entity must use its own documented procurement procedures which reflect applicable State, local, and tribal laws and regulations, provided that the procurements conform to applicable Federal law and the standards identified in this part.

(b) Non-Federal entities must maintain oversight to ensure that contractors perform in accordance with the terms, conditions, and specifications of their contracts or purchase orders.

(c)(1) The non-Federal entity must maintain written standards of conduct covering conflicts of interest and governing the actions of its employees engaged in the selection, award and administration of contracts. No employee, officer, or agent may participate in the selection, award, or administration of a contract supported by a Federal award if he or she has a real or apparent conflict of interest. Such a conflict of interest would arise when the employee, officer, or agent, any member of his or her immediate family, his or her partner, or an organization which employs or is about to employ any of the parties indicated herein, has a financial or other interest in or a tangible personal benefit from a firm considered for a contract. The officers, employees, and agents of the non-Federal entity may neither solicit nor accept gratuities, favors, or anything of monetary value from contractors or parties to subcontracts. However, non-Federal entities may set standards for situations in which the financial interest is not substantial or the gift is an unsolicited item of nominal value. The standards of conduct must provide for disciplinary actions to be applied for violations of such standards by officers, employees, or agents of the non-Federal entity.

(2) If the non-Federal entity has a parent, affiliate, or subsidiary organization that is not a state, local government, or Indian tribe, the non-Federal entity must also maintain written standards of conduct covering organizational conflicts of interest. Organizational conflicts of interest means that because of relationships with a parent company, affiliate, or subsidiary organization, the non-Federal entity is unable or appears to be unable to be impartial in conducting a procurement action involving a related organization.

(d) The non-Federal entity's procedures must avoid acquisition of unnecessary or duplicative items. Consideration should be given to consolidating or breaking out procurements to obtain a more economical purchase. Where appropriate, an analysis will be made of lease versus purchase alternatives, and any other appropriate analysis to determine the most economical approach.

(e) To foster greater economy and efficiency, and in accordance with efforts to promote cost-effective use of shared services across the Federal Government, the non-Federal entity is encouraged to enter into state and local intergovernmental agreements or inter-entity agreements where appropriate for procurement or use of common or shared goods and services.

(f) The non-Federal entity is encouraged to use Federal excess and surplus property in lieu of purchasing new equipment and property whenever such use is feasible and reduces project costs.

(g) The non-Federal entity is encouraged to use value engineering clauses in contracts for construction projects of sufficient size to offer reasonable opportunities for cost reductions. Value engineering is a systematic and creative analysis of each contract item or task to ensure that its essential func-

tion is provided at the overall lower cost.

(h) The non-Federal entity must award contracts only to responsible contractors possessing the ability to perform successfully under the terms and conditions of a proposed procurement. Consideration will be given to such matters as contractor integrity, compliance with public policy, record of past performance, and financial and technical resources. See also §200.213 Suspension and debarment.

(i) The non-Federal entity must maintain records sufficient to detail the history of procurement. These records will include, but are not necessarily limited to the following: rationale for the method of procurement, selection of contract type, contractor selection or rejection, and the basis for the contract price.

(j)(1) The non-Federal entity may use a time and materials type contract only after a determination that no other contract is suitable and if the contract includes a ceiling price that the contractor exceeds at its own risk. Time and materials type contract means a contract whose cost to a non-Federal entity is the sum of:

(i) The actual cost of materials; and

(ii) Direct labor hours charged at fixed hourly rates that reflect wages, general and administrative expenses, and profit.

(2) Since this formula generates an open-ended contract price, a time-and-materials contract provides no positive profit incentive to the contractor for cost control or labor efficiency. Therefore, each contract must set a ceiling price that the contractor exceeds at its own risk. Further, the non-Federal entity awarding such a contract must assert a high degree of oversight in order to obtain reasonable assurance that the contractor is using efficient methods and effective cost controls.

(k) The non-Federal entity alone must be responsible, in accordance with good administrative practice and sound business judgment, for the settlement of all contractual and administrative issues arising out of procurements. These issues include, but are not limited to, source evaluation, protests, disputes, and claims. These standards do not relieve the non-Federal entity of any contractual responsibilities under its contracts. The Federal awarding agency will not substitute its judgment for that of the non-Federal entity unless the matter is primarily a Federal concern. Violations of law will be referred to the local, state, or Federal authority having proper jurisdiction.

[78 FR 78608, Dec. 26, 2013, as amended at 79 FR 75885, Dec. 19, 2014; 80 FR 43309, July 22, 2015]

§ 200.319  Competition.

(a) All procurement transactions must be conducted in a manner providing full and open competition consistent with the standards of this section. In order to ensure objective contractor performance and eliminate unfair competitive advantage, contractors that develop or draft specifications, requirements, statements of work, or invitations for bids or requests for proposals must be excluded from competing for such procurements. Some of the situations considered to be restrictive of competition include but are not limited to:

(1) Placing unreasonable requirements on firms in order for them to qualify to do business;

(2) Requiring unnecessary experience and excessive bonding;

(3) Noncompetitive pricing practices between firms or between affiliated companies;

(4) Noncompetitive contracts to consultants that are on retainer contracts;

(5) Organizational conflicts of interest;

(6) Specifying only a "brand name" product instead of allowing "an equal" product to be offered and describing the performance or other relevant requirements of the procurement; and

(7) Any arbitrary action in the procurement process.

(b) The non-Federal entity must conduct procurements in a manner that prohibits the use of statutorily or administratively imposed state, local, or tribal geographical preferences in the evaluation of bids or proposals, except in those cases where applicable Federal statutes expressly mandate or encourage geographic preference. Nothing in this section preempts state licensing laws. When contracting for architectural and engineering (A/E) services, geographic location may be a selection criterion provided its application leaves an appropriate number of qualified firms, given the nature and size of the project, to compete for the contract.

(c) The non-Federal entity must have written procedures for procurement transactions. These procedures must ensure that all solicitations:

(1) Incorporate a clear and accurate description of the technical requirements for the material, product, or service to be procured. Such description must not, in competitive procurements, contain features which unduly restrict competition. The description may include a statement of the qualitative nature of the material, product or service to be procured and, when necessary, must set forth those minimum essential characteristics and standards to which it must conform if it is to satisfy its intended use. Detailed product specifications should be avoided if at all possible. When it is impractical or uneconomical to make a clear and accurate description of the technical requirements, a "brand name or equivalent" description may be used as a means to define the performance or other salient requirements of procurement. The specific features of the named brand which must be met by offers must be clearly stated; and

(2) Identify all requirements which the offerors must fulfill and all other factors to be used in evaluating bids or proposals.

(d) The non-Federal entity must ensure that all prequalified lists of persons, firms, or products which are used in acquiring goods and services are current and include enough qualified sources to ensure maximum open and free competition. Also, the non-Federal entity must not preclude potential bidders from qualifying during the solicitation period.

[78 FR 78608, Dec. 26, 2013, as amended at 79 FR 75885, Dec. 19, 2014]

§ 200.320  Methods of procurement to be followed.

The non-Federal entity must use one of the following methods of procurement.

(a) Procurement by micro-purchases. Procurement by micro-purchase is the acquisition of supplies or services, the aggregate dollar amount of which does not exceed the micro-purchase threshold (§ 200.67 Micro-purchase). To the extent practicable, the non-Federal entity must distribute micro-purchases equitably among qualified suppliers. Micro-purchases may be awarded without soliciting competitive quotations if the non-Federal entity considers the price to be reasonable.

(b) Procurement by small purchase procedures. Small purchase procedures are those relatively simple and informal procurement methods for securing services, supplies, or other property that do not cost more than the Simplified Acquisition Threshold. If small purchase procedures are used, price or rate quotations must be obtained from an adequate number of qualified sources.

(c) Procurement by sealed bids (formal advertising). Bids are publicly solicited and a firm fixed price contract (lump sum or unit price) is awarded to the responsible bidder whose bid, conforming with all the material terms and conditions of the invitation for bids, is the lowest in price. The sealed bid method is the preferred method for procuring construction, if the conditions in paragraph (c)(1) of this section apply.

(1) In order for sealed bidding to be feasible, the following conditions should be present:

(i) A complete, adequate, and realistic specification or purchase description is available;

(ii) Two or more responsible bidders are willing and able to compete effectively for the business; and

(iii) The procurement lends itself to a firm fixed price contract and the selection of the successful bidder can be made principally on the basis of price.

(2) If sealed bids are used, the following requirements apply:

(i) Bids must be solicited from an adequate number of known suppliers, providing them sufficient response time prior to the date set for opening the bids, for local, and tribal governments, the invitation for bids must be publicly advertised;

(ii) The invitation for bids, which will include any specifications and pertinent attachments, must define the items or services in order for the bidder to properly respond;

(iii) All bids will be opened at the time and place prescribed in the invitation for bids, and for local and tribal governments, the bids must be opened publicly;

(iv) A firm fixed price contract award will be made in writing to the lowest responsive and responsible bidder. Where specified in bidding documents, factors such as discounts, transportation cost, and life cycle costs must be considered in determining which bid is lowest. Payment discounts will only be used to determine the low bid when prior experience indicates that such discounts are usually taken advantage of; and

(v) Any or all bids may be rejected if there is a sound documented reason.

(d) Procurement by competitive proposals. The technique of competitive proposals is normally conducted with more than one source submitting an offer, and either a fixed price or cost-reimbursement type contract is awarded. It is generally used when conditions are not appropriate for the use of sealed bids. If this method is used, the following requirements apply:

(1) Requests for proposals must be publicized and identify all evaluation factors and their relative importance. Any response to publicized requests for proposals must be considered to the maximum extent practical;

(2) Proposals must be solicited from an adequate number of qualified sources;

(3) The non-Federal entity must have a written method for conducting technical evaluations of the proposals received and for selecting recipients;

(4) Contracts must be awarded to the responsible firm whose proposal is most advantageous to the program, with price and other factors considered; and

(5) The non-Federal entity may use competitive proposal procedures for qualifications-based procurement of architectural/engineering (A/E) professional services whereby competitors' qualifications are evaluated and the most qualified competitor is selected,

subject to negotiation of fair and reasonable compensation. The method, where price is not used as a selection factor, can only be used in procurement of A/E professional services. It cannot be used to purchase other types of services though A/E firms are a potential source to perform the proposed effort.

(e) [Reserved]

(f) Procurement by noncompetitive proposals. Procurement by noncompetitive proposals is procurement through solicitation of a proposal from only one source and may be used only when one or more of the following circumstances apply:

(1) The item is available only from a single source;

(2) The public exigency or emergency for the requirement will not permit a delay resulting from competitive solicitation;

(3) The Federal awarding agency or pass-through entity expressly authorizes noncompetitive proposals in response to a written request from the non-Federal entity; or

(4) After solicitation of a number of sources, competition is determined inadequate.

[78 FR 78608, Dec. 26, 2013, as amended at 79 FR 75885, Dec. 19, 2014; 80 FR 54409, Sept. 10, 2015]

### § 200.321 Contracting with small and minority businesses, women's business enterprises, and labor surplus area firms.

(a) The non-Federal entity must take all necessary affirmative steps to assure that minority businesses, women's business enterprises, and labor surplus area firms are used when possible.

(b) Affirmative steps must include:

(1) Placing qualified small and minority businesses and women's business enterprises on solicitation lists;

(2) Assuring that small and minority businesses, and women's business enterprises are solicited whenever they are potential sources;

(3) Dividing total requirements, when economically feasible, into smaller tasks or quantities to permit maximum participation by small and minority businesses, and women's business enterprises;

(4) Establishing delivery schedules, where the requirement permits, which encourage participation by small and minority businesses, and women's business enterprises;

(5) Using the services and assistance, as appropriate, of such organizations as the Small Business Administration and the Minority Business Development Agency of the Department of Commerce; and

(6) Requiring the prime contractor, if subcontracts are to be let, to take the affirmative steps listed in paragraphs (1) through (5) of this section.

### § 200.322 Procurement of recovered materials.

A non-Federal entity that is a state agency or agency of a political subdivision of a state and its contractors must comply with section 6002 of the Solid Waste Disposal Act, as amended by the Resource Conservation and Recovery Act. The requirements of Section 6002 include procuring only items designated in guidelines of the Environmental Protection Agency (EPA) at 40 CFR part 247 that contain the highest percentage of recovered materials practicable, consistent with maintaining a satisfactory level of competition, where the purchase price of the item exceeds $10,000 or the value of the quantity acquired during the preceding fiscal year exceeded $10,000; procuring solid waste management services in a manner that maximizes energy and resource recovery; and establishing an affirmative procurement program for procurement of recovered materials identified in the EPA guidelines.

[78 FR 78608, Dec. 26, 2013, as amended at 79 FR 75885, Dec. 19, 2014]

### § 200.323 Contract cost and price.

(a) The non-Federal entity must perform a cost or price analysis in connection with every procurement action in excess of the Simplified Acquisition Threshold including contract modifications. The method and degree of analysis is dependent on the facts surrounding the particular procurement situation, but as a starting point, the non-Federal entity must make independent estimates before receiving bids or proposals.

(b) The non-Federal entity must negotiate profit as a separate element of the price for each contract in which there is no price competition and in all cases where cost analysis is performed. To establish a fair and reasonable profit, consideration must be given to the complexity of the work to be performed, the risk borne by the contractor, the contractor's investment, the amount of subcontracting, the quality of its record of past performance, and industry profit rates in the surrounding geographical area for similar work.

(c) Costs or prices based on estimated costs for contracts under the Federal award are allowable only to the extent that costs incurred or cost estimates included in negotiated prices would be allowable for the non-Federal entity under Subpart E—Cost Principles of this part. The non-Federal entity may reference its own cost principles that comply with the Federal cost principles.

(d) The cost plus a percentage of cost and percentage of construction cost methods of contracting must not be used.

### §200.324 Federal awarding agency or pass-through entity review.

(a) The non-Federal entity must make available, upon request of the Federal awarding agency or pass-through entity, technical specifications on proposed procurements where the Federal awarding agency or pass-through entity believes such review is needed to ensure that the item or service specified is the one being proposed for acquisition. This review generally will take place prior to the time the specification is incorporated into a solicitation document. However, if the non-Federal entity desires to have the review accomplished after a solicitation has been developed, the Federal awarding agency or pass-through entity may still review the specifications, with such review usually limited to the technical aspects of the proposed purchase.

(b) The non-Federal entity must make available upon request, for the Federal awarding agency or pass-through entity pre-procurement review, procurement documents, such as requests for proposals or invitations for bids, or independent cost estimates, when:

(1) The non-Federal entity's procurement procedures or operation fails to comply with the procurement standards in this part;

(2) The procurement is expected to exceed the Simplified Acquisition Threshold and is to be awarded without competition or only one bid or offer is received in response to a solicitation;

(3) The procurement, which is expected to exceed the Simplified Acquisition Threshold, specifies a "brand name" product;

(4) The proposed contract is more than the Simplified Acquisition Threshold and is to be awarded to other than the apparent low bidder under a sealed bid procurement; or

(5) A proposed contract modification changes the scope of a contract or increases the contract amount by more than the Simplified Acquisition Threshold.

(c) The non-Federal entity is exempt from the pre-procurement review in paragraph (b) of this section if the Federal awarding agency or pass-through entity determines that its procurement systems comply with the standards of this part.

(1) The non-Federal entity may request that its procurement system be reviewed by the Federal awarding agency or pass-through entity to determine whether its system meets these standards in order for its system to be certified. Generally, these reviews must occur where there is continuous high-dollar funding, and third party contracts are awarded on a regular basis;

(2) The non-Federal entity may self-certify its procurement system. Such self-certification must not limit the Federal awarding agency's right to survey the system. Under a self-certification procedure, the Federal awarding agency may rely on written assurances from the non-Federal entity that it is complying with these standards. The non-Federal entity must cite specific policies, procedures, regulations, or standards as being in compliance with these requirements and have its system available for review.

## § 200.325  Bonding requirements.

For construction or facility improvement contracts or subcontracts exceeding the Simplified Acquisition Threshold, the Federal awarding agency or pass-through entity may accept the bonding policy and requirements of the non-Federal entity provided that the Federal awarding agency or pass-through entity has made a determination that the Federal interest is adequately protected. If such a determination has not been made, the minimum requirements must be as follows:

(a) A bid guarantee from each bidder equivalent to five percent of the bid price. The "bid guarantee" must consist of a firm commitment such as a bid bond, certified check, or other negotiable instrument accompanying a bid as assurance that the bidder will, upon acceptance of the bid, execute such contractual documents as may be required within the time specified.

(b) A performance bond on the part of the contractor for 100 percent of the contract price. A "performance bond" is one executed in connection with a contract to secure fulfillment of all the contractor's obligations under such contract.

(c) A payment bond on the part of the contractor for 100 percent of the contract price. A "payment bond" is one executed in connection with a contract to assure payment as required by law of all persons supplying labor and material in the execution of the work provided for in the contract.

## § 200.326  Contract provisions.

The non-Federal entity's contracts must contain the applicable provisions described in Appendix II to Part 200—Contract Provisions for non-Federal Entity Contracts Under Federal Awards.

PERFORMANCE AND FINANCIAL
MONITORING AND REPORTING

## § 200.327  Financial reporting.

Unless otherwise approved by OMB, the Federal awarding agency may solicit only the standard, OMB-approved governmentwide data elements for collection of financial information (at time of publication the Federal Financial Report or such future collections

as may be approved by OMB and listed on the OMB Web site). This information must be collected with the frequency required by the terms and conditions of the Federal award, but no less frequently than annually nor more frequently than quarterly except in unusual circumstances, for example where more frequent reporting is necessary for the effective monitoring of the Federal award or could significantly affect program outcomes, and preferably in coordination with performance reporting.

## 200.328  Monitoring and reporting program performance.

(a) *Monitoring by the non-Federal entity.* The non-Federal entity is responsible for oversight of the operations of the Federal award supported activities. The non-Federal entity must monitor its activities under Federal awards to assure compliance with applicable Federal requirements and performance expectations are being achieved. Monitoring by the non-Federal entity must cover each program, function or activity. See also § 200.331 Requirements for pass-through *entities.*

(b) *Non-construction performance reports.* The Federal awarding agency must use standard, OMB-approved data elements for collection of performance information (including performance progress reports, Research Performance Progress Report, or such future collections as may be approved by OMB and listed on the OMB Web site).

(1) The non-Federal entity must submit performance reports at the interval required by the Federal awarding agency or pass-through entity to best inform improvements in program outcomes and productivity. Intervals must be no less frequent than annually nor more frequent than quarterly except in unusual circumstances, for example where more frequent reporting is necessary for the effective monitoring of the Federal award or could significantly affect program outcomes. Annual reports must be due 90 calendar days after the reporting period; quarterly or semiannual reports must be due 30 calendar days after the reporting period. Alternatively, the Federal awarding agency or pass-through entity may require annual reports before

the anniversary dates of multiple year Federal awards. The final performance report will be due 90 calendar days after the period of performance end date. If a justified request is submitted by a non-Federal entity, the Federal agency may extend the due date for any performance report.

(2) The non-Federal entity must submit performance reports using OMB-approved governmentwide standard information collections when providing performance information. As appropriate in accordance with above mentioned information collections, these reports will contain, for each Federal award, brief information on the following unless other collections are approved by OMB:

(i) A comparison of actual accomplishments to the objectives of the Federal award established for the period. Where the accomplishments of the Federal award can be quantified, a computation of the cost (for example, related to units of accomplishment) may be required if that information will be useful. Where performance trend data and analysis would be informative to the Federal awarding agency program, the Federal awarding agency should include this as a performance reporting requirement.

(ii) The reasons why established goals were not met, if appropriate.

(iii) Additional pertinent information including, when appropriate, analysis and explanation of cost overruns or high unit costs.

(c) *Construction performance reports.* For the most part, onsite technical inspections and certified percentage of completion data are relied on heavily by Federal awarding agencies and pass-through entities to monitor progress under Federal awards and subawards for construction. The Federal awarding agency may require additional performance reports only when considered necessary.

(d) *Significant developments.* Events may occur between the scheduled performance reporting dates that have significant impact upon the supported activity. In such cases, the non-Federal entity must inform the Federal awarding agency or pass-through entity as soon as the following types of conditions become known:

(1) Problems, delays, or adverse conditions which will materially impair the ability to meet the objective of the Federal award. This disclosure must include a statement of the action taken, or contemplated, and any assistance needed to resolve the situation.

(2) Favorable developments which enable meeting time schedules and objectives sooner or at less cost than anticipated or producing more or different beneficial results than originally planned.

(e) The Federal awarding agency may make site visits as warranted by program needs.

(f) The Federal awarding agency may waive any performance report required by this part if not needed.

§ 200.329 **Reporting on real property.**

The Federal awarding agency or pass-through entity must require a non-Federal entity to submit reports at least annually on the status of real property in which the Federal Government retains an interest, unless the Federal interest in the real property extends 15 years or longer. In those instances where the Federal interest attached is for a period of 15 years or more, the Federal awarding agency or pass-through entity, at its option, may require the non-Federal entity to report at various multi-year frequencies (e.g., every two years or every three years, not to exceed a five-year reporting period; or a Federal awarding agency or pass-through entity may require annual reporting for the first three years of a Federal award and thereafter require reporting every five years).

SUBRECIPIENT MONITORING AND MANAGEMENT

§ 200.330 **Subrecipient and contractor determinations.**

The non-Federal entity may concurrently receive Federal awards as a recipient, a subrecipient, and a contractor, depending on the substance of its agreements with Federal awarding agencies and pass-through entities. Therefore, a pass-through entity must make case-by-case determinations whether each agreement it makes for the disbursement of Federal program funds casts the party receiving the funds in the role of a subrecipient or a contractor. The Federal awarding agency may supply and require recipients to comply with additional guidance to support these determinations provided such guidance does not conflict with this section.

(a) *Subrecipients.* A subaward is for the purpose of carrying out a portion of a Federal award and creates a Federal assistance relationship with the subrecipient. See § 200.92 Subaward. Characteristics which support the classification of the non-Federal entity as a subrecipient include when the non-Federal entity:

(1) Determines who is eligible to receive what Federal assistance;

(2) Has its performance measured in relation to whether objectives of a Federal program were met;

(3) Has responsibility for programmatic decision making;

(4) Is responsible for adherence to applicable Federal program requirements specified in the Federal award; and

(5) In accordance with its agreement, uses the Federal funds to carry out a program for a public purpose specified in authorizing statute, as opposed to providing goods or services for the benefit of the pass-through entity.

(b) *Contractors.* A contract is for the purpose of obtaining goods and services for the non-Federal entity's own use and creates a procurement relationship with the contractor. See § 200.22 Contract. Characteristics indicative of a procurement relationship between the non-Federal entity and a contractor are when the contractor:

(1) Provides the goods and services within normal business operations;

(2) Provides similar goods or services to many different purchasers;

(3) Normally operates in a competitive environment;

(4) Provides goods or services that are ancillary to the operation of the Federal program; and

(5) Is not subject to compliance requirements of the Federal program as a result of the agreement, though similar requirements may apply for other reasons.

(c) *Use of judgment in making determination.* In determining whether an agreement between a pass-through entity and another non-Federal entity

casts the latter as a subrecipient or a contractor, the substance of the relationship is more important than the form of the agreement. All of the characteristics listed above may not be present in all cases, and the pass-through entity must use judgment in classifying each agreement as a subaward or a procurement contract.

[78 FR 78608, Dec. 26, 2013, as amended at 80 FR 54409, Sept. 10, 2015]

§ 200.331 Requirements for pass-through entities.

All pass-through entities must:

(a) Ensure that every subaward is clearly identified to the subrecipient as a subaward and includes the following information at the time of the subaward and if any of these data elements change, include the changes in subsequent subaward modification. When some of this information is not available, the pass-through entity must provide the best information available to describe the Federal award and subaward. Required information includes:

(1) Federal Award Identification.

(i) Subrecipient name (which must match the name associated with its unique entity identifier);

(ii) Subrecipient's unique entity identifier;

(iii) Federal Award Identification Number (FAIN);

(iv) Federal Award Date (see § 200.39 Federal award date) of award to the recipient by the Federal agency;

(v) Subaward Period of Performance Start and End Date;

(vi) Amount of Federal Funds Obligated by this action by the pass-through entity to the subrecipient;

(vii) Total Amount of Federal Funds Obligated to the subrecipient by the pass-through entity including the current obligation;

(viii) Total Amount of the Federal Award committed to the subrecipient by the pass-through entity;

(ix) Federal award project description, as required to be responsive to the Federal Funding Accountability and Transparency Act (FFATA);

(x) Name of Federal awarding agency, pass-through entity, and contact information for awarding official of the Pass-through entity;

(xi) CFDA Number and Name; the pass-through entity must identify the dollar amount made available under each Federal award and the CFDA number at time of disbursement;

(xii) Identification of whether the award is R&D; and

(xiii) Indirect cost rate for the Federal award (including if the de minimis rate is charged per § 200.414 Indirect (F&A) costs).

(2) All requirements imposed by the pass-through entity on the subrecipient so that the Federal award is used in accordance with Federal statutes, regulations and the terms and conditions of the Federal award;

(3) Any additional requirements that the pass-through entity imposes on the subrecipient in order for the pass-through entity to meet its own responsibility to the Federal awarding agency including identification of any required financial and performance reports;

(4) An approved federally recognized indirect cost rate negotiated between the subrecipient and the Federal Government or, if no such rate exists, either a rate negotiated between the pass-through entity and the subrecipient (in compliance with this part), or a de minimis indirect cost rate as defined in § 200.414 Indirect (F&A) costs, paragraph (f);

(5) A requirement that the subrecipient permit the pass-through entity and auditors to have access to the subrecipient's records and financial statements as necessary for the pass-through entity to meet the requirements of this part; and

(6) Appropriate terms and conditions concerning closeout of the subaward.

(b) Evaluate each subrecipient's risk of noncompliance with Federal statutes, regulations, and the terms and conditions of the subaward for purposes of determining the appropriate subrecipient monitoring described in paragraphs (d) and (e) of this section, which may include consideration of such factors as:

(1) The subrecipient's prior experience with the same or similar subawards;

(2) The results of previous audits including whether or not the subrecipient receives a Single Audit in accordance with Subpart F—Audit Requirements of this part, and the extent to which the same or similar subaward has been audited as a major program;

(3) Whether the subrecipient has new personnel or new or substantially changed systems; and

(4) The extent and results of Federal awarding agency monitoring (e.g., if the subrecipient also receives Federal awards directly from a Federal awarding agency).

(c) Consider imposing specific subaward conditions upon a subrecipient if appropriate as described in § 200.207 Specific conditions.

(d) Monitor the activities of the subrecipient as necessary to ensure that the subaward is used for authorized purposes, in compliance with Federal statutes, regulations, and the terms and conditions of the subaward; and that subaward performance goals are achieved. Pass-through entity monitoring of the subrecipient must include:

(1) Reviewing financial and performance reports required by the pass-through entity.

(2) Following-up and ensuring that the subrecipient takes timely and appropriate action on all deficiencies pertaining to the Federal award provided to the subrecipient from the pass-through entity detected through audits, on-site reviews, and other means.

(3) Issuing a management decision for audit findings pertaining to the Federal award provided to the subrecipient from the pass-through entity as required by § 200.521 Management decision.

(e) Depending upon the pass-through entity's assessment of risk posed by the subrecipient (as described in paragraph (b) of this section), the following monitoring tools may be useful for the pass-through entity to ensure proper accountability and compliance with program requirements and achievement of performance goals:

(1) Providing subrecipients with training and technical assistance on program-related matters; and

(2) Performing on-site reviews of the subrecipient's program operations;

(3) Arranging for agreed-upon-procedures engagements as described in § 200.425 Audit services.

(f) Verify that every subrecipient is audited as required by Subpart F— Audit Requirements of this part when it is expected that the subrecipient's Federal awards expended during the respective fiscal year equaled or exceeded the threshold set forth in § 200.501 Audit requirements.

(g) Consider whether the results of the subrecipient's audits, on-site reviews, or other monitoring indicate conditions that necessitate adjustments to the pass-through entity's own records.

(h) Consider taking enforcement action against noncompliant subrecipients as described in § 200.338 Remedies for noncompliance of this part and in program regulations.

[78 FR 78608, Dec. 26, 2013, as amended at 79 FR 75885, Dec. 19, 2014; 80 FR 54409, Sept. 10, 2015]

### § 200.332  Fixed amount subawards.

With prior written approval from the Federal awarding agency, a pass-through entity may provide subawards based on fixed amounts up to the Simplified Acquisition Threshold, provided that the subawards meet the requirements for fixed amount awards in § 200.201 Use of grant agreements (including fixed amount awards), cooperative agreements, and contracts.

RECORD RETENTION AND ACCESS

### § 200.333  Retention requirements for records.

Financial records, supporting documents, statistical records, and all other non-Federal entity records pertinent to a Federal award must be retained for a period of three years from the date of submission of the final expenditure report or, for Federal awards that are renewed quarterly or annually, from the date of the submission of the quarterly or annual financial report, respectively, as reported to the Federal awarding agency or pass-through entity in the case of a subrecipient. Federal awarding agencies and pass-through entities must not impose any other record retention requirements upon non-Federal entities. The only exceptions are the following:

(a) If any litigation, claim, or audit is started before the expiration of the 3-year period, the records must be retained until all litigation, claims, or audit findings involving the records have been resolved and final action taken.

(b) When the non-Federal entity is notified in writing by the Federal awarding agency, cognizant agency for audit, oversight agency for audit, cognizant agency for indirect costs, or pass-through entity to extend the retention period.

(c) Records for real property and equipment acquired with Federal funds must be retained for 3 years after final disposition.

(d) When records are transferred to or maintained by the Federal awarding agency or pass-through entity, the 3-year retention requirement is not applicable to the non-Federal entity.

(e) Records for program income transactions after the period of performance. In some cases recipients must report program income after the period of performance. Where there is such a requirement, the retention period for the records pertaining to the earning of the program income starts from the end of the non-Federal entity's fiscal year in which the program income is earned.

(f) Indirect cost rate proposals and cost allocations plans. This paragraph applies to the following types of documents and their supporting records: indirect cost rate computations or proposals, cost allocation plans, and any similar accounting computations of the rate at which a particular group of costs is chargeable (such as computer usage chargeback rates or composite fringe benefit rates).

(1) If submitted for negotiation. If the proposal, plan, or other computation is required to be submitted to the Federal Government (or to the pass-through entity) to form the basis for negotiation of the rate, then the 3-year retention period for its supporting records starts from the date of such submission.

(2) If not submitted for negotiation. If the proposal, plan, or other computation is not required to be submitted to the Federal Government (or to the pass-through entity) for negotiation

130

purposes, then the 3-year retention period for the proposal, plan, or computation and its supporting records starts from the end of the fiscal year (or other accounting period) covered by the proposal, plan, or other computation.

### § 200.334 Requests for transfer of records.

The Federal awarding agency must request transfer of certain records to its custody from the non-Federal entity when it determines that the records possess long-term retention value. However, in order to avoid duplicate recordkeeping, the Federal awarding agency may make arrangements for the non-Federal entity to retain any records that are continuously needed for joint use.

### § 200.335 Methods for collection, transmission and storage of information.

In accordance with the May 2013 Executive Order on Making Open and Machine Readable the New Default for Government Information, the Federal awarding agency and the non-Federal entity should, whenever practicable, collect, transmit, and store Federal award-related information in open and machine readable formats rather than in closed formats or on paper. The Federal awarding agency or pass-through entity must always provide or accept paper versions of Federal award-related information to and from the non-Federal entity upon request. If paper copies are submitted, the Federal awarding agency or pass-through entity must not require more than an original and two copies. When original records are electronic and cannot be altered, there is no need to create and retain paper copies. When original records are paper, electronic versions may be substituted through the use of duplication or other forms of electronic media provided that they are subject to periodic quality control reviews, provide reasonable safeguards against alteration, and remain readable.

### § 200.336 Access to records.

(a) Records of non-Federal entities. The Federal awarding agency, Inspectors General, the Comptroller General of the United States, and the pass-through entity, or any of their authorized representatives, must have the right of access to any documents, papers, or other records of the non-Federal entity which are pertinent to the Federal award, in order to make audits, examinations, excerpts, and transcripts. The right also includes timely and reasonable access to the non-Federal entity's personnel for the purpose of interview and discussion related to such documents.

(b) Only under extraordinary and rare circumstances would such access include review of the true name of victims of a crime. Routine monitoring cannot be considered extraordinary and rare circumstances that would necessitate access to this information. When access to the true name of victims of a crime is necessary, appropriate steps to protect this sensitive information must be taken by both the non-Federal entity and the Federal awarding agency. Any such access, other than under a court order or subpoena pursuant to a bona fide confidential investigation, must be approved by the head of the Federal awarding agency or delegate.

(c) Expiration of right of access. The rights of access in this section are not limited to the required retention period but last as long as the records are retained. Federal awarding agencies and pass-through entities must not impose any other access requirements upon non-Federal entities.

### § 200.337 Restrictions on public access to records.

No Federal awarding agency may place restrictions on the non-Federal entity that limit public access to the records of the non-Federal entity pertinent to a Federal award, except for protected personally identifiable information (PII) or when the Federal awarding agency can demonstrate that such records will be kept confidential and would have been exempted from disclosure pursuant to the Freedom of Information Act (5 U.S.C. 552) or controlled unclassified information pursuant to Executive Order 13556 if the records had belonged to the Federal awarding agency. The Freedom of Information Act (5 U.S.C. 552) (FOIA) does not apply to those records that remain under a non-Federal entity's control except as required under § 200.315 Intangible property. Unless required by Federal, state, local, and tribal statute, non-Federal entities are not required to permit public access to their records. The non-Federal entity's records provided to a Federal agency generally will be subject to FOIA and applicable exemptions.

[78 FR 78608, Dec. 26, 2013, as amended at 79 FR 75885, Dec. 19, 2014]

REMEDIES FOR NONCOMPLIANCE

### § 200.338  Remedies for noncompliance.

If a non-Federal entity fails to comply with Federal statutes, regulations or the terms and conditions of a Federal award, the Federal awarding agency or pass-through entity may impose additional conditions, as described in § 200.207 Specific conditions. If the Federal awarding agency or pass-through entity determines that noncompliance cannot be remedied by imposing additional conditions, the Federal awarding agency or pass-through entity may take one or more of the following actions, as appropriate in the circumstances:

(a) Temporarily withhold cash payments pending correction of the deficiency by the non-Federal entity or more severe enforcement action by the Federal awarding agency or pass-through entity.

(b) Disallow (that is, deny both use of funds and any applicable matching credit for) all or part of the cost of the activity or action not in compliance.

(c) Wholly or partly suspend or terminate the Federal award.

(d) Initiate suspension or debarment proceedings as authorized under 2 CFR part 180 and Federal awarding agency regulations (or in the case of a pass-through entity, recommend such a proceeding be initiated by a Federal awarding agency).

(e) Withhold further Federal awards for the project or program.

(f) Take other remedies that may be legally available.

### § 200.339  Termination.

(a) The Federal award may be terminated in whole or in part as follows:

(1) By the Federal awarding agency or pass-through entity, if a non-Federal entity fails to comply with the terms and conditions of a Federal award;

(2) By the Federal awarding agency or pass-through entity for cause;

(3) By the Federal awarding agency or pass-through entity with the consent of the non-Federal entity, in which case the two parties must agree upon the termination conditions, including the effective date and, in the case of partial termination, the portion to be terminated; or

(4) By the non-Federal entity upon sending to the Federal awarding agency or pass-through entity written notification setting forth the reasons for such termination, the effective date, and, in the case of partial termination, the portion to be terminated. However, if the Federal awarding agency or pass-through entity determines in the case of partial termination that the reduced or modified portion of the Federal award or subaward will not accomplish the purposes for which the Federal award was made, the Federal awarding agency or pass-through entity may terminate the Federal award in its entirety.

(b) When a Federal awarding agency terminates a Federal award prior to the end of the period of performance due to the non-Federal entity's material failure to comply with the Federal award terms and conditions, the Federal awarding agency must report the termination to the OMB-designated integrity and performance system accessible through SAM (currently FAPIIS).

(1) The information required under paragraph (b) of this section is not to be reported to designated integrity and performance system until the non-Federal entity either—

(i) Has exhausted its opportunities to object or challenge the decision, see § 200.341 Opportunities to object, hearings and appeals; or

(ii) Has not, within 30 calendar days after being notified of the termination, informed the Federal awarding agency that it intends to appeal the Federal awarding agency's decision to terminate.

(2) If a Federal awarding agency, after entering information into the

designated integrity and performance system about a termination, subsequently:

(i) Learns that any of that information is erroneous, the Federal awarding agency must correct the information in the system within three business days;

(ii) Obtains an update to that information that could be helpful to other Federal awarding agencies, the Federal awarding agency is strongly encouraged to amend the information in the system to incorporate the update in a timely way.

(3) Federal awarding agencies, shall not post any information that will be made publicly available in the non-public segment of designated integrity and performance system that is covered by a disclosure exemption under the Freedom of Information Act. If the non-Federal entity asserts within seven calendar days to the Federal awarding agency who posted the information, that some of the information made publicly available is covered by a disclosure exemption under the Freedom of Information Act, the Federal awarding agency who posted the information must remove the posting within seven calendar days of receiving the assertion. Prior to reposting the releasable information, the Federal agency must resolve the issue in accordance with the agency's Freedom of Information Act procedures.

(c) When a Federal award is terminated or partially terminated, both the Federal awarding agency or passthrough entity and the non-Federal entity remain responsible for compliance with the requirements in §§ 200.343 Closeout and 200.344 Post-closeout adjustments and continuing responsibilities.

[78 FR 78608, Dec. 26, 2013, as amended at 80 FR 43309, July 22, 2015]

## § 200.340 Notification of termination requirement.

(a) The Federal agency or passthrough entity must provide to the non-Federal entity a notice of termination.

(b) If the Federal award is terminated for the non-Federal entity's material failure to comply with the Federal statutes, regulations, or terms and conditions of the Federal award, the notification must state that—

(1) The termination decision will be reported to the OMB-designated integrity and performance system accessible through SAM (currently FAPIIS);

(2) The information will be available in the OMB-designated integrity and performance system for a period of five years from the date of the termination, then archived;

(3) Federal awarding agencies that consider making a Federal award to the non-Federal entity during that five year period must consider that information in judging whether the non-Federal entity is qualified to receive the Federal award, when the Federal share of the Federal award is expected to exceed the simplified acquisition threshold over the period of performance;

(4) The non-Federal entity may comment on any information the OMB-designated integrity and performance system contains about the non-Federal entity for future consideration by Federal awarding agencies. The non-Federal entity may submit comments to the awardee integrity and performance portal accessible through SAM (currently (CPARS).

(5) Federal awarding agencies will consider non-Federal entity comments when determining whether the non-Federal entity is qualified for a future Federal award.

(c) Upon termination of a Federal award, the Federal awarding agency must provide the information required under FFATA to the Federal Web site established to fulfill the requirements of FFATA, and update or notify any other relevant governmentwide systems or entities of any indications of poor performance as required by 41 U.S.C. 417b and 31 U.S.C. 3321 and implementing guidance at 2 CFR part 77 (forthcoming at time of publication). See also the requirements for Suspension and Debarment at 2 CFR part 180.

[78 FR 78608, Dec. 26, 2013, as amended at 79 FR 75885, Dec. 19, 2014; 80 FR 43310, July 22, 2015]

## § 200.341 Opportunities to object, hearings and appeals.

Upon taking any remedy for noncompliance, the Federal awarding agency must provide the non-Federal entity an opportunity to object and provide information and documentation challenging the suspension or termination action, in accordance with written processes and procedures published by the Federal awarding agency. The Federal awarding agency or pass-through entity must comply with any requirements for hearings, appeals or other administrative proceedings to which the non-Federal entity is entitled under any statute or regulation applicable to the action involved.

[78 FR 78608, Dec. 26, 2013, as amended at 79 FR 75885, Dec. 19, 2014]

**§ 200.342  Effects of suspension and termination.**

Costs to the non-Federal entity resulting from obligations incurred by the non-Federal entity during a suspension or after termination of a Federal award or subaward are not allowable unless the Federal awarding agency or pass-through entity expressly authorizes them in the notice of suspension or termination or subsequently. However, costs during suspension or after termination are allowable if:

(a) The costs result from obligations which were properly incurred by the non-Federal entity before the effective date of suspension or termination, are not in anticipation of it; and

(b) The costs would be allowable if the Federal award was not suspended or expired normally at the end of the period of performance in which the termination takes effect.

CLOSEOUT

**§ 200.343  Closeout.**

The Federal awarding agency or pass-through entity will close-out the Federal award when it determines that all applicable administrative actions and all required work of the Federal award have been completed by the non-Federal entity. This section specifies the actions the non-Federal entity and Federal awarding agency or pass-through entity must take to complete this process at the end of the period of performance.

(a) The non-Federal entity must submit, no later than 90 calendar days after the end date of the period of per-

formance, all financial, performance, and other reports as required by the terms and conditions of the Federal award. The Federal awarding agency or pass-through entity may approve extensions when requested by the non-Federal entity.

(b) Unless the Federal awarding agency or pass-through entity authorizes an extension, a non-Federal entity must liquidate all obligations incurred under the Federal award not later than 90 calendar days after the end date of the period of performance as specified in the terms and conditions of the Federal award.

(c) The Federal awarding agency or pass-through entity must make prompt payments to the non-Federal entity for allowable reimbursable costs under the Federal award being closed out.

(d) The non-Federal entity must promptly refund any balances of unobligated cash that the Federal awarding agency or pass-through entity paid in advance or paid and that are not authorized to be retained by the non-Federal entity for use in other projects. See OMB Circular A–129 and see § 200.345 Collection of amounts due, for requirements regarding unreturned amounts that become delinquent debts.

(e) Consistent with the terms and conditions of the Federal award, the Federal awarding agency or pass-through entity must make a settlement for any upward or downward adjustments to the Federal share of costs after closeout reports are received.

(f) The non-Federal entity must account for any real and personal property acquired with Federal funds or received from the Federal Government in accordance with §§ 200.310 Insurance coverage through 200.316 Property trust relationship and 200.329 Reporting on real property.

(g) The Federal awarding agency or pass-through entity should complete all closeout actions for Federal awards no later than one year after receipt and acceptance of all required final reports.

[78 FR 78608, Dec. 26, 2013, as amended at 79 FR 75885, Dec. 19, 2014]

POST-CLOSEOUT ADJUSTMENTS AND
CONTINUING RESPONSIBILITIES

### § 200.344 Post-closeout adjustments and continuing responsibilities.

(a) The closeout of a Federal award does not affect any of the following:

(1) The right of the Federal awarding agency or pass-through entity to disallow costs and recover funds on the basis of a later audit or other review. The Federal awarding agency or pass-through entity must make any cost disallowance determination and notify the non-Federal entity within the record retention period.

(2) The obligation of the non-Federal entity to return any funds due as a result of later refunds, corrections, or other transactions including final indirect cost rate adjustments.

(3) Audit requirements in Subpart F—Audit Requirements of this part.

(4) Property management and disposition requirements in Subpart D—Post Federal Award Requirements of this part, §§ 200.310 Insurance Coverage through 200.316 Property trust relationship.

(5) Records retention as required in Subpart D—Post Federal Award Requirements of this part, §§ 200.333 Retention requirements for records through 200.337 Restrictions on public access to records.

(b) After closeout of the Federal award, a relationship created under the Federal award may be modified or ended in whole or in part with the consent of the Federal awarding agency or pass-through entity and the non-Federal entity, provided the responsibilities of the non-Federal entity referred to in paragraph (a) of this section, including those for property management as applicable, are considered and provisions made for continuing responsibilities of the non-Federal entity, as appropriate.

[78 FR 78608, Dec. 26, 2013, as amended at 79 FR 75885, Dec. 19, 2014]

COLLECTION OF AMOUNTS DUE

### § 200.345 Collection of amounts due.

(a) Any funds paid to the non-Federal entity in excess of the amount to which the non-Federal entity is finally determined to be entitled under the terms of the Federal award constitute a debt to the Federal Government. If not paid within 90 calendar days after demand, the Federal awarding agency may reduce the debt by:

(1) Making an administrative offset against other requests for reimbursements;

(2) Withholding advance payments otherwise due to the non-Federal entity; or

(3) Other action permitted by Federal statute.

(b) Except where otherwise provided by statutes or regulations, the Federal awarding agency will charge interest on an overdue debt in accordance with the Federal Claims Collection Standards (31 CFR parts 900 through 999). The date from which interest is computed is not extended by litigation or the filing of any form of appeal.

## Subpart E—Cost Principles

GENERAL PROVISIONS

### § 200.400 Policy guide.

The application of these cost principles is based on the fundamental premises that:

(a) The non-Federal entity is responsible for the efficient and effective administration of the Federal award through the application of sound management practices.

(b) The non-Federal entity assumes responsibility for administering Federal funds in a manner consistent with underlying agreements, program objectives, and the terms and conditions of the Federal award.

(c) The non-Federal entity, in recognition of its own unique combination of staff, facilities, and experience, has the primary responsibility for employing whatever form of sound organization and management techniques may be necessary in order to assure proper and efficient administration of the Federal award.

(d) The application of these cost principles should require no significant changes in the internal accounting policies and practices of the non-Federal entity. However, the accounting practices of the non-Federal entity must be consistent with these cost principles and support the accumulation of costs as required by the principles, and must provide for adequate documentation to support costs charged to the Federal award.

(e) In reviewing, negotiating and approving cost allocation plans or indirect cost proposals, the cognizant agency for indirect costs should generally assure that the non-Federal entity is applying these cost accounting principles on a consistent basis during their review and negotiation of indirect cost proposals. Where wide variations exist in the treatment of a given cost item by the non-Federal entity, the reasonableness and equity of such treatments should be fully considered. See § 200.56 Indirect (facilities & administrative (F&A)) costs.

(f) For non-Federal entities that educate and engage students in research, the dual role of students as both trainees and employees (including pre- and post-doctoral staff) contributing to the completion of Federal awards for research must be recognized in the application of these principles.

(g) The non-Federal entity may not earn or keep any profit resulting from Federal financial assistance, unless explicitly authorized by the terms and conditions of the Federal award. See also § 200.307 Program income.

[78 FR 78608, Dec. 26, 2013, as amended at 79 FR 75885, Dec. 19, 2014]

§ 200.401   Application.

(a) *General.* These principles must be used in determining the allowable costs of work performed by the non-Federal entity under Federal awards. These principles also must be used by the non-Federal entity as a guide in the pricing of fixed-price contracts and subcontracts where costs are used in determining the appropriate price. The principles do not apply to:

(1) Arrangements under which Federal financing is in the form of loans, scholarships, fellowships, traineeships, or other fixed amounts based on such items as education allowance or published tuition rates and fees.

(2) For IHEs, capitation awards, which are awards based on case counts or number of beneficiaries according to the terms and conditions of the Federal award.

(3) Fixed amount awards. See also Subpart A—Acronyms and Definitions, §§ 200.45 Fixed amount awards and 200.201 Use of grant agreements (including fixed amount awards), cooperative agreements, and contracts.

(4) Federal awards to hospitals (see Appendix IX to Part 200—Hospital Cost Principles).

(5) Other awards under which the non-Federal entity is not required to account to the Federal Government for actual costs incurred.

(b) *Federal Contract.* Where a Federal contract awarded to a non-Federal entity is subject to the Cost Accounting Standards (CAS), it incorporates the applicable CAS clauses, Standards, and CAS administration requirements per the 48 CFR Chapter 99 and 48 CFR part 30 (FAR Part 30). CAS applies directly to the CAS-covered contract and the Cost Accounting Standards at 48 CFR parts 9904 or 9905 takes precedence over the cost principles in this Subpart E—Cost Principles of this part with respect to the allocation of costs. When a contract with a non-Federal entity is subject to full CAS coverage, the allowability of certain costs under the cost principles will be affected by the allocation provisions of the Cost Accounting Standards (e.g., CAS 414—48 CFR 9904.414, Cost of Money as an Element of the Cost of Facilities Capital, and CAS 417—48 CFR 9904.417, Cost of Money as an Element of the Cost of Capital Assets Under Construction), apply rather the allowability provisions of § 200.449 Interest. In complying with those requirements, the non-Federal entity's application of cost accounting practices for estimating, accumulating, and reporting costs for other Federal awards and other cost objectives under the CAS-covered contract still must be consistent with its cost accounting practices for the CAS-covered contracts. In all cases, only one set of accounting records needs to be maintained for the allocation of costs by the non-Federal entity.

(c) *Exemptions.* Some nonprofit organizations, because of their size and nature of operations, can be considered to be similar to for-profit entities for purpose of applicability of cost principles.

Such nonprofit organizations must operate under Federal cost principles applicable to for-profit entities located at 48 CFR 31.2. A listing of these organizations is contained in Appendix VIII to Part 200—Nonprofit Organizations Exempted From Subpart E—Cost Principles of this part. Other organizations, as approved by the cognizant agency for indirect costs, may be added from time to time.

BASIC CONSIDERATIONS

### § 200.402 Composition of costs.

*Total cost.* The total cost of a Federal award is the sum of the allowable direct and allocable indirect costs less any applicable credits.

### § 200.403 Factors affecting allowability of costs.

Except where otherwise authorized by statute, costs must meet the following general criteria in order to be allowable under Federal awards:

(a) Be necessary and reasonable for the performance of the Federal award and be allocable thereto under these principles.

(b) Conform to any limitations or exclusions set forth in these principles or in the Federal award as to types or amount of cost items.

(c) Be consistent with policies and procedures that apply uniformly to both federally-financed and other activities of the non-Federal entity.

(d) Be accorded consistent treatment. A cost may not be assigned to a Federal award as a direct cost if any other cost incurred for the same purpose in like circumstances has been allocated to the Federal award as an indirect cost.

(e) Be determined in accordance with generally accepted accounting principles (GAAP), except, for state and local governments and Indian tribes only, as otherwise provided for in this part.

(f) Not be included as a cost or used to meet cost sharing or matching requirements of any other federally-financed program in either the current or a prior period. See also § 200.306 Cost sharing or matching paragraph (b).

(g) Be adequately documented. See also §§ 200.300 Statutory and national policy requirements through 200.309 Period of performance of this part.

### § 200.404 Reasonable costs.

A cost is reasonable if, in its nature and amount, it does not exceed that which would be incurred by a prudent person under the circumstances prevailing at the time the decision was made to incur the cost. The question of reasonableness is particularly important when the non-Federal entity is predominantly federally-funded. In determining reasonableness of a given cost, consideration must be given to:

(a) Whether the cost is of a type generally recognized as ordinary and necessary for the operation of the non-Federal entity or the proper and efficient performance of the Federal award.

(b) The restraints or requirements imposed by such factors as: sound business practices; arm's-length bargaining; Federal, state, local, tribal, and other laws and regulations; and terms and conditions of the Federal award.

(c) Market prices for comparable goods or services for the geographic area.

(d) Whether the individuals concerned acted with prudence in the circumstances considering their responsibilities to the non-Federal entity, its employees, where applicable its students or membership, the public at large, and the Federal Government.

(e) Whether the non-Federal entity significantly deviates from its established practices and policies regarding the incurrence of costs, which may unjustifiably increase the Federal award's cost.

[78 FR 78608, Dec. 26, 2013, as amended at 79 FR 75885, Dec. 19, 2014]

### § 200.405 Allocable costs.

(a) A cost is allocable to a particular Federal award or other cost objective if the goods or services involved are chargeable or assignable to that Federal award or cost objective in accordance with relative benefits received. This standard is met if the cost:

(1) Is incurred specifically for the Federal award;

(2) Benefits both the Federal award and other work of the non-Federal entity and can be distributed in proportions that may be approximated using reasonable methods; and

(3) Is necessary to the overall operation of the non-Federal entity and is assignable in part to the Federal award in accordance with the principles in this subpart.

(b) All activities which benefit from the non-Federal entity's indirect (F&A) cost, including unallowable activities and donated services by the non-Federal entity or third parties, will receive an appropriate allocation of indirect costs.

(c) Any cost allocable to a particular Federal award under the principles provided for in this part may not be charged to other Federal awards to overcome fund deficiencies, to avoid restrictions imposed by Federal statutes, regulations, or terms and conditions of the Federal awards, or for other reasons. However, this prohibition would not preclude the non-Federal entity from shifting costs that are allowable under two or more Federal awards in accordance with existing Federal statutes, regulations, or the terms and conditions of the Federal awards.

(d) Direct cost allocation principles. If a cost benefits two or more projects or activities in proportions that can be determined without undue effort or cost, the cost must be allocated to the projects based on the proportional benefit. If a cost benefits two or more projects or activities in proportions that cannot be determined because of the interrelationship of the work involved, then, notwithstanding paragraph (c) of this section, the costs may be allocated or transferred to benefitted projects on any reasonable documented basis. Where the purchase of equipment or other capital asset is specifically authorized under a Federal award, the costs are assignable to the Federal award regardless of the use that may be made of the equipment or other capital asset involved when no longer needed for the purpose for which it was originally required. See also §§ 200.310 Insurance coverage through 200.316 Property trust relationship and 200.439 Equipment and other capital expenditures.

(e) If the contract is subject to CAS, costs must be allocated to the contract pursuant to the Cost Accounting Standards. To the extent that CAS is applicable, the allocation of costs in accordance with CAS takes precedence over the allocation provisions in this part.

[78 FR 78608, Dec. 26, 2013, as amended at 79 FR 75885, Dec. 19, 2014]

§ 200.406   Applicable credits.

(a) Applicable credits refer to those receipts or reduction-of-expenditure-type transactions that offset or reduce expense items allocable to the Federal award as direct or indirect (F&A) costs. Examples of such transactions are: purchase discounts, rebates or allowances, recoveries or indemnities on losses, insurance refunds or rebates, and adjustments of overpayments or erroneous charges. To the extent that such credits accruing to or received by the non-Federal entity relate to allowable costs, they must be credited to the Federal award either as a cost reduction or cash refund, as appropriate.

(b) In some instances, the amounts received from the Federal Government to finance activities or service operations of the non-Federal entity should be treated as applicable credits. Specifically, the concept of netting such credit items (including any amounts used to meet cost sharing or matching requirements) must be recognized in determining the rates or amounts to be charged to the Federal award. (See §§ 200.436 Depreciation and 200.468 Specialized service facilities, for areas of potential application in the matter of Federal financing of activities.)

[78 FR 78608, Dec. 26, 2013, as amended at 79 FR 75885, Dec. 19, 2014]

§ 200.407   Prior written approval (prior approval).

Under any given Federal award, the reasonableness and allocability of certain items of costs may be difficult to determine. In order to avoid subsequent disallowance or dispute based on unreasonableness or nonallocability, the non-Federal entity may seek the prior written approval of the cognizant agency for indirect costs or the Federal awarding agency in advance of the incurrence of special or unusual costs. Prior written approval should include the timeframe or scope of the agreement. The absence of prior written approval on any element of cost will not, in itself, affect the reasonableness or allocability of that element, unless prior approval is specifically required for allowability as described under certain circumstances in the following sections of this part:

(a) §200.201 Use of grant agreements (including fixed amount awards), cooperative agreements, and contracts, paragraph (b)(5);

(b) §200.306 Cost sharing or matching;

(c) §200.307 Program income;

(d) §200.308 Revision of budget and program plans;

(e) §200.311 Real property;

(f) §200.313 Equipment;

(g) §200.332 Fixed amount subawards;

(h) §200.413 Direct costs, paragraph (c);

(i) §200.430 Compensation—personal services, paragraph (h);

(j) §200.431 Compensation—fringe benefits;

(k) §200.438 Entertainment costs;

(l) §200.439 Equipment and other capital expenditures;

(m) §200.440 Exchange rates;

(n) §200.441 Fines, penalties, damages and other settlements;

(o) §200.442 Fund raising and investment management costs;

(p) §200.445 Goods or services for personal use;

(q) §200.447 Insurance and indemnification;

(r) §200.454 Memberships, subscriptions, and professional activity costs, paragraph (c);

(s) §200.455 Organization costs;

(t) §200.456 Participant support costs;

(u) §200.458 Pre-award costs;

(v) §200.462 Rearrangement and reconversion costs;

(w) §200.467 Selling and marketing costs;

(x) §200.470 Taxes (including Value Added Tax); and

(y) §200.474 Travel costs.

[78 FR 78608, Dec. 26, 2013, as amended at 79 FR 75885, Dec. 19, 2014]

### §200.408 Limitation on allowance of costs.

The Federal award may be subject to statutory requirements that limit the allowability of costs. When the maximum amount allowable under a limitation is less than the total amount determined in accordance with the principles in this part, the amount not recoverable under the Federal award may not be charged to the Federal award.

### §200.409 Special considerations.

In addition to the basic considerations regarding the allowability of costs highlighted in this subtitle, other subtitles in this part describe special considerations and requirements applicable to states, local governments, Indian tribes, and IHEs. In addition, certain provisions among the items of cost in this subpart, are only applicable to certain types of non-Federal entities, as specified in the following sections:

(a) Direct and Indirect (F&A) Costs (§§200.412 Classification of costs through 200.415 Required certifications) of this subpart;

(b) Special Considerations for States, Local Governments and Indian Tribes (§§200.416 Cost allocation plans and indirect cost proposals and 200.417 Interagency service) of this subpart; and

(c) Special Considerations for Institutions of Higher Education (§§200.418 Costs incurred by states and local governments and 200.419 Cost accounting standards and disclosure statement) of this subpart.

### §200.410 Collection of unallowable costs.

Payments made for costs determined to be unallowable by either the Federal awarding agency, cognizant agency for indirect costs, or pass-through entity, either as direct or indirect costs, must be refunded (including interest) to the Federal Government in accordance with instructions from the Federal agency that determined the costs are unallowable unless Federal statute or regulation directs otherwise. See also Subpart D—Post Federal Award Requirements of this part, §§200.300 Statutory and national policy requirements through 200.309 Period of performance.

§ 200.411 Adjustment of previously negotiated indirect (F&A) cost rates containing unallowable costs.

(a) Negotiated indirect (F&A) cost rates based on a proposal later found to have included costs that:

(1) Are unallowable as specified by Federal statutes, regulations or the terms and conditions of a Federal award; or

(2) Are unallowable because they are not allocable to the Federal award(s), must be adjusted, or a refund must be made, in accordance with the requirements of this section. These adjustments or refunds are designed to correct the proposals used to establish the rates and do not constitute a reopening of the rate negotiation. The adjustments or refunds will be made regardless of the type of rate negotiated (predetermined, final, fixed, or provisional).

(b) For rates covering a future fiscal year of the non-Federal entity, the unallowable costs will be removed from the indirect (F&A) cost pools and the rates appropriately adjusted.

(c) For rates covering a past period, the Federal share of the unallowable costs will be computed for each year involved and a cash refund (including interest chargeable in accordance with applicable regulations) will be made to the Federal Government. If cash refunds are made for past periods covered by provisional or fixed rates, appropriate adjustments will be made when the rates are finalized to avoid duplicate recovery of the unallowable costs by the Federal Government.

(d) For rates covering the current period, either a rate adjustment or a refund, as described in paragraphs (b) and (c) of this section, must be required by the cognizant agency for indirect costs. The choice of method must be at the discretion of the cognizant agency for indirect costs, based on its judgment as to which method would be most practical.

(e) The amount or proportion of unallowable costs included in each year's rate will be assumed to be the same as the amount or proportion of unallowable costs included in the base year proposal used to establish the rate.

DIRECT AND INDIRECT (F&A) COSTS

§ 200.412 Classification of costs.

There is no universal rule for classifying certain costs as either direct or indirect (F&A) under every accounting system. A cost may be direct with respect to some specific service or function, but indirect with respect to the Federal award or other final cost objective. Therefore, it is essential that each item of cost incurred for the same purpose be treated consistently in like circumstances either as a direct or an indirect (F&A) cost in order to avoid possible double-charging of Federal awards. Guidelines for determining direct and indirect (F&A) costs charged to Federal awards are provided in this subpart.

§ 200.413 Direct costs.

(a) *General.* Direct costs are those costs that can be identified specifically with a particular final cost objective, such as a Federal award, or other internally or externally funded activity, or that can be directly assigned to such activities relatively easily with a high degree of accuracy. Costs incurred for the same purpose in like circumstances must be treated consistently as either direct or indirect (F&A) costs. See also § 200.405 Allocable costs.

(b) *Application to Federal awards.* Identification with the Federal award rather than the nature of the goods and services involved is the determining factor in distinguishing direct from indirect (F&A) costs of Federal awards. Typical costs charged directly to a Federal award are the compensation of employees who work on that award, their related fringe benefit costs, the costs of materials and other items of expense incurred for the Federal award. If directly related to a specific award, certain costs that otherwise would be treated as indirect costs may also include extraordinary utility consumption, the cost of materials supplied from stock or services rendered by specialized facilities or other institutional service operations.

(c) The salaries of administrative and clerical staff should normally be treated as indirect (F&A) costs. Direct charging of these costs may be appropriate only if all of the following conditions are met:

(1) Administrative or clerical services are integral to a project or activity;

(2) Individuals involved can be specifically identified with the project or activity;

(3) Such costs are explicitly included in the budget or have the prior written approval of the Federal awarding agency; and

(4) The costs are not also recovered as indirect costs.

(d) *Minor items.* Any direct cost of minor amount may be treated as an indirect (F&A) cost for reasons of practicality where such accounting treatment for that item of cost is consistently applied to all Federal and non-Federal cost objectives.

(e) The costs of certain activities are not allowable as charges to Federal awards. However, even though these costs are unallowable for purposes of computing charges to Federal awards, they nonetheless must be treated as direct costs for purposes of determining indirect (F&A) cost rates and be allocated their equitable share of the non-Federal entity's indirect costs if they represent activities which:

(1) Include the salaries of personnel,

(2) Occupy space, and

(3) Benefit from the non-Federal entity's indirect (F&A) costs.

(f) For nonprofit organizations, the costs of activities performed by the non-Federal entity primarily as a service to members, clients, or the general public when significant and necessary to the non-Federal entity's mission must be treated as direct costs whether or not allowable, and be allocated an equitable share of indirect (F&A) costs. Some examples of these types of activities include:

(1) Maintenance of membership rolls, subscriptions, publications, and related functions. See also § 200.454 Memberships, subscriptions, and professional activity costs.

(2) Providing services and information to members, legislative or administrative bodies, or the public. See also §§ 200.454 Memberships, subscriptions, and professional activity costs and 200.450 Lobbying.

(3) Promotion, lobbying, and other forms of public relations. See also §§ 200.421 Advertising and public relations and 200.450 Lobbying.

(4) Conferences except those held to conduct the general administration of the non-Federal entity. See also § 200.432 Conferences.

(5) Maintenance, protection, and investment of special funds not used in operation of the non-Federal entity. See also § 200.442 Fund raising and investment management costs.

(6) Administration of group benefits on behalf of members or clients, including life and hospital insurance, annuity or retirement plans, and financial aid. See also § 200.431 Compensation—fringe benefits.

[78 FR 78608, Dec. 26, 2013, as amended at 79 FR 75885, Dec. 19, 2014]

## § 200.414 Indirect (F&A) costs.

(a) *Facilities and Administration Classification.* For major IHEs and major nonprofit organizations, indirect (F&A) costs must be classified within two broad categories: "Facilities" and "Administration." "Facilities" is defined as depreciation on buildings, equipment and capital improvement, interest on debt associated with certain buildings, equipment and capital improvements, and operations and maintenance expenses. "Administration" is defined as general administration and general expenses such as the director's office, accounting, personnel and all other types of expenditures not listed specifically under one of the subcategories of "Facilities" (including cross allocations from other pools, where applicable). For nonprofit organizations, library expenses are included in the "Administration" category; for institutions of higher education, they are included in the "Facilities" category. Major IHEs are defined as those required to use the Standard Format for Submission as noted in Appendix III to Part 200—Indirect (F&A) Costs Identification and Assignment, and Rate Determination for Institutions of Higher Education (IHEs) paragraph C. 11. Major nonprofit organizations are those which receive more than $10 million dollars in direct Federal funding.

(b) *Diversity of nonprofit organizations.* Because of the diverse characteristics and accounting practices of nonprofit organizations, it is not possible to specify the types of cost which may be classified as indirect (F&A) cost in all situations. Identification with a Federal award rather than the nature of the goods and services involved is the determining factor in distinguishing direct from indirect (F&A) costs of Federal awards. However, typical examples of indirect (F&A) cost for many nonprofit organizations may include depreciation on buildings and equipment, the costs of operating and maintaining facilities, and general administration and general expenses, such as the salaries and expenses of executive officers, personnel administration, and accounting.

(c) *Federal Agency Acceptance of Negotiated Indirect Cost Rates.* (See also § 200.306 Cost sharing or matching.)

(1) The negotiated rates must be accepted by all Federal awarding agencies. A Federal awarding agency may use a rate different from the negotiated rate for a class of Federal awards or a single Federal award only when required by Federal statute or regulation, or when approved by a Federal awarding agency head or delegate based on documented justification as described in paragraph (c)(3) of this section.

(2) The Federal awarding agency head or delegate must notify OMB of any approved deviations.

(3) The Federal awarding agency must implement, and make publicly available, the policies, procedures and general decision making criteria that their programs will follow to seek and justify deviations from negotiated rates.

(4) As required under § 200.203 Notices of funding opportunities, the Federal awarding agency must include in the notice of funding opportunity the policies relating to indirect cost rate reimbursement, matching, or cost share as approved under paragraph (e)(1) of this section. As appropriate, the Federal agency should incorporate discussion of these policies into Federal awarding agency outreach activities with non-Federal entities prior to the posting of a notice of funding opportunity.

(d) Pass-through entities are subject to the requirements in § 200.331 Re-

quirements for pass-through entities, paragraph (a)(4).

(e) Requirements for development and submission of indirect (F&A) cost rate proposals and cost allocation plans are contained in Appendices III–VII and Appendix IX as follows:

(1) Appendix III to Part 200—Indirect (F&A) Costs Identification and Assignment, and Rate Determination for Institutions of Higher Education (IHEs);

(2) Appendix IV to Part 200—Indirect (F&A) Costs Identification and Assignment, and Rate Determination for Nonprofit Organizations;

(3) Appendix V to Part 200—State/Local Governmentwide Central Service Cost Allocation Plans;

(4) Appendix VI to Part 200—Public Assistance Cost Allocation Plans;

(5) Appendix VII to Part 200—States and Local Government and Indian Tribe Indirect Cost Proposals; and

(6) Appendix IX to Part 200—Hospital Cost Principles.

(f) In addition to the procedures outlined in the appendices in paragraph (e) of this section, any non-Federal entity that has never received a negotiated indirect cost rate, except for those non-Federal entities described in Appendix VII to Part 200—States and Local Government and Indian Tribe Indirect Cost Proposals, paragraph D.1.b, may elect to charge a de minimis rate of 10% of modified total direct costs (MTDC) which may be used indefinitely. As described in § 200.403 Factors affecting allowability of costs, costs must be consistently charged as either indirect or direct costs, but may not be double charged or inconsistently charged as both. If chosen, this methodology once elected must be used consistently for all Federal awards until such time as a non-Federal entity chooses to negotiate for a rate, which the non-Federal entity may apply to do at any time.

(g) Any non-Federal entity that has a current federally negotiated indirect cost rate may apply for a one-time extension of the rates in that agreement for a period of up to four years. This extension will be subject to the review and approval of the cognizant agency for indirect costs. If an extension is granted the non-Federal entity may not request a rate review until the extension period ends. At the end of the

4-year extension, the non-Federal entity must re-apply to negotiate a rate. Subsequent one-time extensions (up to four years) are permitted if a renegotiation is completed between each extension request.

[78 FR 78608, Dec. 26, 2013, as amended at 79 FR 75886, Dec. 19, 2014]

## § 200.415 Required certifications.

Required certifications include:

(a) To assure that expenditures are proper and in accordance with the terms and conditions of the Federal award and approved project budgets, the annual and final fiscal reports or vouchers requesting payment under the agreements must include a certification, signed by an official who is authorized to legally bind the non-Federal entity, which reads as follows: "By signing this report, I certify to the best of my knowledge and belief that the report is true, complete, and accurate, and the expenditures, disbursements and cash receipts are for the purposes and objectives set forth in the terms and conditions of the Federal award. I am aware that any false, fictitious, or fraudulent information, or the omission of any material fact, may subject me to criminal, civil or administrative penalties for fraud, false statements, false claims or otherwise. (U.S. Code Title 18, Section 1001 and Title 31, Sections 3729–3730 and 3801–3812)."

(b) Certification of cost allocation plan or indirect (F&A) cost rate proposal. Each cost allocation plan or indirect (F&A) cost rate proposal must comply with the following:

(1) A proposal to establish a cost allocation plan or an indirect (F&A) cost rate, whether submitted to a Federal cognizant agency for indirect costs or maintained on file by the non-Federal entity, must be certified by the non-Federal entity using the Certificate of Cost Allocation Plan or Certificate of Indirect Costs as set forth in Appendices III through VII, and Appendix IX. The certificate must be signed on behalf of the non-Federal entity by an individual at a level no lower than vice president or chief financial officer of the non-Federal entity that submits the proposal.

(2) Unless the non-Federal entity has elected the option under § 200.414 Indi-

rect (F&A) costs, paragraph (f), the Federal Government may either disallow all indirect (F&A) costs or unilaterally establish such a plan or rate when the non-Federal entity fails to submit a certified proposal for establishing such a plan or rate in accordance with the requirements. Such a plan or rate may be based upon audited historical data or such other data that have been furnished to the cognizant agency for indirect costs and for which it can be demonstrated that all unallowable costs have been excluded. When a cost allocation plan or indirect cost rate is unilaterally established by the Federal Government because the non-Federal entity failed to submit a certified proposal, the plan or rate established will be set to ensure that potentially unallowable costs will not be reimbursed.

(c) Certifications by non-profit organizations as appropriate that they did not meet the definition of a major non-profit organization as defined in § 200.414 Indirect (F&A) costs, paragraph (a).

(d) See also § 200.450 Lobbying for another required certification.

[78 FR 78608, Dec. 26, 2013, as amended at 79 FR 75886, Dec. 19, 2014]

SPECIAL CONSIDERATIONS FOR STATES, LOCAL GOVERNMENTS AND INDIAN TRIBES

## § 200.416 Cost allocation plans and indirect cost proposals.

(a) For states, local governments and Indian tribes, certain services, such as motor pools, computer centers, purchasing, accounting, etc., are provided to operating agencies on a centralized basis. Since Federal awards are performed within the individual operating agencies, there needs to be a process whereby these central service costs can be identified and assigned to benefitted activities on a reasonable and consistent basis. The central service cost allocation plan provides that process.

(b) Individual operating agencies (governmental department or agency), normally charge Federal awards for indirect costs through an indirect cost rate. A separate indirect cost rate(s) proposal for each operating agency is usually necessary to claim indirect costs under Federal awards. Indirect costs include:

(1) The indirect costs originating in each department or agency of the governmental unit carrying out Federal awards and

(2) The costs of central governmental services distributed through the central service cost allocation plan and not otherwise treated as direct costs.

(c) The requirements for development and submission of cost allocation plans (for central service costs and public assistance programs) and indirect cost rate proposals are contained in appendices IV, V and VI to this part.

## § 200.417  Interagency service.

The cost of services provided by one agency to another within the governmental unit may include allowable direct costs of the service plus a prorated share of indirect costs. A standard indirect cost allowance equal to ten percent of the direct salary and wage cost of providing the service (excluding overtime, shift premiums, and fringe benefits) may be used in lieu of determining the actual indirect costs of the service. These services do not include centralized services included in central service cost allocation plans as described in Appendix V to Part 200—State/Local Government and Indian Tribe-Wide Central Service Cost Allocation Plans.

SPECIAL CONSIDERATIONS FOR
INSTITUTIONS OF HIGHER EDUCATION

## § 200.418  Costs incurred by states and local governments.

Costs incurred or paid by a state or local government on behalf of its IHEs for fringe benefit programs, such as pension costs and FICA and any other costs specifically incurred on behalf of, and in direct benefit to, the IHEs, are allowable costs of such IHEs whether or not these costs are recorded in the accounting records of the institutions, subject to the following:

(a) The costs meet the requirements of §§ 200.402 Composition of costs through 200.411 Adjustment of previously negotiated indirect (F&A) cost rates containing unallowable costs, of this subpart;

(b) The costs are properly supported by approved cost allocation plans in accordance with applicable Federal cost accounting principles in this part; and

(c) The costs are not otherwise borne directly or indirectly by the Federal Government.

## § 200.419  Cost accounting standards and disclosure statement.

(a) An IHE that receives aggregate Federal awards totaling $50 million or more in Federal awards subject to this part in its most recently completed fiscal year must comply with the Cost Accounting Standards Board's cost accounting standards located at 48 CFR 9905.501, 9905.502, 9905.505, and 9905.506. CAS-covered contracts awarded to the IHEs are subject to the CAS requirements at 48 CFR 9900 through 9999 and 48 CFR part 30 (FAR Part 30).

(b) *Disclosure statement.* An IHE that receives aggregate Federal awards totaling $50 million or more subject to this part during its most recently completed fiscal year must disclose their cost accounting practices by filing a Disclosure Statement (DS–2), which is reproduced in Appendix III to Part 200—Indirect (F&A) Costs Identification and Assignment, and Rate Determination for Institutions of Higher Education (IHEs). With the approval of the cognizant agency for indirect costs, an IHE may meet the DS–2 submission by submitting the DS–2 for each business unit that received $50 million or more in Federal awards.

(1) The DS–2 must be submitted to the cognizant agency for indirect costs with a copy to the IHE's cognizant agency for audit.

(2) An IHE is responsible for maintaining an accurate DS–2 and complying with disclosed cost accounting practices. An IHE must file amendments to the DS–2 to the cognizant agency for indirect costs six months in advance of a disclosed practice being changed to comply with a new or modified standard, or when a practice is changed for other reasons. An IHE may proceed with implementing the change only if it has not been notified by the Federal cognizant agency for indirect costs that either a longer period will be needed for review or there are concerns with the potential change within the

six months period. Amendments of a DS–2 may be submitted at any time. Resubmission of a complete, updated DS–2 is discouraged except when there are extensive changes to disclosed practices.

(3) *Cost and funding adjustments.* Cost adjustments must be made by the cognizant agency for indirect costs if an IHE fails to comply with the cost policies in this part or fails to consistently follow its established or disclosed cost accounting practices when estimating, accumulating or reporting the costs of Federal awards, and the aggregate cost impact on Federal awards is material. The cost adjustment must normally be made on an aggregate basis for all affected Federal awards through an adjustment of the IHE's future F&A costs rates or other means considered appropriate by the cognizant agency for indirect costs. Under the terms of CAS covered contracts, adjustments in the amount of funding provided may also be required when the estimated proposal costs were not determined in accordance with established cost accounting practices.

(4) *Overpayments.* Excess amounts paid in the aggregate by the Federal Government under Federal awards due to a noncompliant cost accounting practice used to estimate, accumulate, or report costs must be credited or refunded, as deemed appropriate by the cognizant agency for indirect costs. Interest applicable to the excess amounts paid in the aggregate during the period of noncompliance must also be determined and collected in accordance with applicable Federal agency regulations.

(5) *Compliant cost accounting practice changes.* Changes from one compliant cost accounting practice to another compliant practice that are approved by the cognizant agency for indirect costs may require cost adjustments if the change has a material effect on Federal awards and the changes are deemed appropriate by the cognizant agency for indirect costs.

(6) *Responsibilities.* The cognizant agency for indirect cost must:

(i) Determine cost adjustments for all Federal awards in the aggregate on behalf of the Federal Government. Actions of the cognizant agency for indirect cost in making cost adjustment

determinations must be coordinated with all affected Federal awarding agencies to the extent necessary.

(ii) Prescribe guidelines and establish internal procedures to promptly determine on behalf of the Federal Government that a DS–2 adequately discloses the IHE's cost accounting practices and that the disclosed practices are compliant with applicable CAS and the requirements of this part.

(iii) Distribute to all affected Federal awarding agencies any DS–2 determination of adequacy or noncompliance.

[78 FR 78608, Dec. 26, 2013, as amended at 79 FR 75886, Dec. 19, 2014]

GENERAL PROVISIONS FOR SELECTED ITEMS OF COST

### § 200.420  Considerations for selected items of cost.

This section provides principles to be applied in establishing the allowability of certain items involved in determining cost, in addition to the requirements of Subtitle II. Basic Considerations of this subpart. These principles apply whether or not a particular item of cost is properly treated as direct cost or indirect (F&A) cost. Failure to mention a particular item of cost is not intended to imply that it is either allowable or unallowable; rather, determination as to allowability in each case should be based on the treatment provided for similar or related items of cost, and based on the principles described in §§ 200.402 Composition of costs through 200.411 Adjustment of previously negotiated indirect (F&A) cost rates containing unallowable costs. In case of a discrepancy between the provisions of a specific Federal award and the provisions below, the Federal award governs. Criteria outlined in § 200.403 Factors affecting allowability of *costs* must be applied in determining allowability. See also § 200.102 Exceptions.

### § 200.421  Advertising and public relations.

(a) The term advertising costs means the costs of advertising media and corollary administrative costs. Advertising media include magazines, newspapers, radio and television, direct mail, exhibits, electronic or computer transmittals, and the like.

(b) The only allowable advertising costs are those which are solely for:

(1) The recruitment of personnel required by the non-Federal entity for performance of a Federal award (See also § 200.463 Recruiting costs);

(2) The procurement of goods and services for the performance of a Federal award;

(3) The disposal of scrap or surplus materials acquired in the performance of a Federal award except when non-Federal entities are reimbursed for disposal costs at a predetermined amount; or

(4) Program outreach and other specific purposes necessary to meet the requirements of the Federal award.

(c) The term "public relations" includes community relations and means those activities dedicated to maintaining the image of the non-Federal entity or maintaining or promoting understanding and favorable relations with the community or public at large or any segment of the public.

(d) The only allowable public relations costs are:

(1) Costs specifically required by the Federal award;

(2) Costs of communicating with the public and press pertaining to specific activities or accomplishments which result from performance of the Federal award (these costs are considered necessary as part of the outreach effort for the Federal award); or

(3) Costs of conducting general liaison with news media and government public relations officers, to the extent that such activities are limited to communication and liaison necessary to keep the public informed on matters of public concern, such as notices of funding opportunities, financial matters, etc.

(e) Unallowable advertising and public relations costs include the following:

(1) All advertising and public relations costs other than as specified in paragraphs (b) and (d) of this section;

(2) Costs of meetings, conventions, convocations, or other events related to other activities of the entity (see also § 200.432 Conferences), including:

(i) Costs of displays, demonstrations, and exhibits;

(ii) Costs of meeting rooms, hospitality suites, and other special facilities used in conjunction with shows and other special events; and

(iii) Salaries and wages of employees engaged in setting up and displaying exhibits, making demonstrations, and providing briefings;

(3) Costs of promotional items and memorabilia, including models, gifts, and souvenirs;

(4) Costs of advertising and public relations designed solely to promote the non-Federal entity.

## § 200.422   Advisory councils.

Costs incurred by advisory councils or committees are unallowable unless authorized by statute, the Federal awarding agency or as an indirect cost where allocable to Federal awards. See § 200.444 General costs of government, applicable to states, local governments and Indian tribes.

## § 200.423   Alcoholic beverages.

Costs of alcoholic beverages are unallowable.

## § 200.424   Alumni/ae activities.

Costs incurred by IHEs for, or in support of, alumni/ae activities are unallowable.

## § 200.425   Audit services.

(a) A reasonably proportionate share of the costs of audits required by, and performed in accordance with, the Single Audit Act Amendments of 1996 (31 U.S.C. 7501–7507), as implemented by requirements of this part, are allowable. However, the following audit costs are unallowable:

(1) Any costs when audits required by the Single Audit Act and Subpart F—Audit Requirements of this part have not been conducted or have been conducted but not in accordance therewith; and

(2) Any costs of auditing a non-Federal entity that is exempted from having an audit conducted under the Single Audit Act and Subpart F—Audit Requirements of this part because its expenditures under Federal awards are less than $750,000 during the non-Federal entity's fiscal year.

(b) The costs of a financial statement audit of a non-Federal entity that does not currently have a Federal award may be included in the indirect cost pool for a cost allocation plan or indirect cost proposal.

(c) Pass-through entities may charge Federal awards for the cost of agreed-upon-procedures engagements to monitor subrecipients (in accordance with Subpart D—Post Federal Award Requirements of this part, §§ 200.330 Subrecipient and contractor determinations through 200.332 Fixed Amount Subawards) who are exempted from the requirements of the Single Audit Act and Subpart F—Audit Requirements of this part. This cost is allowable only if the agreed-upon-procedures engagements are:

(1) Conducted in accordance with GAGAS attestation standards;

(2) Paid for and arranged by the pass-through entity; and

(3) Limited in scope to one or more of the following types of compliance requirements: activities allowed or unallowed; allowable costs/cost principles; eligibility; and reporting.

## § 200.426   Bad debts.

Bad debts (debts which have been determined to be uncollectable), including losses (whether actual or estimated) arising from uncollectable accounts and other claims, are unallowable. Related collection costs, and related legal costs, arising from such debts after they have been determined to be uncollectable are also unallowable. See also § 200.428 Collections of improper payments.

## § 200.427   Bonding costs.

(a) Bonding costs arise when the Federal awarding agency requires assurance against financial loss to itself or others by reason of the act or default of the non-Federal entity. They arise also in instances where the non-Federal entity requires similar assurance, including: bonds as bid, performance, payment, advance payment, infringement, and fidelity bonds for employees and officials.

(b) Costs of bonding required pursuant to the terms and conditions of the Federal award are allowable.

(c) Costs of bonding required by the non-Federal entity in the general conduct of its operations are allowable as an indirect cost to the extent that such bonding is in accordance with sound business practice and the rates and premiums are reasonable under the circumstances.

## § 200.428   Collections of improper payments.

The costs incurred by a non-Federal entity to recover improper payments are allowable as either direct or indirect costs, as appropriate. Amounts collected may be used by the non-Federal entity in accordance with cash management standards set forth in § 200.305 *Payment.*

## § 200.429   Commencement and convocation costs.

For IHEs, costs incurred for commencements and convocations are unallowable, except as provided for in Appendix III to Part 200—Indirect (F&A) Costs Identification and Assignment, and Rate Determination for Institutions of Higher Education (IHEs), paragraph (B)(9) Student Administration and Services, as student activity costs.

## § 200.430   Compensation—personal services.

(a) *General.* Compensation for personal services includes all remuneration, paid currently or accrued, for services of employees rendered during the period of performance under the Federal award, including but not necessarily limited to wages and salaries. Compensation for personal services may also include fringe benefits which are addressed in § 200.431 Compensation—fringe benefits. Costs of compensation are allowable to the extent that they satisfy the specific requirements of this part, and that the total compensation for individual employees:

(1) Is reasonable for the services rendered and conforms to the established written policy of the non-Federal entity consistently applied to both Federal and non-Federal activities;

(2) Follows an appointment made in accordance with a non-Federal entity's laws and/or rules or written policies

and meets the requirements of Federal statute, where applicable; and

(3) Is determined and supported as provided in paragraph (i) of this section, Standards for Documentation of Personnel Expenses, when applicable.

(b) *Reasonableness.* Compensation for employees engaged in work on Federal awards will be considered reasonable to the extent that it is consistent with that paid for similar work in other activities of the non-Federal entity. In cases where the kinds of employees required for Federal awards are not found in the other activities of the non-Federal entity, compensation will be considered reasonable to the extent that it is comparable to that paid for similar work in the labor market in which the non-Federal entity competes for the kind of employees involved.

(c) *Professional activities outside the non-Federal entity.* Unless an arrangement is specifically authorized by a Federal awarding agency, a non-Federal entity must follow its written non-Federal entity-wide policies and practices concerning the permissible extent of professional services that can be provided outside the non-Federal entity for non-organizational compensation. Where such non-Federal entity-wide written policies do not exist or do not adequately define the permissible extent of consulting or other non-organizational activities undertaken for extra outside pay, the Federal Government may require that the effort of professional staff working on Federal awards be allocated between:

(1) Non-Federal entity activities, and

(2) Non-organizational professional activities. If the Federal awarding agency considers the extent of non-organizational professional effort excessive or inconsistent with the conflicts-of-interest terms and conditions of the Federal award, appropriate arrangements governing compensation will be negotiated on a case-by-case basis.

(d) *Unallowable costs.* (1) Costs which are unallowable under other sections of these principles must not be allowable under this section solely on the basis that they constitute personnel compensation.

(2) The allowable compensation for certain employees is subject to a ceiling in accordance with statute. For the amount of the ceiling for cost-reimbursement contracts, the covered compensation subject to the ceiling, the covered employees, and other relevant provisions, see 10 U.S.C. 2324(e)(1)(P), and 41 U.S.C. 1127 and 4304(a)(16). For other types of Federal awards, other statutory ceilings may apply.

(e) *Special considerations.* Special considerations in determining allowability of compensation will be given to any change in a non-Federal entity's compensation policy resulting in a substantial increase in its employees' level of compensation (particularly when the change was concurrent with an increase in the ratio of Federal awards to other activities) or any change in the treatment of allowability of specific types of compensation due to changes in Federal policy.

(f) *Incentive compensation.* Incentive compensation to employees based on cost reduction, or efficient performance, suggestion awards, safety awards, etc., is allowable to the extent that the overall compensation is determined to be reasonable and such costs are paid or accrued pursuant to an agreement entered into in good faith between the non-Federal entity and the employees before the services were rendered, or pursuant to an established plan followed by the non-Federal entity so consistently as to imply, in effect, an agreement to make such payment.

(g) *Nonprofit organizations.* For compensation to members of nonprofit organizations, trustees, directors, associates, officers, or the immediate families thereof, determination must be made that such compensation is reasonable for the actual personal services rendered rather than a distribution of earnings in excess of costs. This may include director's and executive committee member's fees, incentive awards, allowances for off-site pay, incentive pay, location allowances, hardship pay, and cost-of-living differentials.

(h) *Institutions of higher education (IHEs).* (1) Certain conditions require special consideration and possible limitations in determining allowable personnel compensation costs under Federal awards. Among such conditions are the following:

(i) Allowable activities. Charges to Federal awards may include reasonable amounts for activities contributing and directly related to work under an agreement, such as delivering special lectures about specific aspects of the ongoing activity, writing reports and articles, developing and maintaining protocols (human, animals, etc.), managing substances/chemicals, managing and securing project-specific data, coordinating research subjects, participating in appropriate seminars, consulting with colleagues and graduate students, and attending meetings and conferences.

(ii) Incidental activities. Incidental activities for which supplemental compensation is allowable under written institutional policy (at a rate not to exceed institutional base salary) need not be included in the records described in paragraph (i) of this section to directly charge payments of incidental activities, such activities must either be specifically provided for in the Federal award budget or receive prior written approval by the Federal awarding agency.

(2) *Salary basis.* Charges for work performed on Federal awards by faculty members during the academic year are allowable at the IBS rate. Except as noted in paragraph (h)(1)(ii) of this section, in no event will charges to Federal awards, irrespective of the basis of computation, exceed the proportionate share of the IBS for that period. This principle applies to all members of faculty at an institution. IBS is defined as the annual compensation paid by an IHE for an individual's appointment, whether that individual's time is spent on research, instruction, administration, or other activities. IBS excludes any income that an individual earns outside of duties performed for the IHE. Unless there is prior approval by the Federal awarding agency, charges of a faculty member's salary to a Federal award must not exceed the proportionate share of the IBS for the period during which the faculty member worked on the award.

(3) *Intra-Institution of Higher Education (IHE) consulting.* Intra-IHE consulting by faculty is assumed to be undertaken as an IHE obligation requiring no compensation in addition to IBS. However, in unusual cases where consultation is across departmental lines or involves a separate or remote operation, and the work performed by the faculty member is in addition to his or her regular responsibilities, any charges for such work representing additional compensation above IBS are allowable provided that such consulting arrangements are specifically provided for in the Federal award or approved in writing by the Federal awarding agency.

(4) Extra Service Pay normally represents overload compensation, subject to institutional compensation policies for services above and beyond IBS. Where extra service pay is a result of Intra-IHE consulting, it is subject to the same requirements of paragraph (b) above. It is allowable if all of the following conditions are met:

(i) The non-Federal entity establishes consistent written policies which apply uniformly to all faculty members, not just those working on Federal awards.

(ii) The non-Federal entity establishes a consistent written definition of work covered by IBS which is specific enough to determine conclusively when work beyond that level has occurred. This may be described in appointment letters or other documentations.

(iii) The supplementation amount paid is commensurate with the IBS rate of pay and the amount of additional work performed. See paragraph (h)(2) of this section.

(iv) The salaries, as supplemented, fall within the salary structure and pay ranges established by and documented in writing or otherwise applicable to the non-Federal entity.

(v) The total salaries charged to Federal awards including extra service pay are subject to the Standards of Documentation as described in paragraph (i) of this section.

(5) *Periods outside the academic year.* (i) Except as specified for teaching activity in paragraph (h)(5)(ii) of this section, charges for work performed by faculty members on Federal awards during periods not included in the base salary period will be at a rate not in excess of the IBS.

(ii) Charges for teaching activities performed by faculty members on Federal awards during periods not included in IBS period will be based on the normal written policy of the IHE governing compensation to faculty members for teaching assignments during such periods.

(6) *Part-time faculty.* Charges for work performed on Federal awards by faculty members having only part-time appointments will be determined at a rate not in excess of that regularly paid for part-time assignments.

(7) *Sabbatical leave costs.* Rules for sabbatical leave are as follow:

(i) Costs of leaves of absence by employees for performance of graduate work or sabbatical study, travel, or research are allowable provided the IHE has a uniform written policy on sabbatical leave for persons engaged in instruction and persons engaged in research. Such costs will be allocated on an equitable basis among all related activities of the IHE.

(ii) Where sabbatical leave is included in fringe benefits for which a cost is determined for assessment as a direct charge, the aggregate amount of such assessments applicable to all work of the institution during the base period must be reasonable in relation to the IHE's actual experience under its sabbatical leave policy.

(8) *Salary rates for non-faculty members.* Non-faculty full-time professional personnel may also earn "extra service pay" in accordance with the non-Federal entity's written policy and consistent with paragraph (h)(1)(i) of this section.

(i) *Standards for Documentation of Personnel Expenses* (1) Charges to Federal awards for salaries and wages must be based on records that accurately reflect the work performed. These records must:

(i) Be supported by a system of internal control which provides reasonable assurance that the charges are accurate, allowable, and properly allocated;

(ii) Be incorporated into the official records of the non-Federal entity;

(iii) Reasonably reflect the total activity for which the employee is compensated by the non-Federal entity, not exceeding 100% of compensated activities (for IHE, this per the IHE's definition of IBS);

(iv) Encompass both federally assisted and all other activities compensated by the non-Federal entity on an integrated basis, but may include the use of subsidiary records as defined in the non-Federal entity's written policy;

(v) Comply with the established accounting policies and practices of the non-Federal entity (See paragraph (h)(1)(ii) above for treatment of incidental work for IHEs.); and

(vi) [Reserved]

(vii) Support the distribution of the employee's salary or wages among specific activities or cost objectives if the employee works on more than one Federal award; a Federal award and non-Federal award; an indirect cost activity and a direct cost activity; two or more indirect activities which are allocated using different allocation bases; or an unallowable activity and a direct or indirect cost activity.

(viii) Budget estimates (i.e., estimates determined before the services are performed) alone do not qualify as support for charges to Federal awards, but may be used for interim accounting purposes, provided that:

(A) The system for establishing the estimates produces reasonable approximations of the activity actually performed;

(B) Significant changes in the corresponding work activity (as defined by the non-Federal entity's written policies) are identified and entered into the records in a timely manner. Short term (such as one or two months) fluctuation between workload categories need not be considered as long as the distribution of salaries and wages is reasonable over the longer term; and

(C) The non-Federal entity's system of internal controls includes processes to review after-the-fact interim charges made to a Federal awards based on budget estimates. All necessary adjustment must be made such that the final amount charged to the Federal award is accurate, allowable, and properly allocated.

(ix) Because practices vary as to the activity constituting a full workload (for IHEs, IBS), records may reflect categories of activities expressed as a percentage distribution of total activities.

(x) It is recognized that teaching, research, service, and administration are often inextricably intermingled in an academic setting. When recording salaries and wages charged to Federal awards for IHEs, a precise assessment of factors that contribute to costs is therefore not always feasible, nor is it expected.

(2) For records which meet the standards required in paragraph (i)(1) of this section, the non-Federal entity will not be required to provide additional support or documentation for the work performed, other than that referenced in paragraph (i)(3) of this section.

(3) In accordance with Department of Labor regulations implementing the Fair Labor Standards Act (FLSA) (29 CFR part 516), charges for the salaries and wages of nonexempt employees, in addition to the supporting documentation described in this section, must also be supported by records indicating the total number of hours worked each day.

(4) Salaries and wages of employees used in meeting cost sharing or matching requirements on Federal awards must be supported in the same manner as salaries and wages claimed for reimbursement from Federal awards.

(5) For states, local governments and Indian tribes, substitute processes or systems for allocating salaries and wages to Federal awards may be used in place of or in addition to the records described in paragraph (1) if approved by the cognizant agency for indirect cost. Such systems may include, but are not limited to, random moment sampling, "rolling" time studies, case counts, or other quantifiable measures of work performed.

(i) Substitute systems which use sampling methods (primarily for Temporary Assistance for Needy Families (TANF), the Supplemental Nutrition Assistance Program (SNAP), Medicaid, and other public assistance programs) must meet acceptable statistical sampling standards including:

(A) The sampling universe must include all of the employees whose salaries and wages are to be allocated based on sample results except as pro-

vided in paragraph (i)(5)(iii) of this section;

(B) The entire time period involved must be covered by the sample; and

(C) The results must be statistically valid and applied to the period being sampled.

(ii) Allocating charges for the sampled employees' supervisors, clerical and support staffs, based on the results of the sampled employees, will be acceptable.

(iii) Less than full compliance with the statistical sampling standards noted in subsection (5)(i) may be accepted by the cognizant agency for indirect costs if it concludes that the amounts to be allocated to Federal awards will be minimal, or if it concludes that the system proposed by the non-Federal entity will result in lower costs to Federal awards than a system which complies with the standards.

(6) Cognizant agencies for indirect costs are encouraged to approve alternative proposals based on outcomes and milestones for program performance where these are clearly documented. Where approved by the Federal cognizant agency for indirect costs, these plans are acceptable as an alternative to the requirements of paragraph (i)(1) of this section.

(7) For Federal awards of similar purpose activity or instances of approved blended funding, a non-Federal entity may submit performance plans that incorporate funds from multiple Federal awards and account for their combined use based on performance-oriented metrics, provided that such plans are approved in advance by all involved Federal awarding agencies. In these instances, the non-Federal entity must submit a request for waiver of the requirements based on documentation that describes the method of charging costs, relates the charging of costs to the specific activity that is applicable to all fund sources, and is based on quantifiable measures of the activity in relation to time charged.

(8) For a non-Federal entity where the records do not meet the standards described in this section, the Federal

Government may require personnel activity reports, including prescribed certifications, or equivalent documentation that support the records as required in this section.

[78 FR 78608, Dec. 26, 2013, as amended at 79 FR 75886, Dec. 19, 2014]

§ 200.431   Compensation—fringe benefits.

(a) Fringe benefits are allowances and services provided by employers to their employees as compensation in addition to regular salaries and wages. Fringe benefits include, but are not limited to, the costs of leave (vacation, family-related, sick or military), employee insurance, pensions, and unemployment benefit plans. Except as provided elsewhere in these principles, the costs of fringe benefits are allowable provided that the benefits are reasonable and are required by law, non-Federal entity-employee agreement, or an established policy of the non-Federal entity.

(b) *Leave.* The cost of fringe benefits in the form of regular compensation paid to employees during periods of authorized absences from the job, such as for annual leave, family-related leave, sick leave, holidays, court leave, military leave, administrative leave, and other similar benefits, are allowable if all of the following criteria are met:

(1) They are provided under established written leave policies;

(2) The costs are equitably allocated to all related activities, including Federal awards; and,

(3) The accounting basis (cash or accrual) selected for costing each type of leave is consistently followed by the non-Federal entity or specified grouping of employees.

(i) When a non-Federal entity uses the cash basis of accounting, the cost of leave is recognized in the period that the leave is taken and paid for. Payments for unused leave when an employee retires or terminates employment are allowable in the year of payment.

(ii) The accrual basis may be only used for those types of leave for which a liability as defined by GAAP exists when the leave is earned. When a non-Federal entity uses the accrual basis of accounting, allowable leave costs are the lesser of the amount accrued or funded.

(c) The cost of fringe benefits in the form of employer contributions or expenses for social security; employee life, health, unemployment, and worker's compensation insurance (except as indicated in § 200.447 Insurance and indemnification); pension plan costs (see paragraph (i) of this section); and other similar benefits are allowable, provided such benefits are granted under established written policies. Such benefits, must be allocated to Federal awards and all other activities in a manner consistent with the pattern of benefits attributable to the individuals or group(s) of employees whose salaries and wages are chargeable to such Federal awards and other activities, and charged as direct or indirect costs in accordance with the non-Federal entity's accounting practices.

(d) Fringe benefits may be assigned to cost objectives by identifying specific benefits to specific individual employees or by allocating on the basis of entity-wide salaries and wages of the employees receiving the benefits. When the allocation method is used, separate allocations must be made to selective groupings of employees, unless the non-Federal entity demonstrates that costs in relationship to salaries and wages do not differ significantly for different groups of employees.

(e) *Insurance.* See also § 200.447 Insurance and indemnification, paragraphs (d)(1) and (2).

(1) Provisions for a reserve under a self-insurance program for unemployment compensation or workers' compensation are allowable to the extent that the provisions represent reasonable estimates of the liabilities for such compensation, and the types of coverage, extent of coverage, and rates and premiums would have been allowable had insurance been purchased to cover the risks. However, provisions for self-insured liabilities which do not become payable for more than one year after the provision is made must not exceed the present value of the liability.

(2) Costs of insurance on the lives of trustees, officers, or other employees holding positions of similar responsibility are allowable only to the extent

that the insurance represents additional compensation. The costs of such insurance when the non-Federal entity is named as beneficiary are unallowable.

(3) Actual claims paid to or on behalf of employees or former employees for workers' compensation, unemployment compensation, severance pay, and similar employee benefits (e.g., post-retirement health benefits), are allowable in the year of payment provided that the non-Federal entity follows a consistent costing policy.

(f) *Automobiles*. That portion of automobile costs furnished by the entity that relates to personal use by employees (including transportation to and from work) is unallowable as fringe benefit or indirect (F&A) costs regardless of whether the cost is reported as taxable income to the employees.

(g) *Pension Plan Costs*. Pension plan costs which are incurred in accordance with the established policies of the non-Federal entity are allowable, provided that:

(1) Such policies meet the test of reasonableness.

(2) The methods of cost allocation are not discriminatory.

(3) For entities using accrual based accounting, the cost assigned to each fiscal year is determined in accordance with GAAP.

(4) The costs assigned to a given fiscal year are funded for all plan participants within six months after the end of that year. However, increases to normal and past service pension costs caused by a delay in funding the actuarial liability beyond 30 calendar days after each quarter of the year to which such costs are assignable are unallowable. Non-Federal entity may elect to follow the "Cost Accounting Standard for Composition and Measurement of Pension Costs" (48 CFR 9904.412).

(5) Pension plan termination insurance premiums paid pursuant to the Employee Retirement Income Security Act (ERISA) of 1974 (29 U.S.C. 1301–1461) are allowable. Late payment charges on such premiums are unallowable. Excise taxes on accumulated funding deficiencies and other penalties imposed under ERISA are unallowable.

(6) Pension plan costs may be computed using a pay-as-you-go method or an acceptable actuarial cost method in accordance with established written policies of the non-Federal entity.

(i) For pension plans financed on a pay-as-you-go method, allowable costs will be limited to those representing actual payments to retirees or their beneficiaries.

(ii) Pension costs calculated using an actuarial cost-based method recognized by GAAP are allowable for a given fiscal year if they are funded for that year within six months after the end of that year. Costs funded after the six month period (or a later period agreed to by the cognizant agency for indirect costs) are allowable in the year funded. The cognizant agency for indirect costs may agree to an extension of the six month period if an appropriate adjustment is made to compensate for the timing of the charges to the Federal Government and related Federal reimbursement and the non-Federal entity's contribution to the pension fund. Adjustments may be made by cash refund or other equitable procedures to compensate the Federal Government for the time value of Federal reimbursements in excess of contributions to the pension fund.

(iii) Amounts funded by the non-Federal entity in excess of the actuarially determined amount for a fiscal year may be used as the non-Federal entity's contribution in future periods.

(iv) When a non-Federal entity converts to an acceptable actuarial cost method, as defined by GAAP, and funds pension costs in accordance with this method, the unfunded liability at the time of conversion is allowable if amortized over a period of years in accordance with GAAP.

(v) The Federal Government must receive an equitable share of any previously allowed pension costs (including earnings thereon) which revert or inure to the non-Federal entity in the form of a refund, withdrawal, or other credit.

(h) *Post-Retirement Health*. Post-retirement health plans (PRHP) refers to costs of health insurance or health services not included in a pension plan covered by paragraph (g) of this section for retirees and their spouses, dependents, and survivors. PRHP costs may be computed using a pay-as-you-go method or an acceptable actuarial cost method in accordance with established written policies of the non-Federal entity.

(1) For PRHP financed on a pay-as-you-go method, allowable costs will be limited to those representing actual payments to retirees or their beneficiaries.

(2) PRHP costs calculated using an actuarial cost method recognized by GAAP are allowable if they are funded for that year within six months after the end of that year. Costs funded after the six month period (or a later period agreed to by the cognizant agency) are allowable in the year funded. The Federal cognizant agency for indirect costs may agree to an extension of the six month period if an appropriate adjustment is made to compensate for the timing of the charges to the Federal Government and related Federal reimbursements and the non-Federal entity's contributions to the PRHP fund. Adjustments may be made by cash refund, reduction in current year's PRHP costs, or other equitable procedures to compensate the Federal Government for the time value of Federal reimbursements in excess of contributions to the PRHP fund.

(3) Amounts funded in excess of the actuarially determined amount for a fiscal year may be used as the non-Federal entity contribution in a future period.

(4) When a non-Federal entity converts to an acceptable actuarial cost method and funds PRHP costs in accordance with this method, the initial unfunded liability attributable to prior years is allowable if amortized over a period of years in accordance with GAAP, or, if no such GAAP period exists, over a period negotiated with the cognizant agency for indirect costs.

(5) To be allowable in the current year, the PRHP costs must be paid either to:

(i) An insurer or other benefit provider as current year costs or premiums, or

(ii) An insurer or trustee to maintain a trust fund or reserve for the sole purpose of providing post-retirement benefits to retirees and other beneficiaries.

(6) The Federal Government must receive an equitable share of any amounts of previously allowed post-retirement benefit costs (including earnings thereon) which revert or inure to the non-Federal entity in the form of a refund, withdrawal, or other credit.

(i) *Severance Pay.* (1) Severance pay, also commonly referred to as dismissal wages, is a payment in addition to regular salaries and wages, by non-Federal entities to workers whose employment is being terminated. Costs of severance pay are allowable only to the extent that in each case, it is required by (a) law, (b) employer-employee agreement, (c) established policy that constitutes, in effect, an implied agreement on the non-Federal entity's part, or (d) circumstances of the particular employment.

(2) Costs of severance payments are divided into two categories as follows:

(i) Actual normal turnover severance payments must be allocated to all activities; or, where the non-Federal entity provides for a reserve for normal severances, such method will be acceptable if the charge to current operations is reasonable in light of payments actually made for normal severances over a representative past period, and if amounts charged are allocated to all activities of the non-Federal entity.

(ii) Measurement of costs of abnormal or mass severance pay by means of an accrual will not achieve equity to both parties. Thus, accruals for this purpose are not allowable. However, the Federal Government recognizes its obligation to participate, to the extent of its fair share, in any specific payment. Prior approval by the Federal awarding agency or cognizant agency for indirect cost, as appropriate, is required.

(3) Costs incurred in certain severance pay packages which are in an amount in excess of the normal severance pay paid by the non-Federal entity to an employee upon termination of employment and are paid to the employee contingent upon a change in management control over, or ownership of, the non-Federal entity's assets, are unallowable.

(4) Severance payments to foreign nationals employed by the non-Federal entity outside the United States, to the extent that the amount exceeds the

customary or prevailing practices for the non-Federal entity in the United States, are unallowable, unless they are necessary for the performance of Federal programs and approved by the Federal awarding agency.

(5) Severance payments to foreign nationals employed by the non-Federal entity outside the United States due to the termination of the foreign national as a result of the closing of, or curtailment of activities by, the non-Federal entity in that country, are unallowable, unless they are necessary for the performance of Federal programs and approved by the Federal awarding agency.

(j)(1) *For IHEs only.* Fringe benefits in the form of undergraduate and graduate tuition or remission of tuition for individual employees are allowable, provided such benefits are granted in accordance with established non-Federal entity policies, and are distributed to all non-Federal entity activities on an equitable basis. Tuition benefits for family members other than the employee are unallowable.

(2) Fringe benefits in the form of tuition or remission of tuition for individual employees not employed by IHEs are limited to the tax-free amount allowed per section 127 of the Internal Revenue Code as amended.

(3) IHEs may offer employees tuition waivers or tuition reductions, provided that the benefit does not discriminate in favor of highly compensated employees. Employees can exercise these benefits at other institutions according to institutional policy. See § 200.466 Scholarships and student aid costs, for treatment of tuition remission provided to students.

(k) For IHEs whose costs are paid by state or local governments, fringe benefit programs (such as pension costs and FICA) and any other benefits costs specifically incurred on behalf of, and in direct benefit to, the non-Federal entity, are allowable costs of such non-Federal entities whether or not these costs are recorded in the accounting records of the non-Federal entities, subject to the following:

(1) The costs meet the requirements of Basic Considerations in §§ 200.402 Composition of costs through 200.411 Adjustment of previously negotiated

indirect (F&A) cost rates containing unallowable costs of this subpart;

(2) The costs are properly supported by approved cost allocation plans in accordance with applicable Federal cost accounting principles; and

(3) The costs are not otherwise borne directly or indirectly by the Federal Government.

[78 FR 78608, Dec. 26, 2013, as amended at 79 FR 75886, Dec. 19, 2014; 80 FR 54409, Sept. 10, 2015]

## § 200.432 Conferences.

A conference is defined as a meeting, retreat, seminar, symposium, workshop or event whose primary purpose is the dissemination of technical information beyond the non-Federal entity and is necessary and reasonable for successful performance under the Federal award. Allowable conference costs paid by the non-Federal entity as a sponsor or host of the conference may include rental of facilities, speakers' fees, costs of meals and refreshments, local transportation, and other items incidental to such conferences unless further restricted by the terms and conditions of the Federal award. As needed, the costs of identifying, but not providing, locally available dependent-care resources are allowable. Conference hosts/sponsors must exercise discretion and judgment in ensuring that conference costs are appropriate, necessary and managed in a manner that minimizes costs to the Federal award. The Federal awarding agency may authorize exceptions where appropriate for programs including Indian tribes, children, and the elderly. See also §§ 200.438 Entertainment costs, 200.456 Participant support costs, 200.474 Travel costs, and 200.475 Trustees.

## § 200.433 Contingency provisions.

(a) Contingency is that part of a budget estimate of future costs (typically of large construction projects, IT systems, or other items as approved by the Federal awarding agency) which is associated with possible events or conditions arising from causes the precise outcome of which is indeterminable at the time of estimate, and that experience shows will likely result, in aggregate, in additional costs for the approved activity or project. Amounts for major project scope changes, unforeseen risks, or extraordinary events may not be included.

(b) It is permissible for contingency amounts other than those excluded in paragraph (a) of this section to be explicitly included in budget estimates, to the extent they are necessary to improve the precision of those estimates. Amounts must be estimated using broadly-accepted cost estimating methodologies, specified in the budget documentation of the Federal award, and accepted by the Federal awarding agency. As such, contingency amounts are to be included in the Federal award. In order for actual costs incurred to be allowable, they must comply with the cost principles and other requirements in this part (see also §§ 200.300 Statutory and national policy requirements through 200.309 Period of performance of Subpart D of this part and 200.403 Factors affecting allowability of costs); be necessary and reasonable for proper and efficient accomplishment of project or program objectives, and be verifiable from the non-Federal entity's records.

(c) Payments made by the Federal awarding agency to the non-Federal entity's "contingency reserve" or any similar payment made for events the occurrence of which cannot be foretold with certainty as to the time or intensity, or with an assurance of their happening, are unallowable, except as noted in §§ 200.431 Compensation—fringe benefits regarding self-insurance, pensions, severance and post-retirement health costs and 200.447 Insurance and indemnification.

[78 FR 78608, Dec. 26, 2013, as amended at 79 FR 75886, Dec. 19, 2014]

### § 200.434  Contributions and donations.

(a) Costs of contributions and donations, including cash, property, and services, from the non-Federal entity to other entities, are unallowable.

(b) The value of services and property donated to the non-Federal entity may not be charged to the Federal award either as a direct or indirect (F&A) cost. The value of donated services and property may be used to meet cost sharing or matching requirements (see § 200.306 Cost sharing or matching). Depreciation on donated assets is permitted in accordance with § 200.436 Depreciation, as long as the donated property is not counted towards cost sharing or matching requirements.

(c) Services donated or volunteered to the non-Federal entity may be furnished to a non-Federal entity by professional and technical personnel, consultants, and other skilled and unskilled labor. The value of these services may not be charged to the Federal award either as a direct or indirect cost. However, the value of donated services may be used to meet cost sharing or matching requirements in accordance with the provisions of § 200.306 Cost sharing or matching.

(d) To the extent feasible, services donated to the non-Federal entity will be supported by the same methods used to support the allocability of regular personnel services.

(e) The following provisions apply to nonprofit organizations. The value of services donated to the nonprofit organization utilized in the performance of a direct cost activity must be considered in the determination of the non-Federal entity's indirect cost rate(s) and, accordingly, must be allocated a proportionate share of applicable indirect costs when the following circumstances exist:

(1) The aggregate value of the services is material;

(2) The services are supported by a significant amount of the indirect costs incurred by the non-Federal entity;

(i) In those instances where there is no basis for determining the fair market value of the services rendered, the non-Federal entity and the cognizant agency for indirect costs must negotiate an appropriate allocation of indirect cost to the services.

(ii) Where donated services directly benefit a project supported by the Federal award, the indirect costs allocated to the services will be considered as a part of the total costs of the project. Such indirect costs may be reimbursed under the Federal award or used to meet cost sharing or matching requirements.

(f) Fair market value of donated services must be computed as described in §200.306 Cost sharing or matching.

(g) Personal Property and Use of Space.

(1) Donated personal property and use of space may be furnished to a non-Federal entity. The value of the personal property and space may not be charged to the Federal award either as a direct or indirect cost.

(2) The value of the donations may be used to meet cost sharing or matching share requirements under the conditions described in §§200.300 Statutory and national policy requirements through 200.309 Period of performance of subpart D of this part. The value of the donations must be determined in accordance with §§200.300 Statutory and national policy requirements through 200.309 Period of performance. Where donations are treated as indirect costs, indirect cost rates will separate the value of the donations so that reimbursement will not be made.

[78 FR 78608, Dec. 26, 2013, as amended at 79 FR 75886, Dec. 19, 2014]

### §200.435 Defense and prosecution of criminal and civil proceedings, claims, appeals and patent infringements.

(a) *Definitions for the purposes of this section.* (1) *Conviction* means a judgment or conviction of a criminal offense by any court of competent jurisdiction, whether entered upon verdict or a plea, including a conviction due to a plea of nolo contendere.

(2) *Costs* include the services of in-house or private counsel, accountants, consultants, or others engaged to assist the non-Federal entity before, during, and after commencement of a judicial or administrative proceeding, that bear a direct relationship to the proceeding.

(3) *Fraud* means:

(i) Acts of fraud or corruption or attempts to defraud the Federal Government or to corrupt its agents,

(ii) Acts that constitute a cause for debarment or suspension (as specified in agency regulations), and

(iii) Acts which violate the False Claims Act (31 U.S.C. 3729–3732) or the Anti-kickback Act (41 U.S.C. 1320a–7b(b)).

(4) *Penalty* does not include restitution, reimbursement, or compensatory damages.

(5) *Proceeding* includes an investigation.

(b) *Costs.* (1) Except as otherwise described herein, costs incurred in connection with any criminal, civil or administrative proceeding (including filing of a false certification) commenced by the Federal Government, a state, local government, or foreign government, or joined by the Federal Government (including a proceeding under the False Claims Act), against the non-Federal entity, (or commenced by third parties or a current or former employee of the non-Federal entity who submits a whistleblower complaint of reprisal in accordance with 10 U.S.C. 2409 or 41 U.S.C. 4712), are not allowable if the proceeding:

(i) Relates to a violation of, or failure to comply with, a Federal, state, local or foreign statute, regulation or the terms and conditions of the Federal award, by the non-Federal entity (including its agents and employees); and

(ii) Results in any of the following dispositions:

(A) In a criminal proceeding, a conviction.

(B) In a civil or administrative proceeding involving an allegation of fraud or similar misconduct, a determination of non-Federal entity liability.

(C) In the case of any civil or administrative proceeding, the disallowance of costs or the imposition of a monetary penalty, or an order issued by the Federal awarding agency head or delegate to the non-Federal entity to take corrective action under 10 U.S.C. 2409 or 41 U.S.C. 4712.

(D) A final decision by an appropriate Federal official to debar or suspend the non-Federal entity, to rescind or void a Federal award, or to terminate a Federal award by reason of a violation or failure to comply with a statute, regulation, or the terms and conditions of the Federal award.

(E) A disposition by consent or compromise, if the action could have resulted in any of the dispositions described in paragraphs (b)(1)(ii)(A) through (D) of this section.

(2) If more than one proceeding involves the same alleged misconduct, the costs of all such proceedings are unallowable if any results in one of the dispositions shown in paragraph (b) of this section.

(c) If a proceeding referred to in paragraph (b) of this section is commenced by the Federal Government and is resolved by consent or compromise pursuant to an agreement by the non-Federal entity and the Federal Government, then the costs incurred may be allowed to the extent specifically provided in such agreement.

(d) If a proceeding referred to in paragraph (b) of this section is commenced by a state, local or foreign government, the authorized Federal official may allow the costs incurred if such authorized official determines that the costs were incurred as a result of:

(1) A specific term or condition of the Federal award, or

(2) Specific written direction of an authorized official of the Federal awarding agency.

(e) Costs incurred in connection with proceedings described in paragraph (b) of this section, which are not made unallowable by that subsection, may be allowed but only to the extent that:

(1) The costs are reasonable and necessary in relation to the administration of the Federal award and activities required to deal with the proceeding and the underlying cause of action;

(2) Payment of the reasonable, necessary, allocable and otherwise allowable costs incurred is not prohibited by any other provision(s) of the Federal award;

(3) The costs are not recovered from the Federal Government or a third party, either directly as a result of the proceeding or otherwise; and,

(4) An authorized Federal official must determine the percentage of costs allowed considering the complexity of litigation, generally accepted principles governing the award of legal fees in civil actions involving the United States, and such other factors as may be appropriate. Such percentage must not exceed 80 percent. However, if an agreement reached under paragraph (c) of this section has explicitly considered this 80 percent limitation and per-mitted a higher percentage, then the full amount of costs resulting from that agreement are allowable.

(f) Costs incurred by the non-Federal entity in connection with the defense of suits brought by its employees or ex-employees under section 2 of the Major Fraud Act of 1988 (18 U.S.C. 1031), including the cost of all relief necessary to make such employee whole, where the non-Federal entity was found liable or settled, are unallowable.

(g) Costs of prosecution of claims against the Federal Government, including appeals of final Federal agency decisions, are unallowable.

(h) Costs of legal, accounting, and consultant services, and related costs, incurred in connection with patent infringement litigation, are unallowable unless otherwise provided for in the Federal award.

(i) Costs which may be unallowable under this section, including directly associated costs, must be segregated and accounted for separately. During the pendency of any proceeding covered by paragraphs (b) and (f) of this section, the Federal Government must generally withhold payment of such costs. However, if in its best interests, the Federal Government may provide for conditional payment upon provision of adequate security, or other adequate assurance, and agreement to repay all unallowable costs, plus interest, if the costs are subsequently determined to be unallowable.

[78 FR 78608, Dec. 26, 2013, as amended at 79 FR 75886, Dec. 19, 2014]

## § 200.436 Depreciation.

(a) Depreciation is the method for allocating the cost of fixed assets to periods benefitting from asset use. The non-Federal entity may be compensated for the use of its buildings, capital improvements, equipment, and software projects capitalized in accordance with GAAP, provided that they are used, needed in the non-Federal entity's activities, and properly allocated to Federal awards. Such compensation must be made by computing depreciation.

(b) The allocation for depreciation must be made in accordance with Appendices III through IX.

(c) Depreciation is computed applying the following rules. The computation of depreciation must be based on the acquisition cost of the assets involved. For an asset donated to the non-Federal entity by a third party, its fair market value at the time of the donation must be considered as the acquisition cost. Such assets may be depreciated or claimed as matching but not both. For the purpose of computing depreciation, the acquisition cost will exclude:

(1) The cost of land;

(2) Any portion of the cost of buildings and equipment borne by or donated by the Federal Government, irrespective of where title was originally vested or where it is presently located;

(3) Any portion of the cost of buildings and equipment contributed by or for the non-Federal entity where law or agreement prohibits recovery; and

(4) Any asset acquired solely for the performance of a non-Federal award.

(d) When computing depreciation charges, the following must be observed:

(1) The period of useful service or useful life established in each case for usable capital assets must take into consideration such factors as type of construction, nature of the equipment, technological developments in the particular area, historical data, and the renewal and replacement policies followed for the individual items or classes of assets involved.

(2) The depreciation method used to charge the cost of an asset (or group of assets) to accounting periods must reflect the pattern of consumption of the asset during its useful life. In the absence of clear evidence indicating that the expected consumption of the asset will be significantly greater in the early portions than in the later portions of its useful life, the straight-line method must be presumed to be the appropriate method. Depreciation methods once used may not be changed unless approved in advance by the cognizant agency. The depreciation methods used to calculate the depreciation amounts for indirect (F&A) rate purposes must be the same methods used by the non-Federal entity for its financial statements.

(3) The entire building, including the shell and all components, may be treated as a single asset and depreciated over a single useful life. A building may also be divided into multiple components. Each component item may then be depreciated over its estimated useful life. The building components must be grouped into three general components of a building: building shell (including construction and design costs), building services systems (e.g., elevators, HVAC, plumbing system and heating and air-conditioning system) and fixed equipment (e.g., sterilizers, casework, fume hoods, cold rooms and glassware/washers). In exceptional cases, a cognizant agency may authorize a non-Federal entity to use more than these three groupings. When a non-Federal entity elects to depreciate its buildings by its components, the same depreciation methods must be used for indirect (F&A) purposes and financial statements purposes, as described in paragraphs (d)(1) and (2) of this section.

(4) No depreciation may be allowed on any assets that have outlived their depreciable lives.

(5) Where the depreciation method is introduced to replace the use allowance method, depreciation must be computed as if the asset had been depreciated over its entire life (i.e., from the date the asset was acquired and ready for use to the date of disposal or withdrawal from service). The total amount of use allowance and depreciation for an asset (including imputed depreciation applicable to periods prior to the conversion from the use allowance method as well as depreciation after the conversion) may not exceed the total acquisition cost of the asset.

(e) Charges for depreciation must be supported by adequate property records, and physical inventories must be taken at least once every two years to ensure that the assets exist and are usable, used, and needed. Statistical sampling techniques may be used in taking these inventories. In addition, adequate depreciation records showing the amount of depreciation taken each period must also be maintained.

[78 FR 78608, Dec. 26, 2013, as amended at 79 FR 75886, Dec. 19, 2014]

## § 200.437 Employee health and welfare costs.

(a) Costs incurred in accordance with the non-Federal entity's documented policies for the improvement of working conditions, employer-employee relations, employee health, and employee performance are allowable.

(b) Such costs will be equitably apportioned to all activities of the non-Federal entity. Income generated from any of these activities will be credited to the cost thereof unless such income has been irrevocably sent to employee welfare organizations.

(c) Losses resulting from operating food services are allowable only if the non-Federal entity's objective is to operate such services on a break-even basis. Losses sustained because of operating objectives other than the above are allowable only:

(1) Where the non-Federal entity can demonstrate unusual circumstances; and

(2) With the approval of the cognizant agency for indirect costs.

## § 200.438 Entertainment costs.

Costs of entertainment, including amusement, diversion, and social activities and any associated costs are unallowable, except where specific costs that might otherwise be considered entertainment have a programmatic purpose and are authorized either in the approved budget for the Federal award or with prior written approval of the Federal awarding agency.

## § 200.439 Equipment and other capital expenditures.

(a) See §§ 200.13 Capital expenditures, 200.33 Equipment, 200.89 Special purpose equipment, 200.48 General purpose equipment, 200.2 Acquisition cost, and 200.12 Capital assets.

(b) The following rules of allowability must apply to equipment and other capital expenditures:

(1) Capital expenditures for general purpose equipment, buildings, and land are unallowable as direct charges, except with the prior written approval of the Federal awarding agency or pass-through entity.

(2) Capital expenditures for special purpose equipment are allowable as direct costs, provided that items with a unit cost of $5,000 or more have the prior written approval of the Federal awarding agency or pass-through entity.

(3) Capital expenditures for improvements to land, buildings, or equipment which materially increase their value or useful life are unallowable as a direct cost except with the prior written approval of the Federal awarding agency, or pass-through entity. See § 200.436 Depreciation, for rules on the allowability of depreciation on buildings, capital improvements, and equipment. See also § 200.465 Rental costs of real property and equipment.

(4) When approved as a direct charge pursuant to paragraphs (b)(1) through (3) of this section, capital expenditures will be charged in the period in which the expenditure is incurred, or as otherwise determined appropriate and negotiated with the Federal awarding agency.

(5) The unamortized portion of any equipment written off as a result of a change in capitalization levels may be recovered by continuing to claim the otherwise allowable depreciation on the equipment, or by amortizing the amount to be written off over a period of years negotiated with the Federal cognizant agency for indirect cost.

(6) Cost of equipment disposal. If the non-Federal entity is instructed by the Federal awarding agency to otherwise dispose of or transfer the equipment the costs of such disposal or transfer are allowable.

(7) Equipment and other capital expenditures are unallowable as indirect costs. See § 200.436 Depreciation.

[78 FR 78608, Dec. 26, 2013, as amended at 79 FR 75886, Dec. 19, 2014]

## § 200.440 Exchange rates.

(a) Cost increases for fluctuations in exchange rates are allowable costs subject to the availability of funding. Prior approval of exchange rate fluctuations is required only when the change results in the need for additional Federal funding, or the increased costs result in the need to significantly reduce the scope of the project. The Federal awarding agency must however ensure that adequate funds are available to cover currency fluctuations in order to avoid a violation of the Anti-Deficiency Act.

(b) The non-Federal entity is required to make reviews of local currency gains to determine the need for additional federal funding before the expiration date of the Federal award. Subsequent adjustments for currency increases may be allowable only when the non-Federal entity provides the Federal awarding agency with adequate source documentation from a commonly used source in effect at the time the expense was made, and to the extent that sufficient Federal funds are available.

[78 FR 78608, Dec. 26, 2013, as amended at 79 FR 75886, Dec. 19, 2014]

### § 200.441 Fines, penalties, damages and other settlements.

Costs resulting from non-Federal entity violations of, alleged violations of, or failure to comply with, Federal, state, tribal, local or foreign laws and regulations are unallowable, except when incurred as a result of compliance with specific provisions of the Federal award, or with prior written approval of the Federal awarding agency. See also § 200.435 Defense and prosecution of criminal and civil proceedings, claims, appeals and patent infringements.

### § 200.442 Fund raising and investment management costs.

(a) Costs of organized fund raising, including financial campaigns, endowment drives, solicitation of gifts and bequests, and similar expenses incurred to raise capital or obtain contributions are unallowable. Fund raising costs for the purposes of meeting the Federal program objectives are allowable with prior written approval from the Federal awarding agency. Proposal costs are covered in § 200.460 Proposal costs.

(b) Costs of investment counsel and staff and similar expenses incurred to enhance income from investments are unallowable except when associated with investments covering pension, self-insurance, or other funds which include Federal participation allowed by this part.

(c) Costs related to the physical custody and control of monies and securities are allowable.

(d) Both allowable and unallowable fund raising and investment activities must be allocated as an appropriate share of indirect costs under the conditions described in § 200.413 Direct costs.

### § 200.443 Gains and losses on disposition of depreciable assets.

(a) Gains and losses on the sale, retirement, or other disposition of depreciable property must be included in the year in which they occur as credits or charges to the asset cost grouping(s) in which the property was included. The amount of the gain or loss to be included as a credit or charge to the appropriate asset cost grouping(s) is the difference between the amount realized on the property and the undepreciated basis of the property.

(b) Gains and losses from the disposition of depreciable property must not be recognized as a separate credit or charge under the following conditions:

(1) The gain or loss is processed through a depreciation account and is reflected in the depreciation allowable under §§ 200.436 Depreciation and 200.439 Equipment and other capital expenditures.

(2) The property is given in exchange as part of the purchase price of a similar item and the gain or loss is taken into account in determining the depreciation cost basis of the new item.

(3) A loss results from the failure to maintain permissible insurance, except as otherwise provided in § 200.447 Insurance and indemnification.

(4) Compensation for the use of the property was provided through use allowances in lieu of depreciation.

(5) Gains and losses arising from mass or extraordinary sales, retirements, or other dispositions must be considered on a case-by-case basis.

(c) Gains or losses of any nature arising from the sale or exchange of property other than the property covered in paragraph (a) of this section, e.g., land, must be excluded in computing Federal award costs.

(d) When assets acquired with Federal funds, in part or wholly, are disposed of, the distribution of the proceeds must be made in accordance with

§§ 200.310 Insurance Coverage through 200.316 Property trust relationship.

[78 FR 78608, Dec. 26, 2013, as amended at 79 FR 75886, Dec. 19, 2014]

§ 200.444  General costs of government.

(a) For states, local governments, and Indian Tribes, the general costs of government are unallowable (except as provided in § 200.474 Travel costs). Unallowable costs include:

(1) Salaries and expenses of the Office of the Governor of a state or the chief executive of a local government or the chief executive of an Indian tribe;

(2) Salaries and other expenses of a state legislature, tribal council, or similar local governmental body, such as a county supervisor, city council, school board, etc., whether incurred for purposes of legislation or executive direction;

(3) Costs of the judicial branch of a government;

(4) Costs of prosecutorial activities unless treated as a direct cost to a specific program if authorized by statute or regulation (however, this does not preclude the allowability of other legal activities of the Attorney General as described in § 200.435 Defense and prosecution of criminal and civil proceedings, claims, appeals and patent infringements); and

(5) Costs of other general types of government services normally provided to the general public, such as fire and police, unless provided for as a direct cost under a program statute or regulation.

(b) For Indian tribes and Councils of Governments (COGs) (see § 200.64 Local government), up to 50% of salaries and expenses directly attributable to managing and operating Federal programs by the chief executive and his or her staff can be included in the indirect cost calculation without documentation.

[78 FR 78608, Dec. 26, 2013, as amended at 79 FR 75886, Dec. 19, 2014]

§ 200.445  Goods or services for personal use.

(a) Costs of goods or services for personal use of the non-Federal entity's employees are unallowable regardless of whether the cost is reported as taxable income to the employees.

(b) Costs of housing (e.g., depreciation, maintenance, utilities, furnishings, rent), housing allowances and personal living expenses are only allowable as direct costs regardless of whether reported as taxable income to the employees. In addition, to be allowable direct costs must be approved in advance by a Federal awarding agency.

§ 200.446  Idle facilities and idle capacity.

(a) As used in this section the following terms have the meanings set forth in this section:

(1) Facilities means land and buildings or any portion thereof, equipment individually or collectively, or any other tangible capital asset, wherever located, and whether owned or leased by the non-Federal entity.

(2) Idle facilities means completely unused facilities that are excess to the non-Federal entity's current needs.

(3) Idle capacity means the unused capacity of partially used facilities. It is the difference between:

(i) That which a facility could achieve under 100 percent operating time on a one-shift basis less operating interruptions resulting from time lost for repairs, setups, unsatisfactory materials, and other normal delays and;

(ii) The extent to which the facility was actually used to meet demands during the accounting period. A multi-shift basis should be used if it can be shown that this amount of usage would normally be expected for the type of facility involved.

(4) Cost of idle facilities or idle capacity means costs such as maintenance, repair, housing, rent, and other related costs, e.g., insurance, interest, and depreciation. These costs could include the costs of idle public safety emergency facilities, telecommunications, or information technology system capacity that is built to withstand major fluctuations in load, e.g., consolidated data centers.

(b) The costs of idle facilities are unallowable except to the extent that:

(1) They are necessary to meet workload requirements which may fluctuate and are allocated appropriately to all benefiting programs; or

(2) Although not necessary to meet fluctuations in workload, they were necessary when acquired and are now idle because of changes in program requirements, efforts to achieve more economical operations, reorganization, termination, or other causes which could not have been reasonably foreseen. Under the exception stated in this subsection, costs of idle facilities are allowable for a reasonable period of time, ordinarily not to exceed one year, depending on the initiative taken to use, lease, or dispose of such facilities.

(c) The costs of idle capacity are normal costs of doing business and are a factor in the normal fluctuations of usage or indirect cost rates from period to period. Such costs are allowable, provided that the capacity is reasonably anticipated to be necessary to carry out the purpose of the Federal award or was originally reasonable and is not subject to reduction or elimination by use on other Federal awards, subletting, renting, or sale, in accordance with sound business, economic, or security practices. Widespread idle capacity throughout an entire facility or among a group of assets having substantially the same function may be considered idle facilities.

### §200.447 Insurance and indemnification.

(a) Costs of insurance required or approved and maintained, pursuant to the Federal award, are allowable.

(b) Costs of other insurance in connection with the general conduct of activities are allowable subject to the following limitations:

(1) Types and extent and cost of coverage are in accordance with the non-Federal entity's policy and sound business practice.

(2) Costs of insurance or of contributions to any reserve covering the risk of loss of, or damage to, Federal Government property are unallowable except to the extent that the Federal awarding agency has specifically required or approved such costs.

(3) Costs allowed for business interruption or other similar insurance must exclude coverage of management fees.

(4) Costs of insurance on the lives of trustees, officers, or other employees holding positions of similar responsibilities are allowable only to the extent that the insurance represents additional compensation (see §200.431 Compensation—fringe benefits). The cost of such insurance when the non-Federal entity is identified as the beneficiary is unallowable.

(5) Insurance against defects. Costs of insurance with respect to any costs incurred to correct defects in the non-Federal entity's materials or workmanship are unallowable.

(6) Medical liability (malpractice) insurance. Medical liability insurance is an allowable cost of Federal research programs only to the extent that the Federal research programs involve human subjects or training of participants in research techniques. Medical liability insurance costs must be treated as a direct cost and must be assigned to individual projects based on the manner in which the insurer allocates the risk to the population covered by the insurance.

(c) Actual losses which could have been covered by permissible insurance (through a self-insurance program or otherwise) are unallowable, unless expressly provided for in the Federal award. However, costs incurred because of losses not covered under nominal deductible insurance coverage provided in keeping with sound management practice, and minor losses not covered by insurance, such as spoilage, breakage, and disappearance of small hand tools, which occur in the ordinary course of operations, are allowable.

(d) Contributions to a reserve for certain self-insurance programs including workers' compensation, unemployment compensation, and severance pay are allowable subject to the following provisions:

(1) The type of coverage and the extent of coverage and the rates and premiums would have been allowed had insurance (including reinsurance) been purchased to cover the risks. However, provision for known or reasonably estimated self-insured liabilities, which do not become payable for more than one year after the provision is made, must not exceed the discounted present value of the liability. The rate used for

discounting the liability must be determined by giving consideration to such factors as the non-Federal entity's settlement rate for those liabilities and its investment rate of return.

(2) Earnings or investment income on reserves must be credited to those reserves.

(3)(i) Contributions to reserves must be based on sound actuarial principles using historical experience and reasonable assumptions. Reserve levels must be analyzed and updated at least biennially for each major risk being insured and take into account any reinsurance, coinsurance, etc. Reserve levels related to employee-related coverages will normally be limited to the value of claims:

(A) Submitted and adjudicated but not paid;

(B) Submitted but not adjudicated; and

(C) Incurred but not submitted.

(ii) Reserve levels in excess of the amounts based on the above must be identified and justified in the cost allocation plan or indirect cost rate proposal.

(4) Accounting records, actuarial studies, and cost allocations (or billings) must recognize any significant differences due to types of insured risk and losses generated by the various insured activities or agencies of the non-Federal entity. If individual departments or agencies of the non-Federal entity experience significantly different levels of claims for a particular risk, those differences are to be recognized by the use of separate allocations or other techniques resulting in an equitable allocation.

(5) Whenever funds are transferred from a self-insurance reserve to other accounts (e.g., general fund or unrestricted account), refunds must be made to the Federal Government for its share of funds transferred, including earned or imputed interest from the date of transfer and debt interest, if applicable, chargeable in accordance with applicable Federal cognizant agency for indirect cost, claims collection regulations.

(e) Insurance refunds must be credited against insurance costs in the year the refund is received.

(f) Indemnification includes securing the non-Federal entity against liabilities to third persons and other losses not compensated by insurance or otherwise. The Federal Government is obligated to indemnify the non-Federal entity only to the extent expressly provided for in the Federal award, except as provided in paragraph (c) of this section.

§ 200.448   Intellectual property.

(a) *Patent costs.* (1) The following costs related to securing patents and copyrights are allowable:

(i) Costs of preparing disclosures, reports, and other documents required by the Federal award, and of searching the art to the extent necessary to make such disclosures;

(ii) Costs of preparing documents and any other patent costs in connection with the filing and prosecution of a United States patent application where title or royalty-free license is required by the Federal Government to be conveyed to the Federal Government; and

(iii) General counseling services relating to patent and copyright matters, such as advice on patent and copyright laws, regulations, clauses, and employee intellectual property agreements (See also § 200.459 Professional service costs).

(2) The following costs related to securing patents and copyrights are unallowable:

(i) Costs of preparing disclosures, reports, and other documents, and of searching the art to make disclosures not required by the Federal award;

(ii) Costs in connection with filing and prosecuting any foreign patent application, or any United States patent application, where the Federal award does not require conveying title or a royalty-free license to the Federal Government.

(b) *Royalties and other costs for use of patents and copyrights.* (1) Royalties on a patent or copyright or amortization of the cost of acquiring by purchase a copyright, patent, or rights thereto, necessary for the proper performance of the Federal award are allowable unless:

(i) The Federal Government already has a license or the right to free use of the patent or copyright.

(ii) The patent or copyright has been adjudicated to be invalid, or has been administratively determined to be invalid.

(iii) The patent or copyright is considered to be unenforceable.

(iv) The patent or copyright is expired.

(2) Special care should be exercised in determining reasonableness where the royalties may have been arrived at as a result of less-than-arm's-length bargaining, such as:

(i) Royalties paid to persons, including corporations, affiliated with the non-Federal entity.

(ii) Royalties paid to unaffiliated parties, including corporations, under an agreement entered into in contemplation that a Federal award would be made.

(iii) Royalties paid under an agreement entered into after a Federal award is made to a non-Federal entity.

(3) In any case involving a patent or copyright formerly owned by the non-Federal entity, the amount of royalty allowed must not exceed the cost which would have been allowed had the non-Federal entity retained title thereto.

[78 FR 78608, Dec. 26, 2013, as amended at 79 FR 75886, Dec. 19, 2014]

### § 200.449 Interest.

(a) *General.* Costs incurred for interest on borrowed capital, temporary use of endowment funds, or the use of the non-Federal entity's own funds, however represented, are unallowable. Financing costs (including interest) to acquire, construct, or replace capital assets are allowable, subject to the conditions in this section.

(b)(1) Capital assets is defined as noted in §200.12 Capital assets. An asset cost includes (as applicable) acquisition costs, construction costs, and other costs capitalized in accordance with GAAP.

(2) For non-Federal entity fiscal years beginning on or after January 1, 2016, intangible assets include patents and computer software. For software development projects, only interest attributable to the portion of the project costs capitalized in accordance with GAAP is allowable.

(c) *Conditions for all non-Federal entities.* (1) The non-Federal entity uses the capital assets in support of Federal awards;

(2) The allowable asset costs to acquire facilities and equipment are limited to a fair market value available to the non-Federal entity from an unrelated (arm's length) third party.

(3) The non-Federal entity obtains the financing via an arm's-length transaction (that is, a transaction with an unrelated third party); or claims reimbursement of actual interest cost at a rate available via such a transaction.

(4) The non-Federal entity limits claims for Federal reimbursement of interest costs to the least expensive alternative. For example, a capital lease may be determined less costly than purchasing through debt financing, in which case reimbursement must be limited to the amount of interest determined if leasing had been used.

(5) The non-Federal entity expenses or capitalizes allowable interest cost in accordance with GAAP.

(6) Earnings generated by the investment of borrowed funds pending their disbursement for the asset costs are used to offset the current period's allowable interest cost, whether that cost is expensed or capitalized. Earnings subject to being reported to the Federal Internal Revenue Service under arbitrage requirements are excludable.

(7) The following conditions must apply to debt arrangements over $1 million to purchase or construct facilities, unless the non-Federal entity makes an initial equity contribution to the purchase of 25 percent or more. For this purpose, "initial equity contribution" means the amount or value of contributions made by the non-Federal entity for the acquisition of facilities prior to occupancy.

(i) The non-Federal entity must reduce claims for reimbursement of interest cost by an amount equal to imputed interest earnings on excess cash flow attributable to the portion of the facility used for Federal awards.

(ii) The non-Federal entity must impute interest on excess cash flow as follows:

(A) Annually, the non-Federal entity must prepare a cumulative (from the inception of the project) report of

165

monthly cash inflows and outflows, regardless of the funding source. For this purpose, inflows consist of Federal reimbursement for depreciation, amortization of capitalized construction interest, and annual interest cost. Outflows consist of initial equity contributions, debt principal payments (less the pro-rata share attributable to the cost of land), and interest payments.

(B) To compute monthly cash inflows and outflows, the non-Federal entity must divide the annual amounts determined in step (i) by the number of months in the year (usually 12) that the building is in service.

(C) For any month in which cumulative cash inflows exceed cumulative outflows, interest must be calculated on the excess inflows for that month and be treated as a reduction to allowable interest cost. The rate of interest to be used must be the three-month Treasury bill closing rate as of the last business day of that month.

(8) Interest attributable to a fully depreciated asset is unallowable.

(d) Additional conditions for states, local governments and Indian tribes. For costs to be allowable, the non-Federal entity must have incurred the interest costs for buildings after October 1, 1980, or for land and equipment after September 1, 1995.

(1) The requirement to offset interest earned on borrowed funds against current allowable interest cost (paragraph (c)(5), above) also applies to earnings on debt service reserve funds.

(2) The non-Federal entity will negotiate the amount of allowable interest cost related to the acquisition of facilities with asset costs of $1 million or more, as outlined in paragraph (c)(7) of this section. For this purpose, a non-Federal entity must consider only cash inflows and outflows attributable to that portion of the real property used for Federal awards.

(e) Additional conditions for IHEs. For costs to be allowable, the IHE must have incurred the interest costs after July 1, 1982, in connection with acquisitions of capital assets that occurred after that date.

(f) Additional condition for nonprofit organizations. For costs to be allowable, the nonprofit organization incurred the interest costs after September 29, 1995, in connection with acquisitions of capital assets that occurred after that date.

(g) The interest allowability provisions of this section do not apply to a nonprofit organization subject to "full coverage" under the Cost Accounting Standards (CAS), as defined at 48 CFR 9903.201–2(a). The non-Federal entity's Federal awards are instead subject to CAS 414 (48 CFR 9904.414), "Cost of Money as an Element of the Cost of Facilities Capital", and CAS 417 (48 CFR 9904.417), "Cost of Money as an Element of the Cost of Capital Assets Under Construction".

[78 FR 78608, Dec. 26, 2013, as amended at 80 FR 54409, Sept. 10, 2015]

§ 200.450   Lobbying.

(a) The cost of certain influencing activities associated with obtaining grants, contracts, cooperative agreements, or loans is an unallowable cost. Lobbying with respect to certain grants, contracts, cooperative agreements, and loans is governed by relevant statutes, including among others, the provisions of 31 U.S.C. 1352, as well as the common rule, "New Restrictions on Lobbying" published at 55 FR 6736 (February 26, 1990), including definitions, and the Office of Management and Budget "Governmentwide Guidance for New Restrictions on Lobbying" and notices published at 54 FR 52306 (December 20, 1989), 55 FR 24540 (June 15, 1990), 57 FR 1772 (January 15, 1992), and 61 FR 1412 (January 19, 1996).

(b) Executive lobbying costs. Costs incurred in attempting to improperly influence either directly or indirectly, an employee or officer of the executive branch of the Federal Government to give consideration or to act regarding a Federal award or a regulatory matter are unallowable. Improper influence means any influence that induces or tends to induce a Federal employee or officer to give consideration or to act regarding a Federal award or regulatory matter on any basis other than the merits of the matter.

(c) In addition to the above, the following restrictions are applicable to nonprofit organizations and IHEs:

(1) Costs associated with the following activities are unallowable:

(i) Attempts to influence the outcomes of any Federal, state, or local election, referendum, initiative, or similar procedure, through in-kind or cash contributions, endorsements, publicity, or similar activity;

(ii) Establishing, administering, contributing to, or paying the expenses of a political party, campaign, political action committee, or other organization established for the purpose of influencing the outcomes of elections in the United States;

(iii) Any attempt to influence:

(A)The introduction of Federal or state legislation;

(B) The enactment or modification of any pending Federal or state legislation through communication with any member or employee of the Congress or state legislature (including efforts to influence state or local officials to engage in similar lobbying activity);

(C) The enactment or modification of any pending Federal or state legislation by preparing, distributing, or using publicity or propaganda, or by urging members of the general public, or any segment thereof, to contribute to or participate in any mass demonstration, march, rally, fund raising drive, lobbying campaign or letter writing or telephone campaign; or

(D) Any government official or employee in connection with a decision to sign or veto enrolled legislation;

(iv) Legislative liaison activities, including attendance at legislative sessions or committee hearings, gathering information regarding legislation, and analyzing the effect of legislation, when such activities are carried on in support of or in knowing preparation for an effort to engage in unallowable lobbying.

(2) The following activities are excepted from the coverage of paragraph (c)(1) of this section:

(i) Technical and factual presentations on topics directly related to the performance of a grant, contract, or other agreement (through hearing testimony, statements, or letters to the Congress or a state legislature, or subdivision, member, or cognizant staff member thereof), in response to a documented request (including a Congressional Record notice requesting testimony or statements for the record at a regularly scheduled hearing) made by the non-Federal entity's member of congress, legislative body or a subdivision, or a cognizant staff member thereof, provided such information is readily obtainable and can be readily put in deliverable form, and further provided that costs under this section for travel, lodging or meals are unallowable unless incurred to offer testimony at a regularly scheduled Congressional hearing pursuant to a written request for such presentation made by the Chairman or Ranking Minority Member of the Committee or Subcommittee conducting such hearings;

(ii) Any lobbying made unallowable by paragraph (c)(1)(iii) of this section to influence state legislation in order to directly reduce the cost, or to avoid material impairment of the non-Federal entity's authority to perform the grant, contract, or other agreement; or

(iii) Any activity specifically authorized by statute to be undertaken with funds from the Federal award.

(iv) Any activity excepted from the definitions of "lobbying" or "influencing legislation" by the Internal Revenue Code provisions that require nonprofit organizations to limit their participation in direct and "grass roots" lobbying activities in order to retain their charitable deduction status and avoid punitive excise taxes, I.R.C. §§501(c)(3), 501(h), 4911(a), including:

(A) Nonpartisan analysis, study, or research reports;

(B) Examinations and discussions of broad social, economic, and similar problems; and

(C) Information provided upon request by a legislator for technical advice and assistance, as defined by I.R.C. §4911(d)(2) and 26 CFR 56.4911–2(c)(1)–(c)(3).

(v) When a non-Federal entity seeks reimbursement for indirect (F&A) costs, total lobbying costs must be separately identified in the indirect (F&A) cost rate proposal, and thereafter treated as other unallowable activity costs in accordance with the procedures of §200.413 Direct costs.

(vi) The non-Federal entity must submit as part of its annual indirect (F&A) cost rate proposal a certification that the requirements and standards of this section have been complied with. (See also § 200.415 Required certifications.)

(vii)(A) Time logs, calendars, or similar records are not required to be created for purposes of complying with the record keeping requirements in § 200.302 Financial management with respect to lobbying costs during any particular calendar month when:

(1) The employee engages in lobbying (as defined in paragraphs (c)(1) and (c)(2) of this section) 25 percent or less of the employee's compensated hours of employment during that calendar month; and

(2) Within the preceding five-year period, the non-Federal entity has not materially misstated allowable or unallowable costs of any nature, including legislative lobbying costs.

(B) When conditions in paragraph (c)(2)(vii)(A)(1) and (2) of this section are met, non-Federal entities are not required to establish records to support the allowability of claimed costs in addition to records already required or maintained. Also, when conditions in paragraphs (c)(2)(vii)(A)(1) and (2) of this section are met, the absence of time logs, calendars, or similar records will not serve as a basis for disallowing costs by contesting estimates of lobbying time spent by employees during a calendar month.

(viii) The Federal awarding agency must establish procedures for resolving in advance, in consultation with OMB, any significant questions or disagreements concerning the interpretation or application of this section. Any such advance resolutions must be binding in any subsequent settlements, audits, or investigations with respect to that grant or contract for purposes of interpretation of this part, provided, however, that this must not be construed to prevent a contractor or non-Federal entity from contesting the lawfulness of such a determination.

### § 200.451 Losses on other awards or contracts.

Any excess of costs over income under any other award or contract of any nature is unallowable. This includes, but is not limited to, the non-Federal entity's contributed portion by reason of cost-sharing agreements or

any under-recoveries through negotiation of flat amounts for indirect (F&A) costs. Also, any excess of costs over authorized funding levels transferred from any award or contract to another award or contract is unallowable. All losses are not allowable indirect (F&A) costs and are required to be included in the appropriate indirect cost rate base for allocation of indirect costs.

### § 200.452 Maintenance and repair costs.

Costs incurred for utilities, insurance, security, necessary maintenance, janitorial services, repair, or upkeep of buildings and equipment (including Federal property unless otherwise provided for) which neither add to the permanent value of the property nor appreciably prolong its intended life, but keep it in an efficient operating condition, are allowable. Costs incurred for improvements which add to the permanent value of the buildings and equipment or appreciably prolong their intended life must be treated as capital expenditures (see § 200.439 Equipment and other capital expenditures). These costs are only allowable to the extent not paid through rental or other agreements.

### § 200.453 Materials and supplies costs, including costs of computing devices.

(a) Costs incurred for materials, supplies, and fabricated parts necessary to carry out a Federal award are allowable.

(b) Purchased materials and supplies must be charged at their actual prices, net of applicable credits. Withdrawals from general stores or stockrooms must be charged at their actual net cost under any recognized method of pricing inventory withdrawals, consistently applied. Incoming transportation charges are a proper part of materials and supplies costs.

(c) Materials and supplies used for the performance of a Federal award may be charged as direct costs. In the specific case of computing devices, charging as direct costs is allowable for devices that are essential and allocable, but not solely dedicated, to the performance of a Federal award.

(d) Where federally-donated or furnished materials are used in performing the Federal award, such materials will be used without charge.

[78 FR 78608, Dec. 26, 2013, as amended at 79 FR 75887, Dec. 19, 2014]

### § 200.454  Memberships, subscriptions, and professional activity costs.

(a) Costs of the non-Federal entity's membership in business, technical, and professional organizations are allowable.

(b) Costs of the non-Federal entity's subscriptions to business, professional, and technical periodicals are allowable.

(c) Costs of membership in any civic or community organization are allowable with prior approval by the Federal awarding agency or pass-through entity.

(d) Costs of membership in any country club or social or dining club or organization are unallowable.

(e) Costs of membership in organizations whose primary purpose is lobbying are unallowable. See also § 200.450 Lobbying.

### § 200.455  Organization costs.

Costs such as incorporation fees, brokers' fees, fees to promoters, organizers or management consultants, attorneys, accountants, or investment counselor, whether or not employees of the non-Federal entity in connection with establishment or reorganization of an organization, are unallowable except with prior approval of the Federal awarding agency.

### § 200.456  Participant support costs.

Participant support costs as defined in § 200.75 Participant support costs are allowable with the prior approval of the Federal awarding agency.

### § 200.457  Plant and security costs.

Necessary and reasonable expenses incurred for protection and security of facilities, personnel, and work products are allowable. Such costs include, but are not limited to, wages and uniforms of personnel engaged in security activities; equipment; barriers; protective (non-military) gear, devices, and equipment; contractual security services; and consultants. Capital expenditures for plant security purposes are subject to § 200.439 Equipment and other capital expenditures.

[78 FR 78608, Dec. 26, 2013, as amended at 79 FR 75887, Dec. 19, 2014]

### § 200.458  Pre-award costs.

Pre-award costs are those incurred prior to the effective date of the Federal award directly pursuant to the negotiation and in anticipation of the Federal award where such costs are necessary for efficient and timely performance of the scope of work. Such costs are allowable only to the extent that they would have been allowable if incurred after the date of the Federal award and only with the written approval of the Federal awarding agency.

### § 200.459  Professional service costs.

(a) Costs of professional and consultant services rendered by persons who are members of a particular profession or possess a special skill, and who are not officers or employees of the non-Federal entity, are allowable, subject to paragraphs (b) and (c) when reasonable in relation to the services rendered and when not contingent upon recovery of the costs from the Federal Government. In addition, legal and related services are limited under § 200.435 Defense and prosecution of criminal and civil proceedings, claims, appeals and patent infringements.

(b) In determining the allowability of costs in a particular case, no single factor or any special combination of factors is necessarily determinative. However, the following factors are relevant:

(1) The nature and scope of the service rendered in relation to the service required.

(2) The necessity of contracting for the service, considering the non-Federal entity's capability in the particular area.

(3) The past pattern of such costs, particularly in the years prior to Federal awards.

(4) The impact of Federal awards on the non-Federal entity's business (i.e., what new problems have arisen).

(5) Whether the proportion of Federal work to the non-Federal entity's total business is such as to influence the non-Federal entity in favor of incurring the cost, particularly where the

services rendered are not of a continuing nature and have little relationship to work under Federal awards.

(6) Whether the service can be performed more economically by direct employment rather than contracting.

(7) The qualifications of the individual or concern rendering the service and the customary fees charged, especially on non-federally funded activities.

(8) Adequacy of the contractual agreement for the service (e.g., description of the service, estimate of time required, rate of compensation, and termination provisions).

(c) In addition to the factors in paragraph (b) of this section, to be allowable, retainer fees must be supported by evidence of bona fide services available or rendered.

§ 200.460  Proposal costs.

Proposal costs are the costs of preparing bids, proposals, or applications on potential Federal and non-Federal awards or projects, including the development of data necessary to support the non-Federal entity's bids or proposals. Proposal costs of the current accounting period of both successful and unsuccessful bids and proposals normally should be treated as indirect (F&A) costs and allocated currently to all activities of the non-Federal entity. No proposal costs of past accounting periods will be allocable to the current period.

§ 200.461  Publication and printing costs.

(a) Publication costs for electronic and print media, including distribution, promotion, and general handling are allowable. If these costs are not identifiable with a particular cost objective, they should be allocated as indirect costs to all benefiting activities of the non-Federal entity.

(b) Page charges for professional journal publications are allowable where:

(1) The publications report work supported by the Federal Government; and

(2) The charges are levied impartially on all items published by the journal, whether or not under a Federal award.

(3) The non-Federal entity may charge the Federal award before close-

out for the costs of publication or sharing of research results if the costs are not incurred during the period of performance of the Federal award.

§ 200.462  Rearrangement and reconversion costs.

(a) Costs incurred for ordinary and normal rearrangement and alteration of facilities are allowable as indirect costs. Special arrangements and alterations costs incurred specifically for a Federal award are allowable as a direct cost with the prior approval of the Federal awarding agency or pass-through entity.

(b) Costs incurred in the restoration or rehabilitation of the non-Federal entity's facilities to approximately the same condition existing immediately prior to commencement of Federal awards, less costs related to normal wear and tear, are allowable.

§ 200.463  Recruiting costs.

(a) Subject to paragraphs (b) and (c) of this section, and provided that the size of the staff recruited and maintained is in keeping with workload requirements, costs of "help wanted" advertising, operating costs of an employment office necessary to secure and maintain an adequate staff, costs of operating an aptitude and educational testing program, travel costs of employees while engaged in recruiting personnel, travel costs of applicants for interviews for prospective employment, and relocation costs incurred incident to recruitment of new employees, are allowable to the extent that such costs are incurred pursuant to the non-Federal entity's standard recruitment program. Where the non-Federal entity uses employment agencies, costs not in excess of standard commercial rates for such services are allowable.

(b) Special emoluments, fringe benefits, and salary allowances incurred to attract professional personnel that do not meet the test of reasonableness or do not conform with the established practices of the non-Federal entity, are unallowable.

(c) Where relocation costs incurred incident to recruitment of a new employee have been funded in whole or in part to a Federal award, and the newly hired employee resigns for reasons within the employee's control within 12 months after hire, the non-Federal entity will be required to refund or credit the Federal share of such relocation costs to the Federal Government. See also § 200.464 Relocation costs of employees.

(d) Short-term, travel visa costs (as opposed to longer-term, immigration visas) are generally allowable expenses that may be proposed as a direct cost. Since short-term visas are issued for a specific period and purpose, they can be clearly identified as directly connected to work performed on a Federal award. For these costs to be directly charged to a Federal award, they must:

(1) Be critical and necessary for the conduct of the project;

(2) Be allowable under the applicable cost principles;

(3) Be consistent with the non-Federal entity's cost accounting practices and non-Federal entity policy; and

(4) Meet the definition of "direct cost" as described in the applicable cost principles.

[78 FR 78608, Dec. 26, 2013, as amended at 79 FR 75887, Dec. 19, 2014]

### § 200.464  Relocation costs of employees.

(a) Relocation costs are costs incident to the permanent change of duty assignment (for an indefinite period or for a stated period of not less than 12 months) of an existing employee or upon recruitment of a new employee. Relocation costs are allowable, subject to the limitations described in paragraphs (b), (c), and (d) of this section, provided that:

(1) The move is for the benefit of the employer.

(2) Reimbursement to the employee is in accordance with an established written policy consistently followed by the employer.

(3) The reimbursement does not exceed the employee's actual (or reasonably estimated) expenses.

(b) Allowable relocation costs for current employees are limited to the following:

(1) The costs of transportation of the employee, members of his or her immediate family and his household, and personal effects to the new location.

(2) The costs of finding a new home, such as advance trips by employees and spouses to locate living quarters and temporary lodging during the transition period, up to maximum period of 30 calendar days.

(3) Closing costs, such as brokerage, legal, and appraisal fees, incident to the disposition of the employee's former home. These costs, together with those described in (4), are limited to 8 per cent of the sales price of the employee's former home.

(4) The continuing costs of ownership (for up to six months) of the vacant former home after the settlement or lease date of the employee's new permanent home, such as maintenance of buildings and grounds (exclusive of fixing-up expenses), utilities, taxes, and property insurance.

(5) Other necessary and reasonable expenses normally incident to relocation, such as the costs of canceling an unexpired lease, transportation of personal property, and purchasing insurance against loss of or damages to personal property. The cost of canceling an unexpired lease is limited to three times the monthly rental.

(c) Allowable relocation costs for new employees are limited to those described in paragraphs (b)(1) and (2) of this section. When relocation costs incurred incident to the recruitment of new employees have been charged to a Federal award and the employee resigns for reasons within the employee's control within 12 months after hire, the non-Federal entity must refund or credit the Federal Government for its share of the cost. However, the costs of travel to an overseas location must be considered travel costs in accordance with § 200.474 Travel costs, and not this § 200.464 Relocation costs of employees, for the purpose of this paragraph if dependents are not permitted at the location for any reason and the costs do not include costs of transporting household goods.

(d) The following costs related to relocation are unallowable:

(1) Fees and other costs associated with acquiring a new home.

(2) A loss on the sale of a former home.

(3) Continuing mortgage principal and interest payments on a home being sold.

(4) Income taxes paid by an employee related to reimbursed relocation costs.

[78 FR 78608, Dec. 26, 2013, as amended at 79 FR 75887, Dec. 19, 2014]

### § 200.465 Rental costs of real property and equipment.

(a) Subject to the limitations described in paragraphs (b) through (d) of this section, rental costs are allowable to the extent that the rates are reasonable in light of such factors as: rental costs of comparable property, if any; market conditions in the area; alternatives available; and the type, life expectancy, condition, and value of the property leased. Rental arrangements should be reviewed periodically to determine if circumstances have changed and other options are available.

(b) Rental costs under "sale and lease back" arrangements are allowable only up to the amount that would be allowed had the non-Federal entity continued to own the property. This amount would include expenses such as depreciation, maintenance, taxes, and insurance.

(c) Rental costs under "less-than-arm's-length" leases are allowable only up to the amount (as explained in paragraph (b) of this section). For this purpose, a less-than-arm's-length lease is one under which one party to the lease agreement is able to control or substantially influence the actions of the other. Such leases include, but are not limited to those between:

(1) Divisions of the non-Federal entity;

(2) The non-Federal entity under common control through common officers, directors, or members; and

(3) The non-Federal entity and a director, trustee, officer, or key employee of the non-Federal entity or an immediate family member, either directly or through corporations, trusts, or similar arrangements in which they hold a controlling interest. For example, the non-Federal entity may establish a separate corporation for the sole purpose of owning property and leasing it back to the non-Federal entity.

(4) Family members include one party with any of the following relationships to another party:

(i) Spouse, and parents thereof;

(ii) Children, and spouses thereof;

(iii) Parents, and spouses thereof;

(iv) Siblings, and spouses thereof;

(v) Grandparents and grandchildren, and spouses thereof;

(vi) Domestic partner and parents thereof, including domestic partners of any individual in 2 through 5 of this definition; and

(vii) Any individual related by blood or affinity whose close association with the employee is the equivalent of a family relationship.

(5) Rental costs under leases which are required to be treated as capital leases under GAAP are allowable only up to the amount (as explained in paragraph (b) of this section) that would be allowed had the non-Federal entity purchased the property on the date the lease agreement was executed. The provisions of GAAP must be used to determine whether a lease is a capital lease. Interest costs related to capital leases are allowable to the extent they meet the criteria in § 200.449 Interest. Unallowable costs include amounts paid for profit, management fees, and taxes that would not have been incurred had the non-Federal entity purchased the property.

(6) The rental of any property owned by any individuals or entities affiliated with the non-Federal entity, to include commercial or residential real estate, for purposes such as the home office workspace is unallowable.

### § 200.466 Scholarships and student aid costs.

(a) Costs of scholarships, fellowships, and other programs of student aid at IHEs are allowable only when the purpose of the Federal award is to provide training to selected participants and the charge is approved by the Federal awarding agency. However, tuition remission and other forms of compensation paid as, or in lieu of, wages to students performing necessary work are allowable provided that:

(1) The individual is conducting activities necessary to the Federal award;

(2) Tuition remission and other support are provided in accordance with established policy of the IHE and consistently provided in a like manner to students in return for similar activities conducted under Federal awards as well as other activities; and

(3) During the academic period, the student is enrolled in an advanced degree program at a non-Federal entity or affiliated institution and the activities of the student in relation to the Federal award are related to the degree program;

(4) The tuition or other payments are reasonable compensation for the work performed and are conditioned explicitly upon the performance of necessary work; and

(5) It is the IHE's practice to similarly compensate students under Federal awards as well as other activities.

(b) Charges for tuition remission and other forms of compensation paid to students as, or in lieu of, salaries and wages must be subject to the reporting requirements in § 200.430 Compensation—personal services, and must be treated as direct or indirect cost in accordance with the actual work being performed. Tuition remission may be charged on an average rate basis. See also § 200.431 Compensation—fringe benefits.

### § 200.467 Selling and marketing costs.

Costs of selling and marketing any products or services of the non-Federal entity (unless allowed under § 200.421 Advertising and public relations.) are unallowable, except as direct costs, with prior approval by the Federal awarding agency when necessary for the performance of the Federal award.

### § 200.468 Specialized service facilities.

(a) The costs of services provided by highly complex or specialized facilities operated by the non-Federal entity, such as computing facilities, wind tunnels, and reactors are allowable, provided the charges for the services meet the conditions of either paragraphs (b) or (c) of this section, and, in addition, take into account any items of income or Federal financing that qualify as applicable credits under § 200.406 Applicable credits.

(b) The costs of such services, when material, must be charged directly to applicable awards based on actual usage of the services on the basis of a schedule of rates or established methodology that:

(1) Does not discriminate between activities under Federal awards and other activities of the non-Federal entity, including usage by the non-Federal entity for internal purposes, and

(2) Is designed to recover only the aggregate costs of the services. The costs of each service must consist normally of both its direct costs and its allocable share of all indirect (F&A) costs. Rates must be adjusted at least biennially, and must take into consideration over/under applied costs of the previous period(s).

(c) Where the costs incurred for a service are not material, they may be allocated as indirect (F&A) costs.

(d) Under some extraordinary circumstances, where it is in the best interest of the Federal Government and the non-Federal entity to establish alternative costing arrangements, such arrangements may be worked out with the Federal cognizant agency for indirect costs.

### § 200.469 Student activity costs.

Costs incurred for intramural activities, student publications, student clubs, and other student activities, are unallowable, unless specifically provided for in the Federal award.

### § 200.470 Taxes (including Value Added Tax).

(a) For states, local governments and Indian tribes:

(1) Taxes that a governmental unit is legally required to pay are allowable, except for self-assessed taxes that disproportionately affect Federal programs or changes in tax policies that disproportionately affect Federal programs.

(2) Gasoline taxes, motor vehicle fees, and other taxes that are in effect user fees for benefits provided to the Federal Government are allowable.

(3) This provision does not restrict the authority of the Federal awarding agency to identify taxes where Federal participation is inappropriate. Where

the identification of the amount of unallowable taxes would require an inordinate amount of effort, the cognizant agency for indirect costs may accept a reasonable approximation thereof.

(b) For nonprofit organizations and IHEs:

(1) In general, taxes which the non-Federal entity is required to pay and which are paid or accrued in accordance with GAAP, and payments made to local governments in lieu of taxes which are commensurate with the local government services received are allowable, except for:

(i) Taxes from which exemptions are available to the non-Federal entity directly or which are available to the non-Federal entity based on an exemption afforded the Federal Government and, in the latter case, when the Federal awarding agency makes available the necessary exemption certificates,

(ii) Special assessments on land which represent capital improvements, and

(iii) Federal income taxes.

(2) Any refund of taxes, and any payment to the non-Federal entity of interest thereon, which were allowed as Federal award costs, will be credited either as a cost reduction or cash refund, as appropriate, to the Federal Government. However, any interest actually paid or credited to an non-Federal entity incident to a refund of tax, interest, and penalty will be paid or credited to the Federal Government only to the extent that such interest accrued over the period during which the non-Federal entity has been reimbursed by the Federal Government for the taxes, interest, and penalties.

(c) Value Added Tax (VAT) Foreign taxes charged for the purchase of goods or services that a non-Federal entity is legally required to pay in country is an allowable expense under Federal awards. Foreign tax refunds or applicable credits under Federal awards refer to receipts, or reduction of expenditures, which operate to offset or reduce expense items that are allocable to Federal awards as direct or indirect costs. To the extent that such credits accrued or received by the non-Federal entity relate to allowable cost, these costs must be credited to the Federal awarding agency either as costs or cash refunds. If the costs are credited back to the Federal award, the non-Federal entity may reduce the Federal share of costs by the amount of the foreign tax reimbursement, or where Federal award has not expired, use the foreign government tax refund for approved activities under the Federal award with prior approval of the Federal awarding agency.

§ 200.471 Termination costs.

Termination of a Federal award generally gives rise to the incurrence of costs, or the need for special treatment of costs, which would not have arisen had the Federal award not been terminated. Cost principles covering these items are set forth in this section. They are to be used in conjunction with the other provisions of this part in termination situations.

(a) The cost of items reasonably usable on the non-Federal entity's other work must not be allowable unless the non-Federal entity submits evidence that it would not retain such items at cost without sustaining a loss. In deciding whether such items are reasonably usable on other work of the non-Federal entity, the Federal awarding agency should consider the non-Federal entity's plans and orders for current and scheduled activity. Contemporaneous purchases of common items by the non-Federal entity must be regarded as evidence that such items are reasonably usable on the non-Federal entity's other work. Any acceptance of common items as allocable to the terminated portion of the Federal award must be limited to the extent that the quantities of such items on hand, in transit, and on order are in excess of the reasonable quantitative requirements of other work.

(b) If in a particular case, despite all reasonable efforts by the non-Federal entity, certain costs cannot be discontinued immediately after the effective date of termination, such costs are generally allowable within the limitations set forth in this part, except that any such costs continuing after termination due to the negligent or willful failure of the non-Federal entity to discontinue such costs must be unallowable.

(c) Loss of useful value of special tooling, machinery, and equipment is generally allowable if:

(1) Such special tooling, special machinery, or equipment is not reasonably capable of use in the other work of the non-Federal entity,

(2) The interest of the Federal Government is protected by transfer of title or by other means deemed appropriate by the Federal awarding agency (see also § 200.313 Equipment, paragraph (d), and

(3) The loss of useful value for any one terminated Federal award is limited to that portion of the acquisition cost which bears the same ratio to the total acquisition cost as the terminated portion of the Federal award bears to the entire terminated Federal award and other Federal awards for which the special tooling, machinery, or equipment was acquired.

(d) Rental costs under unexpired leases are generally allowable where clearly shown to have been reasonably necessary for the performance of the terminated Federal award less the residual value of such leases, if:

(1) The amount of such rental claimed does not exceed the reasonable use value of the property leased for the period of the Federal award and such further period as may be reasonable, and

(2) The non-Federal entity makes all reasonable efforts to terminate, assign, settle, or otherwise reduce the cost of such lease. There also may be included the cost of alterations of such leased property, provided such alterations were necessary for the performance of the Federal award, and of reasonable restoration required by the provisions of the lease.

(e) Settlement expenses including the following are generally allowable:

(1) Accounting, legal, clerical, and similar costs reasonably necessary for:

(i) The preparation and presentation to the Federal awarding agency of settlement claims and supporting data with respect to the terminated portion of the Federal award, unless the termination is for cause (see Subpart D—Post Federal Award Requirements of this part, §§ 200.338 Remedies for Noncompliance through 200.342 Effects of Suspension and termination); and

(ii) The termination and settlement of subawards.

(2) Reasonable costs for the storage, transportation, protection, and disposition of property provided by the Federal Government or acquired or produced for the Federal award.

(f) Claims under subawards, including the allocable portion of claims which are common to the Federal award and to other work of the non-Federal entity, are generally allowable. An appropriate share of the non-Federal entity's indirect costs may be allocated to the amount of settlements with contractors and/or subrecipients, provided that the amount allocated is otherwise consistent with the basic guidelines contained in § 200.414 Indirect (F&A) costs. The indirect costs so allocated must exclude the same and similar costs claimed directly or indirectly as settlement expenses.

## § 200.472  Training and education costs.

The cost of training and education provided for employee development is allowable.

## § 200.473  Transportation costs.

Costs incurred for freight, express, cartage, postage, and other transportation services relating either to goods purchased, in process, or delivered, are allowable. When such costs can readily be identified with the items involved, they may be charged directly as transportation costs or added to the cost of such items. Where identification with the materials received cannot readily be made, inbound transportation cost may be charged to the appropriate indirect (F&A) cost accounts if the non-Federal entity follows a consistent, equitable procedure in this respect. Outbound freight, if reimbursable under the terms and conditions of the Federal award, should be treated as a direct cost.

## § 200.474  Travel costs.

(a) *General.* Travel costs are the expenses for transportation, lodging, subsistence, and related items incurred by employees who are in travel status on official business of the non-Federal entity. Such costs may be charged on an actual cost basis, on a per diem or mileage basis in lieu of actual costs incurred, or on a combination of the two, provided the method used is applied to an entire trip and not to selected days of the trip, and results in charges consistent with those normally allowed in like circumstances in the non-Federal entity's non-federally-funded activities and in accordance with non-Federal entity's written travel reimbursement policies. Notwithstanding the provisions of § 200.444 General costs of government, travel costs of officials covered by that section are allowable with the prior written approval of the Federal awarding agency or pass-through entity when they are specifically related to the Federal award.

(b) *Lodging and subsistence.* Costs incurred by employees and officers for travel, including costs of lodging, other subsistence, and incidental expenses, must be considered reasonable and otherwise allowable only to the extent such costs do not exceed charges normally allowed by the non-Federal entity in its regular operations as the result of the non-Federal entity's written travel policy. In addition, if these costs are charged directly to the Federal award documentation must justify that:

(1) Participation of the individual is necessary to the Federal award; and

(2) The costs are reasonable and consistent with non-Federal entity's established travel policy.

(c)(1) Temporary dependent care costs (as dependent is defined in 26 U.S.C. 152) above and beyond regular dependent care that directly results from travel to conferences is allowable provided that:

(i) The costs are a direct result of the individual's travel for the Federal award;

(ii) The costs are consistent with the non-Federal entity's documented travel policy for all entity travel; and

(iii) Are only temporary during the travel period.

(2) Travel costs for dependents are unallowable, except for travel of duration of six months or more with prior approval of the Federal awarding agency. See also § 200.432 Conferences.

(d) In the absence of an acceptable, written non-Federal entity policy regarding travel costs, the rates and amounts established under 5 U.S.C. 5701–11, ("Travel and Subsistence Expenses; Mileage Allowances"), or by the Administrator of General Services, or by the President (or his or her designee) pursuant to any provisions of such subchapter must apply to travel under Federal awards (48 CFR 31.205–46(a)).

(e) *Commercial air travel.* (1) Airfare costs in excess of the basic least expensive unrestricted accommodations class offered by commercial airlines are unallowable except when such accommodations would:

(i) Require circuitous routing;

(ii) Require travel during unreasonable hours;

(iii) Excessively prolong travel;

(iv) Result in additional costs that would offset the transportation savings; or

(v) Offer accommodations not reasonably adequate for the traveler's medical needs. The non-Federal entity must justify and document these conditions on a case-by-case basis in order for the use of first-class or business-class airfare to be allowable in such cases.

(2) Unless a pattern of avoidance is detected, the Federal Government will generally not question a non-Federal entity's determinations that customary standard airfare or other discount airfare is unavailable for specific trips if the non-Federal entity can demonstrate that such airfare was not available in the specific case.

(f) *Air travel by other than commercial carrier.* Costs of travel by non-Federal entity-owned, -leased, or -chartered aircraft include the cost of lease, charter, operation (including personnel costs), maintenance, depreciation, insurance, and other related costs. The portion of such costs that exceeds the cost of airfare as provided for in paragraph (d) of this section, is unallowable.

[78 FR 78608, Dec. 26, 2013, as amended at 79 FR 75887, Dec. 19, 2014]

## § 200.475 Trustees.

Travel and subsistence costs of trustees (or directors) at IHEs and nonprofit organizations are allowable. See also § 200.474 Travel costs.

## Subpart F—Audit Requirements

GENERAL

### § 200.500  Purpose.

This part sets forth standards for obtaining consistency and uniformity among Federal agencies for the audit of non-Federal entities expending Federal awards.

AUDITS

### § 200.501  Audit requirements.

(a) *Audit required.* A non-Federal entity that expends $750,000 or more during the non-Federal entity's fiscal year in Federal awards must have a single or program-specific audit conducted for that year in accordance with the provisions of this part.

(b) *Single audit.* A non-Federal entity that expends $750,000 or more during the non-Federal entity's fiscal year in Federal awards must have a single audit conducted in accordance with § 200.514 Scope of audit except when it elects to have a program-specific audit conducted in accordance with paragraph (c) of this section.

(c) *Program-specific audit election.* When an auditee expends Federal awards under only one Federal program (excluding R&D) and the Federal program's statutes, regulations, or the terms and conditions of the Federal award do not require a financial statement audit of the auditee, the auditee may elect to have a program-specific audit conducted in accordance with § 200.507 Program-specific audits. A program-specific audit may not be elected for R&D unless all of the Federal awards expended were received from the same Federal agency, or the same Federal agency and the same pass-through entity, and that Federal agency, or pass-through entity in the case of a subrecipient, approves in advance a program-specific audit.

(d) *Exemption when Federal awards expended are less than $750,000.* A non-Federal entity that expends less than $750,000 during the non-Federal entity's fiscal year in Federal awards is exempt from Federal audit requirements for that year, except as noted in § 200.503 Relation to other audit requirements, but records must be available for re-view or audit by appropriate officials of the Federal agency, pass-through entity, and Government Accountability Office (GAO).

(e) *Federally Funded Research and Development Centers (FFRDC).* Management of an auditee that owns or operates a FFRDC may elect to treat the FFRDC as a separate entity for purposes of this part.

(f) *Subrecipients and Contractors.* An auditee may simultaneously be a recipient, a subrecipient, and a contractor. Federal awards expended as a recipient or a subrecipient are subject to audit under this part. The payments received for goods or services provided as a contractor are not Federal awards. Section § 200.330 Subrecipient and contractor determinations sets forth the considerations in determining whether payments constitute a Federal award or a payment for goods or services provided as a contractor.

(g) *Compliance responsibility for contractors.* In most cases, the auditee's compliance responsibility for contractors is only to ensure that the procurement, receipt, and payment for goods and services comply with Federal statutes, regulations, and the terms and conditions of Federal awards. Federal award compliance requirements normally do not pass through to contractors. However, the auditee is responsible for ensuring compliance for procurement transactions which are structured such that the contractor is responsible for program compliance or the contractor's records must be reviewed to determine program compliance. Also, when these procurement transactions relate to a major program, the scope of the audit must include determining whether these transactions are in compliance with Federal statutes, regulations, and the terms and conditions of Federal awards.

(h) *For-profit subrecipient.* Since this part does not apply to for-profit subrecipients, the pass-through entity is responsible for establishing requirements, as necessary, to ensure compliance by for-profit subrecipients. The agreement with the for-profit subrecipient must describe applicable compliance requirements and the for-profit subrecipient's compliance responsibility. Methods to ensure compliance for Federal awards made to for-profit subrecipients may include pre-award audits, monitoring during the agreement, and post-award audits. See also § 200.331 Requirements for pass-through entities.

[78 FR 78608, Dec. 26, 2013, as amended at 79 FR 75887, Dec. 19, 2014]

§ 200.502 Basis for determining Federal awards expended.

(a) *Determining Federal awards expended.* The determination of when a Federal award is expended must be based on when the activity related to the Federal award occurs. Generally, the activity pertains to events that require the non-Federal entity to comply with Federal statutes, regulations, and the terms and conditions of Federal awards, such as: expenditure/expense transactions associated with awards including grants, cost-reimbursement contracts under the FAR, compacts with Indian Tribes, cooperative agreements, and direct appropriations; the disbursement of funds to subrecipients; the use of loan proceeds under loan and loan guarantee programs; the receipt of property; the receipt of surplus property; the receipt or use of program income; the distribution or use of food commodities; the disbursement of amounts entitling the non-Federal entity to an interest subsidy; and the period when insurance is in force.

(b) *Loan and loan guarantees (loans).* Since the Federal Government is at risk for loans until the debt is repaid, the following guidelines must be used to calculate the value of Federal awards expended under loan programs, except as noted in paragraphs (c) and (d) of this section:

(1) Value of new loans made or received during the audit period; plus

(2) Beginning of the audit period balance of loans from previous years for which the Federal Government imposes continuing compliance requirements; plus

(3) Any interest subsidy, cash, or administrative cost allowance received.

(c) *Loan and loan guarantees (loans) at IHEs.* When loans are made to students of an IHE but the IHE does not make the loans, then only the value of loans made during the audit period must be considered Federal awards expended in that audit period. The balance of loans for previous audit periods is not included as Federal awards expended because the lender accounts for the prior balances.

(d) *Prior loan and loan guarantees (loans).* Loans, the proceeds of which were received and expended in prior years, are not considered Federal awards expended under this part when the Federal statutes, regulations, and the terms and conditions of Federal awards pertaining to such loans impose no continuing compliance requirements other than to repay the loans.

(e) *Endowment funds.* The cumulative balance of Federal awards for endowment funds that are federally restricted are considered Federal awards expended in each audit period in which the funds are still restricted.

(f) *Free rent.* Free rent received by itself is not considered a Federal award expended under this part. However, free rent received as part of a Federal award to carry out a Federal program must be included in determining Federal awards expended and subject to audit under this part.

(g) *Valuing non-cash assistance.* Federal non-cash assistance, such as free rent, food commodities, donated property, or donated surplus property, must be valued at fair market value at the time of receipt or the assessed value provided by the Federal agency.

(h) *Medicare.* Medicare payments to a non-Federal entity for providing patient care services to Medicare-eligible individuals are not considered Federal awards expended under this part.

(i) *Medicaid.* Medicaid payments to a subrecipient for providing patient care services to Medicaid-eligible individuals are not considered Federal awards expended under this part unless a state requires the funds to be treated as Federal awards expended because reimbursement is on a cost-reimbursement basis.

(j) *Certain loans provided by the National Credit Union Administration.* For purposes of this part, loans made from the National Credit Union Share Insurance Fund and the Central Liquidity Facility that are funded by contributions from insured non-Federal entities are not considered Federal awards expended.

[78 FR 78608, Dec. 26, 2013, as amended at 79 FR 75887, Dec. 19, 2014]

### § 200.503 Relation to other audit requirements.

(a) An audit conducted in accordance with this part must be in lieu of any financial audit of Federal awards which a non-Federal entity is required to undergo under any other Federal statute or regulation. To the extent that such audit provides a Federal agency with the information it requires to carry out its responsibilities under Federal statute or regulation, a Federal agency must rely upon and use that information.

(b) Notwithstanding subsection (a), a Federal agency, Inspectors General, or GAO may conduct or arrange for additional audits which are necessary to carry out its responsibilities under Federal statute or regulation. The provisions of this part do not authorize any non-Federal entity to constrain, in any manner, such Federal agency from carrying out or arranging for such additional audits, except that the Federal agency must plan such audits to not be duplicative of other audits of Federal awards. Prior to commencing such an audit, the Federal agency or pass-through entity must review the FAC for recent audits submitted by the non-Federal entity, and to the extent such audits meet a Federal agency or pass-through entity's needs, the Federal agency or pass-through entity must rely upon and use such audits. Any additional audits must be planned and performed in such a way as to build upon work performed, including the audit documentation, sampling, and testing already performed, by other auditors.

(c) The provisions of this part do not limit the authority of Federal agencies to conduct, or arrange for the conduct of, audits and evaluations of Federal awards, nor limit the authority of any Federal agency Inspector General or other Federal official. For example, requirements that may be applicable under the FAR or CAS and the terms and conditions of a cost-reimbursement contract may include additional applicable audits to be conducted or arranged for by Federal agencies.

(d) Federal agency to pay for additional audits. A Federal agency that conducts or arranges for additional audits must, consistent with other applicable Federal statutes and regulations, arrange for funding the full cost of such additional audits.

(e) Request for a program to be audited as a major program. A Federal awarding agency may request that an auditee have a particular Federal program audited as a major program in lieu of the Federal awarding agency conducting or arranging for the additional audits. To allow for planning, such requests should be made at least 180 calendar days prior to the end of the fiscal year to be audited. The auditee, after consultation with its auditor, should promptly respond to such a request by informing the Federal awarding agency whether the program would otherwise be audited as a major program using the risk-based audit approach described in § 200.518 Major program determination and, if not, the estimated incremental cost. The Federal awarding agency must then promptly confirm to the auditee whether it wants the program audited as a major program. If the program is to be audited as a major program based upon this Federal awarding agency request, and the Federal awarding agency agrees to pay the full incremental costs, then the auditee must have the program audited as a major program. A pass-through entity may use the provisions of this paragraph for a subrecipient.

### § 200.504 Frequency of audits.

Except for the provisions for biennial audits provided in paragraphs (a) and (b) of this section, audits required by this part must be performed annually. Any biennial audit must cover both years within the biennial period.

(a) A state, local government, or Indian tribe that is required by constitution or statute, in effect on January 1, 1987, to undergo its audits less frequently than annually, is permitted to undergo its audits pursuant to this part biennially. This requirement must still be in effect for the biennial period.

(b) Any nonprofit organization that had biennial audits for all biennial periods ending between July 1, 1992, and January 1, 1995, is permitted to undergo its audits pursuant to this part biennially.

## § 200.505　Sanctions.

In cases of continued inability or unwillingness to have an audit conducted in accordance with this part, Federal agencies and pass-through entities must take appropriate action as provided in § 200.338 Remedies for noncompliance.

## § 200.506　Audit costs.

See § 200.425 Audit services.

## § 200.507　Program-specific audits.

(a) *Program-specific audit guide available.* In many cases, a program-specific audit guide will be available to provide specific guidance to the auditor with respect to internal controls, compliance requirements, suggested audit procedures, and audit reporting requirements. A listing of current program-specific audit guides can be found in the compliance supplement beginning with the 2014 supplement including Federal awarding agency contact information and a Web site where a copy of the guide can be obtained. When a current program-specific audit guide is available, the auditor must follow GAGAS and the guide when performing a program-specific audit.

(b) *Program-specific audit guide not available.* (1) When a current program-specific audit guide is not available, the auditee and auditor must have basically the same responsibilities for the Federal program as they would have for an audit of a major program in a single audit.

(2) The auditee must prepare the financial statement(s) for the Federal program that includes, at a minimum, a schedule of expenditures of Federal awards for the program and notes that describe the significant accounting policies used in preparing the schedule, a summary schedule of prior audit findings consistent with the requirements of § 200.511 Audit findings follow-up, paragraph (b), and a corrective action plan consistent with the requirements

of § 200.511 Audit findings follow-up, paragraph (c).

(3) The auditor must:

(i) Perform an audit of the financial statement(s) for the Federal program in accordance with GAGAS;

(ii) Obtain an understanding of internal controls and perform tests of internal controls over the Federal program consistent with the requirements of § 200.514 Scope of audit, paragraph (c) for a major program;

(iii) Perform procedures to determine whether the auditee has complied with Federal statutes, regulations, and the terms and conditions of Federal awards that could have a direct and material effect on the Federal program consistent with the requirements of § 200.514 Scope of audit, paragraph (d) for a major program;

(iv) Follow up on prior audit findings, perform procedures to assess the reasonableness of the summary schedule of prior audit findings prepared by the auditee in accordance with the requirements of § 200.511 Audit findings follow-up, and report, as a current year audit finding, when the auditor concludes that the summary schedule of prior audit findings materially misrepresents the status of any prior audit finding; and

(v) Report any audit findings consistent with the requirements of § 200.516 Audit findings.

(4) The auditor's report(s) may be in the form of either combined or separate reports and may be organized differently from the manner presented in this section. The auditor's report(s) must state that the audit was conducted in accordance with this part and include the following:

(i) An opinion (or disclaimer of opinion) as to whether the financial statement(s) of the Federal program is presented fairly in all material respects in accordance with the stated accounting policies;

(ii) A report on internal control related to the Federal program, which must describe the scope of testing of internal control and the results of the tests;

(iii) A report on compliance which includes an opinion (or disclaimer of opinion) as to whether the auditee complied with laws, regulations, and the terms and conditions of Federal awards which could have a direct and material effect on the Federal program; and

(iv) A schedule of findings and questioned costs for the Federal program that includes a summary of the auditor's results relative to the Federal program in a format consistent with § 200.515 Audit reporting, paragraph (d)(1) and findings and questioned costs consistent with the requirements of § 200.515 Audit reporting, paragraph (d)(3).

(c) *Report submission for program-specific audits.* (1) The audit must be completed and the reporting required by paragraph (c)(2) or (c)(3) of this section submitted within the earlier of 30 calendar days after receipt of the auditor's report(s), or nine months after the end of the audit period, unless a different period is specified in a program-specific audit guide. Unless restricted by Federal law or regulation, the auditee must make report copies available for public inspection. Auditees and auditors must ensure that their respective parts of the reporting package do not include protected personally identifiable information.

(2) When a program-specific audit guide is available, the auditee must electronically submit to the FAC the data collection form prepared in accordance with § 200.512 Report submission, paragraph (b), as applicable to a program-specific audit, and the reporting required by the program-specific audit guide.

(3) When a program-specific audit guide is not available, the reporting package for a program-specific audit must consist of the financial statement(s) of the Federal program, a summary schedule of prior audit findings, and a corrective action plan as described in paragraph (b)(2) of this section, and the auditor's report(s) described in paragraph (b)(4) of this section. The data collection form prepared in accordance with § 200.512 Report submission, paragraph (b), as applicable to a program-specific audit, and one copy of this reporting package must be electronically submitted to the FAC.

(d) *Other sections of this part may apply.* Program-specific audits are subject to:

(1) 200.500 Purpose through 200.503 Relation to other audit requirements, paragraph (d);

(2) 200.504 Frequency of audits through 200.506 Audit costs;

(3) 200.508 Auditee responsibilities through 200.509 Auditor selection;

(4) 200.511 Audit findings follow-up;

(5) 200.512 Report submission, paragraphs (e) through (h);

(6) 200.513 Responsibilities;

(7) 200.516 Audit findings through 200.517 Audit documentation;

(8) 200.521 Management decision, and

(9) Other referenced provisions of this part unless contrary to the provisions of this section, a program-specific audit guide, or program statutes and regulations.

[78 FR 78608, Dec. 26, 2013, as amended at 79 FR 75887, Dec. 19, 2014]

AUDITEES

## § 200.508   Auditee responsibilities.

The auditee must:

(a) Procure or otherwise arrange for the audit required by this part in accordance with § 200.509 Auditor selection, and ensure it is properly performed and submitted when due in accordance with § 200.512 Report submission.

(b) Prepare appropriate financial statements, including the schedule of expenditures of Federal awards in accordance with § 200.510 Financial statements.

(c) Promptly follow up and take corrective action on audit findings, including preparation of a summary schedule of prior audit findings and a corrective action plan in accordance with § 200.511 Audit findings follow-up, paragraph (b) and § 200.511 Audit findings follow-up, paragraph (c), respectively.

(d) Provide the auditor with access to personnel, accounts, books, records, supporting documentation, and other information as needed for the auditor to perform the audit required by this part.

## § 200.509   Auditor selection.

(a) *Auditor procurement.* In procuring audit services, the auditee must follow the procurement standards prescribed by the Procurement Standards in §§ 200.317 Procurement by states through 20.326 Contract provisions of Subpart D- Post Federal Award Requirements of this part or the FAR (48 CFR part 42), as applicable. When procuring audit services, the objective is to obtain high-quality audits. In requesting proposals for audit services, the objectives and scope of the audit must be made clear and the non-Federal entity must request a copy of the audit organization's peer review report which the auditor is required to provide under GAGAS. Factors to be considered in evaluating each proposal for audit services include the responsiveness to the request for proposal, relevant experience, availability of staff with professional qualifications and technical abilities, the results of peer and external quality control reviews, and price. Whenever possible, the auditee must make positive efforts to utilize small businesses, minority-owned firms, and women's business enterprises, in procuring audit services as stated in § 200.321 Contracting with small and minority businesses, women's business enterprises, and labor surplus area firms, or the FAR (48 CFR part 42), as applicable.

(b) *Restriction on auditor preparing indirect cost proposals.* An auditor who prepares the indirect cost proposal or cost allocation plan may not also be selected to perform the audit required by this part when the indirect costs recovered by the auditee during the prior year exceeded $1 million. This restriction applies to the base year used in the preparation of the indirect cost proposal or cost allocation plan and any subsequent years in which the resulting indirect cost agreement or cost allocation plan is used to recover costs.

(c) *Use of Federal auditors.* Federal auditors may perform all or part of the work required under this part if they comply fully with the requirements of this part.

## § 200.510   Financial statements.

(a) *Financial statements.* The auditee must prepare financial statements that reflect its financial position, results of operations or changes in net assets, and, where appropriate, cash flows for the fiscal year audited. The financial statements must be for the same organizational unit and fiscal year that is chosen to meet the requirements of this part. However, non-Federal entity-wide financial statements may also include departments, agencies, and other organizational units that have separate audits in accordance with § 200.514 Scope of audit, paragraph (a) and prepare separate financial statements.

(b) *Schedule of expenditures of Federal awards.* The auditee must also prepare a schedule of expenditures of Federal awards for the period covered by the auditee's financial statements which must include the total Federal awards expended as determined in accordance with § 200.502 Basis for determining Federal awards expended. While not required, the auditee may choose to provide information requested by Federal awarding agencies and pass-through entities to make the schedule easier to use. For example, when a Federal program has multiple Federal award years, the auditee may list the amount of Federal awards expended for each Federal award year separately. At a minimum, the schedule must:

(1) List individual Federal programs by Federal agency. For a cluster of programs, provide the cluster name, list individual Federal programs within the cluster of programs, and provide the applicable Federal agency name. For R&D, total Federal awards expended must be shown either by individual Federal award or by Federal agency and major subdivision within the Federal agency. For example, the National Institutes of Health is a major subdivision in the Department of Health and Human Services.

(2) For Federal awards received as a subrecipient, the name of the pass-through entity and identifying number assigned by the pass-through entity must be included.

(3) Provide total Federal awards expended for each individual Federal program and the CFDA number or other identifying number when the CFDA information is not available. For a cluster of programs also provide the total for the cluster.

(4) Include the total amount provided to subrecipients from each Federal program.

(5) For loan or loan guarantee programs described in § 200.502 Basis for determining Federal awards expended, paragraph (b), identify in the notes to the schedule the balances outstanding at the end of the audit period. This is in addition to including the total Federal awards expended for loan or loan guarantee programs in the schedule.

(6) Include notes that describe that significant accounting policies used in preparing the schedule, and note whether or not the auditee elected to use the 10% de minimis cost rate as covered in § 200.414 Indirect (F&A) costs.

[78 FR 78608, Dec. 26, 2013, as amended at 79 FR 75887, Dec. 19, 2014]

### § 200.511   Audit findings follow-up.

(a) *General.* The auditee is responsible for follow-up and corrective action on all audit findings. As part of this responsibility, the auditee must prepare a summary schedule of prior audit findings. The auditee must also prepare a corrective action plan for current year audit findings. The summary schedule of prior audit findings and the corrective action plan must include the reference numbers the auditor assigns to audit findings under § 200.516 Audit findings, paragraph (c). Since the summary schedule may include audit findings from multiple years, it must include the fiscal year in which the finding initially occurred. The corrective action plan and summary schedule of prior audit findings must include findings relating to the financial statements which are required to be reported in accordance with GAGAS.

(b) *Summary schedule of prior audit findings.* The summary schedule of prior audit findings must report the status of all audit findings included in the prior audit's schedule of findings and questioned costs. The summary schedule must also include audit findings reported in the prior audit's summary schedule of prior audit findings except audit findings listed as corrected in accordance with paragraph (b)(1) of this section, or no longer valid or not warranting further action in ac-

cordance with paragraph (b)(3) of this section.

(1) When audit findings were fully corrected, the summary schedule need only list the audit findings and state that corrective action was taken.

(2) When audit findings were not corrected or were only partially corrected, the summary schedule must describe the reasons for the finding's recurrence and planned corrective action, and any partial corrective action taken. When corrective action taken is significantly different from corrective action previously reported in a corrective action plan or in the Federal agency's or pass-through entity's management decision, the summary schedule must provide an explanation.

(3) When the auditee believes the audit findings are no longer valid or do not warrant further action, the reasons for this position must be described in the summary schedule. A valid reason for considering an audit finding as not warranting further action is that all of the following have occurred:

(i) Two years have passed since the audit report in which the finding occurred was submitted to the FAC;

(ii) The Federal agency or pass-through entity is not currently following up with the auditee on the audit finding; and

(iii) A management decision was not issued.

(c) *Corrective action plan.* At the completion of the audit, the auditee must prepare, in a document separate from the auditor's findings described in § 200.516 Audit findings, a corrective action plan to address each audit finding included in the current year auditor's reports. The corrective action plan must provide the name(s) of the contact person(s) responsible for corrective action, the corrective action planned, and the anticipated completion date. If the auditee does not agree with the audit findings or believes corrective action is not required, then the corrective action plan must include an explanation and specific reasons.

### § 200.512   Report submission.

(a) *General.* (1) The audit must be completed and the data collection form described in paragraph (b) of this section and reporting package described in paragraph (c) of this section must be submitted within the earlier of 30 calendar days after receipt of the auditor's report(s), or nine months after the end of the audit period. If the due date falls on a Saturday, Sunday, or Federal holiday, the reporting package is due the next business day.

(2) Unless restricted by Federal statutes or regulations, the auditee must make copies available for public inspection. Auditees and auditors must ensure that their respective parts of the reporting package do not include protected personally identifiable information.

(b) *Data Collection.* The FAC is the repository of record for Subpart F—Audit Requirements of this part reporting packages and the data collection form. All Federal agencies, pass-through entities and others interested in a reporting package and data collection form must obtain it by accessing the FAC.

(1) The auditee must submit required data elements described in Appendix X to Part 200—Data Collection Form (Form SF–SAC), which state whether the audit was completed in accordance with this part and provides information about the auditee, its Federal programs, and the results of the audit. The data must include information available from the audit required by this part that is necessary for Federal agencies to use the audit to ensure integrity for Federal programs. The data elements and format must be approved by OMB, available from the FAC, and include collections of information from the reporting package described in paragraph (c) of this section. A senior level representative of the auditee (e.g., state controller, director of finance, chief executive officer, or chief financial officer) must sign a statement to be included as part of the data collection that says that the auditee complied with the requirements of this part, the data were prepared in accordance with this part (and the instructions accompanying the form), the reporting package does not include protected personally identifiable information, the information included in its entirety is accurate and complete, and that the FAC is authorized to make the reporting package and the form publicly available on a Web site.

(2) *Exception for Indian Tribes and Tribal Organizations.* An auditee that is an Indian tribe or a tribal organization (as defined in the Indian Self-Determination, Education and Assistance Act (ISDEAA), 25 U.S.C. 450b(l)) may opt not to authorize the FAC to make the reporting package publicly available on a Web site, by excluding the authorization for the FAC publication in the statement described in paragraph (b)(1) of this section. If this option is exercised, the auditee becomes responsible for submitting the reporting package directly to any pass-through entities through which it has received a Federal award and to pass-through entities for which the summary schedule of prior audit findings reported the status of any findings related to Federal awards that the pass-through entity provided. Unless restricted by Federal statute or regulation, if the auditee opts not to authorize publication, it must make copies of the reporting package available for public inspection.

(3) Using the information included in the reporting package described in paragraph (c) of this section, the auditor must complete the applicable data elements of the data collection form. The auditor must sign a statement to be included as part of the data collection form that indicates, at a minimum, the source of the information included in the form, the auditor's responsibility for the information, that the form is not a substitute for the reporting package described in paragraph (c) of this section, and that the content of the form is limited to the collection of information prescribed by OMB.

(c) *Reporting package.* The reporting package must include the:

(1) Financial statements and schedule of expenditures of Federal awards discussed in § 200.510 Financial statements, paragraphs (a) and (b), respectively;

(2) Summary schedule of prior audit findings discussed in § 200.511 Audit findings follow-up, paragraph (b);

(3) Auditor's report(s) discussed in § 200.515 Audit reporting; and

(4) Corrective action plan discussed in § 200.511 Audit findings follow-up, paragraph (c).

(d) *Submission to FAC.* The auditee must electronically submit to the FAC the data collection form described in paragraph (b) of this section and the reporting package described in paragraph (c) of this section.

(e) *Requests for management letters issued by the auditor.* In response to requests by a Federal agency or pass-through entity, auditees must submit a copy of any management letters issued by the auditor.

(f) *Report retention requirements.* Auditees must keep one copy of the data collection form described in paragraph (b) of this section and one copy of the reporting package described in paragraph (c) of this section on file for three years from the date of submission to the FAC.

(g) *FAC responsibilities.* The FAC must make available the reporting packages received in accordance with paragraph (c) of this section and §200.507 Program-specific audits, paragraph (c) to the public, except for Indian tribes exercising the option in (b)(2) of this section, and maintain a data base of completed audits, provide appropriate information to Federal agencies, and follow up with known auditees that have not submitted the required data collection forms and reporting packages.

(h) *Electronic filing.* Nothing in this part must preclude electronic submissions to the FAC in such manner as may be approved by OMB.

[78 FR 78608, Dec. 26, 2013, as amended at 79 FR 75887, Dec. 19, 2014]

FEDERAL AGENCIES

## §200.513 Responsibilities.

(a)(1) Cognizant agency for audit responsibilities. A non-Federal entity expending more than $50 million a year in Federal awards must have a cognizant agency for audit. The designated cognizant agency for audit must be the Federal awarding agency that provides the predominant amount of direct funding to a non-Federal entity unless OMB designates a specific cognizant agency for audit.

(2) To provide for continuity of cognizance, the determination of the predominant amount of direct funding must be based upon direct Federal awards expended in the non-Federal en-

tity's fiscal years ending in 2009, 2014, 2019 and every fifth year thereafter. For example, audit cognizance for periods ending in 2011 through 2015 will be determined based on Federal awards expended in 2009.

(3) Notwithstanding the manner in which audit cognizance is determined, a Federal awarding agency with cognizance for an auditee may reassign cognizance to another Federal awarding agency that provides substantial funding and agrees to be the cognizant agency for audit. Within 30 calendar days after any reassignment, both the old and the new cognizant agency for audit must provide notice of the change to the FAC, the auditee, and, if known, the auditor. The cognizant agency for audit must:

(i) Provide technical audit advice and liaison assistance to auditees and auditors.

(ii) Obtain or conduct quality control reviews on selected audits made by non-Federal auditors, and provide the results to other interested organizations. Cooperate and provide support to the Federal agency designated by OMB to lead a governmentwide project to determine the quality of single audits by providing a statistically reliable estimate of the extent that single audits conform to applicable requirements, standards, and procedures; and to make recommendations to address noted audit quality issues, including recommendations for any changes to applicable requirements, standards and procedures indicated by the results of the project. This governmentwide audit quality project must be performed once every 6 years beginning in 2018 or at such other interval as determined by OMB, and the results must be public.

(iii) Promptly inform other affected Federal agencies and appropriate Federal law enforcement officials of any direct reporting by the auditee or its auditor required by GAGAS or statutes and regulations.

(iv) Advise the community of independent auditors of any noteworthy or important factual trends related to the quality of audits stemming from quality control reviews. Significant problems or quality issues consistently identified through quality control reviews of audit reports must be referred to appropriate state licensing agencies and professional bodies.

(v) Advise the auditor, Federal awarding agencies, and, where appropriate, the auditee of any deficiencies found in the audits when the deficiencies require corrective action by the auditor. When advised of deficiencies, the auditee must work with the auditor to take corrective action. If corrective action is not taken, the cognizant agency for audit must notify the auditor, the auditee, and applicable Federal awarding agencies and pass-through entities of the facts and make recommendations for follow-up action. Major inadequacies or repetitive substandard performance by auditors must be referred to appropriate state licensing agencies and professional bodies for disciplinary action.

(vi) Coordinate, to the extent practical, audits or reviews made by or for Federal agencies that are in addition to the audits made pursuant to this part, so that the additional audits or reviews build upon rather than duplicate audits performed in accordance with this part.

(vii) Coordinate a management decision for cross-cutting audit findings (as defined in § 200.30 Cross-cutting audit finding) that affect the Federal programs of more than one agency when requested by any Federal awarding agency whose awards are included in the audit finding of the auditee.

(viii) Coordinate the audit work and reporting responsibilities among auditors to achieve the most cost-effective audit.

(ix) Provide advice to auditees as to how to handle changes in fiscal years.

(b) Oversight agency for audit responsibilities. An auditee who does not have a designated cognizant agency for audit will be under the general oversight of the Federal agency determined in accordance with § 200.73 Oversight agency for audit. A Federal agency with oversight for an auditee may reassign oversight to another Federal agency that agrees to be the oversight agency for audit. Within 30 calendar days after any reassignment, both the old and the new oversight agency for audit must provide notice of the change to the FAC, the auditee, and, if

known, the auditor. The oversight agency for audit:

(1) Must provide technical advice to auditees and auditors as requested.

(2) May assume all or some of the responsibilities normally performed by a cognizant agency for audit.

(c) Federal awarding agency responsibilities. The Federal awarding agency must perform the following for the Federal awards it makes (See also the requirements of § 200.210 Information contained in a Federal award):

(1) Ensure that audits are completed and reports are received in a timely manner and in accordance with the requirements of this part.

(2) Provide technical advice and counsel to auditees and auditors as requested.

(3) Follow-up on audit findings to ensure that the recipient takes appropriate and timely corrective action. As part of audit follow-up, the Federal awarding agency must:

(i) Issue a management decision as prescribed in § 200.521 Management decision;

(ii) Monitor the recipient taking appropriate and timely corrective action;

(iii) Use cooperative audit resolution mechanisms (see § 200.25 Cooperative audit resolution) to improve Federal program outcomes through better audit resolution, follow-up, and corrective action; and

(iv) Develop a baseline, metrics, and targets to track, over time, the effectiveness of the Federal agency's process to follow-up on audit findings and on the effectiveness of Single Audits in improving non-Federal entity accountability and their use by Federal awarding agencies in making award decisions.

(4) Provide OMB annual updates to the compliance supplement and work with OMB to ensure that the compliance supplement focuses the auditor to test the compliance requirements most likely to cause improper payments, fraud, waste, abuse or generate audit finding for which the Federal awarding agency will take sanctions.

(5) Provide OMB with the name of a single audit accountable official from among the senior policy officials of the Federal awarding agency who must be:

(i) Responsible for ensuring that the agency fulfills all the requirements of paragraph (c) of this section and effectively uses the single audit process to reduce improper payments and improve Federal program outcomes.

(ii) Held accountable to improve the effectiveness of the single audit process based upon metrics as described in paragraph (c)(3)(iv) of this section.

(iii) Responsible for designating the Federal agency's key management single audit liaison.

(6) Provide OMB with the name of a key management single audit liaison who must:

(i) Serve as the Federal awarding agency's management point of contact for the single audit process both within and outside the Federal Government.

(ii) Promote interagency coordination, consistency, and sharing in areas such as coordinating audit follow-up; identifying higher-risk non-Federal entities; providing input on single audit and follow-up policy; enhancing the utility of the FAC; and studying ways to use single audit results to improve Federal award accountability and best practices.

(iii) Oversee training for the Federal awarding agency's program management personnel related to the single audit process.

(iv) Promote the Federal awarding agency's use of cooperative audit resolution mechanisms.

(v) Coordinate the Federal awarding agency's activities to ensure appropriate and timely follow-up and corrective action on audit findings.

(vi) Organize the Federal cognizant agency for audit's follow-up on cross-cutting audit findings that affect the Federal programs of more than one Federal awarding agency.

(vii) Ensure the Federal awarding agency provides annual updates of the compliance supplement to OMB.

(viii) Support the Federal awarding agency's single audit accountable official's mission.

[78 FR 78608, Dec. 26, 2013, as amended at 79 FR 75887, Dec. 19, 2014]

AUDITORS

## § 200.514 Scope of audit.

(a) *General.* The audit must be conducted in accordance with GAGAS. The audit must cover the entire operations of the auditee, or, at the option of the auditee, such audit must include a series of audits that cover departments, agencies, and other organizational units that expended or otherwise administered Federal awards during such audit period, provided that each such audit must encompass the financial statements and schedule of expenditures of Federal awards for each such department, agency, and other organizational unit, which must be considered to be a non-Federal entity. The financial statements and schedule of expenditures of Federal awards must be for the same audit period.

(b) *Financial statements.* The auditor must determine whether the financial statements of the auditee are presented fairly in all material respects in accordance with generally accepted accounting principles. The auditor must also determine whether the schedule of expenditures of Federal awards is stated fairly in all material respects in relation to the auditee's financial statements as a whole.

(c) *Internal control.* (1) The compliance supplement provides guidance on internal controls over Federal programs based upon the guidance in Standards for Internal Control in the Federal Government issued by the Comptroller General of the United States and the Internal Control—Integrated Framework, issued by the Committee of Sponsoring Organizations of the Treadway Commission (COSO).

(2) In addition to the requirements of GAGAS, the auditor must perform procedures to obtain an understanding of internal control over Federal programs sufficient to plan the audit to support a low assessed level of control risk of noncompliance for major programs.

(3) Except as provided in paragraph (c)(4) of this section, the auditor must:

(i) Plan the testing of internal control over compliance for major programs to support a low assessed level of control risk for the assertions relevant to the compliance requirements for each major program; and

(ii) Perform testing of internal control as planned in paragraph (c)(3)(i) of this section.

(4) When internal control over some or all of the compliance requirements for a major program are likely to be ineffective in preventing or detecting noncompliance, the planning and performing of testing described in paragraph (c)(3) of this section are not required for those compliance requirements. However, the auditor must report a significant deficiency or material weakness in accordance with § 200.516 Audit findings, assess the related control risk at the maximum, and consider whether additional compliance tests are required because of ineffective internal control.

(d) *Compliance.* (1) In addition to the requirements of GAGAS, the auditor must determine whether the auditee has complied with Federal statutes, regulations, and the terms and conditions of Federal awards that may have a direct and material effect on each of its major programs.

(2) The principal compliance requirements applicable to most Federal programs and the compliance requirements of the largest Federal programs are included in the compliance supplement.

(3) For the compliance requirements related to Federal programs contained in the compliance supplement, an audit of these compliance requirements will meet the requirements of this part. Where there have been changes to the compliance requirements and the changes are not reflected in the compliance supplement, the auditor must determine the current compliance requirements and modify the audit procedures accordingly. For those Federal programs not covered in the compliance supplement, the auditor must follow the compliance supplement's guidance for programs not included in the supplement.

(4) The compliance testing must include tests of transactions and such other auditing procedures necessary to provide the auditor sufficient appropriate audit evidence to support an opinion on compliance.

(e) *Audit follow-up.* The auditor must follow-up on prior audit findings, perform procedures to assess the reasonableness of the summary schedule of prior audit findings prepared by the auditee in accordance with § 200.511 Audit findings follow-up paragraph (b), and report, as a current year audit finding, when the auditor concludes that the summary schedule of prior audit findings materially misrepresents the status of any prior audit finding. The auditor must perform audit follow-up procedures regardless of whether a prior audit finding relates to a major program in the current year.

(f) *Data Collection Form.* As required in § 200.512 Report submission paragraph (b)(3), the auditor must complete and sign specified sections of the data collection form.

[78 FR 78608, Dec. 26, 2013, as amended at 79 FR 75887, Dec. 19, 2014]

§ 200.515   Audit reporting.

The auditor's report(s) may be in the form of either combined or separate reports and may be organized differently from the manner presented in this section. The auditor's report(s) must state that the audit was conducted in accordance with this part and include the following:

(a) An opinion (or disclaimer of opinion) as to whether the financial statements are presented fairly in all material respects in accordance with generally accepted accounting principles and an opinion (or disclaimer of opinion) as to whether the schedule of expenditures of Federal awards is fairly stated in all material respects in relation to the financial statements as a whole.

(b) A report on internal control over financial reporting and compliance with provisions of laws, regulations, contracts, and award agreements, noncompliance with which could have a material effect on the financial statements. This report must describe the scope of testing of internal control and compliance and the results of the tests, and, where applicable, it will refer to the separate schedule of findings and questioned costs described in paragraph (d) of this section.

(c) A report on compliance for each major program and a report on internal control over compliance. This report must describe the scope of testing of internal control over compliance, include an opinion or disclaimer of opinion as to whether the auditee complied with Federal statutes, regulations, and the terms and conditions of Federal awards which could have a direct and material effect on each major program and refer to the separate schedule of findings and questioned costs described in paragraph (d) of this section.

(d) A schedule of findings and questioned costs which must include the following three components:

(1) A summary of the auditor's results, which must include:

(i) The type of report the auditor issued on whether the financial statements audited were prepared in accordance with GAAP (i.e., unmodified opinion, qualified opinion, adverse opinion, or disclaimer of opinion);

(ii) Where applicable, a statement about whether significant deficiencies or material weaknesses in internal control were disclosed by the audit of the financial statements;

(iii) A statement as to whether the audit disclosed any noncompliance that is material to the financial statements of the auditee;

(iv) Where applicable, a statement about whether significant deficiencies or material weaknesses in internal control over major programs were disclosed by the audit;

(v) The type of report the auditor issued on compliance for major programs (i.e., unmodified opinion, qualified opinion, adverse opinion, or disclaimer of opinion);

(vi) A statement as to whether the audit disclosed any audit findings that the auditor is required to report under §200.516 Audit findings paragraph (a);

(vii) An identification of major programs by listing each individual major program; however in the case of a cluster of programs only the cluster name as shown on the Schedule of Expenditures of Federal Awards is required;

(viii) The dollar threshold used to distinguish between Type A and Type B programs, as described in §200.518 Major program determination paragraph (b)(1), or (b)(3) when a recalculation of the Type A threshold is required for large loan or loan guarantees; and

(ix) A statement as to whether the auditee qualified as a low-risk auditee under §200.520 Criteria for a low-risk auditee.

(2) Findings relating to the financial statements which are required to be reported in accordance with GAGAS.

(3) Findings and questioned costs for Federal awards which must include audit findings as defined in §200.516 Audit findings, paragraph (a).

(i) Audit findings (e.g., internal control findings, compliance findings, questioned costs, or fraud) that relate to the same issue must be presented as a single audit finding. Where practical, audit findings should be organized by Federal agency or pass-through entity.

(ii) Audit findings that relate to both the financial statements and Federal awards, as reported under paragraphs (d)(2) and (d)(3) of this section, respectively, must be reported in both sections of the schedule. However, the reporting in one section of the schedule may be in summary form with a reference to a detailed reporting in the other section of the schedule.

(e) Nothing in this part precludes combining of the audit reporting required by this section with the reporting required by §200.512 Report submission, paragraph (b) Data Collection when allowed by GAGAS and Appendix X to Part 200—Data Collection Form (Form SF–SAC).

[78 FR 78608, Dec. 26, 2013, as amended at 79 FR 75887, Dec. 19, 2014]

### §200.516 Audit findings.

(a) *Audit findings reported.* The auditor must report the following as audit findings in a schedule of findings and questioned costs:

(1) Significant deficiencies and material weaknesses in internal control over major programs and significant instances of abuse relating to major programs. The auditor's determination of whether a deficiency in internal control is a significant deficiency or material weakness for the purpose of reporting an audit finding is in relation to a type of compliance requirement for a major program identified in the Compliance Supplement.

(2) Material noncompliance with the provisions of Federal statutes, regulations, or the terms and conditions of

Federal awards related to a major program. The auditor's determination of whether a noncompliance with the provisions of Federal statutes, regulations, or the terms and conditions of Federal awards is material for the purpose of reporting an audit finding is in relation to a type of compliance requirement for a major program identified in the compliance supplement.

(3) Known questioned costs that are greater than $25,000 for a type of compliance requirement for a major program. Known questioned costs are those specifically identified by the auditor. In evaluating the effect of questioned costs on the opinion on compliance, the auditor considers the best estimate of total costs questioned (likely questioned costs), not just the questioned costs specifically identified (known questioned costs). The auditor must also report known questioned costs when likely questioned costs are greater than $25,000 for a type of compliance requirement for a major program. In reporting questioned costs, the auditor must include information to provide proper perspective for judging the prevalence and consequences of the questioned costs.

(4) Known questioned costs that are greater than $25,000 for a Federal program which is not audited as a major program. Except for audit follow-up, the auditor is not required under this part to perform audit procedures for such a Federal program; therefore, the auditor will normally not find questioned costs for a program that is not audited as a major program. However, if the auditor does become aware of questioned costs for a Federal program that is not audited as a major program (e.g., as part of audit follow-up or other audit procedures) and the known questioned costs are greater than $25,000, then the auditor must report this as an audit finding.

(5) The circumstances concerning why the auditor's report on compliance for each major program is other than an unmodified opinion, unless such circumstances are otherwise reported as audit findings in the schedule of findings and questioned costs for Federal awards.

(6) Known or likely fraud affecting a Federal award, unless such fraud is otherwise reported as an audit finding in the schedule of findings and questioned costs for Federal awards. This paragraph does not require the auditor to report publicly information which could compromise investigative or legal proceedings or to make an additional reporting when the auditor confirms that the fraud was reported outside the auditor's reports under the direct reporting requirements of GAGAS.

(7) Instances where the results of audit follow-up procedures disclosed that the summary schedule of prior audit findings prepared by the auditee in accordance with § 200.511 Audit findings follow-up, paragraph (b) materially misrepresents the status of any prior audit finding.

(b) *Audit finding detail and clarity.* Audit findings must be presented in sufficient detail and clarity for the auditee to prepare a corrective action plan and take corrective action, and for Federal agencies and pass-through entities to arrive at a management decision. The following specific information must be included, as applicable, in audit findings:

(1) Federal program and specific Federal award identification including the CFDA title and number, Federal award identification number and year, name of Federal agency, and name of the applicable pass-through entity. When information, such as the CFDA title and number or Federal award identification number, is not available, the auditor must provide the best information available to describe the Federal award.

(2) The criteria or specific requirement upon which the audit finding is based, including the Federal statutes, regulations, or the terms and conditions of the Federal awards. Criteria generally identify the required or desired state or expectation with respect to the program or operation. Criteria provide a context for evaluating evidence and understanding findings.

(3) The condition found, including facts that support the deficiency identified in the audit finding.

(4) A statement of cause that identifies the reason or explanation for the condition or the factors responsible for the difference between the situation that exists (condition) and the required

or desired state (criteria), which may also serve as a basis for recommendations for corrective action.

(5) The possible asserted effect to provide sufficient information to the auditee and Federal agency, or pass-through entity in the case of a subrecipient, to permit them to determine the cause and effect to facilitate prompt and proper corrective action. A statement of the effect or potential effect should provide a clear, logical link to establish the impact or potential impact of the difference between the condition and the criteria.

(6) Identification of questioned costs and how they were computed. Known questioned costs must be identified by applicable CFDA number(s) and applicable Federal award identification number(s).

(7) Information to provide proper perspective for judging the prevalence and consequences of the audit findings, such as whether the audit findings represent an isolated instance or a systemic problem. Where appropriate, instances identified must be related to the universe and the number of cases examined and be quantified in terms of dollar value. The auditor should report whether the sampling was a statistically valid sample.

(8) Identification of whether the audit finding was a repeat of a finding in the immediately prior audit and if so any applicable prior year audit finding numbers.

(9) Recommendations to prevent future occurrences of the deficiency identified in the audit finding.

(10) Views of responsible officials of the auditee.

(c) *Reference numbers.* Each audit finding in the schedule of findings and questioned costs must include a reference number in the format meeting the requirements of the data collection form submission required by §200.512 Report submission, paragraph (b) to allow for easy referencing of the audit findings during follow-up.

### §200.517 Audit documentation.

(a) *Retention of audit documentation.* The auditor must retain audit documentation and reports for a minimum of three years after the date of issuance of the auditor's report(s) to the auditee, unless the auditor is notified in writing by the cognizant agency for audit, oversight agency for audit, cognizant agency for indirect costs, or pass-through entity to extend the retention period. When the auditor is aware that the Federal agency, pass-through entity, or auditee is contesting an audit finding, the auditor must contact the parties contesting the audit finding for guidance prior to destruction of the audit documentation and reports.

(b) *Access to audit documentation.* Audit documentation must be made available upon request to the cognizant or oversight agency for audit or its designee, cognizant agency for indirect cost, a Federal agency, or GAO at the completion of the audit, as part of a quality review, to resolve audit findings, or to carry out oversight responsibilities consistent with the purposes of this part. Access to audit documentation includes the right of Federal agencies to obtain copies of audit documentation, as is reasonable and necessary.

### §200.518 Major program determination.

(a) *General.* The auditor must use a risk-based approach to determine which Federal programs are major programs. This risk-based approach must include consideration of: current and prior audit experience, oversight by Federal agencies and pass-through entities, and the inherent risk of the Federal program. The process in paragraphs (b) through (h) of this section must be followed.

(b) *Step one.* (1) The auditor must identify the larger Federal programs, which must be labeled Type A programs. Type A programs are defined as Federal programs with Federal awards expended during the audit period exceeding the levels outlined in the table in this paragraph (b)(1):

| Total Federal awards expended | Type A/B threshold |
|---|---|
| Equal to or exceed $750,000 but less than or equal to $25 million. | $750,000. |
| Exceed $25 million but less than or equal to $100 million. | Total Federal awards expended times .03. |
| Exceed $100 million but less than or equal to $1 billion. | $3 million. |

| Total Federal awards expended | Type A/B threshold |
|---|---|
| Exceed $1 billion but less than or equal to $10 billion. | Total Federal awards expended times .003. |
| Exceed $10 billion but less than or equal to $20 billion. | $30 million. |
| Exceed $20 billion ................. | Total Federal awards expended times .0015. |

(2) Federal programs not labeled Type A under paragraph (b)(1) of this section must be labeled Type B programs.

(3) The inclusion of large loan and loan guarantees (loans) must not result in the exclusion of other programs as Type A programs. When a Federal program providing loans exceeds four times the largest non-loan program it is considered a large loan program, and the auditor must consider this Federal program as a Type A program and exclude its values in determining other Type A programs. This recalculation of the Type A program is performed after removing the total of all large loan programs. For the purposes of this paragraph a program is only considered to be a Federal program providing loans if the value of Federal awards expended for loans within the program comprises fifty percent or more of the total Federal awards expended for the program. A cluster of programs is treated as one program and the value of Federal awards expended under a loan program is determined as described in § 200.502 Basis for determining Federal awards *expended.*

(4) For biennial audits permitted under § 200.504 Frequency of audits, the determination of Type A and Type B programs must be based upon the Federal awards expended during the two-year period.

(c) *Step two.* (1) The auditor must identify Type A programs which are low-risk. In making this determination, the auditor must consider whether the requirements in § 200.519 Criteria for Federal program risk paragraph (c), the results of audit follow-up, or any changes in personnel or systems affecting the program indicate significantly increased risk and preclude the program from being low risk. For a Type A program to be considered low-risk, it must have been audited as a major program in at least one of the two most recent audit periods (in the most re-

cent audit period in the case of a biennial audit), and, in the most recent audit period, the program must have not had:

(i) Internal control deficiencies which were identified as material weaknesses in the auditor's report on internal control for major programs as required under § 200.515 Audit reporting, paragraph (c);

(ii) A modified opinion on the program in the auditor's report on major programs as required under § 200.515 Audit reporting, paragraph (c); or

(iii) Known or likely questioned costs that exceed five percent of the total Federal awards expended for the program.

(2) Notwithstanding paragraph (c)(1) of this section, OMB may approve a Federal awarding agency's request that a Type A program may not be considered low risk for a certain recipient. For example, it may be necessary for a large Type A program to be audited as a major program each year at a particular recipient to allow the Federal awarding agency to comply with 31 U.S.C. 3515. The Federal awarding agency must notify the recipient and, if known, the auditor of OMB's approval at least 180 calendar days prior to the end of the fiscal year to be audited.

(d) *Step three.* (1) The auditor must identify Type B programs which are high-risk using professional judgment and the criteria in § 200.519 Criteria for Federal program risk. However, the auditor is not required to identify more high-risk Type B programs than at least one fourth the number of low-risk Type A programs identified as low-risk under Step 2 (paragraph (c) of this section). Except for known material weakness in internal control or compliance problems as discussed in § 200.519 Criteria for Federal program risk paragraphs (b)(1), (b)(2), and (c)(1), a single criteria in risk would seldom cause a Type B program to be considered high-risk. When identifying which Type B programs to risk assess, the auditor is encouraged to use an approach which provides an opportunity for different high-risk Type B programs to be audited as major over a period of time.

(2) The auditor is not expected to perform risk assessments on relatively

small Federal programs. Therefore, the auditor is only required to perform risk assessments on Type B programs that exceed twenty-five percent (0.25) of the Type A threshold determined in Step 1 (paragraph (b) of this section).

(e) *Step four.* At a minimum, the auditor must audit all of the following as major programs:

(1) All Type A programs not identified as low risk under step two (paragraph (c)(1) of this section).

(2) All Type B programs identified as high-risk under step three (paragraph (d) of this section).

(3) Such additional programs as may be necessary to comply with the percentage of coverage rule discussed in paragraph (f) of this section. This may require the auditor to audit more programs as major programs than the number of Type A programs.

(f) *Percentage of coverage rule.* If the auditee meets the criteria in § 200.520 Criteria for a low-risk auditee, the auditor need only audit the major programs identified in Step 4 (paragraph (e)(1) and (2) of this section) and such additional Federal programs with Federal awards expended that, in aggregate, all major programs encompass at least 20 percent (0.20) of total Federal awards expended. Otherwise, the auditor must audit the major programs identified in Step 4 (paragraphs (e)(1) and (2) of this section) and such additional Federal programs with Federal awards expended that, in aggregate, all major programs encompass at least 40 percent (0.40) of total Federal awards expended.

(g) *Documentation of risk.* The auditor must include in the audit documentation the risk analysis process used in determining major programs.

(h) *Auditor's judgment.* When the major program determination was performed and documented in accordance with this Subpart, the auditor's judgment in applying the risk-based approach to determine major programs must be presumed correct. Challenges by Federal agencies and pass-through entities must only be for clearly improper use of the requirements in this part. However, Federal agencies and pass-through entities may provide auditors guidance about the risk of a particular Federal program and the

auditor must consider this guidance in determining major programs in audits not yet completed.

[78 FR 78608, Dec. 26, 2013, as amended at 79 FR 75887, Dec. 19, 2014]

## § 200.519 Criteria for Federal program risk.

(a) *General.* The auditor's determination should be based on an overall evaluation of the risk of noncompliance occurring that could be material to the Federal program. The auditor must consider criteria, such as described in paragraphs (b), (c), and (d) of this section, to identify risk in Federal programs. Also, as part of the risk analysis, the auditor may wish to discuss a particular Federal program with auditee management and the Federal agency or pass-through entity.

(b) *Current and prior audit experience.* (1) Weaknesses in internal control over Federal programs would indicate higher risk. Consideration should be given to the control environment over Federal programs and such factors as the expectation of management's adherence to Federal statutes, regulations, and the terms and conditions of Federal awards and the competence and experience of personnel who administer the Federal programs.

(i) A Federal program administered under multiple internal control structures may have higher risk. When assessing risk in a large single audit, the auditor must consider whether weaknesses are isolated in a single operating unit (e.g., one college campus) or pervasive throughout the entity.

(ii) When significant parts of a Federal program are passed through to subrecipients, a weak system for monitoring subrecipients would indicate higher risk.

(2) Prior audit findings would indicate higher risk, particularly when the situations identified in the audit findings could have a significant impact on a Federal program or have not been corrected.

(3) Federal programs not recently audited as major programs may be of higher risk than Federal programs recently audited as major programs without audit findings.

(c) *Oversight exercised by Federal agencies and pass-through entities.* (1) Oversight exercised by Federal agencies or pass-through entities could be used to assess risk. For example, recent monitoring or other reviews performed by an oversight entity that disclosed no significant problems would indicate lower risk, whereas monitoring that disclosed significant problems would indicate higher risk.

(2) Federal agencies, with the concurrence of OMB, may identify Federal programs that are higher risk. OMB will provide this identification in the compliance supplement.

(d) *Inherent risk of the Federal program.* (1) The nature of a Federal program may indicate risk. Consideration should be given to the complexity of the program and the extent to which the Federal program contracts for goods and services. For example, Federal programs that disburse funds through third party contracts or have eligibility criteria may be of higher risk. Federal programs primarily involving staff payroll costs may have high risk for noncompliance with requirements of § 200.430 Compensation—personal services, but otherwise be at low risk.

(2) The phase of a Federal program in its life cycle at the Federal agency may indicate risk. For example, a new Federal program with new or interim regulations may have higher risk than an established program with time-tested regulations. Also, significant changes in Federal programs, statutes, regulations, or the terms and conditions of Federal awards may increase risk.

(3) The phase of a Federal program in its life cycle at the auditee may indicate risk. For example, during the first and last years that an auditee participates in a Federal program, the risk may be higher due to start-up or close-out of program activities and staff.

(4) Type B programs with larger Federal awards expended would be of higher risk than programs with substantially smaller Federal awards expended.

## § 200.520  Criteria for a low-risk auditee.

An auditee that meets all of the following conditions for each of the preceding two audit periods must qualify as a low-risk auditee and be eligible for reduced audit coverage in accordance with § 200.518 Major program determination.

(a) Single audits were performed on an annual basis in accordance with the provisions of this Subpart, including submitting the data collection form and the reporting package to the FAC within the timeframe specified in § 200.512 Report submission. A non-Federal entity that has biennial audits does not qualify as a low-risk auditee.

(b) The auditor's opinion on whether the financial statements were prepared in accordance with GAAP, or a basis of accounting required by state law, and the auditor's opinion in relation to opinion on the schedule of expenditures of Federal awards were unmodified.

(c) There were no deficiencies in internal control which were identified as material weaknesses under the requirements of GAGAS.

(d) The auditor did not report a substantial doubt about the auditee's ability to continue as a going concern.

(e) None of the Federal programs had audit findings from any of the following in either of the preceding two audit periods in which they were classified as Type A programs:

(1) Internal control deficiencies that were identified as material weaknesses in the auditor's report on internal control for major programs as required under § 200.515 Audit reporting, paragraph (c);

(2) A modified opinion on a major program in the auditor's report on major programs as required under § 200.515 Audit reporting, paragraph (c); or

(3) Known or likely questioned costs that exceeded five percent of the total Federal awards expended for a Type A program during the audit period.

MANAGEMENT DECISIONS

## § 200.521  Management decision.

(a) *General.* The management decision must clearly state whether or not the audit finding is sustained, the reasons for the decision, and the expected auditee action to repay disallowed costs, make financial adjustments, or take other action. If the auditee has not completed corrective action, a timetable for follow-up should be given. Prior to issuing the management decision, the Federal agency or pass-through entity may request additional information or documentation from the auditee, including a request for auditor assurance related to the documentation, as a way of mitigating disallowed costs. The management decision should describe any appeal process available to the auditee. While not required, the Federal agency or pass-through entity may also issue a management decision on findings relating to the financial statements which are required to be reported in accordance with GAGAS.

(b) *Federal agency.* As provided in § 200.513 Responsibilities, paragraph (a)(7), the cognizant agency for audit must be responsible for coordinating a management decision for audit findings that affect the programs of more than one Federal agency. As provided in § 200.513 Responsibilities, paragraph (c)(3), a Federal awarding agency is responsible for issuing a management decision for findings that relate to Federal awards it makes to non-Federal entities.

(c) *Pass-through entity.* As provided in § 200.331 Requirements for pass-through entities, paragraph (d), the pass-through entity must be responsible for issuing a management decision for audit findings that relate to Federal awards it makes to subrecipients.

(d) *Time requirements.* The Federal awarding agency or pass-through entity responsible for issuing a management decision must do so within six months of acceptance of the audit report by the FAC. The auditee must initiate and proceed with corrective action as rapidly as possible and corrective action should begin no later than upon receipt of the audit report.

(e) *Reference numbers.* Management decisions must include the reference numbers the auditor assigned to each audit finding in accordance with § 200.516 Audit findings paragraph (c).

## APPENDIX I TO PART 200—FULL TEXT OF NOTICE OF FUNDING OPPORTUNITY

The full text of the notice of funding opportunity is organized in sections. The required format outlined in this appendix indicates immediately following the title of each section whether that section is required in every announcement or is a Federal awarding agency option. The format is designed so that similar types of information will appear in the same sections in announcements of different Federal funding opportunities. Toward that end, there is text in each of the following sections to describe the types of information that a Federal awarding agency would include in that section of an actual announcement.

A Federal awarding agency that wishes to include information that the format does not specifically discuss may address that subject in whatever section(s) is most appropriate. For example, if a Federal awarding agency chooses to address performance goals in the announcement, it might do so in the funding opportunity description, the application content, or the reporting requirements.

Similarly, when this format calls for a type of information to be in a particular section, a Federal awarding agency wishing to address that subject in other sections may elect to repeat the information in those sections or use cross references between the sections (there should be hyperlinks for cross-references in any electronic versions of the announcement). For example, a Federal awarding agency may want to include Section A information about the types of non-Federal entities who are eligible to apply. The format specifies a standard location for that information in Section C.1 but does not preclude repeating the information in Section A or creating a cross reference between Section A and C.1, as long as a potential applicant can find the information quickly and easily from the standard location.

The sections of the full text of the announcement are described in the following paragraphs.

### A. PROGRAM DESCRIPTION—REQUIRED

This section contains the full program description of the funding opportunity. It may be as long as needed to adequately communicate to potential applicants the areas in which funding may be provided. It describes the Federal awarding agency's funding priorities or the technical or focus areas in which the Federal awarding agency intends to provide assistance. As appropriate, it may include any program history (e.g., whether this is a new program or a new or changed area of program emphasis). This section may communicate indicators of successful projects (e.g., if the program encourages collaborative efforts) and may include examples of projects that have been funded previously.

This section also may include other information the Federal awarding agency deems necessary, and must at a minimum include citations for authorizing statutes and regulations for the funding opportunity.

B. FEDERAL AWARD INFORMATION—REQUIRED

This section provides sufficient information to help an applicant make an informed decision about whether to submit a proposal. Relevant information could include the total amount of funding that the Federal awarding agency expects to award through the announcement; the anticipated number of Federal awards; the expected amounts of individual Federal awards (which may be a range); the amount of funding per Federal award, on average, experienced in previous years; and the anticipated start dates and periods of performance for new Federal awards. This section also should address whether applications for renewal or supplementation of existing projects are eligible to compete with applications for new Federal awards.

This section also must indicate the type(s) of assistance instrument (e.g., grant, cooperative agreement) that may be awarded if applications are successful. If cooperative agreements may be awarded, this section either should describe the "substantial involvement" that the Federal awarding agency expects to have or should reference where the potential applicant can find that information (e.g., in the funding opportunity description in A. Program Description—Required or Federal award administration information in Section D. Application and Submission Information). If procurement contracts also may be awarded, this must be stated.

C. ELIGIBILITY INFORMATION

This section addresses the considerations or factors that determine applicant or application eligibility. This includes the eligibility of particular types of applicant organizations, any factors affecting the eligibility of the principal investigator or project director, and any criteria that make particular projects ineligible. Federal agencies should make clear whether an applicant's failure to meet an eligibility criterion by the time of an application deadline will result in the Federal awarding agency returning the application without review or, even though an application may be reviewed, will preclude the Federal awarding agency from making a Federal award. Key elements to be addressed are:

1. *Eligible Applicants—Required.* Announcements must clearly identify the types of entities that are eligible to apply. If there are no restrictions on eligibility, this section may simply indicate that all potential applicants are eligible. If there are restrictions on

eligibility, it is important to be clear about the specific types of entities that are eligible, not just the types that are ineligible. For example, if the program is limited to nonprofit organizations subject to 26 U.S.C. 501(c)(3) of the tax code (26 U.S.C. 501(c)(3)), the announcement should say so. Similarly, it is better to state explicitly that Native American tribal organizations are eligible than to assume that they can unambiguously infer that from a statement that nonprofit organizations may apply. Eligibility also can be expressed by exception, (e.g., open to all types of domestic applicants other than individuals). This section should refer to any portion of Section D specifying documentation that must be submitted to support an eligibility determination (e.g., proof of 501(c)(3) status as determined by the Internal Revenue Service or an authorizing tribal resolution). To the extent that any funding restriction in Section D.6 could affect the eligibility of an applicant or project, the announcement must either restate that restriction in this section or provide a cross-reference to its description in Section D.6.

2. *Cost Sharing or Matching—Required.* Announcements must state whether there is required cost sharing, matching, or cost participation without which an application would be ineligible (if cost sharing is not required, the announcement must explicitly say so). Required cost sharing may be a certain percentage or amount, or may be in the form of contributions of specified items or activities (e.g., provision of equipment). It is important that the announcement be clear about any restrictions on the types of cost (e.g., in-kind contributions) that are acceptable as cost sharing. Cost sharing as an eligibility criterion includes requirements based in statute or regulation, as described in § 200.306 Cost sharing or matching of this Part. This section should refer to the appropriate portion(s) of section D. Application and Submission Information stating any preaward requirements for submission of letters or other documentation to verify commitments to meet cost-sharing requirements if a Federal award is made.

3. *Other—Required, if applicable.* If there are other eligibility criteria (i.e., criteria that have the effect of making an application or project ineligible for Federal awards, whether referred to as "responsiveness" criteria, "go-no go" criteria, "threshold" criteria, or in other ways), must be clearly stated and must include a reference to the regulation of requirement that describes the restriction, as applicable. For example, if entities that have been found to be in violation of a particular Federal statute are ineligible, it is important to say so. This section must also state any limit on the number of applications an applicant may submit under the announcement and make clear whether the limitation is on the submitting organization,

individual investigator/program director, or both. This section should also address any eligibility criteria for beneficiaries or for program participants other than Federal award recipients.

D. APPLICATION AND SUBMISSION INFORMATION

1. *Address to Request Application Package—Required.* Potential applicants must be told how to get application forms, kits, or other materials needed to apply (if this announcement contains everything needed, this section need only say so). An Internet address where the materials can be accessed is acceptable. However, since high-speed Internet access is not yet universally available for downloading documents, and applicants may have additional accessibility requirements, there also should be a way for potential applicants to request paper copies of materials, such as a U.S. Postal Service mailing address, telephone or FAX number, Telephone Device for the Deaf (TDD), Text Telephone (TTY) number, and/or Federal Information Relay Service (FIRS) number.

2. *Content and Form of Application Submission—Required.* This section must identify the required content of an application and the forms or formats that an applicant must use to submit it. If any requirements are stated elsewhere because they are general requirements that apply to multiple programs or funding opportunities, this section should refer to where those requirements may be found. This section also should include required forms or formats as part of the announcement or state where the applicant may obtain them.

This section should specifically address content and form or format requirements for:

i. Pre-applications, letters of intent, or white papers required or encouraged (see Section D.4), including any limitations on the number of pages or other formatting requirements similar to those for full applications.

ii. The application as a whole. For all submissions, this would include any limitations on the number of pages, font size and typeface, margins, paper size, number of copies, and sequence or assembly requirements. If electronic submission is permitted or required, this could include special requirements for formatting or signatures.

iii. Component pieces of the application (e.g., if all copies of the application must bear original signatures on the face page or the program narrative may not exceed 10 pages). This includes any pieces that may be submitted separately by third parties (e.g., references or letters confirming commitments from third parties that will be contributing a portion of any required cost sharing).

iv. Information that successful applicants must submit after notification of intent to make a Federal award, but prior to a Federal award. This could include evidence of compliance with requirements relating to human subjects or information needed to comply with the National Environmental Policy Act (NEPA) (42 U.S.C. 4321–4370h).

3. *Unique entity identifier and System for Award Management (SAM)—Required.*

This paragraph must state clearly that each applicant (unless the applicant is an individual or Federal awarding agency that is excepted from those requirements under 2 CFR § 25.110(b) or (c), or has an exception approved by the Federal awarding agency under 2 CFR § 25.110(d)) is required to: (i) Be registered in SAM before submitting its application; (ii) provide a a valid unique entity identifier in its application; and (iii) continue to maintain an active SAM registration with current information at all times during which it has an active Federal award or an application or plan under consideration by a Federal awarding agency. It also must state that the Federal awarding agency may not make a Federal award to an applicant until the applicant has complied with all applicable unique entity identifier and SAM requirements and, if an applicant has not fully complied with the requirements by the time the Federal awarding agency is ready to make a Federal award, the Federal awarding agency may determine that the applicant is not qualified to receive a Federal award and use that determination as a basis for making a Federal award to another applicant.

4. *Submission Dates and Times—Required.* Announcements must identify due dates and times for all submissions. This includes not only the full applications but also any preliminary submissions (e.g., letters of intent, white papers, or pre-applications). It also includes any other submissions of information before Federal award that are separate from the full application. If the funding opportunity is a general announcement that is open for a period of time with no specific due dates for applications, this section should say so. Note that the information on dates that is included in this section also must appear with other overview information in a location preceding the full text of the announcement (see § 200.203 Notices of funding opportunities of this Part).

Each type of submission should be designated as encouraged or required and, if required, any deadline date (or dates, if the Federal awarding agency plans more than one cycle of application submission, review, and Federal award under the announcement) should be specified. The announcement must state (or provide a reference to another document that states):

i. Any deadline in terms of a date and local time. If the due date falls on a Saturday, Sunday, or Federal holiday, the reporting package is due the next business day.

197

ii. What the deadline means (e.g., whether it is the date and time by which the Federal awarding agency must receive the application, the date by which the application must be postmarked, or something else) and how that depends, if at all, on the submission method (e.g., mail, electronic, or personal/courier delivery).

iii. The effect of missing a deadline (e.g., whether late applications are neither reviewed nor considered or are reviewed and considered under some circumstances).

iv. How the receiving Federal office determines whether an application or pre-application has been submitted before the deadline. This includes the form of acceptable proof of mailing or system-generated documentation of receipt date and time.

This section also may indicate whether, when, and in what form the applicant will receive an acknowledgement of receipt. This information should be displayed in ways that will be easy to understand and use. It can be difficult to extract all needed information from narrative paragraphs, even when they are well written. A tabular form for providing a summary of the information may help applicants for some programs and give them what effectively could be a checklist to verify the completeness of their application package before submission.

5. *Intergovernmental Review—Required, if applicable.* If the funding opportunity is subject to Executive Order 12372, "Intergovernmental Review of Federal Programs," the notice must say so. In alerting applicants that they must contact their state's Single Point of Contact (SPOC) to find out about and comply with the state's process under Executive Order 12372, it may be useful to inform potential applicants that the names and addresses of the SPOCs are listed in the Office of Management and Budget's Web site. *www.whitehouse.gov/omb/grants/spoc.html.*

6. *Funding Restrictions—Required.* Notices must include information on funding restrictions in order to allow an applicant to develop an application and budget consistent with program requirements. Examples are whether construction is an allowable activity, if there are any limitations on direct costs such as foreign travel or equipment purchases, and if there are any limits on indirect costs (or facilities and administrative costs). Applicants must be advised if Federal awards will not allow reimbursement of pre-Federal award costs.

7. *Other Submission Requirements— Required.* This section must address any other submission requirements not included in the other paragraphs of this section. This might include the format of submission, i.e., paper or electronic, for each type of required submission. Applicants should not be required to submit in more than one format and this section should indicate whether they may choose whether to submit applications in hard copy or electronically, may submit only in hard copy, or may submit only electronically.

This section also must indicate where applications (and any pre-applications) must be submitted if sent by postal mail, electronic means, or hand-delivery. For postal mail submission, this must include the name of an office, official, individual or function (e.g., application receipt center) and a complete mailing address. For electronic submission, this must include the URL or email address; whether a password(s) is required; whether particular software or other electronic capabilities are required; what to do in the event of system problems and a point of contact who will be available in the event the applicant experiences technical difficulties.[1]

E. APPLICATION REVIEW INFORMATION

1. *Criteria—Required.* This section must address the criteria that the Federal awarding agency will use to evaluate applications. This includes the merit and other review criteria that evaluators will use to judge applications, including any statutory, regulatory, or other preferences (e.g., minority status or Native American tribal preferences) that will be applied in the review process. These criteria are distinct from eligibility criteria that are addressed before an application is accepted for review and any program policy or other factors that are applied during the selection process, after the review process is completed. The intent is to make the application process transparent so applicants can make informed decisions when preparing their applications to maximize fairness of the process. The announcement should clearly describe all criteria, including any subcriteria. If criteria vary in importance, the announcement should specify the relative percentages, weights, or other means used to distinguish among them. For statutory, regulatory, or other preferences, the announcement should provide a detailed explanation of those preferences with an explicit indication of their effect (e.g., whether they result in additional points being assigned).

If an applicant's proposed cost sharing will be considered in the review process (as opposed to being an eligibility criterion described in Section C.2), the announcement must specifically address how it will be considered (e.g., to assign a certain number of additional points to applicants who offer cost sharing, or to break ties among applications with equivalent scores after evaluation

---

[1] With respect to electronic methods for providing information about funding opportunities or accepting applicants' submissions of information, each Federal awarding agency is responsible for compliance with Section 508 of the Rehabilitation Act of 1973 (29 U.S.C. 794d).

against all other factors). If cost sharing will not be considered in the evaluation, the announcement should say so, so that there is no ambiguity for potential applicants. Vague statements that cost sharing is encouraged, without clarification as to what that means, are unhelpful to applicants. It also is important that the announcement be clear about any restrictions on the types of cost (e.g., in-kind contributions) that are acceptable as cost sharing.

2. *Review and Selection Process—Required.* This section may vary in the level of detail provided. The announcement must list any program policy or other factors or elements, other than merit criteria, that the selecting official may use in selecting applications for Federal award (e.g., geographical dispersion, program balance, or diversity). The Federal awarding agency may also include other appropriate details. For example, this section may indicate who is responsible for evaluation against the merit criteria (e.g., peers external to the Federal awarding agency or Federal awarding agency personnel) and/or who makes the final selections for Federal awards. If there is a multi-phase review process (e.g., an external panel advising internal Federal awarding agency personnel who make final recommendations to the deciding official), the announcement may describe the phases. It also may include: the number of people on an evaluation panel and how it operates, the way reviewers are selected, reviewer qualifications, and the way that conflicts of interest are avoided. With respect to electronic methods for providing information about funding opportunities or accepting applicants' submissions of information, each Federal awarding agency is responsible for compliance with Section 508 of the Rehabilitation Act of 1973 (29 U.S.C. 794d).

In addition, if the Federal awarding agency permits applicants to nominate suggested reviewers of their applications or suggest those they feel may be inappropriate due to a conflict of interest, that information should be included in this section.

3. For any Federal award under a notice of funding opportunity, if the Federal awarding agency anticipates that the total Federal share will be greater than the simplified acquisition threshold on any Federal award under a notice of funding opportunity may include, over the period of performance (see §200.88 Simplified Acquisition Threshold), this section must also inform applicants:

i. That the Federal awarding agency, prior to making a Federal award with a total amount of Federal share greater than the simplified acquisition threshold, is required to review and consider any information about the applicant that is in the designated integrity and performance system accessible through SAM (currently FAPIIS) (see 41 U.S.C. 2313);

ii. That an applicant, at its option, may review information in the designated integrity and performance systems accessible through SAM and comment on any information about itself that a Federal awarding agency previously entered and is currently in the designated integrity and performance system accessible through SAM;

iii. That the Federal awarding agency will consider any comments by the applicant, in addition to the other information in the designated integrity and performance system, in making a judgment about the applicant's integrity, business ethics, and record of performance under Federal awards when completing the review of risk posed by applicants as described in §200.205 Federal awarding agency review of risk posed by applicants.

4. *Anticipated Announcement and Federal Award Dates—Optional.* This section is intended to provide applicants with information they can use for planning purposes. If there is a single application deadline followed by the simultaneous review of all applications, the Federal awarding agency can include in this section information about the anticipated dates for announcing or notifying successful and unsuccessful applicants and for having Federal awards in place. If applications are received and evaluated on a "rolling" basis at different times during an extended period, it may be appropriate to give applicants an estimate of the time needed to process an application and notify the applicant of the Federal awarding agency's decision.

F. FEDERAL AWARD ADMINISTRATION INFORMATION

1. *Federal Award Notices—Required.* This section must address what a successful applicant can expect to receive following selection. If the Federal awarding agency's practice is to provide a separate notice stating that an application has been selected before it actually makes the Federal award, this section would be the place to indicate that the letter is not an authorization to begin performance (to the extent that it allows charging to Federal awards of pre-award costs at the non-Federal entity's own risk). This section should indicate that the notice of Federal award signed by the grants officer (or equivalent) is the authorizing document, and whether it is provided through postal mail or by electronic means and to whom. It also may address the timing, form, and content of notifications to unsuccessful applicants. See also §200.210 Information contained in a Federal award.

2. *Administrative and National Policy Requirements—Required.* This section must identify the usual administrative and national policy requirements the Federal awarding

agency's Federal awards may include. Providing this information lets a potential applicant identify any requirements with which it would have difficulty complying if its application is successful. In those cases, early notification about the requirements allows the potential applicant to decide not to apply or to take needed actions before receiving the Federal award. The announcement need not include all of the terms and conditions of the Federal award, but may refer to a document (with information about how to obtain it) or Internet site where applicants can see the terms and conditions. If this funding opportunity will lead to Federal awards with some special terms and conditions that differ from the Federal awarding agency's usual (sometimes called "general") terms and conditions, this section should highlight those special terms and conditions. Doing so will alert applicants that have received Federal awards from the Federal awarding agency previously and might not otherwise expect different terms and conditions. For the same reason, the announcement should inform potential applicants about special requirements that could apply to particular Federal awards after the review of applications and other information, based on the particular circumstances of the effort to be supported (e.g., if human subjects were to be involved or if some situations may justify special terms on intellectual property, data sharing or security requirements).

3. *Reporting—Required.* This section must include general information about the type (*e.g.,* financial or performance), frequency, and means of submission (paper or electronic) of post-Federal award reporting requirements. Highlight any special reporting requirements for Federal awards under this funding opportunity that differ (*e.g.,* by report type, frequency, form/format, or circumstances for use) from what the Federal awarding agency's Federal awards usually require. Federal awarding agencies must also describe in this section all relevant requirements such as those at 2 CFR 180.335 and 2 CFR 180.350.

If the Federal share of any Federal award may include more than $500,000 over the period of performance, this section must inform potential applicants about the post award reporting requirements reflected in Appendix XII—Award Term and Condition for Recipient Integrity and Performance Matters.

G. FEDERAL AWARDING AGENCY CONTACT(S)— REQUIRED

The announcement must give potential applicants a point(s) of contact for answering questions or helping with problems while the funding opportunity is open. The intent of this requirement is to be as helpful as possible to potential applicants, so the Federal

awarding agency should consider approaches such as giving:

i. Points of contact who may be reached in multiple ways (e.g., by telephone, FAX, and/or email, as well as regular mail).

ii. A fax or email address that multiple people access, so that someone will respond even if others are unexpectedly absent during critical periods.

iii. Different contacts for distinct kinds of help (e.g., one for questions of programmatic content and a second for administrative questions).

H. OTHER INFORMATION—OPTIONAL

This section may include any additional information that will assist a potential applicant. For example, the section might:

i. Indicate whether this is a new program or a one-time initiative.

ii. Mention related programs or other upcoming or ongoing Federal awarding agency funding opportunities for similar activities.

iii. Include current Internet addresses for Federal awarding agency Web sites that may be useful to an applicant in understanding the program.

iv. Alert applicants to the need to identify proprietary information and inform them about the way the Federal awarding agency will handle it.

v. Include certain routine notices to applicants (e.g., that the Federal Government is not obligated to make any Federal award as a result of the announcement or that only grants officers can bind the Federal Government to the expenditure of funds).

[78 FR 78608, Dec. 26, 2013, as amended at 80 FR 43310, July 22, 2015]

APPENDIX II TO PART 200—CONTRACT PROVISIONS FOR NON-FEDERAL ENTITY CONTRACTS UNDER FEDERAL AWARDS

In addition to other provisions required by the Federal agency or non-Federal entity, all contracts made by the non-Federal entity under the Federal award must contain provisions covering the following, as applicable.

(A) Contracts for more than the simplified acquisition threshold currently set at $150,000, which is the inflation adjusted amount determined by the Civilian Agency Acquisition Council and the Defense Acquisition Regulations Council (Councils) as authorized by 41 U.S.C. 1908, must address administrative, contractual, or legal remedies in instances where contractors violate or breach contract terms, and provide for such sanctions and penalties as appropriate.

(B) All contracts in excess of $10,000 must address termination for cause and for convenience by the non-Federal entity including the manner by which it will be effected and the basis for settlement.

(C) Equal Employment Opportunity. Except as otherwise provided under 41 CFR Part 60, all contracts that meet the definition of "federally assisted construction contract" in 41 CFR Part 60–1.3 must include the equal opportunity clause provided under 41 CFR 60–1.4(b), in accordance with Executive Order 11246, "Equal Employment Opportunity" (30 FR 12319, 12935, 3 CFR Part, 1964–1965 Comp., p. 339), as amended by Executive Order 11375, "Amending Executive Order 11246 Relating to Equal Employment Opportunity," and implementing regulations at 41 CFR part 60, "Office of Federal Contract Compliance Programs, Equal Employment Opportunity, Department of Labor."

(D) Davis-Bacon Act, as amended (40 U.S.C. 3141–3148). When required by Federal program legislation, all prime construction contracts in excess of $2,000 awarded by non-Federal entities must include a provision for compliance with the Davis-Bacon Act (40 U.S.C. 3141–3144, and 3146–3148) as supplemented by Department of Labor regulations (29 CFR Part 5, "Labor Standards Provisions Applicable to Contracts Covering Federally Financed and Assisted Construction"). In accordance with the statute, contractors must be required to pay wages to laborers and mechanics at a rate not less than the prevailing wages specified in a wage determination made by the Secretary of Labor. In addition, contractors must be required to pay wages not less than once a week. The non-Federal entity must place a copy of the current prevailing wage determination issued by the Department of Labor in each solicitation. The decision to award a contract or subcontract must be conditioned upon the acceptance of the wage determination. The non-Federal entity must report all suspected or reported violations to the Federal awarding agency. The contracts must also include a provision for compliance with the Copeland "Anti-Kickback" Act (40 U.S.C. 3145), as supplemented by Department of Labor regulations (29 CFR Part 3, "Contractors and Subcontractors on Public Building or Public Work Financed in Whole or in Part by Loans or Grants from the United States"). The Act provides that each contractor or subrecipient must be prohibited from inducing, by any means, any person employed in the construction, completion, or repair of public work, to give up any part of the compensation to which he or she is otherwise entitled. The non-Federal entity must report all suspected or reported violations to the Federal awarding agency.

(E) Contract Work Hours and Safety Standards Act (40 U.S.C. 3701–3708). Where applicable, all contracts awarded by the non-Federal entity in excess of $100,000 that involve the employment of mechanics or laborers must include a provision for compliance with 40 U.S.C. 3702 and 3704, as supplemented by Department of Labor regulations (29 CFR Part 5). Under 40 U.S.C. 3702 of the Act, each contractor must be required to compute the wages of every mechanic and laborer on the basis of a standard work week of 40 hours. Work in excess of the standard work week is permissible provided that the worker is compensated at a rate of not less than one and a half times the basic rate of pay for all hours worked in excess of 40 hours in the work week. The requirements of 40 U.S.C. 3704 are applicable to construction work and provide that no laborer or mechanic must be required to work in surroundings or under working conditions which are unsanitary, hazardous or dangerous. These requirements do not apply to the purchases of supplies or materials or articles ordinarily available on the open market, or contracts for transportation or transmission of intelligence.

(F) Rights to Inventions Made Under a Contract or Agreement. If the Federal award meets the definition of "funding agreement" under 37 CFR §401.2 (a) and the recipient or subrecipient wishes to enter into a contract with a small business firm or nonprofit organization regarding the substitution of parties, assignment or performance of experimental, developmental, or research work under that "funding agreement," the recipient or subrecipient must comply with the requirements of 37 CFR Part 401, "Rights to Inventions Made by Nonprofit Organizations and Small Business Firms Under Government Grants, Contracts and Cooperative Agreements," and any implementing regulations issued by the awarding agency.

(G) Clean Air Act (42 U.S.C. 7401–7671q.) and the Federal Water Pollution Control Act (33 U.S.C. 1251–1387), as amended—Contracts and subgrants of amounts in excess of $150,000 must contain a provision that requires the non-Federal award to agree to comply with all applicable standards, orders or regulations issued pursuant to the Clean Air Act (42 U.S.C. 7401–7671q) and the Federal Water Pollution Control Act as amended (33 U.S.C. 1251–1387). Violations must be reported to the Federal awarding agency and the Regional Office of the Environmental Protection Agency (EPA).

(H) Debarment and Suspension (Executive Orders 12549 and 12689)—A contract award (see 2 CFR 180.220) must not be made to parties listed on the governmentwide exclusions in the System for Award Management (SAM), in accordance with the OMB guidelines at 2 CFR 180 that implement Executive Orders 12549 (3 CFR part 1986 Comp., p. 189) and 12689 (3 CFR part 1989 Comp., p. 235), "Debarment and Suspension." SAM Exclusions contains the names of parties debarred, suspended, or otherwise excluded by agencies, as well as parties declared ineligible under statutory or regulatory authority other than Executive Order 12549.

(I) Byrd Anti-Lobbying Amendment (31 U.S.C. 1352)—Contractors that apply or bid for an award exceeding $100,000 must file the required certification. Each tier certifies to the tier above that it will not and has not used Federal appropriated funds to pay any person or organization for influencing or attempting to influence an officer or employee of any agency, a member of Congress, officer or employee of Congress, or an employee of a member of Congress in connection with obtaining any Federal contract, grant or any other award covered by 31 U.S.C. 1352. Each tier must also disclose any lobbying with non-Federal funds that takes place in connection with obtaining any Federal award. Such disclosures are forwarded from tier to tier up to the non-Federal award.

(J) See §200.322 Procurement of recovered materials.

[78 FR 78608, Dec. 26, 2013, as amended at 79 FR 75888, Dec. 19, 2014]

APPENDIX III TO PART 200—INDIRECT (F&A) COSTS IDENTIFICATION AND ASSIGNMENT, AND RATE DETERMINATION FOR INSTITUTIONS OF HIGHER EDUCATION (IHES)

A. GENERAL

This appendix provides criteria for identifying and computing indirect (or indirect (F&A)) rates at IHEs (institutions). Indirect (F&A) costs are those that are incurred for common or joint objectives and therefore cannot be identified readily and specifically with a particular sponsored project, an instructional activity, or any other institutional activity. See subsection B.1, Definition of Facilities and Administration, for a discussion of the components of indirect (F&A) costs.

*1. Major Functions of an Institution*

Refers to instruction, organized research, other sponsored activities and other institutional activities as defined in this section:

a. *Instruction* means the teaching and training activities of an institution. Except for research training as provided in subsection b, this term includes all teaching and training activities, whether they are offered for credits toward a degree or certificate or on a non-credit basis, and whether they are offered through regular academic departments or separate divisions, such as a summer school division or an extension division. Also considered part of this major function are departmental research, and, where agreed to, university research.

(1) *Sponsored instruction and training* means specific instructional or training activity established by grant, contract, or cooperative agreement. For purposes of the cost principles, this activity may be considered a major function even though an institution's

accounting treatment may include it in the instruction function.

(2) *Departmental research* means research, development and scholarly activities that are not organized research and, consequently, are not separately budgeted and accounted for. Departmental research, for purposes of this document, is not considered as a major function, but as a part of the instruction function of the institution.

(3) Only mandatory cost sharing or cost sharing specifically committed in the project budget must be included in the organized research base for computing the indirect (F&A) cost rate or reflected in any allocation of indirect costs. Salary costs above statutory limits are not considered cost sharing.

b. *Organized research* means all research and development activities of an institution that are separately budgeted and accounted for. It includes:

(1) *Sponsored research* means all research and development activities that are sponsored by Federal and non-Federal agencies and organizations. This term includes activities involving the training of individuals in research techniques (commonly called research training) where such activities utilize the same facilities as other research and development activities and where such activities are not included in the instruction function.

(2) *University research* means all research and development activities that are separately budgeted and accounted for by the institution under an internal application of institutional funds. University research, for purposes of this document, must be combined with sponsored research under the function of organized research.

c. *Other sponsored activities* means programs and projects financed by Federal and non-Federal agencies and organizations which involve the performance of work other than instruction and organized research. Examples of such programs and projects are health service projects and community service programs. However, when any of these activities are undertaken by the institution without outside support, they may be classified as other institutional activities.

d. *Other institutional activities* means all activities of an institution except for instruction, departmental research, organized research, and other sponsored activities, as defined in this section; indirect (F&A) cost activities identified in this Appendix paragraph B, Identification and assignment of indirect (F&A) costs; and specialized services facilities described in §200.468 Specialized service facilities of this Part.

Examples of other institutional activities include operation of residence halls, dining halls, hospitals and clinics, student unions, intercollegiate athletics, bookstores, faculty housing, student apartments, guest houses, chapels, theaters, public museums, and other similar auxiliary enterprises. This definition also includes any other categories of activities, costs of which are "unallowable" to Federal awards, unless otherwise indicated in an award.

### 2. Criteria for Distribution

a. *Base period.* A base period for distribution of indirect (F&A) costs is the period during which the costs are incurred. The base period normally should coincide with the fiscal year established by the institution, but in any event the base period should be so selected as to avoid inequities in the distribution of costs.

b. *Need for cost groupings.* The overall objective of the indirect (F&A) cost allocation process is to distribute the indirect (F&A) costs described in Section B, Identification and assignment of indirect (F&A) costs, to the major functions of the institution in proportions reasonably consistent with the nature and extent of their use of the institution's resources. In order to achieve this objective, it may be necessary to provide for selective distribution by establishing separate groupings of cost within one or more of the indirect (F&A) cost categories referred to in subsection B.1, Definition of Facilities and Administration. In general, the cost groupings established within a category should constitute, in each case, a pool of those items of expense that are considered to be of like nature in terms of their relative contribution to (or degree of remoteness from) the particular cost objectives to which distribution is appropriate. Cost groupings should be established considering the general guides provided in subsection c of this section. Each such pool or cost grouping should then be distributed individually to the related cost objectives, using the distribution base or method most appropriate in light of the guidelines set forth in subsection d of this section.

c. *General considerations on cost groupings.* The extent to which separate cost groupings and selective distribution would be appropriate at an institution is a matter of judgment to be determined on a case-by-case basis. Typical situations which may warrant the establishment of two or more separate cost groupings (based on account classification or analysis) within an indirect (F&A) cost category include but are not limited to the following:

(1) If certain items or categories of expense relate solely to one of the major functions of the institution or to less than all functions, such expenses should be set aside as a separate cost grouping for direct assignment or selective allocation in accordance with the guides provided in subsections b and d.

(2) If any types of expense ordinarily treated as general administration or departmental administration are charged to Federal awards as direct costs, expenses applica-

ble to other activities of the institution when incurred for the same purposes in like circumstances must, through separate cost groupings, be excluded from the indirect (F&A) costs allocable to those Federal awards and included in the direct cost of other activities for cost allocation purposes.

(3) If it is determined that certain expenses are for the support of a service unit or facility whose output is susceptible of measurement on a workload or other quantitative basis, such expenses should be set aside as a separate cost grouping for distribution on such basis to organized research, instructional, and other activities at the institution or within the department.

(4) If activities provide their own purchasing, personnel administration, building maintenance or similar service, the distribution of general administration and general expenses, or operation and maintenance expenses to such activities should be accomplished through cost groupings which include only that portion of central indirect (F&A) costs (such as for overall management) which are properly allocable to such activities.

(5) If the institution elects to treat fringe benefits as indirect (F&A) charges, such costs should be set aside as a separate cost grouping for selective distribution to related cost objectives.

(6) The number of separate cost groupings within a category should be held within practical limits, after taking into consideration the materiality of the amounts involved and the degree of precision attainable through less selective methods of distribution.

d. Selection of distribution method.

(1) Actual conditions must be taken into account in selecting the method or base to be used in distributing individual cost groupings. The essential consideration in selecting a base is that it be the one best suited for assigning the pool of costs to cost objectives in accordance with benefits derived; with a traceable cause-and-effect relationship; or with logic and reason, where neither benefit nor a cause-and-effect relationship is determinable.

(2) If a cost grouping can be identified directly with the cost objective benefitted, it should be assigned to that cost objective.

(3) If the expenses in a cost grouping are more general in nature, the distribution may be based on a cost analysis study which results in an equitable distribution of the costs. Such cost analysis studies may take into consideration weighting factors, population, or space occupied if appropriate. Cost analysis studies, however, must (a) be appropriately documented in sufficient detail for subsequent review by the cognizant agency for indirect costs, (b) distribute the costs to the related cost objectives in accordance

with the relative benefits derived, (c) be statistically sound, (d) be performed specifically at the institution at which the results are to be used, and (e) be reviewed periodically, but not less frequently than rate negotiations, updated if necessary, and used consistently. Any assumptions made in the study must be stated and explained. The use of cost analysis studies and periodic changes in the method of cost distribution must be fully justified.

(4) If a cost analysis study is not performed, or if the study does not result in an equitable distribution of the costs, the distribution must be made in accordance with the appropriate base cited in Section B, Identification and assignment of indirect (F&A) costs, unless one of the following conditions is met:

(a) It can be demonstrated that the use of a different base would result in a more equitable allocation of the costs, or that a more readily available base would not increase the costs charged to Federal awards, or

(b) The institution qualifies for, and elects to use, the simplified method for computing indirect (F&A) cost rates described in Section D, Simplified method for small institutions.

(5) Notwithstanding subsection (3), effective July 1, 1998, a cost analysis or base other than that in Section B must not be used to distribute utility or student services costs. Instead, subsections B.4.c Operation and maintenance expenses, may be used in the recovery of utility costs.

e. Order of distribution.

(1) Indirect (F&A) costs are the broad categories of costs discussed in Section B.1, Definitions of Facilities and Administration

(2) Depreciation, interest expenses, operation and maintenance expenses, and general administrative and general expenses should be allocated in that order to the remaining indirect (F&A) cost categories as well as to the major functions and specialized service facilities of the institution. Other cost categories may be allocated in the order determined to be most appropriate by the institutions. When cross allocation of costs is made as provided in subsection (3), this order of allocation does not apply.

(3) Normally an indirect (F&A) cost category will be considered closed once it has been allocated to other cost objectives, and costs may not be subsequently allocated to it. However, a cross allocation of costs between two or more indirect (F&A) cost categories may be used if such allocation will result in a more equitable allocation of costs. If a cross allocation is used, an appropriate modification to the composition of the indirect (F&A) cost categories described in Section B is required.

**B. IDENTIFICATION AND ASSIGNMENT OF INDIRECT (F&A) COSTS**

*1. Definition of Facilities and Administration*

See § 200.414 Indirect (F&A) costs which provides the basis for these indirect cost requirements.

*2. Depreciation*

a. The expenses under this heading are the portion of the costs of the institution's buildings, capital improvements to land and buildings, and equipment which are computed in accordance with § 200.436 Depreciation.

b. In the absence of the alternatives provided for in Section A.2.d, Selection of distribution method, the expenses included in this category must be allocated in the following manner:

(1) Depreciation on buildings used exclusively in the conduct of a single function, and on capital improvements and equipment used in such buildings, must be assigned to that function.

(2) Depreciation on buildings used for more than one function, and on capital improvements and equipment used in such buildings, must be allocated to the individual functions performed in each building on the basis of usable square feet of space, excluding common areas such as hallways, stairwells, and rest rooms.

(3) Depreciation on buildings, capital improvements and equipment related to space (e.g., individual rooms, laboratories) used jointly by more than one function (as determined by the users of the space) must be treated as follows. The cost of each jointly used unit of space must be allocated to benefitting functions on the basis of:

(a) The employee full-time equivalents (FTEs) or salaries and wages of those individual functions benefitting from the use of that space; or

(b) Institution-wide employee FTEs or salaries and wages applicable to the benefitting major functions (see Section A.1) of the institution.

(4) Depreciation on certain capital improvements to land, such as paved parking areas, fences, sidewalks, and the like, not included in the cost of buildings, must be allocated to user categories of students and employees on a full-time equivalent basis. The amount allocated to the student category must be assigned to the instruction function of the institution. The amount allocated to the employee category must be further allocated to the major functions of the institution in proportion to the salaries and wages of all employees applicable to those functions.

### 3. Interest

Interest on debt associated with certain buildings, equipment and capital improvements, as defined in § 200.449 Interest, must be classified as an expenditure under the category Facilities. These costs must be allocated in the same manner as the depreciation on the buildings, equipment and capital improvements to which the interest relates.

### 4. Operation and Maintenance Expenses

a. The expenses under this heading are those that have been incurred for the administration, supervision, operation, maintenance, preservation, and protection of the institution's physical plant. They include expenses normally incurred for such items as janitorial and utility services; repairs and ordinary or normal alterations of buildings, furniture and equipment; care of grounds; maintenance and operation of buildings and other plant facilities; security; earthquake and disaster preparedness; environmental safety; hazardous waste disposal; property, liability and all other insurance relating to property; space and capital leasing; facility planning and management; and central receiving. The operation and maintenance expense category should also include its allocable share of fringe benefit costs, depreciation, and interest costs.

b. In the absence of the alternatives provided for in Section A.2.d, the expenses included in this category must be allocated in the same manner as described in subsection 2.b for depreciation.

c. A utility cost adjustment of up to 1.3 percentage points may be included in the negotiated indirect cost rate of the IHE for organized research, per the computation alternatives in paragraphs (c)(1) and (2) of this section:

(1) Where space is devoted to a single function and metering allows unambiguous measurement of usage related to that space, costs must be assigned to the function located in that space.

(2) Where space is allocated to different functions and metering does not allow unambiguous measurement of usage by function, costs must be allocated as follows:

(i) Utilities costs should be apportioned to functions in the same manner as depreciation, based on the calculated difference between the site or building actual square footage for monitored research laboratory space (site, building, floor, or room), and a separate calculation prepared by the IHE using the "effective square footage" described in subsection (c)(2)(ii) of this section.

(ii) "Effective square footage" allocated to research laboratory space must be calculated as the actual square footage times the relative energy utilization index (REUI) posted on the OMB Web site at the time of a rate determination.

A. This index is the ratio of a laboratory energy use index (lab EUI) to the corresponding index for overall average college or university space (college EUI).

B. In July 2012, values for these two indices (taken respectively from the Lawrence Berkeley Laboratory "Labs for the 21st Century" benchmarking tool *http://labs21benchmarking.lbl.gov/CompareData.php* and the US Department of Energy "Buildings Energy Databook" and *http://buildingsdatabook.eren.doe.gov/CBECS.aspx*) were 310 kBtu/sq ft-yr. and 155 kBtu/sq ft-yr., so that the adjustment ratio is 2.0 by this methodology. To retain currency, OMB will adjust the EUI numbers from time to time (no more often than annually nor less often than every 5 years), using reliable and publicly disclosed data. Current values of both the EUIs and the REUI will be posted on the OMB Web site.

### 5. General Administration and General Expenses

a. The expenses under this heading are those that have been incurred for the general executive and administrative offices of educational institutions and other expenses of a general character which do not relate solely to any major function of the institution; i.e., solely to (1) instruction, (2) organized research, (3) other sponsored activities, or (4) other institutional activities. The general administration and general expense category should also include its allocable share of fringe benefit costs, operation and maintenance expense, depreciation, and interest costs. Examples of general administration and general expenses include: those expenses incurred by administrative offices that serve the entire university system of which the institution is a part; central offices of the institution such as the President's or Chancellor's office, the offices for institution-wide financial management, business services, budget and planning, personnel management, and safety and risk management; the office of the General Counsel; and the operations of the central administrative management information systems. General administration and general expenses must not include expenses incurred within non-university-wide deans' offices, academic departments, organized research units, or similar organizational units. (See subsection 6, Departmental administration expenses.)

b. In the absence of the alternatives provided for in Section A.2.d, the expenses included in this category must be grouped first according to common major functions of the institution to which they render services or provide benefits. The aggregate expenses of each group must then be allocated to serviced or benefitted functions on the modified total cost basis. Modified total costs consist of the same elements as those in Section C.2. When an activity included in this indirect

(F&A) cost category provides a service or product to another institution or organization, an appropriate adjustment must be made to either the expenses or the basis of allocation or both, to assure a proper allocation of costs.

*6. Departmental Administration Expenses*

a. The expenses under this heading are those that have been incurred for administrative and supporting services that benefit common or joint departmental activities or objectives in academic deans' offices, academic departments and divisions, and organized research units. Organized research units include such units as institutes, study centers, and research centers. Departmental administration expenses are subject to the following limitations.

(1) Academic deans' offices. Salaries and operating expenses are limited to those attributable to administrative functions.

(2) Academic departments:

(a) Salaries and fringe benefits attributable to the administrative work (including bid and proposal preparation) of faculty (including department heads) and other professional personnel conducting research and/or instruction, must be allowed at a rate of 3.6 percent of modified total direct costs. This category does not include professional business or professional administrative officers. This allowance must be added to the computation of the indirect (F&A) cost rate for major functions in Section C, Determination and application of indirect (F&A) cost rate or rates; the expenses covered by the allowance must be excluded from the departmental administration cost pool. No documentation is required to support this allowance.

(b) Other administrative and supporting expenses incurred within academic departments are allowable provided they are treated consistently in like circumstances. This would include expenses such as the salaries of secretarial and clerical staffs, the salaries of administrative officers and assistants, travel, office supplies, stockrooms, and the like.

(3) Other fringe benefit costs applicable to the salaries and wages included in subsections (1) and (2) are allowable, as well as an appropriate share of general administration and general expenses, operation and maintenance expenses, and depreciation.

(4) Federal agencies may authorize reimbursement of additional costs for department heads and faculty only in exceptional cases where an institution can demonstrate undue hardship or detriment to project performance.

b. The following guidelines apply to the determination of departmental administrative costs as direct or indirect (F&A) costs.

(1) In developing the departmental administration cost pool, special care should be ex-

ercised to ensure that costs incurred for the same purpose in like circumstances are treated consistently as either direct or indirect (F&A) costs. For example, salaries of technical staff, laboratory supplies (e.g., chemicals), telephone toll charges, animals, animal care costs, computer costs, travel costs, and specialized shop costs must be treated as direct costs wherever identifiable to a particular cost objective. Direct charging of these costs may be accomplished through specific identification of individual costs to benefitting cost objectives, or through recharge centers or specialized service facilities, as appropriate under the circumstances. See §§ 200.413 Direct costs, paragraph (c) and 200.468 Specialized service facilities.

(2) Items such as office supplies, postage, local telephone costs, and memberships must normally be treated as indirect (F&A) costs.

c. In the absence of the alternatives provided for in Section A.2.d, the expenses included in this category must be allocated as follows:

(1) The administrative expenses of the dean's office of each college and school must be allocated to the academic departments within that college or school on the modified total cost basis.

(2) The administrative expenses of each academic department, and the department's share of the expenses allocated in subsection (1) must be allocated to the appropriate functions of the department on the modified total cost basis.

*7. Sponsored Projects Administration*

a. The expenses under this heading are limited to those incurred by a separate organization(s) established primarily to administer sponsored projects, including such functions as grant and contract administration (Federal and non-Federal), special security, purchasing, personnel, administration, and editing and publishing of research and other reports. They include the salaries and expenses of the head of such organization, assistants, and immediate staff, together with the salaries and expenses of personnel engaged in supporting activities maintained by the organization, such as stock rooms, print shops, and the like. This category also includes an allocable share of fringe benefit costs, general administration and general expenses, operation and maintenance expenses, and depreciation. Appropriate adjustments will be made for services provided to other functions or organizations.

b. In the absence of the alternatives provided for in Section A.2.d, the expenses included in this category must be allocated to the major functions of the institution under which the sponsored projects are conducted on the basis of the modified total cost of sponsored projects.

c. An appropriate adjustment must be made to eliminate any duplicate charges to Federal awards when this category includes similar or identical activities as those included in the general administration and general expense category or other indirect (F&A) cost items, such as accounting, procurement, or personnel administration.

### 8. Library Expenses

a. The expenses under this heading are those that have been incurred for the operation of the library, including the cost of books and library materials purchased for the library, less any items of library income that qualify as applicable credits under §200.406 Applicable credits. The library expense category should also include the fringe benefits applicable to the salaries and wages included therein, an appropriate share of general administration and general expense, operation and maintenance expense, and depreciation. Costs incurred in the purchases of rare books (museum-type books) with no value to Federal awards should not be allocated to them.

b. In the absence of the alternatives provided for in Section A.2.d, the expenses included in this category must be allocated first on the basis of primary categories of users, including students, professional employees, and other users.

(1) The student category must consist of full-time equivalent students enrolled at the institution, regardless of whether they earn credits toward a degree or certificate.

(2) The professional employee category must consist of all faculty members and other professional employees of the institution, on a full-time equivalent basis. This category may also include post-doctorate fellows and graduate students.

(3) The other users category must consist of a reasonable factor as determined by institutional records to account for all other users of library facilities.

c. Amount allocated in paragraph b of this section must be assigned further as follows:

(1) The amount in the student category must be assigned to the instruction function of the institution.

(2) The amount in the professional employee category must be assigned to the major functions of the institution in proportion to the salaries and wages of all faculty members and other professional employees applicable to those functions.

(3) The amount in the other users category must be assigned to the other institutional activities function of the institution.

### 9. Student Administration and Services

a. The expenses under this heading are those that have been incurred for the administration of student affairs and for services to students, including expenses of such activities as deans of students, admissions, registrar, counseling and placement services, student advisers, student health and infirmary services, catalogs, and commencements and convocations. The salaries of members of the academic staff whose responsibilities to the institution require administrative work that benefits sponsored projects may also be included to the extent that the portion charged to student administration is determined in accordance with Subpart E—Cost Principles of this Part. This expense category also includes the fringe benefit costs applicable to the salaries and wages included therein, an appropriate share of general administration and general expenses, operation and maintenance, interest expense, and depreciation.

b. In the absence of the alternatives provided for in Section A.2.d, the expenses in this category must be allocated to the instruction function, and subsequently to Federal awards in that function.

### 10. Offset for Indirect (F&A) Expenses Otherwise Provided for by the Federal Government

a. The items to be accumulated under this heading are the reimbursements and other payments from the Federal Government which are made to the institution to support solely, specifically, and directly, in whole or in part, any of the administrative or service activities described in subsections 2 through 9.

b. The items in this group must be treated as a credit to the affected individual indirect (F&A) cost category before that category is allocated to benefitting functions.

### C. DETERMINATION AND APPLICATION OF INDIRECT (F&A) COST RATE OR RATES

#### 1. Indirect (F&A) Cost Pools

a. (1) Subject to subsection b, the separate categories of indirect (F&A) costs allocated to each major function of the institution as prescribed in paragraph B of this paragraph C.1 Identification and assignment of indirect (F&A) costs, must be aggregated and treated as a common pool for that function. The amount in each pool must be divided by the distribution base described in subsection 2 to arrive at a single indirect (F&A) cost rate for each function.

(2) The rate for each function is used to distribute indirect (F&A) costs to individual Federal awards of that function. Since a common pool is established for each major function of the institution, a separate indirect (F&A) cost rate would be established for each of the major functions described in Section A.1 under which Federal awards are carried out.

(3) Each institution's indirect (F&A) cost rate process must be appropriately designed to ensure that Federal sponsors do not in

any way subsidize the indirect (F&A) costs of other sponsors, specifically activities sponsored by industry and foreign governments. Accordingly, each allocation method used to identify and allocate the indirect (F&A) cost pools, as described in Sections A.2, Criteria for distribution, and B.2 through B.9, must contain the full amount of the institution's modified total costs or other appropriate units of measurement used to make the computations. In addition, the final rate distribution base (as defined in subsection 2) for each major function (organized research, instruction, etc., as described in Section A.1, Major functions of an institution) must contain all the programs or activities which utilize the indirect (F&A) costs allocated to that major function. At the time an indirect (F&A) cost proposal is submitted to a cognizant agency for indirect costs, each institution must describe the process it uses to ensure that Federal funds are not used to subsidize industry and foreign government funded programs.

b. In some instances a single rate basis for use across the board on all work within a major function at an institution may not be appropriate. A single rate for research, for example, might not take into account those different environmental factors and other conditions which may affect substantially the indirect (F&A) costs applicable to a particular segment of research at the institution. A particular segment of research may be that performed under a single sponsored agreement or it may consist of research under a group of Federal awards performed in a common environment. The environmental factors are not limited to the physical location of the work. Other important factors are the level of the administrative support required, the nature of the facilities or other resources employed, the scientific disciplines or technical skills involved, the organizational arrangements used, or any combination thereof. If a particular segment of a sponsored agreement is performed within an environment which appears to generate a significantly different level of indirect (F&A) costs, provisions should be made for a separate indirect (F&A) cost pool applicable to such work. The separate indirect (F&A) cost pool should be developed during the regular course of the rate determination process and the separate indirect (F&A) cost rate resulting therefrom should be utilized; provided it is determined that (1) such indirect (F&A) cost rate differs significantly from that which would have been obtained under subsection a, and (2) the volume of work to which such rate would apply is material in relation to other Federal awards at the institution.

### 2. The Distribution Basis

Indirect (F&A) costs must be distributed to applicable Federal awards and other benefitting activities within each major function (see section A.1, Major functions of an institution) on the basis of modified total direct costs (MTDC), consisting of all salaries and wages, fringe benefits, materials and supplies, services, travel, and up to the first $25,000 of each subaward (regardless of the period covered by the subaward). MTDC is defined in §200.68 Modified Total Direct Cost (MTDC). For this purpose, an indirect (F&A) cost rate should be determined for each of the separate indirect (F&A) cost pools developed pursuant to subsection 1. The rate in each case should be stated as the percentage which the amount of the particular indirect (F&A) cost pool is of the modified total direct costs identified with such pool.

### 3. Negotiated Lump Sum for Indirect (F&A) Costs

A negotiated fixed amount in lieu of indirect (F&A) costs may be appropriate for self-contained, off-campus, or primarily subcontracted activities where the benefits derived from an institution's indirect (F&A) services cannot be readily determined. Such negotiated indirect (F&A) costs will be treated as an offset before allocation to instruction, organized research, other sponsored activities, and other institutional activities. The base on which such remaining expenses are allocated should be appropriately adjusted.

### 4. Predetermined Rates for Indirect (F&A) Costs

Public Law 87–638 (76 Stat. 437) as amended (41 U.S.C. 4708) authorizes the use of predetermined rates in determining the "indirect costs" (indirect (F&A) costs) applicable under research agreements with educational institutions. The stated objectives of the law are to simplify the administration of cost-type research and development contracts (including grants) with educational institutions, to facilitate the preparation of their budgets, and to permit more expeditious closeout of such contracts when the work is completed. In view of the potential advantages offered by this procedure, negotiation of predetermined rates for indirect (F&A) costs for a period of two to four years should be the norm in those situations where the cost experience and other pertinent facts available are deemed sufficient to enable the parties involved to reach an informed judgment as to the probable level of indirect (F&A) costs during the ensuing accounting periods.

### 5. Negotiated Fixed Rates and Carry-Forward Provisions

When a fixed rate is negotiated in advance for a fiscal year (or other time period), the over- or under-recovery for that year may be included as an adjustment to the indirect (F&A) cost for the next rate negotiation. When the rate is negotiated before the carry-forward adjustment is determined, the carry-forward amount may be applied to the next subsequent rate negotiation. When such adjustments are to be made, each fixed rate negotiated in advance for a given period will be computed by applying the expected indirect (F&A) costs allocable to Federal awards for the forecast period plus or minus the carry-forward adjustment (over- or under-recovery) from the prior period, to the forecast distribution base. Unrecovered amounts under lump-sum agreements or cost-sharing provisions of prior years must not be carried forward for consideration in the new rate negotiation. There must, however, be an advance understanding in each case between the institution and the cognizant agency for indirect costs as to whether these differences will be considered in the rate negotiation rather than making the determination after the differences are known. Further, institutions electing to use this carry-forward provision may not subsequently change without prior approval of the cognizant agency for indirect costs. In the event that an institution returns to a post-determined rate, any over- or under-recovery during the period in which negotiated fixed rates and carry-forward provisions were followed will be included in the subsequent post-determined rates. Where multiple rates are used, the same procedure will be applicable for determining each rate.

### 6. Provisional and Final Rates for Indirect (F&A) Costs

Where the cognizant agency for indirect costs determines that cost experience and other pertinent facts do not justify the use of predetermined rates, or a fixed rate with a carry-forward, or if the parties cannot agree on an equitable rate, a provisional rate must be established. To prevent substantial overpayment or underpayment, the provisional rate may be adjusted by the cognizant agency for indirect costs during the institution's fiscal year. Predetermined or fixed rates may replace provisional rates at any time prior to the close of the institution's fiscal year. If a provisional rate is not replaced by a predetermined or fixed rate prior to the end of the institution's fiscal year, a final rate will be established and upward or downward adjustments will be made based on the actual allowable costs incurred for the period involved.

### 7. Fixed Rates for the Life of the Sponsored Agreement

7. Except as provided in paragraph (c)(1) of § 200.414 Indirect (F&A) costs, Federal agencies must use the negotiated rates in effect at the time of the initial award throughout the life of the Federal award. Award levels for Federal awards may not be adjusted in future years as a result of changes in negotiated rates. "Negotiated rates" per the rate agreement include final, fixed, and predetermined rates and exclude provisional rates. "Life" for the purpose of this subsection means each competitive segment of a project. A competitive segment is a period of years approved by the Federal awarding agency at the time of the Federal award. If negotiated rate agreements do not extend through the life of the Federal award at the time of the initial award, then the negotiated rate for the last year of the Federal award must be extended through the end of the life of the Federal award.

b. Except as provided in § 200.414 Indirect (F&A) costs, when an educational institution does not have a negotiated rate with the Federal Government at the time of an award (because the educational institution is a new recipient or the parties cannot reach agreement on a rate), the provisional rate used at the time of the award must be adjusted once a rate is negotiated and approved by the cognizant agency for indirect costs.

### 8. Limitation on Reimbursement of Administrative Costs

a. Notwithstanding the provisions of subsection C.1.a, the administrative costs charged to Federal awards awarded or amended (including continuation and renewal awards) with effective dates beginning on or after the start of the institution's first fiscal year which begins on or after October 1, 1991, must be limited to 26% of modified total direct costs (as defined in subsection 2) for the total of General Administration and General Expenses, Departmental Administration, Sponsored Projects Administration, and Student Administration and Services (including their allocable share of depreciation, interest costs, operation and maintenance expenses, and fringe benefits costs, as provided by Section B, Identification and assignment of indirect (F&A) costs, and all other types of expenditures not listed specifically under one of the subcategories of facilities in Section B.

b. Institutions should not change their accounting or cost allocation methods if the effect is to change the charging of a particular type of cost from F&A to direct, or to reclassify costs, or increase allocations from the administrative pools identified in paragraph B.1 of this Appendix to the other F&A cost pools or fringe benefits. Cognizant agencies for indirect cost are authorized to allow changes where an institution's charging practices are at variance with acceptable practices followed by a substantial majority of other institutions.

*9. Alternative Method for Administrative Costs*

a. Notwithstanding the provisions of subsection C.1.a, an institution may elect to claim a fixed allowance for the "Administration" portion of indirect (F&A) costs. The allowance could be either 24% of modified total direct costs or a percentage equal to 95% of the most recently negotiated fixed or predetermined rate for the cost pools included under "Administration" as defined in Section B.1, whichever is less. Under this alternative, no cost proposal need be prepared for the "Administration" portion of the indirect (F&A) cost rate nor is further identification or documentation of these costs required (see subsection c). Where a negotiated indirect (F&A) cost agreement includes this alternative, an institution must make no further charges for the expenditure categories described in Section B.5, General administration and general expenses, Section B.6, Departmental administration expenses, Section B.7, Sponsored projects administration, and Section B.9, Student administration and services.

b. In negotiations of rates for subsequent periods, an institution that has elected the option of subsection a may continue to exercise it at the same rate without further identification or documentation of costs.

c. If an institution elects to accept a threshold rate as defined in subsection a of this section, it is not required to perform a detailed analysis of its administrative costs. However, in order to compute the facilities components of its indirect (F&A) cost rate, the institution must reconcile its indirect (F&A) cost proposal to its financial statements and make appropriate adjustments and reclassifications to identify the costs of each major function as defined in Section A.1, as well as to identify and allocate the facilities components. Administrative costs that are not identified as such by the institution's accounting system (such as those incurred in academic departments) will be classified as instructional costs for purposes of reconciling indirect (F&A) cost proposals to financial statements and allocating facilities costs.

*10. Individual Rate Components*

In order to provide mutually agreed-upon information for management purposes, each indirect (F&A) cost rate negotiation or determination must include development of a rate for each indirect (F&A) cost pool as well as the overall indirect (F&A) cost rate.

*11. Negotiation and Approval of Indirect (F&A) Rate*

a. Cognizant agency for indirect costs is defined in Subpart A—Acronyms and Definitions.

(1) Cost negotiation cognizance is assigned to the Department of Health and Human Services (HHS) or the Department of Defense's Office of Naval Research (DOD), normally depending on which of the two agencies (HHS or DOD) provides more funds to the educational institution for the most recent three years. Information on funding must be derived from relevant data gathered by the National Science Foundation. In cases where neither HHS nor DOD provides Federal funding to an educational institution, the cognizant agency for indirect costs assignment must default to HHS. Notwithstanding the method for cognizance determination described in this section, other arrangements for cognizance of a particular educational institution may also be based in part on the types of research performed at the educational institution and must be decided based on mutual agreement between HHS and DOD. Where a non-Federal entity only receives funds as a subrecipient, see §200.331 Requirements for pass-through entities.

(2) After cognizance is established, it must continue for a five-year period.

b. Acceptance of rates. See §200.414 Indirect (F&A) costs.

c. Correcting deficiencies. The cognizant agency for indirect costs must negotiate changes needed to correct systems deficiencies relating to accountability for Federal awards. Cognizant agencies for indirect costs must address the concerns of other affected agencies, as appropriate, and must negotiate special rates for Federal agencies that are required to limit recovery of indirect costs by statute.

d. Resolving questioned costs. The cognizant agency for indirect costs must conduct any necessary negotiations with an educational institution regarding amounts questioned by audit that are due the Federal Government related to costs covered by a negotiated agreement.

e. Reimbursement. Reimbursement to cognizant agencies for indirect costs for work performed under this Part may be made by reimbursement billing under the Economy Act, 31 U.S.C. 1535.

f. Procedure for establishing facilities and administrative rates must be established by one of the following methods:

(1) Formal negotiation. The cognizant agency for indirect costs is responsible for negotiating and approving rates for an educational institution on behalf of all Federal agencies. Federal awarding agencies that do not have cognizance for indirect costs must notify the cognizant agency for indirect costs of specific concerns (i.e., a need to establish special cost rates) which could affect the negotiation process. The cognizant agency for indirect costs must address the concerns of all interested agencies, as appropriate. A pre-negotiation conference may be scheduled among all interested agencies, if necessary. The cognizant agency for indirect

costs must then arrange a negotiation conference with the educational institution.

(2) Other than formal negotiation. The cognizant agency for indirect costs and educational institution may reach an agreement on rates without a formal negotiation conference; for example, through correspondence or use of the simplified method described in this section D of this Appendix.

g. Formalizing determinations and agreements. The cognizant agency for indirect costs must formalize all determinations or agreements reached with an educational institution and provide copies to other agencies having an interest. Determinations should include a description of any adjustments, the actual amount, both dollar and percentage adjusted, and the reason for making adjustments.

h. Disputes and disagreements. Where the cognizant agency for indirect costs is unable to reach agreement with an educational institution with regard to rates or audit resolution, the appeal system of the cognizant agency for indirect costs must be followed for resolution of the disagreement.

*12. Standard Format for Submission*

For facilities and administrative (indirect (F&A)) rate proposals, educational institutions must use the standard format, shown in section E of this appendix, to submit their indirect (F&A) rate proposal to the cognizant agency for indirect costs. The cognizant agency for indirect costs may, on an institution-by-institution basis, grant exceptions from all or portions of Part II of the standard format requirement. This requirement does not apply to educational institutions that use the simplified method for calculating indirect (F&A) rates, as described in Section D of this Appendix.

As provided in section C.10 of this appendix, each F&A cost rate negotiation or determination must include development of a rate for each F&A cost pool as well as the overall F&A rate.

D. SIMPLIFIED METHOD FOR SMALL INSTITUTIONS

*1. General*

a. Where the total direct cost of work covered by this Part at an institution does not exceed $10 million in a fiscal year, the simplified procedure described in subsections 2 or 3 may be used in determining allowable indirect (F&A) costs. Under this simplified procedure, the institution's most recent annual financial report and immediately available supporting information must be utilized as a basis for determining the indirect (F&A) cost rate applicable to all Federal awards. The institution may use either the salaries and wages (see subsection 2) or modified total direct costs (see subsection 3) as the distribution basis.

b. The simplified procedure should not be used where it produces results which appear inequitable to the Federal Government or the institution. In any such case, indirect (F&A) costs should be determined through use of the regular procedure.

*2. Simplified Procedure—Salaries and Wages Base*

a. Establish the total amount of salaries and wages paid to all employees of the institution.

b. Establish an indirect (F&A) cost pool consisting of the expenditures (exclusive of capital items and other costs specifically identified as unallowable) which customarily are classified under the following titles or their equivalents:

(1) General administration and general expenses (exclusive of costs of student administration and services, student activities, student aid, and scholarships).

(2) Operation and maintenance of physical plant and depreciation (after appropriate adjustment for costs applicable to other institutional activities).

(3) Library.

(4) Department administration expenses, which will be computed as 20 percent of the salaries and expenses of deans and heads of departments.

In those cases where expenditures classified under subsection (1) have previously been allocated to other institutional activities, they may be included in the indirect (F&A) cost pool. The total amount of salaries and wages included in the indirect (F&A) cost pool must be separately identified.

c. Establish a salary and wage distribution base, determined by deducting from the total of salaries and wages as established in subsection a from the amount of salaries and wages included under subsection b.

d. Establish the indirect (F&A) cost rate, determined by dividing the amount in the indirect (F&A) cost pool, subsection b, by the amount of the distribution base, subsection c.

e. Apply the indirect (F&A) cost rate to direct salaries and wages for individual agreements to determine the amount of indirect (F&A) costs allocable to such agreements.

*3. Simplified Procedure—Modified Total Direct Cost Base*

a. Establish the total costs incurred by the institution for the base period.

b. Establish an indirect (F&A) cost pool consisting of the expenditures (exclusive of capital items and other costs specifically identified as unallowable) which customarily are classified under the following titles or their equivalents:

211

(1) General administration and general expenses (exclusive of costs of student administration and services, student activities, student aid, and scholarships).

(2) Operation and maintenance of physical plant and depreciation (after appropriate adjustment for costs applicable to other institutional activities).

(3) Library.

(4) Department administration expenses, which will be computed as 20 percent of the salaries and expenses of deans and heads of departments. In those cases where expenditures classified under subsection (1) have previously been allocated to other institutional activities, they may be included in the indirect (F&A) cost pool. The modified total direct costs amount included in the indirect (F&A) cost pool must be separately identified.

c. Establish a modified total direct cost distribution base, as defined in Section C.2, The distribution basis, that consists of all institution's direct functions.

d. Establish the indirect (F&A) cost rate, determined by dividing the amount in the indirect (F&A) cost pool, subsection b, by the amount of the distribution base, subsection c.

e. Apply the indirect (F&A) cost rate to the modified total direct costs for individual agreements to determine the amount of indirect (F&A) costs allocable to such agreements.

E. DOCUMENTATION REQUIREMENTS

The standard format for documentation requirements for indirect (indirect (F&A)) rate proposals for claiming costs under the regular method is available on the OMB Web site here: *http://www.whitehouse.gov/omb/grants_forms.*

F. CERTIFICATION

*1. Certification of Charges*

To assure that expenditures for Federal awards are proper and in accordance with the agreement documents and approved project budgets, the annual and/or final fiscal reports or vouchers requesting payment under the agreements will include a certification, signed by an authorized official of the university, which reads "By signing this report, I certify to the best of my knowledge and belief that the report is true, complete, and accurate, and the expenditures, disbursements and cash receipts are for the purposes and intent set forth in the award documents. I am aware that any false, fictitious, or fraudulent information, or the omission of any material fact, may subject me to criminal, civil or administrative penalties for fraud, false statements, false claims or otherwise. (U.S. Code, Title 18, Section 1001 and Title 31, Sections 3729–3733 and 3801–3812)".

*2. Certification of Indirect (F&A) Costs*

a. *Policy.* Cognizant agencies must not accept a proposed indirect cost rate unless such costs have been certified by the educational institution using the Certificate of Indirect (F&A) Costs set forth in subsection F.2.c

b. The certificate must be signed on behalf of the institution by the chief financial officer or an individual designated by an individual at a level no lower than vice president or chief financial officer.

An indirect (F&A) cost rate is not binding upon the Federal Government if the most recent required proposal from the institution has not been certified. Where it is necessary to establish indirect (F&A) cost rates, and the institution has not submitted a certified proposal for establishing such rates in accordance with the requirements of this section, the Federal Government must unilaterally establish such rates. Such rates may be based upon audited historical data or such other data that have been furnished to the cognizant agency for indirect costs and for which it can be demonstrated that all unallowable costs have been excluded. When indirect (F&A) cost rates are unilaterally established by the Federal Government because of failure of the institution to submit a certified proposal for establishing such rates in accordance with this section, the rates established will be set at a level low enough to ensure that potentially unallowable costs will not be reimbursed.

c. *Certificate.* The certificate required by this section must be in the following form:

CERTIFICATE OF INDIRECT (F&A) COSTS

This is to certify that to the best of my knowledge and belief:

(1) I have reviewed the indirect (F&A) cost proposal submitted herewith;

(2) All costs included in this proposal [identify date] to establish billing or final indirect (F&A) costs rate for [identify period covered by rate] are allowable in accordance with the requirements of the Federal agreement(s) to which they apply and with the cost principles applicable to those agreements.

(3) This proposal does not include any costs which are unallowable under applicable cost principles such as (without limitation): public relations costs, contributions and donations, entertainment costs, fines and penalties, lobbying costs, and defense of fraud proceedings; and

(4) All costs included in this proposal are properly allocable to Federal agreements on the basis of a beneficial or causal relationship between the expenses incurred and the agreements to which they are allocated in accordance with applicable requirements.

I declare that the foregoing is true and correct.

Institution of Higher Education:
Signature: _____
Name of Official: _____
Title: _____
Date of Execution: _____

[78 FR 78608, Dec. 26, 2013, as amended at 79 FR 75888, Dec. 19, 2014; 80 FR 54409, Sept. 10, 2015]

APPENDIX IV TO PART 200—INDIRECT (F&A) COSTS IDENTIFICATION AND ASSIGNMENT, AND RATE DETERMINATION FOR NONPROFIT ORGANIZATIONS

A. GENERAL

1. Indirect costs are those that have been incurred for common or joint objectives and cannot be readily identified with a particular final cost objective. Direct cost of minor amounts may be treated as indirect costs under the conditions described in § 200.413 Direct costs paragraph (d) of this Part. After direct costs have been determined and assigned directly to awards or other work as appropriate, indirect costs are those remaining to be allocated to benefitting cost objectives. A cost may not be allocated to a Federal award as an indirect cost if any other cost incurred for the same purpose, in like circumstances, has been assigned to a Federal award as a direct cost.

2. "Major nonprofit organizations" are defined in paragraph (a) of § 200.414 Indirect (F&A) costs. See indirect cost rate reporting requirements in sections B.2.e and B.3.g of this Appendix.

B. ALLOCATION OF INDIRECT COSTS AND DETERMINATION OF INDIRECT COST RATES

*1. General*

a. If a nonprofit organization has only one major function, or where all its major functions benefit from its indirect costs to approximately the same degree, the allocation of indirect costs and the computation of an indirect cost rate may be accomplished through simplified allocation procedures, as described in section B.2 of this Appendix.

b. If an organization has several major functions which benefit from its indirect costs in varying degrees, allocation of indirect costs may require the accumulation of such costs into separate cost groupings which then are allocated individually to benefitting functions by means of a base which best measures the relative degree of benefit. The indirect costs allocated to each function are then distributed to individual Federal awards and other activities included in that function by means of an indirect cost rate(s).

c. The determination of what constitutes an organization's major functions will depend on its purpose in being; the types of services it renders to the public, its clients, and its members; and the amount of effort it devotes to such activities as fundraising, public information and membership activities.

d. Specific methods for allocating indirect costs and computing indirect cost rates along with the conditions under which each method should be used are described in section B.2 through B.5 of this Appendix.

e. The base period for the allocation of indirect costs is the period in which such costs are incurred and accumulated for allocation to work performed in that period. The base period normally should coincide with the organization's fiscal year but, in any event, must be so selected as to avoid inequities in the allocation of the costs.

*2. Simplified Allocation Method*

a. Where an organization's major functions benefit from its indirect costs to approximately the same degree, the allocation of indirect costs may be accomplished by (i) separating the organization's total costs for the base period as either direct or indirect, and (ii) dividing the total allowable indirect costs (net of applicable credits) by an equitable distribution base. The result of this process is an indirect cost rate which is used to distribute indirect costs to individual Federal awards. The rate should be expressed as the percentage which the total amount of allowable indirect costs bears to the base selected. This method should also be used where an organization has only one major function encompassing a number of individual projects or activities, and may be used where the level of Federal awards to an organization is relatively small.

b. Both the direct costs and the indirect costs must exclude capital expenditures and unallowable costs. However, unallowable costs which represent activities must be included in the direct costs under the conditions described in § 200.413 Direct costs, paragraph (e) of this Part.

c. The distribution base may be total direct costs (excluding capital expenditures and other distorting items, such as subawards for $25,000 or more), direct salaries and wages, or other base which results in an equitable distribution. The distribution base must exclude participant support costs as defined in § 200.75 Participant support costs.

d. Except where a special rate(s) is required in accordance with section B.5 of this Appendix, the indirect cost rate developed under the above principles is applicable to all Federal awards of the organization. If a special rate(s) is required, appropriate modifications must be made in order to develop the special rate(s).

e. For an organization that receives more than $10 million in direct Federal funding in a fiscal year, a breakout of the indirect cost component into two broad categories, Facilities and Administration as defined in paragraph (a) of § 200.414 Indirect (F&A) costs, is required. The rate in each case must be stated as the percentage which the amount of the particular indirect cost category (i.e., Facilities or Administration) is of the distribution base identified with that category.

### 3. Multiple Allocation Base Method

a. General. Where an organization's indirect costs benefit its major functions in varying degrees, indirect costs must be accumulated into separate cost groupings, as described in subparagraph b. Each grouping must then be allocated individually to benefitting functions by means of a base which best measures the relative benefits. The default allocation bases by cost pool are described in section B.3.c of this Appendix.

b. Identification of indirect costs. Cost groupings must be established so as to permit the allocation of each grouping on the basis of benefits provided to the major functions. Each grouping must constitute a pool of expenses that are of like character in terms of functions they benefit and in terms of the allocation base which best measures the relative benefits provided to each function. The groupings are classified within the two broad categories: "Facilities" and "Administration," as described in section A.3 of this Appendix. The indirect cost pools are defined as follows:

(1) Depreciation. The expenses under this heading are the portion of the costs of the organization's buildings, capital improvements to land and buildings, and equipment which are computed in accordance with § 200.436 Depreciation.

(2) Interest. Interest on debt associated with certain buildings, equipment and capital improvements are computed in accordance with § 200.449 Interest.

(3) Operation and maintenance expenses. The expenses under this heading are those that have been incurred for the administration, operation, maintenance, preservation, and protection of the organization's physical plant. They include expenses normally incurred for such items as: janitorial and utility services; repairs and ordinary or normal alterations of buildings, furniture and equipment; care of grounds; maintenance and operation of buildings and other plant facilities; security; earthquake and disaster preparedness; environmental safety; hazardous waste disposal; property, liability and other insurance relating to property; space and capital leasing; facility planning and management; and central receiving. The operation and maintenance expenses category must also include its allocable share of fringe benefit costs, depreciation, and interest costs.

(4) General administration and general expenses. The expenses under this heading are those that have been incurred for the overall general executive and administrative offices of the organization and other expenses of a general nature which do not relate solely to any major function of the organization. This category must also include its allocable share of fringe benefit costs, operation and maintenance expense, depreciation, and interest costs. Examples of this category include central offices, such as the director's office, the office of finance, business services, budget and planning, personnel, safety and risk management, general counsel, management information systems, and library costs.

In developing this cost pool, special care should be exercised to ensure that costs incurred for the same purpose in like circumstances are treated consistently as either direct or indirect costs. For example, salaries of technical staff, project supplies, project publication, telephone toll charges, computer costs, travel costs, and specialized services costs must be treated as direct costs wherever identifiable to a particular program. The salaries and wages of administrative and pooled clerical staff should normally be treated as indirect costs. Direct charging of these costs may be appropriate as described in § 200.413 Direct Costs. Items such as office supplies, postage, local telephone costs, periodicals and memberships should normally be treated as indirect costs.

c. Allocation bases. Actual conditions must be taken into account in selecting the base to be used in allocating the expenses in each grouping to benefitting functions. The essential consideration in selecting a method or a base is that it is the one best suited for assigning the pool of costs to cost objectives in accordance with benefits derived; a traceable cause and effect relationship; or logic and reason, where neither the cause nor the effect of the relationship is determinable. When an allocation can be made by assignment of a cost grouping directly to the function benefitted, the allocation must be made in that manner. When the expenses in a cost grouping are more general in nature, the allocation must be made through the use of a selected base which produces results that are equitable to both the Federal Government and the organization. The distribution must be made in accordance with the bases described herein unless it can be demonstrated that the use of a different base would result in a more equitable allocation of the costs, or that a more readily available base would not increase the costs charged to Federal awards. The results of special cost studies (such as an engineering utility study) must not be used to determine and allocate the indirect costs to Federal awards.

(1) Depreciation. Depreciation expenses must be allocated in the following manner:

(a) Depreciation on buildings used exclusively in the conduct of a single function, and on capital improvements and equipment used in such buildings, must be assigned to that function.

(b) Depreciation on buildings used for more than one function, and on capital improvements and equipment used in such buildings, must be allocated to the individual functions performed in each building on the basis of usable square feet of space, excluding common areas, such as hallways, stairwells, and restrooms.

(c) Depreciation on buildings, capital improvements and equipment related space (e.g., individual rooms, and laboratories) used jointly by more than one function (as determined by the users of the space) must be treated as follows. The cost of each jointly used unit of space must be allocated to the benefitting functions on the basis of:

(i) the employees and other users on a full-time equivalent (FTE) basis or salaries and wages of those individual functions benefitting from the use of that space; or

(ii) organization-wide employee FTEs or salaries and wages applicable to the benefitting functions of the organization.

(d) Depreciation on certain capital improvements to land, such as paved parking areas, fences, sidewalks, and the like, not included in the cost of buildings, must be allocated to user categories on a FTE basis and distributed to major functions in proportion to the salaries and wages of all employees applicable to the functions.

(2) Interest. Interest costs must be allocated in the same manner as the depreciation on the buildings, equipment and capital equipment to which the interest relates.

(3) Operation and maintenance expenses. Operation and maintenance expenses must be allocated in the same manner as the depreciation.

(4) General administration and general expenses. General administration and general expenses must be allocated to benefitting functions based on modified total costs (MTC). The MTC is the modified total direct costs (MTDC), as described in Subpart A—Acronyms and Definitions of Part 200, plus the allocated indirect cost proportion. The expenses included in this category could be grouped first according to major functions of the organization to which they render services or provide benefits. The aggregate expenses of each group must then be allocated to benefitting functions based on MTC.

d. Order of distribution.

(1) Indirect cost categories consisting of depreciation, interest, operation and maintenance, and general administration and general expenses must be allocated in that order to the remaining indirect cost categories as well as to the major functions of the organization. Other cost categories should be allocated in the order determined to be most appropriate by the organization. This order of allocation does not apply if cross allocation

of costs is made as provided in section B.3.d.2 of this Appendix.

(2) Normally, an indirect cost category will be considered closed once it has been allocated to other cost objectives, and costs must not be subsequently allocated to it. However, a cross allocation of costs between two or more indirect costs categories could be used if such allocation will result in a more equitable allocation of costs. If a cross allocation is used, an appropriate modification to the composition of the indirect cost categories is required.

e. Application of indirect cost rate or rates. Except where a special indirect cost rate(s) is required in accordance with section B.5 of this Appendix, the separate groupings of indirect costs allocated to each major function must be aggregated and treated as a common pool for that function. The costs in the common pool must then be distributed to individual Federal awards included in that function by use of a single indirect cost rate.

f. Distribution basis. Indirect costs must be distributed to applicable Federal awards and other benefitting activities within each major function on the basis of MTDC (see definition in §200.68 Modified Total Direct Cost (MTDC) of Part 200.

g. Individual Rate Components. An indirect cost rate must be determined for each separate indirect cost pool developed. The rate in each case must be stated as the percentage which the amount of the particular indirect cost pool is of the distribution base identified with that pool. Each indirect cost rate negotiation or determination agreement must include development of the rate for each indirect cost pool as well as the overall indirect cost rate. The indirect cost pools must be classified within two broad categories: "Facilities" and "Administration," as described paragraph (a) of §200.414 Indirect (F&) costs.

### 4. Direct Allocation Method

a. Some nonprofit organizations treat all costs as direct costs except general administration and general expenses. These organizations generally separate their costs into three basic categories: (i) General administration and general expenses, (ii) fundraising, and (iii) other direct functions (including projects performed under Federal awards). Joint costs, such as depreciation, rental costs, operation and maintenance of facilities, telephone expenses, and the like are prorated individually as direct costs to each category and to each Federal award or other activity using a base most appropriate to the particular cost being prorated.

b. This method is acceptable, provided each joint cost is prorated using a base which accurately measures the benefits provided to each Federal award or other activity. The bases must be established in accordance with reasonable criteria, and be supported by current data. This method is compatible with the Standards of Accounting and Financial Reporting for Voluntary Health and Welfare Organizations issued jointly by the National Health Council, Inc., the National Assembly of Voluntary Health and Social Welfare Organizations, and the United Way of America.

c. Under this method, indirect costs consist exclusively of general administration and general expenses. In all other respects, the organization's indirect cost rates must be computed in the same manner as that described in section B.2 Simplified allocation method of this Appendix.

*5. Special Indirect Cost Rates*

In some instances, a single indirect cost rate for all activities of an organization or for each major function of the organization may not be appropriate, since it would not take into account those different factors which may substantially affect the indirect costs applicable to a particular segment of work. For this purpose, a particular segment of work may be that performed under a single Federal award or it may consist of work under a group of Federal awards performed in a common environment. These factors may include the physical location of the work, the level of administrative support required, the nature of the facilities or other resources employed, the scientific disciplines or technical skills involved, the organizational arrangements used, or any combination thereof. When a particular segment of work is performed in an environment which appears to generate a significantly different level of indirect costs, provisions should be made for a separate indirect cost pool applicable to such work. The separate indirect cost pool should be developed during the course of the regular allocation process, and the separate indirect cost rate resulting therefrom should be used, provided it is determined that (i) the rate differs significantly from that which would have been obtained under sections B.2, B.3, and B.4 of this Appendix, and (ii) the volume of work to which the rate would apply is material.

C. NEGOTIATION AND APPROVAL OF INDIRECT
COST RATES

*1. Definitions*

As used in this section, the following terms have the meanings set forth in this section:

a. *Cognizant agency for indirect costs* means the Federal agency responsible for negotiating and approving indirect cost rates for a nonprofit organization on behalf of all Federal agencies.

b. *Predetermined rate* means an indirect cost rate, applicable to a specified current or future period, usually the organization's fiscal year. The rate is based on an estimate of the costs to be incurred during the period. A pre-

determined rate is not subject to adjustment.

c. *Fixed rate* means an indirect cost rate which has the same characteristics as a predetermined rate, except that the difference between the estimated costs and the actual costs of the period covered by the rate is carried forward as an adjustment to the rate computation of a subsequent period.

d. *Final rate* means an indirect cost rate applicable to a specified past period which is based on the actual costs of the period. A final rate is not subject to adjustment.

e. *Provisional rate or billing rate* means a temporary indirect cost rate applicable to a specified period which is used for funding, interim reimbursement, and reporting indirect costs on Federal awards pending the establishment of a final rate for the period.

f. *Indirect cost proposal* means the documentation prepared by an organization to substantiate its claim for the reimbursement of indirect costs. This proposal provides the basis for the review and negotiation leading to the establishment of an organization's indirect cost rate.

g. *Cost objective* means a function, organizational subdivision, contract, Federal award, or other work unit for which cost data are desired and for which provision is made to accumulate and measure the cost of processes, projects, jobs and capitalized projects.

*2. Negotiation and Approval of Rates*

a. Unless different arrangements are agreed to by the Federal agencies concerned, the Federal agency with the largest dollar value of Federal awards with an organization will be designated as the cognizant agency for indirect costs for the negotiation and approval of the indirect cost rates and, where necessary, other rates such as fringe benefit and computer charge-out rates. Once an agency is assigned cognizance for a particular nonprofit organization, the assignment will not be changed unless there is a shift in the dollar volume of the Federal awards to the organization for at least three years. All concerned Federal agencies must be given the opportunity to participate in the negotiation process but, after a rate has been agreed upon, it will be accepted by all Federal agencies. When a Federal agency has reason to believe that special operating factors affecting its Federal awards necessitate special indirect cost rates in accordance with section B.5 of this Appendix, it will, prior to the time the rates are negotiated, notify the cognizant agency for indirect costs. (See also § 200.414 Indirect (F&A) costs of Part 200.) Where a non-Federal entity only receives funds as a subrecipient, see the requirements of § 200.331 Requirements for pass-through entities.

b. Except as otherwise provided in § 200.414 Indirect (F&A) costs paragraph (f) of this Part, a nonprofit organization which has not previously established an indirect cost rate with a Federal agency must submit its initial indirect cost proposal immediately after the organization is advised that a Federal award will be made and, in no event, later than three months after the effective date of the Federal award.

c. Unless approved by the cognizant agency for indirect costs in accordance with § 200.414 Indirect (F&A) costs paragraph (g) of this Part, organizations that have previously established indirect cost rates must submit a new indirect cost proposal to the cognizant agency for indirect costs within six months after the close of each fiscal year.

d. A predetermined rate may be negotiated for use on Federal awards where there is reasonable assurance, based on past experience and reliable projection of the organization's costs, that the rate is not likely to exceed a rate based on the organization's actual costs.

e. Fixed rates may be negotiated where predetermined rates are not considered appropriate. A fixed rate, however, must not be negotiated if (i) all or a substantial portion of the organization's Federal awards are expected to expire before the carry-forward adjustment can be made; (ii) the mix of Federal and non-Federal work at the organization is too erratic to permit an equitable carry-forward adjustment; or (iii) the organization's operations fluctuate significantly from year to year.

f. Provisional and final rates must be negotiated where neither predetermined nor fixed rates are appropriate. Predetermined or fixed rates may replace provisional rates at any time prior to the close of the organization's fiscal year. If that event does not occur, a final rate will be established and upward or downward adjustments will be made based on the actual allowable costs incurred for the period involved.

g. The results of each negotiation must be formalized in a written agreement between the cognizant agency for indirect costs and the nonprofit organization. The cognizant agency for indirect costs must make available copies of the agreement to all concerned Federal agencies.

h. If a dispute arises in a negotiation of an indirect cost rate between the cognizant agency for indirect costs and the nonprofit organization, the dispute must be resolved in accordance with the appeals procedures of the cognizant agency for indirect costs.

i. To the extent that problems are encountered among the Federal agencies in connection with the negotiation and approval process, OMB will lend assistance as required to resolve such problems in a timely manner.

D. Certification of Indirect (F&A) Costs

(1) Required Certification. No proposal to establish indirect (F&A) cost rates must be acceptable unless such costs have been certified by the non-profit organization using the Certificate of Indirect (F&A) Costs set forth in section j. of this appendix. The certificate must be signed on behalf of the organization by an individual at a level no lower than vice president or chief financial officer for the organization.

(2) Each indirect cost rate proposal must be accompanied by a certification in the following form:

Certificate of Indirect (F&A) Costs

This is to certify that to the best of my knowledge and belief:

(1) I have reviewed the indirect (F&A) cost proposal submitted herewith;

(2) All costs included in this proposal [identify date] to establish billing or final indirect (F&A) costs rate for [identify period covered by rate] are allowable in accordance with the requirements of the Federal awards to which they apply and with Subpart E—Cost Principles of Part 200.

(3) This proposal does not include any costs which are unallowable under Subpart E—Cost Principles of Part 200 such as (without limitation): public relations costs, contributions and donations, entertainment costs, fines and penalties, lobbying costs, and defense of fraud proceedings; and

(4) All costs included in this proposal are properly allocable to Federal awards on the basis of a beneficial or causal relationship between the expenses incurred and the Federal awards to which they are allocated in accordance with applicable requirements.

I declare that the foregoing is true and correct.

Nonprofit Organization: _____
Signature: _____
Name of Official: _____
Title: _____
Date of Execution: _____

[78 FR 78608, Dec. 26, 2013, as amended at 80 FR 54410, Sept. 10, 2015]

APPENDIX V TO PART 200—STATE/LOCAL GOVERNMENTWIDE CENTRAL SERVICE COST ALLOCATION PLANS

A. GENERAL

1. Most governmental units provide certain services, such as motor pools, computer centers, purchasing, accounting, etc., to operating agencies on a centralized basis. Since federally-supported awards are performed within the individual operating agencies, there needs to be a process whereby these central service costs can be identified and assigned to benefitted activities on a reasonable and consistent basis. The central service cost allocation plan provides that process. All costs and other data used to distribute the costs included in the plan should be supported by formal accounting and other

records that will support the propriety of the costs assigned to Federal awards.

2. Guidelines and illustrations of central service cost allocation plans are provided in a brochure published by the Department of Health and Human Services entitled "*A Guide for State, Local and Indian Tribal Governments: Cost Principles and Procedures for Developing Cost Allocation Plans and Indirect Cost Rates for Agreements with the Federal Government.*" A copy of this brochure may be obtained from the HHS Cost Allocation Services or at their Web site at *https://rates.psc.gov.*

## B. DEFINITIONS

1. *Agency or operating agency* means an organizational unit or sub-division within a governmental unit that is responsible for the performance or administration of Federal awards or activities of the governmental unit.

2. *Allocated central services* means central services that benefit operating agencies but are not billed to the agencies on a fee-for-service or similar basis. These costs are allocated to benefitted agencies on some reasonable basis. Examples of such services might include general accounting, personnel administration, purchasing, etc.

3. *Billed central services* means central services that are billed to benefitted agencies or programs on an individual fee-for-service or similar basis. Typical examples of billed central services include computer services, transportation services, insurance, and fringe benefits.

4. *Cognizant agency for indirect costs* is defined in § 200.19 Cognizant agency for indirect costs of this Part. The determination of cognizant agency for indirect costs for states and local governments is described in section F.1, Negotiation and Approval of Central Service Plans.

5. *Major local government* means local government that receives more than $100 million in direct Federal awards subject to this Part.

## C. SCOPE OF THE CENTRAL SERVICE COST ALLOCATION PLANS

The central service cost allocation plan will include all central service costs that will be claimed (either as a billed or an allocated cost) under Federal awards and will be documented as described in section E. Costs of central services omitted from the plan will not be reimbursed.

## D. SUBMISSION REQUIREMENTS

1. Each state will submit a plan to the Department of Health and Human Services for each year in which it claims central service costs under Federal awards. The plan should include (a) a projection of the next year's allocated central service cost (based either on actual costs for the most recently completed year or the budget projection for the coming year), and (b) a reconciliation of actual allocated central service costs to the estimated costs used for either the most recently completed year or the year immediately preceding the most recently completed year.

2. Each major local government is also required to submit a plan to its cognizant agency for indirect costs annually.

3. All other local governments claiming central service costs must develop a plan in accordance with the requirements described in this Part and maintain the plan and related supporting documentation for audit. These local governments are not required to submit their plans for Federal approval unless they are specifically requested to do so by the cognizant agency for indirect costs. Where a local government only receives funds as a subrecipient, the pass-through entity will be responsible for monitoring the subrecipient's plan.

4. All central service cost allocation plans will be prepared and, when required, submitted within six months prior to the beginning of each of the governmental unit's fiscal years in which it proposes to claim central service costs. Extensions may be granted by the cognizant agency for indirect costs on a case-by-case basis.

## E. DOCUMENTATION REQUIREMENTS FOR SUBMITTED PLANS

The documentation requirements described in this section may be modified, expanded, or reduced by the cognizant agency for indirect costs on a case-by-case basis. For example, the requirements may be reduced for those central services which have little or no impact on Federal awards. Conversely, if a review of a plan indicates that certain additional information is needed, and will likely be needed in future years, it may be routinely requested in future plan submissions. Items marked with an asterisk (*) should be submitted only once; subsequent plans should merely indicate any changes since the last plan.

### 1. General

All proposed plans must be accompanied by the following: an organization chart sufficiently detailed to show operations including the central service activities of the state/local government whether or not they are shown as benefitting from central service functions; a copy of the Comprehensive Annual Financial Report (or a copy of the Executive Budget if budgeted costs are being proposed) to support the allowable costs of each central service activity included in the plan; and, a certification (see subsection 4.) that the plan was prepared in accordance with this Part, contains only allowable costs, and was prepared in a manner that treated similar costs consistently among the various

Federal awards and between Federal and non-Federal awards/activities.

## 2. Allocated Central Services

For each allocated central service*, the plan must also include the following: a brief description of the service, an identification of the unit rendering the service and the operating agencies receiving the service, the items of expense included in the cost of the service, the method used to distribute the cost of the service to benefitted agencies, and a summary schedule showing the allocation of each service to the specific benefitted agencies. If any self-insurance funds or fringe benefits costs are treated as allocated (rather than billed) central services, documentation discussed in subsections 3.b. and c. must also be included.

## 3. Billed Services

a. *General.* The information described in this section must be provided for all billed central services, including internal service funds, self-insurance funds, and fringe benefit funds.

b. Internal service funds.

(1) For each internal service fund or similar activity with an operating budget of $5 million or more, the plan must include: a brief description of each service; a balance sheet for each fund based on individual accounts contained in the governmental unit's accounting system; a revenue/expenses statement, with revenues broken out by source, e.g., regular billings, interest earned, etc.; a listing of all non-operating transfers (as defined by Generally Accepted Accounting Principles (GAAP)) into and out of the fund; a description of the procedures (methodology) used to charge the costs of each service to users, including how billing rates are determined; a schedule of current rates; and, a schedule comparing total revenues (including imputed revenues) generated by the service to the allowable costs of the service, as determined under this Part, with an explanation of how variances will be handled.

(2) Revenues must consist of all revenues generated by the service, including unbilled and uncollected revenues. If some users were not billed for the services (or were not billed at the full rate for that class of users), a schedule showing the full imputed revenues associated with these users must be provided. Expenses must be broken out by object cost categories (e.g., salaries, supplies, etc.).

c. *Self-insurance funds.* For each self-insurance fund, the plan must include: the fund balance sheet; a statement of revenue and expenses including a summary of billings and claims paid by agency; a listing of all non-operating transfers into and out of the fund; the type(s) of risk(s) covered by the fund; the type(s) of risk(s) covered by the fund (e.g., automobile liability, workers'

compensation, etc.); an explanation of how the level of fund contributions are determined, including a copy of the current actuarial report (with the actuarial assumptions used) if the contributions are determined on an actuarial basis; and, a description of the procedures used to charge or allocate fund contributions to benefitted activities. Reserve levels in excess of claims (1) submitted and adjudicated but not paid, (2) submitted but not adjudicated, and (3) incurred but not submitted must be identified and explained.

d. *Fringe benefits.* For fringe benefit costs, the plan must include: a listing of fringe benefits provided to covered employees, and the overall annual cost of each type of benefit; current fringe benefit policies; and procedures used to charge or allocate the costs of the benefits to benefitted activities. In addition, for pension and post-retirement health insurance plans, the following information must be provided: the governmental unit's funding policies, e.g., legislative bills, trust agreements, or state-mandated contribution rules, if different from actuarially determined rates; the pension plan's costs accrued for the year; the amount funded, and date(s) of funding; a copy of the current actuarial report (including the actuarial assumptions); the plan trustee's report; and, a schedule from the activity showing the value of the interest cost associated with late funding.

## 4. Required Certification

Each central service cost allocation plan will be accompanied by a certification in the following form:

### CERTIFICATE OF COST ALLOCATION PLAN

This is to certify that I have reviewed the cost allocation plan submitted herewith and to the best of my knowledge and belief:

(1) All costs included in this proposal [identify date] to establish cost allocations or billings for [identify period covered by plan] are allowable in accordance with the requirements of this Part and the Federal award(s) to which they apply. Unallowable costs have been adjusted for in allocating costs as indicated in the cost allocation plan.

(2) All costs included in this proposal are properly allocable to Federal awards on the basis of a beneficial or causal relationship between the expenses incurred and the Federal awards to which they are allocated in accordance with applicable requirements. Further, the same costs that have been treated as indirect costs have not been claimed as direct costs. Similar types of costs have been accounted for consistently.

I declare that the foregoing is true and correct.

Governmental Unit: _____
Signature: _____
Name of Official: _____

Title: _____

Date of Execution: _____

### F. NEGOTIATION AND APPROVAL OF CENTRAL SERVICE PLANS

#### 1. Federal Cognizant Agency for Indirect Costs Assignments for Cost Negotiation

In general, unless different arrangements are agreed to by the concerned Federal agencies, for central service cost allocation plans, the cognizant agency responsible for review and approval is the Federal agency with the largest dollar value of total Federal awards with a governmental unit. For indirect cost rates and departmental indirect cost allocation plans, the cognizant agency is the Federal agency with the largest dollar value of direct Federal awards with a governmental unit or component, as appropriate. Once designated as the cognizant agency for indirect costs, the Federal agency must remain so for a period of five years. In addition, the following Federal agencies continue to be responsible for the indicated governmental entities:

*Department of Health and Human Services*—Public assistance and state-wide cost allocation plans for all states (including the District of Columbia and Puerto Rico), state and local hospitals, libraries and health districts.

*Department of the Interior*—Indian tribal governments, territorial governments, and state and local park and recreational districts.

*Department of Labor*—State and local labor departments.

*Department of' Education*—School districts and state and local education agencies.

*Department of Agriculture*—State and local agriculture departments.

*Department of Transportation*—State and local airport and port authorities and transit districts.

*Department of Commerce*—State and local economic development districts.

*Department of Housing and Urban Development*—State and local housing and development districts.

*Environmental Protection Agency*—State and local water and sewer districts.

#### 2. Review

All proposed central service cost allocation plans that are required to be submitted will be reviewed, negotiated, and approved by the cognizant agency for indirect costs on a timely basis. The cognizant agency for indirect costs will review the proposal within six months of receipt of the proposal and either negotiate/approve the proposal or advise the governmental unit of the additional documentation needed to support/evaluate the proposed plan or the changes required to make the proposal acceptable. Once an agreement with the governmental unit has

been reached, the agreement will be accepted and used by all Federal agencies, unless prohibited or limited by statute. Where a Federal awarding agency has reason to believe that special operating factors affecting its Federal awards necessitate special consideration, the funding agency will, prior to the time the plans are negotiated, notify the cognizant agency for indirect costs.

#### 3. Agreement

The results of each negotiation must be formalized in a written agreement between the cognizant agency for indirect costs and the governmental unit. This agreement will be subject to re-opening if the agreement is subsequently found to violate a statute or the information upon which the plan was negotiated is later found to be materially incomplete or inaccurate. The results of the negotiation must be made available to all Federal agencies for their use.

#### 4. Adjustments

Negotiated cost allocation plans based on a proposal later found to have included costs that: (a) are unallowable (i) as specified by law or regulation, (ii) as identified in subpart F, General Provisions for selected Items of Cost of this Part, or (iii) by the terms and conditions of Federal awards, or (b) are unallowable because they are clearly not allocable to Federal awards, must be adjusted, or a refund must be made at the option of the cognizant agency for indirect costs, including earned or imputed interest from the date of transfer and debt interest, if applicable, chargeable in accordance with applicable Federal cognizant agency for indirect costs regulations. Adjustments or cash refunds may include, at the option of the cognizant agency for indirect costs, earned or imputed interest from the date of expenditure and delinquent debt interest, if applicable, chargeable in accordance with applicable cognizant agency claims collection regulations. These adjustments or refunds are designed to correct the plans and do not constitute a re-opening of the negotiation.

### G. OTHER POLICIES

#### 1. Billed Central Service Activities

Each billed central service activity must separately account for all revenues (including imputed revenues) generated by the service, expenses incurred to furnish the service, and profit/loss.

#### 2. Working Capital Reserves

Internal service funds are dependent upon a reasonable level of working capital reserve to operate from one billing cycle to the next. Charges by an internal service activity to

provide for the establishment and maintenance of a reasonable level of working capital reserve, in addition to the full recovery
of costs, are allowable. A working capital reserve as part of retained earnings of up to 60
calendar days cash expenses for normal operating purposes is considered reasonable. A
working capital reserve exceeding 60 calendar days may be approved by the cognizant agency for indirect costs in exceptional cases.

*3. Carry-Forward Adjustments of Allocated
Central Service Costs*

Allocated central service costs are usually
negotiated and approved for a future fiscal
year on a "fixed with carry-forward" basis.
Under this procedure, the fixed amounts for
the future year covered by agreement are
not subject to adjustment for that year.
However, when the actual costs of the year
involved become known, the differences between the fixed amounts previously approved
and the actual costs will be carried forward
and used as an adjustment to the fixed
amounts established for a later year. This
"carry-forward" procedure applies to all central services whose costs were fixed in the
approved plan. However, a carry-forward adjustment is not permitted, for a central service activity that was not included in the approved plan, or for unallowable costs that
must be reimbursed immediately.

*4. Adjustments of Billed Central Services*

Billing rates used to charge Federal awards
must be based on the estimated costs of providing the services, including an estimate of
the allocable central service costs. A comparison of the revenue generated by each
billed service (including total revenues
whether or not billed or collected) to the actual allowable costs of the service will be
made at least annually, and an adjustment
will be made for the difference between the
revenue and the allowable costs. These adjustments will be made through one of the
following adjustment methods: (a) a cash refund including earned or imputed interest
from the date of transfer and debt interest, if
applicable, chargeable in accordance with
applicable Federal cognizant agency for indirect costs regulations to the Federal Government for the Federal share of the adjustment, (b) credits to the amounts charged to
the individual programs, (c) adjustments to
future billing rates, or (d) adjustments to allocated central service costs. Adjustments to
allocated central services will not be permitted where the total amount of the adjustment for a particular service (Federal share
and non-Federal) share exceeds $500,000. Ad-
justment methods may include, at the option
of the cognizant agency, earned or imputed
interest from the date of expenditure and delinquent debt interest, if applicable, charge-

able in accordance with applicable cognizant
agency claims collection regulations.

*5. Records Retention*

All central service cost allocation plans
and related documentation used as a basis
for claiming costs under Federal awards
must be retained for audit in accordance
with the records retention requirements contained in Subpart D—Post Federal Award
Requirements, of Part 200.

*6. Appeals*

If a dispute arises in the negotiation of a
plan between the cognizant agency for indirect costs and the governmental unit, the
dispute must be resolved in accordance with
the appeals procedures of the cognizant
agency for indirect costs.

*7. OMB Assistance*

To the extent that problems are encountered among the Federal agencies or governmental units in connection with the negotiation and approval process, OMB will lend assistance, as required, to resolve such problems in a timely manner.

[78 FR 78608, Dec. 26, 2013, as amended at 80
FR 54410, Sept. 10, 2015]

APPENDIX VI TO PART 200—PUBLIC
ASSISTANCE COST ALLOCATION PLANS

A. GENERAL

Federally-financed programs administered
by state public assistance agencies are funded predominately by the Department of
Health and Human Services (HHS). In support of its stewardship requirements, HHS
has published requirements for the development, documentation, submission, negotiation, and approval of public assistance cost
allocation plans in Subpart E of 45 CFR Part
95. All administrative costs (direct and indirect) are normally charged to Federal awards
by implementing the public assistance cost
allocation plan. This Appendix extends these
requirements to all Federal awarding agencies whose programs are administered by a
state public assistance agency. Major federally-financed programs typically administered by state public assistance agencies include: Temporary Aid to Needy Families
(TANF), Medicaid, Food Stamps, Child Support Enforcement, Adoption Assistance and
Foster Care, and Social Services Block
Grant.

B. DEFINITIONS

1. *State public assistance agency* means a
state agency administering or supervising
the administration of one or more public assistance programs operated by the state as
identified in Subpart E of 45 CFR Part 95.

For the purpose of this Appendix, these programs include all programs administered by the state public assistance agency.

2. *State public assistance agency costs* means all costs incurred by, or allocable to, the state public assistance agency, except expenditures for financial assistance, medical contractor payments, food stamps, and payments for services and goods provided directly to program recipients.

### C. POLICY

State public assistance agencies will develop, document and implement, and the Federal Government will review, negotiate, and approve, public assistance cost allocation plans in accordance with Subpart E of 45 CFR Part 95. The plan will include all programs administered by the state public assistance agency. Where a letter of approval or disapproval is transmitted to a state public assistance agency in accordance with Subpart E, the letter will apply to all Federal agencies and programs. The remaining sections of this Appendix (except for the requirement for certification) summarize the provisions of Subpart E of 45 CFR Part 95.

### D. SUBMISSION, DOCUMENTATION, AND APPROVAL OF PUBLIC ASSISTANCE COST ALLOCATION PLANS

1. State public assistance agencies are required to promptly submit amendments to the cost allocation plan to HHS for review and approval.

2. Under the coordination process outlined in section E, Review of Implementation of Approved Plans, affected Federal agencies will review all new plans and plan amendments and provide comments, as appropriate, to HHS. The effective date of the plan or plan amendment will be the first day of the calendar quarter following the event that required the amendment, unless another date is specifically approved by HHS. HHS, as the cognizant agency for indirect costs acting on behalf of all affected Federal agencies, will, as necessary, conduct negotiations with the state public assistance agency and will inform the state agency of the action taken on the plan or plan amendment.

### E. REVIEW OF IMPLEMENTATION OF APPROVED PLANS

1. Since public assistance cost allocation plans are of a narrative nature, the review during the plan approval process consists of evaluating the appropriateness of the proposed groupings of costs (cost centers) and the related allocation bases. As such, the Federal Government needs some assurance that the cost allocation plan has been implemented as approved. This is accomplished by reviews by the Federal awarding agencies, single audits, or audits conducted by the cognizant agency for indirect costs.

2. Where inappropriate charges affecting more than one Federal awarding agency are identified, the cognizant HHS cost negotiation office will be advised and will take the lead in resolving the issue(s) as provided for in Subpart E of 45 CFR Part 95.

3. If a dispute arises in the negotiation of a plan or from a disallowance involving two or more Federal awarding agencies, the dispute must be resolved in accordance with the appeals procedures set out in 45 CFR Part 16. Disputes involving only one Federal awarding agency will be resolved in accordance with the Federal awarding agency's appeal process.

4. To the extent that problems are encountered among the Federal awarding agencies or governmental units in connection with the negotiation and approval process, the Office of Management and Budget will lend assistance, as required, to resolve such problems in a timely manner.

### F. UNALLOWABLE COSTS

Claims developed under approved cost allocation plans will be based on allowable costs as identified in this Part. Where unallowable costs have been claimed and reimbursed, they will be refunded to the program that reimbursed the unallowable cost using one of the following methods: (a) a cash refund, (b) offset to a subsequent claim, or (c) credits to the amounts charged to individual Federal awards. Cash refunds, offsets, and credits may include at the option of the cognizant agency for indirect cost, earned or imputed interest from the date of expenditure and delinquent debt interest, if applicable, chargeable in accordance with applicable cognizant agency for indirect cost claims collection regulations.

### APPENDIX VII TO PART 200—STATES AND LOCAL GOVERNMENT AND INDIAN TRIBE INDIRECT COST PROPOSALS

#### A. GENERAL

1. Indirect costs are those that have been incurred for common or joint purposes. These costs benefit more than one cost objective and cannot be readily identified with a particular final cost objective without effort disproportionate to the results achieved. After direct costs have been determined and assigned directly to Federal awards and other activities as appropriate, indirect costs are those remaining to be allocated to benefitted cost objectives. A cost may not be allocated to a Federal award as an indirect cost if any other cost incurred for the same purpose, in like circumstances, has been assigned to a Federal award as a direct cost.

2. Indirect costs include (a) the indirect costs originating in each department or agency of the governmental unit carrying

out Federal awards and (b) the costs of central governmental services distributed through the central service cost allocation plan (as described in Appendix V to Part 200—State/Local Government and Indian Tribe-Wide Central Service Cost Allocation Plans) and not otherwise treated as direct costs.

3. Indirect costs are normally charged to Federal awards by the use of an indirect cost rate. A separate indirect cost rate(s) is usually necessary for each department or agency of the governmental unit claiming indirect costs under Federal awards. Guidelines and illustrations of indirect cost proposals are provided in a brochure published by the Department of Health and Human Services entitled "*A Guide for States and Local Government Agencies: Cost Principles and Procedures for Establishing Cost Allocation Plans and Indirect Cost Rates for Grants and Contracts with the Federal Government.*" A copy of this brochure may be obtained from HHS Cost Allocation Services or at their Web site at *https://rates.psc.gov.*

4. Because of the diverse characteristics and accounting practices of governmental units, the types of costs which may be classified as indirect costs cannot be specified in all situations. However, typical examples of indirect costs may include certain state/local-wide central service costs, general administration of the non-Federal entity accounting and personnel services performed within the non-Federal entity, depreciation on buildings and equipment, the costs of operating and maintaining facilities.

5. This Appendix does not apply to state public assistance agencies. These agencies should refer instead to Appendix VI to Part 200—Public Assistance Cost Allocation Plans.

### B. DEFINITIONS

1. *Base* means the accumulated direct costs (normally either total direct salaries and wages or total direct costs exclusive of any extraordinary or distorting expenditures) used to distribute indirect costs to individual Federal awards. The direct cost base selected should result in each Federal award bearing a fair share of the indirect costs in reasonable relation to the benefits received from the costs.

2. *Base period* for the allocation of indirect costs is the period in which such costs are incurred and accumulated for allocation to activities performed in that period. The base period normally should coincide with the governmental unit's fiscal year, but in any event, must be so selected as to avoid inequities in the allocation of costs.

3. *Cognizant agency for indirect costs* means the Federal agency responsible for reviewing and approving the governmental unit's indirect cost rate(s) on the behalf of the Federal Government. The cognizant agency for indirect costs assignment is described in Appendix V, section F, Negotiation and Approval of Central Service Plans.

4. *Final rate* means an indirect cost rate applicable to a specified past period which is based on the actual allowable costs of the period. A final audited rate is not subject to adjustment.

5. *Fixed rate* means an indirect cost rate which has the same characteristics as a predetermined rate, except that the difference between the estimated costs and the actual, allowable costs of the period covered by the rate is carried forward as an adjustment to the rate computation of a subsequent period.

6. *Indirect cost pool* is the accumulated costs that jointly benefit two or more programs or other cost objectives.

7. *Indirect cost rate* is a device for determining in a reasonable manner the proportion of indirect costs each program should bear. It is the ratio (expressed as a percentage) of the indirect costs to a direct cost base.

8. *Indirect cost rate proposal* means the documentation prepared by a governmental unit or subdivision thereof to substantiate its request for the establishment of an indirect cost rate.

9. *Predetermined rate* means an indirect cost rate, applicable to a specified current or future period, usually the governmental unit's fiscal year. This rate is based on an estimate of the costs to be incurred during the period. Except under very unusual circumstances, a predetermined rate is not subject to adjustment. (Because of legal constraints, predetermined rates are not permitted for Federal contracts; they may, however, be used for grants or cooperative agreements.) Predetermined rates may not be used by governmental units that have not submitted and negotiated the rate with the cognizant agency for indirect costs. In view of the potential advantages offered by this procedure, negotiation of predetermined rates for indirect costs for a period of two to four years should be the norm in those situations where the cost experience and other pertinent facts available are deemed sufficient to enable the parties involved to reach an informed judgment as to the probable level of indirect costs during the ensuing accounting periods.

10. *Provisional rate* means a temporary indirect cost rate applicable to a specified period which is used for funding, interim reimbursement, and reporting indirect costs on Federal awards pending the establishment of a "final" rate for that period.

### C. ALLOCATION OF INDIRECT COSTS AND DETERMINATION OF INDIRECT COST RATES

#### 1. General

a. Where a governmental unit's department or agency has only one major function, or where all its major functions benefit from the indirect costs to approximately the same degree, the allocation of indirect costs and the computation of an indirect cost rate may be accomplished through simplified allocation procedures as described in subsection 2.

b. Where a governmental unit's department or agency has several major functions which benefit from its indirect costs in varying degrees, the allocation of indirect costs may require the accumulation of such costs into separate cost groupings which then are allocated individually to benefitted functions by means of a base which best measures the relative degree of benefit. The indirect costs allocated to each function are then distributed to individual Federal awards and other activities included in that function by means of an indirect cost rate(s).

c. Specific methods for allocating indirect costs and computing indirect cost rates along with the conditions under which each method should be used are described in subsections 2, 3 and 4.

*2. Simplified Method*

a. Where a non-Federal entity's major functions benefit from its indirect costs to approximately the same degree, the allocation of indirect costs may be accomplished by (1) classifying the non-Federal entity's total costs for the base period as either direct or indirect, and (2) dividing the total allowable indirect costs (net of applicable credits) by an equitable distribution base. The result of this process is an indirect cost rate which is used to distribute indirect costs to individual Federal awards. The rate should be expressed as the percentage which the total amount of allowable indirect costs bears to the base selected. This method should also be used where a governmental unit's department or agency has only one major function encompassing a number of individual projects or activities, and may be used where the level of Federal awards to that department or agency is relatively small.

b. Both the direct costs and the indirect costs must exclude capital expenditures and unallowable costs. However, unallowable costs must be included in the direct costs if they represent activities to which indirect costs are properly allocable.

c. The distribution base may be (1) total direct costs (excluding capital expenditures and other distorting items, such as pass-through funds, subcontracts in excess of $25,000, participant support costs, etc.), (2) direct salaries and wages, or (3) another base which results in an equitable distribution.

*3. Multiple Allocation Base Method*

a. Where a non-Federal entity's indirect costs benefit its major functions in varying degrees, such costs must be accumulated into separate cost groupings. Each grouping must then be allocated individually to benefitted functions by means of a base which best measures the relative benefits.

b. The cost groupings should be established so as to permit the allocation of each grouping on the basis of benefits provided to the major functions. Each grouping should constitute a pool of expenses that are of like character in terms of the functions they benefit and in terms of the allocation base which best measures the relative benefits provided to each function. The number of separate groupings should be held within practical limits, taking into consideration the materiality of the amounts involved and the degree of precision needed.

c. Actual conditions must be taken into account in selecting the base to be used in allocating the expenses in each grouping to benefitted functions. When an allocation can be made by assignment of a cost grouping directly to the function benefitted, the allocation must be made in that manner. When the expenses in a grouping are more general in nature, the allocation should be made through the use of a selected base which produces results that are equitable to both the Federal Government and the governmental unit. In general, any cost element or related factor associated with the governmental unit's activities is potentially adaptable for use as an allocation base provided that: (1) it can readily be expressed in terms of dollars or other quantitative measures (total direct costs, direct salaries and wages, staff hours applied, square feet used, hours of usage, number of documents processed, population served, and the like), and (2) it is common to the benefitted functions during the base period.

d. Except where a special indirect cost rate(s) is required in accordance with paragraph (C)(4) of this Appendix, the separate groupings of indirect costs allocated to each major function must be aggregated and treated as a common pool for that function. The costs in the common pool must then be distributed to individual Federal awards included in that function by use of a single indirect cost rate.

e. The distribution base used in computing the indirect cost rate for each function may be (1) total direct costs (excluding capital expenditures and other distorting items such as pass-through funds, subawards in excess of $25,000, participant support costs, etc.), (2) direct salaries and wages, or (3) another base which results in an equitable distribution. An indirect cost rate should be developed for each separate indirect cost pool developed. The rate in each case should be stated as the percentage relationship between the particular indirect cost pool and the distribution base identified with that pool.

*4. Special Indirect Cost Rates*

a. In some instances, a single indirect cost rate for all activities of a non-Federal entity or for each major function of the agency may not be appropriate. It may not take into account those different factors which may substantially affect the indirect costs applicable to a particular program or group of programs. The factors may include the physical location of the work, the level of administrative support required, the nature of the facilities or other resources employed, the organizational arrangements used, or any combination thereof. When a particular Federal award is carried out in an environment which appears to generate a significantly different level of indirect costs, provisions should be made for a separate indirect cost pool applicable to that Federal award. The separate indirect cost pool should be developed during the course of the regular allocation process, and the separate indirect cost rate resulting therefrom should be used, provided that: (1) The rate differs significantly from the rate which would have been developed under paragraphs (C)(2) and (C)(3) of this Appendix, and (2) the Federal award to which the rate would apply is material in amount.

b. Where Federal statutes restrict the reimbursement of certain indirect costs, it may be necessary to develop a special rate for the affected Federal award. Where a "restricted rate" is required, the same procedure for developing a non-restricted rate will be used except for the additional step of the elimination from the indirect cost pool those costs for which the law prohibits reimbursement.

D. SUBMISSION AND DOCUMENTATION OF PROPOSALS

*1. Submission of Indirect Cost Rate Proposals*

a. All departments or agencies of the governmental unit desiring to claim indirect costs under Federal awards must prepare an indirect cost rate proposal and related documentation to support those costs. The proposal and related documentation must be retained for audit in accordance with the records retention requirements contained in § 200.333 Retention Requirements for Records.

b. A governmental department or agency unit that receives more than $35 million in direct Federal funding must submit its indirect cost rate proposal to its cognizant agency for indirect costs. Other governmental department or agency must develop an indirect cost proposal in accordance with the requirements of this Part and maintain the proposal and related supporting documentation for audit. These governmental departments or agencies are not required to submit their proposals unless they are specifically requested to do so by the cognizant agency for

indirect costs. Where a non-Federal entity only receives funds as a subrecipient, the pass-through entity will be responsible for negotiating and/or monitoring the subrecipient's indirect costs.

c. Each Indian tribal government desiring reimbursement of indirect costs must submit its indirect cost proposal to the Department of the Interior (its cognizant agency for indirect costs).

d. Indirect cost proposals must be developed (and, when required, submitted) within six months after the close of the governmental unit's fiscal year, unless an exception is approved by the cognizant agency for indirect costs. If the proposed central service cost allocation plan for the same period has not been approved by that time, the indirect cost proposal may be prepared including an amount for central services that is based on the latest federally-approved central service cost allocation plan. The difference between these central service amounts and the amounts ultimately approved will be compensated for by an adjustment in a subsequent period.

*2. Documentation of Proposals*

The following must be included with each indirect cost proposal:

a. The rates proposed, including subsidiary work sheets and other relevant data, cross referenced and reconciled to the financial data noted in subsection b. Allocated central service costs will be supported by the summary table included in the approved central service cost allocation plan. This summary table is not required to be submitted with the indirect cost proposal if the central service cost allocation plan for the same fiscal year has been approved by the cognizant agency for indirect costs and is available to the funding agency.

b. A copy of the financial data (financial statements, comprehensive annual financial report, executive budgets, accounting reports, etc.) upon which the rate is based. Adjustments resulting from the use of unaudited data will be recognized, where appropriate, by the Federal cognizant agency for indirect costs in a subsequent proposal.

c. The approximate amount of direct base costs incurred under Federal awards. These costs should be broken out between salaries and wages and other direct costs.

d. A chart showing the organizational structure of the agency during the period for which the proposal applies, along with a functional statement(s) noting the duties and/or responsibilities of all units that comprise the agency. (Once this is submitted, only revisions need be submitted with subsequent proposals.)

## 3. *Required certification.*

Each indirect cost rate proposal must be accompanied by a certification in the following form:

CERTIFICATE OF INDIRECT COSTS

This is to certify that I have reviewed the indirect cost rate proposal submitted herewith and to the best of my knowledge and belief:

(1) All costs included in this proposal [identify date] to establish billing or final indirect costs rates for [identify period covered by rate] are allowable in accordance with the requirements of the Federal award(s) to which they apply and the provisions of this Part. Unallowable costs have been adjusted for in allocating costs as indicated in the indirect cost proposal

(2) All costs included in this proposal are properly allocable to Federal awards on the basis of a beneficial or causal relationship between the expenses incurred and the agreements to which they are allocated in accordance with applicable requirements. Further, the same costs that have been treated as indirect costs have not been claimed as direct costs. Similar types of costs have been accounted for consistently and the Federal Government will be notified of any accounting changes that would affect the predetermined rate.

I declare that the foregoing is true and correct.

Governmental Unit: _____
Signature: _____
Name of Official: _____
Title: _____
Date of Execution: _____

### E. NEGOTIATION AND APPROVAL OF RATES.

1. Indirect cost rates will be reviewed, negotiated, and approved by the cognizant agency on a timely basis. Once a rate has been agreed upon, it will be accepted and used by all Federal agencies unless prohibited or limited by statute. Where a Federal awarding agency has reason to believe that special operating factors affecting its Federal awards necessitate special indirect cost rates, the funding agency will, prior to the time the rates are negotiated, notify the cognizant agency for indirect costs.

2. The use of predetermined rates, if allowed, is encouraged where the cognizant agency for indirect costs has reasonable assurance based on past experience and reliable projection of the non-Federal entity's costs, that the rate is not likely to exceed a rate based on actual costs. Long-term agreements utilizing predetermined rates extending over two or more years are encouraged, where appropriate.

3. The results of each negotiation must be formalized in a written agreement between the cognizant agency for indirect costs and the governmental unit. This agreement will be subject to re-opening if the agreement is subsequently found to violate a statute, or the information upon which the plan was negotiated is later found to be materially incomplete or inaccurate. The agreed upon rates must be made available to all Federal agencies for their use.

4. Refunds must be made if proposals are later found to have included costs that (a) are unallowable (i) as specified by law or regulation, (ii) as identified in § 200.420 Considerations for selected items of cost, of this Part, or (iii) by the terms and conditions of Federal awards, or (b) are unallowable because they are clearly not allocable to Federal awards. These adjustments or refunds will be made regardless of the type of rate negotiated (predetermined, final, fixed, or provisional).

### F. OTHER POLICIES

#### 1. *Fringe Benefit Rates*

If overall fringe benefit rates are not approved for the governmental unit as part of the central service cost allocation plan, these rates will be reviewed, negotiated and approved for individual recipient agencies during the indirect cost negotiation process. In these cases, a proposed fringe benefit rate computation should accompany the indirect cost proposal. If fringe benefit rates are not used at the recipient agency level (i.e., the agency specifically identifies fringe benefit costs to individual employees), the governmental unit should so advise the cognizant agency for indirect costs.

#### 2. *Billed Services Provided by the Recipient Agency*

In some cases, governmental departments or agencies (components of the governmental unit) provide and bill for services similar to those covered by central service cost allocation plans (e.g., computer centers). Where this occurs, the governmental departments or agencies (components of the governmental unit)should be guided by the requirements in Appendix V relating to the development of billing rates and documentation requirements, and should advise the cognizant agency for indirect costs of any billed services. Reviews of these types of services (including reviews of costing/billing methodology, profits or losses, etc.) will be made on a case-by-case basis as warranted by the circumstances involved.

#### 3. *Indirect Cost Allocations Not Using Rates*

In certain situations, governmental departments or agencies (components of the governmental unit), because of the nature of their Federal awards, may be required to develop a cost allocation plan that distributes indirect (and, in some cases, direct) costs to the specific funding sources. In these cases, a narrative cost allocation methodology should be developed, documented, maintained for audit, or submitted, as appropriate, to the cognizant agency for indirect costs for review, negotiation, and approval.

*4. Appeals*

If a dispute arises in a negotiation of an indirect cost rate (or other rate) between the cognizant agency for indirect costs and the governmental unit, the dispute must be resolved in accordance with the appeals procedures of the cognizant agency for indirect costs.

*5. Collection of Unallowable Costs and Erroneous Payments*

Costs specifically identified as unallowable and charged to Federal awards either directly or indirectly will be refunded (including interest chargeable in accordance with applicable Federal cognizant agency for indirect costs regulations).

*6. OMB Assistance*

To the extent that problems are encountered among the Federal agencies or governmental units in connection with the negotiation and approval process, OMB will lend assistance, as required, to resolve such problems in a timely manner.

[78 FR 78608, Dec. 26, 2013, as amended at 79 FR 75889, Dec. 19, 2014]

APPENDIX VIII TO PART 200—NONPROFIT ORGANIZATIONS EXEMPTED FROM SUBPART E—COST PRINCIPLES OF PART 200

1. Advance Technology Institute (ATI), Charleston, South Carolina
2. Aerospace Corporation, El Segundo, California
3. American Institutes of Research (AIR), Washington, DC
4. Argonne National Laboratory, Chicago, Illinois
5. Atomic Casualty Commission, Washington, DC
6. Battelle Memorial Institute, Headquartered in Columbus, Ohio
7. Brookhaven National Laboratory, Upton, New York
8. Charles Stark Draper Laboratory, Incorporated, Cambridge, Massachusetts
9. CNA Corporation (CNAC), Alexandria, Virginia
10. Environmental Institute of Michigan, Ann Arbor, Michigan
11. Georgia Institute of Technology/Georgia Tech Applied Research Corporation/Georgia Tech Research Institute, Atlanta, Georgia

12. Hanford Environmental Health Foundation, Richland, Washington
13. IIT Research Institute, Chicago, Illinois
14. Institute of Gas Technology, Chicago, Illinois
15. Institute for Defense Analysis, Alexandria, Virginia
16. LMI, McLean, Virginia
17. Mitre Corporation, Bedford, Massachusetts
18. Noblis, Inc., Falls Church, Virginia
19. National Radiological Astronomy Observatory, Green Bank, West Virginia
20. National Renewable Energy Laboratory, Golden, Colorado
21. Oak Ridge Associated Universities, Oak Ridge, Tennessee
22. Rand Corporation, Santa Monica, California
23. Research Triangle Institute, Research Triangle Park, North Carolina
24. Riverside Research Institute, New York, New York
25. South Carolina Research Authority (SCRA), Charleston, South Carolina
26. Southern Research Institute, Birmingham, Alabama
27. Southwest Research Institute, San Antonio, Texas
28. SRI International, Menlo Park, California
29. Syracuse Research Corporation, Syracuse, New York
30. Universities Research Association, Incorporated (National Accelerator Lab), Argonne, Illinois
31. Urban Institute, Washington DC
32. Non-profit insurance companies, such as Blue Cross and Blue Shield Organizations
33. Other non-profit organizations as negotiated with Federal awarding agencies

APPENDIX IX TO PART 200—HOSPITAL COST PRINCIPLES

Based on initial feedback, OMB proposes to establish a review process to consider existing hospital cost determine how best to update and align them with this Part. Until such time as revised guidance is proposed and implemented for hospitals, the existing principles located at 45 CFR Part 75 Appendix E, entitled "Principles for Determining Cost Applicable to Research and Development Under Grants and Contracts with Hospitals," remain in effect.

[78 FR 78608, Dec. 26, 2013, as amended at 79 FR 75889, Dec. 19, 2014]

APPENDIX X TO PART 200—DATA COLLECTION FORM (FORM SF–SAC)

The Data Collection Form SF–SAC is available on the FAC Web site.

APPENDIX XI TO PART 200—COMPLIANCE
SUPPLEMENT

The compliance supplement is available on
the OMB Web site: (e.g. for 2013 here *http://
www.whitehouse.gov/omb/circulars/*)

APPENDIX XII TO PART 200—AWARD
TERM AND CONDITION FOR RECIPIENT
INTEGRITY AND PERFORMANCE MAT-
TERS

A. REPORTING OF MATTERS RELATED TO
RECIPIENT INTEGRITY AND PERFORMANCE

*1. General Reporting Requirement*

If the total value of your currently active
grants, cooperative agreements, and procurement contracts from all Federal awarding
agencies exceeds $10,000,000 for any period of
time during the period of performance of this
Federal award, then you as the recipient during that period of time must maintain the
currency of information reported to the System for Award Management (SAM) that is
made available in the designated integrity
and performance system (currently the Federal Awardee Performance and Integrity Information System (FAPIIS)) about civil,
criminal, or administrative proceedings described in paragraph 2 of this award term
and condition. This is a statutory requirement under section 872 of Public Law 110–417,
as amended (41 U.S.C. 2313). As required by
section 3010 of Public Law 111–212, all information posted in the designated integrity
and performance system on or after April 15,
2011, except past performance reviews required for Federal procurement contracts,
will be publicly available.

*2. Proceedings About Which You Must Report*

Submit the information required about
each proceeding that:
a. Is in connection with the award or performance of a grant, cooperative agreement,
or procurement contract from the Federal
Government;
b. Reached its final disposition during the
most recent five year period; and
c. Is one of the following:
(1) A criminal proceeding that resulted in a
conviction, as defined in paragraph 5 of this
award term and condition;
(2) A civil proceeding that resulted in a
finding of fault and liability and payment of
a monetary fine, penalty, reimbursement,
restitution, or damages of $5,000 or more;
(3) An administrative proceeding, as defined in paragraph 5. of this award term and
condition, that resulted in a finding of fault
and liability and your payment of either a
monetary fine or penalty of $5,000 or more or
reimbursement, restitution, or damages in
excess of $100,000; or

(4) Any other criminal, civil, or administrative proceeding if:
(i) It could have led to an outcome described in paragraph 2.c.(1), (2), or (3) of this
award term and condition;
(ii) It had a different disposition arrived at
by consent or compromise with an acknowledgment of fault on your part; and
(iii) The requirement in this award term
and condition to disclose information about
the proceeding does not conflict with applicable laws and regulations.

*3. Reporting Procedures*

Enter in the SAM Entity Management area
the information that SAM requires about
each proceeding described in paragraph 2 of
this award term and condition. You do not
need to submit the information a second
time under assistance awards that you received if you already provided the information through SAM because you were required
to do so under Federal procurement contracts that you were awarded.

*4. Reporting Frequency*

During any period of time when you are
subject to the requirement in paragraph 1 of
this award term and condition, you must report proceedings information through SAM
for the most recent five year period, either
to report new information about any pro-
ceeding(s) that you have not reported previously or affirm that there is no new information to report. Recipients that have Federal contract, grant, and cooperative agreement awards with a cumulative total value
greater than $10,000,000 must disclose semi-
annually any information about the criminal, civil, and administrative proceedings.

*5. Definitions*

For purposes of this award term and condition:
a. Administrative proceeding means a non-
judicial process that is adjudicatory in nature in order to make a determination of
fault or liability (*e.g.*, Securities and Exchange Commission Administrative proceedings, Civilian Board of Contract Appeals
proceedings, and Armed Services Board of
Contract Appeals proceedings). This includes
proceedings at the Federal and State level
but only in connection with performance of a
Federal contract or grant. It does not include audits, site visits, corrective plans, or
inspection of deliverables.
b. Conviction, for purposes of this award
term and condition, means a judgment or
conviction of a criminal offense by any court
of competent jurisdiction, whether entered
upon a verdict or a plea, and includes a conviction entered upon a plea of nolo
contendere.

c. Total value of currently active grants, cooperative agreements, and procurement contracts includes—

(1) Only the Federal share of the funding under any Federal award with a recipient cost share or match; and

(2) The value of all expected funding increments under a Federal award and options, even if not yet exercised.

B. [Reserved]

[80 FR 43310, July 22, 2015]

## PARTS 201–299 [RESERVED]

# Subtitle B—Federal Agency Regulations for Grants and Agreements

# CHAPTER III—DEPARTMENT OF HEALTH AND HUMAN SERVICES

# PART 300—UNIFORM ADMINISTRATIVE REQUIREMENTS, COST PRINCIPLES, AND AUDIT REQUIREMENTS FOR FEDERAL AWARDS

AUTHORITY: 5 U.S.C. 301, 2 CFR part 200.

SOURCE: 79 FR 75889, Dec. 19, 2014, unless otherwise noted.

## § 300.1 Adoption of 2 CFR Part 200.

Under the authority listed above, the Department of Health and Human Services adopts the Office of Management and Budget (OMB) Guidance in 2 CFR part 200, and has codified the text, with HHS-specific amendments in 45 CFR part 75. Thus, this part gives regulatory effect to the OMB guidance and supplements the guidance as needed for the Department.

## PARTS 301–375 [RESERVED]

## PART 376—NONPROCUREMENT DEBARMENT AND SUSPENSION

AUTHORITY: 5 U.S.C. 301; 31 U.S.C. 6101 (note); E.O. 12689 (3 CFR, 1989 Comp., p. 235); E.O. 12549 (3 CFR, 1986 Comp., p. 189); E.O. 11738 (3 CFR, 1973 Comp., p. 799).

SOURCE: 72 FR 9234, Mar. 1, 2007, unless otherwise noted.

## § 376.10   What does this part do?

This part adopts the Office of Management and Budget (OMB) guidance in subparts A through I of 2 CFR part 180, as supplemented by this part, as the Department of Health and Human Services (HHS or Department) policies and procedures for nonprocurement debarment and suspension. HHS thereby gives regulatory effect to the OMB guidance as supplemented by this part. This part satisfies the requirements in 2 CFR 180.20, section 3 of Executive Order 12549, "Debarment and Suspension" (3 CFR 1986 Comp., p. 189), Executive Order 12689, "Debarment and Suspension" (3 CFR 1989 Comp., p. 235) and 31 U.S.C. 6101 note (Section 2455, Pub. L. 103–355, 108 Stat. 3327).

## § 376.20   Does this part apply to me?

This part and, through this part, pertinent portions of the OMB guidance in subparts A through I of 2 CFR part 180 (see table at 2 CFR 180.100(b)), apply to you if you are a—

(a) Participant or principal in a "covered transaction" under subpart B of 2 CFR part 180, as supplemented by this part, and the definition of non-procurement transaction" at 2 CFR 180.970.

(b) Respondent in HHS suspension or debarment action;

(c) HHS debarment or suspension official;

(d) HHS grants officer, agreements officer, or other HHS official authorized to enter into any type of non-procurement transaction that is a covered transaction.

### § 376.30 What policies and procedures must I follow?

The policies and procedures that you must follow are the policies and procedures specified in each applicable section of the OMB guidance in subparts A through I of 2 CFR part 180, including the corresponding section that HHS published in 2 CFR part 376 identified by the same section number. The contracts under a nonprocurement transaction, that are covered transactions, for example, are specified by section 220 of the OMB guidance (i.e., 2 CFR 180.220) as supplemented by section 220 in this part (i.e., 2 CFR 376.220). For any section of OMB guidance in subparts A through I of 2 CFR part 180 that has no corresponding section in this part, HHS policies and procedures are those in the OMB guidance at 2 CFR part 180.

## Subpart A—General

### § 376.137 Who in the Department of Health and Human Services (HHS) may grant an exception to let an excluded person participate in a covered transaction?

The HHS Debarring/Suspension Official has the authority to grant an exception to let an excluded person participate in a covered transaction as provided at 2 CFR 180.135.

### § 376.147 Does an exclusion from participation in Federal health care programs under Title XI of the Social Security Act affect a person's eligibility to participate in nonprocurement and procurement transactions?

Any individual or entity excluded from participation in Medicare, Medicaid, and other Federal health care programs under Title XI of the Social Security Act, 42 U.S.C. 1320a–7, 1320a–7a, 1320c–5, or 1395ccc, and implementing regulation at 42 CFR part 1001, will be subject to the prohibitions against participating in covered transactions, as set forth in this part and part 180, and is prohibited from participating in all Federal Government procurement programs and nonprocurement programs. For example, if an individual or entity is excluded by the HHS Office of the Inspector General from participation in Medicare, Medicaid, and/or other Federal health care programs, in accordance with 42 U.S.C. 1320a–7, then that individual or entity is prohibited from participating in all Federal Government procurement and nonprocurement programs (42 CFR part 1001).

## Subpart B—Covered Transactions

### § 376.220 What contracts and subcontracts, in addition to those listed in 2 CFR 180.220, are covered transactions?

In addition to the contracts covered under 2 CFR 180.220(b), this part also applies to all lower tiers of subcontracts under covered nonprocurement transactions, as permitted under the OMB guidance at 2 CFR 180.220(c). (See optional lower tier coverage in the diagram in the appendix to 2 CFR part 180.)

## Subpart C—Responsibilities of Participants Regarding Transactions

### § 376.332 What methods must I use to pass requirements down to participants at lower tiers with whom I intend to do business?

To communicate the requirements to lower-tier participants, you must include a term or condition in the lower-tier transaction requiring the lower-tier participant's compliance with 2 CFR part 180, as supplemented by this subpart.

### § 376.370 What are the obligations of Medicare carriers and inter-mediaries?

Because Medicare carriers, inter-mediaries and other Medicare contractors undertake responsibilities on behalf of the Medicare program (Title XVIII of the Social Security Act), these entities assume the same obligations and responsibilities as the HHS Medicare officials responsible for the Medicare Program with respect to actions under 2 CFR part 376. This would include the requirement for these entities to check the Excluded Parties List System (EPLS) and take necessary steps to effect this part.

## Subpart D—Responsibilities of Federal Agency Officials Regarding Transactions

### § 376.437 What method do I use to communicate to a participant the requirements described in the OMB guidance at 2 CFR 180.435?

To communicate to a participant the requirements described in 2 CFR 180.435, you must include a term or condition in the transaction that requires the participant's compliance with subpart C of 2 CFR part 180, as supplemented by subpart C of this part, and require the participant to include a similar term or condition in lower-tier covered transactions.

## Subpart E—Excluded Parties List System [Reserved]

## Subpart F—General Principles Relating to Suspension and Debarment Actions [Reserved]

## Subpart G—Suspension [Reserved]

## Subpart H—Debarment [Reserved]

## Subpart I—Definitions

### § 376.935 Disqualified. (HHS supplement to government-wide definition at 2 CFR 180.935).

*Disqualified* means persons prohibited from participating in specified federal procurement and nonprocurement transactions pursuant to the statutes listed in 2 CFR 180.935, and pursuant to Title XI of the Social Security Act (42 U.S.C. 1320a–7, 1320a–7a, 1320c–5, and 1395ccc) as enforced by the HHS Office of the Inspector General.

### § 376.995 Principal (HHS supplement to government-wide definition at 2 CFR 180.995).

*Principal* means individuals, in addition to those listed at 2 CFR 180.995, who participate in HHS covered transactions including:

(a) Providers of federally required audit services; and

(b) Researchers.

## Subpart J [Reserved]

## PART 382—REQUIREMENTS FOR DRUG-FREE WORKPLACE (FINANCIAL ASSISTANCE)

## Subpart E—Violations of This Part and Consequences

382.500 Who in HHS determines that a recipient other than an individual violated the requirements of this part?
382.505 Who in HHS determines that a recipient who is an individual violated the requirements of this part?

## Subpart F [Reserved]

AUTHORITY: 41 U.S.C. 701–707.

SOURCE: 74 FR 58190, Nov. 12, 2009, unless otherwise noted.

### § 382.10 What does this part do?

This part requires that the award and administration of HHS grants and cooperative agreements comply with Office of Management and Budget (OMB) guidance implementing the portion of the Drug-Free Workplace Act of 1988 (41 U.S.C. 701–707, as amended, hereafter referred to as "the Act") that applies to grants. It thereby—

(a) Gives regulatory effect to the OMB guidance (Subparts A through F of 2 CFR part 182) for the HHS grants and cooperative agreements; and

(b) Establishes HHS policies and procedures for compliance with the Act that are the same as those of other Federal agencies, in conformance with the requirement in 41 U.S.C. 705 for Governmentwide implementing regulations.

### § 382.20 Does this part apply to me?

This part and, through this part, pertinent portions of the OMB guidance in subparts A through F of 2 CFR part 182 (see table at 2 CFR 182.115(b)) apply to you if you are a—

(a) Recipient of an HHS grant or cooperative agreement; or

(b) HHS awarding official.

### § 382.30 What policies and procedures must I follow?

(a) *General.* You must follow the policies and procedures specified in applicable sections of the OMB guidance in subparts A through F of 2 CFR part 182, as implemented by this part.

(b) *Specific sections of OMB guidance that this part supplements.* In implementing the OMB guidance in 2 CFR part 182, this part supplements four sections of the guidance, as shown in the following table. For each of those sections, you must follow the policies and procedures in the OMB guidance, as supplemented by this part.

| Section of OMB guidance | Section in this part where supplemented | What the supplementation clarifies |
|---|---|---|
| (1) 2 CFR 182.225(a) | § 382.225 ............... | Whom in HHS a recipient other than an individual must notify if an employee is convicted for a violation of a criminal drug statute in the workplace. |
| (2) 2 CFR 182.300(b) | § 382.300 ............... | Whom in HHS a recipient who is an individual must notify if he or she is convicted of a criminal drug offense resulting from a violation occurring during the conduct of any award activity. |
| (3) 2 CFR 182.500 ... | § 382.500 ............... | Who in HHS is authorized to determine that a recipient other than an individual is in violation of the requirements of 2 CFR part 182, as implemented by this part. |
| (4) 2 CFR 182.505 ... | § 382.505 ............... | Who in HHS is authorized to determine that a recipient who is an individual is in violation of the requirements of 2 CFR part 182, as implemented by this part. |

(c) *Sections of the OMB guidance that this part does not supplement.* For any section of OMB guidance in subparts A through F of 2 CFR part 182 that is not listed in paragraph (b) of this section, HHS policies and procedures are the same as those in the OMB guidance.

## Subpart A [Reserved]

## Subpart B—Requirements for Recipients Other Than Individuals

### § 382.225 Whom in HHS does a recipient other than an individual notify about a criminal drug conviction?

A recipient other than an individual that is required under 2 CFR 182.225(a) to notify Federal agencies about an employee's conviction for a criminal drug offense must notify each HHS office from which it currently has an award.

## Subpart C—Requirements for Recipients Who Are Individuals

**§382.300  Whom in HHS does a recipient who is an individual notify about a criminal drug conviction?**

A recipient who is an individual and is required under 2 CFR 182.300(b) to notify Federal agencies about a conviction for a criminal drug offense must notify each HHS office from which it currently has an award.

## Subpart D—Responsibilities of Agency Awarding Officials

**§382.400  What method do I use as an agency awarding official to obtain a recipient's agreement to comply with the OMB guidance?**

To obtain a recipient's agreement to comply with applicable requirements in the OMB guidance at 2 CFR part 182, you must include the following term or condition in the award:

*Drug-free workplace.* You as the recipient must comply with drug-free workplace requirements in Subpart B (or Subpart C, if the recipient is an individual) of part 382, which adopts the Governmentwide implementation (2 CFR part 182) of sec. 5152–5158 of the Drug-Free Workplace Act of 1988 (Pub. L. 100–690, Title V, Subtitle D; 41 U.S.C. 701–707).

## Subpart E—Violations of This Part and Consequences

**§382.500  Who in HHS determines that a recipient other than an individual violated the requirements of this part?**

The agency head is the official authorized to make the determination under 2 CFR 182.500.

**§382.505  Who in HHS determines that a recipient who is an individual violated the requirements of this part?**

The agency head is the official authorized to make the determination under 2 CFR 182.505.

## Subpart F [Reserved]

## PARTS 383–399 [RESERVED]

# CHAPTER IV—DEPARTMENT OF AGRICULTURE

---

# PART 400—UNIFORM ADMINISTRATIVE REQUIREMENTS, COST PRINCIPLES, AND AUDIT REQUIREMENTS FOR FEDERAL AWARDS

Sec.
400.1  What does this part do?
400.2  Conflict of interest.

AUTHORITY: 31 U.S.C. 503.

SOURCE: 79 FR 75982, Dec. 19, 2014, unless otherwise noted.

## § 400.1  What does this part do?

This part adopts the OMB guidance in subparts A through F of 2 CFR part 200, as supplemented by this part, as USDA policies and procedures for uniform administrative requirements, cost principles, and audit requirements for Federal awards. It thereby gives regulatory effect for the USDA to the OMB guidance, as supplemented by this part.

## § 400.2  Conflict of interest.

(a) Each USDA awarding agency must establish conflict of interest policies for its Federal awards.

(b) Non-Federal entities must disclose in writing any potential conflicts of interest to the USDA awarding agency or pass-through entity.

(1) The non-Federal entity must maintain written standards of conduct covering conflicts of interest and governing the performance of its employees in the selection, award and administration of Federal awards. No employee, officer or agent may participate in the selection, award, or administration of a Federal award if he or she has a real or apparent conflict of interest. Such a conflict of interest would arise when the employee, officer, or agent, any member of his or her immediate family, his or her partner, or an organization which employs or is about to employ any of the parties indicated herein, has a financial or other interest in or a tangible personal benefit from a non-Federal entity considered for a Federal award. The non-Federal entity may set standards for situations in which the financial interest is not substantial or the gift is an unsolicited item of nominal value. The standards of conduct must provide for disciplinary actions to be applied for violations of such standards by officers, employees, or agents of the non-Federal entity.

(2) If the non-Federal entity has a parent, affiliate, or subsidiary organization that is not a state, local government, or Indian tribe, the non-Federal entity must also maintain written standards of conduct covering organizational conflicts of interest. Organizational conflicts of interest means that because of the relationships with a parent company, affiliate, or subsidiary organization, is unable or appears to be unable to be impartial in conducting a Federal award action involving a related organization.

# PARTS 401–414 [RESERVED]

# PART 415—GENERAL PROGRAM ADMINISTRATIVE REGULATIONS

## Subpart A—Application for Federal Assistance

Sec.
415.1  Competition in the awarding of discretionary grants and cooperative agreements.

## Subpart B—Miscellaneous

415.2  Acknowledgement of Support on Publications and Audiovisuals.

## Subpart C—Intergovernmental Review of Department of Agriculture Programs and Activities

415.3  Purpose.
415.4  Definitions.
415.5  Applicability.
415.6  Secretary's general responsibilities.
415.7  Federal interagency coordination.
415.8  State selection of programs and activities.
415.9  Communication with State and local elected officials.
415.10  State comments on proposed Federal financial assistance and direct Federal development.
415.11  Processing comments.
415.12  Accommodation of intergovernmental concerns.
415.13  Interstate situations.
415.14  Simplification, consolidation, or substitution of State plans.
415.15  Waivers.

AUTHORITY: 5 U.S.C. 301.

SOURCE: 79 FR 75982, Dec. 19, 2014, unless otherwise noted.

## Subpart A—Application for Federal Assistance

**§ 415.1 Competition in the awarding of discretionary grants and cooperative agreements.**

(a) *Standards for competition.* Except as provided in paragraph (d) of this section, awarding agencies shall enter into discretionary grants and cooperative agreements only after competition. An awarding agency's competitive award process shall adhere to the following standards:

(1) Potential applicants must be invited to submit proposals through publications such as the FEDERAL REGISTER, OMB-designated government-wide Web site as described in 2 CFR 200.203, professional trade journals, agency or program handbooks, the Catalog of Federal Domestic Assistance, or any other appropriate means of solicitation. In so doing, awarding agencies should consider the broadest dissemination of project solicitations in order to reach the highest number of potential applicants.

(2) Proposals are to be evaluated objectively by independent reviewers in accordance with written criteria set forth by the awarding agency. Reviewers should make written comments, as appropriate, on each application. Independent reviewers may be from the private sector, another agency, or within the awarding agency, as long as they do not include anyone who has approval authority for the applications being reviewed or anyone who might appear to have a conflict of interest in the role of reviewer of applications. A conflict of interest might arise when the reviewer or the reviewer's immediate family members have been associated with the applicant or applicant organization within the past two years as an owner, partner, officer, director, employee, or consultant; has any financial interest in the applicant or applicant organization; or is negotiating for, or has any arrangement, concerning prospective employment.

(3) An unsolicited application, which is not unique and innovative, shall be competed under the project solicitation it comes closest to fitting. Awarding agency officials will determine the solicitation under which the application is to be evaluated. When the awarding agency official decides that the unsolicited application does not fall under a recent, current, or planned solicitation, a noncompetitive award may be made, if appropriate to do so under the criteria of this section. Otherwise, the application should be returned to the applicant.

(b) *Project solicitations.* A project solicitation by the awarding agency shall include or reference the following, as appropriate:

(1) A description of the eligible activities which the awarding agency proposes to support and the program priorities;

(2) Eligible applicants;

(3) The dates and amounts of funds expected to be available for awards;

(4) Evaluation criteria and weights, if appropriate, assigned to each;

(5) Methods for evaluating and ranking applications;

(6) Name and address where proposals should be mailed or emailed and submission deadline(s);

(7) Any required forms and how to obtain them;

(8) Applicable cost principles and administrative requirements;

(9) Type of funding instrument intended to be used (grant or cooperative agreement); and

(10) The Catalog of Federal Domestic Assistance number and title.

(c) *Approval of applications.* The final decision to award is at the discretion of the awarding/approving official in each agency. The awarding/approving official shall consider the ranking, comments, and recommendations from the independent review group, and any other pertinent information before deciding which applications to approve and their order of approval. Any appeals by applicants regarding the award decision shall be handled by the awarding agency using existing agency appeal procedures or good administrative practice and sound business judgment.

(d) *Exceptions.* The awarding/approving official may make a determination in writing that competition is not deemed appropriate for a particular transaction. Such determination shall be limited to transactions where it can be adequately justified that a non-competitive award is in the best interest of the Government and necessary to the accomplishment of the goals of the program. Reasons for considering non-competitive awards may include, but are not necessarily limited to, the following:

(1) Nonmonetary awards of property or services;

(2) Awards of less than $75,000;

(3) Awards to fund continuing work already started under a previous award;

(4) Awards which cannot be delayed due to an emergency or a substantial danger to health or safety;

(5) Awards when it is impracticable to secure competition; or

(6) Awards to fund unique and innovative unsolicited applications.

## Subpart B—Miscellaneous

### §415.2 Acknowledgement of USDA Support on Publications and Audiovisuals.

(a) *Definitions.* (1) "Audiovisual" means a product containing visual imagery or sound or both. Examples of audiovisuals are motion pictures, live or prerecorded radio or television programs, slide shows, filmstrips, audio recordings, and multimedia presentations.

(2) "Production of an audiovisual" means any of the steps that lead to a finished audiovisual, including design, layout, script-writing, filming, editing, fabrication, sound recording or taping. The term does not include the placing of captions for the hearing impaired on films or videotapes not originally produced for use with the hearing impaired.

(3) "Publication" means a published book, periodical, pamphlet, brochure, flier, or similar item. It does not include any audiovisuals.

(b) *Publications.* Recipients shall have an acknowledgement of USDA awarding agency support placed on any publications written or published with grant support and, if feasible, on any publication reporting the results of, or describing, a grant-supported activity.

(c) *Audiovisuals.* Recipients shall have an acknowledgement of USDA awarding agency support placed on any audiovisual which is produced with grant support and which has a direct production cost to the recipient of over $5,000. Unless the other provisions of the grant award make it apply, this requirement does not apply to:

(1) Audiovisuals produced as research instruments or for documenting experimentation or findings and not intended for presentation or distribution to the general public.

(2) [Reserved]

(d) *Waivers.* USDA awarding agencies may waive any requirement of this section.

## Subpart C—Intergovernmental Review of Department of Agriculture Programs and Activities

### §415.3 Purpose.

(a) The regulations in this part implement Executive Order 12372, "Intergovernmental Review of Federal Programs", issued July 14, 1982, and amended on April 8, 1983. These regulations also implement applicable provisions of section 401 of the Intergovernmental Cooperation Act of 1968 and section 204 of the Demonstration Cities and Metropolitan Development Act of 1966.

(b) These regulations are intended to foster an intergovernmental partnership and a strengthened Federalism by relying on State processes and on State, areawide, regional and local coordination for review of proposed Federal financial assistance and direct Federal development.

(c) The regulations are intended to aid the internal management of the Department, and are not intended to create any right or benefit enforceable at law by a party against the Department or its officers.

### §415.4 Definitions.

As used in this part, the following definitions apply:

*Department* means the U.S. Department of Agriculture.

*Order* means Executive Order 12372, issued July 14, 1982, and amended April 8, 1983, and titled Intergovernmental Review of Federal Programs.

*Secretary* means the Secretary of the U.S. Department of Agriculture or an official or employee of the Department acting for the Secretary under a delegation of authority.

*State* means any of the 50 states, the District of Columbia, the Commonwealth of Puerto Rico, the Commonwealth of the Northern Mariana Islands, Guam, American Samoa, and the U.S. Virgin Islands.

## § 415.5 Applicability.

The Secretary publishes in the FEDERAL REGISTER a list of the Department's programs and activities that are subject to these regulations and identifies which of these are subject to the requirements of section 204 of the Demonstration Cities and Metropolitan Development Act.

## § 415.6 Secretary's general responsibilities.

(a) The Secretary provides opportunities for consultation by elected officials of those State and local governments that would provide the non-Federal funds for, or that would be directly affected by, proposed Federal financial assistance from, or direct Federal development by, the Department.

(b) If a State adopts a process under the Order to review and coordinate proposed Federal financial assistance and direct Federal development, the Secretary, to the extent permitted by law:

(1) Uses the State process to determine official views of State and local elected officials;

(2) Communicates with State and local elected officials as early in a program planning cycle as is reasonably feasible to explain specific plans and actions;

(3) Makes efforts to accommodate State and local elected officials' concerns with proposed Federal financial assistance and direct Federal development that are communicated through the State process;

(4) Allows the States to simplify and consolidate existing Federally required State plan submissions;

(5) Where State planning and budgeting systems are sufficient and where permitted by law, encourages the substitution of State plans for Federally required State plans;

(6) Seeks the coordination of views of affected State and local elected officials in one State with those of another State when proposed Federal financial assistance or direct Federal development has an impact on interstate metropolitan urban centers or other interstate areas; and

(7) Supports State and local governments by discouraging the reauthorization or creation of any planning organization which is Federally-funded, which has a limited purpose, and which is not adequately representative of, or accountable to, State or local elected officials.

## § 415.7 Federal interagency coordination.

The Secretary, to the extent practicable, consults with and seeks advice from all other substantially affected Federal departments and agencies in an effort to assure full coordination between such agencies and the Department regarding programs and activities covered under these regulations.

## § 415.8 State selection of programs and activities.

(a) A State may select any program or activity published in the FEDERAL REGISTER in accordance with § 415.5 for intergovernmental review under these regulations. Each State, before selecting programs and activities, shall consult with local elected officials.

(b) Each State that adopts a process shall notify the secretary of the Department's programs and activities selected for that process.

(c) A State may notify the Secretary of changes in its selections at any time. For each change, the State shall submit to the Secretary an assurance that the State has consulted with elected local officials regarding the change. The Department may establish deadlines by which States are required to inform the Secretary of changes in their program selections.

(d) The Secretary uses a State's process as soon as feasible, depending on individual programs and activities, after the Secretary is notified of its selections.

### §415.9 Communication with State and local elected officials.

(a) The Secretary provides notice to directly affected State, areawide, regional, and local entities in a State of proposed Federal financial assistance or direct Federal development if:

(1) The State has not adopted a process under the Order; or

(2) The assistance or development involves a program or an activity that is not covered under the State process.

(b) This notice may be made by publication in the FEDERAL REGISTER or other appropriate means, which the Department in its discretion deems appropriate.

(c) In order to facilitate communication with State and local officials the Secretary has established an office within the Department to receive all communications pertinent to this Order. All communications should be sent to the Office of the Chief Financial Officer, Room 143–W, 1400 Independence Avenue SW., Washington, DC 20250, Attention: E.O. 12372.

### §415.10 State comments on proposed Federal financial assistance and direct Federal development.

(a) Except in unusual circumstances, the Secretary gives State processes or directly affected State, areawide, regional, and local officials and entities:

(1) At least 30 days from the date established by the Secretary to comment on proposed Federal financial assistance in the form of noncompeting continuation awards; and

(2) At least 60 days from the date established by the Secretary to comment on proposed direct Federal development or Federal financial assistance other than noncompeting continuation awards.

(b) This section also applies to comments in cases in which the review, coordination and communication with the Department have been delegated.

(c) Applicants for programs and activities subject to section 204 of the Demonstration Cities and Metropolitan Development Act shall allow areawide agencies a 60-day opportunity for review and comment.

### §415.11 Processing comments.

(a) The Secretary follows the procedures in §415.12 if:

(1) A State office or official is designated to act as a single point of contact between a State process and all Federal agencies; and

(2) That office or official transmits a State process recommendation for a program selected under §415.8.

(b)(1) The single point of contact is not obligated to transmit comments from State, areawide, regional or local officials and entities where there is no State process recommendation.

(2) If a State process recommendation is transmitted by a single point of contact, all comments from State, areawide, regional and local officials and entities that differ from it must also be transmitted.

(c) If a State has not established a process, or is unable to submit a State process recommendation, State, areawide, regional and local officials and entities may submit comments either to the applicant or to the Department.

(d) If a program or activity is not selected by a State process, State, areawide, regional and local officials and entities may submit comments either to the applicant or to the Department. In addition, if a State process recommendation for a non-selected program or activity is transmitted to the Department by the single point of contact, the Secretary follows the procedures of §415.12.

(e) The Secretary considers comments which do not constitute a State process recommendation submitted under these regulations and for which the Secretary is not required to apply the procedures of §415.12, when such comments are provided by a single point of contact by the applicant, or directly to the Department by a commenting party.

### §415.12 Accommodation of intergovernmental concerns.

(a) If a State process provides a State process recommendation to the Department through its single point of contact, the Secretary either—

(1) Accepts the recommendations;

(2) Reaches a mutually agreeable solution with the State process; or

(3) Provides the single point of contact with a written explanation of the decision, as the Secretary in his or her discretion deems appropriate. The Secretary may also supplement the written explanation by also providing the explanation to the single point of contact by telephone, other telecommunication, or other means.

(b) In any explanation under paragraph (a)(3) of this section, the Secretary informs the single point of contact that:

(1) The Department will not implement its decision for at least ten days after the single point of contact receives the explanation; or

(2) The Secretary has reviewed the decision and determined that, because of unusual circumstances, the waiting period of at least ten days is not feasible.

(c) For purposes of computing the waiting period under paragraph (b)(1) of this section, a single point of contact is presumed to have received written notification five days after the date of mailing of such notification.

### §415.13   Interstate situations.

(a) The Secretary is responsible for:

(1) Identifying proposed Federal financial assistance and direct Federal development that have an impact on interstate areas;

(2) Notifying appropriate officials in States which have adopted a process and which selected the Department's program or activity;

(3) Making efforts to identify and notify the affected State, areawide, regional and local officials and entities in those States that have not adopted a process under the Order or do not select the Department's program or activity; and

(4) Responding, pursuant to §415.12, if the Secretary receives a recommendation from a designated areawide agency transmitted by a single point of contact, in cases in which the review, coordination, and communication with the Department have been delegated.

(b) The Secretary uses the procedures in §415.12 if a State process provides a State process recommendation to the Department through a single point of contact.

### §415.14   Simplification, consolidation, or substitution of State plans.

(a) As used in this section:

(1) Simplify means that a State may develop its own format, choose its own submission date, and select the planning period for a State plan.

(2) Consolidate means that a State may meet statutory and regulatory requirements by combining two or more plans into one document and that the State can select the format, submission date, and the planning period for the consolidated plan.

(3) Substitute means that a State may use a plan or other document that it has developed for its own purposes to meet Federal requirements.

(b) If not inconsistent with law, a State may decide to try to simplify, consolidate, or substitute Federally required State plans without prior approval by the Secretary.

(c) The Secretary reviews each State plan a State has simplified, consolidated or substituted and accepts the plan only if its contents meet Federal requirements.

### §415.15   Waivers.

In an emergency, the Secretary may waive any provision in Subpart C—Intergovernmental Review of Department of Agriculture Programs and Activities, 2 CFR 415.3 to 415.14.

## PART 416—GENERAL PROGRAM ADMINISTRATIVE REGULATIONS FOR GRANTS AND COOPERATIVE AGREEMENTS TO STATE AND LOCAL GOVERNMENTS

AUTHORITY: 5 U.S.C. 301.

SOURCE: 79 FR 75985, Dec. 19, 2014, unless otherwise noted.

### §416.1   Special Procurement Provisions.

(a) In order to ensure objective contractor performance and eliminate unfair competitive advantage, a prospective contractor that develops or drafts specifications, requirements, statements of work, invitations for bids, request for proposals, contract term and conditions or other documents for use by a State in conducting a procurement under the USDA entitlement programs specified in 2 CFR 200.101(e)(4) through (6) shall be excluded from competing for such procurements. Such prospective contractors are ineligible for contract awards resulting from such procurements regardless of the procurement method used. However, prospective contractors may provide States with specification information related to a State procurement under the USDA entitlement programs specified in 2 CFR 200.101(e)(4) through (6) and still compete for the procurement if the State, and not the prospective contractor, develops or drafts the specifications, requirements, statements of work, invitations for bid, and/or requests for proposals used to conduct the procurement.

(b) Procurements by States under USDA entitlement programs specified in 2 CFR 200.101(e)(4) through (6) shall be conducted in a manner that prohibits the use of statutorily or administratively imposed in-State or local geographic preferences except as provided for in 2 CFR 200.319(b).

## PART 417—NONPROCUREMENT DEBARMENT AND SUSPENSION

AUTHORITY: 5 U.S.C. 301; Pub. L. 101–576, 104 Stat. 2838; Sec. 2455, Pub. L. 103–355, 108 Stat. 3327 (31 U.S.C. 6101 note); 7 U.S.C. 2209j; E.O. 12549 (3 CFR, 1986 Comp., p. 189); E.O. 12698 (3 CFR, Comp., p. 235); 7 CFR 2.28.

SOURCE: 75 FR 29185, May 25, 2010, unless otherwise noted.

### §417.10  What does this part do?

This part adopts the OMB guidance in subparts A through I of 2 CFR part 180, as supplemented by this part, as the USDA policies and procedures for nonprocurement debarment and suspension. It thereby gives regulatory effect for the USDA to the OMB guidance, as supplemented by this part. This part satisfies the requirements in section 3 of Executive Order 12549, "Debarment and Suspension" (3 CFR 1986 Comp., p. 189), Executive Order 12689, "Debarment and Suspension" (3

CFR 1989 Comp., p. 235) and 31 U.S.C. 6101 note (Section 2455, Pub. L. 103–355, 108 Stat. 3327).

### § 417.20 Does this part apply to me?

Through this part, pertinent portions of the OMB guidance in subparts A through I of 2 CFR part 180 (*see* table at 2 CFR 180.100(b)) apply to you if you are a:

(a) Participant or principal in a "covered transaction" (*see* subpart B of 2 CFR part 180 and the definition of "nonprocurement transaction" at 2 CFR 180.970, as supplemented by §§ 417.215 and 417.220 of this part);

(b) Respondent in a USDA debarment and suspension action;

(c) USDA debarment or suspension official; or

(d) USDA grants officer, agreements officer, or other official authorized to enter into any type of nonprocurement transaction that is a covered transaction.

### § 417.30 What policies and procedures must I follow?

The USDA policies and procedures that you must follow are the policies and procedures specified in this regulation and each applicable section of the OMB guidance in subparts A through I of 2 CFR part 180, as that section is supplemented by the section in this part with the same section number. The contracts that are covered transactions, for example, are specified by section 220 of the OMB guidance (*i.e.*, 2 CFR 180.220) as supplemented by section 220 in this part (*i.e.*, § 417.220). For any section of OMB guidance in subparts A through I of 2 CFR part 180 that has no corresponding section in this part, USDA policies and procedures are those in the OMB guidance.

## Subpart A—General

### § 417.137 Who in the USDA may grant an exception to let an excluded person participate in a covered transaction?

Within the USDA, a debarring official may grant an exception to let an excluded person participate in a covered transaction as provided under 2 CFR 180.135.

## Subpart B—Covered Transactions

### § 417.210 Which nonprocurement transactions are covered transactions?

All nonprocurement transactions, as defined in § 417.970, are covered transactions unless listed in § 417.215.

### § 417.215 Which nonprocurement transactions, in addition to those listed in 2 CFR 180.215, are not covered transactions?

(a) *Transactions not covered.* In addition to the nonprocurement transactions listed in 2 CFR 180.215, the following nonprocurement transactions are not covered transactions:

(1) An entitlement or mandatory award required by a statute, including a lower tier entitlement or mandatory award that is required by a statute.

(2) The export or substitution of Federal timber governed by the Forest Resources Conservation and Shortage Relief Act of 1990, 16 U.S.C. 620 *et seq.* (The "Export Act"), which prevents a debarred person from entering into any contract for the purchase of unprocessed timber from Federal lands. *See* 16 U.S.C. 620d(d)(1)(A).

(3) The receipt of licenses, permits, certificates, and indemnification under regulatory programs conducted in the interest of public health and safety, and animal and plant health and safety.

(4) The receipt of official grading and inspection services, animal damage control services, public health and safety inspection services, and animal and plant health and safety inspection services.

(5) If the person is a State or local government, the provision of official grading and inspection services, animal damage control services, animal and plant health and safety inspection services.

(6) The receipt of licenses, permits, or certificates under regulatory programs conducted in the interest of ensuring fair trade practices.

(7) Permits, licenses, exchanges and other acquisitions of real property, rights of way, and easements under natural resource management programs.

(8) Any transaction to be implemented outside the United States that is below the primary tier covered transaction in a USDA foreign assistance program.

(9) Any transaction to be implemented outside the United States that is below the primary tier covered transaction in a USDA export credit guarantee program or direct credit program.

(b) *Limited requirement to check EPLS.* Notwithstanding the fact that transactions to be implemented outside the United States that are below the primary tier covered transaction in a USDA foreign assistance program, export credit guarantee program or direct credit program are not covered transactions, pursuant to paragraphs (a)(8) and (9) of this section, primary tier participants under these programs must check the EPLS prior to entering into any transaction with a person at the first lower tier and shall not enter into such a transaction if the person is excluded or disqualified under the EPLS.

(c) *Exception.* A cause for suspension or debarment under §180.700 or §180.800 of this title (as supplemented by §417.800) may be based on the actions of a person with respect to a procurement or nonprocurement transaction under a USDA program even if such transaction has been excluded from covered transaction status by this section or §417.220.

## §417.220 Are any procurement contracts included as covered transactions?

(a) Covered transactions under this part:

(1) Do not include any procurement contracts awarded directly by a Federal agency; but

(2) Do include some procurement contracts awarded by non-Federal participants in nonprocurement covered transactions (*see* appendix to this part).

(b) Specifically, a contract for goods or services is a covered transaction if any of the following applies:

(1) The contract is awarded by a participant in a nonprocurement transaction that is covered under §417.210, and the amount of the contract is expected to equal or exceed $25,000.

(2) The contract requires the consent of a USDA official. In that case, the contract, regardless of the amount, always is a covered transaction, and it does not matter who awarded it. For example, it could be a subcontract awarded by a contractor at a tier below a nonprocurement transaction, as shown in the appendix to this part.

(3) The contract is for federally-required audit services.

(c) Any procurement contract to be implemented outside the United States that is below the primary tier covered transaction in a USDA foreign assistance program is not a covered transaction, notwithstanding the provisions in paragraphs (a) and (b) of this section.

(d) Any procurement contract to be implemented outside the United States that is below the primary tier covered transaction in a USDA export credit guarantee program or direct credit program is not a covered transaction, notwithstanding the provisions in paragraphs (a) and (b) of this section.

(e) Notwithstanding the fact that procurement contracts to be implemented outside the United States that are below the primary tier covered transaction in a USDA foreign assistance program, export credit guarantee program or direct credit program are not covered transactions, pursuant to paragraphs (c) and (d) of this section, primary tier participants under these programs must check the EPLS prior to entering into any procurement contract that is expected to equal or exceed $25,000 with a person at the first lower tier and shall not enter into such a procurement contract if the person is excluded or disqualified under the EPLS.

## §417.221 How would the exclusions from coverage for the USDA's foreign assistance programs apply?

The primary tier covered transaction would be the food aid grant agreement entered into between USDA and a program participant, such as a U.S. private voluntary organization. USDA would have to check the EPLS before entering into the food aid grant agreement to ensure that the U.S. private voluntary organization that would be

251

the primary tier participant is not excluded or disqualified. A transaction at the first lower tier might be a subrecipient agreement between the U.S. private voluntary organization and a foreign subrecipient of the commodities that were provided under the food aid grant agreement. Pursuant to § 417.215(a)(8), this nonprocurement transaction would not be a covered transaction. In addition, a transaction at the first lower tier might be a procurement contract entered into between the U.S. private voluntary organization and a foreign entity to provide supplies or services that are expected to equal or exceed $25,000 in value and that are needed by such organization to implement activities under the food aid grant agreement. Pursuant to § 417.220(c), this procurement contract would not be a covered transaction. However, pursuant to §§ 417.215(b) and 417.220(e), the U.S. private voluntary organization would be prohibited from entering into, at the first lower tier, an agreement with a subrecipient or a procurement contract that is expected to equal or exceed $25,000 with an entity that appears on the EPLS as excluded or disqualified.

§ 417.222 How would the exclusions from coverage for USDA's export credit guarantee and direct credit programs apply?

(a) *Export credit guarantee program.* In the case of the export credit guarantee program, the primary tier covered transaction would be the guarantee issued by the USDA to a U.S. exporter. The U.S. exporter usually assigns the guarantee to a U.S. financial institution, and this would create another primary tier covered transaction between USDA and the U.S. financial institution. USDA would have to check the EPLS before issuing a guarantee or accepting a guarantee assignment to ensure that the U.S. exporter or financial institution that would be the primary tier participant is not excluded or disqualified. A transaction at the first lower tier under the export credit guarantee program might be a payment obligation of a foreign bank to the U.S. exporter to pay on behalf of the importer for the exported U.S. commodities that are covered by the guarantee.

Similarly, a transaction at the first lower tier might be a payment obligation of a foreign bank under an instrument, such as a loan agreement or letter of credit, to the U.S. financial institution assigned the guarantee, which has paid the exporter for the exported U.S. commodities and, in so doing, issued a loan to the foreign bank, which the foreign bank is obligated to repay on deferred payment terms. Pursuant to § 417.215(a)(9), these nonprocurement transactions would not be covered transactions. In addition, a transaction at the first lower tier under the export credit guarantee program might be a procurement contract (*i.e.,* a contract for the purchase and sale of goods) that is expected to equal or exceed $25,000 entered into between the U.S. exporter and the foreign importer for the U.S. commodities, the payment for which is covered by the guarantee. Pursuant to § 417.220(d), this procurement contract would not be a covered transaction. However, pursuant to §§ 417.215(b) and 417.220(e), the U.S. exporter or U.S. financial institution would be prohibited from entering into, at the first lower tier, an agreement with an importer (or intervening purchaser) or foreign bank or a procurement contract that is expected to equal or exceed $25,000 with an entity that appears on the EPLS as excluded or disqualified.

(b) *Direct credit program.* In the case of the direct credit program, the primary tier covered transaction would be the financing agreement between the USDA and the U.S. exporter. USDA purchases the exporter's account receivable in a particular transaction pursuant to the financing agreement. On occasion, such transaction may contemplate a payment obligation of a U.S. or foreign bank to make the required payments. USDA would have to check the EPLS before entering into a financing agreement or accepting such a payor to ensure that the U.S. exporter or the bank, if any, that would be the primary tier participant is not excluded or disqualified. A transaction at the first lower tier might be a payment obligation of the importer to pay the exporter for the exported U.S. commodities that are covered by the financing agreement. Pursuant to

§ 417.215(a)(9), this nonprocurement transaction would not be a covered transaction. In addition, a transaction at the first lower tier might be a procurement contract that is expected to equal or exceed $25,000 entered into between the U.S. exporter and the foreign importer for the U.S. commodities, the payment for which is covered by the financing agreement. Pursuant to § 417.220(d), this procurement contract would not be a covered transaction. However, pursuant to §§ 417.215(b) and 417.220(e), the U.S. exporter would be prohibited from entering into, at the first lower tier, an agreement with an importer (or intervening purchaser) or bank, or a procurement contract that is expected to equal or exceed $25,000 with an entity that appears on the EPLS as excluded or disqualified.

## Subpart C—Responsibilities of Participants Regarding Transactions

### § 417.332 What methods must I use to pass down requirements to participants in lower tier covered transactions with whom I intend to do business?

You as a participant must include a term or condition in lower tier covered transactions requiring lower tier participants to comply with subpart C of the OMB guidance in 2 CFR part 180, as supplemented by subpart C of this part.

## Subpart D—Responsibilities of Department of Agriculture Officials Regarding Transactions

### § 417.437 What method do I use to communicate to a participant the requirements described in the OMB guidance at 2 CFR 180.435?

To communicate to a participant the requirements described in 2 CFR 180.435, you must include a term or condition in the transaction that requires the participant's compliance with subpart C of 2 CFR part 180, as supplemented by subpart C of this part, and requires the participant to include a similar term or condition in lower tier covered transactions.

## Subparts E–F [Reserved]

## Subpart G—Suspension

### § 417.755 When will I know whether the USDA suspension is continued or terminated?

The suspending official must make a written decision whether to continue, modify, or terminate your suspension within 45 days of closing the official record. The official record closes upon the suspending official's receipt of final submissions, information and findings of fact, if any. The suspending official may extend that period for good cause. However, the record will remain open for the full 30 days, as called for in § 180.725, even when you make a submission before the 30 days expire.

## Subpart H—Debarment

### § 417.800 What are the USDA causes for debarment?

A Federal agency may debar a person for—

(a) Conviction of or civil judgment for—

(1) Commission of fraud or a criminal offense in connection with obtaining, attempting to obtain, or performing a public or private agreement or transaction;

(2) Violation of Federal or State antitrust statutes, including those proscribing price fixing between competitors, allocation of customers between competitors, and bid rigging;

(3) Commission of embezzlement, theft, forgery, bribery, falsification or destruction of records, making false statements, tax evasion, receiving stolen property, making false claims, or obstruction of justice; or

(4) Commission of any other offense indicating a lack of business integrity or business honesty that seriously and directly affects your present responsibility;

(b) Violation of the terms of a public agreement or transaction so serious as to affect the integrity of an agency program, such as—

(1) A willful failure to perform in accordance with the terms of one or more public agreements or transactions;

(2) A history of failure to perform or of unsatisfactory performance of one or more public agreements or transactions; or

253

(3) A willful violation of a statutory or regulatory provision or requirement applicable to a public agreement or transaction;

(c) Any of the following causes:

(1) A nonprocurement debarment by any Federal agency taken before March 1, 1989, or a procurement debarment by any Federal agency taken pursuant to 48 CFR part 9, subpart 9.4, before August 25, 1995;

(2) Knowingly doing business with an ineligible person, except as permitted under §180.135;

(3) Failure to pay a single substantial debt, or a number of outstanding debts (including disallowed costs and overpayments, but not including sums owed the Federal Government under the Internal Revenue Code) owed to any Federal agency or instrumentality, provided the debt is uncontested by the debtor or, if contested, provided that the debtor's legal and administrative remedies have been exhausted;

(4) Violation of a material provision of a voluntary exclusion agreement entered into under §180.640 or of any settlement of a debarment or suspension action; or

(5) Violation of the provisions of the Drug-Free Workplace Act of 1988 (41 U.S.C. 701); or

(d) Any other cause of so serious or compelling a nature that it affects your present responsibility.

## §417.865  How long may my debarment last?

(a) If the debarring official decides to debar you, your period of debarment will be based on the seriousness of the cause(s) upon which your debarment is based. Generally, debarment should not exceed 3 years. However, if circumstances warrant, the debarring official may impose a longer period of debarment.

(b) In determining the period of debarment, the debarring official may consider the factors in 2 CFR 180.860. If a suspension has preceded your debarment, the debarring official must consider the time you were suspended.

(c) If the debarment is for a violation of the provisions of the Drug-Free Workplace Act of 1988, your period of debarment may not exceed 5 years.

(d) The Secretary shall permanently debar from participation in USDA programs any individual, organization, corporation, or other entity convicted of a felony for knowingly defrauding the United States in connection with any program administered by USDA.

(1) *Reduction.* If the Secretary considers it appropriate s/he may reduce a debarment under this subsection to a period of not less than 10 years.

(2) *Exemption.* A debarment under this subsection shall not apply with regard to participation in USDA domestic food assistance programs. For purposes of this paragraph, participation in a domestic food assistance program does not include acting as an authorized retail food store in the Supplemental Nutrition Assistance Program (SNAP), the Special Supplemental Nutrition Assistance Program for Women, Infants, and Children (WIC), or as a nonbeneficiary entity in any of the domestic food assistance programs. The programs include:

(i) Special Nutrition Assistance Program, 7 U.S.C. 2011, *et seq.;*

(ii) Food Distribution Program on Indian Reservations, 7 U.S.C. 2013(b);

(iii) National School Lunch Program, 42 U.S.C. 1751, *et seq.;*

(iv) Summer Food Service Program for Children, 42 U.S.C. 1761; Child and Adult Care Food Program, 42 U.S.C. 1766;

(v) Special Milk Program for Children, 42 U.S.C. 1772; School Breakfast Program, 42 U.S.C. 1773;

(vi) Special Supplemental Nutrition Program for Women, Infants, and Children, 42 U.S.C. 1786;

(vii) Commodity Supplemental Food Program, 42 U.S.C. 612c note;

(viii) WIC Farmers Market Nutrition Program, 42 U.S.C. 1786;

(ix) Senior Farmers' Market Nutrition Program, 7 U.S.C. 3007; and

(x) Emergency Food Assistance Program, 7 U.S.C. 7501, *et. seq.*

## §417.870  When do I know if the USDA debarring official debars me?

(a) The debarring official must make a written decision whether to debar within 45 days of closing the official record. The official record closes upon the debarring official's receipt of final submissions, information and findings of fact, if any. The debarring official may extend that period for good cause. However, the record will remain open for the full 30 days, as called for in § 180.820, even when you make a submission before the 30 days expire.

(b) The debarring official sends you written notice, pursuant to § 180.615, that the official decided, either:

(1) Not to debar you; or

(2) To debar you. In this event, the notice:

(i) Refers to the Notice of Proposed Debarment;

(ii) Specifies the reasons for your debarment;

(iii) States the period of your debarment, including the effective dates; and

(iv) Advises you that your debarment is effective for covered transactions and contracts that are subject to the Federal Acquisition Regulation (48 CFR chapter 1), throughout the Executive Branch of the Federal Government unless an agency head or an authorized designee grants an exception.

## Subpart I—Definitions

### § 417.930  Debarring  official  (USDA supplement to governmentwide definition at 2 CFR 180.930).

(a) Debarring official means an agency official who is authorized to impose debarment. The debarring official is either:

(1) The agency head; or

(2) An official designated by the agency head.

(b) The head of an organizational unit within USDA (e.g., Administrator, Food and Nutrition Service), who has been delegated authority in 7 CFR part 2 to carry out a covered transaction, is delegated authority to act as the debarring official in connection with such transaction. This authority to act as a debarring official may not be redelegated below the head of the organizational unit, except that, in the case of the Forest Service, the Chief may redelegate the authority to act as a debarring official to the Deputy Chief for the National Forest System or an Associate Deputy Chief for the National Forest System.

### § 417.1010  Suspending  official  (USDA supplement to governmentwide definition at 2 CFR 180.1010).

(a) Suspending official means an agency official who is authorized to impose suspension. The suspending official is either:

(1) The agency head; or

(2) An official designated by the agency head.

(b) The head of an organizational unit within USDA (e.g., Administrator, Food and Nutrition Service), who has been delegated authority in 7 CFR part 2 of this title to carry out a covered transaction, is delegated authority to act as the suspending official in connection with such transaction. This authority to act as a suspending official may not be redelegated below the head of the organizational unit, except that, in the case of the Forest Service, the Chief may redelegate the authority to act as a suspending official to the Deputy Chief for the National Forest System or an Associate Deputy Chief for the National Forest System.

## Subpart J [Reserved]

## PART 418—NEW RESTRICTIONS ON LOBBYING

### Subpart A—General

AUTHORITY: 31 U.S.C. 1352; 5 U.S.C. 301.

SOURCE: 79 FR 75985, Dec. 19, 2014, unless
otherwise noted.

## Subpart A—General

### § 418.100  Conditions on use of funds.

(a) No appropriated funds may be expended by the recipient of a Federal contract, grant, loan, or cooperative agreement to pay any person for influencing or attempting to influence an officer or employee of any agency, a Member of Congress, an officer or employee of Congress, or an employee of a Member of Congress in connection with any of the following covered Federal actions: the awarding of any Federal contract, the making of any Federal grant, the making of any Federal loan, the entering into of any cooperative agreement, and the extension, continuation, renewal, amendment, or modification of any Federal contract, grant, loan, or cooperative agreement.

(b) Each person who requests or receives from an agency a Federal contract, grant, loan, or cooperative agreement shall file with that agency a certification, set forth in Appendix A, that the person has not made, and will not make, any payment prohibited by paragraph (a) of this section.

(c) Each person who requests or receives from an agency a Federal contract, grant, loan, or a cooperative agreement shall file with that agency a disclosure form, set forth in Appendix B, if such person has made or has agreed to make any payment using nonappropriated funds (to include profits from any covered Federal action), which would be prohibited under paragraph (a) of this section if paid for with appropriated funds.

(d) Each person who requests or receives from an agency a commitment providing for the United States to insure or guarantee a loan shall file with that agency a statement, set forth in Appendix A, whether that person has made or has agreed to make any payment to influence or attempt to influence an officer or employee of any agency, a Member of Congress, an officer or employee of Congress, or an employee of a Member of Congress in connection with that loan insurance or guarantee.

(e) Each person who requests or receives from an agency a commitment providing for the United States to insure or guarantee a loan shall file with that agency a disclosure form, set forth in Appendix B, if that person has made or has agreed to make any payment to influence or attempt to influence an officer or employee of any agency, a Member of Congress, an officer or employee of Congress, or an employee of a Member of Congress in connection with that loan insurance or guarantee.

### § 418.105  Definitions.

For purposes of this part:

(a) *Agency*, as defined in 5 U.S.C. 552(f), includes Federal executive departments and agencies as well as independent regulatory commissions and Government corporations, as defined in 31 U.S.C. 9101(1).

(b) *Covered Federal action.* (1) Covered Federal action means any of the following Federal actions:

(i) The awarding of any Federal contract;

(ii) The making of any Federal grant;

(iii) The making of any Federal loan;

(iv) The entering into of any cooperative agreement; and,

(v) The extension, continuation, renewal, amendment, or modification of any Federal contract, grant, loan, or cooperative agreement.

(2) Covered Federal action does not include receiving from an agency a commitment providing for the United States to insure or guarantee a loan. Loan guarantees and loan insurance are addressed independently within this part.

(c) *Federal contract* means an acquisition contract awarded by an agency, including those subject to the Federal Acquisition Regulation (FAR), and any other acquisition contract for real or personal property or services not subject to the FAR.

(d) *Federal cooperative agreement* means a cooperative agreement entered into by an agency.

(e) *Federal grant* means an award of financial assistance in the form of money, or property in lieu of money, by the Federal Government or a direct appropriation made by law to any person. The term does not include technical assistance which provides services instead of money, or other assistance in the form of revenue sharing, loans, loan guarantees, loan insurance, interest subsidies, insurance, or direct United States cash assistance to an individual.

(f) *Federal loan* means a loan made by an agency. The term does not include loan guarantee or loan insurance.

(g) *Indian tribe* and *tribal organization* have the meaning provided in section 4 of the Indian Self-Determination and Education Assistance Act (25 U.S.C. 450B). Alaskan Natives are included under the definitions of Indian tribes in that Act.

(h) *Influencing or attempting to influence* means making, with the intent to influence, any communication to or appearance before an officer or employee or any agency, a Member of Congress, an officer or employee of Congress, or an employee of a Member of Congress in connection with any covered Federal action.

(i) *Loan guarantee* and *loan insurance* means an agency's guarantee or insurance of a loan made by a person.

(j) *Local government* means a unit of government in a State and, if chartered, established, or otherwise recognized by a State for the performance of a governmental duty, including a local public authority, a special district, an intrastate district, a council of governments, a sponsor group representative organization, and any other instrumentality of a local government.

(k) *Officer or employee of an agency* includes the following individuals who are employed by an agency:

(1) An individual who is appointed to a position in the Government under title 5, U.S. Code, including a position under a temporary appointment;

(2) A member of the uniformed services as defined in section 101(3), title 37, U.S. Code;

(3) A special Government employee as defined in section 202, title 18, U.S. Code; and,

(4) An individual who is a member of a Federal advisory committee, as defined by the Federal Advisory Committee Act, title 5, U.S. Code appendix 2.

(l) *Person* means an individual, corporation, company, association, authority, firm, partnership, society, State, and local government, regardless of whether such entity is operated for profit or not for profit. This term excludes an Indian tribe, tribal organization, or any other Indian organization with respect to expenditures specifically permitted by other Federal law.

(m) *Reasonable compensation* means, with respect to a regularly employed officer or employee of any person, compensation that is consistent with the normal compensation for such officer or employee for work that is not furnished to, not funded by, or not furnished in cooperation with the Federal Government.

(n) *Reasonable payment* means, with respect to professional and other technical services, a payment in an amount that is consistent with the amount normally paid for such services in the private sector.

(o) *Recipient* includes all contractors, subcontractors at any tier, and subgrantees at any tier of the recipient of funds received in connection with a Federal contract, grant, loan, or cooperative agreement. The term excludes an Indian tribe, tribal organization, or any other Indian organization with respect to expenditures specifically permitted by other Federal law.

(p) *Regularly employed* means, with respect to an officer or employee of a person requesting or receiving a Federal contract, grant, loan, or cooperative agreement or a commitment providing for the United States to insure or guarantee a loan, an officer or employee who is employed by such person for at least 130 working days within one year immediately preceding the date of the submission that initiates agency consideration of such person for receipt of such contract, grant, loan, cooperative agreement, loan insurance commitment, or loan guarantee commitment. An officer or employee who is employed by such person for less than 130 working days within one year immediately preceding the date of the submission that initiates agency consideration of such person shall be considered to be regularly employed as soon as he or she is employed by such person for 130 working days.

(q) *State* means a State of the United States, the District of Columbia, the Commonwealth of Puerto Rico, a territory or possession of the United States, an agency or instrumentality of a State, and a multi-State, regional, or interstate entity having governmental duties and powers.

### §418.110  Certification and disclosure.

(a) Each person shall file a certification, and a disclosure form, if required, with each submission that initiates agency consideration of such person for:

(1) Award of a Federal contract, grant, or cooperative agreement exceeding $100,000; or

(2) An award of a Federal loan or a commitment providing for the United States to insure or guarantee a loan exceeding $150,000.

(b)(1) Each person shall file a certification, and a disclosure form, if required, upon receipt by such person of:

(i) A Federal contract, grant, or cooperative agreement exceeding $100,000; or

(ii) A Federal loan or a commitment providing for the United States to insure or guarantee a loan exceeding $150,000,

(2) Unless such person previously filed a certification, and a disclosure form, if required, under paragraph (a) of this section.

(c) Each person shall file a disclosure form at the end of each calendar quarter in which there occurs any event that requires disclosure or that materially affects the accuracy of the information contained in any disclosure form previously filed by such person under paragraphs (a) or (b) of this section. An event that materially affects the accuracy of the information reported includes:

(1) A cumulative increase of $25,000 or more in the amount paid or expected to be paid for influencing or attempting to influence a covered Federal action; or

(2) A change in the person(s) or individual(s) influencing or attempting to influence a covered Federal action; or,

(3) A change in the officer(s), employee(s), or Member(s) contacted to influence or attempt to influence a covered Federal action.

(d) Any person shall file a certification, and a disclosure form, if required, to the next tier above who requests or receives from a person referred to in paragraphs (a) or (b) of this section:

(1) A subcontract exceeding $100,000 at any tier under a Federal contract;

(2) A subgrant, contract, or subcontract exceeding $100,000 at any tier under a Federal grant;

(3) A contract or subcontract exceeding $100,000 at any tier under a Federal loan exceeding $150,000; or,

(4) A contract or subcontract exceeding $100,000 at any tier under a Federal cooperative agreement.

(e) All disclosure forms, but not certifications, shall be forwarded from tier to tier until received by the person referred to in paragraphs (a) or (b) of this section. That person shall forward all disclosure forms to the agency.

(f) Any certification or disclosure form filed under paragraph (e) of this section shall be treated as a material representation of fact upon which all receiving tiers shall rely. All liability arising from an erroneous representation shall be borne solely by the tier filing that representation and shall not be shared by any tier to which the erroneous representation is forwarded. Submitting an erroneous certification or disclosure constitutes a failure to file the required certification or disclosure, respectively. If a person fails to file a required certification or disclosure, the United States may pursue all available remedies, including those authorized by section 1352, title 31, U.S. Code.

(g) For awards and commitments in process prior to December 23, 1989, but not made before that date, certifications shall be required at award or commitment, covering activities occurring between December 23, 1989, and the date of award or commitment.

However, for awards and commitments in process prior to the December 23, 1989 effective date of these provisions, but not made before December 23, 1989, disclosure forms shall not be required at time of award or commitment but shall be filed within 30 days.

(h) No reporting is required for an activity paid for with appropriated funds if that activity is allowable under either Subpart B or C of this part.

## Subpart B—Activities by Own Employees

### §418.200 Agency and legislative liaison.

(a) The prohibition on the use of appropriated funds, in §418.100 (a), does not apply in the case of a payment of reasonable compensation made to an officer or employee of a person requesting or receiving a Federal contract, grant, loan, or cooperative agreement if the payment is for agency and legislative liaison activities not directly related to a covered Federal action.

(b) For purposes of paragraph (a) of this section, providing any information specifically requested by an agency or Congress is allowable at any time.

(c) For purposes of paragraph (a) of this section, the following agency and legislative liaison activities are allowable at any time only where they are not related to a specific solicitation for any covered Federal action:

(1) Discussing with an agency (including individual demonstrations) the qualities and characteristics of the person's products or services, conditions or terms of sale, and service capabilities; and,

(2) Technical discussions and other activities regarding the application or adaptation of the person's products or services for an agency's use.

(d) For purposes of paragraph (a) of this section, the following agencies and legislative liaison activities are allowable only where they are prior to formal solicitation of any covered Federal action:

(1) Providing any information not specifically requested but necessary for an agency to make an informed decision about initiation of a covered Federal action;

(2) Technical discussions regarding the preparation of an unsolicited proposal prior to its official submission; and,

(3) Capability presentations by persons seeking awards from an agency pursuant to the provisions of the Small Business Act, as amended by Public Law 95–507 and other subsequent amendments.

(e) Only those activities expressly authorized by this section are allowable under this section.

### §418.205 Professional and technical services.

(a) The prohibition on the use of appropriated funds, in §418.100 (a), does not apply in the case of a payment of reasonable compensation made to an officer or employee of a person requesting or receiving a Federal contract, grant, loan, or cooperative agreement or an extension, continuation, renewal, amendment, or modification of a Federal contract, grant, loan, or cooperative agreement if payment is for professional or technical services rendered directly in the preparation, submission, or negotiation of any bid, proposal, or application for that Federal contract, grant, loan, or cooperative agreement or for meeting requirements imposed by or pursuant to law as a condition for receiving that Federal contract, grant, loan, or cooperative agreement.

(b) For purposes of paragraph (a) of this section, "professional and technical services" shall be limited to advice and analysis directly applying any professional or technical discipline. For example, drafting of a legal document accompanying a bid or proposal by a lawyer is allowable. Similarly, technical advice provided by an engineer on the performance or operational capability of a piece of equipment rendered directly in the negotiation of a contract is allowable. However, communications with the intent to influence made by a professional (such as a licensed lawyer) or a technical person (such as a licensed accountant) are not allowable under this section unless they provide advice and analysis directly applying their professional or technical expertise and unless the advice or analysis is rendered directly

259

and solely in the preparation, submission or negotiation of a covered Federal action. Thus, for example, communications with the intent to influence made by a lawyer that do not provide legal advice or analysis directly and solely related to the legal aspects of his or her client's proposal, but generally advocate one proposal over another are not allowable under this section because the lawyer is not providing professional legal services. Similarly, communications with the intent to influence made by an engineer providing an engineering analysis prior to the preparation or submission of a bid or proposal are not allowable under this section since the engineer is providing technical services but not directly in the preparation, submission or negotiation of a covered Federal action.

(c) Requirements imposed by or pursuant to law as a condition for receiving a covered Federal award include those required by law or regulation, or reasonably expected to be required by law or regulation, and any other requirements in the actual award documents.

(d) Only those services expressly authorized by this section are allowable under this section.

### § 418.210  Reporting.

No reporting is required with respect to payments of reasonable compensation made to regularly employed officers or employees of a person.

## Subpart C—Activities by Other Than Own Employees

### § 418.300  Professional and technical services.

(a) The prohibition on the use of appropriated funds, in § 418.100 (a), does not apply in the case of any reasonable payment to a person, other than an officer or employee of a person requesting or receiving a covered Federal action, if the payment is for professional or technical services rendered directly in the preparation, submission, or negotiation of any bid, proposal, or application for that Federal contract, grant, loan, or cooperative agreement or for meeting requirements imposed by or pursuant to law as a condition for re-ceiving that Federal contract, grant, loan, or cooperative agreement.

(b) The reporting requirements in § 418.110 (a) and (b) regarding filing a disclosure form by each person, if required, shall not apply with respect to professional or technical services rendered directly in the preparation, submission, or negotiation of any commitment providing for the United States to insure or guarantee a loan.

(c) For purposes of paragraph (a) of this section, "professional and technical services" shall be limited to advice and analysis directly applying any professional or technical discipline. For example, drafting of a legal document accompanying a bid or proposal by a lawyer is allowable. Similarly, technical advice provided by an engineer on the performance or operational capability of a piece of equipment rendered directly in the negotiation of a contract is allowable. However, communications with the intent to influence made by a professional (such as a licensed lawyer) or a technical person (such as a licensed accountant) are not allowable under this section unless they provide advice and analysis directly applying their professional or technical expertise and unless the advice or analysis is rendered directly and solely in the preparation, submission or negotiation of a covered Federal action. Thus, for example, communications with the intent to influence made by a lawyer that do not provide legal advice or analysis directly and solely related to the legal aspects of his or her client's proposal, but generally advocate one proposal over another are not allowable under this section because the lawyer is not providing professional legal services. Similarly, communications with the intent to influence made by an engineer providing an engineering analysis prior to the preparation or submission of a bid or proposal are not allowable under this section since the engineer is providing technical services but not directly in the preparation, submission or negotiation of a covered Federal action.

(d) Requirements imposed by or pursuant to law as a condition for receiving a covered Federal award include those required by law or regulation, or reasonably expected to be required by law or regulation, and any other requirements in the actual award documents.

(e) Persons other than officers or employees of a person requesting or receiving a covered Federal action include consultants and trade associations.

(f) Only those services expressly authorized by this section are allowable under this section.

## Subpart D—Penalties and Enforcement

### § 418.400  Penalties.

(a) Any person who makes an expenditure prohibited herein shall be subject to a civil penalty of not less than $10,000 and not more than $100,000 for each such expenditure.

(b) Any person who fails to file or amend the disclosure form (see Appendix B) to be filed or amended if required herein, shall be subject to a civil penalty of not less than $10,000 and not more than $100,000 for each such failure.

(c) A filing or amended filing on or after the date on which an administrative action for the imposition of a civil penalty is commenced does not prevent the imposition of such civil penalty for a failure occurring before that date. An administrative action is commenced with respect to a failure when an investigating official determines in writing to commence an investigation of an allegation of such failure.

(d) In determining whether to impose a civil penalty, and the amount of any such penalty, by reason of a violation by any person, the agency shall consider the nature, circumstances, extent, and gravity of the violation, the effect on the ability of such person to continue in business, any prior violations by such person, the degree of culpability of such person, the ability of the person to pay the penalty, and such other matters as may be appropriate.

(e) First offenders under paragraphs (a) or (b) of this section shall be subject to a civil penalty of $10,000, absent aggravating circumstances. Second and subsequent offenses by persons shall be subject to an appropriate civil penalty between $10,000 and $100,000, as deter-

mined by the agency head or his or her designee.

(f) An imposition of a civil penalty under this section does not prevent the United States from seeking any other remedy that may apply to the same conduct that is the basis for the imposition of such civil penalty.

### § 418.405  Penalty procedures.

Agencies shall impose and collect civil penalties pursuant to the provisions of the Program Fraud and Civil Remedies Act, 31 U.S.C.s 3803 (except subsection (c)), 3804, 3805, 3806, 3807, 3808, and 3812, insofar as these provisions are not inconsistent with the requirements herein.

### § 418.410  Enforcement.

The head of each agency shall take such actions as are necessary to ensure that the provisions herein are vigorously implemented and enforced in that agency.

## Subpart E—Exemptions

### § 418.500  Secretary of Defense.

(a) The Secretary of Defense may exempt, on a case-by-case basis, a covered Federal action from the prohibition whenever the Secretary determines, in writing, that such an exemption is in the national interest. The Secretary shall transmit a copy of each such written exemption to Congress immediately after making such a determination.

(b) The Department of Defense may issue supplemental regulations to implement paragraph (a) of this section.

## Subpart F—Agency Reports

### § 418.600  Semi-annual compilation.

(a) The head of each agency shall collect and compile the disclosure reports (see appendix B) and, on May 31 and November 30 of each year, submit to the Secretary of the Senate and the Clerk of the House of Representatives a report containing a compilation of the information contained in the disclosure reports received during the six-month period ending on March 31 or September 30, respectively, of that year.

(b) The report, including the compilation, shall be available for public inspection 30 days after receipt of the report by the Secretary and the Clerk.

(c) Information that involves intelligence matters shall be reported only to the Select Committee on Intelligence of the Senate, the Permanent Select Committee on Intelligence of the House of Representatives, and the Committees on Appropriations of the Senate and the House of Representatives in accordance with procedures agreed to by such committees. Such information shall not be available for public inspection.

(d) Information that is classified under Executive Order 12356 or any successor order shall be reported only to the Committee on Foreign Relations of the Senate and the Committee on Foreign Affairs of the House of Representatives or the Committees on Armed Services of the Senate and the House of Representatives (whichever such committees have jurisdiction of matters involving such information) and to the Committees on Appropriations of the Senate and the House of Representatives in accordance with procedures agreed to by such committees. Such information shall not be available for public inspection.

(e) The first semi-annual compilation shall be submitted on May 31, 1990, and shall contain a compilation of the disclosure reports received from December 23, 1989 to March 31, 1990.

(f) Major agencies, designated by the Office of Management and Budget (OMB), are required to provide machine-readable compilations to the Secretary of the Senate and the Clerk of the House of Representatives no later than with the compilations due on May 31, 1991. OMB shall provide detailed specifications in a memorandum to these agencies.

(g) Non-major agencies are requested to provide machine-readable compilations to the Secretary of the Senate and the Clerk of the House of Representatives.

(h) Agencies shall keep the originals of all disclosure reports in the official files of the agency.

## § 418.605 Inspector General report.

(a) The Inspector General, or other official as specified in paragraph (b) of this section, of each agency shall prepare and submit to Congress each year, commencing with submission of the President's Budget in 1991, an evaluation of the compliance of that agency with, and the effectiveness of, the requirements herein. The evaluation may include any recommended changes that may be necessary to strengthen or improve the requirements.

(b) In the case of an agency that does not have an Inspector General, the agency official comparable to an Inspector General shall prepare and submit the annual report, or, if there is no such comparable official, the head of the agency shall prepare and submit the annual report.

(c) The annual report shall be submitted at the same time the agency submits its annual budget justifications to Congress.

(d) The annual report shall include the following: All alleged violations relating to the agency's covered Federal actions during the year covered by the report, the actions taken by the head of the agency in the year covered by the report with respect to those alleged violations and alleged violations in previous years, and the amounts of civil penalties imposed by the agency in the year covered by the report.

APPENDIX A TO PART 418—
CERTIFICATION REGARDING LOBBYING

*Certification for Contracts, Grants, Loans, and Cooperative Agreements*

The undersigned certifies, to the best of his or her knowledge and belief, that:

(1) No Federal appropriated funds have been paid or will be paid, by or on behalf of the undersigned, to any person for influencing or attempting to influence an officer or employee of an agency, a Member of Congress, an officer or employee of Congress, or an employee of a Member of Congress in connection with the awarding of any Federal contract, the making of any Federal grant, the making of any Federal loan, the entering into of any cooperative agreement, and the extension, continuation, renewal, amendment, or modification of any Federal contract, grant, loan, or cooperative agreement.

(2) If any funds other than Federal appropriated funds have been paid or will be paid to any person for influencing or attempting

to influence an officer or employee of any agency, a Member of Congress, an officer or employee of Congress, or an employee of a Member of Congress in connection with this Federal contract, grant, loan, or cooperative agreement, the undersigned shall complete and submit Standard Form-LLL, "Disclosure Form to Report Lobbying," in accordance with its instructions.

(3) The undersigned shall require that the language of this certification be included in the award documents for all subawards at all tiers (including subcontracts, subgrants, and contracts under grants, loans, and cooperative agreements) and that all subrecipients shall certify and disclose accordingly.

This certification is a material representation of fact upon which reliance was placed when this transaction was made or entered into. Submission of this certification is a prerequisite for making or entering into this transaction imposed by section 1352, title 31, U.S. Code. Any person who fails to file the required certification shall be subject to a

civil penalty of not less than $10,000 and not more than $100,000 for each such failure.

*Statement for Loan Guarantees and Loan Insurance*

The undersigned states, to the best of his or her knowledge and belief, that:

If any funds have been paid or will be paid to any person for influencing or attempting to influence an officer or employee of any agency, a Member of Congress, an officer or employee of Congress, or an employee of a Member of Congress in connection with this commitment providing for the United States to insure or guarantee a loan, the undersigned shall complete and submit Standard Form-LLL, "Disclosure Form to Report Lobbying," in accordance with its instructions.

Submission of this statement is a prerequisite for making or entering into this transaction imposed by section 1352, title 31, U.S. Code. Any person who fails to file the required statement shall be subject to a civil penalty of not less than $10,000 and not more than $100,000 for each such failure.

APPENDIX B TO PART 418—DISCLOSURE FORM TO REPORT LOBBYING

## DISCLOSURE OF LOBBYING ACTIVITIES
Complete this form to disclose lobbying activities pursuant to 31 U.S.C. 1352
(See reverse for public burden disclosure.)

Approved by OMB
0348-0046

**1. Type of Federal Action:**
- a. contract
- b. grant
- c. cooperative agreement
- d. loan
- e. loan guarantee
- f. loan insurance

**2. Status of Federal Action:**
- a. bid/offer/application
- b. initial award
- c. post-award

**3. Report Type:**
- a. initial filing
- b. material change

**For Material Change Only:**
year _____ quarter _____
date of last report _____

**4. Name and Address of Reporting Entity:**
☐ Prime    ☐ Subawardee
Tier _____, if known:

Congressional District, if known:

**5. If Reporting Entity in No. 4 is a Subawardee, Enter Name and Address of Prime:**

Congressional District, if known:

**6. Federal Department/Agency:**

**7. Federal Program Name/Description:**

CFDA Number, if applicable: _____

**8. Federal Action Number, if known:**

**9. Award Amount, if known:**
$

**10. a. Name and Address of Lobbying Entity**
(if individual, last name, first name, MI):

**b. Individuals Performing Services** (including address if different from No. 10a)
(last name, first name, MI):

(attach Continuation Sheet(s) SF-LLLA, if necessary)

**11. Amount of Payment** (check all that apply):
$ _____   ☐ actual   ☐ planned

**12. Form of Payment** (check all that apply):
- ☐ a. cash
- ☐ b. in-kind; specify:   nature _____
                            value _____

**13. Type of Payment** (check all that apply):
- ☐ a. retainer
- ☐ b. one-time fee
- ☐ c. commission
- ☐ d. contingent fee
- ☐ e. deferred
- ☐ f. other; specify: _____

**14. Brief Description of Services Performed or to be Performed and Date(s) of Service, including officer(s), employee(s), or Member(s) contacted, for Payment Indicated in Item 11:**

(attach Continuation Sheet(s) SF-LLLA, if necessary)

**15. Continuation Sheet(s) SF-LLLA attached:**   ☐ Yes   ☐ No

**16.** Information requested through this form is authorized by title 31 U.S.C. section 1352. This disclosure of lobbying activities is a material representation of fact upon which reliance was placed by the tier above when this transaction was made or entered into. This disclosure is required pursuant to 31 U.S.C. 1352. This information will be reported to the Congress semi-annually and will be available for public inspection. Any person who fails to file the required disclosure shall be subject to a civil penalty of not less that $10,000 and not more than $100,000 for each such failure.

Signature: _____
Print Name: _____
Title: _____
Telephone No.: _____   Date: _____

**Federal Use Only:**

Authorized for Local Reproduction
Standard Form LLL (Rev. 7-97)

## INSTRUCTIONS FOR COMPLETION OF SF-LLL, DISCLOSURE OF LOBBYING ACTIVITIES

This disclosure form shall be completed by the reporting entity, whether subawardee or prime Federal recipient, at the initiation or receipt of a covered Federal action, or a material change to a previous filing, pursuant to title 31 U.S.C. section 1352. The filing of a form is required for each payment or agreement to make payment to any lobbying entity for influencing or attempting to influence an officer or employee of any agency, a Member of Congress, an officer or employee of Congress, or an employee of a Member of Congress in connection with a covered Federal action. Use the SF-LLLA Continuation Sheet for additional information if the space on the form is inadequate. Complete all items that apply for both the initial filing and material change report. Refer to the implementing guidance published by the Office of Management and Budget for additional information.

1. Identify the type of covered Federal action for which lobbying activity is and/or has been secured to influence the outcome of a covered Federal action.

2. Identify the status of the covered Federal action.

3. Identify the appropriate classification of this report. If this is a followup report caused by a material change to the information previously reported, enter the year and quarter in which the change occurred. Enter the date of the last previously submitted report by this reporting entity for this covered Federal action.

4. Enter the full name, address, city, State and zip code of the reporting entity. Include Congressional District, if known. Check the appropriate classification of the reporting entity that designates if it is, or expects to be, a prime or subaward recipient. Identify the tier of the subawardee, e.g., the first subawardee of the prime is the 1st tier. Subawards include but are not limited to subcontracts, subgrants and contract awards under grants.

5. If the organization filing the report in item 4 checks "Subawardee," then enter the full name, address, city, State and zip code of the prime Federal recipient. Include Congressional District, if known.

6. Enter the name of the Federal agency making the award or loan commitment. Include at least one organizational level below agency name, if known. For example, Department of Transportation, United States Coast Guard.

7. Enter the Federal program name or description for the covered Federal action (item 1). If known, enter the full Catalog of Federal Domestic Assistance (CFDA) number for grants, cooperative agreements, loans, and loan commitments.

8. Enter the most appropriate Federal identifying number available for the Federal action identified in item 1 (e.g., Request for Proposal (RFP) number; Invitation for Bid (IFB) number; grant announcement number; the contract, grant, or loan award number; the application/proposal control number assigned by the Federal agency). Include prefixes, e.g., "RFP-DE-90-001."

9. For a covered Federal action where there has been an award or loan commitment by the Federal agency, enter the Federal amount of the award/loan commitment for the prime entity identified in item 4 or 5.

10. (a) Enter the full name, address, city, State and zip code of the lobbying entity engaged by the reporting entity identified in item 4 to influence the covered Federal action.

    (b) Enter the full names of the individual(s) performing services, and include full address if different from 10 (a). Enter Last Name, First Name, and Middle Initial (MI).

11. Enter the amount of compensation paid or reasonably expected to be paid by the reporting entity (item 4) to the lobbying entity (item 10). Indicate whether the payment has been made (actual) or will be made (planned). Check all boxes that apply. If this is a material change report, enter the cumulative amount of payment made or planned to be made.

12. Check the appropriate box(es). Check all boxes that apply. If payment is made through an in-kind contribution, specify the nature and value of the in-kind payment.

13. Check the appropriate box(es). Check all boxes that apply. If other, specify nature.

14. Provide a specific and detailed description of the services that the lobbyist has performed, or will be expected to perform, and the date(s) of any services rendered. Include all preparatory and related activity, not just time spent in actual contact with Federal officials. Identify the Federal official(s) or employee(s) contacted or the officer(s), employee(s), or Member(s) of Congress that were contacted.

15. Check whether or not a SF-LLLA Continuation Sheet(s) is attached.

16. The certifying official shall sign and date the form, print his/her name, title, and telephone number.

**DISCLOSURE OF LOBBYING ACTIVITIES**

**CONTINUATION SHEET**

Approved by OMB
0348-0046

Reporting Entity: _____　Page _____ of _____

EF　Created by: PSC Media Arts (301) 443-2454

Authorized for Local Reproduction
Standard Form - LLL-A

# PART 421—REQUIREMENTS FOR DRUG-FREE WORKPLACE (FINANCIAL ASSISTANCE)

Sec.
421.10   What does this part do?
421.20   Does this part apply to me?
421.30   What policies and procedures must I follow?

### Subpart A—Purpose and Coverage [Reserved]

### Subpart B—Requirements for Recipients Other Than Individuals

421.225   Whom in the USDA does a recipient other than an individual notify about a criminal drug conviction?

### Subpart C—Requirements for Recipients Who Are Individuals

421.300   Whom in the USDA does a recipient who is an individual notify about a criminal drug conviction?

### Subpart D—Responsibilities of Agency Awarding Officials

421.400   What method do I use as an agency awarding official to obtain a recipient's agreement to comply with the OMB guidance?

### Subpart E—Violations of This Part and Consequences

421.500   Who in the USDA determines that a recipient other than an individual violated the requirements of this part?
421.505   Who in the USDA determines that a recipient who is an individual violated the requirements of this part?

AUTHORITY: 41 U.S.C. 701–707.

SOURCE: 76 FR 76610, Dec. 8, 2011, unless otherwise noted.

## §421.10   What does this part do?

This part requires that the award and administration of USDA grants and co-operative agreements comply with Office of Management and Budget (OMB) guidance implementing the portion of the Drug-Free Workplace Act of 1988 (41 U.S.C. 701–707, as amended, hereafter referred to as "the Act") that applies to grants. It thereby—

(a) Gives regulatory effect to the OMB guidance (Subparts A through F of 2 CFR part 182) for USDA's grants and cooperative agreements; and

(b) Establishes USDA policies and procedures for compliance with the Act that are the same as those of other Federal agencies, in conformance with the requirement in 41 U.S.C. 705 for Governmentwide implementing regulations.

## §421.20   Does this part apply to me?

This part and, through this part, pertinent portions of the OMB guidance in Subparts A through F of 2 CFR part 182 (see table at 2 CFR 182.115(b)) apply to you if you are a—

(a) Recipient of a USDA grant or co-operative agreement; or

(b) USDA awarding official.

## §421.30   What policies and procedures must I follow?

(a) *General.* You must follow the policies and procedures specified in applicable sections of the OMB guidance in Subparts A through F of 2 CFR part 182, as implemented by this part.

(b) *Specific sections of OMB guidance that this part supplements.* In implementing the OMB guidance in 2 CFR part 182, this part supplements four sections of the guidance, as shown in the following table. For each of those sections, you must follow the policies and procedures in the OMB guidance, as supplemented by this part.

| Section of OMB guidance | Section in this part where supplemented | What the supplementation clarifies |
|---|---|---|
| (1) 2 CFR 182.225(a) | §421.225 | Whom in the USDA a recipient other than an individual must notify if an employee is convicted for a violation of a criminal drug statute in the workplace. |
| (2) 2 CFR 182.300(b) | §421.300 | Whom in the USDA a recipient who is an individual must notify if he or she is convicted of a criminal drug offense resulting from a violation occurring during the conduct of any award activity. |
| (3) 2 CFR 182.500 | §421.500 | Who in the USDA is authorized to determine that a recipient other than an individual is in violation of the requirements of 2 CFR part 182, as implemented by this part. |

| Section of OMB guidance | Section in this part where supplemented | What the supplementation clarifies |
|---|---|---|
| (4) 2 CFR 182.505 .......... | § 421.505 ...................... | Who in the USDA is authorized to determine that a recipient who is an individual is in violation of the requirements of 2 CFR part 182, as implemented by this part. |

(c) *Sections of the OMB guidance that this part does not supplement.* For any section of OMB guidance in Subparts A through F of 2 CFR part 182 that is not listed in paragraph (b) of this section, USDA policies and procedures are the same as those in the OMB guidance.

## Subpart A—Purpose and Coverage [Reserved]

## Subpart B—Requirements for Recipients Other Than Individuals

**§ 421.225 Whom in the USDA does a recipient other than an individual notify about a criminal drug conviction?**

A recipient other than an individual that is required under 2 CFR 182.225(a) to notify Federal agencies about an employee's conviction for a criminal drug offense must notify the awarding official for each USDA agency from which the recipient currently has an award.

## Subpart C—Requirements for Recipients Who Are Individuals

**§ 421.300 Whom in the USDA does a recipient who is an individual notify about a criminal drug conviction?**

A recipient who is an individual that is required under 2 CFR 182.300(b) to notify Federal agencies about a conviction for a criminal drug offense must notify the awarding official for each USDA agency from which the recipient currently has an award.

## Subpart D—Responsibilities of Agency Awarding Officials

**§ 421.400 What method do I use as an agency awarding official to obtain a recipient's agreement to comply with the OMB guidance?**

To obtain a recipient's agreement to comply with applicable requirements in the OMB guidance at 2 CFR part 182,

you must include the following term or condition in the award:

*Drug-free workplace.* You as the recipient must comply with drug-free workplace requirements in Subpart B (or Subpart C, if the recipient is an individual) of part 421, which adopts the Governmentwide implementation (2 CFR part 182) of sec. 5152–5158 of the Drug-Free Workplace Act of 1988 (Pub. L. 100–690, Title V, Subtitle D; 41 U.S.C. 701–707).

## Subpart E—Violations of This Part and Consequences

**§ 421.500 Who in the USDA determines that a recipient other than an individual violated the requirements of this part?**

The Secretary of Agriculture and the Secretary's designee or designees are authorized to make the determination under 2 CFR 182.500.

**§ 421.505 Who in the USDA determines that a recipient who is an individual violated the requirements of this part?**

The Secretary of Agriculture and the Secretary's designee or designees are authorized to make the determination under 2 CFR 182.505.

## PART 422—RESEARCH INSTITUTIONS CONDUCTING USDA-FUNDED EXTRAMURAL RESEARCH; RESEARCH MISCONDUCTS

Sec.
422.1  Definitions.
422.2  Procedures.
422.3  Inquiry, investigation, and adjudication.
422.4  USDA Panel to determine appropriateness of research misconduct policy.
422.5  Reservation of right to conduct subsequent inquiry, investigation, and adjudication.
422.6  Notification of USDA of allegations of research misconduct.
422.7  Notification of ARIO during an inquiry of investigation.

422.8 Communication of research misconduct policies and procedures.
422.9 Documents required.
422.10 Reporting to USDA.
422.11 Research records and evidence.
422.12 Remedies for noncompliance.
422.13 Appeals.
422.14 Relationship to other requirements.

AUTHORITY: 5 U.S.C. 301; Office of Science and Technology Policy (65 FR 76260); USDA Secretary's Memorandum (SM) 2400–007; and USDA OIG, 7 CFR 2610.1(c)(4)(ix).

SOURCE: 79 FR 75992, Dec. 19, 2014, unless otherwise noted.

§ 422.1 Definitions.

The following definitions apply to this part:

*Adjudication.* The stage in response to an allegation of research misconduct when the outcome of the investigation is reviewed, and appropriate corrective actions, if any, are determined. Corrective actions generally will be administrative in nature, such as termination of an award, debarment, award restrictions, recovery of funds, or correction of the research record. However, if there is an indication of violation of civil or criminal statutes, civil or criminal sanctions may be pursued.

*Agency Research Integrity Officer (ARIO).* The individual appointed by a USDA agency that conducts research and who is responsible for:

(1) Receiving and processing allegations of research misconduct as assigned by the USDA RIO;

(2) Informing OIG and the USDA RIO and the research institution associated with the alleged research misconduct, of allegations of research misconduct in the event it is reported to the USDA agency;

(3) Ensuring that any records, documents and other materials relating to a research misconduct allegation are provided to OIG when requested;

(4) Coordinating actions taken to address allegations of research misconduct with respect to extramural research with the research institution(s) at which time the research misconduct is alleged to have occurred, and with the USDA RIO;

(5) Overseeing proceedings to address allegations of extramurally funded research misconduct at intramural research institutions and research insti-

tutions where extramural research occurs;

(6) Ensuring that agency action to address allegations of research misconduct at USDA agencies performing extramurally funded research is performed at an organizational level that allows an independent, unbiased, and equitable process;

(7) Immediately notifying OIG, the USDA RIO, and the applicable research institution if:

(i) Public health or safety is at risk;

(ii) USDA's resources, reputation, or other interests need protecting;

(iii) Research activities should be suspended;

(iv) Federal action may be needed to protect the interest of a subject of the investigation or of others potentially affected;

(v) A premature public disclosure of the inquiry into or investigation of the allegation may compromise the process;

(vi) The scientific community or the public should be informed; or

(vii) Behavior that is or may be criminal in nature is discovered at any point during the inquiry, investigation, or adjudication phases of the research misconduct proceedings;

(8) Documenting the dismissal of the allegation, and ensuring that the name of the accused individual and/or institution is cleared if an allegation of research misconduct is dismissed at any point during the inquiry or investigation phase of the proceedings;

(9) Other duties relating to research misconduct proceedings as assigned.

*Allegation.* A disclosure of possible research misconduct through any means of communication. The disclosure may be by written or oral statement, or by other means of communication to an institutional or USDA official.

*Applied research.* Systematic study to gain knowledge or understanding necessary to determine the means by which a recognized and specific need may be met.

*Assistant Inspector General for Investigations.* The individual in OIG who is responsible for OIG's domestic and foreign investigative operations through a headquarters office and the six regional offices.

*Basic research.* Systematic study directed toward fuller knowledge or understanding of the fundamental aspects of phenomena and of observable facts without specific applications towards processes or products in mind.

*Extramural research.* Research conducted by any research institution other than the Federal agency to which the funds supporting the research were appropriated. Research institutions conducting extramural research may include Federal research facilities.

*Fabrication.* Making up data or results and recording or reporting them.

*Falsification.* Manipulating research materials, equipment, or processes, or changing or omitting data or results such that the research is not accurately represented in the research record.

*Finding of research misconduct.* The conclusion, proven by a preponderance of the evidence, that research misconduct occurred, that such research misconduct represented a significant departure from accepted practices of the relevant research community, and that such research misconduct was committed intentionally, knowingly, or recklessly.

*Inquiry.* The stage in the response to an allegation of research misconduct when an assessment is made to determine whether the allegation has substance and whether an investigation is warranted.

*Intramural research.* Research conducted by a Federal Agency, to which funds were appropriated for the purpose of conducting research.

*Investigation.* The stage in the response to an allegation of research misconduct when the factual record is formally developed and examined to determine whether to dismiss the case, recommend a finding of research misconduct, and/or take other appropriate remedies.

*Office of Inspector General (OIG).* The Office of Inspector General of the United States Department of Agriculture.

*Office of Science and Technology Policy (OSTP).* The Office of Science and Technology Policy of the Executive Office of the President.

*Plagiarism.* The appropriation of another person's ideas, processes, results, or words without giving appropriate credit.

*Preponderance of the evidence.* Proof by information that, compared with that opposing it, leads to the conclusion that the fact at issue is more probably true than not.

*Research.* All basic, applied, and demonstration research in all fields of science, engineering, and mathematics. This includes, but is not limited to, research in economics, education, linguistics, medicine, psychology, social sciences, statistics, and research involving human subjects or animals regardless of the funding mechanism used to support it.

*Research institution.* All organizations using Federal funds for research, including, for example, colleges and universities, Federally funded research and development centers, national user facilities, industrial laboratories, or other research institutes.

*Research misconduct.* Fabrication, falsification, or plagiarism in proposing, performing, or reviewing research, or in reporting research results. Research misconduct does not include honest error or differences of opinion.

*Research record.* The record of data or results that embody the facts resulting from scientific inquiry, and includes, but is not limited to, research proposals, research records (including data, notes, journals, laboratory records (both physical and electronic)), progress reports, abstracts, theses, oral presentations, internal reports, and journal articles.

*USDA.* United States Department of Agriculture.

*USDA Research Integrity Officer (USDA RIO).* The individual designated by the Office of the Under Secretary for Research, Education, and Economics (REE) who is responsible for:

(1) Overseeing USDA agency responses to allegations of research misconduct;

(2) Ensuring that agency research misconduct procedures are consistent with this part;

(3) Receiving and assigning allegations of research misconduct reported by the public;

(4) Developing Memoranda of Understanding with agencies that elect not

to develop their own research misconduct procedures;

(5) Monitoring the progress of all research misconduct cases; and

(6) Serving as liaison with OIG to receive allegations of research misconduct when they are received via the OIG Hotline.

## §422.2 Procedures.

Research institutions that conduct extramural research funded by USDA must foster an atmosphere conducive to research integrity. They must develop or have procedures in place to respond to allegations of research misconduct that ensure:

(a) Appropriate separations of responsibility for inquiry, investigation, and adjudication;

(b) Objectivity;

(c) Due process;

(d) Whistleblower protection;

(e) Confidentiality. To the extent possible and consistent with a fair and thorough investigation and as allowed by law, knowledge about the identity of subjects and informants is limited to those who need to know; and

(f) Timely resolution.

## §422.3 Inquiry, investigation, and adjudication.

A research institution that conducts extramural research funded by USDA bears primary responsibility for prevention and detection of research misconduct and for the inquiry, investigation, and adjudication of research misconduct allegations reported directly to it. The research institution must perform an inquiry in response to an allegation, and must follow the inquiry with an investigation if the inquiry determines that the allegation or apparent instance of research misconduct has substance. The responsibilities for adjudication must be separate from those for inquiry and investigation. In most instances, USDA will rely on a research institution conducting extramural research to promptly:

(a) Initiate an inquiry into any suspected or alleged research misconduct;

(b) Conduct a subsequent investigation, if warranted;

(c) Acquire, prepare, and maintain appropriate records of allegations of extramural research misconduct and all related inquiries, investigations, and findings; and

(d) Take action to ensure the following:

(1) The integrity of research;

(2) The rights and interests of the subject of the investigation and the public are protected;

(3) The observance of legal requirements or responsibilities including cooperation with criminal investigations; and

(4) Appropriate safeguards for subjects of allegations, as well as informants (see §422.6). These safeguards should include timely written notification of subjects regarding substantive allegations made against them; a description of all such allegations; reasonable access to the data and other evidence supporting the allegations; and the opportunity to respond to allegations, the supporting evidence and the proposed findings of research misconduct, if any.

## §422.4 USDA Panel to determine appropriateness of research misconduct policy.

Before USDA will rely on a research institution to conduct an inquiry, investigation, and adjudication of an allegation in accordance with this part, the research institution where the research misconduct is alleged must provide the ARIO its policies and procedures related to research misconduct at the institution. The research institution has the option of providing either a written copy of such policies and procedures or a Web site address where such policies and procedures can be accessed. The ARIO to whom the policies and procedures were made available shall convene a panel comprised of the USDA RIO and ARIOs from the Forest Service, the Agricultural Research Service, and the National Institute of Food and Agriculture. The Panel will review the research institution's policies and procedures for compliance with the OSTP Policy and render a decision regarding the research institution's ability to adequately resolve research misconduct allegations. The ARIO will inform the research institution of the Panel's determination that its inquiry, investigation, and adjudication procedures are sufficient. If the Panel determines that the research institution does not have sufficient policies and procedures in place to conduct inquiry, investigation, and adjudication proceedings, or that the research institution is in any way unfit or unprepared to handle the inquiry, investigation, and adjudication in a prompt, unbiased, fair, and independent manner, the ARIO will inform the research institution in writing of the Panel's decision. An appropriate USDA agency, as determined by the Panel, will then conduct the inquiry, investigation, and adjudication of research misconduct in accordance with this part. If an allegation of research misconduct is made regarding extramural research conducted at a Federal research institution (whether USDA or not), it is presumed that the Federal research institution has research misconduct procedures consistent with the OSTP Policy. USDA reserves the right to convene the Panel to assess the sufficiency of a Federal agency's research misconduct procedures, should there be any question whether the agency's procedures will ensure a fair, unbiased, equitable, and independent inquiry, investigation, and adjudication process.

§ 422.5 Reservation of right to conduct subsequent inquiry, investigation, and adjudication.

(a) USDA reserves the right to conduct its own inquiry, investigation, and adjudication into allegations of research misconduct at a research institution conducting extramural research subsequent to the proceedings of the research institution related to the same allegation. This may be necessary if the USDA RIO or ARIO believes, in his or her sound discretion, that despite the Panel's finding that the research institution in question had appropriate and OSTP-compliant research misconduct procedures in place, the research institution conducting the extramural research at issue:

(1) Did not adhere to its own research misconduct procedures;

(2) Did not conduct research misconduct proceedings in a fair, unbiased, or independent manner; or

(3) Has not completed research misconduct inquiry, investigation, or adjudication in a timely manner.

(b) Additionally, USDA reserves the right to conduct its own inquiry, investigation, and adjudication into allegations of research misconduct at a research institution conducting extramural research subsequent to the proceedings of the research institution related to the same allegation for any other reason that the USDA RIO or ARIO considers it appropriate to conduct research misconduct proceedings in lieu of the research institution's conducting the extramural research at issue. This right is subject to paragraph (c) of this section.

(c) In cases where the USDA RIO or ARIO believes it is necessary for USDA to conduct its own inquiry, investigation, and adjudication subsequent to the proceedings of the research institution related to the same allegation, the USDA RIO or ARIO shall reconvene the Panel, which will determine whether it is appropriate for the relevant USDA agency to conduct the research misconduct proceedings related to the allegation(s) of research misconduct. If the Panel determines that it is appropriate for a USDA agency to conduct the proceedings, the ARIO will immediately notify the research institution in question. The research institution must then promptly provide the relevant USDA agency with documentation of the research misconduct proceedings the research institution has conducted to that point, and the USDA agency will conduct research misconduct proceedings in accordance with the Agency research misconduct procedures.

§ 422.6 Notification of USDA of allegations of research misconduct.

(a) Research institutions that conduct USDA-funded extramural research must promptly notify OIG and the USDA RIO of all allegations of research misconduct involving USDA funds when the institution inquiry into the allegation warrants the institution moving on to an investigation.

(b) Individuals at research institutions who suspect research misconduct at the institution should report allegations in accordance with the institution's research misconduct policies and procedures. Anyone else who suspects that researchers or research institutions performing Federally-funded research may have engaged in research misconduct is encouraged to make a formal allegation of research misconduct to OIG.

(1) OIG may be notified using any of the following methods:

(i) Via the OIG Hotline: Telephone: (202) 690–1622, (800) 424–9121, (202) 690–1202 (TDD).

(ii) Email: usda_hotline@oig.usda.gov.

(iii) U.S. Mail: United States Department of Agriculture, Office of Inspector General, P.O. Box 23399, Washington, DC 20026–3399.

(2) The USDA RIO may be reached at: USDA Research Integrity Officer, 214W Whitten Building, Washington, DC 20250; telephone: 202–720–5923; Email: researchintegrity@usda.gov.

(c) To the extent known, the following details should be included in any formal allegation:

(1) The name of the research projects involved, the nature of the alleged misconduct, and the names of the individual or individuals alleged to be involved in the misconduct;

(2) The source or sources of funding for the research project or research projects involved in the alleged misconduct;

(3) Important dates;

(4) Any documentation that bears upon the allegation; and

(5) Any other potentially relevant information.

(d) Safeguards for informants give individuals the confidence that they can bring allegations of research misconduct made in good faith to the attention of appropriate authorities or serve as informants to an inquiry or an investigation without suffering retribution. Safeguards include protection against retaliation for informants who make good faith allegations, fair and objective procedures for the examination and resolution of allegations of research misconduct, and diligence in protecting the positions and reputations of those persons who make allegations of research misconduct in good faith. The identity of informants who wish to remain anonymous will be kept confidential to the extent permitted by law or regulation.

## §422.7 Notification of ARIO during an inquiry or investigation.

(a) Research institutions that conduct USDA-funded extramural research must promptly notify the ARIO should the institution become aware during an inquiry or investigation that:

(1) Public health or safety is at risk;

(2) The resources, reputation, or other interests of USDA are in need of protection;

(3) Research activities should be suspended;

(4) Federal action may be needed to protect the interest of a subject of the investigation or of others potentially affected;

(5) A premature public disclosure of the inquiry into or investigation of the allegation may compromise the process;

(6) The scientific community or the public should be informed; or

(7) There is reasonable indication of possible violations of civil or criminal law.

(b) If research misconduct proceedings reveal behavior that may be criminal in nature at any point during the proceedings, the institution must promptly notify the ARIO.

## §422.8 Communication of research misconduct policies and procedures.

Institutions that conduct USDA-funded extramural research are to maintain and effectively communicate to their staffs policies and procedures relating to research misconduct, including the guidelines in this part. The institution is to inform their researchers and staff members who conduct USDA-funded extramural research when and under what circumstances USDA is to be notified of allegations of research misconduct, and when and under what circumstances USDA is to be updated on research misconduct proceedings.

## §422.9 Documents required.

(a) A research institution that conducts USDA-funded extramural research must maintain the following documents related to an allegation of research misconduct at the research institution:

(1) A written statement describing the original allegation;

(2) A copy of the formal notification presented to the subject of the allegation;

(3) A written report describing the inquiry stage and its outcome including copies of all supporting documentation;

(4) A description of the methods and procedures used to gather and evaluate information pertinent to the alleged misconduct during inquiry and investigation stages;

(5) A written report of the investigation, including the evidentiary record and supporting documentation;

(6) A written statement of the findings; and

(7) If applicable, a statement of recommended corrective actions, and any response to such a statement by the subject of the original allegation, and/or other interested parties, including any corrective action plan.

(b) The research institution must retain the documents specified in paragraph (a) of this section for at least 3 years following the final adjudication of the alleged research misconduct.

## § 422.10   Reporting to USDA.

Following completion of an investigation into allegations of research misconduct, the institution conducting extramural research must provide to the ARIO a copy of the evidentiary record, the report of the investigation, recommendations made to the institution's adjudicating official, the adjudicating official's determination, the institution's corrective action taken or planned, and the written response of the individual who is the subject of the allegation to any recommendations.

## § 422.11   Research records and evidence.

(a) A research institution that conducts extramural research supported by USDA funds, as the responsible legal entity for the USDA-supported research, has a continuing obligation to create and maintain adequate records (including documents and other evidentiary matter) as may be required by any subsequent inquiry, investigation, finding, adjudication, or other proceeding.

(b) Whenever an investigation is initiated, the research institution must promptly take all reasonable and practical steps to obtain custody of all relevant research records and evidence as may be necessary to conduct the research misconduct proceedings. This must be accomplished before the research institution notifies the researcher/respondent of the allegation, or immediately thereafter.

(c) The original research records and evidence taken into custody by the research institution shall be inventoried and stored in a secure place and manner. Research records involving raw data shall include the devices or instruments on which they reside. However, if deemed appropriate by the research institution or investigator, research data or records that reside on or in instruments or devices may be copied and removed from those instruments or devices as long as the copies are complete, accurate, and have substantially equivalent evidentiary value as the data or records have when the data or records reside on the instruments or devices. Such copies of data or records shall be made by a disinterested, qualified technician and not by the subject of the original allegation or other interested parties. When the relevant data or records have been removed from the devices or instruments, the instruments or devices need not be maintained as evidence.

## § 422.12   Remedies for noncompliance.

USDA agencies' implementation procedures identify the administrative actions available to remedy a finding of research misconduct. Such actions may include the recovery of funds, correction of the research record, debarment of the researcher(s) that engaged in the research misconduct, proper attribution, or any other action deemed appropriate to remedy the instance(s) of research misconduct. The agency should consider the seriousness of the misconduct, including, but not limited to, the degree to which the misconduct was knowingly conducted, intentional, or reckless; was an isolated event or part of a pattern; or had significant impact on the research record, research subjects, other researchers, institutions, or the public welfare. In determining the appropriate administrative action, the appropriate agency must impose a remedy that is commensurate with the infraction as described in the finding of research misconduct.

### §422.13 Appeals.

(a) If USDA relied on an institution to conduct an inquiry, investigation, and adjudication, the alleged person(s) should first follow the institution's appeal policy and procedures.

(b) USDA agencies' implementation procedures identify the appeal process when a finding of research misconduct is elevated to the agency.

### §422.14 Relationship to other requirements.

Some of the research covered by this part also may be subject to regulations of other governmental agencies (*e.g.*, a university that receives funding from a USDA agency and also under a grant from another Federal agency). If more than one agency of the Federal Government has jurisdiction, USDA will cooperate with the other agency(ies) in designating a lead agency. When USDA is not the lead agency, it will rely on the lead agency following its policies and procedures in determining whether there is a finding of research misconduct. Further, USDA may, in consultation with the lead agency, take action to protect the health and safety of the public, to promote the integrity of the USDA-supported research and research process, or to conserve public funds. When appropriate, USDA will seek to resolve allegations jointly with the other agency or agencies.

## PARTS 423–499 [RESERVED]

# CHAPTER VI—DEPARTMENT OF STATE

## PART 600—THE UNIFORM ADMINIS-TRATIVE REQUIREMENTS, COST PRINCIPLES, AND AUDIT RE-QUIREMENTS FOR FEDERAL AWARDS

Sec.
600.101  Applicability.
600.205  Federal awarding agency review of risk posed by applicants.
600.315  Intangible property.
600.407  Prior written approval (prior approval).

AUTHORITY: 5 U.S.C. 301; 22 U.S.C 2651a, 22 U.S.C. 2151, 22 U.S.C. 2451, 22 U.S.C. 1461, 2 CFR part 200.

SOURCE: 79 FR 76019, Dec. 19, 2014, unless otherwise noted.

### § 600.101  Applicability.

Under the authority listed above, the Department of State adopts the Office of Management and Budget (OMB) Guidance in 2 CFR part 200, except for:

(a) The Uniform Administrative Requirements, Cost Principles, and Audit Requirements for Federal Awards set forth in 2 CFR part 200 (Subparts A through F) shall apply to all non-Federal entities, except as noted below.

(b) Subparts A through E of 2 CFR part 200 shall apply to all foreign organizations not recognized as Foreign Public Entities and Subparts A through D of 2 CFR part 200 shall apply to all U.S. and foreign for-profit entities, except where the Federal awarding agency determines that the application of these subparts would be inconsistent with the international obligations of the United States or the statute or regulations of a foreign government. The Federal Acquisition Regulation (FAR) at 48 CFR part 30, Cost Accounting Standards, and Part 31 Contract Cost Principles and Procedures takes precedence over the cost principles in Subpart E for Federal awards to U.S. and foreign for-profit entities. Thus, this part gives regulatory effect to the OMB guidance and supplements the guidance as needed for the Department.

### § 600.205  Federal awarding agency review of risk posed by applicants.

Use of 2 CFR 200.205 (the DOS review of risk posed by applicants) is required for all selected competitive and non-competitive awards.

### § 600.315  Intangible property.

If the DOS obtains research data solely in response to a FOIA request, the DOS may charge the requester fees consistent with the FOIA and applicable DOS regulations and policies.

### § 600.407  Prior written approval (prior approval).

The non-Federal entity must seek the prior written approval for indirect or special or unusual costs prior to incurring such costs where DOS is the cognizant agency.

## PART 601—NONPROCUREMENT DEBARMENT AND SUSPENSION

Sec.
601.10  What does this part do?
601.20  Does this part apply to me?
601.30  What policies and procedures must I follow?

#### Subpart A—General

601.137  Who in the Department of State may grant an exception to let an excluded person participate in a covered transaction?

#### Subpart B—Covered Transactions

601.220  What contracts and subcontracts, in addition to those listed in 2 CFR 180.220, are covered transactions?

#### Subpart C—Responsibilities of Participants Regarding Transactions

601.332  What methods must I use to pass requirements down to participants at lower tiers with whom I intend to do business?

#### Subpart D—Responsibilities of Federal Agency Officials Regarding Transactions

601.437  What method do I use to communicate to a participant the requirements described in the OMB guidance at 2 CFR 180.435?

#### Subparts E–H [Reserved]

#### Subpart I—Definitions

601.930  Debarring Official (Department of State supplement to government-wide definition at 2 CFR 180.930).

279

601.1010 Suspending Official (Department of State supplement to government-wide definition at 2 CFR 180.1010).

### Subpart J [Reserved]

AUTHORITY: Sec. 2455, Pub. L. 103–355, 108; Stat. 3327 (31 U.S.C. 6101 note); E.O. 12549; (3 CFR, 1986 Comp., p. 189); E.O. 12689 (3); CFR, 1989 Comp., p. 235).

SOURCE: 72 FR 10034, Mar. 7, 2007, unless otherwise noted.

### § 601.10  What does this part do?

This part adopts the Office of Management and Budget (OMB) guidance in subparts A through I of 2 CFR part 180, as supplemented by this part, as the DOS policies and procedures for nonprocurement debarment and suspension. It thereby gives regulatory effect for DOS to the OMB guidance as supplemented by this part. This part satisfies the requirements in section 3 of Executive Order 12549, "Debarment and Suspension" (3 CFR 1986 Comp., p. 189); Executive Order 12689, "Debarment and Suspension" (3 CFR 1989 Comp., p. 235); and section 2455 of the Federal Acquisition Streamlining Act of 1994, Pub. L. 103–355 (31 U.S.C. 6101 note).

### § 601.20  Does this part apply to me?

This part and, through this part, pertinent portions of the OMB guidance in subparts A through I of 2 CFR part 180 (see table at 2 CFR 180.100(b)) apply to you if you are a—

(a) Participant or principal in a "covered transaction" (see subpart B of 2 CFR part 180 and the definition of "nonprocurement transaction" at 2 CFR 180.970);

(b) Respondent in a DOS suspension or debarment action;

(c) DOS debarment or suspension official; and

(d) DOS grants officer, agreements officer, or other official authorized to enter into any type of nonprocurement transaction that is a covered transaction.

### § 601.30  What policies and procedures must I follow?

The DOS policies and procedures that you must follow are the policies and procedures specified in each applicable section of the OMB guidance in subparts A through I of 2 CFR part 180 and any supplemental policies and procedures set forth in this part.

## Subpart A—General

### § 601.137  Who in the Department of State may grant an exception to let an excluded person participate in a covered transaction?

The Procurement Executive, Office of the Procurement Executive, DOS, may grant an exception permitting an excluded person to participate in a particular covered transaction. If the Procurement Executive, Office of the Procurement Executive, DOS, grants an exception, the exception must be in writing and state the reason(s) for deviating from the government-wide policy in Executive Order 12549.

## Subpart B—Covered Transactions

### § 601.220  What contracts and subcontracts, in addition to those listed in 2 CFR 180.220, are covered transactions?

In addition to the contracts covered under 2 CFR 180.220(b) of the OMB guidance, this part applies to any contract, regardless of tier, that is awarded by a contractor, subcontractor, supplier, consultant, or its agent or representative in any transaction, if the contract is to be funded or provided by the DOS under a covered nonprocurement transaction and the amount of the contract is expected to equal or exceed $25,000. This extends the coverage of the DOS nonprocurement suspension and debarment requirements to all lower tiers of subcontracts under covered nonprocurement transactions, as permitted under the OMB guidance at 2 CFR 180.220(c) (see optional lower tier coverage in the figure in the appendix to 2 CFR part 180).

## Subpart C—Responsibilities of Participants Regarding Transactions

**§ 601.332 What methods must I use to pass requirements down to participants at lower tiers with whom I intend to do business?**

You, as a participant, must include a term or condition in lower-tier transactions requiring lower-tier participants to comply with subpart C of the OMB guidance in 2 CFR part 180, as supplemented by this subpart.

## Subpart D—Responsibilities of Federal Agency Officials Regarding Transactions

**§ 601.437 What method do I use to communicate to a participant the requirements described in the OMB guidance at 2 CFR 180.435?**

To communicate to a participant the requirements described in 2 CFR 180.435 of the OMB guidance, you must include a term or condition in the transaction that requires the participant's compliance with subpart C of 2 CFR part 180, as supplemented by subpart C of this part, and requires the participant to include a similar term or condition in lower-tier covered transactions.

## Subparts E–H [Reserved]

## Subpart I—Definitions

**§ 601.930 Debarring Official (Department of State supplement to government-wide definition at 2 CFR 180.930).**

The Debarring Official for the Department of State is the Procurement Executive, Office of the Procurement Executive (A/OPE).

**§ 601.1010 Suspending Official (Department of Energy supplement to government-wide definition at 2 CFR 180.1010).**

The Debarring Official for the Department of State is the Procurement Executive, Office of the Procurement Executive (A/OPE).

## Subpart J [Reserved]

## PARTS 602–699 [RESERVED]

# CHAPTER VII—AGENCY FOR INTERNATIONAL DEVELOPMENT

# PART 700—UNIFORM ADMINISTRATIVE REQUIREMENTS, COST PRINCIPLES, AND AUDIT REQUIREMENTS FOR FEDERAL AWARDS

Sec.

## Subpart A—Acronyms and Definitions

700.1   Definitions.

## Subpart B—General Provisions

700.2   Adoption of 2 CFR part 200.
700.3   Applicability.
700.4   Exceptions.
700.5   Supersession.

## Subpart C—Pre-Federal Award Requirements and Contents of Federal Awards

700.6   Metric system of measurement.
700.7   Advance payment.

## Subpart D—Post Federal Award Requirements

700.8   Payment.
700.9   Property standards.
700.10   Cost sharing or matching.
700.11   Contracting with small and minority businesses, women's business enterprises, and labor surplus area firms.
700.12   Contract provisions.
700.13   Additional provisions for awards to for-profit entities.

TERMINATION AND DISPUTES

700.14   Termination.
700.15   Disputes.

USAID—SPECIFIC REQUIREMENTS

700.16   Marking.

AUTHORITY: Sec. 621, Public L. 87–195, 75 Stat 445, (22 U.S.C. 2381) as amended, E.O. 12163, Sept 29, 1979, 44 FR 56673; 2 CFR 1979 Comp., p. 435.

SOURCE: 80 FR 55722, Sept. 17, 2015, unless otherwise noted.

## Subpart A—Acronyms and Definitions

### § 700.1   Definitions.

These are the definitions for terms used in this part. Different definitions may be found in Federal statutes or regulations that apply more specifically to particular programs or activities.

*Activity* means a set of actions through which inputs—such as commodities, technical assistance, training, or resource transfers—are mobilized to produce specific outputs, such as vaccinations given, schools built, microenterprise loans issued, or policies changed. Activities are undertaken to achieve objectives that have been formally approved and notified to Congress.

*Agreement Officer* means a person with the authority to enter into, administer, terminate and/or closeout assistance agreements subject to this part, and make related determinations and findings on behalf of USAID. An Agreement Officer can only act within the scope of a duly authorized warrant or other valid delegation of authority. The term "Agreement Officer" includes persons warranted as "Grant Officers." It also includes certain authorized representatives of the Agreement Officer acting within the limits of their authority as delegated by the Agreement Officer.

*Apparently successful applicant(s)* means the applicant(s) for USAID funding recommended for an award after merit review, but who has not yet been awarded a grant, cooperative agreement or other assistance award by the Agreement Officer. Apparently successful applicant status confers no right and constitutes no USAID commitment to an award, which still must be executed by the Agreement Officer.

*Award* means financial assistance that provides support or stimulation to accomplish a public purpose. Awards include grants, cooperative agreements, and other agreements in the form of money or property in lieu of money, by the Federal Government to an eligible recipient. The term does not include: Technical assistance, which provides services instead of money; other assistance in the form of loans, loan guarantees, interest subsidies, or insurance; direct payments of any kind to individuals; contracts which are required to be entered into and administered under procurement laws and regulations.

*Branding strategy* means a strategy the apparently successful applicant submits at the specific request of an USAID Agreement Officer after merit review of an application for USAID funding, describing how the program,

285

project, or activity is named and positioned, as well as how it is promoted and communicated to beneficiaries and cooperating country citizens. It identifies all donors and explains how they will be acknowledged. A Branding Strategy is required even if a Presumptive Exception is approved in the Marking Plan.

*Commodities* mean any material, article, supply, goods or equipment, excluding recipient offices, vehicles, and non-deliverable items for recipient's internal use in administration of the USAID-funded grant, cooperative agreement, or other agreement or sub-agreement.

*Date of completion* means the date on which all work under an award is completed or the date on the award document, or any supplement or amendment, on which USAID sponsorship ends.

*Marking plan* means a plan that the apparently successful applicant submits at the specific request of a USAID Agreement Officer after merit review of an application for USAID funding, detailing the public communications, commodities, and program materials and other items that will visibly bear the USAID Identity. Recipients may request approval of Presumptive Exceptions to marking requirements in the Marking Plan.

*Principal officer* means the most senior officer in an USAID Operating Unit in the field, *e.g.*, USAID Mission Director or USAID Representative. For global programs managed from Washington but executed across many countries such as disaster relief and assistance to internally displaced persons, humanitarian emergencies or immediate post conflict and political crisis response, the cognizant Principal Officer may be an Office Director, for example, the Directors of USAID/W/Office of Foreign Disaster Assistance and Office of Transition Initiatives. For non-presence countries, the cognizant Principal Officer is the Senior USAID officer in a regional USAID Operating Unit responsible for the non-presence country, or in the absence of such a responsible operating unit, the Principle U.S Diplomatic Officer in the non-presence country exercising delegated authority from USAID.

*Program* means an organized set of activities and allocation of resources directed toward a common purpose, objective, or goal undertaken or proposed by an organization to carry out the responsibilities assigned to it. Projects include all the marginal costs of inputs (including the proposed investment) technically required to produce a discrete marketable output or a desired result (for example, services from a fully functional water/sewage treatment facility).

*Public communications* are documents and messages intended for distribution to audiences external to the recipient's organization. They include, but are not limited to, correspondence, publications, studies, reports, audio visual productions, and other informational products; applications, forms, press and promotional materials used in connection with USAID funded programs, projects or activities, including signage and plaques; Web sites/Internet activities; and events such as training courses, conferences, seminars, press conferences and the like.

*Suspension* means an action by USAID that temporarily withdraws Federal sponsorship under an award, pending corrective action by the recipient or pending a decision to terminate the award. Suspension of an award is a separate action from suspension under USAID regulations implementing E.O.'s 12549 and 12689, "Debarment and Suspension." See 2 CFR part 780.

*Unrecovered indirect cost* means the difference between the amount awarded and the amount which could have been awarded under the recipient's approved negotiated indirect cost rate.

*USAID* means the United States Agency for International Development.

*USAID Identity* (Identity) means the official marking for the United States Agency for International Development (USAID) comprised of the USAID logo or seal and new brandmark with the tagline that clearly communicates our assistance is "from the American people." In exceptional circumstances, upon a written determination by the USAID Administrator, the definition of the USAID Identity may be amended to include additional or substitute use of a logo or seal and tagline representing a presidential initiative or other high level interagency Federal initiative that requires consistent and uniform branding and marking by all participating agencies. The USAID Identity (including any required presidential initiative or related identity) is available on the USAID Web site at *http://www.usaid.gov/branding* and is provided without royalty, license or other fee to recipients of USAID funded grants or cooperative agreements or other assistance awards.

## Subpart B—General Provisions

### §700.2  Adoption of 2 CFR Part 200.

Under the authority listed above the Agency for International Development adopts the Office of Management and Budget (OMB) guidance Uniform Administrative Requirements, Cost Principles, and Audit Requirements for Federal Awards to Non-Federal Entities (subparts A through F of 2 CFR part 200), as supplemented by this part, as the Agency for International Development (USAID) policies and procedures for financial assistance administration. This part satisfies the requirements of 2 CFR 200.110(a) and gives regulatory effect to the OMB guidance as supplemented by this part.

### §700.3  Applicability.

(a) Subparts A through D of 2 CFR part 200 apply to for-profit entities. The Federal Acquisition Regulation (FAR) at 48 CFR part 30, Cost Accounting Standards, and Part 31, Contract Cost Principles and Procedures, takes precedence over the cost principles in Subpart E for Federal awards to for-profit entities.

(b) Subpart E applies to foreign organizations and foreign public entities, except where the Federal awarding agency determines that the application of these subparts would be inconsistent with the international obligations of the United States or the statute or regulations of a foreign government.

### §700.4  Exceptions.

Consistent with 2 CFR 200.102(b):

(a) Exceptions on a case-by-case basis for individual non-Federal entities may be authorized by USAID's Assistant Administrator, Bureau for Management, or designee as delegated in Agen-

cy policy, except where otherwise required by law or where OMB or other approval is expressly required by this Part. No case-by-case exceptions may be granted to the provisions of Subpart F—Audit Requirements of this Part.

(b) USAID's Assistant Administrator, Bureau for Management, or designee as delegated in Agency policy, is also authorized to approve exceptions, on a class or an individual case basis, to USAID program specific assistance regulations other than those which implement statutory and executive order requirements.

(c) The Federal awarding agency may apply more restrictive requirements to a class of Federal awards or non-Federal entities when approved by OMB, required by Federal statutes or regulations except for the requirements in Subpart F—Audit Requirements of this part. A Federal awarding agency may apply less restrictive requirements when making awards at or below the simplified acquisition threshold, or when making fixed amount awards as defined in Subpart A—Acronyms and Definitions of 2 CFR part 200, except for those requirements imposed by statute or in Subpart F—Audit Requirements of this part.

### §700.5  Supersession.

Effective December 26, 2014, this part supersedes the following regulations under Title 22 of the Code of Federal Regulations: 22 CFR part 226, "Administration of Assistance Awards To U.S. Non-Governmental Organizations."

## Subpart C—Pre-Federal Award Requirements and Contents of Federal Awards

### §700.6  Metric system of measurement.

(a) The Metric Conversion Act, as amended by the Omnibus Trade and Competitiveness Act (15 U.S.C. 205) declares that the metric system is the preferred measurement system for U.S. trade and commerce.

(b) Wherever measurements are required or authorized, they must be made, computed, and recorded in metric system units of measurement, unless otherwise authorized by the Agreement Officer in writing when it has been found that such usage is impractical or is likely to cause U.S. firms to experience significant inefficiencies or the loss of markets. Where the metric system is not the predominant standard for a particular application, measurements may be expressed in both the metric and the traditional equivalent units, provided the metric units are listed first.

### § 700.7 Advance payment.

Advance payment mechanisms include, but are not limited to, Letter of Credit, Treasury check and electronic funds transfer and must comply with applicable guidance in 31 CFR part 205.

## Subpart D—Post Federal Award Requirements

### § 700.8 Payment.

(a) Use of resources before requesting advance payments. To the extent available, the non-Federal entity must disburse funds available from program income (including repayments to a revolving fund), rebates, refunds, contract settlements, audit recoveries, and interest earned on such funds before requesting additional cash payments. This paragraph is not applicable to such earnings which are generated as foreign currencies.

(b) Standards governing the use of banks and other institutions as depositories of advance payments under Federal awards are as follows:

(1) Except for situations described in paragraph (b)(2) of this section, USAID does not require separate depository accounts for funds provided to a non-Federal entity or establish any eligibility requirements for depositories for funds provided to the non-Federal entity. However, the non-Federal entity must be able to account for receipt, obligation and expenditure of funds.

(2) Advance payments of Federal funds must be deposited and maintained in insured accounts whenever possible.

### § 700.9 Property standards.

(a) *Real property.* Unless the agreement provides otherwise, title to real property will vest in accordance with 2 CFR 200.311.

(b) *Equipment.* Unless the agreement provides otherwise, title to equipment will vest in accordance with 2 CFR 200.313.

### § 700.10 Cost sharing or matching.

Unrecovered indirect costs, including indirect costs on cost sharing or matching may be included as part of cost sharing or matching. Unrecovered indirect cost means the difference between the amount charged to the Federal award and the amount which would have been charged to the Federal award under the non-Federal entity's approved negotiated indirect cost rate.

### § 700.11 Contracting with small and minority businesses, women's business enterprises, and labor surplus area firms.

(a) Make information on forthcoming opportunities available and arrange time frames for purchases and contracts to encourage and facilitate participation by small businesses, minority-owned firms, and women's business enterprises. To permit USAID, in accordance with the small business provisions of the Foreign Assistance Act of 1961, as amended, to give United States small business firms an opportunity to participate in supplying commodities and services procured under the award, the recipient must to the maximum extent possible provide the following information to the Office of Small Disadvantaged Business Utilization (OSDBU), USAID, Washington, DC 20523, at least 45 days prior to placing any order or contract in excess of the simplified acquisition threshold:

(1) Brief general description and quantity of goods or services;

(2) Closing date for receiving quotations, proposals or bids; and

(3) Address where solicitations or specifications can be obtained.

(b) [Reserved]

### § 700.12 Contract provisions.

(a) The non-Federal entity's contracts must contain the applicable provisions described in Appendix II to Part 200—Contract Provisions for non-Federal Entity Contracts Under Federal Awards.

(b) All negotiated contracts (except those for less than the simplified acquisition threshold) awarded by the non-Federal entity must include a provision to the effect that the non-Federal Entity, USAID, the Comptroller General of the United States, or any of their duly authorized representatives, must have access to any books, documents, papers and records of the contractor which are directly pertinent to a specific program for the purpose of making audits, examinations, excerpts and transcriptions.

§700.13 Additional provisions for awards to for-profit entities.

(a) This paragraph contains additional provisions that apply to awards to for-profit entities. These provisions supplement and make exceptions for awards to for-profit entities from other provisions of this part.

(1) Prohibition against profit. No funds will be paid as profit to any for-profit entity receiving or administering Federal financial assistance as a recipient or subrecipient. Federal financial assistance does not include contracts as defined at 2 CFR 200.22, other contracts a Federal agency uses to buy goods or services from a contractor, or contracts to operate Federal government owned, contractor operated facilities (GOCOs). Profit is any amount in excess of allowable direct and indirect costs.

(2) Program income. As described in §200.307(e)(2), program income earned by a for-profit entity may not be added to the Federal award.

(b) [Reserved]

TERMINATION AND DISPUTES

§700.14 Termination.

If at any time USAID determines that continuation of all or part of the funding for a program should be suspended or terminated because such assistance would not be in the national interest of the United States or would be in violation of an applicable law, then USAID may, following notice to the recipient, suspend or terminate the award in whole or in part and prohibit the recipient from incurring additional obligations chargeable to the award other than those costs specified in the notice of suspension. If a suspension is put into effect and the situation causing the suspension continues for 60 calendar days or more, then USAID may terminate the award in whole or in part on written notice to the recipient and cancel any portion of the award which has not been disbursed or irrevocably committed to third parties.

§700.15 Disputes.

(a) Any dispute under or relating to a grant or agreement will be decided by the USAID Agreement Officer. The Agreement Officer must furnish the recipient a written copy of the decision.

(b) Decisions of the USAID Agreement Officer will be final unless, within 30 calendar days of receipt of the decision, the recipient appeals the decision to USAID's Assistant Administrator, Bureau for Management, or designee as delegated in Agency policy. Appeals must be in writing with a copy concurrently furnished to the Agreement Officer.

(c) In order to facilitate review of the record by the USAID's Assistant Administrator, Bureau for Management, or designee as delegated in Agency policy, the recipient will be given an opportunity to submit written evidence in support of its appeal. No hearing will be provided.

(d) Decisions by the Assistant Administrator, Bureau for Management, or designee as delegated in Agency policy, will be final.

USAID—SPECIFIC REQUIREMENTS

§700.16 Marking.

(a) USAID policy is that all programs, projects, activities, public communications, and commodities, specified further at paragraphs (c) through (f) of this section, partially or fully funded by a USAID grant or cooperative agreement or other assistance award or subaward must be marked appropriately overseas with the USAID Identity, of a size and prominence equivalent to or greater than the recipient's, other donor's or any other third party's identity or logo.

(1) USAID reserves the right to require the USAID Identity to be larger

and more prominent if it is the majority donor, or to require that a cooperating country government's identity be larger and more prominent if circumstances warrant; any such requirement will be on a case-by-case basis depending on the audience, program goals and materials produced.

(2) USAID reserves the right to request pre-production review of USAID funded public communications and program materials for compliance with the approved Marking Plan.

(3) USAID reserves the right to require marking with the USAID Identity in the event the recipient does not choose to mark with its own identity or logo.

(4) To ensure that the marking requirements "flow down" to subrecipients of subawards, recipients of USAID funded grants and cooperative agreements or other assistance awards are required to include a USAID-approved marking provision in any USAID funded subaward, to read as follows:

As a condition of receipt of this subaward, marking with the USAID Identity of a size and prominence equivalent to or greater than the recipient's, subrecipient's, other donor's or third party's is required. In the event the recipient chooses not to require marking with its own identity or logo by the subrecipient, USAID may, at its discretion, require marking by the subrecipient with the USAID Identity.

(b) Subject to § 700.16(a), (h), and (j), program, project, or activity sites funded by USAID, including visible infrastructure projects (for example, roads, bridges, buildings) or other programs, projects, or activities that are physical in nature (for example, agriculture, forestry, water management), must be marked with the USAID Identity. Temporary signs or plaques should be erected early in the construction or implementation phase. When construction or implementation is complete, a permanent, durable sign, plaque or other marking must be installed.

(c) Subject to § 700.16(a), (h), and (j), technical assistance, studies, reports, papers, publications, audio-visual productions, public service announcements, Web sites/Internet activities and other promotional, informational, media, or communications products

funded by USAID must be marked with the USAID Identity.

(1) Any "public communications" as defined in § 700.1, funded by USAID, in which the content has not been approved by USAID, must contain the following disclaimer:

This study/report/audio/visual/other information/media product (specify) is made possible by the generous support of the American people through the United States Agency for International Development (USAID). The contents are the responsibility of [insert recipient name] and do not necessarily reflect the views of USAID or the United States Government.

(2) The recipient must provide the Agreement Officer's Representative (AOR) or other USAID personnel designated in the grant or cooperative agreement with at least two copies of all program and communications materials produced under the award. In addition, the recipient must submit one electronic and/or one hard copy of all final documents to USAID's Development Experience Clearinghouse.

(d) Subject to § 700.16(a), (h), and (j), events financed by USAID such as training courses, conferences, seminars, exhibitions, fairs, workshops, press conferences and other public activities, must be marked appropriately with the USAID Identity. Unless directly prohibited and as appropriate to the surroundings, recipients should display additional materials such as signs and banners with the USAID Identity. In circumstances in which the USAID Identity cannot be displayed visually, recipients are encouraged otherwise to acknowledge USAID and the American people's support.

(e) Subject to § 700.16(a), (h), and (j), all commodities financed by USAID, including commodities or equipment provided under humanitarian assistance or disaster relief programs, and all other equipment, supplies and other materials funded by USAID, and their export packaging, must be marked with the USAID Identity.

(f) After merit review of applications for USAID funding, USAID Agreement Officers will request apparently successful applicants to submit a Branding Strategy, defined in § 700.1. The proposed Branding Strategy will not be evaluated competitively. The Agreement Officer will review for adequacy the proposed Branding Strategy, and will negotiate, approve and include the Branding Strategy in the award. Failure to submit or negotiate a Branding Strategy within the time specified by the Agreement Officer will make the apparently successful applicant ineligible for award.

(g) After merit review of applications for USAID funding, USAID Agreement Officers will request apparently successful applicants to submit a Marking Plan, defined in §700.1. The Marking Plan may include requests for approval of Presumptive Exceptions, paragraph (h) of this section. All estimated costs associated with branding and marking USAID programs, such as plaques, labels, banners, press events, promotional materials, and the like, must be included in the total cost estimate of the grant or cooperative agreement or other assistance award, and are subject to revision and negotiation with the Agreement Officer upon submission of the Marking Plan. The Marking Plan will not be evaluated competitively. The Agreement Officer will review for adequacy the proposed Marking Plan, and will negotiate, approve and include the Marking Plan in the award. Failure to submit or negotiate a Marking Plan within the time specified by the Agreement Officer will make the apparently successful applicant ineligible for award. Agreement Officers have the discretion to suspend the implementation requirements of the Marking Plan if circumstances warrant. Recipients of USAID funded grant or cooperative agreement or other assistance award or subaward should retain copies of any specific marking instructions or waivers in their project, program or activity files. Agreement Officer's Representatives will be assigned responsibility to monitor marking requirements on the basis of the approved Marking Plan.

(h) Presumptive exceptions:

(1) The above marking requirements in §700.16(a) through (e) may not apply if marking would:

(i) Compromise the intrinsic independence or neutrality of a program or materials where independence or neutrality is an inherent aspect of the program and materials, such as election monitoring or ballots, and voter information literature; political party support or public policy advocacy or reform; independent media, such as television and radio broadcasts, newspaper articles and editorials; public service announcements or public opinion polls and surveys.

(ii) Diminish the credibility of audits, reports, analyses, studies, or policy recommendations whose data or findings must be seen as independent.

(iii) Undercut host-country government "ownership" of constitutions, laws, regulations, policies, studies, assessments, reports, publications, surveys or audits, public service announcements, or other communications better positioned as "by" or "from" a cooperating country ministry or government official.

(iv) Impair the functionality of an item, such as sterilized equipment or spare parts.

(v) Incur substantial costs or be impractical, such as items too small or other otherwise unsuited for individual marking, such as food in bulk.

(vi) Offend local cultural or social norms, or be considered inappropriate on such items as condoms, toilets, bed pans, or similar commodities.

(vii) Conflict with international law.

(2) These exceptions are presumptive, not automatic and must be approved by the Agreement Officer. Apparently successful applicants may request approval of one or more of the presumptive exceptions, depending on the circumstances, in their Marking Plan. The Agreement Officer will review requests for presumptive exceptions for adequacy, along with the rest of the Marking Plan. When reviewing a request for approval of a presumptive exception, the Agreement Officer may review how program materials will be marked (if at all) if the USAID identity is removed. Exceptions approved will apply to subrecipients unless otherwise provided by USAID.

(i) In cases where the Marking Plan has not been complied with, the Agreement Officer will initiate corrective action. Such action may involve informing the recipient of a USAID grant or cooperative agreement or other assistance award or subaward of instances of noncompliance and requesting that the recipient carry out its responsibilities as set forth in the Marking Plan and award. Major or repeated non-compliance with the Marking Plan will be governed by the uniform suspension and termination procedures set forth at 2 CFR 200.338 through 2 CFR 200.342, and 2 CFR 700.14.

(j)(1) *Waivers.* USAID Principal Officers, defined for purposes of this provision at §700.1, may at any time after award waive in whole or in part the USAID approved Marking Plan, including USAID marking requirements for each USAID funded program, project, activity, public communication or commodity, or in exceptional circumstances may make a waiver by region or country, if the Principal Officer determines that otherwise USAID required marking would pose compelling political, safety, or security concerns, or marking would have an adverse impact in the cooperating country. USAID recipients may request waivers of the Marking Plan in whole or in part, through the AOR. No marking is required while a waiver determination is pending. The waiver determination on safety or security grounds must be made in consultation with U.S. Government security personnel if available, and must consider the same information that applies to determinations of the safety and security of U.S. Government employees in the cooperating country, as well as any information supplied by the AOR or the recipient for whom the waiver is sought. When reviewing a request for approval of a waiver, the Principal Officer may review how program materials will be marked (if at all) if the USAID Identity is removed. Approved waivers are not limited in duration but are subject to Principal Officer review at any time due to changed circumstances. Approved waivers "flow down" to recipients of subawards unless specified otherwise. Principal Officers may also authorize the removal of USAID markings already affixed if circumstances warrant. Principal Officers' determinations regarding waiver requests are subject to appeal to the Principal Officer's cognizant Assistant Administrator. Recipients may appeal by submitting a written request to reconsider the Principal Officer's waiver determination to the cognizant Assistant Administrator.

(2) *Non-retroactivity.* Marking requirements apply to any obligation of USAID funds for new awards as of January 2, 2006. Marking requirements also will apply to new obligations under existing awards, such as incremental funding actions, as of January 2, 2006, when the total estimated cost of the existing award has been increased by USAID or the scope of effort is changed to accommodate any costs associated with marking. In the event a waiver is rescinded, the marking requirements will apply from the date forward that the waiver is rescinded. In the event a waiver is rescinded after the period of performance as defined in 2 CFR 200.77 but before closeout as defined in 2 CFR 200.16., the USAID mission or operating unit with initial responsibility to administer the marking requirements must make a cost benefit analysis as to requiring USAID marking requirements after the date of completion of the affected programs, projects, activities, public communications or commodities.

(k) The USAID Identity and other guidance will be provided at no cost or fee to recipients of USAID grants, cooperative agreements or other assistance awards or subawards. Additional costs associated with marking requirements will be met by USAID if reasonable, allowable, and allocable under 2 CFR part 200, subpart E. The standard cost reimbursement provisions of the grant, cooperative agreement, other assistance award or subaward must be followed when applying for reimbursement of additional marking costs.

(End of award term)

# PART 701—PARTNER VETTING IN USAID ASSISTANCE

AUTHORITY: 22 U.S.C. 2251 *et seq.*; 22 U.S.C. 2151t, 22 U.S.C. 2151a, 2151b, 2151c, and 2151d; 22 U.S.C. 2395(b).

SOURCE: 80 FR 36705, June 26, 2015, unless otherwise noted.

## §701.1 Definitions.

This section contains the definitions for terms used in this part. Other terms used in the part are defined at 2 CFR part 200. Different definitions may be found in Federal statutes or regulations that apply more specifically to particular programs or activities.

*Key individual* means the principal officer of the organization's governing body (for example, chairman, vice chairman, treasurer and secretary of the board of directors or board of trustees); the principal officer and deputy principal officer of the organization (for example, executive director, deputy director, president, vice president); the program manager or chief of party for the USG-financed program; and any other person with significant responsibilities for administration of the USG-financed activities or resources, such as key personnel as identified in the solicitation or resulting cooperative agreement. Key personnel, whether or not they are employees of the prime recipient, must be vetted.

*Key personnel* means those individuals identified for approval as part of substantial involvement in a cooperative agreement whose positions are essential to the successful implementation of an award. *Vetting official* means the USAID employee identified in the application or award as having responsibility for receiving vetting information, responding to questions about information to be included on the Partner Information Form, coordinating with the USAID Office of Security (SEC), and conveying the vetting determination to each applicant, potential subrecipients and contractors subject to vetting, and the agreement officer. The vetting official is not part of the office making the award selection and has no involvement in the selection process.

## §701.2 Applicability.

The requirements established in this part apply to non-Federal entities, non-profit organizations, for-profit entities, and foreign organizations.

## §701.3 Partner vetting.

(a) It is USAID policy that USAID may determine that a particular award is subject to vetting in the interest of national security. In that case, USAID may require vetting of the key individuals of applicants, including key personnel, whether or not they are employees of the applicant, first tier subrecipients, contractors, and any other class of subawards and procurements as identified in the assistance solicitation and resulting award. When USAID conducts partner vetting, it will not award to any applicant who determined ineligible by the vetting process.

(b) When USAID determines an award to be subject to vetting, the agreement officer determines the appropriate stage of the award cycle to require applicants to submit the completed USAID Partner Information Form, USAID Form 500–13, to the vetting official identified in the assistance solicitation. The agreement officer must specify in the assistance solicitation the stage at which the applicants will be required to submit the USAID Partner Information Form, USAID Form 500–13. As a general matter those applicants who will be vetted will be typically the applicants that have been determined to be apparently successful.

(c) Selection of the successful applicant proceeds separately from vetting. The agreement officer makes the selection determination separately from the vetting process and without knowledge of vetting-related information other than that, based on the vetting results, the apparently successful applicant is eligible or ineligible for an award. However, no applicants will be excluded from an award until after vetting has been completed.

(d) For those awards the agency has determined are subject to vetting, the agreement officer may only award to an applicant that has been determined to be eligible after completion of the vetting process.

(e)(1) For those awards the agency has determined are subject to vetting, the recipient must submit the completed USAID Partner Information Form any time it changes:

(i) Key individuals; or

(ii) Subrecipients and contractors for which vetting is required.

(2) The recipient must submit the completed Partner Information Form within 15 days of the change in either paragraph (e)(1)(i) or (ii) of this section.

(f) USAID may vet key individuals of the recipient, subrecipients and contractors periodically during program implementation using information already submitted on the Form.

(g) When the prime recipient is subject to vetting, vetting may be required for key individuals of subawards when the prime recipient requests prior approval in accordance with 2 CFR 200.308(c)(6) for the subaward, transfer, or contracting out of any work.

(h) When the prime recipient is subject to vetting, vetting may be required for key individuals of contractors of certain services. The agreement officer must identify these services in the assistance solicitation and any resulting award.

(i) When vetting of subawards is required, the agreement officer must not approve the subaward, transfer, or contracting out, or the procurement of certain classes of items until the organization subject to vetting has been determined eligible. When vetting of contractors is required, the recipient may not procure the identified services until the contractor has been determined to be eligible.

(j) The recipient may instruct prospective subrecipients or, when applicable contractors who are subject to vetting to submit the USAID Partner Information Form to the vetting official as soon as the recipient submits the USAID Partner Information Form for its key individuals.

(k) *Pre-award provision and award term.* (1) The agreement officer must insert the pre-award provision Partner Vetting Pre-Award Requirements in Appendix B of this part in all assistance solicitations USAID identifies as subject to vetting.

(2) The agreement officer must insert the award term Partner Vetting in Appendix B in all assistance solicitations and awards USAID identifies as subject to vetting.

APPENDIX B TO PART 701—PARTNER VETTING PRE-AWARD REQUIREMENTS AND AWARD TERM

*Partner Vetting Pre-Award Requirements*

(a) USAID has determined that any award resulting from this assistance solicitation is subject to vetting. An applicant that has not passed vetting is ineligible for award.

(b) The following are the vetting procedures for this solicitation:

(1) Prospective applicants review the attached USAID Partner Information Form, USAID Form 500–13, and submit any questions about the USAID Partner Information Form or these procedures to the agreement officer by the deadline in the solicitation.

(2) The agreement officer notifies the applicant when to submit the USAID Partner Information Form. For this solicitation, USAID will vet [insert in the provision the applicable stage of the selection process at which the Agreement Officer will notify the applicant(s) who must be vetted]. Within the timeframe set by the agreement officer in the notification, the applicant must complete and submit the USAID Partner Information Form to the vetting official. The designated vetting official is:

Vetting official: _____

Address: _____

Email: _____
(for inquiries only).

(3) The applicants must notify proposed subrecipients and contractors of this requirement when the subrecipients or contractors are subject to vetting.

NOTE: Applicants who submit using non-secure methods of transmission do so at their own risk.

(c) Selection proceeds separately from vetting. Vetting is conducted independently from any discussions the agreement officer may have with an applicant. The applicant and any proposed subrecipient or contractor subject to vetting must not provide vetting information to anyone other than the vetting official. The applicant and any proposed subrecipient or contractor subject to vetting will communicate only with the vetting official regarding their vetting submission(s) and not with any other USAID or USG personnel, including the agreement officer or the agreement officer's representatives. The agreement officer designates the vetting official as the only individual authorized to clarify the applicant's and proposed subrecipient's and contractor's vetting information.

(d)(1) The vetting official notifies the applicant that it: (i) Is eligible based on the vetting results, (ii) is ineligible based on the vetting results, or (iii) must provide additional information, and resubmit the USAID

Partner Information Form with the additional information within the number of days the vetting official specified in the notification.

(2) The vetting official will coordinate with the agency that provided the data being used for vetting prior to notifying the applicant or releasing any information. In any determination for release of information, the classification and sensitivity of the information, the need to protect sources and methods, and the status of ongoing law enforcement and intelligence community investigations or operations will be taken into consideration.

(e) Reconsideration: (1) Within 7 calendar days after the date of the vetting official's notification, an applicant that vetting has determined to be ineligible may request in writing to the vetting official that the Agency reconsider the vetting determination. The request should include any written explanation, legal documentation and any other relevant written material for reconsideration.

(2) Within 7 calendar days after the vetting official receives the request for reconsideration, the Agency will determine whether the applicant's additional information merits a revised decision.

(3) The Agency's determination of whether reconsideration is warranted is final.

(f) Revisions to vetting information: (1) Applicants who change key individuals, whether the applicant has previously been determined eligible or not, must submit a revised USAID Partner Information Form to the vetting official. This includes changes to key personnel resulting from revisions to the technical portion of the application.

(2) The vetting official will follow the vetting process of this provision for any revision of the applicant's Form.

(g) Award. At the time of award, the agreement officer will confirm with the vetting official that the apparently successful applicant is eligible after vetting. The agreement officer may award only to an apparently successful applicant that is eligible after vetting.

*Partner Vetting*

(a) The recipient must comply with the vetting requirements for key individuals under this award.

(b) Definitions: As used in this provision, "key individual," "key personnel," and "vetting official" have the meaning contained in 22 CFR 701.1.

(c) The Recipient must submit within 15 days a USAID Partner Information Form, USAID Form 500–13, to the vetting official identified below when the Recipient replaces key individuals with individuals who have not been previously vetted for this award. Note: USAID will not approve any key personnel who are not eligible for approval after vetting. The designated vetting official is:

Vetting official: _____
Address: _____
Email: _____
(for inquiries only).

(d)(1) The vetting official will notify the Recipient that it—
(i) Is eligible based on the vetting results,
(ii) Is ineligible based on the vetting results, or
(iii) Must provide additional information, and resubmit the USAID Partner Information Form with the additional information within the number of days the vetting official specifies.

(2) The vetting official will include information that USAID determines releasable. USAID will determine what information may be released consistent with applicable law and Executive Orders, and with the concurrence of relevant agencies.

(e) The inability to be deemed eligible as described in this award term may be determined to be a material failure to comply with the terms and conditions of the award and may subject the recipient to suspension or termination as specified in the subpart "Remedies for Noncompliance" at 2 CFR part 200.

(f) Reconsideration: (1) Within 7 calendar days after the date of the vetting official's notification, the recipient or prospective subrecipient or contractor that has not passed vetting may request in writing to the vetting official that the Agency reconsider the vetting determination. The request should include any written explanation, legal documentation and any other relevant written material for reconsideration.

(2) Within 7 calendar days after the vetting official receives the request for reconsideration, the Agency will determine whether the recipient's additional information merits a revised decision.

(3) The Agency's determination of whether reconsideration is warranted is final.

(g) A notification that the Recipient has passed vetting does not constitute any other approval under this award.

Alternate I. When subrecipients will be subject to vetting, add the following paragraphs to the basic award term:

(h) When the prime recipient anticipates that it will require prior approval for a subaward in accordance with 2 CFR 200.308(c)(6) the subaward is subject to vetting. The prospective subrecipient must submit a USAID Partner Information Form, USAID Form 500–13, to the vetting official identified in paragraph (c) of this provision. The agreement officer must not approve a subaward to any organization that has not passed vetting when required.

(i) The recipient agrees to incorporate the substance of paragraphs (a) through (i) of this award term in all first tier subawards under this award.

Alternate II. When specific classes of services are subject to vetting, add the following paragraph:

(j) Prospective contractors at any tier providing the following classes of services

_____

_____

must pass vetting. Recipients must not pro cure these services until they receive confirmation from the vetting official that the prospective contractor has passed vetting. (End of award term)

## PARTS 702-779 [RESERVED]

## PART 780—NONPROCUREMENT DEBARMENT AND SUSPENSION

AUTHORITY: Sec. 2455, Pub. L. 103–355, 108 Stat. 3327; E.O. 12549, 3 CFR, 1986 Comp., p. 189; E.O. 12689, 3 CFR, 1989 Comp., p. 235.

SOURCE: 76 FR 34144, June 13, 2011, unless otherwise noted.

### § 780.10  What does this part do?

This part adopts the Office of Management and Budget (OMB) guidance in subparts A through I of 2 CFR part 180, as supplemented by this part, as the USAID policies and procedures for nonprocurement debarment and suspension. It thereby gives regulatory effect for USAID to the OMB guidance as supplemented by this part. This part satisfies the requirements in section 3 of Executive Order 12549, "Debarment and Suspension" (3 CFR 1986 Comp., p. 189); Executive Order 12689, "Debarment and Suspension" (3 CFR 1989 Comp., p. 235); and section 2455 of the Federal Acquisition Streamlining Act of 1994, Public Law 103–355 (31 U.S.C. 6101 note).

### § 780.20  Does this part apply to me?

This part and, through this part, pertinent portions of the OMB guidance in subparts A through I of 2 CFR part 180 (see table at 2 CFR 180.100(b)) apply to you if you are a—

(a) Participant or principal in a "covered transaction" (see subpart B of 2 CFR part 180 and the definition of "non-procurement transaction" at 2 CFR 180.970);

(b) Respondent in a USAID suspension or debarment action;

(c) USAID debarment or suspension official; and

(d) USAID grants officer, agreements officer, or other official authorized to enter into any type of non-procurement transaction that is a covered transaction.

### § 780.30  What policies and procedures must I follow?

The USAID policies and procedures that you must follow are the policies and procedures specified in each applicable section of the OMB guidance in subparts A through I of 2 CFR part 180 and any supplemental policies and procedures set forth in this part.

## Subpart A—General

### § 780.137 Who in USAID may grant an exception to let an excluded person participate in a covered transaction?

The Assistant Administrator, Bureau for Management, or designee as delegated in Agency policy found in ADS 103—Delegations of Authority, may grant an exception permitting an excluded person to participate in a particular covered transaction. If the Assistant Administrator, Bureau for Management or designee, grants an exception, the exception must be in writing and state the reason(s) for deviating from the government-wide policy in Executive Order 12549.

[80 FR 12915, Mar. 12, 2015]

## Subpart B—Covered Transactions

### § 780.220 What contracts and subcontracts, in addition to those listed in 2 CFR 180.220, are covered transactions?

In addition to the contracts covered under 2 CFR 180.220(b) of the OMB guidance, this part applies to any contract, regardless of tier, that is awarded by a contractor, subcontractor, supplier, consultant, or its agent or representative in any transaction, if the contract is to be funded or provided by the USAID under a covered non-procurement transaction and the amount of the contract is expected to equal or exceed $25,000. This extends the coverage of the USAID non-procurement suspension and debarment requirements to all lower tiers of subcontracts under covered non-procurement transactions, as permitted under the OMB guidance at 2 CFR 180.220(c) (see optional lower tier coverage in the figure in the appendix to 2 CFR part 180).

## Subpart C—Responsibilities of Participants Regarding Transactions

### § 780.332 What requirements must I pass down to persons at lower tiers with whom I intend to do business?

You, as a participant, must include a term or condition in lower-tier transactions requiring lower-tier partici-pants to comply with subpart C of the OMB guidance in 2 CFR part 180, as supplemented by this subpart.

## Subpart D—Responsibilities of Federal Agency Officials Regarding Transactions

### § 780.437 What method do I use to communicate to a participant the requirements described in the OMB guidance at 2 CFR 180.435?

To communicate to a participant the requirements described in 2 CFR 180.435 of the OMB guidance, you must include a term or condition in the transaction that requires the participant's compliance with subpart C of 2 CFR part 180, and supplemented by subpart C of this part, and requires the participant to include a similar term or condition in lower-tier covered transactions.

## Subparts E–H [Reserved]

## Subpart I—Definitions

### § 780.930 Debarring Official (Agency for International Development supplement to government-wide definition at 2 CFR 180.930).

The *Debarring Official* for USAID is the Assistant Administrator, Bureau for Management, or designee as delegated in Agency policy found in ADS 103—Delegations of Authority.

[80 FR 12916, Mar. 12, 2015]

### § 780.1010 Suspending Official (Agency for International Development supplement to government-wide definition at 2 CFR 180.1010).

The *Suspending Official* for USAID is the Assistant Administrator, Bureau for Management, or designee as delegated in Agency policy found in ADS 103—Delegations of Authority.

[80 FR 12916, Mar. 12, 2015]

## Subpart J [Reserved]

## PART 782—REQUIREMENTS FOR DRUG-FREE WORKPLACE (FINANCIAL ASSISTANCE)

Sec.
782.10  What does this part do?
782.20  Does this part apply to me?

782.30 What policies and procedures must I follow?

### Subpart A—Purpose and Coverage [Reserved]

### Subpart B—Requirements for Recipients Other Than Individuals

782.225 Whom in USAID does a recipient other than an individual notify about a criminal drug conviction?

### Subpart C—Requirements for Recipients Who Are Individuals

782.300 Whom in USAID does a recipient who is an individual notify about a criminal drug conviction?

### Subpart D—Responsibilities of Agency Awarding Officials

782.400 What method do I use as an agency awarding official to obtain a recipient's agreement to comply with the OMB guidance?

### Subpart E—Violations of This Part and Consequences

782.500 Who in USAID determines that a recipient other than an individual violated the requirements of this part?
782.505 Who in USAID determines that a recipient who is an individual violated the requirements of this part?

### Subpart F—Definitions

782.605 Award (USAID Supplement to Government Wide Definition at 2 CFR 182.605).

AUTHORITY: 41 U.S.C. 701–707.

SOURCE: 76 FR 34574, June 14, 2011, unless otherwise noted.

### § 782.10 What does this part do?

This part requires that the award and administration of USAID grants and cooperative agreements comply with Office of Management and Budget (OMB) guidance implementing the portion of the Drug-Free Workplace Act of 1988 (41 U.S.C. 701–707, as amended, hereafter referred to as "the Act") that applies to grants. It thereby—

(a) Gives regulatory effect to the OMB guidance (Subparts A through F of 2 CFR Part 182) for USAID's grants and cooperative agreements; and

(b) Establishes USAID policies and procedures for compliance with the Act that are the same as those of other Federal agencies, in conformance with the requirement in 41 U.S.C. 705 for Government wide implementing regulations.

### § 782.20 Does this part apply to me?

This part and, through this part, pertinent portions of the OMB guidance in subparts A through F of 2 CFR part 182 (see table at 2 CFR 182.115(b)) apply to you if you are a—

(a) Recipient of a USAID grant or cooperative agreement; or

(b) USAID awarding official.

### § 782.30 What policies and procedures must I follow?

(a) *General.* You must follow the policies and procedures specified in applicable sections of the OMB guidance in Subparts A through F of 2 CFR part 182, as implemented by this part.

(b) *Specific sections of OMB guidance that this part supplements.* In implementing the OMB guidance in 2 CFR part 182, this part supplements four sections of the guidance, as shown in the following table. For each of those sections, you must follow the policies and procedures in the OMB guidance, as supplemented by this part.

| Section of OMB guidance | Section in this part where supplemented | What the supplementation clarifies |
|---|---|---|
| (1) 2 CFR 182.225(a) ..................... | § 782.225 | Whom in USAID a recipient other than an individual must notify if an employee is convicted for a violation of a criminal drug statute in the workplace. |
| (2) 2 CFR 182.300(b) ..................... | § 782.300 | Whom in USAID a recipient who is an individual must notify if he or she is convicted of a criminal drug offense resulting from a violation occurring during the conduct of any award activity. |
| (3) 2 CFR 182.500 .......................... | § 782.500 | Who in USAID is authorized to determine that a recipient other than an individual is in violation of the requirements of 2 CFR part 182, as implemented by this part. |
| (4) 2 CFR 182.505 .......................... | § 782.505 | Who in USAID is authorized to determine that a recipient who is an individual is in violation of the requirements of 2 CFR part 182, as implemented by this part. |

(c) *Sections of the OMB guidance that this part does not supplement.* For any section of OMB guidance in Subparts A through F of 2 CFR part 182 that is not listed in paragraph (b) of this section, USAID policies and procedures are the same as those in the OMB guidance.

## Subpart A—Purpose and Coverage [Reserved]

## Subpart B—Requirements for Recipients Other Than Individuals

**§ 782.225 Whom in USAID does a recipient other than an individual notify about a criminal drug conviction?**

A recipient other than an individual that is required under 2 CFR 182.225(a) to notify Federal agencies about an employee's conviction for a criminal drug offense must notify—

(a) Federal agencies if an employee who is engaged in the performance of an award informs you about a conviction, or you otherwise learn of the conviction. Your notification to the Federal agencies must—

(1) Be in writing;

(2) Include the employee's position title;

(3) Include the identification number(s) of each affected award;

(4) Be sent within ten calendar days after you learn of the conviction; and

(5) Be sent to every Federal agency on whose award the convicted employee was working. It must be sent to every awarding official or his or her official designee, unless the Federal agency has specified a central point for the receipt of the notices.

(b) Within 30 calendar days of learning about an employee's conviction, you must either—

(1) Take appropriate personnel action against the employee, up to and including termination, consistent with the requirements of the Rehabilitation Act of 1973 (29 U.S.C. 794), as amended; or

(2) Require the employee to participate satisfactorily in a drug abuse assistance or rehabilitation program approved for these purposes by a Federal, State or local health, law enforcement, or other appropriate agency.

## Subpart C—Requirements for Recipients Who Are Individuals

**§ 782.300 Whom in USAID does a recipient who is an individual notify about a criminal drug conviction?**

A recipient who is an individual and is required under 2 CFR 182.300(b) to notify Federal agencies about a conviction for a criminal drug offense must notify each USAID office from which it currently has an award.

## Subpart D—Responsibilities of Agency Awarding Officials

**§ 782.400 What method do I use as an agency awarding official to obtain a recipient's agreement to comply with the OMB guidance?**

To obtain a recipient's agreement to comply with applicable requirements in the OMB guidance at 2 CFR part 182, you must include the following term or condition in the award:

*Drug-free workplace.* You as the recipient must comply with drug-free workplace requirements in subpart B (or subpart C, if the recipient is an individual) of 782, which adopts the Government-wide implementation (2 CFR part 182) of sec. 5152–5158 of the Drug-Free Workplace Act of 1988 (Pub. L. 100–690, Title V, Subtitle D; 41 U.S.C. 701–707).

## Subpart E—Violations of This Part and Consequences

**§ 782.500 Who in USAID determines that a recipient other than an individual violated the requirements of this part?**

The Director of the Office of Acquisition and Assistance is the official authorized to make the determination under 2 CFR 182.500.

**§ 782.505 Who in USAID determines that a recipient who is an individual violated the requirements of this part?**

The Director of the Office of Acquisition and Assistance is the official authorized to make the determination under 2 CFR 182.505.

## Subpart F—Definitions

### § 782.605 Award (USAID supplement to Government-wide definition at 2 CFR 182.605)

*Award* means an award of financial assistance by the U.S. Agency for International Development or other Federal agency directly to a recipient.

(a) The term award includes:

(1) A Federal grant or cooperative agreement, in the form of money or property in lieu of money.

(2) A block grant or a grant in an entitlement program, whether or not the grant is exempted from coverage under the Government-wide rule that implements OMB Circular A–102 (for availability, see 5 CFR 1310.3) and specifies uniform administrative requirements.

(b) The term award does not include:

(1) Technical assistance that provides services instead of money.

(2) Loans.

(3) Loan guarantees.

(4) Interest subsidies.

(5) Insurance.

(6) Direct appropriations.

(7) Veterans' benefits to individuals (i.e., any benefit to veterans, their families, or survivors by virtue of the service of a veteran in the Armed Forces of the United States).

(c) Notwithstanding paragraph (a)(2) of this section, this paragraph is not applicable to AID.

## PARTS 783–799 [RESERVED]

# CHAPTER VIII—DEPARTMENT OF VETERANS AFFAIRS

---

# PART 800 [RESERVED]

# PART 801—NONPROCUREMENT DEBARMENT AND SUSPENSION

Sec.
801.10 What does this part do?
801.20 Does this part apply to me?
801.30 What policies and procedures must I follow?

## Subpart A—General

801.137 Who in the Department of Veterans Affairs may grant an exception to allow an excluded person to participate in a covered transaction?

## Subpart B—Covered Transactions

801.220 What contracts and subcontracts, in addition to those listed in 2 CFR 180.220, are covered transactions?

## Subpart C—Responsibilities of Participants Regarding Transactions

801.332 What methods must I use to pass requirements down to participants at lower tiers with whom I intend to do business?

## Subpart D—Responsibilities of Federal Agency Officials Regarding Transactions

801.437 What method do I use to communicate to a participant the requirements described in the OMB guidance at 2 CFR 180.435?

## Subparts E–H [Reserved]

## Subpart I—Definitions

801.930 Debarring official (Department of Veterans Affairs supplement to government-wide definition at 2 CFR 180.930).
801.995 Principal (Department of Veterans Affairs supplement to government-wide definition at 2 CFR 180.995).
801.1010 Suspending official (Department of Veterans Affairs supplement to government-wide definition at 2 CFR 180.1010).

## Subpart J—Limited Denial of Participation (Department of Veterans Affairs Optional Subpart for OMB Guidance at 2 CFR Part 180).

801.1100 General.
801.1105 Cause for a limited denial of participation.
801.1110 Scope and period of a limited denial of participation.
801.1111 Notice.
801.1112 Conference.
801.1113 Appeal.

AUTHORITY: Sec. 2455, Pub. L. 103–355, 108 Stat. 3327; E.O. 12549, 3 CFR, 1986 Comp., p. 189; E.O. 12689, 3 CFR, 1989 Comp., p. 235; 38 U.S.C. 501(a) and 3703(c).

SOURCE: 72 FR 30240, May 31, 2007, unless otherwise noted.

## § 801.10  What does this part do?

This part adopts the Office of Management and Budget (OMB) guidance in subparts A through I of 2 CFR part 180, as supplemented by this part, as the Department of Veterans Affairs (VA) policies and procedures for nonprocurement debarment and suspension. It thereby gives regulatory effect for the Department of Veterans Affairs to the OMB guidance as supplemented by this part. This part satisfies the requirements in section 3 of Executive Order 12549, "Debarment and Suspension" (3 CFR 1986 Comp., p. 189), Executive Order 12689, "Debarment and Suspension" (3 CFR 1989 Comp., p. 235) and 31 U.S.C. 6101 note (Section 2455, Pub. L. 103–355, 108 Stat. 3327).

## § 801.20  Does this part apply to me?

This part and, through this part, pertinent portions of the OMB guidance in subparts A through I of 2 CFR part 180 (see table at 2 CFR 180.100(b)) apply to you if you are a—

(a) Participant or principal in a "covered transaction" (see Subpart B of 2 CFR part 180 and the definition of "nonprocurement transaction" at 2 CFR 180.970, as supplemented by Subpart B of this part);

(b) Respondent in a Department of Veterans Affairs debarment or suspension action;

(c) Department of Veterans Affairs debarment or suspension official; or

(d) Department of Veterans affairs grants officer, agreements officer, or other official authorized to enter into any type of nonprocurement transaction that is a covered transaction.

## § 801.30  What policies and procedures must I follow?

For any section of OMB guidance in subparts A through I of 2 CFR part 180 that has no corresponding section in this part, Department of Veterans Affairs policies and procedures are those in the OMB guidance. For any such section where there is a corresponding

section in this part, the Department of
Veterans Affairs policies and procedures that you must follow are the
policies and procedures specified in
each applicable section of the OMB
guidance in subparts A through I of 2
CFR part 180, and as supplemented by
the section in this part with the same
section number. The contracts that are
covered transactions, for example, are
specified by § 180.220 of the OMB guidance (2 CFR 180.220) as supplemented
by § 801.220 in this part (2 CFR 801.220).

## Subpart A—General

**§ 801.137  Who in the Department of
Veterans Affairs may grant an exception to allow an excluded person
to participate in a covered transaction?**

Within the Department of Veterans
Affairs, the Secretary of Veterans Affairs, the Under Secretary for Health,
the Under Secretary for Benefits, and
the Under Secretary for Memorial Affairs each has the authority to grant
an exception to allow an excluded person to participate in a covered transaction, as provided in the OMB guidance at 2 CFR 180.135.

## Subpart B—Covered Transactions

**§ 801.220  What contracts and sub-
contracts, in addition to those listed
in 2 CFR 180.220, are covered transactions?**

VA does not extend coverage of nonprocurement suspension and debarment
requirements beyond first-tier procurement contracts under a covered nonprocurement transaction, although the
OMB guidance at 2 CFR 180.220(c) allows a Federal agency to do so (also see
optional lower tier coverage in the figure in the appendix to 2 CFR part 180).

## Subpart C—Responsibilities of Par-
ticipants Regarding Transactions

**§ 801.332  What methods must I use to
pass requirements down to participants at lower tiers with whom I intend to do business?**

You as a participant must include a
term or condition in lower-tier transactions requiring lower-tier partici-

pants to comply with subpart C of the
OMB guidance in 2 CFR part 180, as
supplemented by this subpart.

## Subpart D—Responsibilities of Fed-
eral Agency Officials Regarding Transactions

**§ 801.437  What method do I use to com-
municate to a participant the requirements described in the OMB
guidance at 2 CFR 180.435?**

To communicate to a participant the
requirements described in 2 CFR 180.435
of the OMB guidance, you must include
a term or condition in the transaction
that requires the participant's compliance with subpart C of 2 CFR part 180
(as supplemented by subpart C of this
part) and requires the participant to
include a similar term or condition in
lower-tier covered transactions.

## Subparts E–H [Reserved]

## Subpart I—Definitions

**§ 801.930  Debarring official (Depart-
ment of Veterans Affairs supplement to government-wide definition
at 2 CFR 180.930).**

In addition to the debarring official
listed at 2 CFR 180.930, the debarring
official for the Department of Veterans
Affairs is:

(a) For the Veterans Health Administration, the Under Secretary for
Health;

(b) For the Veterans Benefits Administration, the Under Secretary for Benefits; and

(c) For the National Cemetery Administration, the Under Secretary for
Memorial Affairs.

**§ 801.995  Principal (Department of
Veterans Affairs supplement to government-wide definition at 2 CFR
180.995.)**

In addition to the principals identified at 2 CFR 180.995, for the Department of Veterans Affairs loan guaranty
program, principals include, but are
not limited to the following:

(a) Loan officers.
(b) Loan solicitors.
(c) Loan processors.
(d) Loan servicers.
(e) Loan supervisors.

(f) Mortgage brokers.
(g) Office managers.
(h) Staff appraisers and inspectors.
(i) Fee Appraisers and inspectors.
(j) Underwriters.
(k) Bonding companies.
(l) Real estate agents and brokers.
(m) Management and marketing agents.
(n) Accountants, consultants, investment bankers, architects, engineers, attorneys, and others in a business relationship with participants in connection with a covered transaction under the Department of Veterans Affairs loan guaranty program.
(o) Contractors involved in the construction, improvement or repair of properties financed with Department of Veterans Affairs guaranteed loans.
(p) Closing agents.

**§801.1010  Suspending official (Department of Veterans Affairs supplement to government-wide definition at 2 CFR 180.1010).**

In addition to the suspending official listed at 2 CFR 180.1010, the suspending official for the Department of Veterans Affairs is:
(a) For the Veterans Health Administration, the Under Secretary for Health;
(b) For the Veterans Benefits Administration, the Under Secretary for Benefits; and
(c) For the National Cemetery Administration, the Under Secretary for Memorial Affairs.

## Subpart J—Limited Denial of Participation (Department of Veterans Affairs Optional Subpart for OMB Guidance at 2 CFR Part 180).

**§801.1100  General.**

Field facility directors are authorized to order a limited denial of participation affecting any participant or contractor and its affiliates except lenders and manufactured home manufacturers. In each case, even if the offense or violation is of a criminal, fraudulent or other serious nature, the decision to order a limited denial of participation shall be discretionary and in the best interests of the Government.

**§801.1105  Cause for a limited denial of participation.**

(a) *Causes.* A limited denial of participation shall be based upon adequate evidence of any of the following causes:
(1) Irregularities in a participant's or contractor's performance in the VA loan guaranty program;
(2) Denial of participation in programs administered by the Department of Housing and Urban Development or the Department of Agriculture, Rural Housing Service;
(3) Failure to satisfy contractual obligations or to proceed in accordance with contract specifications;
(4) Failure to proceed in accordance with VA requirements or to comply with VA regulations;
(5) Construction deficiencies deemed by VA to be the participant's responsibility;
(6) Falsely certifying in connection with any VA program, whether or not the certification was made directly to VA;
(7) Commission of an offense or other cause listed in §180.800;
(8) Violation of any law, regulation, or procedure relating to the application for guaranty, or to the performance of the obligations incurred pursuant to a commitment to guaranty;
(9) Making or procuring to be made any false statement for the purpose of influencing in any way an action of the Department.
(10) Imposition of a limited denial of participation by any other VA field facility.
(b) *Indictment.* A criminal indictment or information shall constitute adequate evidence for the purpose of limited denial of participation actions.
(c) *Limited denial of participation.* Imposition of a limited denial of participation by a VA field facility shall, at the discretion of any other VA field facility, constitute adequate evidence for a concurrent limited denial of participation. Where such a concurrent limited denial of participation is imposed, participation may be restricted on the same basis without the need for an additional conference or further hearing.

## § 801.1110  Scope and period of a limited denial of participation.

(a) *Scope and period.* The scope of a limited denial of participation shall be as follows:

(1) A limited denial of participation extends only to participation in the VA Loan Guaranty Program and shall be effective only within the geographic jurisdiction of the office or offices imposing it.

(2) The sanction may be imposed for a period not to exceed 12 months except for unresolved construction deficiencies. In cases involving construction deficiencies, the builder may be excluded for either a period not to exceed 12 months or for an indeterminate period which ends when the deficiency has been corrected or otherwise resolved in a manner acceptable to VA.

(b) *Effectiveness.* The sanction shall be effective immediately upon issuance and shall remain effective for the prescribed period. If the cause for the limited denial of participation is resolved before the expiration of the prescribed period, the official who imposed the sanction may terminate it. The imposition of a limited denial of participation shall not affect the right of the Department to suspend or debar any person under this part.

(c) *Affiliates.* An affiliate or organizational element may be included in a limited denial of participation solely on the basis of its affiliation, and regardless of its knowledge of or participation in the acts providing cause for the sanction. The burden of proving that a particular affiliate or organizational element is capable of meeting VA requirements and is currently a responsible entity and not controlled by the primary sanctioned party (or by an entity that itself is controlled by the primary sanctioned party) is on the affiliate or organizational element.

## § 801.1111  Notice.

(a) *Generally.* A limited denial of participation shall be initiated by advising a participant or contractor, and any specifically named affiliate, by certified mail, return receipt requested:

(1) That the sanction is effective as of the date of the notice;

(2) Of the reasons for the sanction in terms sufficient to put the participant or contractor on notice of the conduct or transaction(s) upon which it is based;

(3) Of the cause(s) relied upon under § 801.1105 for imposing the sanction;

(4) Of the right to request in writing, within 30 days of receipt of the notice, a conference on the sanction, and the right to have such conference held within 10 business days of receipt of the request;

(5) Of the potential effect of the sanction and the impact on the participant's or contractor's participation in Departmental programs, specifying the program(s) involved and the geographical area affected by the action.

(b) *Notification of action.* After 30 days, if no conference has been requested, the official imposing the limited denial of participation will notify VA Central Office of the action taken and of the fact that no conference has been requested. If a conference is requested within the 30-day period, VA Central Office need not be notified unless a decision to affirm all or a portion of the remaining period of exclusion is issued. VA Central Office will notify all VA field offices of sanctions imposed and still in effect under this subpart.

## § 801.1112  Conference.

Upon receipt of a request for a conference, the official imposing the sanction shall arrange such a conference with the participant or contractor and may designate another official to conduct the conference. The participant shall be given the opportunity to be heard within 10 business days of receipt of the request. This conference precedes, and is in addition to, the formal hearing provided if an appeal is taken under § 801.1113. Although formal rules of procedure do not apply to the conference, the participant or contractor may be represented by counsel and may present all relevant information and materials to the official or designee. After consideration of the information and materials presented, the official shall, in writing, advise the participant or contractor of the decision to withdraw, modify or affirm the limited denial of participation. If the decision is made to affirm all or a portion of the remaining period of exclusion, the participant shall be advised of the right to request a formal hearing in writing within 30 days of receipt of the notice of decision. This decision shall be issued promptly, but in no event later than 20 days after the conference and receipt of materials.

### §801.1113  Appeal.

Where the decision is made to affirm all or a portion of the remaining period of exclusion, any participant desiring an appeal shall file a written request for a hearing with the Under Secretary for Benefits, Department of Veterans Affairs, 810 Vermont Avenue, NW., Washington, DC 20420. This request shall be filed within 30 days of receipt of the decision to affirm. If a hearing is requested, it shall be held in accordance with the procedures in §§108.825 through 108.855. Where a limited denial of participation is followed by a suspension or debarment, the limited de-nial of participation shall be super-seded and the appeal shall be heard solely as an appeal of the suspension or debarment.

## PART 802—UNIFORM ADMINISTRATIVE REQUIREMENTS, COST PRINCIPLES, AND AUDIT REQUIREMENTS FOR FEDERAL AWARDS

AUTHORITY: 5 U.S.C. 301; 38 U.S.C. 501, 2 CFR part 200, and as noted in specific sections.

SOURCE: 79 FR 76024, Dec. 19, 2014, unless otherwise noted.

### §802.101  Applicable regulations.

The Uniform Administrative Requirements, Cost Principles, and Audit Requirements for Federal Awards set forth in 2 CFR part 200 shall apply to the Department of Veterans Affairs.

## PARTS 803–899 [RESERVED]

# CHAPTER IX—DEPARTMENT OF ENERGY

# PART 900 [RESERVED]

# PART 901—NONPROCUREMENT DEBARMENT AND SUSPENSION

Sec.
901.10  What does this part do?
901.20  Does this part apply to me?
901.30  What policies and procedures must I follow?

## Subpart A—General

901.137  Who in the Department of Energy may grant an exception to let an excluded person participate in a covered transaction?

## Subpart B—Covered Transactions

901.220  What contracts and subcontracts, in addition to those listed in 2 CFR 180.220, are covered transactions?

## Subpart C—Responsibilities of Participants Regarding Transactions

901.332  What methods must I use to pass requirements down to participants at lower tiers with whom I intend to do business?

## Subpart D—Responsibilities of Federal Agency Officials Regarding Transactions

901.437  What method do I use to communicate to a participant the requirements described in the OMB guidance at 2 CFR 180.435?

## Subparts E–H [Reserved]

## Subpart I—Definitions

901.930  Debarring official (Department of Energy supplement to government-wide definition at 2 CFR 180.935).
901.950  Federal agency (Department of Energy supplement to government-wide definition at 2 CFR 180.910).
901.1010  Suspending official (Department of Energy supplement to government-wide definition at 2 CFR 180.1010).

## Subpart J [Reserved]

AUTHORITY: Sec. 2455, Pub. L. 103–355, 108 Stat. 3327 (31 U.S.C. 6101 note); E.O. 12549 (3 CFR, 1986 Comp., p. 189); E.O. 12689 (3 CFR, 1989 Comp., p. 235); 42 U.S.C. 7101 *et seq.*; 50 U.S.C. 2401 *et seq.*

SOURCE: 71 FR 70459, Dec. 5, 2006, unless otherwise noted.

## § 901.10  What does this part do?

This part adopts the Office of Management and Budget (OMB) guidance in subparts A through I of 2 CFR part 180, as supplemented by this part, as the DOE policies and procedures for nonprocurement debarment and suspension. It thereby gives regulatory effect for DOE to the OMB guidance as supplemented by this part. This part satisfies the requirements in section 3 of Executive Order 12549, "Debarment and Suspension" (3 CFR 1986 Comp., p. 189); Executive Order 12689, "Debarment and Suspension" (3 CFR 1989 Comp., p. 235); and section 2455 of the Federal Acquisition Streamlining Act of 1994, Pub. L. 103–355 (31 U.S.C. 6101 note).

## § 901.20  Does this part apply to me?

This part and, through this part, pertinent portions of the OMB guidance in subparts A through I of 2 CFR part 180 (see table at 2 CFR 180.100(b)) apply to you if you are a—

(a) Participant or principal in a "covered transaction" (see subpart B of 2 CFR part 180 and the definition of "nonprocurement transaction" at 2 CFR 180.970);

(b) Respondent in a DOE suspension or debarment action;

(c) DOE debarment or suspension official; and

(d) DOE grants officer, agreements officer, or other official authorized to enter into any type of nonprocurement transaction that is a covered transaction.

## § 901.30  What policies and procedures must I follow?

The DOE policies and procedures that you must follow are the policies and procedures specified in each applicable section of the OMB guidance in subparts A through I of 2 CFR part 180 and any supplemental policies and procedures set forth in this part.

## Subpart A—General

**§ 901.137 Who in the Department of Energy may grant an exception to let an excluded person participate in a covered transaction?**

The Director, Office of Procurement and Assistance Management, DOE, for DOE actions, and the Director, Office of Acquisition and Supply Management, NNSA, for NNSA actions, may grant an exception permitting an excluded person to participate in a particular covered transaction. If the Director, Office of Procurement and Assistance Management, DOE, for DOE actions, and Director, Office of Acquisition and Supply Management, NNSA, for NNSA actions, grants an exception, the exception must be in writing and state the reason(s) for deviating from the government-wide policy in Executive Order 12549.

## Subpart B—Covered Transactions

**§ 901.220 What contracts and subcontracts, in addition to those listed in 2 CFR 180.220, are covered transactions?**

Although the OMB guidance at 2 CFR 180.220(c) allows a Federal agency to do so (also see optional lower tier coverage in the figure in the appendix to 2 CFR part 180), DOE does not extend coverage of nonprocurement suspension and debarment requirements beyond first-tier procurement contracts under a covered nonprocurement transaction.

## Subpart C—Responsibilities of Participants Regarding Transactions

**§ 901.332 What methods must I use to pass requirements down to participants at lower tiers with whom I intend to do business?**

You, as a participant, must include a term or condition in lower-tier transactions requiring lower-tier participants to comply with subpart C of the OMB guidance in 2 CFR part 180, as supplemented by this subpart.

## Subpart D—Responsibilities of Federal Agency Officials Regarding Transactions

**§ 901.437 What method do I use to communicate to a participant the requirements described in the OMB guidance at 2 CFR 180.435?**

To communicate to a participant the requirements described in 2 CFR 180.435 of the OMB guidance, you must include a term or condition in the transaction that requires the participant's compliance with subpart C of 2 CFR part 180, as supplemented by subpart C of this part, and requires the participant to include a similar term or condition in lower-tier covered transactions.

## Subparts E–H [Reserved]

## Subpart I—Definitions

**§ 901.930 Debarring official (Department of Energy supplement to government-wide definition at 2 CFR 180.930).**

The Debarring Official for the Department of Energy, exclusive of NNSA, is the Director, Office of Procurement and Assistance Management, DOE. The Debarring Official for NNSA is the Director, Office of Acquisition and Supply Management, NNSA.

**§ 901.950 Federal agency (Department of Energy supplement to government-wide definition at 2 CFR 180.950).**

*DOE* means the U.S. Department of Energy, including the NNSA.

*NNSA* means the National Nuclear Security Administration.

**§ 901.1010 Suspending official (Department of Energy supplement to government-wide definition at 2 CFR 180.1010).**

The suspending official for the Department of Energy, exclusive of NNSA, is the Director, Office of Procurement and Assistance Management, DOE. The suspending official for NNSA is the Director, Office of Acquisition and Supply Management, NNSA.

## Subpart J [Reserved]

# PART 902—REQUIREMENTS FOR DRUG-FREE WORKPLACE (FINANCIAL ASSISTANCE)

Sec.
902.10 What does this part do?
902.20 Does this part apply to me?
902.30 What policies and procedures must I follow?

### Subpart A—Purpose and Coverage [Reserved]

### Subpart B—Requirements for Recipients Other Than Individuals

902.225 Whom in the DOE does a recipient other than an individual notify about a criminal drug conviction?

### Subpart C—Requirements for Recipients Who Are Individuals

902.300 Whom in the DOE does a recipient who is an individual notify about a criminal drug conviction?

### Subpart D—Responsibilities of Agency Awarding Officials

902.400 What method do I use as an agency awarding official to obtain a recipient's agreement to comply with the OMB guidance?

### Subpart E—Violations of this Part and Consequences

902.500 Who in the DOE determines that a recipient other than an individual violated the requirements of this part?
902.505 Who in the DOE determines that a recipient who is an individual violated the requirements of this part?

### Subpart F—Definitions

902.605 Award (DOE supplement to Governmentwide definition at 2 CFR 182.605).
902.645 Federal agency or agency.

AUTHORITY: 41 U.S.C. 701; 42 U.S.C. 7101 *et seq.*; 50 U.S.C. 2401 *et seq.*

SOURCE: 75 FR 39444, July 9, 2010, unless otherwise noted.

## §902.10 What does this part do?

This part requires that the award and administration of DOE grants and cooperative agreements comply with Office of Management and Budget (OMB) guidance implementing the portion of the Drug-Free Workplace Act of 1988 (41 U.S.C. 701–707, as amended, hereafter referred to as "the Act") that applies to grants. It thereby—

(a) Gives regulatory effect to the OMB guidance (Subparts A through F of 2 CFR part 182) for the DOE's grants and cooperative agreements; and

(b) Establishes DOE policies and procedures for compliance with the Act that are the same as those of other Federal agencies, in conformance with the requirement in 41 U.S.C. 705 for Governmentwide implementing regulations.

## §902.20 Does this part apply to me?

This part and, through this part, pertinent portions of the OMB guidance in Subparts A through F of 2 CFR part 182 (see table at 2 CFR 182.115(b)) apply to you if you are a—

(a) Recipient of a DOE grant or cooperative agreement; or

(b) DOE awarding official.

## §902.30 What policies and procedures must I follow?

(a) *General.* You must follow the policies and procedures specified in applicable sections of the OMB guidance in Subparts A through F of 2 CFR part 182, as implemented by this part.

(b) *Specific sections of OMB guidance that this part supplements.* In implementing the OMB guidance in 2 CFR part 182, this part supplements four sections of the guidance, as shown in the following table. For each of those sections, you must follow the policies and procedures in the OMB guidance, as supplemented by this part.

| Section of OMB guidance | Section in this part where supplemented | What the supplementation clarifies |
|---|---|---|
| (1) 2 CFR 182.225(a) ........................ | §902.225 | Whom in the DOE a recipient other than an individual must notify if an employee is convicted for a violation of a criminal drug statute in the workplace. |
| (2) 2 CFR 182.300(b) ........................ | §902.300 | Whom in the DOE a recipient who is an individual must notify if he or she is convicted of a criminal drug offense resulting from a violation occurring during the conduct of any award activity. |

| Section of OMB guidance | Section in this part where supplemented | What the supplementation clarifies |
|---|---|---|
| (3) 2 CFR 182.500 .............................. | § 902.500 | Who in the DOE is authorized to determine that a recipient other than an individual is in violation of the requirements of 2 CFR part 182, as implemented by this part. |
| (4) 2 CFR 182.505 .............................. | § 902.505 | Who in the DOE is authorized to determine that a recipient who is an individual is in violation of the requirements of 2 CFR part 182, as implemented by this part. |
| (5) 2 CFR 182.605 .............................. | § 902.605 | Definition of "Award". |
| (6) 2 CFR 182.645 .............................. | § 902.645 | Definition of "Federal agency or agency". |

(c) *Sections of the OMB guidance that this part does not supplement.* For any section of OMB guidance in Subparts A through F of 2 CFR part 182 that is not listed in paragraph (b) of this section, DOE policies and procedures are the same as those in the OMB guidance.

## Subpart A—Purpose and Coverage [Reserved]

## Subpart B—Requirements for Recipients Other Than Individuals

**§ 902.225 Whom in the DOE does a recipient other than an individual notify about a criminal drug conviction?**

A recipient other than an individual that is required under 2 CFR 182.225(a) to notify Federal agencies about an employee's conviction for a criminal drug offense must notify each DOE office from which it currently has an award.

## Subpart C—Requirements for Recipients Who Are Individuals

**§ 902.300 Whom in the DOE does a recipient who is an individual notify about a criminal drug conviction?**

A recipient who is an individual and is required under 2 CFR 182.300(b) to notify Federal agencies about a conviction for a criminal drug offense must notify each DOE office from which it currently has an award.

## Subpart D—Responsibilities of Agency Awarding Officials

**§ 902.400 What method do I use as an agency awarding official to obtain a recipient's agreement to comply with the OMB guidance?**

To obtain a recipient's agreement to comply with applicable requirements in the OMB guidance at 2 CFR part 182, you must include the following term or condition in the award:

Drug-free workplace. You as the recipient must comply with drug-free workplace requirements in Subpart B (or Subpart C, if the recipient is an individual) of Part 902, which adopts the Governmentwide implementation (2 CFR part 182) of sec. 5152–5158 of the Drug-Free Workplace Act of 1988 (Pub. L. 100–690, Title V, Subtitle D; 41 U.S.C. 701–707).

## Subpart E—Violations of this Part and Consequences

**§ 902.500 Who in the DOE determines that a recipient other than an individual violated the requirements of this part?**

The Secretary of the Department of Energy and the Secretary's designee or designees are authorized to make the determinations under 2 CFR 182.500 for DOE, including NNSA.

**§ 902.505 Who in the DOE determines that a recipient who is an individual violated the requirements of this part?**

The Secretary of the Department of Energy and the Secretary's designee or designees are authorized to make the determinations under 2 CFR 182.500 for DOE, including NNSA.

## Subpart F—Definitions

### § 902.605 Award (DOE supplement to Governmentwide definition at 2 CFR 182.605).

The term *award* also includes Technology Investment Agreements (TIA). A TIA is a special type of assistance instrument used to increase the involvement of commercial firms in the Department's RD&D programs. A TIA may be either a type of cooperative agreement or a type of assistance transaction other than a cooperative agreement, depending on the intellectual property provisions. A TIA may be either expenditure based or fixed support.

### § 902.645 Federal agency or agency.

*Department of Energy* means the U.S. Department of Energy (DOE), including the National Nuclear Security Administration (NNSA).

## PARTS 903–909 [RESERVED]

## PART 910—UNIFORM ADMINISTRATIVE REQUIREMENTS, COST PRINCIPLES, AND AUDIT REQUIREMENTS FOR FEDERAL AWARDS

### Subpart A [Reserved]

### Subpart B—General Provisions

### Subpart C [Reserved]

### Subpart D—Post Award Federal Requirements for For-Profit Entities

### Subpart E—Cost Principles

### Subpart F—Audit Requirements for For-Profit Entities

#### GENERAL

#### AUDITS

#### AUDITEES

#### FEDERAL AGENCIES

#### AUDITORS

#### MANAGEMENT DECISIONS

AUTHORITY: 42 U.S.C. 7101, *et seq.*; 31 U.S.C. 6301–6308; 50 U.S.C. 2401 *et seq.*; 2 CFR part 200.

SOURCE: 79 FR 76024, Dec. 19, 2014, unless otherwise noted.

### Subpart A [Reserved]

### Subpart B—General Provisions

#### § 910.120 Adoption of 2 CFR part 200.

(a) Under the authority listed above, the Department of Energy adopts the

Office of Management and Budget (OMB) Guidance in 2 CFR part 200, with the following additions. Thus, this part gives regulatory effect to the OMB guidance and supplements the guidance as needed for the Department.

(b) The additions include: Expanding the definition of non-Federal entity for DOE to include For-profit entities; adding back additional coverage from 10 CFR part 600 required by DOE statute; adding back coverage specific for For-Profit entities which existed in 10 CFR part 600 which still applies.

## § 910.122  Applicability.

(a) For DOE, unless otherwise noted in Part 910, the definition of Non-Federal entity found in 2 CFR 200.69 is expanded to include for-profit organizations in addition to states, local governments, Indian tribes, institutions of higher education (IHE), and nonprofit organizations.

(b) A for-profit organization is defined as one that distributes any profit not reinvested into the business as profit or dividends to its employees or shareholders.

## § 910.124  Eligibility.

(a) *Purpose and scope.* This section implements section 2306 of the Energy Policy Act of 1992, 42 U.S.C. 13525, and sets forth a general statement of policy, including procedures and interpretations, for the guidance of implementing DOE officials in making mandatory pre-award determinations of eligibility for financial assistance under Titles XX through XXIII of that Act.

(b) *Definitions.* The definitions in Subpart A of 2 CFR part 200, including the definition of the term "Federal financial assistance," are applicable to this section. In addition, as used in this section:

*Act* means the Energy Policy Act of 1992.

*Company* means any business entity other than an organization of the type described in section 501(c) (3) of the Internal Revenue Code of 1954 (26 U.S.C. 501(c)(3)).

*Covered program* means a program under Titles XX through XXIII of the Act. (A list of covered programs, updated periodically as appropriate, is maintained and published by the Department of Energy.)

*Parent company* means a company that:

(1) Exercises ultimate ownership of the applicant company either directly, by ownership of a majority of that company's voting securities, or indirectly, by control over a majority of that company's voting securities through one or more intermediate subsidiary companies or otherwise, and

(2) Is not itself subject to the ultimate ownership control of another company.

*United States* means the several States, the District of Columbia, and all commonwealths, territories, and possessions of the United States.

*United States-owned company* means:

(1) A company that has majority ownership by individuals who are citizens of the United States, or

(2) A company organized under the laws of a State that either has no parent company or has a parent company organized under the laws of a State.

*Voting security* has the meaning given the term in the Public Utility Holding Company Act (15 U.S.C. 15b(17)).

(c) *What must DOE determine.* A company shall be eligible to receive an award of financial assistance under a covered program only if DOE finds that—

(1) Consistent with § 910.124(d), the company's participation in a covered program would be in the economic interest of the United States; and

(2) The company is either—

(i) A United States-owned company; or

(ii) Incorporated or organized under the laws of any State and has a parent company which is incorporated or organized under the laws of a country which—

(A) Affords to the United States-owned companies opportunities, comparable to those afforded to any other company, to participate in any joint venture similar to those authorized under the Act;

(B) Affords to United States-owned companies local investment opportunities comparable to those afforded to any other company; and

(C) Affords adequate and effective protection for the intellectual property rights of United States-owned companies.

(d) *Determining the economic interest of the United States.* In determining whether participation of an applicant company in a covered program would be in the economic interest of the United States under §910.124(c)(1), DOE may consider any evidence showing that a financial assistance award would be in the economic interest of the United States including, but not limited to—

(1) Investments by the applicant company and its affiliates in the United States in research, development, and manufacturing (including, for example, the manufacture of major components or subassemblies in the United States);

(2) Significant contributions to employment in the United States by the applicant company and its affiliates; and

(3) An agreement by the applicant company, with respect to any technology arising from the financial assistance being sought—

(i) To promote the manufacture within the United States of products resulting from that technology (taking into account the goals of promoting the competitiveness of United States industry); and

(ii) To procure parts and materials from competitive suppliers.

(e) Information an applicant must submit.

(1) Any applicant for Federal financial assistance under a covered program shall submit with the application for Federal financial assistance, or at such later time as may be specified by DOE, evidence for DOE to consider in making findings required under §910.124 (c)(1) and findings concerning ownership status under §910.124(c)(2).

(2) If an applicant for Federal financial assistance is submitting evidence relating to future undertakings, such as an agreement under §910.124(d)(3) to promote manufacture in the United States of products resulting from a technology developed with financial assistance or to procure parts and materials from competitive suppliers, the applicant shall submit a representation affirming acceptance of these undertakings. The applicant should also briefly describe its plans, if any, for any manufacturing of products arising from the program-supported research and development, including the location where such manufacturing is expected to occur.

(3) If an applicant for Federal financial assistance is claiming to be a United States-owned company, the applicant must submit a representation affirming that it falls within the definition of that term provided in §910.124(b).

(4) DOE may require submission of additional information deemed necessary to make any portion of the determination required by §910.124(b) 2.

(f) Other information DOE may consider.

In making the determination under §910.124(c)(2)(ii), DOE may—

(1) Consider information on the relevant international and domestic law obligations of the country of incorporation of the parent company of an applicant;

(2) Consider information relating to the policies and practices of the country of incorporation of the parent company of an applicant with respect to:

(i) The eligibility criteria for, and the experience of United States-owned company participation in, energy-related research and development programs;

(ii) Local investment opportunities afforded to United States-owned companies; and

(iii) Protection of intellectual property rights of United States-owned companies;

(3) Seek and consider advice from other federal agencies, as appropriate; and

(4) Consider any publicly available information in addition to the information provided by the applicant.

**§910.126 Competition.**

(a) *General.* DOE shall solicit applications for Federal financial assistance in a manner which provides for the maximum amount of competition feasible.

(b) *Restricted eligibility.* If DOE restricts eligibility, an explanation of why the restriction of eligibility is considered necessary shall be included in the notice of funding opportunity or, program rule. Such restriction of eligibility shall be:

(1) Supported by a written determination initiated by the program office;

(2) Concurred in by legal counsel and the Contracting Officer; and

(3) Approved, prior to award, by an approver at least one level above the Contracting Officer.

(c) *Noncompetitive Federal financial assistance.* DOE may award a grant or cooperative agreement on a noncompetitive basis only if the application satisfies one or more of the follow selection criteria:

(1) The activity to be funded is necessary to the satisfactory completion of, or is a continuation or renewal of, an activity presently being funded by DOE or another Federal agency, and for which competition for support would have a significant adverse effect on continuity or completion of the activity.

(2) The activity is being or would be conducted by the applicant using its own resources or those donated or provided by third parties; however, DOE support of that activity would enhance the public benefits to be derived and DOE knows of no other entity which is conducting or is planning to conduct such an activity.

(3) The applicant is a unit of government and the activity to be supported is related to performance of a governmental function within the subject jurisdiction, thereby precluding DOE provision of support to another entity.

(4) The applicant has exclusive domestic capability to perform the activity successfully, based upon unique equipment, proprietary data, technical expertise, or other such unique qualifications.

(5) The award implements an agreement between the United States Government and a foreign government to fund a foreign applicant.

(6) Time constraints associated with a public health, safety, welfare or national security requirement preclude competition.

(7) The proposed project was submitted as an unsolicited proposal and represents a unique or innovative idea, method, or approach that would not be eligible for financial assistance under a

recent, current, or planned notice of funding opportunity, and if, as determined by DOE, a competitive notice of funding opportunity would not be appropriate.

(8) The responsible program Assistant Secretary, Deputy Administrator, or other official of equivalent authority has determined that making the award non-competitively is in the public interest. This authority cannot not be delegated.

(d) *Approval requirements.* Determinations of noncompetitive awards shall be:

(1) Documented in writing;

(2) Concurred in by the responsible program technical official and local legal counsel; and

(3) Approved, prior to award, by the Contracting Officer and an approver at least one level above the CO.

(e) *Definitions.* For purposes of this section, the following definitions are applicable:

*Continuation Award*—A financial assistance award authorizing a second or subsequent budget period within an existing project period.

*Renewal Award*—A financial assistance award authorizing the first budget period of an extended project period.

[79 FR 76024, Dec. 19, 2014, as amended at 80 FR 57511, Sept. 24, 2015]

## § 910.127 Legal authority and effect.

(a) A DOE financial assistance award is valid only if it is in writing and is signed, either in writing or electronically, by a DOE Contracting Officer.

(b) Recipients are free to accept or reject the award. A request to draw down DOE funds constitutes the Recipient's acceptance of the terms and conditions of this Award.

[80 FR 57511, Sept. 24, 2015]

## § 910.128 Disputes and appeals.

(a) *Informal dispute resolution.* Whenever practicable, DOE shall attempt to resolve informally any dispute over the award or administration of Federal financial assistance. Informal resolution, including resolution through an alternative dispute resolution mechanism, shall be preferred over formal procedures, to the extent practicable.

(b) *Alternative dispute resolution (ADR).* Before issuing a final determination in any dispute in which informal resolution has not been achieved, the Contracting Officer shall suggest that the other party consider the use of voluntary consensual methods of dispute resolution, such as mediation. The DOE dispute resolution specialist is available to provide assistance for such disputes, as are trained mediators of other federal agencies. ADR may be used at any stage of a dispute.

(c) *Final determination.* Whenever a dispute is not resolved informally or through an alternative dispute resolution process, DOE shall mail (by certified mail) a brief written determination signed by a Contracting Officer, setting forth DOE's final disposition of such dispute. Such determination shall contain the following information:

(1) A summary of the dispute, including a statement of the issues and of the positions taken by DOE and the party or parties to the dispute; and

(2) The factual, legal and, if appropriate, policy reasons for DOE's disposition of the dispute.

(d) *Right of appeal.* Except as provided in paragraph (f)(1) of this section, the final determination under paragraph (c) of this section may be appealed to the cognizant Senior Procurement Executive (SPE) for either DOE or the National Nuclear Security Administration (NNSA). The appeal must be received by DOE within 90 days of the receipt of the final determination. The mailing address for the DOE SPE is Office of Acquisition and Project Management, 1000 Independence Ave., SW., Washington, DC 20585. The mailing address for the NNSA SPE is Office of Acquisition Management, National Nuclear Security Administration (NNSA), 1000 Independence Ave. SW., Washington, DC 20585.

(e) *Effect of appeal.* The filing of an appeal with the SPE shall not stay any determination or action taken by DOE which is the subject of the appeal. Consistent with its obligation to protect the interests of the Federal Government, DOE may take such authorized actions as may be necessary to preserve the status quo pending decision by the SPE, or to preserve its ability to provide relief in the event the SPE decides in favor of the appellant.

(f) *Review on appeal.* (1) The SPE shall have no jurisdiction to review:

(i) Any preaward dispute (except as provided in paragraph (f)(2)(ii) of this section), including use of any special restrictive condition pursuant to 2 CFR 200.207 Specific Conditions ;

(ii) DOE denial of a request for an Exception under 2 CFR 200.102;

(iii) DOE denial of a request for a budget revision or other change in the approved project under 2 CFR 200.308 or 200.403 or under another term or condition of the award;

(iv) Any DOE action authorized under 2 CFR 200.338, Remedies for Non-compliance, or such actions authorized by program rule;

(v) Any DOE decision about an action requiring prior DOE approval under 2 CFR 200.324 or under another term or condition of the award;

(2) In addition to any right of appeal established by program rule, or by the terms and conditions (not inconsistent with paragraph (f)(1) of this section) of an award, the SPE shall have jurisdiction to review:

(i) A DOE determination that the recipient has failed to comply with the applicable requirements of this part, the program statute or rules, or other terms and conditions of the award;

(ii) A DOE decision not to make a continuation award based on any of the determinations described in paragraph (f)(2)(i) of this section;

(iii) Termination of an award, in whole or in part, by DOE under 2 CFR 200.339 (a)(1)–(2);

(iv) A DOE determination that an award is void or invalid;

(v) The application by DOE of an indirect cost rate; and

(vi) DOE disallowance of costs.

(3) In reviewing disputes authorized under paragraph (f)(2) of this section, the SPE shall be bound by the applicable law, statutes, and rules, including the requirements of this part, and by the terms and conditions of the award.

(4) The decision of the SPE shall be the final decision of DOE.

## § 910.130   Cost sharing (EPACT).

In addition to the requirements of 2 CFR 200.306 the following requirements

319

apply to research, development, demonstration and commercial application activities:

(a) Cost sharing is required for most financial assistance awards for research, development, demonstration and commercial applications activities initiated after the enactment of the Energy Policy Act of 2005 on August 8, 2005. This requirement does not apply to:

(1) An award under the small business innovation research program (SBIR) or the small business technology transfer program (STTR); or

(2) A program with cost sharing requirements defined by other than Section 988 of the Energy Policy Act of 2005 including other sections of the 2005 Act and the Energy Policy Act of 1992.

(b) A cost share of at least 20 percent of the cost of the activity is required for research and development except where:

(1) A research or development activity of a basic or fundamental nature has been excluded by an appropriate officer of DOE, generally an Under Secretary; or

(2) The Secretary has determined it is necessary and appropriate to reduce or eliminate the cost sharing requirement for a research and development activity of an applied nature.

(c) A cost share of at least 50 percent of the cost of a demonstration or commercial application activity is required unless the Secretary has determined it is necessary and appropriate to reduce the cost sharing requirements, taking into consideration any technological risk relating to the activity.

(d) Cost share shall be provided by non-Federal funds unless otherwise authorized by statute. In calculating the amount of the non-Federal contribution:

(1) Base the non-Federal contribution on total project costs, including the cost of work where funds are provided directly to a partner, consortium member or subrecipient, such as a Federally Funded Research and Development Center;

(2) Include the following costs as allowable in accordance with the applicable cost principles:

(i) Cash;

(ii) Personnel costs;

(iii) The value of a service, other resource, or third party in-kind contribution determined in accordance with Subpart E—Cost Principles—of 2 CFR part 200. For recipients that are for-profit organizations as defined by 2 CFR 910.122, the Cost Principles which apply are contained in 48 CFR 31.2. See § 910.352 for further information;

(iv) Indirect costs or facilities and administrative costs; and/or

(v) Any funds received under the power program of the Tennessee Valley Authority (except to the extent that such funds are made available under an annual appropriation Act);

(3) Exclude the following costs:

(i) Revenues or royalties from the prospective operation of an activity beyond the time considered in the award;

(ii) Proceeds from the prospective sale of an asset of an activity; or

(iii) Other appropriated Federal funds.

(iv) Repayment of the Federal share of a cost-shared activity under Section 988 of the Energy Policy Act of 2005 shall not be a condition of the award.

(e) For purposes of this section, the following definitions are applicable:

*Demonstration* means a project designed to determine the technical feasibility and economic potential of a technology on either a pilot or prototype scale.

*Development* is defined in 2 CFR 200.87.

*Research* is also defined in 2 CFR 200.87.

## § 910.132  Research misconduct.

(a) A recipient is responsible for maintaining the integrity of research of any kind under an award from DOE including the prevention, detection, and remediation of research misconduct, and the conduct of inquiries, investigations, and adjudication of allegations of research misconduct in accordance with the requirements of this section.

(b) For purposes of this section, the following definitions are applicable:

*Adjudication* means a formal review of a record of investigation of alleged research misconduct to determine whether and what corrective actions and sanctions should be taken.

*Fabrication* means making up data or results and recording or reporting them.

*Falsification* means manipulating research materials, equipment, or processes, or changing or omitting data or results such that the research is not accurately represented in the research record.

*Finding of Research Misconduct* means a determination, based on a preponderance of the evidence, that research misconduct has occurred. Such a finding requires a conclusion that there has been a significant departure from accepted practices of the relevant research community and that it be knowingly, intentionally, or recklessly committed.

*Inquiry* means information gathering and initial fact-finding to determine whether an allegation or apparent instance of misconduct warrants an investigation.

*Investigation* means the formal examination and evaluation of the relevant facts.

*Plagiarism* means the appropriation of another person's ideas, processes, results, or words without giving appropriate credit.

*Research misconduct* means fabrication, falsification, or plagiarism in proposing, performing, or reviewing research, or in reporting research results, but does not include honest error or differences of opinion.

*Research record* means the record of all data or results that embody the facts resulting from scientists' inquiries, including, but not limited to, research proposals, laboratory records, both physical and electronic, progress reports, abstracts, theses, oral presentations, internal reports, and journal articles.

(c) Unless otherwise instructed by the Contracting Officer, the recipient must conduct an initial inquiry into any allegation of research misconduct. If the recipient determines that there is sufficient evidence to proceed to an investigation, it must notify the Contracting Officer and, unless otherwise instructed, the recipient must:

(1) Conduct an investigation to develop a complete factual record and an examination of such record leading to either a finding of research misconduct and an identification of appropriate remedies or a determination that no further action is warranted;

(2) Inform the Contracting Officer if an initial inquiry supports an investigation and, if requested by the Contracting Officer thereafter, keep the Contracting Officer informed of the results of the investigation and any subsequent adjudication. When an investigation is complete, the recipient will forward to the Contracting Officer a copy of the evidentiary record, the investigative report, any recommendations made to the recipient's adjudicating official, and the adjudicating official's decision and notification of any corrective action taken or planned, and the subject's written response to the recommendations (if any).

(3) If the investigation leads to a finding of research misconduct, conduct an adjudication by a responsible official who was not involved in the inquiry or investigation and is separated organizationally from the element which conducted the investigation. The adjudication must include a review of the investigative record and, as warranted, a determination of appropriate corrective actions and sanctions.

(d) DOE may elect to act in lieu of the recipient in conducting an inquiry or investigation into an allegation of research misconduct if the Contracting Officer finds that:

(1) The research organization is not prepared to handle the allegation in a manner consistent with this section;

(2) The allegation involves an entity of sufficiently small size that it cannot reasonably conduct the inquiry;

(3) DOE involvement is necessary to ensure the public health, safety, and security, or to prevent harm to the public interest; or,

(4) The allegation involves possible criminal misconduct.

(e) DOE reserves the right to pursue such remedies and other actions as it deems appropriate, consistent with the terms and conditions of the award instrument and applicable laws and regulations. However, the recipient's good faith administration of this section and the effectiveness of its remedial actions and sanctions shall be positive considerations and shall be taken into account as mitigating factors in assessing the need for such actions. If DOE pursues any such action, it will inform the subject of the action of the outcome and any applicable appeal procedures.

(f) In conducting the activities in paragraph (c) of this section, the recipient and DOE, if it elects to conduct the inquiry or investigation, shall adhere to the following guidelines:

(1) *Safeguards for information and subjects of allegations.* The recipient shall provide safeguards to ensure that individuals may bring allegations of research misconduct made in good faith to the attention of the recipient without suffering retribution. Safeguards include: Protection against retaliation; fair and objective procedures for examining and resolving allegations; and diligence in protecting positions and reputations. The recipient shall also provide the subjects of allegations confidence that their rights are protected and that the mere filing of an allegation of research misconduct will not result in an adverse action. Safeguards include timely written notice regarding substantive allegations against them, a description of the allegation and reasonable access to any evidence submitted to support the allegation or developed in response to an allegation and notice of any findings of research misconduct.

(2) *Objectivity and expertise.* The recipient shall select individual(s) to inquire, investigate, and adjudicate allegations of research misconduct who have appropriate expertise and have no unresolved conflict of interest. The individual(s) who conducts an adjudication must not be the same individual(s) who conducted the inquiry or investigation, and must be separate organizationally from the element that conducted the inquiry or investigation.

(3) *Timeliness.* The recipient shall coordinate, inquire, investigate and adjudicate allegations of research misconduct promptly, but thoroughly. Generally, an investigation should be completed within 120 days of initiation, and adjudication should be complete within 60 days of receipt of the record of investigation.

(4) *Confidentiality.* To the extent possible, consistent with fair and thorough processing of allegations of research misconduct and applicable law and regulation, knowledge about the identity of the subjects of allegations and informants should be limited to those with a need to know.

(5) *Remediation and sanction.* If the recipient finds that research misconduct has occurred, it shall assess the seriousness of the misconduct and its impact on the research completed or in process. The recipient must take all necessary corrective actions. Such action may include but are not limited to, correcting the research record and as appropriate imposing restrictions, controls, or other parameters on research in process or to be conducted in the future. The recipient must coordinate remedial actions with the Contracting Officer. The recipient must also consider whether personnel sanctions are appropriate. Any such sanction must be consistent with any applicable personnel laws, policies, and procedures, and must take into account the seriousness of the misconduct and its impact, whether it was done knowingly or intentionally, and whether it was an isolated event or pattern of conduct.

(g) By executing this agreement, the recipient provides its assurance that it has established an administrative process for performing an inquiry, mediating if possible, investigating, and reporting allegations of research misconduct; and that it will comply with its own administrative process and the requirements and definitions of 10 CFR part 733 for performing an inquiry, possible mediation, investigation and reporting of allegations of research misconduct.

(h) The recipient must insert or have inserted the substance of this section, including paragraph (g), in subawards at all tiers that involve research.

## Subpart C [Reserved]

## Subpart D—Post Award Federal Requirements for For-Profit Entities

**§ 910.350  Applicability of 2 CFR part 200.**

(a) As stated in 2 CFR 910.122, unless otherwise noted in part 910, the definition of Non-Federal entity found in 2

CFR 200.69 is expanded for DOE to include for-profit organizations in addition to states, local governments, Indian tribes, institutions of higher education (IHE), and nonprofit organizations.

(b) A for-profit organization is defined as one that distributes any profit not reinvested into the business as profit or dividends to its employees or shareholders.

(c) Subpart D of 2 CFR part 910 contains specific changes to 2 CFR part 200 that apply only to For-Profit Recipients and, unless otherwise specified, subrecipients. In some cases, the coverage in Subpart D will replace the language in a specific section of 2 CFR part 200.

### §910.352   Cost Principles.

For For-Profit Entities, the Cost Principles contained in 48 CFR 31.2 (Contracts with Commercial Organizations) must be followed in lieu of the Cost principles contained in 2 CFR 200.400 through 200.475, except that patent prosecution costs are not allowable unless specifically authorized in the award document. This applies to For-Profit entities whether they are recipients or subrecipients.

### §910.354   Payment.

(a) For-Profit Recipients are an exception to 2 CFR 200.305(b)(1) which requires that non-Federal entities be paid in advance as long as certain conditions are met.

(b) For For-Profit Recipients who are paid directly by DOE, reimbursement is the preferred method of payment. Under the reimbursement method of payment, the Federal awarding agency must reimburse the non-Federal entity for its actual cash disbursements. When the reimbursement method is used, the Federal awarding agency must make payment within 30 calendar days after receipt of the billing, unless the Federal awarding agency reasonably believes the request to be improper.

### §910.356   Audits.

See Subpart F of this part (Sections 910.500 through 910.521) for specific DOE regulations which apply to audits of DOE's For-Profit Recipients. For-Prof-

it entities are an exception to the Single Audit requirements contained in Subpart F of 2 CFR 200 and therefore the regulations contained in 2 CFR 910 Subpart F apply instead.

### §910.358   Profit or fee for SBIR/STTR.

(a) As authorized by 2 CFR 200.400 (g), DOE may expressly allow non-federal entities to earn a profit or fee resulting from Federal financial assistance.

(b) DOE allows a profit or fee to be paid under two of its financial assistance programs only: Small Business Innovation Research (SBIR) and Small Business Technology Transfer Research (STTR).

(c) Awards under these programs will contain a specific provision which allows a profit or fee to be paid.

(d) Profit or Fee is unallowable for all other DOE programs which award grants and cooperative agreements.

### §910.360   Real property and equipment.

(a) *Prior approvals for acquisition with Federal funds.* Recipients may purchase real property or equipment with an acquisition cost per unit of $5,000 or more in whole or in part with Federal funds only with the prior written approval of the contracting officer or in accordance with express award terms.

(b) *Title.* Unless a statute specifically authorizes and the award specifies that title to property vests unconditionally in the recipient, title to real property or equipment vests in the recipient, subject to all terms and conditions of the award and that the recipient shall:

(1) Use the real property or equipment for the authorized purposes of the project until funding for the project ceases, or until the real property or equipment is no longer needed for the purposes of the project, as may be determined by the contracting officer;

(2) Not encumber or permit any encumbrance on the real property or equipment without the prior written approval of the contracting officer;

(3) Use and dispose of the real property or equipment in accordance with paragraphs (e), (f), and (g) of this section; and

(4) Properly record, and consent to the Department's ability to properly record if the recipient fails to do so,

UCC financing statement(s) for all equipment purchased with Federal funds (Financial assistance awards made under the Small Business Innovation Research/Small Business Technology Transfer (SBIR/STTR) program are exempt from this requirement unless otherwise specified within the grant agreement); such a filing is required when the Federal share of the financial assistance agreement is more than $1,000,000, and the Contracting Officer may require it in his or her discretion when the Federal share is less than $1,000,000. These financing statement(s) must be approved in writing by the contracting officer prior to the recording, and they shall provide notice that the recipient's title to all equipment (not real property) purchased with Federal funds under the financial assistance agreement is conditional pursuant to the terms of this section, and that the Government retains an undivided reversionary interest in the equipment. The UCC financing statement(s) must be filed before the contracting officer may reimburse the recipient for the Federal share of the equipment unless otherwise provided for in the relevant financial assistance agreement. The recipient shall further make any amendments to the financing statements or additional recordings, including appropriate continuation statements, as necessary or as the contracting officer may direct.

(c) *Remedies.* If the recipient fails at any time to comply with any of the conditions or requirements of paragraph (b) of this section, then the contracting officer may:

(1) Notify the recipient of noncompliance in accordance with 2 CFR 200.338, which may lead to suspension or termination of the award;

(2) Impose special award conditions pursuant to 2 CFR 200.205 and 200.207 as amended by 2 CFR 910.372;

(3) Issue instructions to the recipient for disposition of the property in accordance with paragraph (g) of this section;

(4) In the case of a failure to properly record UCC financing statement(s) in accordance with paragraph (b)(4) of this section, effect such a recording; and

(5) Apply other remedies that may be legally available.

(d) *Title to and Federal interest in real property or equipment offered as cost-share.* As provided in 2 CFR 200.306(h), depending upon the purpose of the Federal award, a recipient may offer the fair market value of real property or equipment that is purchased with recipient's funds or that is donated by a third party to meet a portion of any required cost sharing or matching. If a resulting award includes such property as a portion of the recipient's cost share, the recipient holds conditional title to the property and the Government has an undivided reversionary interest in the share of the property value equal to the Federal participation in the project. The property is treated as if it had been acquired in part with Federal funds, and is subject to the provisions of paragraph (b) of this section and to the provisions of 2 CFR 200.311 and 200.313.

(e) *Insurance.* Recipients must, at a minimum, provide the equivalent insurance coverage for real property and equipment acquired with Federal funds as provided to property owned by the recipient.

(f) *Additional uses during and after the project period.* Unless a statute and the award terms expressly provide for the vesting of unconditional title to real property or equipment with the recipient, the real property or equipment acquired wholly or in part with Federal funds is subject to the following:

(1) During the Project Period, the recipient must make real property and equipment available for use on other projects or programs, if such other use does not interfere with the work on the project or program for which the real property or equipment was originally acquired. Use of the real property or equipment on other projects is subject to the following order of priority:

(i) Activities sponsored by DOE grants, cooperative agreements, or other assistance awards;

(ii) Activities sponsored by other Federal agencies' grants, cooperative agreements, or other assistance awards;

(iii) Activities under Federal procurement contracts or activities not sponsored by any Federal agency. If so used, use charges must be assessed to those activities. For real property or equipment, the use charges must be at rates equivalent to those for which comparable real property or equipment may be leased.

(2) After Federal funding for the project ceases, or if, as may be determined by the contracting officer, the real property or equipment is no longer needed for the purposes of the project, or if the recipient suspends work on the project, the recipient may use the real property or equipment for other projects, if:

(i) There are Federally sponsored projects for which the real property or equipment may be used;

(ii) The recipient obtains written approval from the contracting officer to do so. The contracting officer must ensure that there is a formal change of accountability for the real property or equipment to a currently funded Federal award; and

(iii) The recipient's use of the real property or equipment for other projects is in the same order of priority as described in paragraph (e)(1) of this section.

(iv) If the only use for the real property or equipment is for projects that have no Federal sponsorship, the recipient must proceed with disposition of the real property or equipment in accordance with paragraph (g) of this section.

(g) *Disposition.* (1) If, as determined by the contracting officer, an item of real property or equipment is no longer needed for Federally sponsored projects, or if the recipient has suspended work on the project, the recipient has the following options:

(i) If the property is equipment with a current per unit fair market value of less than $5,000, it may be retained, sold, or otherwise disposed of with no further obligation to DOE.

(ii) If the property is equipment (rather than real property) and with the written approval of the contracting officer, the recipient may replace it with an item that is needed currently for the project by trading in or selling to offset the costs of the replacement equipment.

(iii) The recipient may elect to retain title, without further obligation to the Federal Government, by compensating the Federal Government for that percentage of the current fair market value of the real property or equipment that is attributable to the Federal participation in the project.

(iv) If the recipient does not elect to retain title to real property or equipment or does not request approval to use equipment as trade-in or offset for replacement equipment, the recipient must request disposition instructions from the responsible agency.

(2) If a recipient requests disposition instructions, the contracting officer must:

(i) For either real property or equipment, issue instructions to the recipient for disposition of the property no later than 120 calendar days after the recipient's request. The contracting officer's options for disposition are to direct the recipient to:

(A) Transfer title to the real property or equipment to the Federal Government or to a third party designated by the contracting officer provided that, in such cases, the recipient is entitled to compensation for its attributable percentage of the current fair market value of the real property or equipment, plus any reasonable shipping or interim storage costs incurred; or

(B) Sell the real property or equipment and pay the Federal Government for that percentage of the current fair market value of the property that is attributable to the Federal participation in the project (after deducting actual and reasonable selling and fix-up expenses, if any, from the sale proceeds). If the recipient is authorized or required to sell the real property or equipment, the recipient must use competitive procedures that result in the highest practicable return.

(3) If the contracting officer fails to issue disposition instructions within 120 calendar days of the recipient's request, the recipient must dispose of the real property or equipment through the option described in paragraph (g)(2)(i)(B) of this section.

[80 FR 53237, Sept. 3, 2015]

§910.362   **Intellectual property.**

(a) *Scope.* This section sets forth the policies with regard to disposition of rights to data and to inventions conceived or first actually reduced to practice in the course of, or under, a grant or cooperative agreement made to a For-Profit entity by DOE.

(b) *Patents right—small business concerns.* In accordance with 35 U.S.C. 202, if the recipient is a small business concern and receives a grant, cooperative agreement, subaward, or contract for research, developmental, or demonstration activities, then, unless there are "exceptional circumstances" as described in 35 U.S.C. 202(e), the award must contain the standard clause in appendix A to this subpart, entitled "Patents Rights (Small Business Firms and Nonprofit Organizations" which provides to the recipient the right to elect ownership of inventions made under the award.

(c) *Patent rights—other than small business concerns, e.g., large businesses—*

(1) *No Patent Waiver.* Except as provided by paragraph (c)(2) of this section, if the recipient is a for-profit organization other than a small business concern, as defined in 35 U.S.C. 201(h) and receives an award or a subaward for research, development, and demonstration activities, then, pursuant to statute, the award must contain the standard clause in appendix A to this subpart, entitled "Patent Rights (Large Business Firms)—No Waiver" which provides that DOE owns the patent rights to inventions made under the award.

(2) *Patent Waiver Granted.* Paragraph (c)(1) of this section does not apply if:

(i) DOE grants a class waiver for a particular program under 10 CFR part 784;

(ii) The applicant requests and receives an advance patent waiver under 10 CFR part 784; or

(iii) A subaward is covered by a waiver granted under the prime award.

(3) *Special Provision.* Normally, an award will not include a background patent and data provision. However, under special circumstances, in order to provide heightened assurance of commercialization, a provision providing for a right to require licensing of third parties to background inventions, limited rights data and/or restricted computer software, may be included. Inclusion of a background patent and/or a data provision to assure commercialization will be done only with the written concurrence of the DOE program official setting forth the need for such assurance. An award may include the right to license the Government and third party contractors for special Government purposes when future availability of the technology would also benefit the government, *e.g.,* clean-up of DOE facilities. The scope of any such background patent and/or data licensing provision is subject to negotiation.

(d) *Rights in data—general rule.* (1) Subject to paragraphs (d)(2) and (3) of this section, and except as otherwise provided by paragraphs (e) and (f) of this section or other law, any award under this subpart must contain the standard clause in appendix A to this subpart, entitled "Rights in Data—General".

(2) Normally, an award will not require the delivery of limited rights data or restricted computer software. However, if the contracting officer, in consultation with DOE patent counsel and the DOE program official, determines that delivery of limited rights data or restricted computer software is necessary, the contracting officer, after negotiation with the applicant, may insert in the award the standard clause as modified by Alternates I and/or II set forth in appendix A to this subpart.

(3) If software is specified for delivery to DOE, or if other special circumstances exist, *e.g.,* DOE specifying "open-source" treatment of software, then the contracting officer, after negotiation with the recipient, may include in the award special provisions requiring the recipient to obtain written approval of the contracting officer prior to asserting copyright in the software, modifying the retained Government license, and/or otherwise altering the copyright provisions.

(e) *Rights in data—programs covered under special protected data statutes.* (1) If a statute, other than those providing for the Small Business Innovation Research (SBIR) and Small Business Technology Transfer Research (STTR) programs, provides for a period of time, typically up to five years, during which data produced under an award for research, development, and demonstration may be protected from public disclosure, then the contracting officer must insert in the award the standard clause in appendix A to this subpart entitled "Rights in Data—Programs Covered Under Special Protected Data Statutes" or, as determined in consultation with DOE patent counsel and the DOE program official, a modified version of such clause which may identify data or categories of data that the recipient must make available to the public.

(2) An award under paragraph (e)(1) of this section is subject to the provisions of paragraphs (d)(2) and (3) of this section.

(f) *Rights in data—SBIR/STTR programs.* If an applicant receives an award under the SBIR or STTR program, then the contracting officer must insert in the award the standard data clause in the General Terms and Conditions for SBIR Grants, entitled "Rights in Data—SBIR Program".

(g) *Authorization and consent.* (1) Work performed by a recipient under a grant is not subject to authorization and consent to the use of a patented invention, and the Government assumes no liability for patent infringement by the recipient under 28 U.S.C. 1498.

(2) Work performed by a recipient under a cooperative agreement is subject to authorization and consent to the use of a patented invention consistent with the principles set forth in 48 CFR 27.201–1.

(3) The contracting officer, in consultation with patent counsel, may also include clauses in the cooperative agreement addressing other patent matters related to authorization and consent, such as patent indemnification of the Government by recipient and notice and assistance regarding patent and copyright infringement. The policies and clauses for these other patent matters will be the same or consistent with those in 48 CFR part 927.

**§910.364 Reporting on utilization of subject inventions.**

(a) Unless otherwise instructed, a recipient that obtains title to an invention made under an award shall submit annual reports on the utilization or efforts to obtain utilization of the invention for at least 10 years from the date the invention was first disclosed to DOE (Utilization Reports). Utilization Reports shall include at least the following information:

(1) Status of development;

(2) Date of first commercial sale or use;

(3) Gross royalties received by the recipient;

(4) The location of any manufacture of products embodying the subject invention; and

(5) Any such other data and information as DOE may reasonably specify.

(b) To the extent data or information supplied in a Utilization Report is considered by the recipient to be privileged and confidential and is so marked by the recipient, DOE agrees that, to the extent permitted by law, it shall not disclose such information to persons outside the Government.

[80 FR 53238, Sept. 3, 2015]

**§910.366 Export Control and U.S. Manufacturing and Competitiveness.**

(a) *Export Control.* Any recipient of any award for research, development and/or demonstration must comply with all applicable U.S. laws regarding export control.

(b) *U.S. Manufacturing and Competitiveness.* It is the policy of DOE to ensure that DOE-funded research, development, and/or demonstration projects foster domestic manufacturing. Funding opportunity announcements (FOAs), therefore, may require that applicants submit a "U.S. Manufacturing Plan" in their applications. Such FOAs may encourage U.S. Manufacturing Plans to include proposals by recipients and any sub-recipients to manufacture DOE-funded technologies in the United States; however, the FOAs will also state that these plans should not include requirements regarding the source of inputs used during the manufacturing process. Regardless of whether such plans will be part of the merit review criteria or a program policy factor, and to the extent legally permissible, all awards subject to this subpart, including subawards, for research, development, and/or demonstration, must include a provision that provides plans by the recipient and any subrecipients to support manufacturing in the United States of technology developed under the award. The recipient and any subrecipients must agree to make those plans binding on any assignee or licensee or any entity otherwise acquiring rights to any subject invention or developed technology covered under the award. A recipient, subrecipient, assignee, licensee, or any entity otherwise acquiring the rights to any subject invention or developed technology may request a waiver or modification of U.S. manufacturing plans from DOE. DOE will determine whether to approve such a waiver in light of equitable considerations, including, for example, whether the requester satisfactorily shows that the planned support is not economically feasible and whether there is a satisfactory alternative net benefit to the U.S. economy if the requested waiver or modification is approved.

[80 FR 53239, Sept. 3, 2015]

### § 910.368  Change of control.

(a) Change of control is defined as any of the following:

(1) Any event by which any individual or entity other than the recipient becomes the beneficial owner of more than 50% of the total voting power of the voting stock of the recipient;

(2) The recipient merges with or into any entity other than in a transaction in which the shares of the recipient's voting stock are converted into a majority of the voting stock of the surviving entity;

(3) The sale, lease or transfer of all or substantially all of the assets of the recipient to any individual or entity other than the recipient in one or a series of related transactions;

(4) The adoption of a plan relating to the liquidation or dissolution of the recipient; or

(5) Where the recipient is a wholly-owned subsidiary at the time of award or novation, and the recipient's parent entity undergoes a change of control as defined in this section.

(b) When the Federal share of the financial assistance agreement is more than $10,000,000 or DOE requests the information in writing, the recipient must provide the contracting officer with documentation identifying all parties who exercise control in the recipient at the time of award.

(c) When there is a change of control of a recipient, or the recipient has reason to know a change of control is likely, the recipient must notify the contracting officer within 30 days of its knowledge of such change of control. Such notification must include, at a minimum, copies of documents necessary to reflect the transaction that resulted or will result in the change of control, and identification of all entities, individuals or other parties to such transaction. Failure to notify the contracting officer of a change of control is grounds for suspension or termination of the award for failure to comply with the terms and conditions of the award.

(d) The contracting officer must authorize a change of control for the purposes of the award. Failure to receive the contracting officer's authorization for a change of control may lead to a suspension of the award, termination for failure to comply with the terms and conditions of the award, or imposition of special award conditions pursuant to 2 CFR 910.372. Special award conditions may include but are not limited to:

(1) Additional reporting requirements related to the change of control; and

(2) Suspension of payments due to the recipient.

[80 FR 53239, Sept. 3, 2015]

### § 910.370  Novation of financial assistance agreements.

(a) Financial assistance agreements are not assignable absent written consent from the contracting officer. At his or her sole discretion, the contracting officer may, through novation, recognize a third party as the successor in interest to a financial assistance agreement if such recognition is in the Government's interest, conforms with all applicable laws and the third party's interest in the agreement arises out of the transfer of:

(1) All of the recipient's assets; or

(2) The entire portion of the assets necessary to perform the project described in the agreement.

(b) When the contracting officer determines that it is not in the Government's interest to consent to the novation of a financial assistance agreement from the original recipient to a third party, the original recipient remains subject to the terms of the financial assistance agreement, and the Department may exercise all legally available remedies under 2 CFR 200.338 through 200.342, or that may be otherwise available, should the original recipient not perform.

(c) The contracting officer may require submission of any documentation in support of a request for novation, including but not limited to documents identified in 48 CFR Subpart 42.12. The contracting officer may use the format in 48 CFR 42.1204 as guidance for novation agreements identified in paragraph (a) of this section.

[80 FR 53239, Sept. 3, 2015]

### § 910.372 Special award conditions.

(a) In addition to the requirements of 2 CFR 200.205, the following actions may require the use of Specific Conditions as identified in 2 CFR 200.207:

(1) Has not conformed to the terms and conditions of a previous award;

(2) Has a change of control as defined in § 910.368;

(3) Fails to comply with real property and equipment requirements at § 910.360; or

(4) Is not otherwise responsible.

[80 FR 53239, Sept. 3, 2015]

APPENDIX A TO SUBPART D—PATENT AND DATA PROVISIONS

1. Patent Rights (Small Business Firms and Nonprofit Organizations)
2. Patent Rights (Large Business Firms)—No Waiver
3. Rights in Data—General
4. Rights in Data—Programs Covered Under Special Protected Data Statutes

1. Patent Rights (Small Business Firms and Nonprofit Organizations)

(a) Definitions

*Invention* means any invention or discovery which is or may be patentable or otherwise protectable under title 35 of the United States Code, or any novel variety of plant which is or may be protected under the Plant Variety Protection Act (7 U.S.C. 2321 *et seq.*).

*Made* when used in relation to any invention means the conception or first actual reduction to practice of such invention.

*Nonprofit organization* is defined in 2 CFR 200.70.

*Practical application* means to manufacture in the case of a composition or product, to practice in the case of a process or method, or to operate in the case of a machine or system; and, in each case, under such conditions as to establish that the invention is being utilized and that its benefits are to the extent permitted by law or Government regulations available to the public on reasonable terms.

*Small business firm* means a small business concern as defined at section 2 of Public Law 85–536 (16 U.S.C. 632) and implementing regulations of the Administrator of the Small Business Administration. For the purpose of this clause, the size standards for small business concerns involved in Government procurement and subcontracting at 13 CFR 121.3 through 121.8 and 13 CFR 121.3 through 121.12, respectively, will be used.

*Subject invention* means any invention of the Recipient conceived or first actually reduced to practice in the performance of work under this award, provided that in the case of a variety of plant, the date of determination (as defined in section 41(d) of the Plant Variety Protection Act, 7 U.S.C. 2401(d) must also occur during the period of award performance.

(b) Allocation of Principal Rights

The Recipient may retain the entire right, title, and interest throughout the world to each subject invention subject to the provisions of this Patent Rights clause and 35 U.S.C. 203. With respect to any subject invention in which the Recipient retains title, the Federal Government shall have a non-exclusive, nontransferable, irrevocable, paid-up license to practice or have practiced for or on behalf of the U.S. the subject invention throughout the world.

(c) Invention Disclosure, Election of Title and Filing of Patent Applications by Recipient

(1) The Recipient will disclose each subject invention to DOE within two months after the inventor discloses it in writing to Recipient personnel responsible for the administration of patent matters. The disclosure to DOE shall be in the form of a written report and shall identify the award under which the invention was made and the inventor(s). It shall be sufficiently complete in technical detail to convey a clear understanding to the extent known at the time of disclosure, of the nature, purpose, operation, and the physical, chemical, biological or electrical characteristics of the invention. The disclosure shall also identify any publication, on sale or public use of the invention and whether a manuscript describing the invention has been submitted for publication and, if so,

whether it has been accepted for publication at the time of disclosure. In addition, after disclosure to DOE, the Recipient will promptly notify DOE of the acceptance of any manuscript describing the invention for publication or of any on sale or public use planned by the Recipient.

(2) The Recipient will elect in writing whether or not to retain title to any such invention by notifying DOE within two years of disclosure to DOE. However, in any case where publication, on sale, or public use has initiated the one-year statutory period wherein valid patent protection can still be obtained in the U.S., the period for election of title may be shortened by the agency to a date that is no more than 60 days prior to the end of the statutory period.

(3) The Recipient will file its initial patent application on an invention to which it elects to retain title within one year after election of title or, if earlier, prior to the end of any statutory period wherein valid patent protection can be obtained in the U.S. after a publication, on sale, or public use. The Recipient will file patent applications in additional countries or international patent offices within either ten months of the corresponding initial patent application, or six months from the date when permission is granted by the Commissioner of Patents and Trademarks to file foreign patent applications when such filing has been prohibited by a Secrecy Order.

(4) Requests for extension of the time for disclosure to DOE, election, and filing under subparagraphs (c)(1), (2), and (3) of this clause may, at the discretion of DOE, be granted.

(d) Conditions When the Government May Obtain Title

The Recipient will convey to DOE, upon written request, title to any subject invention:

(1) If the Recipient fails to disclose or elect the subject invention within the times specified in paragraph (c) of this patent rights clause, or elects not to retain title; provided that DOE may only request title within 60 days after learning of the failure of the Recipient to disclose or elect within the specified times;

(2) In those countries in which the Recipient fails to file patent applications within the times specified in paragraph (c) of this Patent Rights clause; provided, however, that if the Recipient has filed a patent application in a country after the times specified in paragraph (c) of this Patent Rights clause, but prior to its receipt of the written request of DOE, the Recipient shall continue to retain title in that country; or

(3) In any country in which the Recipient decides not to continue the prosecution of any application for, to pay the maintenance fees on, or defend in a reexamination or opposition proceeding on, a patent on a subject invention.

(e) Minimum Rights to Recipient and Protection of the Recipient Right To File

(1) The Recipient will retain a non-exclusive royalty-free license throughout the world in each subject invention to which the Government obtains title, except if the Recipient fails to disclose the subject invention within the times specified in paragraph (c) of this Patent Rights clause. The Recipient's license extends to its domestic subsidiaries and affiliates, if any, within the corporate structure of which the Recipient is a party and includes the right to grant sublicenses of the same scope to the extent the Recipient was legally obligated to do so at the time the award was awarded. The license is transferable only with the approval of DOE except when transferred to the successor of that part of the Recipient's business to which the invention pertains.

(2) The Recipient's domestic license may be revoked or modified by DOE to the extent necessary to achieve expeditious practical application of the subject invention pursuant to an application for an exclusive license submitted in accordance with applicable provisions at 37 CFR part 404 and the agency's licensing regulation, if any. This license will not be revoked in that field of use or the geographical areas in which the Recipient has achieved practical application and continues to make the benefits of the invention reasonably accessible to the public. The license in any foreign country may be revoked or modified at discretion of the funding Federal agency to the extent the Recipient, its licensees, or its domestic subsidiaries or affiliates have failed to achieve practical application in that foreign country.

(3) Before revocation or modification of the license, the funding Federal agency will furnish the Recipient a written notice of its intention to revoke or modify the license, and the Recipient will be allowed thirty days (or such other time as may be authorized by DOE for good cause shown by the Recipient) after the notice to show cause why the license should not be revoked or modified. The Recipient has the right to appeal, in accordance with applicable regulations in 37 CFR part 404 and the agency's licensing regulations, if any, concerning the licensing of Government-owned inventions, any decision concerning the revocation or modification of its license.

(f) Recipient Action To Protect Government's Interest

(1) The Recipient agrees to execute or to have executed and promptly deliver to DOE all instruments necessary to:

(i) Establish or confirm the rights the Government has throughout the world in those subject inventions for which the Recipient retains title; and

(ii) Convey title to DOE when requested under paragraph (d) of this Patent Rights clause, and to enable the government to obtain patent protection throughout the world in that subject invention.

(2) The Recipient agrees to require, by written agreement, its employees, other than clerical and non-technical employees, to disclose promptly in writing to personnel identified as responsible for the administration of patent matters and in a format suggested by the Recipient each subject invention made under this award in order that the Recipient can comply with the disclosure provisions of paragraph (c) of this Patent Rights clause, and to execute all papers necessary to file patent applications on subject inventions and to establish the Government's rights in the subject inventions. The disclosure format should require, as a minimum, the information requested by paragraph (c)(1) of this Patent Rights clause. The Recipient shall instruct such employees through the employee agreements or other suitable educational programs on the importance of reporting inventions in sufficient time to permit the filing of patent applications prior to U.S. or foreign statutory bars.

(3) The Recipient will notify DOE of any decision not to continue prosecution of a patent application, pay maintenance fees, or defend in a reexamination or opposition proceeding on a patent, in any country, not less than 30 days before the expiration of the response period required by the relevant patent office.

(4) The Recipient agrees to include, within the specification of any U.S. patent application and any patent issuing thereon covering a subject invention, the following statement: "This invention was made with Government support under (identify the award) awarded by (identify DOE). The Government has certain rights in this invention."

(g) Subaward/Contract

(1) The Recipient will include this Patent Rights clause, suitably modified to identify the parties, in all subawards/contracts, regardless of tier, for experimental, developmental or research work to be performed by a small business firm or nonprofit organization. The subrecipient/contractor will retain all rights provided for the Recipient in this Patent Rights clause, and the Recipient will not, as part of the consideration for awarding the subcontract, obtain rights in the subcontractors' subject inventions.

(2) The Recipient will include in all other subawards/contracts, regardless of tier, for experimental, developmental or research work, the patent rights clause required by 2 CFR 910.362(c).

(3) In the case of subawards/contracts at any tier, DOE, the Recipient, and the subrecipient/contractor agree that the mutual obligations of the parties created by this clause constitute a contract between the subrecipient/contractor and DOE with respect to those matters covered by the clause.

(h) Reporting on Utilization of Subject Inventions

The Recipient agrees to submit on request periodic reports no more frequently than annually on the utilization of a subject invention or on efforts at obtaining such utilization that are being made by the Recipient or its licensees or assignees. Such reports shall include information regarding the status of development, date of first commercial sale or use, gross royalties received by the Recipient and such other data and information as DOE may reasonably specify. The Recipient also agrees to provide additional reports in connection with any march-in proceeding undertaken by DOE in accordance with paragraph (j) of this Patent Rights clause. As required by 35 U.S.C. 202(c)(5), DOE agrees it will not disclose such information to persons outside the Government without the permission of the Recipient.

(i) Preference for United States Industry.

Notwithstanding any other provision of this Patent Rights clause, the Recipient agrees that neither it nor any assignee will grant to any person the exclusive right to use or sell any subject invention in the U.S. unless such person agrees that any products embodying the subject invention or produced through the use of the subject invention will be manufactured substantially in the U.S. However, in individual cases, the requirement for such an agreement may be waived by DOE upon a showing by the Recipient or its assignee that reasonable but unsuccessful efforts have been made to grant licenses on similar terms to potential licensees that would be likely to manufacture substantially in the U.S. or that under the circumstances domestic manufacture is not commercially feasible.

(j) March-in-Rights

The Recipient agrees that with respect to any subject invention in which it has acquired title, DOE has the right in accordance with procedures at 37 CFR 401.6 and any supplemental regulations of the Agency to require the Recipient, an assignee or exclusive licensee of a subject invention to grant a non-exclusive, partially exclusive, or exclusive license in any field of use to a responsible applicant or applicants, upon terms that are reasonable under the circumstances and if the Recipient, assignee, or exclusive licensee refuses such a request, DOE has the right to grant such a license itself if DOE determines that:

(1) Such action is necessary because the Recipient or assignee has not taken or is not expected to take within a reasonable time, effective steps to achieve practical application of the subject invention in such field of use;

(2) Such action is necessary to alleviate health or safety needs which are not reasonably satisfied by the Recipient, assignee, or their licensees;

(3) Such action is necessary to meet requirements for public use specified by Federal regulations and such requirements are not reasonably satisfied by the Recipient, assignee, or licensee; or

(4) Such action is necessary because the agreement required by paragraph (i) of this Patent Rights clause has not been obtained or waived or because a licensee of the exclusive right to use or sell any subject invention in the U.S. is in breach of such agreement.

(k) Special Provisions for Awards With Nonprofit Organizations

If the Recipient is a nonprofit organization, it agrees that:

(1) Rights to a subject invention in the U.S. may not be assigned without the approval of DOE, except where such assignment is made to an organization which has as one of its primary functions the management of inventions, provided that such assignee will be subject to the same provisions as the Recipient;

(2) The Recipient will share royalties collected on a subject invention with the inventor, including Federal employee co-inventors (when DOE deems it appropriate) when the subject invention is assigned in accordance with 35 U.S.C. 202(e) and 37 CFR 401.10;

(3) The balance of any royalties or income earned by the Recipient with respect to subject inventions, after payment of expenses (including payments to inventors) incidental to the administration of subject inventions, will be utilized for the support of scientific or engineering research or education; and

(4) It will make efforts that are reasonable under the circumstances to attract licensees of subject inventions that are small business firms and that it will give preference to a small business firm if the Recipient determines that the small business firm has a plan or proposal for marketing the invention which, if executed, is equally likely to bring the invention to practical application as any plans or proposals from applicants that are not small business firms; provided that the Recipient is also satisfied that the small business firm has the capability and resources to carry out its plan or proposal. The decision whether to give a preference in any specific case will be at the discretion of the Recipient. However, the Recipient agrees that the Secretary of Commerce may review the Recipient's licensing program and decisions regarding small business applicants, and the Recipient will negotiate changes to its licensing policies, procedures or practices with the Secretary when the Secretary's review discloses that the Recipient could take reasonable steps to implement more effectively the requirements of this paragraph (k)(4).

(l) Communications

All communications required by this Patent Rights clause should be sent to the DOE Patent Counsel address listed in the Award Document.

(m) Electronic Filing

Unless otherwise specified in the award, the information identified in paragraphs (f)(2) and (f)(3) may be electronically filed.

(End of clause)

2. Patent Rights (Large Business Firms)—No Waiver

(a) Definitions

*DOE patent waiver regulations,* as used in this clause, means the Department of Energy patent waiver regulations in effect on the date of award. See 10 CFR part 784.

*Invention,* as used in this clause, means any invention or discovery which is or may be patentable or otherwise protectable under title 35 of the United States Code or any novel variety of plant that is or may be protectable under the Plant Variety Protection Act (7 U.S.C. 2321, *et seq.*).

*Patent Counsel,* as used in this clause, means the Department of Energy Patent Counsel assisting the awarding activity.

*Subject invention,* as used in this clause, means any invention of the Recipient conceived or first actually reduced to practice in the course of or under this agreement.

(b) Allocations of Principal Rights

(1) Assignment to the Government. The Recipient agrees to assign to the Government the entire right, title, and interest throughout the world in and to each subject invention, except to the extent that rights are retained by the Recipient under subparagraph (b)(2) and paragraph (d) of this clause.

(2) Greater rights determinations. The Recipient, or an employee-inventor after consultation with the Recipient, may request greater rights than the nonexclusive license and the foreign patent rights provided in paragraph (d) of this clause on identified inventions in accordance with the DOE patent waiver regulation. Each determination of greater rights under this agreement shall be subject to paragraph (c) of this clause, unless otherwise provided in the greater rights determination, and to the reservations and conditions deemed to be appropriate by the Secretary of Energy or designee.

(c) Minimum Rights Acquired by the Government

With respect to each subject invention to which the Department of Energy grants the Recipient principal or exclusive rights, the Recipient agrees to grant to the Government: A nonexclusive, nontransferable, irrevocable, paid-up license to practice or have practiced each subject invention throughout the world by or on behalf of the Government of the United States (including any Government agency); "march-in rights" as set forth in 37 CFR 401.14(a)(J)); preference for U.S. industry as set forth in 37 CFR 401.14(a)(I); periodic reports upon request, no more frequently than annually, on the utilization or intent of utilization of a subject invention in a manner consistent with 35 U.S.C. 202(c)(50); and such Government rights in any instrument transferring rights in a subject invention.

(d) Minimum Rights to the Recipient

(1) The Recipient is hereby granted a revocable, nonexclusive, royalty-free license in each patent application filed in any country on a subject invention and any resulting patent in which the Government obtains title, unless the Recipient fails to disclose the subject invention within the times specified in subparagraph (e)(2) of this clause. The Recipient's license extends to its domestic subsidiaries and affiliates, if any, within the corporate structure of which the Recipient is a part and includes the right to grant sublicenses of the same scope to the extent the Recipient was legally obligated to do so at the time the agreement was awarded. The license is transferable only with the approval of DOE except when transferred to the successor of that part of the Recipient's business to which the invention pertains.

(2) The Recipient may request the right to acquire patent rights to a subject invention in any foreign country where the Government has elected not to secure such rights, subject to the minimum rights acquired by the Government similar to paragraph (c) of this clause. Such request must be made in writing to the Patent Counsel as part of the disclosure required by subparagraph (e)(2) of this clause, with a copy to the DOE Contracting Officer. DOE approval, if given, will be based on a determination that this would best serve the national interest.

(e) Invention Identification, Disclosures, and Reports

(1) The Recipient shall establish and maintain active and effective procedures to assure that subject inventions are promptly identified and disclosed to Recipient personnel responsible for patent matters within 6 months of conception and/or first actual reduction to practice, whichever occurs first in the performance of work under this agreement. These procedures shall include the maintenance of laboratory notebooks or equivalent records and other records as are reasonably necessary to document the conception and/or the first actual reduction to practice of subject inventions, and records that show that the procedures for identifying and disclosing the inventions are followed. Upon request, the Recipient shall furnish the Contracting Officer a description of such procedures for evaluation and for determination as to their effectiveness.

(2) The Recipient shall disclose each subject invention to the DOE Patent Counsel with a copy to the Contracting Officer within 2 months after the inventor discloses it in writing to Recipient personnel responsible for patent matters or, if earlier, within 6 months after the Recipient becomes aware that a subject invention has been made, but in any event before any on sale, public use, or publication of such invention known to the Recipient. The disclosure to DOE shall be in the form of a written report and shall identify the agreement under which the invention was made and the inventor(s). It shall be sufficiently complete in technical detail to convey a clear understanding, to the extent known at the time of the disclosure, of the nature, purpose, operation, and physical, chemical, biological, or electrical characteristics of the invention. The disclosure shall also identify any publication, on sale, or public use of the invention and whether a manuscript describing the invention has been submitted for publication and, if so, whether it has been accepted for publication at the time of disclosure. In addition, after disclosure to DOE, the Recipient shall promptly notify Patent Counsel of the acceptance of any manuscript describing the invention for publication or of any on sale or public use planned by the Recipient. The report should also include any request for a greater rights determination in accordance with subparagraph (b)(2) of this clause. When an invention is disclosed to DOE under this paragraph, it shall be deemed to have been made in the manner specified in Sections (a)(1) and (a)(2) of 42 U.S.C. 5908, unless the Recipient contends in writing at the time the invention is disclosed that it was not so made.

(3) The Recipient shall furnish the Contracting Officer a final report, within 3 months after completion of the work listing all subject inventions or containing a statement that there were no such inventions, and listing all subawards/contracts at any tier containing a patent rights clause or containing a statement that there were no such subawards/contracts.

(4) The Recipient agrees to require, by written agreement, its employees, other than clerical and nontechnical employees, to disclose promptly in writing to personnel identified as responsible for the administration of patent matters and in a format suggested by the Recipient each subject invention made under subaward/contract in order that the Recipient can comply with the disclosure provisions of paragraph (c) of this clause, and to execute all papers necessary to file patent applications on subject inventions and to establish the Government's rights in the subject inventions. This disclosure format should require, as a minimum, the information required by subparagraph (e)(2) of this clause.

333

(5) The Recipient agrees, subject to FAR 27.302(j), that the Government may duplicate and disclose subject invention disclosures and all other reports and papers furnished or required to be furnished pursuant to this clause.

(f) Examination of Records Relating to Inventions

(1) The Contracting Officer or any authorized representative shall, until 3 years after final payment under this agreement, have the right to examine any books (including laboratory notebooks), records, and documents of the Recipient relating to the conception or first actual reduction to practice of inventions in the same field of technology as the work under this agreement to determine whether—(i) Any such inventions are subject inventions; (ii) The Recipient has established and maintains the procedures required by subparagraphs (e)(1) and (4) of this clause; (iii) The Recipient and its inventors have complied with the procedures.

(2) If the Contracting Officer learns of an unreported Recipient invention which the Contracting Officer believes may be a subject invention, the Recipient may be required to disclose the invention to DOE for a determination of ownership rights.

(3) Any examination of records under this paragraph will be subject to appropriate conditions to protect the confidentiality of the information involved.

(g) Subaward/Contract

(1) The recipient shall include the clause PATENT RIGHTS (SMALL BUSINESS FIRMS AND NONPROFIT ORGANIZATIONS) (suitably modified to identify the parties) in all subawards/contracts, regardless of tier, for experimental, developmental, demonstration, or research work to be performed by a small business firm or domestic nonprofit organization, except where the work of the subaward/contract is subject to an Exceptional Circumstances Determination by DOE. In all other subawards/contracts, regardless of tier, for experimental, developmental, demonstration, or research work, the Recipient shall include this clause (suitably modified to identify the parties), or an alternate clause as directed by the contracting officer. The Recipient shall not, as part of the consideration for awarding the subaward/contract, obtain rights in the subrecipient's/contractor's subject inventions.

(2) In the event of a refusal by a prospective subrecipient/contractor to accept such a clause the Recipient: (i) Shall promptly submit a written notice to the Contracting Officer setting forth the subrecipient/contractor's reasons for such refusal and other pertinent information that may expedite disposition of the matter; and (ii) Shall not proceed with such subaward/contract without the written authorization of the Contracting Officer.

(3) In the case of subawards/contracts at any tier, DOE, the subrecipient/contractor, and Recipient agree that the mutual obligations of the parties created by this clause constitute a contract between the subrecipient/contractor and DOE with respect to those matters covered by this clause.

(4) The Recipient shall promptly notify the Contracting Officer in writing upon the award of any subaward/contract at any tier containing a patent rights clause by identifying the subrecipient/contractor, the applicable patent rights clause, the work to be performed under the subaward/contract, and the dates of award and estimated completion. Upon request of the Contracting Officer, the Recipient shall furnish a copy of such subaward/contract, and, no more frequently than annually, a listing of the subawards/contracts that have been awarded.

(5) The Recipient shall identify all subject inventions of a subrecipient/contractor of which it acquires knowledge in the performance of this agreement and shall notify the Patent Counsel, with a copy to the contracting officer, promptly upon identification of the inventions.

(h) Atomic Energy

(1) No claim for pecuniary award of compensation under the provisions of the Atomic Energy Act of 1954, as amended, shall be asserted with respect to any invention or discovery made or conceived in the course of or under this agreement.

(2) Except as otherwise authorized in writing by the Contracting Officer, the Recipient will obtain patent agreements to effectuate the provisions of subparagraph (h)(1) of this clause from all persons who perform any part of the work under this agreement, except nontechnical personnel, such as clerical employees and manual laborers.

(i) Publication

It is recognized that during the course of the work under this agreement, the Recipient or its employees may from time to time desire to release or publish information regarding scientific or technical developments conceived or first actually reduced to practice in the course of or under this agreement. In order that public disclosure of such information will not adversely affect the patent interests of DOE or the Recipient, patent approval for release of publication shall be secured from Patent Counsel prior to any such release or publication.

(j) Forfeiture of Rights in Unreported Subject Inventions

(1) The Recipient shall forfeit and assign to the Government, at the request of the Secretary of Energy or designee, all rights in any subject invention which the Recipient fails to report to Patent Counsel within six months after the time the Recipient: (i) Files

or causes to be filed a United States or foreign patent application thereon; or (ii) Submits the final report required by subparagraph (e)(3) of this clause, whichever is later.

(2) However, the Recipient shall not forfeit rights in a subject invention if, within the time specified in subparagraph (e)(2) of this clause, the Recipient: (i) Prepares a written decision based upon a review of the record that the invention was neither conceived nor first actually reduced to practice in the course of or under the agreement and delivers the decision to Patent Counsel, with a copy to the Contracting Officer, or (ii) Contending that the invention is not a subject invention, the Recipient nevertheless discloses the invention and all facts pertinent to this contention to the Patent Counsel, with a copy of the Contracting Officer; or (iii) Establishes that the failure to disclose did not result from the Recipient's fault or negligence.

(3) Pending written assignment of the patent application and patents on a subject invention determined by the Secretary of Energy or designee to be forfeited (such determination to be a final decision under the Disputes clause of this agreement), the Recipient shall be deemed to hold the invention and the patent applications and patents pertaining thereto in trust for the Government. The forfeiture provision of this paragraph (j) shall be in addition to and shall not supersede other rights and remedies which the Government may have with respect to subject inventions.

(End of clause)

3. Rights in Data—General

(a) Definitions

*Computer Data Bases,* as used in this clause, means a collection of data in a form capable of, and for the purpose of, being stored in, processed, and operated on by a computer. The term does not include computer software.

*Computer software,* as used in this clause, means (i) computer programs which are data comprising a series of instructions, rules, routines or statements, regardless of the media in which recorded, that allow or cause a computer to perform a specific operation or series of operations and (ii) data comprising source code listings, design details, algorithms, processes, flow charts, formulae, and related material that would enable the computer program to be produced, created or compiled. The term does not include computer data bases.

*Data,* as used in this clause, means recorded information, regardless of form or the media on which it may be recorded. The term includes technical data and computer software. The term does not include information incidental to administration, such as financial, administrative, cost or pricing, or management information.

*Form, fit, and function data,* as used in this clause, means data relating to items, components, or processes that are sufficient to enable physical and functional interchangeability, as well as data identifying source, size, configuration, mating, and attachment characteristics, functional characteristics, and performance requirements; except that for computer software it means data identifying source, functional characteristics, and performance requirements but specifically excludes the source code, algorithm, process, formulae, and flow charts of the software.

*Limited rights,* as used in this clause, means the rights of the Government in limited rights data as set forth in the Limited Rights Notice of subparagraph (g)(2) if included in this clause.

*Limited rights data,* as used in this clause, means data (other than computer software) developed at private expense that embody trade secrets or are commercial or financial and confidential or privileged.

*Restricted computer software,* as used in this clause, means computer software developed at private expense and that is a trade secret; is commercial or financial and is confidential or privileged; or is published copyrighted computer software; including minor modifications of such computer software.

*Restricted rights,* as used in this clause, means the rights of the Government in restricted computer software, as set forth in a Restricted Rights Notice of subparagraph (g)(3) if included in this clause, or as otherwise may be provided in a collateral agreement incorporated in and made part of this contract, including minor modifications of such computer software.

*Technical data,* as used in this clause, means data (other than computer software) which are of a scientific or technical nature. Technical data does not include computer software, but does include manuals and instructional materials and technical data formatted as a computer data base.

*Unlimited rights,* as used in this clause, means the right of the Government to use, disclose, reproduce, prepare derivative works, distribute copies to the public, and perform publicly and display publicly, in any manner and for any purpose, and to have or permit others to do so.

(b) Allocations of Rights

(1) Except as provided in paragraph (c) of this clause regarding copyright, the Government shall have unlimited rights in—

(i) Data first produced in the performance of this agreement;

(ii) Form, fit, and function data delivered under this agreement;

(iii) Data delivered under this agreement (except for restricted computer software) that constitute manuals or instructional and training material for installation, operation, or routine maintenance and repair of items, components, or processes delivered or furnished for use under this agreement; and

(iv) All other data delivered under this agreement unless provided otherwise for limited rights data or restricted computer software in accordance with paragraph (g) of this clause.

(2) The Recipient shall have the right to—

(i) Use, release to others, reproduce, distribute, or publish any data first produced or specifically used by the Recipient in the performance of this agreement, unless provided otherwise in paragraph (d) of this clause;

(ii) Protect from unauthorized disclosure and use those data which are limited rights data or restricted computer software to the extent provided in paragraph (g) of this clause;

(iii) Substantiate use of, add or correct limited rights, restricted rights, or copyright notices and to take over appropriate action, in accordance with paragraphs (e) and (f) of this clause; and

(iv) Establish claim to copyright subsisting in data first produced in the performance of this agreement to the extent provided in paragraph (c)(1) of this clause.

(c) Copyright

(1) Data first produced in the performance of this agreement. Unless provided otherwise in paragraph (d) of this clause, the Recipient may establish, without prior approval of the Contracting Officer, claim to copyright subsisting in data first produced in the performance of this agreement. When claim to copyright is made, the Recipient shall affix the applicable copyright notices of 17 U.S.C. 401 or 402 and acknowledgement of Government sponsorship (including agreement number) to the data when such data are delivered to the Government, as well as when the data are published or deposited for registration as a published work in the U.S. Copyright Office. For such copyrighted data, including computer software, the Recipient grants to the Government, and others acting on its behalf, a paid-up nonexclusive, irrevocable worldwide license in such copyrighted data to reproduce, prepare derivative works, distribute copies to the public, and perform publicly and display publicly, by or on behalf of the Government.

(2) Data not first produced in the performance of this agreement. The Recipient shall not, without prior written permission of the Contracting Officer, incorporate in data delivered under this agreement any data not first produced in the performance of this agreement and which contains the copyright notice of 17 U.S.C. 401 or 402, unless the Recipient identifies such data and grants to the Government, or acquires on its behalf, a license of the same scope as set forth in paragraph (c)(1) of this clause; provided, however, that if such data are computer software the Government shall acquire a copyright li-

cense as set forth in paragraph (g)(3) of this clause if included in this agreement or as otherwise may be provided in a collateral agreement incorporated in or made part of this agreement.

(3) Removal of copyright notices. The Government agrees not to remove any copyright notices placed on data pursuant to this paragraph (c), and to include such notices on all reproductions of the data.

(d) Release, Publication and Use of Data

(1) The Recipient shall have the right to use, release to others, reproduce, distribute, or publish any data first produced or specifically used by the Recipient in the performance of this agreement, except to the extent such data may be subject to the Federal export control or national security laws or regulations, or unless otherwise provided in this paragraph of this clause or expressly set forth in this agreement.

(2) The Recipient agrees that to the extent it receives or is given access to data necessary for the performance of this award, which contain restrictive markings, the Recipient shall treat the data in accordance with such markings unless otherwise specifically authorized in writing by the contracting officer.

(e) Unauthorized Marking of Data

(1) Notwithstanding any other provisions of this agreement concerning inspection or acceptance, if any data delivered under this agreement are marked with the notices specified in paragraph (g)(2) or (g)(3) of this clause and use of such is not authorized by this clause, or if such data bears any other restrictive or limiting markings not authorized by this agreement, the Contracting Officer may at any time either return the data to the Recipient or cancel or ignore the markings. However, the following procedures shall apply prior to canceling or ignoring the markings.

(i) The Contracting Officer shall make written inquiry to the Recipient affording the Recipient 30 days from receipt of the inquiry to provide written justification to substantiate the propriety of the markings;

(ii) If the Recipient fails to respond or fails to provide written justification to substantiate the propriety of the markings within the 30-day period (or a longer time not exceeding 90 days approved in writing by the Contracting Officer for good cause shown), the Government shall have the right to cancel or ignore the markings at any time after said period and the data will no longer be made subject to any disclosure prohibitions.

(iii) If the Recipient provides written justification to substantiate the propriety of the markings within the period set in paragraph (e)(1)(i) of this clause, the Contracting Officer shall consider such written justification and determine whether or not the markings are to be cancelled or ignored. If the Contracting Officer determines that the markings are authorized, the Recipient shall be so notified in writing. If the Contracting Officer determines, with concurrence of the head of the contracting activity, that the markings are not authorized, the Contracting Officer shall furnish the Recipient a written determination, which determination shall become the final agency decision regarding the appropriateness of the markings unless the Recipient files suit in a court of competent jurisdiction within 90 days of receipt of the Contracting Officer's decision. The Government shall continue to abide by the markings under this paragraph (e)(1)(iii) until final resolution of the matter either by the Contracting Officer's determination becoming final (in which instance the Government shall thereafter have the right to cancel or ignore the markings at any time and the data will no longer be made subject to any disclosure prohibitions), or by final disposition of the matter by court decision if suit is filed.

(2) The time limits in the procedures set forth in paragraph (e)(1) of this clause may be modified in accordance with agency regulations implementing the Freedom of Information Act (5 U.S.C. 552) if necessary to respond to a request thereunder.

(f) Omitted or Incorrect Markings

(1) Data delivered to the Government without either the limited rights or restricted rights notice as authorized by paragraph (g) of this clause, or the copyright notice required by paragraph (c) of this clause, shall be deemed to have been furnished with unlimited rights, and the Government assumes no liability for the disclosure, use, or reproduction of such data. However, to the extent the data has not been disclosed without restriction outside the Government, the Recipient may request, within 6 months (or a longer time approved by the Contracting Officer for good cause shown) after delivery or such data, permission to have notices placed on qualifying data at the Recipient's expense, and the Contracting Officer may agree to do so if the Recipient:

(i) Identifies the data to which the omitted notice is to be applied;

(ii) Demonstrates that the omission of the notice was inadvertent;

(iii) Establishes that the use of the proposed notice is authorized; and

(iv) Acknowledges that the Government has no liability with respect to the disclosure, use, or reproduction of any such data made prior to the addition of the notice or resulting from the omission of the notice.

(2) The Contracting Officer may also:

(i) Permit correction at the Recipient's expense of incorrect notices if the Recipient identifies the data on which correction of the notice is to be made, and demonstrates that the correct notice is authorized, or

(ii) Correct any incorrect notices.

(g) Protection of Limited Rights Data and Restricted Computer Software

When data other than that listed in paragraphs (b)(1)(i), (ii), and (iii) of this clause are specified to be delivered under this agreement and qualify as either limited rights data or restricted computer software, if the Recipient desires to continue protection of such data, the Recipient shall withhold such data and not furnish them to the Government under this agreement. As a condition to this withholding, the Recipient shall identify the data being withheld and furnish form, fit, and function data in lieu thereof. Limited rights data that are formatted as a computer data base for delivery to the Government are to be treated as limited rights data and not restricted computer software.

(h) Subaward/Contract

The Recipient has the responsibility to obtain from its subrecipients/contractors all data and rights therein necessary to fulfill the Recipient's obligations to the Government under this agreement. If a subrecipient/contractor refuses to accept terms affording the Government such rights, the Recipient shall promptly bring such refusal to the attention of the Contracting Officer and not proceed with the subaward/contract award without further authorization.

(i) Additional Data Requirements

In addition to the data specified elsewhere in this agreement to be delivered, the Contracting Officer may, at any time during agreement performance or within a period of 3 years after acceptance of all items to be delivered under this agreement, order any data first produced or specifically used in the performance of this agreement. This clause is applicable to all data ordered under this subparagraph. Nothing contained in this subparagraph shall require the Recipient to deliver any data the withholding of which is authorized by this clause, or data which are specifically identified in this agreement as not subject to this clause. When data are to be delivered under this subparagraph, the Recipient will be compensated for converting the data into the prescribed form, for reproduction, and for delivery.

(j) The recipient agrees, except as may be otherwise specified in this award for specific data items listed as not subject to this paragraph, that the Contracting Officer or an authorized representative may, up to three years after acceptance of all items to be delivered under this award, inspect at the Recipient's facility any data withheld pursuant to paragraph (g) of this clause, for purposes of verifying the Recipient's assertion pertaining to the limited rights or restricted rights status of the data or for evaluating work performance. Where the Recipient whose data are to be inspected demonstrates to the Contracting Officer that there would be a possible conflict of interest if the inspection were made by a particular representative, the Contracting Officer shall designate an alternate inspector.

As prescribed in 2 CFR 910.362(d)(1), the following Alternate I and/or II may be inserted in the clause in the award instrument.

*Alternate I:*

(g)(2) Notwithstanding paragraph (g)(1) of this clause, the agreement may identify and specify the delivery of limited rights data, or the Contracting Officer may require by written request the delivery of limited rights data that has been withheld or would otherwise be withholdable. If delivery of such data is so required, the Recipient may affix the following "Limited Rights Notice" to the data and the Government will thereafter treat the data, in accordance with such Notice:

*Limited Rights Notice*

(a) These data are submitted with limited rights under Government agreement No. ____ (and subaward/contract No. ____, if appropriate). These data may be reproduced and used by the Government with the express limitation that they will not, without written permission of the Recipient, be used for purposes of manufacture nor disclosed outside the Government; except that the Government may disclose these data outside the Government for the following purposes, if any, provided that the Government makes such disclosure subject to prohibition against further use and disclosure:

(1) Use (except for manufacture) by Federal support services contractors within the scope of their contracts;

(2) This "limited rights data" may be disclosed for evaluation purposes under the restriction that the "limited rights data" be retained in confidence and not be further disclosed;

(3) This "limited rights data" may be disclosed to other contractors participating in the Government's program of which this Recipient is a part for information or use (except for manufacture) in connection with the work performed under their awards and under the restriction that the "limited rights data" be retained in confidence and not be further disclosed;

(4) This "limited rights data" may be used by the Government or others on its behalf for emergency repair or overhaul work under the restriction that the "limited rights data" be retained in confidence and not be further disclosed; and

(5) Release to a foreign government, or instrumentality thereof, as the interests of the United States Government may require, for information or evaluation, or for emergency repair or overhaul work by such government.

This Notice shall be marked on any reproduction of this data in whole or in part.

(b) This Notice shall be marked on any reproduction of these data, in whole or in part.

(End of notice)

*Alternate II:*

(g)(3)(i) Notwithstanding paragraph (g)(1) of this clause, the agreement may identify and specify the delivery of restricted computer software, or the Contracting Officer may require by written request the delivery of restricted computer software that has been withheld or would otherwise be withholdable. If delivery of such computer software is so required, the Recipient may affix the following "Restricted Rights Notice" to the computer software and the Government will thereafter treat the computer software, subject to paragraphs (e) and (f) of this clause, in accordance with the Notice.

*Restricted Rights Notice*

(a) This computer software is submitted with restricted rights under Government Agreement No.____ (and subaward/contract ____, if appropriate). It may not be used, reproduced, or disclosed by the Government except as provided in paragraph (b) of this Notice or as otherwise expressly stated in the agreement.

(b) This computer software may be—

(1) Used or copies for use in or with the computer or computers for which it was acquired, including use at any Government installation to which such computer or computers may be transferred;

(2) Used or copied for use in a backup computer if any computer or in which it was acquired is inoperative;

(3) Reproduced for safekeeping (archives) or backup purposes;

(4) Modified, adapted, or combined with other computer software, provided that the modified, combined, or adapted portions of the derivative software are made subject to the same restricted rights;

(5) Disclosed to and reproduced for use by support service Recipients in accordance with paragraph (b)(1) through (4) of this clause, provided the Government makes such disclosure or reproduction subject to these restricted rights; and

(6) Used or copied for use in or transferred to a replacement computer.

(c) Notwithstanding the foregoing, if this computer software is published copyrighted computer software, it is licensed to the Government, without disclosure prohibitions, with the minimum rights set forth in paragraph (b) of this clause.

(d) Any other rights or limitations regarding the use, duplication, or disclosure of this computer software are to be expressly stated in, or incorporated in, the agreement.

(e) This Notice shall be marked on any reproduction of this computer software, in whole or in part.

(End of notice)

(ii) Where it is impractical to include the Restricted Rights Notice on restricted computer software, the following short-form Notice may be used in lieu thereof:

Restricted Rights Notice

Use, reproduction, or disclosure is subject to restrictions set forth in agreement No. _____ (and subaward/contract_____, If appropriate) with _____(name of Recipient and subrecipient/contractor).

(End of notice)

(iii) If restricted computer software is delivered with the copyright notice of 17 U.S.C. 401, it will be presumed to be published copyrighted computer software licensed to the government without disclosure prohibitions, with the minimum rights set forth in paragraph (b) of this clause, unless the Recipient includes the following statement with such copyright notice: "Unpublished—rights reserved under the Copyright Laws of the United States."

(End of clause)

4. Rights in Data—Programs Covered Under Special Data Statutes

(a) Definitions

*Computer Data Bases,* as used in this clause, means a collection of data in a form capable of, and for the purpose of, being stored in, processed, and operated on by a computer. The term does not include computer software.

*Computer software,* as used in this clause, means

(i) computer programs which are data comprising a series of instructions, rules, routines, or statements, regardless of the media in which recorded, that allow or cause a computer to perform a specific operation or series of operations and

(ii) data comprising source code listings, design details, algorithms, processes, flow charts, formulae and related material that would enable the computer program to be produced, created or compiled. The term does not include computer data bases.

*Data,* as used in this clause, means recorded information, regardless of form or the media on which it may be recorded. The term includes technical data and computer software. The term does not include information incidental to administration, such as financial, administrative, cost or pricing or management information.

*Form, fit, and function data,* as used in this clause, means data relating to items, components, or processes that are sufficient to enable physical and functional interchangeability as well as data identifying source, size, configuration, mating and attachment characteristics, functional characteristics, and performance requirements except that for computer software it means data identifying source, functional characteristics, and performance requirements but specifically excludes the source code, algorithm, process, formulae, and flow charts of the software.

*Limited rights data,* as used in this clause, means data (other than computer software) developed at private expense that embody trade secrets or are commercial or financial and confidential or privileged.

*Restricted computer software,* as used in this clause, means computer software developed at private expense and that is a trade secret; is commercial or financial and confidential or privileged; or is published copyrighted computer software; including modifications of such computer software.

*Protected data,* as used in this clause, means technical data or commercial or financial data first produced in the performance of the award which, if it had been obtained from and first produced by a non-federal party, would be a trade secret or commercial or financial information that is privileged or confidential under the meaning of 5 U.S.C. 552(b)(4) and which data is marked as being protected data by a party to the award.

*Protected rights,* as used in this clause, mean the rights in protected data set forth in the Protected Rights Notice of paragraph (g) of this clause.

*Technical data,* as used in this clause, means that data which are of a scientific or technical nature. Technical data does not include computer software, but does include manuals and instructional materials and technical data formatted as a computer data base.

*Unlimited rights,* as used in this clause, means the right of the Government to use, disclose, reproduce, prepare derivative works, distribute copies to the public, and perform publicly and display publicly, in any manner and for any purpose whatsoever, and to have or permit others to do so.

(b) Allocation of Rights

(1) Except as provided in paragraph (c) of this clause regarding copyright, the Government shall have unlimited rights in—

(i) Data specifically identified in this agreement as data to be delivered without restriction;

(ii) Form, fit, and function data delivered under this agreement;

(iii) Data delivered under this agreement (except for restricted computer software) that constitute manuals or instructional and training material for installation, operation, or routine maintenance and repair of items, components, or processes delivered or furnished for use under this agreement; and

(iv) All other data delivered under this agreement unless provided otherwise for protected data in accordance with paragraph (g) of this clause or for limited rights data or restricted computer software in accordance with paragraph (h) of this clause.

(2) The Recipient shall have the right to—

(i) Protect rights in protected data delivered under this agreement in the manner and to the extent provided in paragraph (g) of this clause;

(ii) Withhold from delivery those data which are limited rights data or restricted computer software to the extent provided in paragraph (h) of this clause;

(iii) Substantiate use of, add, or correct protected rights or copyrights notices and to take other appropriate action, in accordance with paragraph (e) of this clause; and

(iv) Establish claim to copyright subsisting in data first produced in the performance of this agreement to the extent provided in paragraph (c)(1) of this clause.

(c) Copyright

(1) Data first produced in the performance of this agreement. Except as otherwise specifically provided in this agreement, the Recipient may establish, without the prior approval of the Contracting Officer, claim to copyright subsisting in any data first produced in the performance of this agreement. If claim to copyright is made, the Recipient shall affix the applicable copyright notice of 17 U.S.C. 401 or 402 and acknowledgment of Government sponsorship (including agreement number) to the data when such data are delivered to the Government, as well as when the data are published or deposited for registration as a published work in the U.S. Copyright Office. For such copyrighted data, including computer software, the Recipient grants to the Government, and others acting on its behalf, a paid-up nonexclusive, irrevocable, worldwide license to reproduce, prepare derivative works, distribute copies to the public, and perform publicly and display publicly, by or on behalf of the Government, for all such data.

(2) Data not first produced in the performance of this agreement. The Recipient shall not, without prior written permission of the Contracting Officer, incorporate in data delivered under this agreement any data that are not first produced in the performance of this agreement and that contain the copyright notice of 17 U.S.C. 401 or 402, unless the Recipient identifies such data and grants to the Government, or acquires on its behalf, a license of the same scope as set forth in paragraph (c)(1) of this clause; provided, however, that if such data are computer software, the Government shall acquire a copyright license as set forth in paragraph (h)(3) of this clause if included in this agreement or as otherwise may be provided in a collateral agreement incorporated or made a part of this agreement.

(3) Removal of copyright notices. The Government agrees not to remove any copyright notices placed on data pursuant to this paragraph (c), and to include such notices on all reproductions of the data.

(d) Release, Publication and Use of Data

(1) The Receipt shall have the right to use, release to others, reproduce, distribute, or publish any data first produced or specifically used by the Recipient in the performance of this contract, except to the extent such data may be subject to the Federal export control or national security laws or regulations, or unless otherwise provided in this paragraph of this clause or expressly set forth in this contract.

(2) The Recipient agrees that to the extent it receives or is given access to data necessary for the performance of this agreement which contain restrictive markings, the Recipient shall treat the data in accordance with such markings unless otherwise specifically authorized in writing by the Contracting Officer.

(e) Unauthorized Marking of Data

(1) Notwithstanding any other provisions of this agreement concerning inspection or acceptance, if any data delivered under this agreement are marked with the notices specified in paragraph (g)(2) or (g)(3) of this clause and use of such is not authorized by this clause, or if such data bears any other restrictive or limiting markings not authorized by this agreement, the Contracting Officer may at any time either return the data to the Recipient or cancel or ignore the markings. However, the following procedures shall apply prior to canceling or ignoring the markings.

(i) The Contracting Officer shall make written inquiry to the Recipient affording the Recipient 30 days from receipt of the inquiry to provide written justification to substantiate the propriety of the markings;

(ii) If the Recipient fails to respond or fails to provide written justification to substantiate the propriety of the markings within the 30-day period (or a longer time not exceeding 90 days approved in writing by the Contracting Officer for good cause shown), the Government shall have the right to cancel or ignore the markings at any time after said period and the data will no longer be made subject to any disclosure prohibitions.

(iii) If the Recipient provides written justification to substantiate the propriety of the markings within the period set in subdivision (e)(1)(i) of this clause, the Contracting Officer shall consider such written justification and determine whether or not the markings are to be cancelled or ignored. If the Contracting Officer determines that the markings are authorized, the Recipient shall be so notified in writing. If the Contracting Officer determines, with concurrence of the head of the contracting activity, that the markings are not authorized, the

Contracting Officer shall furnish the Recipient a written determination, which determination shall become the final agency decision regarding the appropriateness of the markings unless the Recipient files suit in a court of competent jurisdiction within 90 days of receipt of the Contracting Officer's decision. The Government shall continue to abide by the markings under this subdivision (e)(1)(iii) until final resolution of the matter either by the Contracting Officer's determination become final (in which instance the Government shall thereafter have the right to cancel or ignore the markings at any time and the data will no longer be made subject to any disclosure prohibitions), or by final disposition of the matter by court decision if suit is filed.

(2) The time limits in the procedures set forth in paragraph (e)(1) of this clause may be modified in accordance with agency regulations implementing the Freedom of Information Act (5 U.S.C. 552) if necessary to respond to a request thereunder.

(f) Omitted or Incorrect Markings

(1) Data delivered to the Government without either the limited rights or restricted rights notice as authorized by paragraph (g) of this clause, or the copyright notice required by paragraph (c) of this clause, shall be deemed to have been furnished with unlimited rights, and the Government assumes no liability for the disclosure, use, or reproduction of such data. However, to the extent the data has not been disclosed without restriction outside the Government, the Recipient may request, within 6 months (or a longer time approved by the Contracting Officer for good cause shown) after delivery of such data, permission to have notices placed on qualifying data at the Recipient's expense, and the Contracting Officer may agree to do so if the Recipient—

(i) Identifies the data to which the omitted notice is to be applied;

(ii) Demonstrates that the omission of the notice was inadvertent;

(iii) Establishes that the use of the proposed notice is authorized; and

(iv) Acknowledges that the Government has no liability with respect to the disclosure, use, or reproduction of any such data made prior to the addition of the notice or resulting from the omission of the notice.

(2) The Contracting Officer may also:

(i) Permit correction at the Recipient's expense of incorrect notices if the Recipient identifies the data on which correction of the notice is to be made, and demonstrates that the correct notice is authorized; or

(ii) Correct any incorrect notices.

(g) Rights to Protected Data

(1) The Recipient may, with the concurrence of DOE, claim and mark as protected data, any data first produced in the performance of this award that would have been treated as a trade secret if developed at private expense. Any such claimed "protected data" will be clearly marked with the following Protected Rights Notice, and will be treated in accordance with such Notice, subject to the provisions of paragraphs (e) and (f) of this clause.

Protected Rights Notice

These protected data were produced under agreement no. _____ with the U.S. Department of Energy and may not be published, disseminated, or disclosed to others outside the Government until (Note:) The period of protection of such data is fully negotiable, but cannot exceed the applicable statutorily authorized maximum), unless express written authorization is obtained from the recipient. Upon expiration of the period of protection set forth in this Notice, the Government shall have unlimited rights in this data. This Notice shall be marked on any reproduction of this data, in whole or in part.

(End of notice)

(2) Any such marked Protected Data may be disclosed under obligations of confidentiality for the following purposes:

(a) For evaluation purposes under the restriction that the "Protected Data" be retained in confidence and not be further disclosed; or

(b) To subcontractors or other team members performing work under the Government's (insert name of program or other applicable activity) program of which this award is a part, for information or use in connection with the work performed under their activity, and under the restriction that the Protected Data be retained in confidence and not be further disclosed.

(3) The obligations of confidentiality and restrictions on publication and dissemination shall end for any Protected Data.

(a) At the end of the protected period;

(b) If the data becomes publicly known or available from other sources without a breach of the obligation of confidentiality with respect to the Protected Data;

(c) If the same data is independently developed by someone who did not have access to the Protected Data and such data is made available without obligations of confidentiality; or

(d) If the Recipient disseminates or authorizes another to disseminate such data without obligations of confidentiality.

(4) However, the Recipient agrees that the following types of data are not considered to be protected and shall be provided to the Government when required by this award without any claim that the data are Protected Data. The parties agree that notwithstanding the following lists of types of data, nothing precludes the Government from seeking delivery of additional data in accordance with this award, or from making

publicly available additional non-protected data, nor does the following list constitute any admission by the Government that technical data not on the list is Protected Data. (Note: It is expected that this paragraph will specify certain types of mutually agreed upon data that will be available to the public and will not be asserted by the recipient/contractor as limited rights or protected data).

(5) The Government's sole obligation with respect to any protected data shall be as set forth in this paragraph (g).

(h) Protection of Limited Rights Data

When data other than that listed in paragraphs (b)(1)(i), (ii), and (iii) of this clause are specified to be delivered under this agreement and such data qualify as either limited rights data or restricted computer software, the Recipient, if the Recipient desires to continue protection of such data, shall withhold such data and not furnish them to the Government under this agreement. As a condition to this withholding the Recipient shall identify the data being withheld and furnish form, fit, and function data in lieu thereof.

(i) Subaward/Contract

The Recipient has the responsibility to obtain from its subrecipients/contractors all data and rights therein necessary to fulfill the Recipient's obligations to the Government under this agreement. If a subrecipient/contractor refuses to accept terms affording the Government such rights, the Recipient shall promptly bring such refusal to the attention of the Contracting Officer and not proceed with subaward/contract award without further authorization.

(j) Additional Data Requirements

In addition to the data specified elsewhere in this agreement to be delivered, the Contracting Officer may, at any time during agreement performance or within a period of 3 years after acceptance of all items to be delivered under this agreement, order any data first produced or specifically used in the performance of this agreement. This clause is applicable to all data ordered under this subparagraph. Nothing contained in this subparagraph shall require the Recipient to deliver any data the withholding of which is authorized by this clause or data which are specifically identified in this agreement as not subject to this clause. When data are to be delivered under this subparagraph, the Recipient will be compensated for converting the data into the prescribed form, for reproduction, and for delivery.

(k) The Recipient agrees, except as may be otherwise specified in this agreement for specific data items listed as not subject to this paragraph, that the Contracting Officer or an authorized representative may, up to three years after acceptance of all items to be delivered under this contract, inspect at the Recipient's facility any data withheld pursuant to paragraph (h) of this clause, for purposes of verifying the Recipient's assertion pertaining to the limited rights or restricted rights status of the data or for evaluating work performance. Where the Recipient whose data are to be inspected demonstrates to the Contracting Officer that there would be a possible conflict of interest if the inspection were made by a particular representative, the Contracting Officer shall designate an alternate inspector.

As prescribed in 2 CFR 910.362(e)(2), the following Alternate I and/or II may be inserted in the clause in the award instrument.

### Alternate I

(h)(2) Notwithstanding paragraph (h)(1) of this clause, the agreement may identify and specify the delivery of limited rights data, or the Contracting Officer may require by written request the delivery of limited rights data that has been withheld or would otherwise be withholdable. If delivery of such data is so required, the Recipient may affix the following "Limited Rights Notice" to the data and the Government will thereafter treat the data, in accordance with such Notice:

### Limited Rights Notice

(a) These data are submitted with limited rights under Government agreement No._____ (and subaward/contract No. _____, if appropriate). These data may be reproduced and used by the Government with the express limitation that they will not, without written permission of the Recipient, be used for purposes of manufacture nor disclosed outside the Government; except that the Government may disclose these data outside the Government for the following purposes, if any, provided that the Government makes such disclosure subject to prohibition against further use and disclosure:

(1) Use (except for manufacture) by Federal support services contractors within the scope of their contracts;

(2) This "limited rights data" may be disclosed for evaluation purposes under the restriction that the "limited rights data" be retained in confidence and not be further disclosed;

(3) This "limited rights data" may be disclosed to other contractors participating in the Government's program of which this Recipient is a part for information or use (except for manufacture) in connection with the work performed under their awards and under the restriction that the "limited rights data" be retained in confidence and not be further disclosed;

(4) This "limited rights data" may be used by the Government or others on its behalf for emergency repair or overhaul work under the restriction that the "limited rights

data" be retained in confidence and not be further disclosed; and

(5) Release to a foreign government, or instrumentality thereof, as the interests of the United States Government may require, for information or evaluation, or for emergency repair or overhaul work by such government. This Notice shall be marked on any reproduction of this data in whole or in part.

(b) This Notice shall be marked on any reproduction of these data, in whole or in part.

(End of notice)

Alternate II

(h)(3)(i) Notwithstanding paragraph (h)(1) of this clause, the agreement may identify and specify the delivery of restricted computer software, or the Contracting Officer may require by written request the delivery of restricted computer software that has been withheld or would otherwise be withholdable. If delivery of such computer software is so required, the Recipient may affix the following "Restricted Rights Notice" to the computer software and the Government will thereafter treat the computer software, subject to paragraphs (d) and (e) of this clause, in accordance with the Notice:

Restricted Rights Notice

(a) This computer software is submitted with restricted rights under Government Agreement No._____ (and subaward/contract _____, if appropriate). It may not be used, reproduced, or disclosed by the Government except as provided in paragraph (c) of this Notice or as otherwise expressly stated in the agreement.

(b) This computer software may be—

(1) Used or copied for use in or with the computer or computers for which it was acquired, including use at any Government installation to which such computer or computers may be transferred;

(2) Used or copies for use in a backup computer if any computer for which it was acquired is inoperative

(3) Reproduced for safekeeping (archives) or backup purposes;

(4) Modified, adapted, or combined with other computer software, provided that the modified, combined, or adapted portions of the derivative software are made subject to the same restricted rights;

(5) Disclosed to and reproduced for use by Federal support service Contractors in accordance with paragraphs (b)(1) through (4) of this clause, provided the Government makes such disclosure or reproduction subject to these restricted rights; and

(6) Used or copies for use in or transferred to a replacement computer.

(c) Notwithstanding the foregoing, if this computer software is published copyrighted computer software, it is licensed to the Government, without disclosure prohibitions,

with the minimum rights set forth in paragraph (b) of this clause.

(d) Any other rights or limitations regarding the use, duplication, or disclosure of this computer software are to be expressly stated in, or incorporated in, the agreement.

(e) This Notice shall be marked on any reproduction of this computer software, in whole or in part.

(End of notice)

(ii) Where it is impractical to include the Restricted Rights Notice on restricted computer software, the following short-form Notice may be used in lieu thereof:

Restricted Rights Notice

Use, reproduction, or disclosure is subject to restrictions set forth in Agreement No._____ (and subaward/contract_____, if appropriate) with_____ (name of Recipient and subrecipient/contractor).

(End of notice)

(iii) If restricted computer software is delivered with the copyright notice of 17 U.S.C. 401, it will be presumed to be published copyrighted computer software licensed to the Government without disclosure prohibitions, with the minimum rights set forth in paragraph (b) of this clause, unless the Recipient includes the following statement with such copyright notice: "Unpublished—rights reserved under the Copyright Laws of the United States."

(End of clause)

# Subpart E—Cost Principles

### §910.401 Application to M&O's.

In accordance with 48 CFR 970.3002–1 and 970.3101–00–70, a Federally Funded Research Center (FFRDC) which is also a designated DOE Management and Operating (M&O) contract must follow the cost accounting standards (CAS) contained in 48 CFR part 30 and must follow the appropriate Cost Principles contained in 48 CFR part 31.

# Subpart F—Audit Requirements for For-Profit Entities

GENERAL

### §910.500 Purpose.

This Part follows the same format as 2 CFR 200.500. We purposely did not renumber the paragraphs within this part so that auditors and recipients can compare this to the single audit requirements contained in 2 CFR 200.500.

AUDITS

### § 910.501 Audit requirements.

(a) *Audit required.* A for–profit entity that expends $750,000 or more during the non-Federal entity's fiscal year in DOE awards must have a compliance audit conducted for that year in accordance with the provisions of this Part.

(b) *Compliance audit.* (1) If a for-profit entity has one or more DOE awards with expenditures of $750,000 or more during the for-profit entity's fiscal year, they must have a compliance audit for each of the awards with $750,000 or more in expenditures. A compliance audit should comply with the applicable provisions in § 910.514—Scope of Audit. The remaining awards do not require, individually or in the aggregate, a compliance audit.

(2) If a for-profit entity receives more than one award from DOE with a sum total of expenditures of $750,000 or more during the for-profit entity's fiscal year, but does not have any single award with expenditures of $750,000 or more; the entity must determine whether any or all of the awards have common compliance requirements (*i.e.,* are considered a cluster of awards) and determine the total expenditures of the awards with common compliance requirements. A compliance audit is required for the largest cluster of awards (if multiple clusters of awards exist) or the largest award not in a cluster of awards, whichever corresponding expenditure total is greater. A compliance audit should comply with the applicable provisions in § 910.514—Scope of Audit. The remaining awards do not require, individually or in the aggregate, a compliance audit;

(3) If a for-profit entity receives one or more awards from DOE with a sum total of expenditures less than $750,000, no compliance audit is required;

(4) If the for-profit entity is a sub-recipient, 2 CFR 200.501(h) requires that the pass-through entity establish appropriate monitoring and controls to ensure the sub-recipient complies with award requirements. These compliance audits must be conducted in accordance with 2 CFR 200.514 Scope of audit

(c) *Program-specific audit election.* Not applicable.

(d) *Exemption when Federal awards expended are less than $750,000.* A for-profit entity that expends less than $750,000 during the for-profit's fiscal year in DOE awards is exempt from DOE audit requirements for that year, except as noted in § 910.503 Relation to other audit requirements, but records must be available for review or audit by appropriate officials of the Federal agency, pass-through entity, and Government Accountability Office (GAO).

(e) *Federally Funded Research and Development Centers (FFRDC).* Management of an auditee that owns or operates a FFRDC may elect to treat the FFRDC as a separate entity for purposes of this Part.

(f) *Subrecipients and Contractors.* An auditee may simultaneously be a recipient, a subrecipient, and a contractor. Federal awards expended as a recipient are subject to audit under this Part. The payments received for goods or services provided as a contractor are not Federal awards. Section 2 CFR 200.330 Subrecipient and contractor determinations should be considered in determining whether payments constitute a Federal award or a payment for goods or services provided as a contractor.

(g) *Compliance responsibility for contractors.* In most cases, the auditee's compliance responsibility for contractors is only to ensure that the procurement, receipt, and payment for goods and services comply with Federal statutes, regulations, and the terms and conditions of Federal awards. Federal award compliance requirements normally do not pass through to contractors. However, the auditee is responsible for ensuring compliance for procurement transactions which are structured such that the contractor is responsible for program compliance or the contractor's records must be reviewed to determine program compliance. Also, when these procurement transactions relate to a major program, the scope of the audit must include determining whether these transactions are in compliance with Federal statutes, regulations, and the terms and conditions of Federal awards.

(h) *For-profit subrecipient*. Since this Part does not apply to for-profit subrecipients, the pass-through entity is responsible for establishing requirements, as necessary, to ensure compliance by for-profit subrecipients to DOE Federal award requirements. The agreement with the for-profit subrecipient should describe applicable compliance requirements and the for-profit subrecipient's compliance responsibility. Methods to ensure compliance for Federal awards made to for-profit subrecipients may include pre-award audits, monitoring during the agreement, and post-award audits. See also 2 CFR 200.331 Requirements for pass- through entities.

[79 FR 76024, Dec. 19, 2014, as amended at 80 FR 57511, Sept. 24, 2015]

### §910.502 Basis for determining DOE awards expended.

*Determining Federal awards expended.* The determination of when a Federal award is expended must be based on when the activity related to the DOE award occurs. Generally, the activity pertains to events that require the non-Federal entity to comply with Federal statutes, regulations, and the terms and conditions of DOE awards, such as: expenditure/expense transactions associated with awards including grants, cost-reimbursement contracts under the FAR, compacts with Indian Tribes, cooperative agreements, and direct appropriations; the disbursement of funds to subrecipients; the use of loan proceeds under loan and loan guarantee programs; the receipt of property; the receipt of surplus property; the receipt or use of program income; the distribution or use of food commodities; the disbursement of amounts entitling the for-profit entity to an interest subsidy; and the period when insurance is in force.

(a) *Loan and loan guarantees (loans).* Loan and loan guarantees issued by the DOE Loan Program Office corresponding to Title XVII of the Energy Policy Act of 2005, as amended, 42 U.S.C. 16511–16516 ("Title XVII") are exempt from these provisions.

(1) Not applicable.

(2) Not applicable.

(3) Not applicable.

(b) Not applicable.

(c) Not applicable.

(d) *Endowment funds.* The cumulative balance of DOE awards for endowment funds that are federally restricted are considered DOE awards expended in each audit period in which the funds are still restricted.

(e) *Free rent.* Free rent received by itself is not considered a DOE award expended under this Part. However, free rent received as part of a DOE award to carry out a DOE program must be included in determining DOE awards expended and subject to audit under this Part.

(f) *Valuing non-cash assistance.* DOE non-cash assistance, such as free rent, food commodities, donated property, or donated surplus property, must be valued at fair market value at the time of receipt or the assessed value provided by DOE.

(g) Not applicable.

(h) Not applicable.

(i) Not applicable.

[79 FR 76024, Dec. 19, 2014, as amended at 80 FR 57512, Sept. 24, 2015]

### §910.503 Relation to other audit requirements.

(a) An audit conducted in accordance with this Part must be in lieu of any financial audit of DOE awards which a for-profit entity is required to undergo under any other Federal statute or regulation. To the extent that such audit provides DOE with the information it requires to carry out its responsibilities under Federal statute or regulation, DOE must rely upon and use that information.

(b) Notwithstanding paragraph (a) of this section, DOE, Inspectors General, or GAO may conduct or arrange for additional audits which are necessary to carry out its responsibilities under Federal statute or regulation. The provisions of this Part do not authorize any for-profit entity to constrain, in any manner, DOE from carrying out or arranging for such additional audits, except that DOE must plan such audits to not be duplicative of other audits of DOE. Any additional audits must be planned and performed in such a way as to build upon work performed, including the audit documentation, sampling, and testing already performed, by other auditors.

(c) The provisions of this Part do not limit the authority of DOE to conduct, or arrange for the conduct of, audits and evaluations of DOE awards, nor limit the authority of any Federal agency Inspector General or other Federal official.

(d) DOE to pay for additional audits. If DOE conducts or arranges for additional audits it must, consistent with other applicable Federal statutes and regulations, arrange for funding the full cost of such additional audits.

(e) Not applicable.

### § 910.504   Frequency of audits.

Audits required by this Part must be performed annually.

(a) Not applicable.

(b) Not applicable.

### § 910.505   Sanctions.

In cases of continued inability or unwillingness to have an audit conducted in accordance with this Part, DOE and pass-through entities must take appropriate action as provided in 2 CFR 200.338 Remedies for noncompliance.

### § 910.506   Audit costs.

See 2 CFR 200.425 Audit services.

### § 910.507   Compliance audits.

(a) *Program-specific audit guide available.* In many cases, a program-specific audit guide will be available to provide specific guidance to the auditor with respect to internal controls, compliance requirements, suggested audit procedures, and audit reporting requirements. A listing of current program-specific audit guides can be found in the compliance supplement beginning with the 2014 supplement including Federal awarding agency contact information and a Web site where a copy of the guide can be obtained. When a current program- specific audit guide is available, the auditor must follow GAGAS and the guide when performing a compliance audit.

(1) *Program-specific audit guide not available.* When a program-specific audit guide is not available, the auditee and auditor must conduct the compliance audit in accordance with GAAS and GAGAS.

(2) If audited financial statements are available, for-profit recipients should submit audited financial statements to DOE as a part of the compliance audit. (If the recipient is a subsidiary for which separate financial statements are not available, the recipient may submit the financial statements of the consolidated group.)

(3) The auditor must:

(i) Not applicable.

(ii) Obtain an understanding of internal controls and perform tests of internal controls over the DOE program consistent with the requirements of § 910.514 Scope of audit.,

(iii) Perform procedures to determine whether the auditee has complied with Federal statutes, regulations, and the terms and conditions of DOE awards that could have a direct and material effect on the DOE program consistent with the requirements of § 910.514 Scope of audit.

(iv) Follow up on prior audit findings, perform procedures to assess the reasonableness of the summary schedule of prior audit findings prepared by the auditee in accordance with the requirements of § 910.511 Audit findings follow-up, and report, as a current year audit finding, when the auditor concludes that the summary schedule of prior audit findings materially misrepresents the status of any prior audit finding; and

(v) Report any audit findings consistent with the requirements of § 910.516 Audit findings.

(4) The auditor's report(s) may be in the form of either combined or separate reports and may be organized differently from the manner presented in this section. The auditor's report(s) must state that the audit was conducted in accordance with this Part and include the following:

(i) An opinion (or disclaimer of opinion) as to whether the financial statement(s) (if available) of the DOE program is presented fairly in all material respects in accordance with the stated accounting policies;

(ii) A report on internal control related to the DOE program, which must describe the scope of testing of internal control and the results of the tests;

(iii) A report on compliance which includes an opinion (or disclaimer of opinion) as to whether the auditee complied with laws, regulations, and the terms and conditions of DOE awards which could have a direct and material effect on the DOE program; and

(iv) A schedule of findings and questioned costs for the DOE program that includes a summary of the auditor's results relative to the DOE program in a format consistent with § 910.515 Audit reporting, paragraph (d)(1) and findings and questioned costs consistent with the requirements of § 910.515 Audit reporting, paragraph (d)(3).

(5) *Report submission for program-specific audits.* The audit must be completed and the reporting required by paragraph (c)(2) or (c)(3) of this section submitted within the earlier of 30 calendar days after receipt of the auditor's report(s), or nine months after the end of the audit period, unless a different period is specified in a program-specific audit guide. Unless restricted by Federal law or regulation, the auditee must make report copies available for public inspection. Auditees and auditors must ensure that their respective parts of the reporting package do not include protected personally identifiable information.

(6) When a program-specific audit guide is available, the compliance audits must be submitted (along with audited financial statements if audited financial statements are available), to the appropriate DOE Contracting Officer as well as to the DOE Office of the Chief Financial Officer.

(7) When a program-specific audit guide is not available, the reporting package for a program-specific audit must consist of, a summary schedule of prior audit findings, and a corrective action plan as described in paragraph (b)(2) of this section, and the auditor's report(s) described in paragraph (b)(4) of this section. The compliance audit must be submitted (along with audited financial statements if audited financial statements are available), to the appropriate DOE Contracting Officer as well as to the DOE Office of the Chief Financial Officer.

(b) Other sections of this Part may apply. Compliance audits are subject to:

(1) 910.500 Purpose through 910.503 Relation to other audit requirements, paragraph (d);

(2) 910.504 Frequency of audits through 910.506 Audit costs;

(3) 910.508 Auditee responsibilities through 910.509 Auditor selection;

(4) 910.511 Audit findings follow-up;

(5) 910.512 Report submission, paragraphs (e) through (h);

(6) 910.513 Responsibilities;

(7) 910.516 Audit findings through 910.517 Audit documentation;

(8) 910.521 Management decision, and

(9) Other referenced provisions of this Part unless contrary to the provisions of this section, a program-specific audit guide, or program statutes and regulations.

[79 FR 76024, Dec. 19, 2014, as amended at 80 FR 57512, Sept. 24, 2015]

AUDITEES

### § 910.508  Auditee responsibilities.

The auditee must:

(a) Procure or otherwise arrange for the audit required by this Part in accordance with § 910.509 Auditor selection, and ensure it is properly performed and submitted when due in accordance with § 910.512 Report submission.

(b) Submit appropriate financial statements (if available).

(c) Submit the schedule of expenditures of DOE awards in accordance with § 910.510 Financial statements.

(d) Promptly follow up and take corrective action on audit findings, including preparation of a summary schedule of prior audit findings and a corrective action plan in accordance with § 910.511 Audit findings follow- up, paragraph (b) and § 910.511 Audit findings follow-up, paragraph (c), respectively.

(e) Provide the auditor with access to personnel, accounts, books, records, supporting documentation, and other information as needed for the auditor to perform the audit required by this Part.

## § 910.509  Auditor selection.

(a) *Auditor procurement.* When procuring audit services, the objective is to obtain high-quality audits. In requesting proposals for audit services, the objectives and scope of the audit must be made clear and the for-profit entity must request a copy of the audit organization's peer review report which the auditor is required to provide under GAGAS. Factors to be considered in evaluating each proposal for audit services include the responsiveness to the request for proposal, relevant experience, availability of staff with professional qualifications and technical abilities, the results of peer and external quality control reviews, and price. Whenever possible, the auditee must make positive efforts to utilize small businesses, minority-owned firms, and women's business enterprises, in procuring audit services as stated in 2 CFR 200.321 Contracting with small and minority businesses, women's business enterprises, and labor surplus area firms, or the FAR (48 CFR part 42), as applicable.

(b) *Restriction on auditor preparing indirect cost proposals.* An auditor who prepares the indirect cost proposal or cost allocation plan may not also be selected to perform the audit required by this Part when the indirect costs recovered by the auditee during the prior year exceeded $1 million. This restriction applies to the base year used in the preparation of the indirect cost proposal or cost allocation plan and any subsequent years in which the resulting indirect cost agreement or cost allocation plan is used to recover costs.

(c) *Use of Federal auditors.* Federal auditors may perform all or part of the work required under this Part if they comply fully with the requirements of this Part.

## § 910.510  Financial statements.

(a) *Financial statements.* If available, the auditee must submit financial statements that reflect its financial position, results of operations or changes in net assets, and, where appropriate, cash flows for the fiscal year audited. The financial statements must be for the same organizational unit and fiscal year that is chosen to meet the requirements of this Part. However,

for-profit entity-wide financial statements may also include departments, agencies, and other organizational units that have separate audits in accordance with § 910.514 Scope of audit, paragraph (a) and prepare separate financial statements.

(b) *Schedule of expenditures of DOE awards.* The auditee must prepare a schedule of expenditures of DOE awards for the period covered by the auditee's fiscal year which must include the total DOE awards expended as determined in accordance with § 910.502 Basis for determining DOE awards expended. While not required, the auditee may choose to provide information requested by DOE and pass-through entities to make the schedule easier to use. For example, when a DOE program has multiple DOE award years, the auditee may list the amount of DOE awards expended for each DOE award year separately. At a minimum, the schedule must:

(1) List individual DOE programs. For a cluster of programs, provide the cluster name, list individual DOE programs within the cluster of programs. For R&D, total DOE awards expended must be shown by individual DOE award and major subdivision within DOE. For example, the National Institutes of Health is a major subdivision in the Department of Health and Human Services.

(2) Not applicable.

(3) Provide total DOE awards expended for each individual DOE program and the CFDA number For a cluster of programs also provide the total for the cluster.

(4) Not applicable.

(5) Not applicable.

(6) Include notes that describe that significant accounting policies used in preparing the schedule, and note whether or not the for-profit entity elected to use the 10% de minimis cost rate as covered in 2 CFR 200.414 Indirect (F&A) costs.

## § 910.511  Audit findings follow-up.

(a) *General.* The auditee is responsible for follow-up and corrective action on all audit findings. As part of this responsibility, the auditee must prepare a summary schedule of prior audit findings. The auditee must also prepare a corrective action plan for current year audit findings. The summary schedule of prior audit findings and the corrective action plan must include the reference numbers the auditor assigns to audit findings under § 910.516 Audit findings, paragraph (c). Since the summary schedule may include audit findings from multiple years, it must include the fiscal year in which the finding initially occurred. The corrective action plan and summary schedule of prior audit findings must include findings relating to the financial statements which are required to be reported in accordance with GAGAS.

(b) *Summary schedule of prior audit findings.* The summary schedule of prior audit findings must report the status of all audit findings included in the prior audit's schedule of findings and questioned costs. The summary schedule must also include audit findings reported in the prior audit's summary schedule of prior audit findings except audit findings listed as corrected in accordance with paragraph (b)(1) of this section, or no longer valid or not warranting further action in accordance with paragraph (b)(3) of this section.

(1) When audit findings were fully corrected, the summary schedule need only list the audit findings and state that corrective action was taken.

(2) When audit findings were not corrected or were only partially corrected, the summary schedule must describe the reasons for the finding's recurrence and planned corrective action taken, and any partial corrective action taken is significantly different from corrective action previously reported in a corrective action plan or in DOE's or pass-through entity's management decision, the summary schedule must provide an explanation.

(3) When the auditee believes the audit findings are no longer valid or do not warrant further action, the reasons for this position must be described in the summary schedule. A valid reason for considering an audit finding as not warranting further action is that all of the following have occurred:

(i) Two years have passed since the audit report in which the finding occurred was submitted to DOE;

(ii) DOE is not currently following up with the auditee on the audit finding; and

(iii) A management decision was not issued.

(c) *Corrective action plan.* At the completion of the audit, the auditee must prepare, in a document separate from the auditor's findings described in § 910.516 Audit findings, a corrective action plan to address each audit finding included in the current year auditor's reports. The corrective action plan must provide the name(s) of the contact person(s) responsible for corrective action, the corrective action planned, and the anticipated completion date. If the auditee does not agree with the audit findings or believes corrective action is not required, then the corrective action plan must include an explanation and specific reasons.

### § 910.512  Report submission.

(a) *General.* (1) The audit must be completed and the reporting package described in paragraph (c) of this section must be submitted within the earlier of 30 calendar days after receipt of the auditor's report(s), or nine months after the end of the audit period. If the due date falls on a Saturday, Sunday, or Federal holiday, the reporting package is due the next business day.

(2) Unless restricted by Federal statutes or regulations, the auditee must make copies available for public inspection. Auditees and auditors must ensure that their respective parts of the reporting package do not include protected personally identifiable information.

(b) *Data collection.* See paragraph (b)(1) of this section:

(1) A senior level representative of the auditee (*e.g.*, director of finance, chief executive officer, or chief financial officer) must sign a statement to be included as part of the reporting package that says that the auditee complied with the requirements of this Part, the reporting package does not include protected personally identifiable information, and the information included in its entirety is accurate and complete.

(2) Not applicable.

(3) Not applicable.

(c) *Reporting package.* The reporting package must include the:

(1) Financial statements (if available) and schedule of expenditures of DOE awards discussed in § 910.510 Financial statements, paragraphs (a) and (b), respectively;

(2) Summary schedule of prior audit findings discussed in § 910.511 Audit findings follow-up, paragraph (b);

(3) Auditor's report(s) discussed in § 910.515 Audit reporting; and

(4) Corrective action plan discussed in § 910.511 Audit findings follow-up, paragraph (c).

(d) *Submission to DOE.* The auditee must electronically submit the compliance reporting package described in paragraph (c) of this section compliance audits must be submitted (along with audited financial statements if audited financial statements are available), to the appropriate DOE Contracting Officer as well as to the DOE Office of the Chief Financial Officer.

(e) *Requests for management letters issued by the auditor.* In response to requests by a Federal agency, auditees must submit a copy of any management letters issued by the auditor.

(f) *Report retention requirements.* Auditees must keep one copy of the reporting package described in paragraph (c) of this section on file for three years from the date of submission to DOE.

(g) Not applicable.

(h) Not applicable.

FEDERAL AGENCIES

### § 910.513  Responsibilities.

(a)(1) Not applicable.
(2) Not applicable.
(3) Not applicable.
(i) Not applicable.
(ii) Not applicable.
(iii) Not applicable.
(iv) Not applicable.
(v) Not applicable.
(vi) Not applicable.
(vii) Not applicable.
(viii) Not applicable.
(ix) Not applicable.
(b) Not applicable
(1) Not applicable
(2) Not applicable
(c) *DOE responsibilities.* DOE must perform the following for the awards it makes (See also the requirements of 2 CFR 200.210 Information contained in a Federal award):

(1) Ensure that audits are completed and reports are received in a timely manner and in accordance with the requirements of this Part.

(2) Provide technical advice and counsel to auditees and auditors as requested.

(3) Follow-up on audit findings to ensure that the recipient takes appropriate and timely corrective action. As part of audit follow-up, the DOE must:

(i) Issue a management decision as prescribed in § 910.521 Management decision;

(ii) Monitor the recipient taking appropriate and timely corrective action;

(iii) Use cooperative audit resolution mechanisms (see 2 CFR 200.25 Cooperative audit resolution) to improve DOE program outcomes through better audit resolution, follow-up, and corrective action; and

(iv) Develop a baseline, metrics, and targets to track, over time, the effectiveness of the DOE's process to follow-up on audit findings and on the effectiveness of Compliance Audits in improving non-Federal entity accountability and their use by DOE in making award decisions.

(4) Not applicable.
(5) Not applicable:
(i) Not applicable
(ii) Not applicable
(6) Not applicable
(7) Not applicable
(i) Not applicable
(ii) Not applicable.
(iii) Not applicable.
(iv) Not applicable
(v) Not applicable
(vi) Not applicable
(vii) Not applicable.
(viii) Not applicable

AUDITORS

### § 910.514  Scope of audit.

(a) *General.* The audit must be conducted in accordance with GAGAS. The audit must cover the entire operations of the auditee, or, at the option of the auditee, such audit must include a series of audits that cover departments, agencies, and other organizational units that expended or otherwise administered DOE awards during such audit period, provided that each such audit must encompass the schedule of expenditures of DOE awards for each such department, agency, and other organizational unit, which must be considered to be a for-profit entity. The financial statements (if available) and schedule of expenditures of DOE awards must be for the same audit period.

(b) *Financial statements.* If financial statements are available, the auditor must determine whether the schedule of expenditures of DOE awards is stated fairly in all material respects in relation to the auditee's financial statements as a whole.

(1) *Internal control.* The compliance supplement provides guidance on internal controls over Federal programs based upon the guidance in Standards for Internal Control in the Federal Government issued by the Comptroller General of the United States and the Internal Control— Integrated Framework, issued by the Committee of Sponsoring Organizations of the Treadway Commission (COSO).

(2) In addition to the requirements of GAGAS the auditor must perform procedures to obtain an understanding of internal control over DOE programs sufficient to plan the audit to support a low assessed level of control risk of noncompliance for major programs.

(3) Except as provided in paragraph (c)(4) of this section, the auditor must:

(i) Plan the testing of internal control over compliance to support a low assessed level of control risk for the assertions relevant to the compliance requirements.

(ii) Perform testing of internal control as planned in paragraph (c)(3)(i) of this section.

(4) When internal control over some or all of the compliance requirements are likely to be ineffective in preventing or detecting noncompliance, the planning and performing of testing described in paragraph (c)(3) of this section are not required for those compliance requirements. However, the auditor must report a significant deficiency or material weakness in accordance with §910.516 Audit findings, assess the related control risk at the maximum, and consider whether additional compliance tests are required because of ineffective internal control.

(5) *Compliance.* In addition to the requirements of GAGAS, the auditor must determine whether the auditee has complied with Federal statutes, regulations, and the terms and conditions of Federal awards that may have a direct and material effect.

(6) The principal compliance requirements applicable to most Federal programs and the compliance requirements of the largest Federal programs are included in the compliance supplement.

(7) For the compliance requirements related to Federal programs contained in the compliance supplement, an audit of these compliance requirements will meet the requirements of this Part. Where there have been changes to the compliance requirements and the changes are not reflected in the compliance supplement, the auditor must determine the current compliance requirements and modify the audit procedures accordingly. For those Federal programs not covered in the compliance supplement, the auditor should follow the compliance supplement's guidance for programs not included in the supplement.

(8) The compliance testing must include tests of transactions and such other auditing procedures necessary to provide the auditor sufficient appropriate audit evidence to support an opinion on compliance.

(c) *Audit follow-up.* The auditor must follow-up on prior audit findings, perform procedures to assess the reasonableness of the summary schedule of prior audit findings prepared by the auditee in accordance with §910.511 Audit findings follow-up paragraph (b), and report, as a current year audit finding, when the auditor concludes that the summary schedule of prior audit findings materially misrepresents the status of any prior audit finding. The auditor must perform audit follow-up procedures.

### §910.515  Audit reporting.

The auditor's report(s) may be in the form of either combined or separate reports and may be organized differently from the manner presented in this section. The auditor's report(s) must state that the audit was conducted in accordance with this Part and include the following:

(a) An opinion (or disclaimer of opinion) as to whether the financial statements (if available) are presented fairly in all material respects in accordance with generally accepted accounting principles and an opinion (or disclaimer of opinion) as to whether the schedule of expenditures of DOE awards is fairly stated in all material respects in relation to the financial statements (if available) as a whole.

(b) A report on internal control over financial reporting and compliance with Federal statutes, regulations, and the terms and conditions of the DOE award, noncompliance with which could have a material effect on the financial statements. This report must describe the scope of testing of internal control and compliance and the results of the tests, and, where applicable, it will refer to the separate schedule of findings and questioned costs described in paragraph (d) of this section.

(c) A report on compliance and report and internal control over compliance. This report must describe the scope of testing of internal control over compliance, include an opinion or modified opinion as to whether the auditee complied with Federal statutes, regulations, and the terms and conditions of DOE awards which could have a direct and material effect and refer to the separate schedule of findings and questioned costs described in paragraph (d) of this section.

(d) A schedule of findings and questioned costs which must include the following three components:

(1) A summary of the auditor's results, which must include:

(i) The type of report the auditor issued (if applicable)on whether the financial statements (if available) audited were prepared in accordance with GAAP (*i.e.*, unmodified opinion, qualified opinion, adverse opinion, or disclaimer of opinion);

(ii) Where applicable, a statement about whether significant deficiencies or material weaknesses in internal control were disclosed by the audit of the financial statements (if available);

(iii) A statement (if applicable) as to whether the audit disclosed any non-compliance that is material to the financial statements (if available) of the auditee;

(iv) Where applicable, a statement about whether significant deficiencies or material weaknesses in internal control over major programs were disclosed by the audit;

(v) The type of report the auditor issued on compliance (*i.e.*, unmodified opinion, qualified opinion, adverse opinion, or disclaimer of opinion);

(vi) A statement as to whether the audit disclosed any audit findings that the auditor is required to report under §910.516 Audit findings paragraph (a);

(vii) Not applicable.

(viii) Not applicable.

(ix) Not applicable.

(2) Findings relating to the financial Statements (if available) which are required to be reported in accordance with GAGAS.

(i) Findings and questioned costs for DOE awards which must include audit findings as defined in §910.516 Audit findings, paragraph (a).Audit findings (*e.g.*, internal control findings, compliance findings, questioned costs, or fraud) that relate to the same issue should be presented as a single audit finding.

(ii) Audit findings that relate to both the financial statements (if available) and DOE awards, as reported under paragraphs (d)(2) and (d)(3) of this section, respectively, should be reported in both sections of the schedule. However, the reporting in one section of the schedule may be in summary form with a reference to a detailed reporting in the other section of the schedule.

(e) Nothing in this Part precludes combining of the audit reporting required by this section with the reporting required by §910.512 Report submission, paragraph (b) Data Collection when allowed by GAGAS.

§910.516  Audit findings.

(a) *Audit findings reported.* The auditor must report the following as audit findings in a schedule of findings and questioned costs:

(1) Significant deficiencies and material weaknesses in internal control over major programs and significant instances of abuse relating to major programs. The auditor's determination

of whether a deficiency in internal control is a significant deficiency or material weakness for the purpose of reporting an audit finding is in relation to a type of compliance requirement for a major program identified in the Compliance Supplement.

(2) Material noncompliance with the provisions of Federal statutes, regulations, or the terms and conditions of DOE awards related to a major program. The auditor's determination of whether a noncompliance with the provisions of Federal statutes, regulations, or the terms and conditions of DOE awards is material for the purpose of reporting an audit finding is in relation to a type of compliance requirement for a major program identified in the compliance supplement.

(3) Known questioned costs that are greater than $25,000 for a type of compliance requirement for a major program. Known questioned costs are those specifically identified by the auditor. In evaluating the effect of questioned costs on the opinion on compliance, the auditor considers the best estimate of total costs questioned (likely questioned costs), not just the questioned costs specifically identified (known questioned costs). The auditor must also report known questioned costs when likely questioned costs are greater than $25,000 for a type of compliance requirement for a major program. In reporting questioned costs, the auditor must include information to provide proper perspective for judging the prevalence and consequences of the questioned costs.

(4) Known questioned costs that are greater than $25,000 for a DOE program. which is not audited as a major program. Except for audit follow-up, the auditor is not required under this Part to perform audit procedures for such a DOE program; therefore, the auditor will normally not find questioned costs for a program that is not audited as a major program. However, if the auditor does become aware of questioned costs for a DOE program that is not audited as a major program (e.g., as part of audit follow-up or other audit procedures) and the known questioned costs are greater than $25,000, then the auditor must report this as an audit finding.

(5) Not applicable.

(6) Known or likely fraud affecting a DOE award, unless such fraud is otherwise reported as an audit finding in the schedule of findings and questioned costs for DOE awards. This paragraph does not require the auditor to report publicly information which could compromise investigative or legal proceedings or to make an additional reporting when the auditor confirms that the fraud was reported outside the auditor's reports under the direct reporting requirements of GAGAS.

(7) Instances where the results of audit follow-up procedures disclosed that the summary schedule of prior audit findings prepared by the auditee in accordance with §910.511 Audit findings follow-up, paragraph (b) materially misrepresents the status of any prior audit finding.

(b) *Audit finding detail and clarity.* Audit findings must be presented in sufficient detail and clarity for the auditee to prepare a corrective action plan and take corrective action, and for DOE to arrive at a management decision. The following specific information must be included, as applicable, in audit findings:

(1) Federal program and specific Federal award identification including the CFDA title and number, and Federal award identification number and year. When information, such as the CFDA title and number or DOE award identification number, is not available, the auditor must provide the best information available to describe the Federal award.

(2) The criteria or specific requirement upon which the audit finding is based, including the Federal statutes, regulations, or the terms and conditions of the DOE awards. Criteria generally identify the required or desired state or expectation with respect to the program or operation. Criteria provide a context for evaluating evidence and understanding findings.

(3) The condition found, including facts that support the deficiency identified in the audit finding.

(4) A statement of cause that identifies the reason or explanation for the condition or the factors responsible for the difference between the situation that exists (condition) and the required

or desired state (criteria), which may also serve as a basis for recommendations for corrective action.

(5) The possible asserted effect to provide sufficient information to the auditee and DOE to permit them to determine the cause and effect to facilitate prompt and proper corrective action. A statement of the effect or potential effect should provide a clear, logical link to establish the impact or potential impact of the difference between the condition and the criteria.

(6) Identification of questioned costs and how they were computed. Known questioned costs must be identified by applicable CFDA number(s) and applicable DOE award identification number(s).

(7) Information to provide proper perspective for judging the prevalence and consequences of the audit findings, such as whether the audit findings represent an isolated instance or a systemic problem. Where appropriate, instances identified must be related to the universe and the number of cases examined and be quantified in terms of dollar value. The auditor should report whether the sampling was a statistically valid sample.

(8) Identification of whether the audit finding was a repeat of a finding in the immediately prior audit and if so any applicable prior year audit finding numbers.

(9) Recommendations to prevent future occurrences of the deficiency identified in the audit finding.

(10) Views of responsible officials of the auditee.

(c) *Reference numbers.* Each audit finding in the schedule of findings and questioned costs must include a reference number in the format meeting the requirements of the data collection form submission required by §910.512 Report submission, paragraph (b) to allow for easy referencing of the audit findings during follow-up.

## §910.517   Audit documentation.

(a) *Retention of audit documentation.* The auditor must retain audit documentation and reports for a minimum of three years after the date of issuance of the auditor's report(s) to the auditee, unless the auditor is notified in writing by DOE or the cognizant

agency for indirect costs to extend the retention period. When the auditor is aware that the Federal agency or auditee is contesting an audit finding, the auditor must contact the parties contesting the audit finding for guidance prior to destruction of the audit documentation and reports.

(b) *Access to audit documentation.* Audit documentation must be made available upon request to the cognizant agency for indirect cost, DOE, or GAO at the completion of the audit, as part of a quality review, to resolve audit findings, or to carry out oversight responsibilities consistent with the purposes of this Part. Access to audit documentation includes the right of Federal agencies to obtain copies of audit documentation, as is reasonable and necessary.

## §910.518   [Reserved]

## §910.519   Criteria for Federal program risk.

(a) *General.* The auditor's determination should be based on an overall evaluation of the risk of noncompliance occurring that could be material to the DOE program. The auditor must consider criteria, such as described in paragraphs (b), (c), and (d) of this section, to identify risk in Federal programs. Also, as part of the risk analysis, the auditor may wish to discuss a particular DOE program with auditee management and DOE.

(1) *Current and prior audit experience.* Weaknesses in internal control over DOE programs would indicate higher risk. Consideration should be given to the control environment over DOE programs and such factors as the expectation of management's adherence to Federal statutes, regulations, and the terms and conditions of DOE awards and the competence and experience of personnel who administer the DOE programs.

(i) A DOE program administered under multiple internal control structures may have higher risk. The auditor must consider whether weaknesses are isolated in a single operating unit (*e.g.*, one college campus) or pervasive throughout the entity.

(ii) When significant parts of a DOE program are passed through to subrecipients, a weak system for monitoring subrecipients would indicate higher risk.

(2) Prior audit findings would indicate higher risk, particularly when the situations identified in the audit findings could have a significant impact on a DOE program or have not been corrected.

(3) DOE programs not recently audited as major programs may be of higher risk than Federal programs recently audited as major programs without audit findings.

(4) *Oversight exercised by DOE.* Oversight exercised by DOE could be used to assess risk. For example, recent monitoring or other reviews performed by an oversight entity that disclosed no significant problems would indicate lower risk, whereas monitoring that disclosed significant problems would indicate higher risk.

(5) Federal agencies, with the concurrence of OMB, may identify Federal programs that are higher risk. OMB will provide this identification in the compliance supplement.

(6) *Inherent risk of the Federal program.* The nature of a Federal program may indicate risk. Consideration should be given to the complexity of the program and the extent to which the Federal program contracts for goods and services. For example, Federal programs that disburse funds through third party contracts or have eligibility criteria may be of higher risk. Federal programs primarily involving staff payroll costs may have high risk for noncompliance with requirements of 2 CFR 200.430 Compensation—personal services, but otherwise be at low risk.

(7) The phase of a Federal program in its life cycle at the Federal agency may indicate risk. For example, a new Federal program with new or interim regulations may have higher risk than an established program with time-tested regulations. Also, significant changes in Federal programs, statutes, regulations, or the terms and conditions of Federal awards may increase risk.

(8) The phase of a Federal program in its life cycle at the auditee may indicate risk. For example, during the first and last years that an auditee participates in a Federal program, the risk may be higher due to start-up or close-out of program activities and staff.

(9) Programs with larger Federal awards expended would be of higher risk than programs with substantially smaller Federal awards expended.

§910.520 **Criteria for a low-risk auditee.**

(a) An auditee that meets all of the following conditions for each of the preceding two audit periods may qualify as a low-risk auditee and be eligible for reduced audit coverage. Compliance audits were performed on an annual basis in accordance with the provisions of this Subpart, including submitting the data collection form to DOE within the timeframe specified in §910.512 Report submission. A for-profit entity that has biennial audits does not qualify as a low-risk auditee.

(b) The auditor's opinion on whether the financial statements (if available) were prepared in accordance with GAAP, or a basis of accounting required by state law, and the auditor's in relation to opinion on the schedule of expenditures of DOE awards were unmodified.

(c) There were no deficiencies in internal control which were identified as material weaknesses under the requirements of GAGAS.

(d) The auditor did not report a substantial doubt about the auditee's ability to continue as a going concern.

(e) None of the DOE programs had audit findings from any of the following in either of the preceding two audit periods:

(1) Internal control deficiencies that were identified as material weaknesses in the auditor's report on internal control as required under §910.515 Audit reporting, paragraph (c);

(2) Not applicable.

(3) Not applicable.

MANAGEMENT DECISIONS

§910.521 **Management decision.**

(a) *General.* The management decision must clearly state whether or not the audit finding is sustained, the reasons for the decision, and the expected auditee action to repay disallowed costs, make financial adjustments, or take other action. If the auditee has not completed corrective action, a timetable for follow-up should be given. Prior to issuing the management decision, the Federal agency may request additional information or documentation from the auditee, including a request for auditor assurance related to the documentation, as a way of mitigating disallowed costs. The management decision should describe any appeal process available to the auditee. While not required, DOE agency may also issue a management decision on findings relating to the financial statements (if they were available) which are required to be reported in accordance with GAGAS.

(b) As provided in § 910.513 Responsibilities, paragraph (c)(3), DOE is responsible for issuing a management decision for findings that relate to DOE awards it makes to for-profit entities.

(c) Not applicable.

(d) *Time requirements.* DOE must issue a management decision within six months of acceptance of the audit report. The auditee must initiate and proceed with corrective action as rapidly as possible and corrective action should begin no later than upon receipt of the audit report.

(e) *Reference numbers.* Management decisions must include the reference numbers the auditor assigned to each audit finding in accordance with § 910.516 Audit findings paragraph (c).

## PARTS 911–999 [RESERVED]

# CHAPTER X—DEPARTMENT OF TREASURY

# PART 1000—UNIFORM ADMINIS-TRATIVE REQUIREMENTS, COST PRINCIPLES, AND AUDIT RE-QUIREMENTS FOR FEDERAL AWARDS

Sec.
1000.10   Applicable regulations.
1000.306   Cost sharing or matching.
1000.336   Access to records.

AUTHORITY: 5 U.S.C. 301; 31 U.S.C. 301; 2 CFR part 200.

SOURCE: 79 FR 76047, Dec. 19, 2014, unless otherwise noted.

## § 1000.10   Applicable regulations.

Except for the deviations set forth elsewhere in this Part, the Department of the Treasury adopts the Uniform Administrative Requirements, Cost Principles, and Audit Requirements for Federal Awards, set forth at 2 CFR part 200.

## § 1000.306   Cost sharing or matching.

Notwithstanding 2 CFR 200.306(e), Low Income Taxpayer Clinic grantees may use the rates found in 26 U.S.C. 7430 so long as:

(a) The grantee is funded to provide controversy representation;

(b) The services are provided by a qualified representative, which includes any individual, whether or not an attorney, who is authorized to represent taxpayers before the Internal Revenue Service or an applicable court;

(c) The qualified representative is not a student; and

(d) The qualified representative is acting in a representative capacity and is advocating for a taxpayer.

## § 1000.336   Access to records.

The right of access under 2 CFR 200.336 shall not extend to client information held by attorneys or federally authorized tax practitioners under the Low Income Taxpayer Clinic program.

# PARTS 1201–1299 [RESERVED]

# CHAPTER XI—DEPARTMENT OF DEFENSE

# PARTS 1100–1102 [RESERVED]

# PART 1103—INTERIM GRANTS AND COOPERATIVE AGREEMENTS IMPLEMENTATION OF GUIDANCE IN 2 CFR PART 200, "UNIFORM ADMINISTRATIVE REQUIREMENTS, COST PRINCIPLES, AND AUDIT REQUIREMENTS FOR FEDERAL AWARDS"

### Subpart A—Interim Implementation of Guidance in 2 CFR Part 200

Sec.
1103.100 Applicability of 2 CFR part 200 to requirements for recipients in DoD Components' terms and conditions.

### Subpart B—Pre-Existing Policies Continuing in Effect During Interim Implementation

1103.200 Exception for small awards.
1103.205 Timing of payments made using the reimbursement method.
1103.210 Management of federally owned property for which a recipient is accountable.
1103.215 Intangible property developed or produced under an award or subaward.
1103.220 Debarment and suspension requirements related to recipients' procurements.
1103.225 Debt collection.

### Subpart C—Definitions of Terms Used in This Part

1103.300 DoD Components.
1103.305 DoD Grant and Agreement Regulations.
1103.310 Small award.

AUTHORITY: 5 U.S.C. 301 and 10 U.S.C. 113.

SOURCE: 79 FR 76047, Dec. 19, 2014, unless otherwise noted.

## Subpart A—Interim Implementation of Guidance in 2 CFR Part 200

§ 1103.100 Applicability of 2 CFR part 200 to requirements for recipients in DoD Components' terms and conditions.

Effective December 26, 2014, and on an interim basis pending update of the DoD Grant and Agreement Regulations to implement Office of Management and Budget (OMB) guidance published in 2 CFR part 200:

(a) The guidance in 2 CFR part 200 as modified and supplemented by provisions of Subpart B of this part governs the administrative requirements, cost principles, and audit requirements to be included in terms and conditions of DoD Components' new grant and cooperative agreement awards to:

(1) Institutions of higher education, hospitals, and other nonprofit organizations included in the definition of "recipient" in part 32 of the DoD Grant and Agreement Regulations (32 CFR part 32).

(2) States, local governments, and Indian tribal governments.

(b) The following class deviations from selected provisions of the DoD Grant and Agreement Regulations therefore are approved for DoD Components' new grant and cooperative agreement awards made on or after December 26, 2014:

(1) Awards to institutions of higher education, hospitals, and other nonprofit organizations included in the definition of "recipient" in part 32 of the DoD Grant and Agreement Regulations (32 CFR part 32) are not subject to the administrative requirements, cost principles, and audit requirements specified in 32 CFR part 32.

(2) Awards to States, local governments, and Indian tribal governments are not subject to the administrative requirements, cost principles, and audit requirements specified in part 33 of the DoD Grant and Agreement Regulations (32 CFR part 33).

(3) References in other parts of the DoD Grant and Agreement Regulations that cite part 32 or part 33 as the source of administrative requirements, cost principles, and audit requirements for awards to the types of recipient entities described in paragraphs (b)(1) and (2) of this section therefore do not apply to those new awards.

(c) Provisions of the DoD Grant and Agreement Regulations other than those listed in paragraph (b) of this section continue to be in effect, with applicability as stated in those provisions.

363

## Subpart B—Pre-Existing Policies Continuing in Effect During Interim Implementation

### § 1103.200  Exception for small awards.

For small awards to institutions of higher education, hospitals, and other nonprofit organizations, DoD Components' terms and conditions may apply less restrictive requirements to recipients than the OMB guidance in 2 CFR part 200 specifies, except for requirements that are statutory. This exception maintains long-standing policy established in 32 CFR 32.4.

### § 1103.205  Timing of payments made using the reimbursement method.

In DoD Components' awards to institutions of higher education, hospitals, and other nonprofit organizations, the terms and conditions implementing the provisions of 2 CFR 200.305(b)(3) concerning timing of payments when the reimbursement method is used must specify that the DoD payment office generally makes payment within 30 calendar days after receipt of the request for reimbursement by the office designated to receive the request, unless the request is reasonably believed to be improper. This substitution of "generally makes payment" for "must make payment" maintains long-standing policy established in 32 CFR 32.22(e)(1).

### § 1103.210  Management of federally owned property for which a recipient is accountable.

In award terms and conditions implementing the guidance in 2 CFR 200.313(d) on procedural requirements for a recipient's equipment management system, DoD Components must:

(a) For any award to an institution of higher education, hospital, or other nonprofit organization, broaden the requirements of 2 CFR 200.313(d) to also apply to any federally owned property for which the recipient is accountable under its award. Doing so maintains long-standing policy established in 32 CFR 32.34(f).

(b) For any award to a State, local government, or Indian tribal government (as defined in 32 CFR part 33), specify that the recipient must manage federally owned equipment in accordance with the DoD Components' rules and procedures. Doing so maintains long-standing policy established in 32 CFR 33.32(f).

### § 1103.215  Intangible property developed or produced under an award or subaward.

In DoD Components' awards to institutions of higher education, hospitals, and other nonprofit organizations, the award terms and conditions implementing the guidance in 2 CFR 200.315(a) on intangible property must exclude intangible property developed or produced under an award or subaward. Doing so maintains long-standing policy established in 32 CFR 32.36(e).

### § 1103.220  Debarment and suspension requirements related to recipients' procurements.

In award terms and conditions implementing the guidance in 2 CFR 200.318(h) on awarding contracts only to responsible entities, DoD Components must require recipients to comply with DoD's implementation in 2 CFR part 1125 of OMB guidance on nonprocurement debarment and suspension (2 CFR part 180). Doing so maintains long-standing policy established in 2 CFR parts 180 and 1125 and in 32 CFR 32.44(d), as well as compliance with Executive Orders 12549 and 12689.

### § 1103.225  Debt collection.

In award terms and conditions implementing the guidance in 2 CFR 200.345 on collection of amounts due, DoD Components must inform recipients that DoD post-award administration offices follow procedures set forth in 32 CFR 22.820 for issuing demands for payment and transferring debts for collection, and that a recipient will be informed about specific procedures and timeframes affecting it through the written notices of grants officers' decisions and demands for payment. Doing so maintains long-standing policy established in 32 CFR 32.73(c).

## Subpart C—Definitions of Terms Used in This Part

### § 1103.300  DoD Components.

The Office of the Secretary of Defense, the Military Departments, and all Defense Agencies, DoD Field Activities, and other entities within the Department of Defense that are authorized to award or administer grants, cooperative agreements, and other nonprocurement transactions subject to the DoD Grants and Agreement Regulations.

### § 1103.305  DoD Grant and Agreement Regulations.

The regulations in Chapter I, Subchapter C of Title 32, Code of Federal Regulations, and Chapter XI of Title 2, Code of Federal Regulations.

### § 1103.310  Small award.

An award not exceeding the simplified acquisition threshold.

## PARTS 1104–1124 [RESERVED]

## PART 1125—NONPROCUREMENT DEBARMENT AND SUSPENSION

Sec.
1125.10   What does this part do?
1125.20   Does this part implement the OMB guidance in 2 CFR part 180 for all DoD nonprocurement transactions?
1125.30   Does this part apply to me?
1125.40   What policies and procedures must I follow?

### Subpart A—General

1125.137   Who in the Department of Defense may grant an exception to let an excluded person participate in a covered transaction?

### Subpart B—Covered Transactions

1125.220   What contracts and subcontracts, in addition to those listed in 2 CFR 180.220, are covered transactions?

### Subpart C—Responsibilities of Participants Regarding Transactions

1125.332   What method must I use to pass requirements down to participants at lower tiers with whom I intend to do business?

### Subpart D—Responsibilities of DoD Officials Regarding Transactions

1125.425   When do I check to see if a person is excluded or disqualified?
1125.437   What method do I use to communicate to a participant the requirements described in the OMB guidance at 2 CFR 180.435?

### Subparts E–H [Reserved]

### Subpart I—Definitions

1125.930   Debarring official (DoD supplement to Governmentwide definition at 2 CFR 180.930).
1125.937   DoD Component.
1125.1010   Suspending official (DoD supplement to Governmentwide definition at 2 CFR 180.1010).

AUTHORITY: Sec. 2455, Pub. L. 103–355, 108 Stat. 3327; E.O. 12549, 3 CFR, 1986 Comp., p. 189; E.O. 12689, 3 CFR, 1989 Comp., p. 235; 5 U.S.C. 301 and 10 U.S.C. 113.

SOURCE: 72 FR 34984, June 26, 2007, unless otherwise noted.

### § 1125.10  What does this part do?

This part adopts the Office of Management and Budget (OMB) guidance in subparts A through I of 2 CFR part 180, as supplemented by this part, as the Department of Defense (DoD) policies and procedures for nonprocurement debarment and suspension. It thereby gives regulatory effect for the Department of Defense to the OMB guidance as supplemented by this part. This part satisfies the requirements in section 3 of Executive Order 12549, "Debarment and Suspension" (3 CFR 1986 Comp., p. 189), Executive Order 12689, "Debarment and Suspension" (3 CFR 1989 Comp., p. 235) and 31 U.S.C. 6101 note (Section 2455, Public Law 103–355, 108 Stat. 3327).

### § 1125.20  Does this part implement the OMB guidance in 2 CFR part 180 for all DoD nonprocurement transactions?

This part implements the OMB guidelines in 2 CFR part 180 for most DoD nonprocurement transactions. However, it does not implement the guidelines as they apply to prototype projects under the authority of Section 845 of the National Defense Authorization Act for Fiscal Year 1994 (Pub. L. 103–160), as amended. The Director of Defense Procurement and Acquisition

Policy maintains a DoD issuance separate from this part that addresses section 845 transactions.

### § 1125.30 Does this part apply to me?

This part and, through this part, pertinent portions of the OMB guidance in subparts A through I of 2 CFR part 180 (see table at 2 CFR 180.100(b)) apply to you if you are a—

(a) Participant or principal in a "covered transaction" (see subpart B of 2 CFR part 180 and the definition of "nonprocurement transaction" at 2 CFR 180.970, as supplemented by subpart B of this part), other than a section 845 transaction described in § 1125.20;

(b) Respondent in a DoD Component's nonprocurement suspension or debarment action;

(c) DoD Component's debarment or suspension official; or

(d) DoD Component's grants officer, agreements officer, or other official authorized to enter into a nonprocurement transaction that is a covered transaction.

### § 1125.40 What policies and procedures must I follow?

(a) *General.* You must follow the policies and procedures specified in applicable sections of the OMB guidance in subparts A through I of 2 CFR part 180, as implemented by this part.

(b) *Specific sections of OMB guidance that this part supplements.* In implementing the OMB guidance in 2 CFR part 180, this part supplements eight sections of the guidance, as shown in the following table. For each of those sections, you must follow the policies and procedures in the OMB guidance, as supplemented by this part.

| Section of OMB guidance | Section in this part where supplemented | What the supplementation clarifies |
|---|---|---|
| (1) 2 CFR 180.135 | § 1125.137 | Who in DoD may grant an exception for an excluded person to participate in a covered transaction. |
| (2) 2 CFR 180.220 | § 1125.220 | Which lower-tier contracts under a nonprocurement transaction are covered transactions. |
| (3) 2 CFR 180.330 | § 1125.332 | What method a participant must use to communicate requirements to a lower-tier participant. |
| (4) 2 CFR 180.425 | § 1125.425 | When a DoD awarding official must check to see if a person is excluded or disqualified. |
| (5) 2 CFR 180.435 | § 1125.437 | What method a DoD official must use to communicate requirements to a participant. |
| (6) 2 CFR 180.930 | § 1125.930 | Which DoD officials are debarring officials. |
| (7) 2 CFR 180.1010 | § 1125.1010 | Which DoD officials are suspending officials. |

(c) *Sections of the OMB guidance that this part does not supplement.* For any section of OMB guidance in subparts A through I of 2 CFR 180 that is not listed in paragraph (b) of this section, DoD policies and procedures are the same as those in the OMB guidance.

## Subpart A—General

### § 1125.137 Who in the Department of Defense may grant an exception to let an excluded person participate in a covered transaction?

Within the Department of Defense, the Secretary of Defense, Secretary of a Military Department, Head of a Defense Agency, Head of the Office of Economic Adjustment, and Head of the Special Operations Command have the authority to grant an exception to let an excluded person participate in a covered transaction, as provided in the OMB guidance at 2 CFR 180.135.

## Subpart B—Covered Transactions

### § 1125.220 What contracts and subcontracts, in addition to those listed in 2 CFR 180.220, are covered transactions?

Although the OMB guidance at 2 CFR 180.220(c) allows a Federal agency to do so (also see optional lower tier coverage in the figure in the appendix to 2 CFR part 180), the Department of Defense does not extend coverage of nonprocurement suspension and debarment requirements beyond first-tier procurement contracts under a covered nonprocurement transaction.

## Subpart C—Responsibilities of Participants Regarding Transactions

### §1125.332 What method must I use to pass requirements down to participants at lower tiers with whom I intend to do business?

You as a participant in a covered transaction must include a term or condition in any lower-tier covered transaction into which you enter, to require the participant of that transaction to—

(a) Comply with subpart C of the OMB guidance in 2 CFR part 180; and

(b) Include a similar term or condition in any covered transaction into which it enters at the next lower tier.

## Subpart D—Responsibilities of DoD Officials Regarding Transactions

### §1125.425 When do I check to see if a person is excluded or disqualified?

In addition to the four instances identified in the OMB guidance at 2 CFR 180.425, you as a DoD Component official must check to see if a person is excluded or disqualified before you obligate additional funding (e.g., through an incremental funding action) for a pre-existing grant or cooperative agreement with an institution of higher education, as provided in 32 CFR 22.520(e)(5).

### §1125.437 What method do I use to communicate to a participant the requirements described in the OMB guidance at 2 CFR 180.435?

You as a DoD Component official must include a term or condition in each covered transaction into which you enter, to communicate to the participant the requirements to—

(a) Comply with subpart C of 2 CFR part 180, as supplemented by subpart C of this part; and

(b) Include a similar term or condition in any lower-tier covered transactions into which the participant enters.

## Subparts E–H [Reserved]

## Subpart I—Definitions

### §1125.930 Debarring official (DoD supplement to Governmentwide definition at 2 CFR 180.930).

DoD Components' debarring officials for nonprocurement transactions are the same officials identified in 48 CFR part 209, subpart 209.4, as debarring officials for procurement contracts.

### §1125.937 DoD Component.

In this part, DoD Component means the Office of the Secretary of Defense, a Military Department, a Defense Agency, a DoD Field Activity, or any other organizational entity of the Department of Defense that is authorized to award or administer grants, cooperative agreements, or other nonprocurement transactions.

### §1125.1010 Suspending official (DoD supplement to Governmentwide definition at 2 CFR 180.1010).

DoD Components' suspending officials for nonprocurement transactions are the same officials identified in 48 CFR part 209, subpart 209.4, as suspending officials for procurement contracts.

## PARTS 1126–1199 [RESERVED]

# CHAPTER XII—DEPARTMENT OF TRANSPORTATION

369

# PART 1200—NONPROCUREMENT SUSPENSION AND DEBARMENT

Sec.
1200.10  What does this part do?
1200.20  Does this part apply to me?
1200.30  What policies and procedures must I follow?

## Subpart A—General

1200.137  Who in the Department of Transportation may grant an exception to let an excluded person participate in a covered transaction?

## Subpart B—Covered Transactions

1200.220  What contracts and subcontracts, in addition to those listed in 2 CFR 180.220, are covered transactions?

## Subpart C—Responsibilities of Participants Regarding Transactions

1200.332  What methods must I use to pass requirements down to participants at lower tiers with whom I intend to do business?

## Subpart D—Responsibilities of Federal Agency Officials Regarding Transactions

1200.437  What method do I use to communicate to a participant the requirements described in the OMB guidance at 2 CFR 180.435?

## Subparts E–J [Reserved]

AUTHORITY: 49 U.S.C. 322; Sec. 2455, Public Law 103–355, 108 Stat. 3327 (31 U.S.C. 6101 note); E.O. 12549 (3 CFR, 1986 Comp., p. 189); E.O. 12689 (3 CFR, 1989 Comp., p. 235).

SOURCE: 73 FR 24140, May 2, 2008, unless otherwise noted.

## § 1200.10  What does this part do?

This part adopts the Office of Management and Budget (OMB) guidance in subparts A through I of 2 CFR part 180, as supplemented by this part, as the Department of Transportation policies and procedures for nonprocurement suspension and debarment. It thereby gives regulatory effect for the Department of Transportation to the OMB guidance as supplemented by this part. This part satisfies the requirements in section 3 of Executive Order 12549, "Supension and Debarment" (3 CFR 1986 Comp., p. 189), Executive Order 12689, "Suspension and Debarment" (3

CFR 1989 Comp., p. 235) and 31 U.S.C. 6101 note (Section 2455, Public Law 103–355, 108 Stat. 3327).

## § 1200.20  Does this part apply to me?

This part and, through this part, pertinent portions of the OMB guidance in subparts A through I of 2 CFR part 180 (see table at 2 CFR 180.100(b)) apply to you if you are a—

(a) Participant or principal in a "covered transaction" (see subpart B of 2 CFR part 180 and the definition of "nonprocurement transaction" at 2 CFR 180.970;

(b) Respondent in a Department of Transportation suspension or debarment action;

(c) Department of Transportation debarment or suspension official;

(d) Department of Transportation grants officer, agreements officer, or other official authorized to enter into any type of nonprocurement transaction that is a covered transaction.

## § 1200.30  What policies and procedures must I follow?

The Department of Transportation policies and procedures that you must follow are the policies and procedures specified in each applicable section of the OMB guidance in subparts A through I of 2 CFR part 180, as that section is supplemented by the section in this part with the same section number. The contracts that are covered transactions, for example, are specified by section 220 of the OMB guidance (i.e., 2 CFR 180.220), as supplemented by section 220 in this part (i.e., §1200.220). For any section of OMB guidance in subparts A through I of 2 CFR 180 that has no corresponding section in this part, Department of Transportation policies and procedures are those in the OMB guidance.

## Subpart A—General

## § 1200.137  Who in the Department of Transportation may grant an exception to let an excluded person participate in a covered transaction?

Within the Department of Transportation, Office of the Secretary, the Secretary or an official designated by the

371

Secretary may grant an exception permitting an excluded person to participate in a particular covered transaction. Within an Operating Administration of the Department of Transportation, the head of the operating administration may grant an exception permitting an excluded person to participate in a particular covered transaction. The head of an operating administration may delegate this function and authorize successive delegations.

## Subpart B—Covered Transactions

**§ 1200.220 What contracts and subcontracts, in addition to those listed in 2 CFR 180.220, are covered transactions?**

In addition to the contracts covered under 2 CFR 180.220(b) of the OMB guidance, this part applies to any contract, regardless of tier, that is awarded by a contractor, subcontractor, supplier, consultant, or its agent or representative in any transaction, if the contract is to be funded or provided by the Department of Transportation under a covered nonprocurement transaction and the amount of the contract is expected to equal or exceed $25,000. This extends the coverage of the Department of Transportation nonprocurement suspension and debarment requirements to all lower tiers of subcontracts under covered nonprocurement transactions, as permitted under the OMB guidance at 2 CFR 180.220(c) (see optional lower-tier coverage in the figure in the appendix to 2 CFR part 180).

## Subpart C—Responsibilities of Participants Regarding Transactions

**§ 1200.332 What methods must I use to pass requirements down to participants at lower tiers with whom I intend to do business?**

You as a participant must include a term or condition in lower-tier transactions requiring lower-tier participants to comply with subpart C of the OMB guidance in 2 CFR part 180, as supplemented by this subpart.

## Subpart D—Responsibilities of Federal Agency Officials Regarding Transactions

**§ 1200.437 What method do I use to communicate to a participant the requirements described in the OMB guidance at 2 CFR 180.435?**

To communicate to a participant the requirements described in 2 CFR 180.435 of the OMB guidance, you must include a term or condition in the transaction that requires the participant's compliance with subpart C of 2 CFR part 180 and requires the participant to include a similar term or condition in lower-tier covered transactions.

## Subparts E–J [Reserved]

# PART 1201—UNIFORM ADMINISTRATIVE REQUIREMENTS, COST PRINCIPLES, AND AUDIT REQUIREMENTS FOR FEDERAL AWARDS

Sec.
1201.1   What does this part do?
1201.2   Definitions.
1201.80   Program income.
1201.102   Exceptions.
1201.106   DOT Component implementation.
1201.107   DOT Headquarters responsibilities.
1201.108   Inquiries.
1201.109   Review date.
1201.112   Conflict of interest.
1201.206   Standard application requirements.
1201.313   Equipment.
1201.317   Procurements by States.
1201.319   Competition.
1201.327   Financial reporting.

AUTHORITY: 49 U.S.C. 322(a); 2 CFR 200.106.

SOURCE: 79 FR 76049, Dec. 19, 2014, unless otherwise noted.

**§ 1201.1 What does this part do?**

Except as otherwise provided in this part, the Department of Transportation adopts the Office of Management and Budget Uniform Administrative Requirements, Cost Principles, and Audit Requirements for Federal Awards (2 CFR part 200). This part supersedes and repeals the requirements of the Department of Transportation Common Rules (49 CFR part 18—Uniform Administrative Requirements for Grants and Cooperative Agreements to State and Local Governments and 49

CFR part 19—Uniform Administrative Requirements—Uniform Administrative Requirements for Grants and Agreements with Institutions of Higher Education, Hospitals, and other Non-Profit Organizations), except that grants and cooperative agreements executed prior to December 26, 2014 shall continue to be subject to 49 CFR parts 18 and 19 as in effect on the date of such grants or agreements. New parts with terminology specific to the Department of Transportation follow.

§1201.2 Definitions.

Throughout this part, the term "DOT Component" refers to any Division, Office, or Mode (e.g., the Federal Aviation Administration (FAA), Federal Highway Administration (FHWA), Federal Motor Carrier Safety Administration (FMCSA), Federal Railroad Administration (FRA), Federal Transit Administration (FTA), Maritime Administration (MARAD), National Highway Traffic Safety Administration (NHTSA), Office of Inspector General (OIG), Office of the Secretary of Transportation (OST), Pipeline and Hazardous Materials Safety Administration (PHMSA), St. Lawrence Seaway Development Corporation (SLSDC), and the Surface Transportation Board (STB)) within the Department of Transportation awarding Federal financial assistance. In addition, the term "DOT Headquarters" refers to the Secretary of Transportation or any office designated by the Secretary to fulfill headquarters' functions within any office under the Secretary's immediate supervision.

§1201.80 Program income.

Notwithstanding 2 CFR 200.80, *program income* means gross income earned by the non-Federal entity that is directly generated by a supported activity or earned as a result of the Federal award during the period of performance. (See 2 CFR 200.77 Period of performance.) Program income includes but is not limited to income from fees for services performed, the use or rental or real or personal property acquired under Federal awards, the sale of commodities or items fabricated under a Federal award, license fees and royalties on patents and copyrights, and

principal and interest on loans made with Federal award funds. Interest earned on advances of Federal funds is not program income. Except as otherwise provided in Federal statutes, regulations, or the terms and conditions of the Federal award, program income does not include rebates, credits, discounts, taxes, special assessments, levies, and fines raised by a grantee and subgrantee, and interest earned on any of them.

§1201.102 Exceptions.

DOT Headquarters may grant exceptions to Part 1201 on a case-by-case basis. Such exceptions will be granted only as determined by the Secretary of Transportation.

§1201.106 DOT Component implementation.

The specific requirements and responsibilities for grant-making DOT Components are set forth in this part. DOT Components must implement the language in this part unless different provisions are required by Federal statute or are approved by DOT Headquarters. DOT Components making Federal awards to non-Federal entities must implement the language in the Subpart C—Pre-Federal Award Requirements and Contents of Federal Awards of this Part through Subpart F—Audit Requirements of this Part in codified regulations unless different provisions are required by Federal statute or are approved by DOT Headquarters.

§1201.107 DOT Headquarters responsibilities.

DOT Headquarters will review DOT Component implementation of this part, and will provide interpretations of policy requirements and assistance to ensure effective and efficient implementation. Any exceptions will be subject to approval by DOT Headquarters. Exceptions will only be made in particular cases where adequate justification is presented.

§1201.108 Inquiries.

Inquiries regarding Part 1201 should be addressed to the DOT Component making the award, cognizant agency for indirect costs, cognizant or oversight agency for audit, or pass-through entities as appropriate. DOT Components will, in turn, direct the inquiry to the Office of Chief Financial Officer, Department of Transportation.

### § 1201.109  Review date.

DOT Headquarters will review this part at least every five years after December 26, 2014.

### § 1201.112  Conflict of interest.

The DOT Component making a financial assistance award must establish conflict of interest policies for Federal awards, including policies from DOT Headquarters. The non-Federal entity must disclose in writing any potential conflict of interest to the DOT Component or pass-through entity in accordance with applicable Federal awarding agency policy.

### § 1201.206  Standard  application  requirements.

The requirements of 2 CFR 200.206 do not apply to formula grant programs, which do not require applicants to apply for funds on a project basis.

### § 1201.313  Equipment.

Notwithstanding 2 CFR 200.313, subrecipients of States shall follow such policies and procedures allowed by the State with respect to the use, management and disposal of equipment acquired under a Federal award.

### § 1201.317  Procurements by States.

Notwithstanding 2 CFR 200.317, subrecipients of States shall follow such policies and procedures allowed by the State when procuring property and services under a Federal award.

### § 1201.327  Financial reporting.

Notwithstanding 2 CFR 200.327, recipients of FHWA and NHTSA financial assistance may use FHWA, NHTSA or State financial reports.

## PARTS 1202–1299 [RESERVED]

# CHAPTER XIII—DEPARTMENT OF COMMERCE

# PARTS 1300–1325 [RESERVED]

# PART 1326—NONPROCUREMENT DEBARMENT AND SUSPENSION

Sec.
1326.10 What does this part do?
1326.20 Does this part apply to me?
1326.30 What policies and procedures must I follow?

## Subpart A—General

1326.137 Who in the Department of Commerce may grant an exception to let an excluded person participate in a covered transaction?

## Subpart B—Covered Transactions

1326.215 Which nonprocurement transactions, in addition to those listed in 2 CFR 180.215, are not covered transactions?
1326.220 What contracts and subcontracts, in addition to those listed in 2 CFR 180.220, are covered transactions?

## Subpart C—Responsibilities of Participants Regarding Transactions

1326.332 What methods must I use to pass requirements down to participants at lower tiers with whom I intend to do business?

## Subpart D—Responsibilities of Federal Agency Officials Regarding Transactions

1326.437 What method do I use to communicate to a participant the requirements described in the OMB guidance at 2 CFR 180.435?

## Subparts E–H [Reserved]

## Subpart I—Definitions

1326.970 Nonprocurement transaction (Department of Commerce supplement to government-wide definition at 2 CFR 180.970).

## Subpart J [Reserved]

AUTHORITY: 5 U.S.C. 301; Sec. 2455, Pub. L. 103–355, 108 Stat. 3327; E.O. 12549, 3 CFR, 1986 Comp., p. 189; E.O. 12689, 3 CFR, 1989 Comp., p. 235.

SOURCE: 71 FR 76574, Dec. 21, 2006, unless otherwise noted.

## § 1326.10  What does this part do?

This part adopts the Office of Management and Budget (OMB) guidance in subparts A through I of 2 CFR part 180, as supplemented by this part, as the Department of Commerce policies and procedures for nonprocurement debarment and suspension. It thereby gives regulatory effect to the OMB guidance as supplemented by this part. This part satisfies the requirements in section 3 of Executive Order 12549, "Debarment and Suspension" (3 CFR 1986 Comp., p. 189), Executive Order 12689, "Debarment and Suspension" (3 CFR 1989 Comp., p. 235) and 31 U.S.C. 6101 note (Section 2455, Public Law 103–355, 108 Stat. 3327).

## § 1326.20  Does this part apply to me?

This part and, through this part, pertinent portions of the OMB guidance in subparts A through I of 2 CFR part 180 (see table at 2 CFR 180.100(b)) apply to you if you are a—

(a) Participant or principal in a "covered transaction" (see subpart B of 2 CFR part 180 and the definition of "nonprocurement transaction" at 2 CFR 180.970, as supplemented by subpart B and § 1326.970 of this part).

(b) Respondent in a Department of Commerce suspension or debarment action.

(c) Department of Commerce debarment or suspension official;

(d) Department of Commerce grants officer, agreements officer, or other official authorized to enter into any type of nonprocurement transaction that is a covered transaction;

## § 1326.30  What policies and procedures must I follow?

The Department of Commerce policies and procedures that you must follow are the policies and procedures specified in each applicable section of the OMB guidance in subparts A through I of 2 CFR part 180, as that section is supplemented by the section in this part with the same section number. The contracts that are covered transactions, for example, are specified by section 220 of the OMB guidance (i.e., 2 CFR 180.220) as supplemented by section 220 in this part (i.e., § 1326.220). For any section of OMB guidance in subparts A through I of 2 CFR 180 that has no corresponding section in this part, Department of Commerce policies

377

and procedures are those in the OMB guidance.

## Subpart A—General

**§ 1326.137 Who in the Department of Commerce may grant an exception to let an excluded person participate in a covered transaction?**

Within the Department of Commerce, the Secretary of Commerce or designee has the authority to grant an exception to let an excluded person participate in a covered transaction, as provided in the OMB guidance at 2 CFR 180.135.

## Subpart B—Covered Transactions

**§ 1326.215 Which nonprocurement transactions, in addition to those listed in 2 CFR 180.215, are not covered transactions?**

(a) For purposes of the Department of Commerce, a transaction that the Department needs to respond to a national or agency-recognized emergency or disaster includes the Fisherman's Contingency Fund.

(b) For purposes of the Department of Commerce, an incidental benefit that results from ordinary governmental operations includes:

(1) Export Promotion, Trade Information and Counseling, and Trade policy.

(2) Geodetic Surveys and Services (Specialized Services).

(3) Fishery Products Inspection Certification.

(4) Standard Reference Materials.

(5) Calibration, Measurement, and Testing.

(6) Critically Evaluated Data (Standard Reference Data).

(7) Phoenix Data System.

(8) The sale or provision of products, information, and services to the general public.

(c) For purposes of the Department of Commerce, any other transaction if the application of an exclusion to the transaction is prohibited by law includes:

(1) The Administration of the Antidumping and Countervailing Duty Statutes.

(2) The export Trading Company Act Certification of Review Program.

(3) Trade Adjustment Assistance Program Certification.

(4) Foreign Trade Zones Act of 1934, as amended.

(5) Statutory Import Program.

**§ 1326.220 What contracts and subcontracts, in addition to those listed in 2 CFR 180.220, are covered transactions?**

In addition to the contracts covered under 2 CFR 180.220(b) of the OMB guidance, this part applies to a subcontract that is awarded by a participant in a procurement transaction covered under 2 CFR 180.220(a), if the amount of the subcontract exceeds or is expected to exceed $25,000. This extends the coverage of the Department of Commerce nonprocurement suspension and debarment requirements to one additional tier of contracts under covered nonprocurement transactions, as permitted under the OMB guidance at 2 CFR 180.220(c) (see optional lower tier coverage in the figure in the appendix to 2 CFR part 180).

## Subpart C—Responsibilities of Participants Regarding Transactions

**§ 1326.332 What methods must I use to pass requirements down to participants at lower tiers with whom I intend to do business?**

You as a participant must include a term or condition in lower-tier transactions requiring lower-tier participants to comply with subpart C of the OMB guidance in 2 CFR Part 180, as supplemented by this subpart.

## Subpart D—Responsibilities of Federal Agency Officials Regarding Transactions

**§ 1326.437 What method do I use to communicate to a participant the requirements described in the OMB guidance at 2 CFR 180.435?**

To communicate to a participant the requirements described in 2 CFR 180.435 of the OMB guidance, you must include a term or condition in the transaction that requires the participant's compliance with subpart C of 2 CFR part 180, as supplemented by subpart C of this part, and requires the participant to include a similar term or condition in lower-tier covered transactions.

## Subparts E–H [Reserved]

## Subpart I—Definitions

**§ 1326.970 Nonprocurement transaction (Department of Commerce supplement to government-wide definition at 2 CFR 180.970).**

For purposes of the Department of Commerce, nonprocurement transaction includes the following:

(a) Joint project Agreements under 15 U.S.C. 1525.

(b) Cooperative research and development agreements.

(c) Joint statistical agreements.

(d) Patent licenses under 35 U.S.C. 207.

(e) NTIS joint ventures, 15 U.S.C. 3704b.

## Subpart J [Reserved]

## PART 1327—UNIFORM ADMINISTRATIVE REQUIREMENTS, COST PRINCIPLES, AND AUDIT REQUIREMENTS FOR FEDERAL AWARDS

AUTHORITY: 5 U.S.C. 301; 38 U.S.C. 501; 2 CFR part 200.

SOURCE: 79 FR 76050, Dec. 19, 2014, unless otherwise noted.

**§ 1327.101 Adoption of 2 CFR Part 200.**

Under the authority listed above, the Department of Commerce adopts the Office of Management and Budget (OMB) Guidance in 2 CFR part 200. Thus, this part gives regulatory effect to the OMB guidance and supplements the guidance as needed for the Department.

## PART 1328 [RESERVED]

## PART 1329—REQUIREMENTS FOR DRUG-FREE WORKPLACE (FINANCIAL ASSISTANCE)

Sec.
1329.10 What does this part do?
1329.20 Does this part apply to me?
1329.30 What policies and procedures must I follow?

## Subpart A—Purpose and Coverage [Reserved]

## Subpart B—Requirements for Recipients Other Than Individuals

1329.225 Whom in the Department of Commerce does a recipient other than an individual notify about a criminal drug conviction?

## Subpart C—Requirements for Recipients Who Are Individuals

1329.300 Whom in the Department of Commerce does a recipient who is an individual notify about a criminal drug conviction?

## Subpart D—Responsibilities of Agency Awarding Officials

1329.400 What method do I use as an agency awarding official to obtain a recipient's agreement to comply with the OMB guidance?

## Subpart E—Violations of This Part and Consequences

1329.500 Who in the Department of Commerce determines that a recipient other than an individual violated the requirements of this part?
1329.505 Who in the Department of Commerce determines that a recipient who is an individual violated the requirements of this part?

## Subpart F—Definitions [Reserved]

AUTHORITY: 5 U.S.C. 301; 41 U.S.C. 701–707.

SOURCE: 81 FR 3700, Jan. 22, 2016, unless otherwise noted.

**§ 1329.10 What does this part do?**

This part requires that the award and administration of Department of Commerce grants and cooperative agreements comply with Office of Management and Budget (OMB) guidance implementing the portion of the Drug-Free Workplace Act of 1988 (41 U.S.C. 701–707, as amended, hereafter referred to as "the Act") that applies to grants. It thereby—

(a) Gives regulatory effect to the OMB guidance (subparts A through F of 2 CFR part 182) for the Department of Commerce's grants and cooperative agreements; and

(b) Establishes Department of Commerce policies and procedures for compliance with the Act that are the same

379

as those of other Federal agencies, in conformance with the requirement in 41 U.S.C. 705 for Governmentwide implementing regulations.

## § 1329.20   Does this part apply to me?

This part and, through this part, pertinent portions of the OMB guidance in subparts A through F of 2 CFR part 182 (see table at 2 CFR 182.115(b)) apply to you if you are a—

(a) Recipient of a Department of Commerce grant or cooperative agreement; or

(b) Department of Commerce awarding official.

## § 1329.30   What policies and procedures must I follow?

(a) *General.* You must follow the policies and procedures specified in applicable sections of the OMB guidance in subparts A through F of 2 CFR part 182, as implemented by this part.

(b) *Specific sections of OMB guidance that this part supplements.* In implementing the OMB guidance in 2 CFR part 182, this part supplements four sections of the guidance, as shown in the following table. For each of those sections, you must follow the policies and procedures in the OMB guidance, as supplemented by this part.

| Section of OMB guidance | Section in this part where supplemented | What the supplementation clarifies |
|---|---|---|
| (1) 2 CFR 182.225(a) ............ | § 1329.225 | Whom in the Department of Commerce a recipient other than an individual must notify if an employee is convicted for a violation of a criminal drug statute in the workplace. |
| (2) 2 CFR 182.300(b) ............ | § 1329.300 | Whom in the Department of Commerce a recipient who is an individual must notify if he or she is convicted of a criminal drug offense resulting from a violation occurring during the conduct of any award activity. |
| (3) 2 CFR 182.500 ................ | § 1329.500 | Who in the Department of Commerce is authorized to determine that a recipient other than an individual is in violation of the requirements of 2 CFR part 182, as implemented by this part. |
| (4) 2 CFR 182.505 ................ | § 1329.505 | Who in the Department of Commerce is authorized to determine that a recipient who is an individual is in violation of the requirements of 2 CFR part 182, as implemented by this part. |

(c) *Sections of the OMB guidance that this part does not supplement.* For any section of OMB guidance in subparts A through F of 2 CFR part 182 that is not listed in paragraph (b) of this section, Department of Commerce policies and procedures are the same as those in the OMB guidance.

## Subpart A—Purpose and Coverage [Reserved]

## Subpart B—Requirements for Recipients Other Than Individuals

## § 1329.225   Whom in the Department of Commerce does a recipient other than an individual notify about a criminal drug conviction?

A recipient other than an individual that is required under 2 CFR 182.225(a) to notify Federal agencies about an employee's conviction for a criminal drug offense must notify each Department of Commerce office from which it currently has an award.

## Subpart C—Requirements for Recipients Who Are Individuals

## § 1329.300   Whom in the Department of Commerce does a recipient who is an individual notify about a criminal drug conviction?

A recipient who is an individual and is required under 2 CFR 182.300(b) to notify Federal agencies about a conviction for a criminal drug offense must notify each Department of Commerce office from which it currently has an award.

## Subpart D—Responsibilities of Agency Awarding Officials

## § 1329.400   What method do I use as an agency awarding official to obtain a recipient's agreement to comply with the OMB guidance?

To obtain a recipient's agreement to comply with applicable requirements in the OMB guidance at 2 CFR part 182, you must include the following term or condition in the award: Drug-free workplace. You as the recipient must comply with drug-free workplace requirements in Subpart B (or Subpart C, if the recipient is an individual) of 2 CFR part 1329, which adopts the Governmentwide implementation (2 CFR part 182) of sec. 5152–5158 of the Drug-Free Workplace Act of 1988 (Pub. L. 100–690, Title V, Subtitle D; 41 U.S.C. 701–707).

## Subpart E—Violations of This Part and Consequences

**§ 1329.500 Who in the Department of Commerce determines that a recipient other than an individual violated the requirements of this part?**

The Secretary of Commerce or designee determines that a recipient other than an individual violated the requirements of this part.

**§ 1329.505 Who in the Department of Commerce determines that a recipient who is an individual violated the requirements of this part?**

The Secretary of Commerce or designee determines that a recipient who is an individual violated the requirements of this part.

## Subpart F—Definitions [Reserved]

## PARTS 1330–1399 [RESERVED]

# CHAPTER XIV—DEPARTMENT OF THE INTERIOR

# PART 1400—NONPROCUREMENT DEBARMENT AND SUSPENSION

AUTHORITY: Section 2455, Pub. L. 103–355, 108 Stat. 3327 (31 U.S.C. 6101 note); 5 U.S.C. 301; E.O. 12549 (3 CFR, 1986 Comp., p. 189); and E.O. 12689 (3 CFR, 1989 Comp., p. 235).

SOURCE: 72 FR 33384, June 18, 2007, unless otherwise noted.

## § 1400.10   What does this part do?

This part provides procedures for the Department of the Interior nonprocurement suspension and debarment actions.

[81 FR 65855, Sept. 26, 2016]

## § 1400.20   When does this part apply to me?

This part and, through this part, pertinent portions of the OMB guidance in subparts A through I of 2 CFR part 180 (see table at 2 CFR 180.100(b)) apply to you if you are—

(a) Participant or principal in a "covered transaction" (see subpart B of 2 CFR part 180 and the definition of "nonprocurement transaction" at 2 CFR 180.970, as supplemented by subpart B and § 1400.970);

(b) Respondent in a Department of the Interior suspension or debarment action;

(c) Department of the Interior debarment or suspension official, i.e., the Director, Office of Acquisition and Property Management; or

(d) Department of the Interior grants officer, agreements officer, or other official authorized to enter into any type of nonprocurement transaction that is a covered transaction.

### § 1400.30 What policies and procedures must I follow?

(a) The Department of the Interior policies and procedures that you must follow are specified in:

(1) Each applicable section of the OMB guidance in subparts A through I of 2 CFR part 180; and

(2) The supplement to each section of the OMB guidance that is found in this part under the same section number. (The contracts that are covered transactions, for example, are specified by section 220 of the OMB guidance (i.e., 2 CFR 180.220) as supplemented by section 220 in this part (i.e., Sec. 1400.220)).

(b) For any section of OMB guidance in subparts A through I of 2 CFR part 180 that has no corresponding section in this part, Department of the Interior policies and procedures are those in the OMB guidance.

## Subpart A—General

### § 1400.137 Who in the Department of the Interior may grant an exception to let an excluded person participate in a covered transaction?

Within the Department of the Interior, the Director, Office of Acquisition and Property Management has the authority to grant an exception to let an excluded person participate in a covered transaction, as provided in the OMB guidance at 2 CFR 180.135.

## Subpart B—Covered Transactions

### § 1400.215 Which nonprocurement transactions, in addition to those listed in 2 CFR 180.215, are not covered transactions?

(a) Transactions entered into pursuant to Public Law 93–638, 88 Stat. 2203.

(b) Under natural resource management programs, permits, licenses, exchanges, and other acquisitions of real property, rights-of-way, and easements.

(c) Transactions concerning mineral patent claims entered into pursuant to 30 U.S.C. 22 *et seq.*; and

(d) Water service contracts and repayments entered into pursuant to 43 U.S.C. 485.

### § 1400.220 What contracts and subcontracts, in addition to those listed in 2 CFR 180.220, are covered transactions?

Although the OMB guidance at 2 CFR 180.220(c) allows a Federal agency to do so (also see optional lower tier coverage in the figure in the appendix to 2 CFR part 180), the Department of the Interior does not extend coverage of nonprocurement suspension and debarment requirements beyond first-tier procurement contracts under a covered nonprocurement transaction.

## Subpart C—Responsibilities of Participants Regarding Transactions

### § 1400.332 What methods must I use to pass requirements down to participants at lower tiers with whom I intend to do business?

You as a participant must include a term or condition in lower-tier transactions requiring lower-tier participants to comply with subpart C of the OMB guidance in 2 CFR part 180.

## Subpart D—Responsibilities of Federal Agency Officials Regarding Transactions

### § 1400.437 What method do I use to communicate to a participant the requirements described in the OMB guidance at 2 CFR 180.435?

To communicate to a participant the requirements described in 2 CFR 180.435

of the OMB guidance, you must include a term or condition in the transaction that requires the participant's compliance with subpart C of 2 CFR part 180, as supplemented by subpart C of this part, and requires the participant to include a similar term or condition in lower-tier covered transactions.

## Subpart E—System for Award Management Exclusions

SOURCE: 81 FR 65855, Sept. 26, 2016, unless otherwise noted.

### § 1400.526 Who at DOI Places Exclusions Information into SAM?

The Office of Acquisition and Property Management (PAM) Debarment Program personnel enter information about persons suspended or debarred by DOI into the GSA Web-based System for Award Management (SAM) within 3 working days of the effective date of the action.

## Subpart F—General Principles Relating to Suspension and Debarment Actions

SOURCE: 81 FR 65855, Sept. 26, 2016, unless otherwise noted.

### § 1400.600 How does a DOI suspension or debarment action begin?

(a) Federal officials, DOI award officials, employees, or other sources will forward information indicating the potential existence of a cause for suspension or debarment, as listed in 2 CFR 180.700 and 180.800, to:

(1) The DOI Office of Inspector General Administrative Remedies Division (OIG ARD); or

(2) The Suspending and Debarring Official.

(b) If forwarded to the OIG ARD, that office will conduct a review to determine if a recommendation for administrative action is warranted. If warranted, the OIG ARD will prepare and submit to the Suspending and Debarring Official an Action Referral Memorandum (ARM) with supporting documentation for the administrative record.

(c) OIG ARD will also identify potential matters for case development and conduct a review to determine if a recommendation for administrative action is warranted. If warranted, the OIG ARD will prepare and submit to the Suspending and Debarring Official an ARM with supporting documentation for the administrative record.

(d) The Suspending and Debarring Official will review the ARM to determine the adequacy of evidence to support and initiate:

(1) A suspension by taking the actions listed in 2 CFR 180.615 and 180.715; or

(2) A debarment by taking the actions listed in 2 CFR 180.615 and 2 CFR 180.805; and

(3) Notification of the respondent on how the respondent may contest the action.

### § 1400.635 May DOI settle a debarment or suspension action?

Under 2 CFR 180.635, the Suspending and Debarring Official may resolve a suspension or debarment action through an administrative agreement if it is in the best interest of the Government at any stage of proceedings, where the respondent agrees to appropriate terms. The specific effect of administrative agreements that incorporate terms regarding award eligibility will vary with the terms of the agreements. Where the Suspending and Debarring Official enters into an administrative agreement, PAM will notify the award officials by:

(a) Entering any appropriate information regarding an exclusion or the termination of an exclusion into SAM; and

(b) Entering the agreement into the Federal Awardee Performance Integrity Information System (FAPIIS) or its successor system.

## Subpart G—Suspension

SOURCE: 81 FR 65855, Sept. 26, 2016, unless otherwise noted.

### § 1400.751 What does the Suspending and Debarring Official consider in making a decision on whether to continue a suspension following notice issuance?

(a) In the event a respondent does not contest the suspension in writing within the time period provided at 2 CFR 180.715 through 180.725, the suspension will remain in place without further proceedings.

(b) Where a suspension is contested, the Suspending and Debarring Official follows the provisions at 2 CFR 180.730 through 180.755 in reaching a decision on whether to continue or terminate the suspension.

(c) The contested suspension proceeding will include an oral Presentation of Matters in Opposition (PMIO), where one is requested by a respondent. The PMIO is conducted in an informal business meeting format and electronically recorded for inclusion in the administrative record.

(d) Where fact-finding occurs as part of the suspension proceeding, after receiving the findings of fact and the hearing record from the fact-finding official, the Suspending and Debarring Official completes suspension proceedings, including a PMIO if one has been requested and did not occur before the fact-finding proceeding. Following completion of suspension proceedings, the Suspending and Debarring Official issues a written decision under the provisions of 2 CFR 180.750 and 180.755.

### § 1400.752 When does a contested suspension action include a fact-finding proceeding?

(a) Fact-finding to resolve genuine disputes over facts material to the suspension occurs where the conditions listed in 2 CFR 180.735(b) are satisfied.

(b) The fact-finding official for DOI suspension proceedings is the DOI Debarment Program Director, unless the Suspending and Debarring Official designates another DOI official to serve as the fact-finding official.

### § 1400.753 How is the fact-finding proceeding conducted?

(a) The fact-finding proceeding is conducted in accordance with PAM's suspension and debarment program fact-finding procedures, a copy of which is provided to the respondent.

(b) The fact-finding proceeding is undertaken in accordance with 2 CFR 180.745.

(1) The reporters' fees and other direct costs associated with the fact-finding proceeding are borne by the bureau(s) or office(s) initiating the suspension action, except in the case of actions initiated by the OIG ARD.

(2) For actions initiated by the OIG ARD, the costs are borne by bureau(s) and/or office(s) out of which the matter arose.

(3) A transcribed record transcript of the fact-finding proceedings is available to the respondent as provided at 2 CFR 180.745(b).

(c) The fact-finding official provides findings of fact and the hearing record to the Suspending and Debarring Official. The fact-finding official files the original copy of the transcribed record of the fact-finding proceedings transcript with the administrative record.

### § 1400.756 May a respondent request administrative review of the Suspending and Debarring Official's decision?

A respondent may seek administrative reconsideration of the Suspending and Debarring Official's decision by following the procedures in this section.

(a) Within 30 days of receiving the decision, the respondent may ask the Suspending and Debarring Official to reconsider the decision for clear and material errors of fact or law that would change the outcome of the matter. The respondent bears the burden of demonstrating the existence of the asserted clear and material errors of fact or law.

(b) A respondent's request for reconsideration must be submitted in writing to the Suspending and Debarring Official and include:

(1) The specific findings of fact and conclusions of law believed to be in error; and

(2) The reasons or legal basis for the respondent's position.

(c) The Suspending and Debarring Official may, in the exercise of discretion, stay the suspension pending reconsideration. The Suspending and Debarring Official will:

(1) Notify the respondent in writing of the decision on whether to reconsider the decision; and

(2) If reconsideration occurs, notify the respondent in writing of the results of the reconsideration.

## Subpart H—Debarment

SOURCE: 81 FR 65855, Sept. 26, 2016, unless otherwise noted.

### §1400.861 What procedures does the Suspending and Debarring Official follow to make a decision on whether to impose debarment following notice issuance?

(a) In the event a respondent does not contest the proposed debarment in writing within the time period provided at 2 CFR 180.815 through 180.825, the debarment as proposed in the notice will be imposed without further proceedings.

(b) Where a proposed debarment is contested, the Suspending and Debarring Official will follow the provisions at 2 CFR 180.830 through 180.870 in reaching a decision on whether to impose a period of debarment.

(c) The administrative record will include an oral PMIO, in those actions where the respondent requests one. The PMIO is conducted in an informal business meeting format and electronically recorded for the record.

(d) Where fact-finding occurs as part of the proposed debarment proceeding, after receiving the findings of fact and the hearing record from the fact-finding official, the Suspending and Debarring Official completes debarment proceedings, including a PMIO if one has been requested and did not occur before the fact-finding proceeding. Following completion of proposed debarment proceedings, the Suspending and Debarring Official issues a written decision under the provisions of 2 CFR 180.870.

### §1400.862 When does a contested proposed debarment action include a fact-finding proceeding?

Fact-finding to resolve genuine disputes over facts material to the proposed debarment occurs where the conditions at 2 CFR 180.830(b) are satisfied.

### §1400.863 How is the fact-finding proceeding conducted?

(a) The fact-finding proceeding is conducted in accordance with PAM's suspension and debarment program fact-finding procedures, a copy of which is provided to the respondent.

(b) The fact-finding official for DOI debarment proceedings is the DOI Debarment Program Director, unless the Suspending and Debarring Official designates another DOI official to serve as the fact-finding official.

(c) The fact-finding proceeding is undertaken in accordance with 2 CFR 180.840.

(1) The reporters' fees and other direct costs associated with the fact-finding proceeding are borne by the bureau(s) or office(s) initiating the debarment action, except in the case of actions initiated by the OIG.

(2) For actions initiated by the OIG, the costs are borne by the bureau(s) and/or office(s) out of which the matter arose.

(3) A transcribed record of the fact-finding proceedings is available to the respondent as provided at 2 CFR 180.840(b).

(d) The fact-finding official provides written findings of fact and the hearing record to the Suspending and Debarring Official. The fact-finding official files the original copy of the transcribed record of the fact-finding proceedings with the administrative record.

### §1400.876 May a respondent request administrative reconsideration of a decision?

A respondent may request the Suspending and Debarring Official to review a decision under this part as follows:

(a) Within 30 days of receiving the decision, the respondent may ask the Suspending and Debarring Official to reconsider the decision based on clear and material error(s) of fact or conclusion(s) of law that would change the outcome of the matter. The respondent bears the burden of demonstrating the existence of the asserted clear and material error(s) of fact or conclusion(s) of law.

(b) The respondent's request for reconsideration must be submitted in writing to the Suspending and Debarring Official and include:

(1) The specific finding(s) of fact and conclusion(s) of law the respondent believes are in error; and

(2) The reasons or legal bases for the respondent's position.

(c) The Suspending and Debarring Official may in the exercise of discretion stay the debarment pending reconsideration. The Suspending and Debarring Official will review the request for reconsideration and:

(1) Notify the respondent in writing whether the Suspending and Debarring Official will reconsider the decision; and

(2) If reconsideration occurs, notify the respondent in writing of the results of the reconsideration.

**§ 1400.881 May a respondent seek award eligibility reinstatement at any time before the end of the period of debarment?**

In addition to a petition for reconsideration based on a clear error of material fact or law, a respondent may, at any time following imposition of debarment, request the Suspending and Debarring Official to reduce or terminate the period of debarment based upon the factors under the provisions of 2 CFR 180.880.

## Subpart I—Definitions

**§ 1400.930 Debarring official (Department of the Interior supplement to the definition at 2 CFR 180.930).**

The Debarring Official for the Department of the Interior is the Director, Office of Acquisition and Property Management.

**§ 1400.970 Nonprocurement transaction (Department of the Interior supplement to the definition at 2 CFR 180.970).**

In addition to those listed in 2 CFR 180.970, the Department of the Interior includes the following as nonprocurement transactions:

(a) Federal acquisition of a leasehold interest or any other interest in real property;

(b) Concession contracts;

(c) Disposition of Federal real and personal property and natural resources; and

(d) Any other nonprocurement transactions between the Department and a person.

**§ 1400.1010 Suspending official (Department of the Interior supplement to the definition at 2 CFR 180.930).**

The Suspending Official for the Department of the Interior is the Director, Office of Acquisition and Property Management.

**§ 1400.1011 The DOI Debarment Program Director.**

The Debarment Program Director is the individual in PAM who advises the Suspending and Debarring Official on DOI suspension and debarment practices and procedures, manages the suspension and debarment process, and acts as the DOI suspension and debarment program fact-finding official.

[81 FR 65857, Sept. 26, 2016]

**§ 1400.1012 The OIG Administrative Remedies Division (ARD).**

The OIG ARD prepares and forwards suspension and/or debarment action referral memoranda to the Suspending and Debarring Official and may provide additional assistance, in the course of action proceedings.

[81 FR 65857, Sept. 26, 2016]

**§ 1400.1013 The administrative record.**

The administrative record for DOI suspension and debarment actions consists of the initiating action referral memorandum and its attached documents; the action notice; contested action scheduling correspondence; written information, arguments and supporting documents submitted by a respondent in opposition to the action notice; written information, arguments and supporting documents submitted by the OIG ARD in response to information provided by a respondent; the electronic recording of the PMIO, where a PMIO is held as part of the proceeding; where fact-finding is conducted, the transcribed record of the fact-finding proceedings, and findings of fact; and the final written determination by the Suspending and Debarring Official on the action; or, alternatively, the administrative agreement endorsed by the respondent and the Suspending and Debarring Official that resolves an action.

[81 FR 65857, Sept. 26, 2016]

### § 1400.1014 Respondent.

Respondent means a person who is the subject of a DOI suspension or proposed debarment action.

[81 FR 65857, Sept. 26, 2016]

## Subpart J [Reserved]

## PART 1401—REQUIREMENTS FOR DRUG-FREE WORKPLACE (FINANCIAL ASSISTANCE)

### Subpart A—Purpose and Coverage

AUTHORITY: 5 U.S.C. 301; 31 U.S.C. 6101 note, 7501; 41 U.S.C. 252a; 41 U.S.C. 701–707.

SOURCE: 75 FR 71008, Nov. 22, 2010, unless otherwise noted.

## Subpart A—Purpose and Coverage

### § 1401.100 What does this part do?

This part requires that the award and administration of the DOI grants and cooperative agreements comply with Office of Management and Budget (OMB) guidance implementing the portion of the Drug-Free Workplace Act of 1988, 41 U.S.C. 701–707, as amended (hereinafter, "the Act") that applies to grants. It thereby—

(a) Gives regulatory effect to the OMB guidance (Subparts A through F of 2 CFR Part 182) for DOI's grants and cooperative agreements; and

(b) Establishes DOI policies and procedures for compliance with the Act that are the same as those of other Federal agencies, in conformance with the requirement in 41 U.S.C. 705 for government-wide implementing regulations.

## § 1401.105  Does this part apply to me?

This part and, through this part, pertinent portions of the OMB guidance in Subparts A through F of 2 CFR part 182 apply if you are—

(a) A recipient of an assistance award from the Department of the Interior; or

(b) The Department of the Interior awarding official.

The following table (will be incorporated into 2 CFR part 182) shows the subparts that apply to you:

| If you are | *See* subparts |
|---|---|
| (1) A recipient who is not an individual ... | A, C and F. |
| (2) A recipient who is an individual ......... | A, D and F. |

| If you are | *See* subparts |
|---|---|
| (3) A Department of the Interior awarding official. | A, E and F. |

## § 1401.110  What policies and procedures must I follow?

(a) *General.* You must follow the policies and procedures specified in applicable sections of the OMB guidance in Subparts A through F of 2 CFR part 182, as implemented by this part.

(b) In implementing OMB guidance in 2 CFR part 182, this part supplements four sections of the guidance, as shown in the following table. For each of those sections, you must follow the policies and procedures set forth in the OMB guidance, as supplemented by this part.

| Section of OMB guidance | Section in this part where supplemented | What the supplementation clarifies |
|---|---|---|
| (1) 2 CFR 182.225(a) ..................... | § 1401.335 | Whom in the DOI a recipient other than an individual must notify if an employee is convicted for a violation of a criminal drug statute in the workplace. |
| (2) 2 CFR 182.300(b) ..................... | § 1401.401 | Whom in the DOI a recipient who is an individual must notify if he or she is convicted of a criminal drug offense resulting from a violation occurring during the conduct of any award activity. |
| (3) 2 CFR 182.500 .......................... | § 1401.600 | Who in the DOI is authorized to determine that a recipient other than an individual is in violation of the requirements of 2 CFR Part 182, as implemented by this part. |
| (4) 2 CFR 182.505 .......................... | § 1401.605 | Who in the DOI is authorized to determine that a recipient who is an individual is in violation of the requirements of 2 CFR Part 182, as implemented by this part. |

(c) *Sections of the OMB guidance that this part does not supplement.* For any section of OMB guidance in Subparts A through F of 2 CFR Part 182 that is not listed in paragraph (b) of this section, DOI policies and procedures are the same as those in the OMB guidance.

## § 1401.115  Are any of my Federal assistance awards exempt from this part?

This part does not apply to any award if the Director, Office of Acquisition and Property Management (PAM), determines that the application of this part would be inconsistent with the international obligations of the United States or the laws or regulations of a foreign government.

## § 1401.120  Does this part affect the Federal contracts that I receive?

It will affect future contract awards indirectly if you are debarred or sus-

pended for a violation of the requirements of this part, as described in § 1401.610(c). However, this part does not directly apply to procurement contracts. The portion of the Drug-Free Workplace Act of 1988 that applies to Federal procurement contracts is carried out through the Federal Acquisition Regulation in 48 CFR part 23, subpart 23.5.

## Subpart F—Definitions

### § 1401.205  Award.

*Award* means an award of financial assistance by DOI or other Federal agency directly to a recipient.

(a) The term award includes:

(1) A Federal grant or cooperative agreement, in the form of money or property in lieu of money.

(2) A block grant or a grant in an entitlement program, whether or not the

grant is exempted from coverage under the Departmental rules at 43 CFR part 12, subpart C, "Uniform Administrative Requirements for Grants and Cooperative Agreements to State and Local Governments."

(b) The term award does not include:

(1) Technical assistance that provides services instead of money.

(2) Loans.

(3) Loan guarantees.

(4) Interest subsidies.

(5) Insurance.

(6) Direct appropriations.

(7) Veterans' benefits to individuals (*i.e.*, any benefit to veterans, their families, or survivors by virtue of the service of a veteran in the Armed Forces of the United States).

### § 1401.210  Controlled substance.

*Controlled substance* means any controlled substance identified in schedules I through V of the Controlled Substances Act, 21 U.S.C. 812, and as further defined by regulations at 21 CFR 1308.11 through 1308.15.

### § 1401.215  Conviction.

*Conviction* means a finding of guilt (including a plea of nolo contendere) or imposition of sentence, or both, by any judicial body charged with the responsibility to determine violations of the Federal or State criminal drug statutes.

### § 1401.220  Cooperative agreement.

*Cooperative agreement* means an award of financial assistance that, consistent with 31 U.S.C. 6305, is used to enter into the same kind of relationship as a grant (*see* definition of grant in section 1401.250), except that substantial involvement is expected between the Federal agency and the recipient when carrying out the activity contemplated by the award. The term does not include cooperative research and development agreements as defined in 15 U.S.C. 3710a.

### § 1401.225  Criminal drug statute.

*Criminal drug statute* means a Federal or non-Federal criminal statute involving the manufacture, distribution, dispensing, use, or possession of any controlled substance.

### § 1401.230  Debarment.

*Debarment* means an action taken by a Federal agency to prohibit a recipient from participating in Federal Government procurement contracts and covered non-procurement transactions. A recipient so prohibited is debarred, in accordance with the Federal Acquisition Regulation for procurement contracts (48 CFR part 9, subpart 9.4) and 2 CFR part 180.

### § 1401.235  Drug-free workplace.

*Drug-free workplace* means a site for the performance of work done in connection with a specific award at which employees of the recipient are prohibited from engaging in the unlawful manufacture, distribution, dispensing, possession, or use of a controlled substance.

### § 1401.240  Employee.

(a) *Employee* means the employee of a recipient directly engaged in the performance of work under the award, including—

(1) All direct charge employees;

(2) All indirect charge employees, unless their impact or involvement in the performance of work under the award is insignificant to the performance of the award; and

(3) Temporary personnel and consultants who are directly engaged in the performance of work under the award and who are on the recipient's payroll.

(b) This definition does not include workers not on the payroll of the recipient (*e.g.*, volunteers, even if used to meet a matching requirement; consultants or independent contractors not on the payroll; or employees of sub-recipients or subcontractors in covered workplaces).

### § 1401.245  Federal agency or agency.

*Federal agency* or *agency* means any United States executive department, military department, government corporation, government controlled corporation, any other establishment in the executive branch (including the Executive Office of the President), or any independent regulatory agency.

## § 1401.250  Grant.

*Grant* means an award of financial assistance that, consistent with 31 U.S.C. 6304, is used to enter into a relationship whereby—

(a) The principal purpose of which is to transfer a thing of value to the recipient to carry out a public purpose of support or stimulation authorized by a law of the United States, rather than to acquire property or services for the Federal Government's direct benefit or use; and

(b) In which substantial involvement is not expected between the Federal agency and the recipient when carrying out the activity contemplated by the award.

## § 1401.255  Individual.

*Individual* means a natural person.

## § 1401.260  Recipient.

*Recipient* means any individual, corporation, partnership, association, unit of government (except a Federal agency) or legal entity, however organized, that receives an award directly from a Federal agency.

## § 1401.265  State.

*State* means any of the States of the United States, the District of Columbia, the Commonwealth of Puerto Rico, or any territory or possession of the United States.

## § 1401.270  Suspension.

*Suspension* means an action taken by a Federal agency that immediately prohibits a recipient from participating in Federal Government procurement contracts and covered non-procurement transactions for a temporary period, pending completion of an investigation and any judicial or administrative proceedings that may ensue. A recipient so prohibited is suspended, in accordance with the Federal Acquisition Regulation for procurement contracts (48 CFR part 9, subpart 9.4) and 2 CFR part 180. Suspension of a recipient is a distinct and separate action from suspension of an award or suspension of payments under an award.

## Subpart C—Requirements for Recipients Other Than Individuals

### § 1401.300  What must I do to comply with this part?

There are two general requirements if you are a recipient other than an individual.

(a) First, you must make a good faith effort, on a continuing basis, to maintain a drug-free workplace. You must agree to do so as a condition for receiving any award covered by this part. The specific measures that you must take in this regard are described in more detail in subsequent sections of this subpart. Briefly, those measures are to—

(1) Publish a drug-free workplace statement and establish a drug-free awareness program for your employees; and

(2) Take actions concerning employees who are convicted of violating drug statutes in the workplace.

(b) Second, you must identify all known workplaces under your Federal awards.

### § 1401.305  What must I include in my drug-free workplace statement?

You must publish a statement that—

(a) Tells your employees that the unlawful manufacture, distribution, dispensing, possession, or use of a controlled substance is prohibited in your workplace;

(b) Specifies the actions that you will take against employees for violating that prohibition; and

(c) Lets each employee know that, as a condition of employment under any award, he or she:

(1) Will abide by the terms of the statement; and

(2) Must notify you in writing if he or she is convicted for a violation of a criminal drug statute occurring in the workplace and must do so no more than five calendar days after the conviction.

### § 1401.310  To whom must I distribute my drug-free workplace statement?

You must require that a copy of the statement described in § 1401.305 be given to each employee who will be engaged in the performance of any Federal award.

## § 1401.315 What must I include in my drug-free awareness program?

You must establish an ongoing drug-free awareness program to inform employees about—

(a) The dangers of drug abuse in the workplace;

(b) Your policy of maintaining a drug-free workplace;

(c) Any available drug counseling, rehabilitation, and employee assistance programs; and

(d) The penalties that you may impose upon them for drug abuse violations occurring in the workplace.

## § 1401.320 By when must I publish my drug-free workplace statement and establish my drug-free awareness program?

If you are a new recipient that does not already have a policy statement as described in § 1401.305 and an ongoing awareness program as described in § 1401.315, you must publish the statement and establish the program by the time given in the following table:

| If . . . | then you . . . |
|---|---|
| (a) The performance period of the award is less than 30 days | must have the policy statement and program in place as soon as possible, but before the date on which performance is expected to be completed. |
| (b) The performance period of the award is 30 days or more ... | must have the policy statement and program in place within 30 days after award. |
| (c) You believe there are extraordinary circumstances that will require more than 30 days for you to publish the policy statement and establish the awareness program. | may ask the Department of the Interior awarding official to give you more time to do so. The amount of additional time, if any, to be given is at the discretion of the awarding official. |

## § 1401.325 What actions must I take concerning employees who are convicted of drug violations in the workplace?

There are two actions you must take if an employee is convicted of a drug violation in the workplace:

(a) First, you must notify Federal agencies if an employee who is engaged in the performance of an award informs you about a conviction, as required by § 1401.305(c)(2), or you otherwise learn of the conviction. Your notification to the Federal agencies must—

(1) Be in writing;

(2) Include the employee's position title;

(3) Include the identification number(s) of each affected award;

(4) Be sent within ten calendar days after you learn of the conviction; and

(5) Be sent to every Federal agency on whose award the convicted employee was working. It must be sent to every awarding official or his or her official designee, unless the Federal agency has specified a central point for the receipt of the notices.

(b) Second, within 30 calendar days of learning about an employee's conviction, you must either—

(1) Take appropriate personnel action against the employee, up to and including termination, consistent with the requirements of the Rehabilitation Act of 1973, 29 U.S.C. 794, as amended; or

(2) Require the employee to participate satisfactorily in a drug abuse assistance or rehabilitation program approved for these purposes by a Federal, State or local health, law enforcement, or other appropriate agency.

## § 1401.330 How and when must I identify workplaces?

(a) You must identify all known workplaces under each DOI award. A failure to do so is a violation of your drug-free workplace requirements. You may identify the workplaces—

(1) To the DOI official that is making the award, either at the time of application or upon award; or

(2) In documents that you keep on file in your offices during the performance of the award, in which case you must make the information available for inspection upon request by DOI officials or their designated representatives.

(b) Your workplace identification for an award must include the actual address of buildings (or parts of buildings) or other sites where work under the award takes place. Categorical descriptions may be used (e.g., all vehicles of a mass transit authority or State highway department while in operation, State employees in each local unemployment office, performers in concert halls or radio studios).

(c) If you identified workplaces to the DOI awarding official at the time of application or award, as described in paragraph (a)(1) of this section, and any workplace that you identified changes during the performance of the award, you must inform the DOI awarding official.

§ 1401.335 Whom in the DOI does a recipient other than an individual notify about a criminal drug conviction?

The DOI is not designating a central location for the receipt of these reports. Therefore you shall provide this report to every grant officer, or other designee within a bureau or office of the Department on whose grant activity the convicted employee was working.

## Subpart D—Requirements for Recipients Who Are Individuals

§ 1401.400 What must I do to comply with this part if I am an individual recipient?

As a condition of receiving a DOI award, if you are an individual recipient, you must agree that—

(a) You will not engage in the unlawful manufacture, distribution, dispensing, possession, or use of a controlled substance in conducting any activity related to the award; and

(b) If you are convicted of a criminal drug offense resulting from a violation occurring during the conduct of any award activity, you will report the conviction:

(1) In writing.

(2) Within 10 calendar days of the conviction.

(3) To the Department of the Interior awarding official or other designee for each award that you currently have, unless § 1401.401 or the award document designates a central point for the receipt of the notices. When notice is made to a central point, it must in-

clude the identification number(s) of each affected award.

§ 1401.401 Whom in the DOI does a recipient who is an individual notify about a criminal drug conviction?

The DOI is not designating a central location for the receipt of these reports. Therefore you shall provide this report to every grant officer, or other designee within a bureau or office of the Department on whose grant activity the convicted employee was working.

## Subpart E—Responsibilities of Department of Interior Awarding Officials

§ 1401.500 What are my responsibilities as a DOI awarding official?

To obtain a recipient's agreement to comply with applicable requirements in the OMB guidance at 2 CFR part 182, you must include the following term or condition in the award:

*Drug-free workplace.* You, as the recipient, must comply with drug-free workplace requirements in subpart B (or subpart C, if the recipient is an individual) of part 1401, which adopts the government-wide implementation of 2 CFR part 182; sections 5152–5158 of the Drug-Free Workplace Act of 1988, Pub. L. 100–690, Title V, Subtitle D; 41 U.S.C. 701–707.

## Subpart F—Violations of this Part and Consequences

§ 1401.600 How are violations of this part determined for recipients other than individuals?

A recipient other than an individual is in violation of the requirements of this part if the Director, PAM determines, in writing, that—

(a) The recipient has violated the requirements of subpart B of this part; or

(b) The number of convictions of the recipient's employees for violating criminal drug statutes in the workplace is large enough to indicate that the recipient has failed to make a good faith effort to provide a drug-free workplace.

## § 1401.605 How are violations of this part determined for recipients who are individuals?

An individual recipient is in violation of the requirements of this part if the Director, PAM determines, in writing, that—

(a) The recipient has violated the requirements of subpart C of this part; or

(b) The recipient is convicted of a criminal drug offense resulting from a violation occurring during the conduct of any award activity.

## § 1401.610 What actions will the Federal Government take against a recipient determined to have violated this part?

If a recipient is determined to have violated this part, as described in § 1401.600 or § 1401.605, DOI may take one or more of the following actions—

(a) Suspension of payments under the award;

(b) Suspension or termination of the award; and

(c) Suspension or debarment of the recipient under 2 CFR part 180, for a period not to exceed five years.

## § 1401.615 Are there any exceptions to those actions?

The Secretary of the Interior may waive with respect to a particular award, in writing, a suspension of payments under an award, suspension or termination of an award, or suspension or debarment of a recipient if the Secretary of the Interior determines that such a waiver would be in the public interest. This exception authority cannot be delegated to any other official.

## PART 1402—UNIFORM ADMINISTRATIVE REQUIREMENTS, COST PRINCIPLES, AND AUDIT REQUIREMENTS FOR FEDERAL AWARDS

Sec.

AUTHORITY: 5 U.S.C. 301; 38 U.S.C. 501, 2 CFR part 200.

SOURCE: 79 FR 76050, Dec. 19, 2014, unless otherwise noted.

## § 1402.100  Purpose.

The Uniform Administrative Requirements, Cost Principles, and Audit Requirements for Federal Awards set forth in 2 CFR part 200 apply to the Department of the Interior. This part adopts, as the Department of the Interior (DOI) policies and procedures, the Office of Management and Budget's (OMB) Uniform Administrative Requirements, Cost Principles, and Audit Requirements set forth in 2 CFR part 200. The Uniform guidance applies in full except as stated in §§ 1402.102 and 1402.103.

## § 1402.101  To whom does this part apply?

This part, and through it 2 CFR part 200, subparts A through E. applies to any non-Federal entity that applies for, receives, operates, or expends funds from a DOI Federal financial assistance award, cooperative agreement or grant after the effective date of December 26, 2014.

## § 1402.102  Do DOI financial assistance policies include any exceptions to 2 CFR part 200?

This chapter applies to Federally recognized Indian tribal governments, except for those awards made pursuant to the authority of the Indian Self-Determination and Education Assistance Act (P.L. 93–638, 88 Stat. 2204), as amended. However, Sec. 9 of P.L. 93–638 does provide for use of a grant agreement or cooperative agreement when mutually agreed to by the Secretary of the Interior and the tribal organization involved.

## § 1402.103  Does DOI have any other policies or procedures award recipients must follow?

Award recipients must follow bureau/office program specific or technical merit policies and procedures that will be published in the FEDERAL REGISTER, Grants.gov, or bureau Web site.

## PARTS 1403–1499 [RESERVED]

# CHAPTER XV—ENVIRONMENTAL PROTECTION AGENCY

---

# PART 1500—UNIFORM ADMINIS-TRATIVE REQUIREMENTS, COST PRINCIPLES, AND AUDIT RE-QUIREMENTS FOR FEDERAL AWARDS

### Subpart A—Acronyms and Definitions [Reserved]

### Subpart B—General Provisions

Sec.
1500.1 Adoption of 2 CFR part 200.
1500.2 Applicability.
1500.3 Exceptions.
1500.4 Supersession.

### Subpart C—Pre-Federal Award Requirements and Contents of Federal Awards.

1500.5 Fixed Amount Awards.

### Subpart D—Post Federal Award Requirements.

STANDARDS FOR FINANCIAL AND PROGRAM MANAGEMENT

1500.6 Retention requirements for records.
1500.7 Program Income.
1500.8 Revision of budget and program plans.

PROCUREMENT STANDARDS

1500.9 General Procurement Standards.
1500.10 Use of the same architect or engineer during construction.

PERFORMANCE AND FINANCIAL MONITORING AND REPORTING

1500.11 Quality Assurance.

### Subpart E—Disputes.

1500.12 Purpose and scope of this subpart.
1500.13 Definitions.
1500.14 Submission of Appeal.
1500.15 Notice of receipt of Appeal to Affected Entity.
1500.16 Determination of Appeal.
1500.17 Request for review.
1500.18 Notice of receipt of request for review.
1500.19 Determination of request for review.

AUTHORITY: 5 U.S.C. 301, 42 U.S.C. 241, 242b, 243, 246, 1857 *et seq.*, 33 U.S.C. 1251 *et seq.*, 42 U.S.C. 7401 *et seq.*, 42 U.S.C. 6901 *et seq.*, 42 U.S.C. 300f *et seq.*, 7 U.S.C. 136 *et seq.*, 15 U.S.C. 2601 *et seq.*, 42 U.S.C. 9601 *et seq.*, 20 U.S.C. 4011 *et seq.*, and 33 U.S.C. 1401 *et seq.*; 2 CFR part 200.

SOURCE: 79 FR 76050, Dec. 19, 2014, unless otherwise noted.

## Subpart A—Acronyms and Definitions [Reserved]

## Subpart B—General Provisions

### § 1500.1  Adoption of 2 CFR Part 200.

Under the authority listed above the Environmental Protection Agency adopts the Office of Management and Budget (OMB) guidance Uniform Administrative Requirements, Cost Principles, and Audit Requirements for Federal Awards to Non-Federal Entities (subparts A through F of 2 CFR part 200), as supplemented by this part, as the Environmental Protection Agency (EPA) policies and procedures for financial assistance administration. This part satisfies the requirements of 2 CFR 200.110(a) and gives regulatory effect to the OMB guidance as supplemented by this part. EPA also has programmatic regulations located in 40 CFR Chapter 1 Subchapter B.

### § 1500.2  Applicability.

Uniform administrative requirements and cost principles (Subparts A through E of 2 CFR part 200 as supplemented by this part) apply to foreign public entities or foreign organizations, except where EPA determines that the application of these subparts would be inconsistent with the international obligations of the United States or the statute or regulations of a foreign government.

### § 1500.3  Exceptions.

Consistent with 2 CFR 200.102(b):

(a) In the EPA, the Director, Office of Grants and Debarment or designee, is authorized to grant exceptions on a case-by-case basis for non-Federal entities.

(b) The EPA Director or designee is also authorized to approve exceptions, on a class or an individual case basis, to EPA program specific assistance regulations other than those which implement statutory and executive order requirements.

### § 1500.4  Supersession.

Effective December 26, 2014, this part supersedes the following regulations under Title 40 of the Code of Federal Regulations:

(a) 40 CFR part 30, "Uniform Administrative Requirements for Grants and Agreements with Institutions of Higher Education, Hospitals, and other Nonprofit Organizations."

(b) 40 CFR part 31, "Uniform Administrative Requirements for Grants and Cooperative Agreements to State and Local Governments."

## Subpart C—Pre-Federal Award Requirements and Contents of Federal Awards

### § 1500.5 Fixed Amount Awards.

In the EPA, programs awarding fixed amount awards will do so in accordance with guidance issued from the Office of Grants and Debarment. (See 2 CFR 200.201(b)).

## Subpart D—Post Federal Award Requirements.

STANDARDS FOR FINANCIAL AND PROGRAM MANAGEMENT

### § 1500.6 Retention requirements for records.

(a) In the EPA, some programs require longer retention requirements for records by statute.

(b) When there is a difference between the retention requirements for records of the Uniform Administrative Requirements, Cost Principles, and Audit Requirements for Federal Awards (2 CFR 200.333) and the applicable statute, the non-federal entity will follow to the retention requirements for records in the statute.

### § 1500.7 Program Income.

(a) Governmental revenues. Permit fees are governmental revenue and not program income. (See 2 CFR 200.307(c))

(b) Use of Program Income. The default use of program income for EPA awards is addition. The program income shall be used for the purposes and under the conditions of the assistance agreement. (See 2 CFR 200.307(e)(2))

(c) Brownfields Revolving Loan. To continue the mission of the Brownfields Revolving Loan fund, recipients may use grant funding prior to using program income funds generated by the revolving loan fund. Recipients may also keep program income at the end of the assistance agreement as long as they use these funds to continue to operate the revolving loan fund or some other brownfield purpose as outlined in their closeout agreement.

### § 1500.8 Revision of budget and program plans.

Pre-award Costs. EPA award recipients may incur allowable project costs 90 calendar days before the Federal awarding agency makes the Federal award. Expenses more than 90 calendar days pre-award require prior approval of EPA. All costs incurred before EPA makes the award are at the recipient's risk. EPA is under no obligation to reimburse such costs if for any reason the recipient does not receive a Federal award or if the Federal award is less than anticipated and inadequate to cover such costs.

PROCUREMENT STANDARDS

### § 1500.9 General Procurement Standards.

(a) Payment to consultants. EPA will limit its participation in the salary rate (excluding overhead) paid to individual consultants retained by recipients or by a recipient's contractors or subcontractors to the maximum daily rate for level 4 of the Executive Schedule unless a greater amount is authorized by law. (Recipient's may, however, pay consultants more than this amount with non EPA funds.) This limitation applies to consultation services of designated individuals with specialized skills who are paid at a daily or hourly rate. This rate does not include transportation and subsistence costs for travel performed; recipients will pay these in accordance with their normal travel reimbursement practices. Contracts with firms for services which are awarded using the procurement standards in Subpart D of 2 CFR part 200 are not affected by this limitation.

(b) Subawards with firms for services which are awarded using the procurement standards in 2 CFR 200.317 through 2 CFR 200.326 are not affected by this limitation.

## § 1500.10 Use of the same architect or engineer during construction.

(a) If the recipient is satisfied with the qualifications and performance of the architect or engineer who provided any or all of the facilities planning or design services for a waste-water treatment works project and wishes to retain that firm or individual during construction of the project, it may do so without further public notice and evaluation of qualifications, provided:

(1) The recipient received a facilities planning (Step 1) or design grant (Step 2), and selected the architect or engineer in accordance with EPA's procurement regulations in effect when EPA awarded the grant; or

(2) The award official approves non-competitive procurement under 2 CFR 200.320(f) for reasons other than simply using the same individual or firm that provided facilities planning or design services for the project; or

(3) The recipient attests that:

(i) The initial request for proposals clearly stated the possibility that the firm or individual selected could be awarded a subaward for services during construction; and

(ii) The firm or individual was selected for facilities planning or design services in accordance with procedures specified in this section.

(iii) No employee, officer or agent of the recipient, any member of their immediate families, or their partners have financial or other interest in the firm selected for award; and

(iv) None of the recipient's officers, employees or agents solicited or accepted gratuities, favors or anything of monetary value from contractors or other parties to subawards.

(b) However, if the recipient uses the procedures in paragraph (a) of this section to retain an architect or engineer, any Step 3 subawards between the architect or engineer and the grantee must meet all of the other procurement provisions in 2 CFR 200.317 through 200.326.

PERFORMANCE AND FINANCIAL MONITORING AND REPORTING

## § 1500.11 Quality Assurance.

(a) Quality assurance applies to all assistance agreements that involve environmentally related data operations, including environmental data collection, production or use.

(b) Recipients shall develop a written quality assurance system commensurate with the degree of confidence needed for the environmentally related data operations.

(c) If the recipient complies with EPA's quality policy, the system will be presumed to be in compliance with the quality assurance system requirement. The recipient may also comply with the quality assurance system requirement by complying with American National Standard ASQ/ANSI E4:2014: Quality management systems for environmental information and technology programs.

(d) The recipient shall submit the written quality assurance system for EPA review. Upon EPA's written approval, the recipient shall implement the EPA-approved quality assurance system.

(e) EPA Quality Policy is available at: *http://www.epa.gov/quality*.

(f) The standards required in this section are incorporated by reference into this section with the approval of the Director of the Federal Register under 5 U.S.C. 552(a) and 1 CFR part 51. The material is available for inspection at the Environmental Protection Agency's Headquarters Library, Room 3340, EPA West Building, 1301 Constitution Avenue NW., Washington, DC 20004, (202) 566–0556. A copy is also available for inspection at the National Archives and Records Administration (NARA). For information on the availability of this material at NARA, call 202–741–6030, or go to: *http://www.archives.gov/federal_register/code_of_federal_regulations/ibrlocations.html*.

(1) American Society for Quality, 600 North Plankinton Avenue, Milwaukee, WI 53201, 1–800–248–1946, *http://asq.org*.

(i) American National Standard ASQ/ANSI E4:2014: Quality management systems for environmental information and technology programs—Requirements with guidance for use, approved February 4, 2014.

(ii) Reserved.

(2) Reserved.

[79 FR 76050, Dec. 19, 2014, as amended at 80 FR 61088, Oct. 9, 2015]

## Subpart E—Disputes

**§ 1500.12 Purpose and scope of this subpart.**

(a) This section provides the process for the resolution of pre-award and post-award assistance agreement disputes as described in § 1500.13, except for:

(1) Assistance agreement competition-related disputes; and

(2) Any appeal process relating to an award official's determination that an entity is not qualified for award that may be developed pursuant to guidance implementing Section 872 of the Duncan Hunter National Defense Authorization Act for Fiscal Year 2009 (Pub. L. 110–417, as amended).

(b) Pre-award and post-award disagreements between affected entities and EPA related to an assistance agreement should be resolved at the lowest level possible. If an agreement cannot be reached, absent any other applicable statutory or regulatory dispute provisions, affected entities must follow the dispute procedures outlined in this subpart.

(c) Determinations affecting assistance agreements made under other Agency decision-making processes are not subject to review under the procedures in this Subpart or the Agency's procedures for resolving assistance agreement competition-related disputes. These determinations include, but are not limited to:

(1) Decisions on requests for exceptions under § 1500.3;

(2) Bid protest decisions under 2 CFR 200.318(k);

(3) National Environmental Policy Act decisions under 40 CFR part 6;

(4) Policy decisions of the EPA Internal Audit Dispute Resolution Process (formerly known as Audit Resolution Board); and

(5) Suspension and Debarment Decisions under 2 CFR parts 180 and 1532.

**§ 1500.13 Definitions.**

As used in this subpart:

(a) *Action Official (AO)* is the EPA official who authors the Agency Decision to the Affected Entity regarding a pre-award or post-award matter.

(b) *Affected Entity* is an entity that applies for and/or receives Federal financial assistance from EPA including but not limited to: State and local governments, Indian Tribes, Intertribal Consortia, Institutions of Higher Education, Hospitals, and other Non-profit Organizations, and Individuals.

(c) *Agency Decision* is the Agency's initial pre-award or post-award determination. The Agency Decision is sent by the Action Official (AO) to the Affected Entity electronically and informs them of their dispute rights including appealing the Agency Decision to the DDO. Assistance Agreement Appeal (or Appeal) is the letter an Affected Entity submits to the DDO to challenge an Agency Decision.

(d) *Dispute* is a disagreement by an Affected Entity with a specific Agency Decision regarding a pre-award or post-award action.

(e) *Disputes Decision Official (DDO)* is the designated agency official responsible for issuing a decision resolving an Appeal.

(1) The DDO for a Headquarters Assistance Agreement Appeal is the Director of the Grants and Interagency Agreement Management Division in the Office of Grants and Debarment or designee. To help provide for a fair and impartial review, the AO for the challenged Agency Decision may not serve as the Headquarters DDO and the DDO cannot serve as the Review Official for the Appeal decision.

(2) The DDO for a Regional Assistance Agreement Appeal is the official designated by the Regional Administrator to issue the written decision resolving the Appeal. To help provide for a fair and impartial review, the AO for the challenged Agency Decision may not serve as the Regional DDO and the DDO cannot serve as the Review Official for the Appeal decision. Request for Review is the letter an Affected Entity submits to the designated Review Official to challenge the DDO's Appeal decision.

(f) *Review Official* is the EPA official responsible for issuing a decision resolving an Affected Entity's request for review of a DDO's Appeal decision.

(1) For a Headquarters DDO Appeal decision, the Review Official is the Director of the Office of Grants and Debarment or designee.

(2) For a Regional DDO Appeal decision, the Review Official is the Regional Administrator or designee.

## § 1500.14 Submission of Appeal.

An Affected Entity or its authorized representative may dispute an Agency Decision by electronically submitting an Appeal to the DDO identified in the Agency Decision. In order for the DDO to consider the Appeal, it must satisfy the following requirements:

(a) *Timeliness.* The DDO must receive the Appeal no later than 30 calendar days from the date the Agency Decision is electronically sent to the Affected Entity. The DDO will dismiss any Appeal received after the 30-day period unless the DDO grants an extension of time to submit the Appeal. The Affected Entity must submit a written request for extension to the DDO before the expiration of the 30-day period. The DDO may grant a one-time extension of up to 30 calendar days when justified by the situation, which may include the unusual complexity of the Appeal or because of exigent circumstances.

(b) *Method of submission.* The Affected Entity must submit the Appeal electronically via email to the DDO, with a copy to the AO, using the email addresses specified in the Agency Decision within the 30-day period stated in paragraph (a) of this section.

(c) *Contents of Appeal.* The Appeal submitted to the DDO must include:

(1) A copy of the disputed Agency Decision;

(2) A detailed statement of the specific legal and factual grounds for the Appeal, including copies of any supporting documents;

(3) The specific remedy or relief the Affected Entity seeks under the Appeal; and

(4) The name and contact information, including email address, of the Affected Entity's designated point of contact for the Appeal.

## § 1500.15 Notice of receipt of Appeal to Affected Entity.

Within 15 calendar days of receiving the Appeal, the DDO will provide the Affected Entity a written notice, sent electronically, acknowledging receipt of the Appeal.

(a) *Timely Appeals.* If the Appeal was timely submitted, the notice of acknowledgement may identify any additional information or documentation that is required for a thorough consideration of the Appeal. The notice should provide no more than 30 calendar days for the Affected Entity to provide the requested information. If it is not feasible to identify such information or documentation in the notice the DDO may request it at a later point in time prior to Appeal resolution.

(b) *Untimely Appeals.* If the DDO did not receive the Appeal within the required 30-day period, or any extension of it, the DDO will notify the Affected Entity that the Appeal is being dismissed as untimely and the Agency Decision of the AO becomes final. The notification will also identify the Review Official. The dismissal of an untimely Appeal constitutes the final agency action, unless further review is sought in accordance with the requirements of § 1500.16. In limited circumstances, the DDO may, as a matter of discretion, consider an untimely Appeal if doing so would be in the interests of fairness and equity.

## § 1500.16 Determination of Appeal.

(a) *Record on Appeal.* In determining the merits of the Appeal, the DDO will consider the record related to the Agency Decision, any documentation that the Affected Entity submits with its Appeal, any additional documentation submitted by the Affected Entity in response to the DDO's request under § 1500.14(a), and any other information the DDO determines is relevant to the Appeal provided the DDO gives notice of that information to the Affected Entity. The Affected Entity may not on its own initiative submit any additional documents.

(b) *Appeal decision.* The DDO will issue the Appeal decision within 180 calendar days from the date the Appeal is received by the DDO unless a longer period is necessary based on the complexity of the legal, technical and factual issues presented. The DDO will notify the Affected Entity if the expected decision will not be issued within the 180 day period and if feasible will indicate when the decision is expected to be issued. The Appeal decision will also identify the Review Official. The DDO will issue the Appeal decision electronically. The DDO's decision will constitute the final agency action unless the Affected Entity files a timely request for review in accordance with the Request for Review procedures in § 1500.17.

## § 1500.17 Request for review.

An Affected Entity may file an electronic written request for review of the DDO's Appeal decision to the appropriate Review Official within 15 calendar days from the date the Appeal decision is electronically sent to the Affected Entity. The request for review must comply with the following requirements:

(a) *Submission of request for review.* The request must be submitted to the Review Official identified in the Appeal decision as follows:

(1) If a Headquarters DDO issued the Appeal decision, the request must be electronically submitted to the Director of the Office of Grants and Debarment, or designee, at the email address identified in the Appeal decision, with a copy to the DDO.

(2) If the Appeal decision was issued by a DDO located in an agency Regional Office, the request for review must be electronically submitted to the Regional Administrator, or designee, at the email address identified in the Appeal decision, with a copy to the DDO.

(b) *Contents and grounds of request for review.* The request for review must include a copy of the DDO's Appeal decision and provide a detailed statement of the factual and legal grounds warranting reversal or modification of the Appeal decision. The only ground for review of a DDO's Appeal decision is that there was a clear and prejudicial error of law, fact or application of agency policy in deciding the Appeal.

(c) *Conducting the review.* In reviewing the Appeal decision, the Review Official will only consider the information that was part of the Appeal decision unless:

(1) The Affected Entity provides new information in the request for review that was not available to the DDO for the Appeal decision; and

(2) The Review Official determines that the new information is relevant and should be considered in the interests of fairness and equity.

## § 1500.18 Notice of receipt of request for review.

*Timeliness.* The Review Official will provide the Affected Entity electronic written notice acknowledging receipt of the review request within 15 calendar days of receiving the request. The Review Official will further provide a copy of the notice to the DDO.

(a) If the request was submitted in accordance with § 1500.17, the notice of acknowledgment will also advise the Affected Entity that the Review Official expects to issue a decision within 45 calendar days from the date they received the request.

(b) If the request for review was not submitted within the required 15 calendar day period, or does not allege reviewable grounds consistent with § 1500.17, the Review Official will notify the Affected Entity that the request is denied as untimely and/or for failing to state a valid basis for review. In limited circumstances, the Review Official may, as a matter of discretion, consider an untimely review if doing so would be in the interest of fairness and equity.

## § 1500.19 Determination of request for review.

(a) Within 15 calendar days of receiving a copy of the notice acknowledging the receipt of a timely and reviewable Request for Review, the DDO will submit the Appeal record to the Review Official.

(b) The Review Official will issue a final written decision within 45 calendar days of the submission of the request for review unless a longer period is necessary based on the complexity of the legal, technical and factual issues presented.

(1) The Review Official will notify the Affected Entity if the expected decision will not be issued within the 45-day period and if feasible will indicate when the decision is expected to be issued.

(2) The Review Official's decision constitutes the final agency action and

is not subject to further review within the agency.

# PARTS 1501–1531 [RESERVED]

# PART 1532—NONPROCUREMENT DEBARMENT AND SUSPENSION

AUTHORITY: 33 U.S.C. 1251 *et seq.*; 42 U.S.C. 7401 *et seq.*; Sec. 2455, Pub. L. 103–355, 108 Stat. 3327 (31 U.S.C. 6101 note); E.O. 11738 (3 CFR, 1973 Comp., p. 799); E.O. 12549 (3 CFR, 1986 Comp., p. 189); E.O. 12689 (3 CFR, 1989 Comp., p. 235).

SOURCE: 72 FR 2422, Jan. 19, 2007, unless otherwise noted.

### § 1532.10  What does this part do?

This part adopts the Office of Management and Budget (OMB) guidance in subparts A through I of 2 CFR part 180, as supplemented by this part, as the Environmental Protection Agency (EPA) policies and procedures for nonprocurement debarment and suspension. It thereby gives regulatory effect for the EPA to the OMB guidance as supplemented by this part. This part satisfies the requirements in section 3 of Executive Order 12549, "Debarment and Suspension" (3 CFR 1986 Comp., p. 189), Executive Order 12689, "Debarment and Suspension" (3 CFR 1989 Comp., p. 235) and 31 U.S.C. 6101 note (Section 2455, Pub. L. 103-355, 108 Stat. 3327).

### § 1532.20  Does this part apply to me?

This part and, through this part, pertinent portions of the OMB guidance in subparts A through I of 2 CFR part 180 (see table at 2 CFR 180.100(b)) apply to you if you are a—

(a) Participant or principal in a "covered transaction" (see subpart B of 2 CFR part 180 and the definition of "nonprocurement transaction" at 2 CFR 180.970;

(b) Respondent in an EPA suspension or debarment action;

(c) EPA debarment or suspension official; or

(d) EPA grants officer, agreements officer, or other official authorized to enter into any type of nonprocurement transaction that is a covered transaction.

### § 1532.30  What policies and procedures must I follow?

The EPA policies and procedures that you must follow are the policies and procedures specified in each applicable section of the OMB guidance in subparts A through I of 2 CFR part 180, as that section is supplemented by the section in this part with the same section number. The contracts that are covered transactions, for example, are specified by section 220 of the OMB guidance (i.e., 2 CFR 180.220) as supplemented by section 220 in this part (i.e., § 1532.220). For any section of OMB guidance in subparts A through I of 2 CFR 180 that has no corresponding sec-

tion in this part, EPA policies and procedures are those in the OMB guidance.

## Subpart A—General

### § 1532.137  Who in the EPA may grant an exception to let an excluded person participate in a covered transaction?

The EPA Debarring Official has the authority to grant an exception to let an excluded person participate in a covered transaction, as provided in the OMB guidance at 2 CFR 180.135. If the EPA Debarring Official grants an exception, the exception must be in writing and state the reason(s) for deviating from the governmentwide policy in Executive Order 12549.

## Subpart B—Covered Transactions

### § 1532.220  What contracts and subcontracts, in addition to those listed in 2 CFR 180.220, are covered transactions?

In addition to the contracts covered under 2 CFR 180.220(b) of the OMB guidance, this part applies to any contract, regardless of tier, that is awarded by a contractor, subcontractor, supplier, consultant, or its agent or representative in any transaction, if the contract is to be funded or provided by the EPA under a covered nonprocurement transaction and the amount of the contract is expected to equal or exceed $25,000. This extends the coverage of the EPA nonprocurement suspension and debarment requirements to all lower tiers of subcontracts under covered nonprocurement transactions, as permitted under the OMB guidance at 2 CFR 180.220(c) (see optional lower tier coverage in the figure in the appendix to 2 CFR part 180).

## Subpart C—Responsibilities of Participants Regarding Transactions

### § 1532.332  What methods must I use to pass requirements down to participants at lower tiers with whom I intend to do business?

You as a participant must include a term or condition in lower-tier transactions requiring lower-tier participants to comply with subpart C of the

OMB guidance in 2 CFR part 180, as supplemented by this subpart.

## Subpart D—Responsibilities of Federal Agency Officials Regarding Transactions

### §1532.437 What method do I use to communicate to a participant the requirements described in the OMB guidance at 2 CFR 180.435?

To communicate to a participant the requirements described in 2 CFR 180.435 of the OMB guidance, you must include a term or condition in the transaction that requires the participant's compliance with subpart C of 2 CFR part 180, as supplemented by subpart C of this part, and requires the participant to include a similar term or condition in lower-tier covered transactions.

## Subparts E–F [Reserved]

## Subpart G—Suspension

### §1532.765 How may I appeal my EPA suspension?

(a) If the EPA suspending official issues a decision under 2 CFR 180.755 to continue your suspension after you present information in opposition to that suspension under 2 CFR 180.720, you can ask for review of the suspending official's decision in two ways:

(1) You may ask the suspending official to reconsider the decision for material errors of fact or law that you believe will change the outcome of the matter; and/or

(2) You may request the Director, Office of Grants and Debarment (OGD Director), to review the suspending official's decision to continue your suspension within 30 days of your receipt of the suspending official's decision under 2 CFR 180.755 or paragraph (a)(1) of this section. However, the OGD Director can reverse the suspending official's decision only where the OGD Director finds that the decision is based on a clear error of material fact or law, or where the OGD Director finds that the suspending official's decision was arbitrary, capricious, or an abuse of discretion.

(b) A request for review under this section must be in writing; state the specific findings you believe to be in error; and include the reasons or legal bases for your position.

(c) A review under paragraph (a)(2) of this section is solely within the discretion of the OGD Director who may also stay the suspension pending review of the suspending official's decision.

(d) The EPA suspending official and the OGD Director must notify you of their decisions under this section, in writing, using the notice procedures at 2 CFR 180.615 and 180.975.

## Subpart H—Debarment

### §1532.890 How may I appeal my EPA debarment?

(a) If the EPA debarring official issues a decision under 2 CFR 180.870 to debar you after you present information in opposition to a proposed debarment under 2 CFR 180.815, you can ask for review of the debarring official's decision in two ways:

(1) You may ask the debarring official to reconsider the decision for material errors of fact or law that you believe will change the outcome of the matter; and/or

(2) You may request the Director, Office of Grants and Debarment (OGD Director), to review the debarring official's decision to debar you within 30 days of your receipt of the debarring official's decision under 2 CFR 180.870 or paragraph (a)(1) of this section. However, the OGD Director can reverse the debarring official's decision only where the OGD Director finds that the decision is based on a clear error of material fact or law, or where the OGD Director finds that the debarring official's decision was arbitrary, capricious, or an abuse of discretion.

(b) A request for review under this section must be in writing; state the specific findings you believe to be in error; and include the reasons or legal bases for your position.

(c) A review under paragraph (a)(2) of this section is solely within the discretion of the OGD Director who may also stay the debarment pending review of the debarring official's decision.

(d) The EPA debarring official and the OGD Director must notify you of their decisions under this section, in writing, using the notice procedures at 2 CFR 180.615 and 180.975.

## Subpart I—Definitions

### § 1532.995 Principal (EPA supplement to government-wide definition at 2 CFR 180.995).

In addition to those listed in 2 CFR 180.995, other examples of individuals who are principals in EPA covered transactions include:

(a) Principal investigators;

(b) Technical or management consultants;

(c) Individuals performing chemical or scientific analysis or oversight;

(d) Professional service providers such as doctors, lawyers, accountants, engineers, etc.;

(e) Individuals responsible for the inspection, sale, removal, transportation, storage or disposal of solid or hazardous waste or materials;

(f) Individuals whose duties require special licenses;

(g) Individuals that certify, authenticate or authorize billings; and

(h) Individuals that serve in positions of public trust.

## Subpart J—Statutory Disqualification and Reinstatement Under the Clean Air Act and Clean Water Act

### § 1532.1100  What does this subpart do?

This subpart explains how the EPA administers section 306 of the Clean Air Act (CAA) (42 U.S.C. 7606) and section 508 of the Clean Water Act (CWA) (33 U.S.C. 1368), which disqualify persons convicted for certain offenses under those statutes (see § 1532.1105), from eligibility to receive certain contracts, subcontracts, assistance, loans and other benefits (see coverage under the Federal Acquisition Regulation (FAR), 48 CFR part 9, subpart 9.4 and subparts A through I of 2 CFR part 180). It also explains: the procedures for seeking reinstatement of a person's eligibility under the CAA or CWA; the criteria and standards that apply to EPA's decision-making process; and requirements of award officials and others involved in Federal procurement and nonprocurement activities in carrying out their responsibilities under the CAA and CWA.

### § 1532.1105  Does this subpart apply to me?

(a) Portions of this subpart apply to you if you are convicted, or likely to be convicted, of any offense under section 7413(c) of the CAA or section 1319(c) of the CWA.

(b) Portions of this subpart apply to you if you are the EPA debarring official, a Federal procurement or nonprocurement award official, a participant in a Federal procurement or nonprocurement program that is precluded from entering into a covered transaction with a person disqualified under the CAA or CWA, or if you are a Federal department or agency anticipating issuing an exception to a person otherwise disqualified under the CAA or CWA.

### § 1532.1110  How will a CAA or CWA conviction affect my eligibility to participate in Federal contracts, subcontracts, assistance, loans and other benefits?

If you are convicted of any offense described in § 1532.1105, you are automatically disqualified from eligibility to receive any contract, subcontract, assistance, sub-assistance, loan or other nonprocurement benefit or transaction that is prohibited by a Federal department or agency under the Governmentwide debarment and suspension system (i.e. covered transactions under subpart A through I of 2 CFR part 180, or prohibited awards under 48 CFR part 9, subpart 9.4), if you:

(a) Will perform any part of the transaction or award at the facility giving rise to your conviction (called the violating facility); and

(b) You own, lease or supervise the violating facility.

### § 1532.1115  Can the EPA extend a CAA or CWA disqualification to other facilities?

The CAA specifically authorizes the EPA to extend a CAA disqualification to other facilities that are owned or operated by the convicted person. The EPA also has authority under subparts A through I of 2 CFR part 180, or under 48 CFR part 9, subpart 9.4, to take discretionary suspension and debarment actions on the basis of misconduct leading to a CAA or CWA conviction, or for activities that the EPA debarring official believes were designed to improperly circumvent a CAA or CWA disqualification.

### §1532.1120 What is the purpose of CAA or CWA disqualification?

As provided for in Executive Order 11738 (3 CFR, 1973 Comp., p. 799), the purpose of CAA and CWA disqualification is to enforce the Federal Government's policy of undertaking Federal procurement and nonprocurement activities in a manner that improves and enhances environmental quality by promoting effective enforcement of the CAA or CWA.

### §1532.1125 How do award officials and others know if I am disqualified?

If you are convicted under these statutes, the EPA enters your name and address and that of the violating facility into the Excluded Parties List System (EPLS) as soon as possible after the EPA learns of your conviction. In addition, the EPA enters other information describing the nature of your disqualification. Federal award officials and others who administer Federal programs consult the EPLS before entering into or approving procurement and nonprocurement transactions. Anyone may access the EPLS through the internet, currently at *http://www.epls.gov.*

### §1532.1130 How does disqualification under the CAA or CWA differ from a Federal discretionary suspension or debarment action?

(a) CAA and CWA disqualifications are exclusions mandated by statute. In contrast, suspensions and debarments imposed under subparts A through I of 2 CFR part 180 or under 48 CFR part 9, subpart 9.4, are exclusions imposed at the discretion of Federal suspending or debarring officials. This means that if you are convicted of violating the CAA or CWA provisions described under §1532.1105, ordinarily your name and that of the violating facility is placed into the EPLS before you receive a confirmation notice of the listing, or have the opportunity to discuss the disqualification with, or seek reinstatement from, the EPA.

(b) CAA or CWA disqualification applies to both the person convicted of the offense, and to the violating facility during performance of an award or covered transaction under the Federal procurement and nonprocurement suspension and debarment system. It is the EPA's policy to carry out CAA and CWA disqualifications in a manner which integrates the disqualifications into the Governmentwide suspension and debarment system. Whenever the EPA determines that the risk presented to Federal procurement and nonprocurement activities on the basis of the misconduct which gives rise to a person's CAA or CWA conviction exceeds the coverage afforded by mandatory disqualification, the EPA may use its discretionary authority to suspend or debar a person under subparts A through I of 2 CFR part 180, or under 48 CFR part 9, subpart 9.4.

### §1532.1135 Does CAA or CWA disqualification mean that I must remain ineligible?

You must remain ineligible until the EPA debarring official certifies that the condition giving rise to your conviction has been corrected. If you desire to have your disqualification terminated, you must submit a written request for reinstatement to the EPA debarring official and support your request with persuasive documentation. For information about the process for reinstatement see §§1532.1205 and 1532.1300.

### §1532.1140 Can an exception be made to allow me to receive an award even though I may be disqualified?

(a) After consulting with the EPA debarring official, the head of any Federal department or agency (or designee) may exempt any particular award or a class of awards with that department or agency from CAA or CWA disqualification. In the event an exemption is granted, the exemption must:

(1) Be in writing; and

(2) State why the exemption is in the paramount interests of the United States.

(b) In the event an exemption is granted, the exempting department or agency must send a copy of the exemption decision to the EPA debarring official for inclusion in the official record.

### § 1532.1200 How will I know if I am disqualified under the CAA or CWA?

There may be several ways that you learn about your disqualification. You are legally on notice by the statutes that a criminal conviction the CAA or CWA automatically disqualifies you. As a practical matter, you may learn about your disqualification from your defense counsel, a Federal contract or award official, or from someone else who sees your name in the EPLS. As a courtesy, the EPA will attempt to notify you and the owner, lessor or supervisor of the violating facility that your names have been entered into the EPLS. The EPA will inform you of the procedures for seeking reinstatement and give you the name of a person you can contact to discuss your reinstatement request.

### § 1532.1205 What procedures must I follow to have my procurement and nonprocurement eligibility reinstated under the CAA or CWA?

(a) You must submit a written request for reinstatement to the EPA debarring official stating what you believe the conditions were that led to your conviction, and how those conditions have been corrected, relieved or addressed. Your request must include documentation sufficient to support all material assertions you make. The debarring official must determine that all the technical and non-technical causes, conditions and consequences of your actions have been sufficiently addressed so that the Government can confidently conduct future business activities with you, and that your future operations will be conducted in compliance with the CAA and CWA.

(b) You may begin the reinstatement process by having informal discussions with the EPA representative named in your notification of listing. Having informal dialogue with that person will make you aware of the EPA concerns that must be addressed. The EPA representative is not required to negotiate conditions for your reinstatement. However, beginning the reinstatement process with informal dialogue in-

creases the chance of achieving a favorable outcome, and avoids unnecessary delay that may result from an incomplete or inadequate reinstatement request. It may also allow you to resolve your disqualification by reaching an agreement with the EPA debarring official under informal procedures. Using your informal option first does not prevent you from submitting a formal reinstatement request with the debarring official at any time.

### § 1532.1210 Will anyone else provide information to the EPA debarring official concerning my reinstatement request?

If you request reinstatement under § 1532.1205, the EPA debarring official may obtain review and comment on your request by anyone who may have information about, or an official interest in, the matter. For example, the debarring official may consult with the EPA Regional offices, the Department of Justice or other Federal agencies, or state, tribal or local governments. The EPA debarring official will make sure that you have an opportunity to address important allegations or information contained in the administrative record before making a final decision on your request for reinstatement.

### § 1532.1215 What happens if I disagree with the information provided by others to the EPA debarring official on my reinstatement request?

(a) If your reinstatement request is based on factual information (as opposed to a legal matter or discretionary conclusion) that is different from the information provided by others or otherwise contained in the administrative record, the debarring official will decide whether those facts are genuinely in dispute, and material to making a decision. If so, a fact-finding proceeding will be conducted in accordance with 2 CFR 180.830 through 180.840, and the debarring official will consider the findings when making a decision on your reinstatement request.

(b) If the basis for your disagreement with the information contained in the administrative record relates to a legal issue or discretionary conclusion, or is not a genuine dispute over a material fact, you will not have a fact-finding proceeding. However, the debarring official will allow you ample opportunity to support your position for the record and present matters in opposition to your continued disqualification. A summary of any information you provide orally, if not already recorded, should also be submitted to the debarring official in writing to assure that it is preserved for the debarring official's consideration and the administrative record.

§1532.1220 What will the EPA debarring official consider in making a decision on my reinstatement request?

(a) The EPA debarring official will consider all information and arguments contained in the administrative record in support of, or in opposition to, your request for reinstatement, including any findings of material fact.

(b) The debarring official will also consider any mitigating or aggravating factors that may relate to your conviction or the circumstances surrounding it, including any of those factors that appear in 2 CFR 180.860 that may apply to your situation.

(c) Finally, if disqualification applies to a business entity, the debarring official will consider any corporate or business attitude, policies, practices and procedures that contributed to the events leading to conviction, or that may have been implemented since the date of the misconduct or conviction. You can obtain any current policy directives issued by the EPA that apply to CAA or CWA disqualification or reinstatement by contacting the Office of the EPA Debarring Official, U.S. EPA, Office of Grants and Debarment (3901R), 1200 Pennsylvania Avenue, NW., Washington, DC 20460.

§1532.1225 When will the EPA debarring official make a decision on my reinstatement request?

(a) The EPA debarring official will make a decision regarding your reinstatement request under §1532.1205(a), when the administrative record is complete, and he or she can determine whether the condition giving rise to the CAA or CWA conviction has been corrected-usually within 45 days of closing the administrative record.

(b) A reinstatement request is not officially before the debarring official while you are having informal discussions under §1532.1205(b).

§1532.1230 How will the EPA debarring official notify me of the reinstatement decision?

The EPA debarring official will notify you of the reinstatement decision in writing, using the same methods for communicating debarment or suspension action notices under 2 CFR 180.615.

§1532.1300 Can I resolve my eligibility status under terms of an administrative agreement without having to submit a formal reinstatement request?

(a) The EPA debarring official may, at any time, resolve your CAA or CWA eligibility status under the terms of an administrative agreement. Ordinarily, the debarring official will not make an offer to you for reinstatement until after the administrative record for decision is complete, or contains enough information to enable him or her to make an informed decision in the matter.

(b) Any resolution of your eligibility status under the CAA or CWA resulting from an administrative agreement must include a certification that the condition giving rise to the conviction has been corrected.

(c) The EPA debarring official may enter into an administrative agreement to resolve CAA or CWA disqualification issues as part of a comprehensive criminal plea, civil or administrative agreement when it is in the best interest of the United States to do so.

§1532.1305 What are the consequences if I mislead the EPA in seeking reinstatement or fail to comply with my administrative agreement?

(a) Any certification of correction issued by the EPA debarring official whether the certification results from a reinstatement decision under §§1532.1205(a) and 1532.1230, or from an administrative agreement under §§1532.1205(b) and 1532.1300, is conditioned upon the accuracy of the information, representations or assurances made during development of the administrative record.

(b) If the EPA debarring official finds that he or she has certified correction of the condition giving rise to a CAA or CWA conviction or violation on the basis of a false, misleading, incomplete or inaccurate information; or if a person fails to comply with material condition of an administrative agreement, the EPA debarring official may take suspension or debarment action against the person(s) responsible for the misinformation or noncompliance with the agreement as appropriate. If anyone provides false, inaccurate, incomplete or misleading information to EPA in an attempt to obtain reinstatement, the EPA debarring official will refer the matter to the EPA Office of Inspector General for potential criminal or civil action.

§ 1532.1400 How may I appeal a decision denying my request for reinstatement?

(a) If the EPA debarring official denies your request for reinstatement under the CAA or CWA, you can ask for review of the debarring official's decision in two ways:

(1) You may ask the debarring official to reconsider the decision for material errors of fact or law that you believe will change the outcome of the matter; and/ or

(2) You may request the Director, Office of Grants and Debarment (OGD Director), to review the debarring official's denial within 30 days of your receipt of the debarring official's decision under § 1532.1230 or paragraph (a)(1) of this section. However, the OGD Director can reverse the debarring official's decision denying reinstatement only where the OGD Director finds that there is a clear error of material fact or law, or where the OGD Director finds that the debarring official's decision was arbitrary, capricious, or an abuse of discretion.

(b) A request for review under this section must be in writing and state the specific findings you believe to be in error and include the reasons or legal bases for your position.

(c) A review under this section is solely within the discretion of the OGD Director.

(d) The OGD Director must notify you of his or her decision under this section, in writing, using the notice procedures at 2 CFR 180.615 and 180.975.

§ 1532.1500 If I am reinstated, when will my name be removed from the EPLS?

If your eligibility for procurement and nonprocurement participation is restored under the CAA or CWA, whether by decision, appeal, or by administrative agreement, the EPA will remove your name and that of the violating facility from the EPLS, generally within 5 working days of your reinstatement.

§ 1532.1600 What definitions apply specifically to actions under this subpart?

In addition to definitions under subpart A through I of 2 CFR part 180 that apply to this part as a whole, the following two definitions apply specifically to CAA and CWA disqualifications under this subpart:

(a) Person means an individual, corporation, partnership, association, state, municipality, commission, or political subdivision of a state, or any interstate body.

(b) Violating facility means any building, plant, installation, structure, mine, vessel, floating craft, location or site of operations that gives rise to a CAA or CWA conviction, and is a location at which or from which a Federal contract, subcontract, loan, assistance award or other covered transactions may be performed. If a site of operations giving rise to a CAA or CWA conviction contains or includes more than one building, plant, installation, structure, mine, vessel, floating craft, or other operational element, the entire location or site of operation is regarded as the violating facility unless otherwise limited by the EPA.

# PART 1536—REQUIREMENTS FOR DRUG-FREE WORKPLACE (FINANCIAL ASSISTANCE)

Sec.
1536.10 What does this part do?
1536.20 Does this part apply to me?
1536.30 What policies and procedures must I follow?

### Subpart A—Purpose and Coverage
### [Reserved]

## Subpart B—Requirements for Recipients Other Than Individuals

1536.225 Whom in the Environmental Protection Agency does a recipient other than an individual notify about a criminal drug conviction?

## Subpart C—Requirements for Recipients Who Are Individuals

1536.300 Whom in the Environmental Protection Agency does a recipient who is an individual notify about a criminal drug conviction?

## Subpart D—Responsibilities of Agency Awarding Officials

1536.400 What method do I use as an agency awarding official to obtain a recipient's agreement to comply with the OMB guidance?

## Subpart E—Violations of This Part and Consequences

1536.500 Who in the Environmental Protection Agency determines that a recipient other than an individual violated the requirements of this part?
1536.505 Who in the Environmental Protection Agency determines that a recipient who is an individual violated the requirements of this part?

AUTHORITY: 41 U.S.C. 701–707.

SOURCE: 75 FR 80288, Dec. 22, 2010, unless otherwise noted.

### § 1536.10   What does this part do?

This part requires that the award and administration of Environmental Protection Agency grants and cooperative agreements comply with Office of Management and Budget (OMB) guidance implementing the portion of the Drug-Free Workplace Act of 1988 (41 U.S.C. 701–707, as amended, hereafter referred to as "the Act") that applies to grants. It thereby—

(a) Gives regulatory effect to the OMB guidance (Subparts A through F of 2 CFR part 182) for the Environmental Protection Agency's grants and cooperative agreements; and

(b) Establishes Environmental Protection Agency policies and procedures for compliance with the Act that are the same as those of other Federal agencies, in conformance with the requirement in 41 U.S.C. 705 for Governmentwide implementing regulations.

### § 1536.20   Does this part apply to me?

This part and, through this part, pertinent portions of the OMB guidance in Subparts A through F of 2 CFR part 182 (*see* table at 2 CFR 182.115(b)) apply to you if you are a—

(a) Recipient of a Environmental Protection Agency grant or cooperative agreement; or

(b) Environmental Protection Agency awarding official.

### § 1536.30   What policies and procedures must I follow?

(a) *General.* You must follow the policies and procedures specified in applicable sections of the OMB guidance in Subparts A through F of 2 CFR part 182, as implemented by this part.

(b) *Specific sections of OMB guidance that this part supplements.* In implementing the OMB guidance in 2 CFR part 182, this part supplements four sections of the guidance, as shown in the following table. For each of those sections, you must follow the policies and procedures in the OMB guidance, as supplemented by this part.

| Section of OMB guidance | Section in this part where supplemented | What the supplementation clarifies |
|---|---|---|
| (1) 2 CFR 182.225(a) .................................... | § 1536.225 | Whom in the Environmental Protection Agency a recipient other than an individual must notify if an employee is convicted for a violation of a criminal drug statute in the workplace. |
| (2) 2 CFR 182.300(b) .................................... | § 1536.300 | Whom in the Environmental Protection Agency a recipient who is an individual must notify if he or she is convicted of a criminal drug offense resulting from a violation occurring during the conduct of any award activity. |
| (3) 2 CFR 182.500 ......................................... | § 1536.500 | Who in the Environmental Protection Agency is authorized to determine that a recipient other than an individual is in violation of the requirements of 2 CFR part 182, as implemented by this part. |

| Section of OMB guidance | Section in this part where supplemented | What the supplementation clarifies |
|---|---|---|
| (4) 2 CFR 182.505 ......................................... | § 1536.505 | Who in the Environmental Protection Agency is authorized to determine that a recipient who is an individual is in violation of the requirements of 2 CFR part 182, as implemented by this part. |

(c) *Sections of the OMB guidance that this part does not supplement.* For any section of OMB guidance in Subparts A through F of 2 CFR part 182 that is not listed in paragraph (b) of this section, Environmental Protection Agency policies and procedures are the same as those in the OMB guidance.

## Subpart A—Purpose and Coverage [Reserved]

## Subpart B—Requirements for Recipients Other Than Individuals

**§ 1536.225  Whom in the Environmental Protection Agency does a recipient other than an individual notify about a criminal drug conviction?**

A recipient other than an individual that is required under 2 CFR 182.225(a) to notify Federal agencies about an employee's conviction for a criminal drug offense must notify the EPA award official from each Environmental Protection Agency office from which it currently has an award.

## Subpart C—Requirements for Recipients Who Are Individuals

**§ 1536.300  Whom in the Environmental Protection Agency does a recipient who is an individual notify about a criminal drug conviction?**

A recipient who is an individual and is required under 2 CFR 182.300(b) to notify Federal agencies about a conviction for a criminal drug offense must notify the EPA award official from each Environmental Protection Agency office from which it currently has an award.

## Subpart D—Responsibilities of Agency Awarding Officials

**§ 1536.400  What method do I use as an agency awarding official to obtain a recipient's agreement to comply with the OMB guidance?**

To obtain a recipient's agreement to comply with applicable requirements in the OMB guidance at 2 CFR part 182, you must include the following term or condition in the award:

Drug-free workplace. You as the recipient must comply with drug-free workplace requirements in Subpart B (or Subpart C, if the recipient is an individual) of 2 CFR Subtitle B, Chapter XV, Part 1536, which adopts the Governmentwide implementation (2 CFR part 182) of sec. 5152–5158 of the Drug-Free Workplace Act of 1988 (Pub. L. 100–690, Title V, Subtitle D; 41 U.S.C. 701–707).

## Subpart E—Violations of This Part and Consequences

**§ 1536.500  Who in the Environmental Protection Agency determines that a recipient other than an individual violated the requirements of this part?**

The EPA Administrator or designee is the official authorized to make the determination under 2 CFR 182.500.

**§ 1536.505  Who in the Environmental Protection Agency determines that a recipient who is an individual violated the requirements of this part?**

The EPA Administrator or designee is the official authorized to make the determination under 2 CFR 182.505.

## PARTS 1537–1599 [RESERVED]

# CHAPTER XVIII—NATIONAL AERONAUTICS AND SPACE ADMINISTRATION

# PART 1800—UNIFORM ADMINIS-TRATIVE REQUIREMENTS, COST PRINCIPLES, AND AUDIT RE-QUIREMENTS FOR FEDERAL AWARDS

AUTHORITY: 51 U.S.C. 20113 (e), Pub. L. 97–258, 96 Stat. 1003 (31 U.S.C. 6301 *et seq.*), and 2 CFR part 200.

SOURCE: 80 FR 54701, Sept. 11, 2015, unless otherwise noted.

## § 1800.1  Authority.

The National Aeronautics and Space Administration (NASA) awards grants and cooperative agreements under the authority of 51 U.S.C. 20113 (e), the National Aeronautics and Space Act. This part 1800 is issued under the authority of 51 U.S.C. 20113 (e), Pub. L. 97–258, 96 Stat. 1003 (31 U.S.C. 6301 *et seq.*), and 2 CFR part 200.

## § 1800.2  Purpose.

This part adopts the Office of Management and Budget (OMB) guidance in subparts A through F of 2 CFR part 200, as supplemented by this part, as the NASA policies and procedures for uniform administrative requirements, cost principles, and audit requirements for Federal awards. It thereby gives regulatory effect for NASA to the OMB guidance as supplemented by this part.

## § 1800.3  Applicability.

(a) This part establishes policies and procedures for grants and cooperative agreements awarded by NASA to non-Federal entities, commercial firms (when cost sharing is not required), and foreign organizations as allowed by 2 CFR 200.101 Applicability. The policies and procedures that you must follow are those appearing in subparts A through F of 2 CFR part 200 and as supplemented by 2 CFR part 1800. For supplemental guidance, NASA has adopted section numbers that correspond to those in the OMB guidance in 2 CFR part 200.

(b) Throughout this part, the term "award" refers to both "grant" and "cooperative agreement" unless otherwise indicated.

(c) When commercial firms are required to provide cost sharing pursuant to 2 CFR 200.306, Cost Sharing, the regulations at 14 CFR part 1274 apply.

(d)(1) In general, research with foreign organizations will not be conducted through grants or cooperative agreements, but instead will be accomplished on a no-exchange-of-funds basis. In these cases, NASA enters into agreements undertaking projects of international scientific collaboration. NASA policy on performing research with foreign organizations on a no-exchange-of-funds basis is set forth at NASA FAR Supplement (NFS) 1835.016–70. In rare instances, NASA may enter into an international agreement under which funds will be transferred to a foreign recipient.

(2) Grants or cooperative agreements awarded to foreign organizations are made on an exceptional basis only. Awards require the prior approval of

419

the Headquarters Office of International and Interagency Relations and the Headquarters Office of the General Counsel. Requests to issue awards to foreign organizations are to be coordinated through the Office of Procurement, Program Operations Division.

§ 1800.4 Amendment.

This part will be amended by publication of changes in the FEDERAL REGISTER. Changes will be issued as final rules.

§ 1800.5 Publication.

The official site for accessing the NASA Grant and Cooperative Agreement Regulation, including notices, internal guidance, certifications, Grants and Cooperative Agreements Manual and other source information is on the internet at *https://prod.nais.nasa.gov/ pub/pub_library/srba*.

§ 1800.6 Deviations.

(a) A deviation is required for any of the following—

(1) When a prescribed term or condition set forth verbatim in this Part 1800 is modified or omitted.

(2) When a term or condition is set forth in this Part, but not for use verbatim, and the Center substitutes a term or condition which is inconsistent with the intent, principle, and substance of the term or condition.

(3) When a form prescribed by this Part is altered or another form is used in its place.

(4) When limitations, imposed by this regulation upon the use of an award term or condition, form, procedure, or any other award action, are changed.

(5) When a form is created for recipient use that constitutes a "Collection of Information" within the meaning of the Paperwork Reduction Act (44 U.S.C. 35) and its implementation in 5 CFR part 1320.

(b) Requests for authority to deviate from this part shall be submitted, by appropriate NASA staff, to the Office of Procurement, NASA Headquarters, Program Operations Division. Requests, signed by the procurement officer, shall contain the following—

(1) A full description of the deviation, the circumstances in which it will be used, and identification of the requirement from which a deviation is sought;

(2) The rationale for the request, pertinent background information, and the intended effect of the deviation;

(3) The name of the recipient, identification of the award affected, and the dollar value;

(4) A statement as to whether the deviation has been requested previously, and, if so, details of that request; and

(5) A copy of legal counsel's concurrence or comments.

(c) Where it is necessary to obtain an exception from 2 CFR part 200, the Program Operations Division will process all necessary documents. (See 2 CFR 200.102.)

## Subpart A—Acronyms and Definitions

§ 1800.10 Acronyms.

The following acronyms are a supplement to the acronyms set forth at 2 CFR 200.0

ACH  Automated Clearing House
AO  Announcement of Opportunity
CAN  Cooperative Agreement Notice
CFR  Code of Federal Regulations
CNSI  Classified National Security Information
EPA  Environmental Protection Agency
HBCU  Historically Black Colleges and Universities
LEP  Limited English Proficiency
MI  Minority Institutions
MYA  Multiple Year Award
NASA  National Aeronautics and Space Administration
NFS  NASA FAR Supplement
NPR  NASA Procedural Requirements
NRA  NASA Research Announcement
NSSC  NASA Shared Services Center
OMB  Office of Management and Budget
ONR  Office of Naval Research
RPPR  Research Performance Progress Report
STIP  NASA Scientific and Technical Information Program

§ 1800.11 Definitions.

(a) The following definitions are a supplement to the subpart A definitions set forth at 2 CFR 200.2 through 200.99.

*Administrative Grant Officer* means a Federal employee delegated responsibility for award administration; *e.g.*, a NASA Grant Officer who has retained award administration responsibilities, or an Office of Naval Research (ONR) Grant Officer delegated award administration by a NASA Grant Officer.

*Commercial firm* means any corporation, trust or other organization which is organized primarily for profit.

*Effective date* means the date work can begin. This date is the beginning of the period of performance and can be earlier or later than the date of signature on a basic award. Expenditures made prior to the effective date are incurred at the recipient's risk.

*Grant Officer* means a Federal employee responsible for the signing of the grant award documents.

*Historically Black Colleges and Universities (HBCUs)* means institutions determined by the Secretary of Education to meet the requirements of 34 CFR 608.2 and listed therein.

*Minority Institutions (MIs)* means an institution of higher education whose enrollment of a single minority or a combination of minorities (minority meaning American Indian, Alaskan Native, Black (not of Hispanic origin), Hispanic (including persons of Mexican, Puerto Rican, Cuban, and Central or South American origin), Pacific Islander or other ethnic group under-represented in science and engineering.) exceeds 50 percent of the total enrollment.

*NASA Technical Officer* means the NASA official responsible for the programmatic, scientific, and/or technical aspects of assigned applications and awards.

*Original signature* means an authorized signature as follows. If the system (such as NSPIRS) used to submit required documents allows for electronic signatures, then the submission of the documents, by the authorized representative of the organization serves as the required original signature. If, however, a paper copy submission is required, all documents submitted shall be appropriately signed in ink with an actual signature by the authorized representative of the organization.

*Prescription* is defined as the written instructions, to the Grants Officer, for the application of terms and conditions.

*Research misconduct* is defined in 14 CFR 1275.101. NASA policies and procedures regarding Research misconduct

are set out in 14 CFR part 1275, "Investigation of Research Misconduct."

*Summary of research* means a document summarizing the results of the entire project, which includes bibliographies, abstracts, and lists of other media in which the research was discussed. Terms and conditions replace the provisions cited in the former Grant Handbook. They may be modified as noted in each section.

## Subpart B—Pre-Federal Award Requirements and Contents of Federal Awards

### § 1800.208   Certifications and representations.

The certifications and representations for NASA may be found at Appendix A of this part and *https:// prod.nais.nasa.gov/pub/pub_library/srba*.

### § 1800.209   Pre-award costs.

NASA waives the approval requirement for pre-award costs of 90 days or less.

### § 1800.210   Information contained in a Federal award.

NASA waives the requirement for the inclusion of indirect cost rates on any notice of Federal award for commercial firms with no cost sharing requirement. The terms and conditions for NASA may be found at appendix B of this part and *https://prod.nais.nasa.gov/ pub/pub_library/srba*.

[81 FR 74659, Oct. 27, 2016]

## Subpart C—Post Federal Award Requirements

STANDARDS FOR FINANCIAL AND PROGRAM MANAGEMENT

### § 1800.305   Payment.

Payments under awards with commercial firms will be made based on incurred costs. Standard Form 425 is not required. Commercial firms shall not submit invoices more frequently than quarterly. Payments to be made on a more frequent basis require the written approval of the Grant Officer.

## § 1800.306   Cost sharing or matching.

In some cases NASA research projects require cost sharing/match. Where cost sharing/match is required, recipients must secure and document matching funds, to receive the Federal award.

PROPERTY STANDARDS

## § 1800.312   Federally owned and exempt property.

Under the authority of the Childs Act, 31 U.S.C. 6301 to 6308, NASA has determined to vest title to property acquired with Federal funds in the recipient without further obligation to NASA, including reporting requirements.

## § 1800.315   Intangible property.

Due to the substantial involvement on the part of NASA under a cooperative agreement, intellectual property may be produced by Federal employees and NASA contractors tasked to perform NASA assigned activities. Title to intellectual property created under the cooperative agreement by NASA or its contractors will initially vest with the creating party or parties. Certain rights may be exchanged with the recipient.

REMEDIES FOR NONCOMPLIANCE

## § 1800.339   Termination.

NASA reserves the ability to terminate a Federal award in accordance with § 200.338 through § 200.342 and as set forth in 2 CFR 1800.921.

## § 1800.400   Policy guide.

Payment of fee or profit is consistent with an activity whose principal purpose is the acquisition of goods and services for the direct benefit or use of the United States Government, rather than an activity whose principal purpose is assistance. Therefore, the Grants Officer shall use a procurement contract, rather than assistance instrument, in all cases where fee or profit is to be paid to the recipient of the instrument or the instrument is to be used to carry out a program where fee or profit is necessary to achieving program objectives. Grants and Cooperative Agreements shall not provide for the payment of fee or profit to the recipient.

APPENDIX A TO PART 1800—CERTIFICATIONS, ASSURANCES, AND REPRESENTATIONS

These Certifications, Assurances, and Representations apply to all awards and are required at time of application.
A.1 Certifications, Assurances, and Representations.
A.2 Certification of Compliance on Proposal Cover Page.
A.3 Assurance of Compliance with the National Aeronautics and Space Administration Regulations Pursuant to Nondiscrimination in Federally Assisted Programs.
A.4 Certification Regarding Lobbying.
A.5 Certification Regarding Debarment, Suspension, and Other Matters of Responsibility.
A.6 Certifications to Implement Restrictions in Appropriations Acts.

A.1 CERTIFICATIONS, ASSURANCES, AND REPRESENTATIONS

Unless prohibited by statute or codified regulation, NASA will allow recipients to submit certain certifications and representations required by statute, executive order, or regulation on an annual basis, if the recipients have ongoing and continuing relationships with the agency. Annual certifications and representations shall be signed by responsible officials with the authority to ensure recipients' compliance with the pertinent requirements. Recipients determine how annual representations affect their responsibility to obtain required certifications from pass-through entities. All Certification required for an application can be found at *https://prod.nais.nasa.gov/pub/pub_library/srba.*

A.2 CERTIFICATION OF COMPLIANCE ON PROPOSAL COVER PAGE

By submitting the proposal identified in the Cover Sheet/Proposal Summary in response to this Research Announcement, the Authorizing Official of the proposing organization (or the individual Proposer if there is no proposing organization) as identified below—
(a) Certifies that the statements made in this proposal are true and complete to the best of his/her knowledge;
(b) Agrees to accept the obligation to comply with NASA award terms and conditions if an award is made as a result of this proposal; and
(c) Confirms compliance with all applicable terms and conditions, rules, and stipulations set forth in the Certifications, Assurances, and Representations contained in this NRA

or CAN. Willful inclusion of false information in this proposal and/or its supporting documents, or in reports required under an ensuing award, is a criminal offense (U.S. Code, Title 18, Section 1001).

A.3 ASSURANCE OF COMPLIANCE WITH THE NATIONAL AERONAUTICS AND SPACE ADMINISTRATION REGULATIONS PURSUANT TO NON-DISCRIMINATION IN FEDERALLY ASSISTED PROGRAMS

The Organization, corporation, firm, or other organization on whose behalf this assurance is made, hereinafter called "Applicant"

"HEREBY acknowledges and agrees that it must comply (and require any subawardees, contractors, successors, transferees, and assignees to comply) with applicable provisions of National laws and policies prohibiting discrimination, including but not limited to—

1. Title VI of the Civil Rights Act of 1964, as amended, which prohibits recipients of Federal financial assistance from discriminating on the basis of race, color, or national origin (42 U.S.C. 2000d *et seq.*), as implemented by NASA Title VI regulations, 14 CFR part 1250. As clarified by Executive Order 13166, Improving Access to Services for Persons with Limited English Proficiency, and resulting agency guidance, national origin discrimination includes discrimination on the basis of limited English proficiency (LEP). To ensure compliance with Title VI, the Applicant must take reasonable steps to ensure that LEP persons have meaningful access to its programs in accordance with NASA Title VI LEP Guidance to Grant (Award) Recipients (68 FR 70039). Meaningful access may entail providing language assistance services, including oral and written translation, where necessary. The Applicant is encouraged to consider the need for language services for LEP persons served or encountered both in developing budgets and in conducting programs and activities. Assistance and information regarding LEP obligations may be found at *http://www.lep.gov*.

2. Title IX of the Education Amendments of 1972, as amended, which prohibits discrimination on the basis of sex in education programs or activities (20 U.S.C. 1681 *et seq.*) as implemented by NASA Title IX regulations, 14 CFR part 1253. If the Applicant is an educational institution—

a. The Applicant is required to designate at least one employee to serve as its Title IX coordinator (14 CFR 1253.135(a)).

b. The Applicant is required to notify all of its program beneficiaries of the name, office, address, and telephone number of the employee(s) designated to serve as the Title IX coordinators (14 CFR 1253.135(a)).

c. The Applicant is required to publish internal grievance procedures to promptly and equitably resolve complaints alleging illegal discrimination in its programs or activities (14 CFR 1253.135(b)).

d. The Applicant is required to take specific steps to regularly and consistently notify program beneficiaries that The Applicant does not discriminate in the operation of its programs and activities (14 CFR 1253.140).

3. Section 504 of the Rehabilitation Act of 1973, as amended, which prohibits The Applicant from discriminating on the basis of disability (29 U.S.C. 794) as implemented by NASA Section 504 regulations, 14 CFR part 1251.

a. The Applicant is required to designate at least one employee to serve as its Section 504 coordinator (14 CFR 1251.106(a)).

b. The Applicant is required to notify all its program beneficiaries of the name, office, address, and telephone number of the employee(s) designated to serve as the Section 504 coordinator (14 CFR 1251.106(a)).

c. The Applicant is required to publish internal grievance procedures to promptly and equitably resolve complaints alleging illegal discrimination in its programs or activities (14 CFR 1251.106(b)).

d. The Applicant is required to take specific steps to regularly and consistently notify program beneficiaries that the Applicant does not discriminate in the operation of its programs and activities (14 CFR 1251.107).

4. The Age Discrimination Act of 1975, as amended, which prohibits the Applicant from discriminating on the basis of age (42 U.S.C. 6101 *et seq.*) as implemented by NASA Age Discrimination Act regulations, 14 CFR part 1252.

The Applicant also acknowledges and agrees that it must cooperate with any compliance review or complaint investigation conducted by NASA and comply (and require any subawardees, contractors, successors, transferees, and assignees to comply) with applicable terms and conditions governing NASA access to records, accounts, documents, information, facilities, and staff. The Applicant must keep such records and submit to the responsible NASA official or designee timely, complete, and accurate compliance reports at such times, and in such form and containing such information, as the responsible NASA official or his designee may determine to be necessary to ascertain whether the Applicant has complied or is complying with relevant obligations and must immediately take any measure determined necessary to effectuate this agreement. The Applicant must comply with all other reporting, data collection, and evaluation requirements, as prescribed by law or detailed in program guidance.

The United States shall have the right to seek judicial enforcement of these obligations. This assurance is binding on the Applicant, its successors, transferees, and assignees, and the person or persons whose signatures appear below are authorized to sign on behalf of the Applicant.''

Under penalty of perjury, the undersigned officials certify that they have read and understand their obligations as herein described, that the information submitted in conjunction with this document is accurate and complete, and that the recipient is in compliance with the nondiscrimination requirements set out above.

[End of Assurance]

A.4 CERTIFICATION REGARDING LOBBYING

No Federal appropriated funds have been paid or will be paid, by or on behalf of the undersigned, to any person for influencing or attempting to influence an officer or employee of any agency, a Member of Congress, an officer or employee of Congress, or an employee of a Member of Congress in connection with the awarding of any Federal contract, the making of any Federal award, the making of any Federal loan, the entering into of any cooperative agreement, and the extension, continuation, renewal, amendment, or modification of any Federal contract, grant, loan, or cooperative agreement.

If any funds other than Federal appropriated funds have been paid or will be paid to any person for influencing or attempting to influence an officer or employee of any agency, a Member of Congress, an officer or employee of Congress, or an employee of a Member of Congress in connection with this Federal contract, grant, loan, or cooperative agreement, the undersigned shall complete and submit Standard Form-LLL, "Disclosure Form to Report Lobbying," in accordance with its instructions. The undersigned shall require that the language of this certification be included in the award documents for all subawards at all tiers (including subcontracts, subgrants, and contracts under grants, loans, and cooperative agreements) and that all subrecipients shall certify and disclose accordingly. This certification is a material representation of fact upon which reliance was placed when this transaction was made or entered into. Submission of this certification is a prerequisite for making or entering into this transaction imposed by section 1352, title 31, U.S. Code. Any person who fails to file the required certification shall be subject to a civil penalty of not less than $10,000, and not more than $100,000 for each such failure.

[End of Certification]

A.5 CERTIFICATION REGARDING DEBARMENT, SUSPENSION, AND OTHER MATTERS OF RESPONSIBILITY

Pursuant to Executive Order 12549, Debarment and Suspension, and implemented at 2 CFR parts 180 and 1880—

(1) The prospective primary participant certifies to the best of its knowledge and belief, that it and its principals—

(a) Are not presently debarred, suspended, proposed for debarment, declared ineligible, or voluntarily excluded from covered transactions by any Federal department or agency;

(b) Have not within a three-year period preceding this proposal been convicted of or had a civil judgment rendered against them for commission of fraud or a criminal offense in connection with obtaining, attempting to obtain, or performing a public (Federal, State, or local) transaction or contract under a public transaction; violation of Federal or State antitrust statues or commission of embezzlement theft, forgery, bribery, falsification or destruction of records, making false statements, or receiving stolen property;

(c) Are not presently indicted for or otherwise criminally or civilly charged by a governmental entity (Federal, State or local) with commission of any of the offenses enumerated in paragraph (1)(b) of this certification; and

(d) Have not within a three-year period preceding this application/proposal had one or more public transactions (Federal, State, or local) terminated for cause or default.

(2) Where the prospective primary participant is unable to certify to any of the statements in this certification, such prospective participant shall attach an explanation to this proposal.

[End of Certification]

A.6 CERTIFICATIONS TO IMPLEMENT RESTRICTIONS IN APPROPRIATIONS ACTS

The text of these certifications is found at *https://prod.nais.nasa.gov/pub/pub_library/srba.*

APPENDIX B TO PART 1800—TERMS AND CONDITIONS

#### 1800.900  TERMS AND CONDITIONS

(a) Unless otherwise noted in the prescriptive language awards with Non-Federal entities shall incorporate by reference the terms and conditions set forth in sections §§ 1800.901 through 1800.918 of this appendix. Any of the terms and conditions in sections §§ 1800.919 through 1800.928 shall be referenced in full text. The program office may need to include information required for certain terms and conditions to allow for additional information, or permit minor modifications. For example, the Grant Officer may substitute appropriate sections of § 1800.902, Technical Publications and Reports," with reporting requirements specified by the program office.

(b) Additional special terms and conditions may be included to the extent they are required and are not inconsistent with the other terms and conditions in this Appendix B. A deviation in accordance with 2 CFR 1800.6 is required before a new term and condition inconsistent with the standard terms and conditions can be included in an award.

(c) Whenever the word "award" appears in this Appendix, it shall be deemed to include, both grants and cooperative agreements, as appropriate.

(d) Terms and conditions for research awards awarded to foreign organizations, when approved by Headquarters, will be provided in full text. Referenced handbooks, statutes, or other regulations, which the re-

cipient may not have access to, must be made available when requested by the foreign organization.

(e) Awards issued by NASA to commercial organizations where cost sharing is not required shall incorporate the terms and conditions set forth in this appendix.

(f) Terms and conditions do not supersede state laws.

1800.901  COMPLIANCE WITH OMB GUIDANCE ON UNIFORM ADMINISTRATIVE REQUIREMENTS, COST PRINCIPLES, AND AUDIT REQUIREMENTS FOR FEDERAL AWARDS

Prescription—This term and condition implements 2 CFR part 200, Uniform Administrative Requirements, Cost Principles, and Audit Requirements for Federal awards herein referred to as the "OMB Uniform Guidance." The Grant Officer shall use this term and condition in all awards with recipients that are other than commercial firms. The Grant Office shall use Alternate 1 for awards with commercial firms.

*Compliance With OMB Guidance*

This award is subject to the requirements set forth in 2 CFR part 200, Uniform Administrative Requirements, Cost Principles, and Audit Requirements for Federal awards as adopted by NASA in Part 1800 of Title 2 of the Code of Federal Regulations. Specific terms and conditions set forth in this award document are provided to supplement and clarify, not replace, the OMB Uniform Guidance, except in circumstances where a waiver from OMB Uniform Guidance requirements has been obtained by NASA.

(End of Term and Condition)

*Alternate 1*

(a) With the exception of Subpart E and F, this award is subject to the requirements set forth in OMB Guidance on Uniform Administrative Requirements, Cost Principles, and Audit Requirements for Federal awards at 2 CFR Chapter 1, and Chapter II Part 200 as adopted by NASA in Part 1800 of Title 2 of the Code of Federal Regulations. Specific terms and conditions set forth in this award document are provided to supplement and clarify, not replace, the Guidance, except in circumstances where a waiver from the OMB Uniform Guidance requirements has been obtained by NASA.

(b) In lieu of Subparts E and F of 2 CFR part 200, the expenditure of Government funds by the recipient and the allowability of costs recognized as a resource contribution by the recipient shall be governed by the FAR cost principles implemented by FAR Parts 30, 31, and 48 CFR part 99. (If the recipient is a consortium which includes noncommercial firm members, cost allowability for those members will be determined by the

OMB Uniform Guidance at Subpart E and F of 2 CFR 200.)

(End of Term and Condition)

1800.902  TECHNICAL PUBLICATIONS AND REPORTS

Prescription—The Grant Officer shall include on a "substantially as" basis in all awards. The requirements set forth under this term and condition may be modified by the Grant Officer based on specific report needs for the award.

*Technical Publications and Reports*

(a) NASA encourages the widest practicable dissemination of research results at any time during the course of the investigation.

(1) All information disseminated as a result of the award shall contain a statement which acknowledges NASA's support and identifies the award by number (*e.g.*, "the material is based upon work supported by NASA under award No(s) XXXXX (as shown on the award notice).)

(2) Except for articles or papers published in scientific, technical, or professional journals, the exposition of results from NASA supported research should also include the following disclaimer— "Any opinions, findings, and conclusions or recommendations expressed in this material are those of the author(s) and do not necessarily reflect the views of the National Aeronautics and Space Administration."

(3) As a courtesy, any release of a NASA photograph or illustration should list NASA first on the credit line followed by the name of the Principal Investigator's Institution. As an example— "Photograph or illustration, figure, etc. courtesy of NASA or NASA Center managing the mission or program and the Principal Investigator's institution."

(4) For research and research-related awards, see additional reporting requirements at 1800.930 Access to Research Results.

(b) Reports shall be in the English language, informal in nature, and ordinarily not exceed three pages (not counting bibliographies, abstracts, and lists of other media). The recipient shall submit the following reports—

(1) A Progress Report for all but the final year of the award. Each report is due 60 days before the anniversary date of the award and shall briefly describe what was accomplished during the reporting period. A term or condition specifying more frequent reporting may be required.

(2) A Summary of Research or Educational Activity Report is due within 90 days after the end date for the period of performance, regardless of whether or not support is continued under another award. This report shall be a comprehensive summary of signifi-

cant accomplishments during the duration of the award.

(c) Progress Reports, Summaries of Research, and Educational Activity Reports shall include the following on the first page:

(1) Title of the award.

(2) Type of report.

(3) Name of the principal investigator.

(4) Period covered by the report.

(5) Name and address of the recipient's institution.

(6) Award number.

(d) Progress Reports, Summaries of Research, and Educational Activity Reports shall be distributed as follows:

(1) The original report, in both hard copy and electronic format, to the Technical Officer.

(2) One copy to the NASA Technical Officer and New Technology Officer with a notice to the Grant Officer, that a report was sent.

(End of Term and Condition)

1800.903  EXTENSIONS

Prescription—The Grant Officer shall include this term and condition in all awards except awards with commercial firms. If included, minor modifications to the term and condition, such as the time frame for cost extensions, is permissible.

*Extensions*

(a) It is NASA's policy to provide maximum possible continuity in funding award-supported research and educational activities, therefore, awards may be extended for additional periods of time when necessary to complete work that was part of the original award. NASA generally only approves such extensions within funds already made available. Any extension that would require additional funding must be supported by a proposal submitted at least three months in advance of the end date of the period of performance.

(b) Recipients may extend the expiration date of an award if additional time beyond the established end date is required to assure adequate completion of the original scope of work within the funds already made available. For this purpose, the recipient may make a one-time no-cost extension, not to exceed 12 months, prior to the established expiration date. Written notification of such an extension, with the supporting reasons, must be received by the NASA Grant Officer at least ten days prior to the expiration of the award. A copy of the extension must also be forwarded to cognizant Office of Naval Research (ONR) office, if administration has been delegated to ONR. NASA reserves the right to disapprove the extension if the requirements set forth at §200.308(d) (2) are not met.

(c) Requests for approval for all other no-cost extensions must be submitted in writing to the NASA Grant Officer. A copy of this request must also be forwarded to cognizant Office of Naval Research (ONR) office, if administration has been delegated to ONR.

(End of Term and Condition)

1800.904 TERMINATION AND ENFORCEMENT

Prescription—This term and condition implements § 200.338 through § 200.342. The Grant Officer shall include this term and condition in all awards.

*Termination and Enforcement*

Termination and enforcement conditions of this award are specified in § 200.338 through § 200.342.

(End of Term and Condition)

1800.905 CHANGE IN PRINCIPAL INVESTIGATOR OR SCOPE

Prescription—The Grant Officer shall include this term and condition in all awards.

*Change in Principal Investigator or Scope*

(a) The recipient shall obtain the approval of the NASA Grant Officer for a change of the Principal Investigator, or for a significant absence of the Principal Investigator from the project, defined as a three month absence from the program or a 25 percent reduction in time devoted to the project. Significantly reduced availability of the services of the Principal Investigator(s) named in the award instrument could be grounds for termination, unless alternative arrangements are made and approved in writing by the Grant Officer.

(b) Prior written approval is required from NASA if there is to be a significant change in the objective or scope of the project.

(End of Term and Condition)

1800.906 FINANCIAL MANAGEMENT

Prescription—This term and condition implements § 200.302. The Grant Officer shall include this term and condition in all awards except when the recipient is a commercial firm.

*Financial Management*

(a) Advance payments will be made by the Financial Management Office of the NASA Center assigned financial cognizance of the award, using the Department of Health and Human Services' Payment Management System (DHHS/PMS), in accordance with procedures provided to the recipient. The recipient shall submit a Federal Financial Report (SF 425), and, when applicable, a Federal Financial Report Attachment (SF 425A) electronically to DHHS/PMS within 30 days following the end of each Federal fiscal quarter

(*i.e.*, December 31, March 31, June 30, and September 30).

(b) In addition, the recipient shall submit a final SF 425 in electronic or paper form to NASA within 90 calendar days after the end date of the period of performance. The final SF 425 shall pertain only to the completed award and shall include total disbursements from inception through completion. The report shall be marked "Final." The final SF 425 shall be submitted to NASA per the Grants and Cooperative Agreement Manual (GCAM) Exhibit E, Required Publications and Reports, A copy of the GCAM is located at *https://prod.nais.nasa.gov/pub/pub_library/srba.*

(c) By signing any report delivered under the award, the authorizing official for the recipient certifies to the best of his or her knowledge and belief that the report is true, complete, and accurate, and the expenditures, disbursements and cash receipts are for the purposes and intent set forth in the award documents. The authorizing official by signing the report also certified he or she is aware that any false, fictitious, or fraudulent information, or the omission of any material fact, may subject him or her to criminal, civil or administrative penalties for fraud, false statements, false claims or otherwise. (U.S. Code, Title 18, Section 1001 and Title 31 Section 3729–3733 and 3801–3812.)

(d) Unless otherwise directed by the Grant Officer, any unexpended balance of funds which remains at the end of any funding period, except the final funding period of the award, may be carried over to the next funding period, and may be used to defray costs of any funding period of the award. This includes allowing the carryover of funds to the second and subsequent years of a multiple year award. Unexpended funds from one award may not be carried over to a new or different award. This term and condition also applies to subawardees/subcontractors performing substantive work under the award. NASA reserves the right to remove unexpended balances from awards when insufficient efforts have been made by the awardee to liquidate funding balances in a timely fashion.

(End of Term and Condition)

1800.907 EQUIPMENT AND OTHER PROPERTY

Prescription—The Grant Officer shall include this term and condition in all awards except when recipient is a commercial firm.

*Equipment and Other Property*

(a) NASA permits acquisition of special purpose and general purpose equipment specifically required for use exclusively for research activities.

(1) Acquisition of special purpose or general purpose equipment costing in excess of

$5,000 (unless a lower threshold has been established by the recipient) and not included in the approved proposal budget, requires the prior approval of the NASA Grant Officer. Requests to the Grant Officer for the acquisition of equipment shall be supported by written documentation setting forth the description, purpose, and acquisition value of the equipment, and including a written certification that the equipment will be used exclusively for research, activities. (A change in the model number of a prior approved piece of equipment does not require resubmission for that item.) Research awards are exempt from the prior approval requirement.

(2) Special purpose and general purpose equipment costing in excess of $5,000 (unless a lower threshold has been established by the recipient) acquired by the recipient under an award for the purpose of research shall be titled to the recipient as "exempt" without further obligation to NASA, including reporting of the equipment, in accordance with § 200.312(c) and § 1800.312. Special purpose or general purpose equipment costing in excess of $5,000 (unless a lower threshold has been established by the recipient) acquired by the recipient under an award for non-research work shall be titled to the recipient in accordance with § 200.313.

(3) Special purpose or general purpose equipment acquired by the recipient with award funds, valued under $5,000 (unless a lower threshold is established by the recipient) are classified as "supplies," do not require the prior approval of the NASA Grant Officer, shall vest in the recipient and will be titled to the recipient in accordance with § 200.314.

(4) Award funds may be expended for the acquisition of land or interests therein or for the acquisition and construction of facilities only under a facilities award.

(b) As required the recipient shall submit an annual Inventory Report, to be received no later than October 15 of each year, which lists all reportable non-exempt equipment and/or Federally owned property in its custody as of September 30. Negative responses for annual Inventory Reports (when there is no reportable equipment) are not required. A Final Inventory Report of Federally Owned Property, including equipment where title was taken by the Government, will be submitted by the recipient no later than 60 days after the end date of the period of performance. Negative responses for Final Inventory Reports are required.

(1) All reports will include the information listed in paragraph (d)(1) of § 200.313, Equipment. No specific report form or format is required, provided that all necessary information is provided.

(2) The original of each report shall be submitted to the Deputy Chief Financial Officer (Finance). Copies shall be furnished to the Center Industrial Property Officer and to ONR.

(End of Term and Condition)

1800.908   PATENT RIGHTS

Prescription—The Grant Officer shall include this term and condition in all awards, except awards with large businesses.

*Patent Rights*

As stated at § 200.315(c), this award is subject to the provisions of 37 CFR 401.3(a) which requires use of the standard clause set out at 37 CFR 401.14 "Patent Rights (Small Business Firms and Nonprofit Organizations)" and the following:

(a) Definitions.

The words "contract" or "Contractor" are used in 37 CFR 401.14. Those words shall be replaced by the words "award" or "recipient," respectively.

The term "Federal Agency," "agency," or "funding Federal agency" is used 37 CFR 401.14, the term shall be replaced by the term "NASA."

The term "award," as used in this term and condition, means any actual or proposed grant, cooperative agreement, understanding, or other arrangement, and includes any assignment, substitution of parties, subaward, or subcontract executed or entered into thereunder.

(b) The below items are added to the end of paragraph (c) of 37 CFR 401.14 are as follows:

"(5) The recipient may use whatever format is convenient to disclose subject invention required in subparagraph (c)(1). NASA prefers that the recipient use either the electronic or paper version of NASA Form 1679, Disclosure of Invention and New Technology (Including Software), to disclose subject inventions. Both the electronic and paper version of the NASA Form 1679 may be accessed at the electronic New Technology Reporting Web site *https://invention.nasa.gov.*

"(6) In addition to the above, the recipient shall provide the New Technology Representative, as designated under term and condition "Designation of New Technology Representative and Patent Representative" at 1800.924 of this award, the following:

(i) A yearly interim new technology summary report listing any subject inventions required to be disclosed during the preceding year (or a statement certifying there were none).

(ii) A final new technology summary report listing all subject inventions (or a statement certifying there were none) for the entire award period; which report shall be submitted within 90 days after the end date for the period of performance within the designated system noted within the award document."

(c) The below item is added to the end of paragraph (f)(1) of 37 CFR 401.14 "Patent Rights" as follows:

"(iii) The recipient shall through employee agreements or other suitable recipient policy, require that its employees "will assign and do hereby assign" to the recipient all right, title and interest in any subject invention under this award."

(d) The term "subcontract" in paragraph (g) of 37 CFR 401.14 shall include purchase orders.

(f) The following constitutes paragraph "(1)" of in 37 CFR 404.14—

"(1) Communications. A copy of all submissions or requests required 37 CFR 401.14, plus a copy of any reports, manuscripts, publications or similar material bearing on patent matters, shall be sent to the Center Patent Counsel and the NASA Grant Officer in addition to any other submission requirements in the award terms and conditions (e.g., as specified in this term and condition and in term and condition 1800.924 "Designation of New Technology Representative and Patent Representative"). If any reports contain information describing a "subject invention" for which the recipient has elected or may elect to retain title, NASA will use reasonable efforts to delay public release by NASA or publication by NASA in a NASA technical series until an application filing date has been established, provided that the recipient identify the information and the "subject invention" to which it relates at the time of submittal. If required by the Patent Representative or requested by the New Technology Representative, as designated under 1800.924 "Designation of New Technology Representative and Patent Representative," the recipient shall provide the filing date, serial number and title, a copy of the patent application, and a patent number and issue date for any "subject invention" in any country in which the recipient has applied for patents. Additionally, the NASA shall have an irrevocable power to inspect and make copies of the patent application file, when a Federal Government employee is a co-inventor."

(g) NASA Inventions. NASA will use reasonable efforts to report inventions made by NASA employees as a consequence of, or which bear a direct relation to, the performance of specified NASA activities under this agreement and, upon timely request, will use reasonable efforts to grant the recipient an exclusive, or partially exclusive, revocable, royalty-bearing license, subject to the retention of a royalty-free right of the Government to practice or have practiced the invention by or on behalf of the Government.

(h) The recipient agrees, subject to (g)(1) below, that the Government may duplicate and disclose subject invention disclosures and all other reports and papers furnished or required to be furnished pursuant to this term and condition.

(1) Publishing information concerning an invention before a patent application is filed on a subject invention may create a bar to a valid patent. To avoid this bar, agencies may withhold information from the public that discloses any invention in which the Government owns or may own a right, title, or interest (including a nonexclusive license) (see 35 U.S.C. 205 and 37 CFR part 401). Agencies may only withhold information concerning inventions for a reasonable time in order for a patent application to be filed. Once filed in any patent office, agencies are not required to release copies of any document that is a part of a patent application for those subject inventions.

(2) In the event NASA contractors are tasked to perform work in support of specified activities under a cooperative agreement and inventions are made by contractor employees, the contractor will normally retain title to its employee inventions in accordance with 35 U.S.C. 202, 14 CFR part 1245, and/or Executive Order 12591. In the event the contractor decides not to pursue rights to title in any such invention and NASA obtains or retains title to such inventions, NASA will use reasonable efforts to report such inventions and, upon timely request, will use reasonable efforts to grant the recipient an exclusive, or partially exclusive, revocable, royalty-bearing license, subject to the retention of a royalty-free right of the Government to practice or have practiced the invention by or on behalf of the Government.

(End of Term and Condition)

1800.909   RIGHTS IN DATA

Prescription—The Grant Officer may revise the language under this term and condition to modify each party's rights based on the particular circumstances of the program and/or the recipient's need to protect specific proprietary information. Any modification to the standard language set forth under the term and condition requires the concurrence of the Center's Patent Counsel and that the term and condition be printed in full text.

*Rights in Data*

(a) "Data," as used in this term and condition, means recorded information, regardless of form, the media on which it may be recorded, or the method of recording. The term includes, but is not limited to, data of a scientific or technical nature, and any copyrightable work, including computer software and documentation thereof.

(b) As to data first produced by recipient in carrying out recipient's responsibilities under this award in which the recipient asserts copyright, or data for which copyright ownership was acquired under the grant, the recipient grants to the Federal Government (Government), a royalty-free, nonexclusive and irrevocable license to use, reproduce, distribute (including distribution by transmission) to the public, perform publicly, prepare derivative works, and display publicly, data in whole or in part and in any manner for Federal purposes and to have or permit others to do so for Federal purposes only.

(c) In order that the Government may exercise its license rights in data, the Government, upon request to the recipient, shall have the right to review and/or obtain delivery of data resulting from the performance of work under this award or acquired under this award, and authorize others to receive such data to use for Federal purposes.

(d) Cost Sharing and/or Matching Efforts. When the recipient cost shares with the Government on the effort, the following paragraph also applies—

"(1) In the event data first produced by the recipient in carrying out recipient's responsibilities under this award is furnished to NASA, and recipient considers such data to embody trade secrets or to comprise commercial or financial information which is privileged or confidential, and such data is so identified with a suitable notice or legend, the data will be maintained in confidence and disclosed and used by the Government and its contractors (under suitable protective conditions) only for experimental, evaluation, research and development purposes, by or on behalf of the Government for an agreed to period of time, and thereafter for Federal purposes as defined in § 1800.909(b)."

(e) For Cooperative Agreements, the following paragraph also applies—

"(1) As to data first produced by NASA in carrying out NASA's responsibilities under a cooperative agreement and which data would embody trade secrets or would comprise commercial or financial information that is privileged or confidential if it has been obtained from the recipient, such data will be marked with an appropriate legend and maintained in confidence for 5 years (unless a shorter period has been agreed to between the Government and recipient) after development of the information, with the express understanding that during the aforesaid period such data may be disclosed and used (under suitable protective conditions) by or on behalf of the Government for Government purposes only, and thereafter for any purpose whatsoever without restriction on disclosure and use. Recipient agrees not to disclose such data to any third party without NASA's written approval until the aforementioned restricted period expires."

(End of Term and Condition)

1800.910  NATIONAL SECURITY

Prescription—This term and condition implements Executive Order 12829. The Grant Officer shall include in all awards.

*National Security*

NASA awards normally do not involve classified information. However, if it is known in advance that an award involves classified information or if the work on the award is likely to develop classified information, individuals performing on the award who will have access to the information must obtain the appropriate security clearance in advance of performing on the award, in accordance with NASA Procedural Requirements (NPR) 1600.2, NASA Classified National Security Information (CNSI) w/ Change 2. When access to classified information is not originally anticipated in the performance of an award, but such information is subsequently sought or potentially developed by the award recipient, the NASA Grant Officer who issued the award shall be notified immediately, and prior to work under the award proceeding, to implement the appropriate clearance requirements.

(End of Term and Condition)

1800.911  NONDISCRIMINATION

Prescription—This term and condition implements Executive Order 11246. The Grant Officer shall include in all awards.

*Nondiscrimination*

(a) To the extent provided by law and any applicable agency regulations, this award and any program assisted thereby are subject to the provisions of Title VI of the Civil Rights Act of 1964 (Pub. L. 88–352), Title IX of the Education amendments of 1972 (Pub. L. 92–318, 20 U.S.C. 1681 *et seq.*), section 504 of the Rehabilitation Act of 1973 (29 U.S.C. 794), the Age Discrimination Act of 1975 (Pub. L. 94–135), the implementing regulations issued pursuant thereto by NASA, and the assurance of compliance which the recipient has filed with NASA.

(b) Except for commercially available supplies, materials, equipment, or general support services, the recipient shall obtain an assurance of compliance as required by NASA regulations from each organization that applies or serves as a subrecipient, subawardee, contractor or subcontractor under this award.

(c) Work on NASA awards is subject to the provisions of Title VI of the Civil Rights Act of 1964 (Pub. L. 88–352; 42 U.S.C. 2000d-1), Title IX of the Education Amendments of 1972 (20 U.S.C. 1680 *et seq.*), section 504 of the Rehabilitation Act of 1973, as amended (29 U.S.C. 794), the Age Discrimination Act of

1975 (42 U.S.C. 6101 *et seq.*), and the NASA implementing regulations (14 CFR parts 1250, 1251, 1252, and 1253).

(End of Term and Condition)

1800.912  CLEAN AIR AND WATER

Prescription—This term and condition implements the Clean Air Act at 42 U.S.C. 7401 *et seq.* The Grant Officer shall include this term and condition on all awards.

*Clean Air and Water*

The recipient agrees to the following:

(a) Comply with applicable standards, orders or regulations issued pursuant to the Clean Air Act, as amended (42 U.S.C. 7401 *et seq.*) and of the Federal Water Pollution Control Act (33 U.S.C. 1251 *et seq.*).

(b) Ensure that no portion of the work under this award will be performed in a facility listed on the Environmental Protection Agency (EPA) List of Violating Facilities on the date that this award was effective unless and until the EPA eliminates the name of such facility or facilities from such listings.

(c) Use its best efforts to comply with clean air standards and clean water standards at the facility in which the award is being performed.

(d) Insert the substance of these terms and conditions into any nonexempt subaward or contract under the award.

(e) Report violations to NASA and to EPA.

(End of Term and Condition)

1800.913  INVESTIGATIVE REQUIREMENTS

Prescription—This term and condition implements Executive Order 12829. The Grant Officer shall include this term and condition in all awards. The term and condition must be augmented to conform to the requirements of OMB Guidance M–05–24 "Implementation of Homeland Security Presidential Directive (HSPD) 12—Policy for a Common Identification Standard for Federal Employees and Contractors" when a recipient will require routine access to a Federal-controlled facility and/or information system.

*Investigative Requirements*

(a) NASA reserves the right to perform security checks and to deny or restrict access to a NASA Center, facility, or computer system, or to NASA technical information, as NASA deems appropriate. To the extent the recipient needs such access for performance of the work, the recipient shall ensure that individuals needing such access provide the personal background and biographical information requested by NASA. Individuals failing to provide the requested information may be denied such access.

(b) All requests to visit a NASA Center or facility must be submitted in a timely manner in accordance with instructions provided by that Center or facility.

(End of Term and Condition)

1800.914  TRAVEL AND TRANSPORTATION

Prescription—This term and condition implements The Fly American Act, 49 U.S.C. 1517 and the Department of Transportation regulations on hazardous materials. The Grant Officer will include this term and condition in all awards.

*Travel and Transportation*

(a) The Fly American Act, 49 U.S.C. 1517, requires the recipient to use U.S. flag air carriers for international air transportation of personnel and property to the extent that service by those carriers is available.

(b) Department of Transportation regulations, 49 CFR 173, govern recipient shipment of hazardous materials and other items.

(End of Term and Condition)

1800.915  SAFETY

Prescription—This term and condition implements NPR 8715.3C or its successor requirements document. The Grant Officer will include this term and condition in all awards.

*Safety*

(a) The recipient shall act responsibly in matters of safety and shall take all reasonable safety measures in performing under this award. The recipient shall comply with all applicable Federal, state, and local laws relating to safety. The recipient shall maintain a record of, and will notify the NASA Grant Officer immediately (within one workday) of any accident involving death, disabling injury or substantial loss of property in performing this award. The recipient will immediately (within one workday) advise NASA of hazards that come to its attention as a result of the work performed.

(b) Where the work under this award involves flight hardware, the hazardous aspects, if any, of such hardware will be identified, in writing, by the recipient. Compliance with this term and condition by sub-awardees/subcontractors shall be the responsibility of the recipient.

(End of Term and Condition)

1800.916  BUY AMERICAN ENCOURAGEMENT

Prescription—This term and condition implements section 319 of Public Law 106–391, the NASA Authorization Act. The Grant Officer will include this term and condition in all awards, except awards with foreign recipients.

*Buy American Encouragement*

As stated in Section 319 of Public Law 106–391, the NASA Authorization Act as amended recipients are encouraged to purchase only American-made equipment and products.

(End of Term and Condition)

1800.917   INVESTIGATION OF RESEARCH MISCONDUCT

Prescription—This term and condition implements § 200.336, The Grant Officer shall include this term and condition in all awards.

*Investigation of Research Misconduct*

Recipients of this award are subject to the requirements of 14 CFR 1275, "Investigation of Research Misconduct."

(End of Term and Condition)

1800.918   ALLOCATION OF RISK/LIABILITY

Prescription—The Grant Officer shall include this term and condition in all awards.

*Allocation of Risk/Liability*

(a) With respect to activities undertaken under this award, the recipient agrees not to make any claim against NASA or the U.S. Government with respect to the injury or death of its employees or its subawardees/contractors and subaward/subcontractor employees, or to the loss of its property or that of its subawardeees/contractors and subawardees/subcontractors, whether such injury, death, damage or loss arises through negligence or otherwise, except in the case of willful misconduct.

(b) In addition, as applicable, the recipient agrees to indemnify and hold the U.S. Government and its contractors and subcontractors harmless from any third party claim, judgment, or cost arising from the injury to or death of any person, or for damage to or loss of any property, arising as a result of its possession or use of any U.S. Government property. If State law prohibits the recipient from accepting indemnification, then the recipient shall ensure this term and condition applies to all subrecipients, subawardees, contractors or subcontractors under this award.

(End of Term and Condition)

1800.919   COOPERATIVE AGREEMENT

Prescription—The Grant Officer shall include this term and condition in all cooperative agreement awards.

*Cooperative Agreement*

(a) This award is a cooperative agreement and it is anticipated there will be substantial NASA involvement during performance of the effort. NASA and the recipient mutually agree to the following statement of antici-pated cooperative interactions which may occur during the performance of this effort—

(Reference the approved proposal that contains a detailed description of the work and insert a concise statement of the exact nature of the cooperative interactions NASA and the recipient will provide.)

(b) The terms "award" and "recipient" mean "cooperative agreement" and "recipient of cooperative agreement," respectively, wherever the language appears in terms and conditions included in this agreement.

(c) NASA's ability to participate and perform its collaborative effort under this cooperative agreement is subject to the availability of appropriated funds and nothing in this cooperative agreement commits the United States Congress to appropriate funds therefore.

(End of Term and Condition)

1800.920   MULTIPLE YEAR AWARD

Prescription—The Grant Officer shall include this term and condition in multi-year awards. This term and condition does not have to be included in awards with commercial firms. If included, minor modifications to the term and condition, such as the time frame for cost extensions, are permissible.

*Multiple Year Award*

This is a multiple-year award contingent on the availability of funds, scientific progress of the project, and continued relevance to NASA programs. NASA anticipates continuing support at approximately the following levels—

Second year $ ___, Anticipated funding date ___.

Third year $ ___, Anticipated funding date ___.

(Periods may be added or omitted, as applicable)

End of Term and Condition)

1800.921   INCREMENTAL FUNDING

Prescription—The Grant Officer shall include this term and condition when incremental funding is used, changes as needed are permissible.

*Incremental Funding*

(a) Only $XXX of the amount indicated on the face of this award is available for payment and allotted to this award. NASA contemplates making additional allotments of funds during performance of this effort. It is anticipated that these funds will be obligated as appropriated funds become available without any action required by the recipient. The recipient will be given written notification by the NASA Grant Officer.

(b) The recipient agrees to perform work up to the point at which the total amount paid or payable by the Government approximates but does not exceed the total amount actually allotted to this award. NASA is not obligated to reimburse the recipient for the expenditure of amounts in excess of the total funds allotted by NASA to this grant or cooperative agreement. The recipient is not authorized to continue performance beyond the amount allotted to this award.

Special Note—Balance is contingent on availability of funds. The remaining balance to fully fund this year is $XXX.

(End of Term and Condition)

### 1800.922 COST SHARING

Prescription—The Grant Officer shall include this term and condition when an award involves cost sharing, changes as need are permissible.

*Cost Sharing*

(a) NASA and the recipient will share in providing the resources necessary to perform the award. NASA funding and non-cash contributions (personnel, equipment, facilities, etc.) and the dollar value of the recipient's cash and/or non-cash contribution will be on a ___ percent recipient basis.

(b) The funding and non-cash contributions by both parties are represented by the following dollar amounts—

Government Share

_____

Recipient Share

_____

Total Amount    _____

(c) Criteria and procedures for allowable and allocable costs of cash and non-cash contributions shall be governed by § 200.306, Cost Sharing or Matching. The applicable Federal cost principles are cited in 2 CFR 200 Subpart E.

(d) The Recipient's share shall not be charged to the Government under this award or under any other contract or award.

(End of Term and Condition)

### 1800.923 NEW TECHNOLOGY

Prescription— The Grant Officer shall include this term and condition in all grants with commercial firms other than those with small businesses. This term and condition is used in lieu of the term and condition at 2 CFR 1800.908, Patent Rights.

*New Technology*

(a) Definitions.

Administrator, as used in this term and condition, means the Administrator of the National Aeronautics and Space Administration (NASA) or duly authorized representative.

The term "award," as used in this term and condition, means any actual or proposed grant, cooperative agreement, understanding, or other arrangement, and includes any assignment, substitution of parties, subaward, or subcontract executed or entered into thereunder.

Made, as used in this term and condition, means conception or first actual reduction to practice; provided, that in the case of a variety of plant, the date of determination (as defined in section 41(d) of the Plant Variety Protection Act, 7 U.S.C. 2401(d)) must also occur during the period of performance.

Nonprofit organization, as used in this term and condition, means a domestic university or other institution of higher education or an organization of the type described in section 501(c)(3) of the Internal Revenue Code of 1954 (26 U.S.C. 501(c)) and exempt from taxation under section 501(a) of the Internal Revenue Code (26 U.S.C. 501(a)), or any domestic nonprofit scientific or educational organization qualified under a State nonprofit organization statute.

Practical application, as used in this term and condition, means to manufacture, in the case of a composition or product; to practice, in the case of a process or method; or to operate, in case of a machine or system; and, in each case, under such conditions as to establish that the invention is being utilized and that its benefits are, to the extent permitted by law or Government regulations, available to the public on reasonable terms.

Reportable item, as used in this term and condition, means any invention, discovery, improvement, or innovation of the awardee, whether or not patentable or otherwise protectable under Title 35 of the United States Code, made in the performance of any work under any NASA award or in the performance of any work that is reimbursable under any term and condition in any NASA award providing for reimbursement of costs incurred before the effective date of the award. Reportable items include, but are not limited to, new processes, machines, manufactures, and compositions of matter, and improvements to, or new applications of, existing processes, machines, manufactures, and compositions of matter. Reportable items also include new computer programs, and improvements to, or new applications of, existing computer programs, whether or not copyrightable or otherwise protectable under Title 17 of the United States Code.

Small business firm, as used in this term and condition, means a domestic small business concern as defined at 15 U.S.C. 632 and implementing regulations (see 13 CFR 121.401 *et seq.*) of the Administrator of the Small Business Administration.

Subject invention, as used in this term and condition, means any reportable item which is or may be patentable or otherwise protectable under Title 35 of the United

States Code, or any novel variety of plant that is or may be protectable under the Plant Variety Protection Act (7 U.S.C. 2321 *et seq.*).

(b) Allocation of principal rights.

(1) Presumption of title.

(i) Any reportable item that the Administrator considers to be a subject invention shall be presumed to have been made in the manner specified in paragraph (A) or (B) of section 20135(b)(1) of the National Aeronautics and Space Act of 1958 (51 U.S.C. 20135) (hereinafter called "the Act"), and that presumption shall be conclusive unless at the time of reporting the reportable item the recipient submits to the Grant Officer a written statement, containing supporting details, demonstrating that the reportable item was not made in the manner specified in paragraph (A) or (B) of section 20135(b)(1) of the Act.

(ii) Regardless of whether title to a given subject invention would otherwise be subject to an advance waiver or is the subject of a petition for waiver, the recipient may nevertheless file the statement described in paragraph (b)(1)(i) of this term and condition. The Administrator will review the information furnished by the recipient in any such statement and any other available information relating to the circumstances surrounding the making of the subject invention and will notify the recipient whether the Administrator has determined that the subject invention was made in the manner specified in paragraph (A) or (B) of section 20135(b)(1) of the Act.

(2) Property rights in subject inventions. Each subject invention for which the presumption of paragraph (b)(1)(i) of this term and condition is conclusive or for which there has been a determination that it was made in the manner specified in paragraph (A) or (B) of section 20135(b)(1) of the Act shall be the exclusive property of the United States as represented by NASA unless the Administrator waives all or any part of the rights of the United States, as provided in paragraph (b)(3) of this term and condition.

(3) Waiver of rights.

(i) Section 20135(g) of the Act provides for the promulgation of regulations by which the Administrator may waive the rights of the United States with respect to any invention or class of inventions made or that may be made under conditions specified in paragraph (A) or (B) of section 20135(b)(1) of the Act.

(ii) As provided in 14 CFR part 1245, subpart 1, recipients may petition, either prior to execution of the award or within 30 days after execution of the award, for advance waiver of rights to any or all of the inventions that may be made under an award. If such a petition is not submitted, or if after submission it is denied, the recipient (or an employee inventor of the recipient) may pe-

tition for waiver of rights to an identified subject invention within eight months of first disclosure of the invention in accordance with paragraph (e)(2) of this term and condition, or within such longer period as may be authorized in accordance with 14 CFR 1245.105.

(c) Minimum rights reserved by the Government.

(1) With respect to each subject invention for which a waiver of rights is applicable in accordance with 14 CFR part 1245, subpart 1, the Government reserves—

(i) An irrevocable, nonexclusive, nontransferable, royalty-free license for the practice of such invention throughout the world by or on behalf of the United States or any foreign government in accordance with any treaty or agreement with the United States; and

(ii) Such other rights as stated in 14 CFR 1245.107.

(2) Nothing contained in this paragraph (c) shall be considered to grant to the Government any rights with respect to any invention other than a subject invention.

(d) Minimum rights to the Recipient.

(1) The recipient is hereby granted a revocable, nonexclusive, royalty-free license in each patent application filed in any country on a subject invention and any resulting patent in which the Government acquires title, unless the recipient fails to disclose the subject invention within the times specified in paragraph (e)(2) of this term and condition. The recipient's license extends to its domestic subsidiaries and affiliates, if any, within the corporate structure of which the recipient is a party and includes the right to grant sublicenses of the same scope to the extent the recipient was legally obligated to do so at the time the award was issued. The license is transferable only with the approval of the Administrator except when transferred to the successor of that part of the recipient's business to which the invention pertains.

(2) The recipient's domestic license may be revoked or modified by the Administrator to the extent necessary to achieve expeditious practical application of the subject invention pursuant to an application for an exclusive license submitted in accordance with 37 CFR part 404, Licensing of Government Owned Inventions. This license will not be revoked in that field of use or the geographical areas in which the recipient has achieved practical application and continues to make the benefits of the invention reasonably accessible to the public. The license in any foreign country may be revoked or modified at the discretion of the Administrator to the extent the recipient, its licensees, or its domestic subsidiaries or affiliates have failed to achieve practical application in that foreign country.

(3) Before revocation or modification of the license, the recipient will be provided a written notice of the Administrator's intention to revoke or modify the license, and the recipient will be allowed 30 days (or such other time as may be authorized by the Administrator for good cause shown by the recipient) after the notice to show cause why the license should not be revoked or modified. The recipient has the right to appeal to the Administrator any decision concerning the revocation or modification of its license.

(e) Invention identification, disclosures, and reports.

(1) The recipient shall establish and maintain active and effective procedures to assure that reportable items are promptly identified and disclosed to recipient personnel responsible for the administration of this New Technology term and condition within six months of conception and/or first actual reduction to practice, whichever occurs first in the performance of work under this award. These procedures shall include the maintenance of laboratory notebooks or equivalent records and other records as are reasonably necessary to document the conception and/or the first actual reduction to practice of the reportable items, and records that show that the procedures for identifying and disclosing reportable items are followed. Upon request, the recipient shall furnish the Grant Officer a description of such procedures for evaluation and for determination as to their effectiveness.

(2) The recipient will disclose each reportable item to the New Technology Representative, with notice to the Grant Officer, within two months after the inventor discloses it in writing to recipient personnel responsible for the administration of this New Technology term and condition or, if earlier, within six months after the recipient becomes aware that a reportable item has been made, but in any event for subject inventions before any on sale, public use, or publication of such invention known to the recipient. The disclosure to the agency shall be in the form of a written report and shall identify the award under which the reportable item was made and the inventor(s) or innovator(s). It shall be sufficiently complete in technical detail to convey a clear understanding, to the extent known at the time of the disclosure, of the nature, purpose, operation, and physical, chemical, biological, or electrical characteristics of the reportable item. The disclosure shall also identify any publication, on sale, or public use of any subject invention and whether a manuscript describing such invention has been submitted for publication and, if so, whether it has been accepted for publication at the time of disclosure. In addition, after disclosure to the agency, the recipient will promptly notify the agency of the acceptance of any manuscript describing a subject invention

for publication or of any on sale or public use planned by the recipient for such invention.

(3) The recipient shall furnish the New Technology Representative, with notice to the Grants Officer, the following:

(i) Interim new technology summary reports every 12 months from the date of award, listing reportable items during that period, and certifying that all reportable items have been disclosed (or that there are no such inventions) and that the procedures required by paragraph (e)(1) of this term and condition have been followed.

(ii) A final new technology summary report within 90 days after the end of the period of performance, listing all reportable items or certifying that there were no such reportable items, and listing all research subawardees/subcontractors at any tier containing a patent rights clause or certifying that there were no such subcontractors.

(4) The recipient agrees, upon written request of the Patent Representative, to furnish additional technical and other information available to the recipient as is necessary for the preparation of a patent application on a subject invention and for the prosecution of the patent application, and to execute all papers necessary to file patent applications on subject inventions and to establish the Government's rights in the subject inventions.

(5) The recipient agrees, subject to 5(a) below, the Government may duplicate and disclose subject invention disclosures and all other reports and papers furnished or required to be furnished pursuant to this term and condition.

(a) Publishing information concerning an invention before a patent application is filed on a subject invention may create a bar to a valid patent. To avoid this bar, agencies may withhold information from the public that discloses any invention in which the Government owns or may own a right, title, or interest (including a nonexclusive license) (see 35 U.S.C. 205 and 37 CFR part 401). Agencies may only withhold information concerning inventions for a reasonable time in order for a patent application to be filed. Once filed in any patent office, agencies are not required to release copies of any document that is a part of a patent application for those subject inventions.

(f) Examination of records relating to inventions.

(1) The Grant Officer or any authorized representative shall, until 3 years after final payment under this award, have the right to examine any books (including laboratory notebooks), records, and documents of the recipient relating to the conception or first actual reduction to practice of inventions in the same field of technology as the work under this award to determine whether—

(i) Any such inventions are subject inventions;

(ii) The recipient has established and maintained the procedures required by paragraph (e)(1) of this term and condition; and

(iii) The recipient and its inventors have complied with the procedures.

(2) If the New Technology Representative or Patent Representative learns of an unreported recipient invention, the recipient may be required to disclose the invention to the agency for a determination of ownership rights.

(3) Any examination of records under this paragraph will be subject to appropriate conditions to protect the confidentiality of the information involved.

(h) Subawards/Subcontracts.

(1) Unless otherwise authorized or directed by the Grant Officer, the recipient shall—

(i) Include the clause at NASA FAR Supplement (NFS) 1852.227-70, New Technology, (suitably modified to identify the parties) in any subaward/subcontract hereunder (regardless of tier) with other than a small business firm or nonprofit organization for the performance of experimental, developmental, or research work; and

(ii) Include the FAR clause 52.227-11, as modified by the NASA FAR Supplement (NFS) 1852.227-11, "Patent Right-Retention by the Contractor (Short Form)" (suitably modified to identify the parties) in any subaward/subcontract hereunder (regardless of tier) with a small business firm or nonprofit organization for the performance of experimental, developmental, or research work.

(2) In the event of a refusal by a prospective subrecipient to accept such a clause the recipient—

(i) Shall promptly submit a written notice to the Grant Officer setting forth the subrecipient's reasons for such refusal and other pertinent information that may expedite disposition of the matter; and

(ii) Shall not proceed with such subaward/subcontract without the written authorization of the Grant Officer.

(3) The recipient shall promptly notify the Grant Officer in writing upon the award of any subaward/subcontract at any tier containing a patent rights clause by identifying the subrecipient, the applicable patent rights term and condition/clause, the work to be performed under the subrecipient and the dates of award and estimated completion. Upon request of the Grant Officer, the recipient shall furnish a copy of such subaward/subcontract, and, no more frequently than annually, a listing of the subawards/subcontracts that have been awarded.

(4) The subrecipient will retain all rights provided for the recipient in paragraph (h)(1)(i) or (ii) of this term and condition, whichever is included in the subaward/subcontracts, and the recipient will not, as part of the consideration for awarding the subaward/subcontract, obtain rights in the subrecipients's subject inventions.

(i) Preference for United States industry. Unless provided otherwise, no recipient that receives title to any subject invention and no assignee of any such recipient shall grant to any person the exclusive right to use or sell any subject invention in the United States unless such person agrees that any products embodying the subject invention will be manufactured substantially in the United States. However, in individual cases, the requirement may be waived by the Administrator upon a showing by the recipient or assignee that reasonable but unsuccessful efforts have been made to grant licenses on similar terms to potential licensees that would be likely to manufacture substantially in the United States or that under the circumstances domestic manufacture is not commercially feasible.

(End of Term and Condition)

1800.924 DESIGNATION OF NEW TECHNOLOGY REPRESENTATIVE AND PATENT REPRESENTATIVE

Prescription—The Grant Officer shall include this term and condition all awards containing the term and condition "Patent Rights" at 1800.908 or the term and condition "New Technology" at 1800.923.

*Designation of New Technology Representative and Patent Representative*

(a) For purposes of administration of the term and condition entitled "New Technology," or "Patent Rights" whichever is included, the following named representatives are hereby designated by the Grant Officer to administer such term and condition—

• New Technology Representative
• Patent Representative

(b) Reports of reportable items, and disclosure of subject inventions, interim reports, final reports, utilization reports, and other reports required by the term and condition, as well as any correspondence with respect to such matters, should be directed to the New Technology Representative, with notification to the Grant Officer, unless transmitted in response to correspondence or request from the Patent Representative. Inquires or requests regarding disposition of rights, election of rights, or related matters should be directed to the Patent Representative. This term and condition shall be included in any subaward/subcontract hereunder requiring a "New Technology" term and condition or "Patent Rights—Retention by the Contractor (Short Form)" term and condition unless otherwise authorized or directed by the Grant Officer. The respective responsibilities and authorities of the above named representatives are set forth in the Grants and Cooperative Agreement Manual.

(End of Term and Condition)

1800.925  EQUIPMENT AND OTHER PROPERTY UNDER AWARDS WITH COMMERCIAL FIRMS

Prescription—The Grant Officer shall include this term and condition in awards with commercial firms that have property.

*Equipment and Other Property Under Awards With Commercial Firms*

(a) This award permits acquisition of special purpose equipment required for the conduct of research. Acquisition of special purpose equipment costing in excess of $5,000 and not included in the approved proposal budget requires the prior approval of the Grant Officer unless the item is merely a different model of an item shown in the approved proposal budget.

(b) Recipients may not purchase, as a direct cost to the award, items of general purpose equipment, examples of which include but are not limited to office equipment and furnishings, air conditioning equipment, reproduction and printing equipment, motor vehicles, and automatic data processing equipment. If the recipient requests an exception, the recipient shall submit a written request for Grant Officer approval, prior to purchase by the recipient, stating why the recipient cannot charge the general purpose equipment to indirect costs.

(c) Under no circumstances shall award funds be used to acquire land or any interest therein, to acquire or construct facilities (as defined in 48 CFR (FAR) 45.301), or to procure passenger carrying vehicles.

(d) The Government shall have title to equipment and other personal property acquired with Government funds. Such property shall be disposed of pursuant to 48 CFR (FAR) 45.603.

(e) Title to Government furnished equipment (including equipment, title to which has been transferred to the Government prior to completion of the work) will remain with the Government.

(f) The recipient shall establish and maintain property management standards for Government property and otherwise manage such property as set forth in 48 CFR (FAR) 45.5 and 48 CFR (NFS) 1845.5.

(g) Recipients shall submit annually a NASA Form 1018, NASA Property in the Custody of Contractors, in accordance with the instructions on the form, the provisions of 48 CFR (NFS) 1845.71 and any supplemental instructions that may be issued by NASA for the current reporting period. The original NF 1018 shall be submitted to the Center Deputy Chief Financial Officer (Finance) with three copies sent concurrently to the Center Industrial Property Officer. The annual reporting period shall be from October 1

of each year through September 30 of the following year. The report shall be submitted in time to be received by October 15. Negative reports (*i.e.* no reportable property) are required. The information contained in the reports is entered into the NASA accounting system to reflect current asset values for agency financial statement purposes. Therefore, it is essential that required reports be received no later than October 15. A final report is required within 30 days after the end of the period of performance.

(h) The requirements set forth in this term and condition supersedes award term and condition 1800.907, Equipment and Other Property.

(End of Term and Condition)

1800.926  LISTING OF REPORTABLE EQUIPMENT AND OTHER PROPERTY.

Prescription—The Grant Officer shall include this term and condition in awards with property.

*Listing of Reportable Equipment and Other Property*

(a) Title to Federally-owned property provided to the recipient remains vested in the Federal Government, and shall be managed in accordance with § 200.312. The following items of Federally-owned property are being provided to the recipient for use in performance of the work under this award—

List property or state "not applicable.

(b) The following specific items of equipment acquired by the recipient have been identified by NASA for transfer of title to the Government when no longer required for performance under this award. This equipment will be managed in accordance with 200.313, and shall be transferred to NASA or NASA's designee in accordance with the procedures set forth at 200.313(e)—

(List property or state "not applicable.")

(End of Term and Condition)

1800.927  INVOICES AND PAYMENTS UNDER AWARDS WITH COMMERCIAL FIRMS

Prescription—The Grant Officer shall include this term and condition in all awards with commercial firms.

*Invoices and Payments Under Awards With Commercial Firms*

(a) Invoices for payment of actual incurred costs shall be submitted by the recipient no more frequently than on a__XX___basis.

(b) Invoices shall be submitted by the recipient to the following offices:

(1) The original invoice shall be sent directly to the payment office designated on the award cover page.

(2) Copies of the invoice shall be sent to the NASA Technical Officer and NASA Grant Officer.

(c) All invoices shall reference the award number.

(d) The final invoice shall be marked "Final" and shall be submitted within 90 days of the end date of the period of performance.

(e) The requirements set forth in this term and condition shall govern to the extent these requirements are inconsistent with the requirements in term and condition "Financial Management" at 1800.906.

(End of Term and Condition)

1800.928   ELECTRONIC FUNDS TRANSFER PAYMENT METHODS

Prescription—The Grant Officer shall include this term and condition in all awards with commercial firms.

*Electronic Funds Transfer Payment Methods*

(a) Payments under this award will be made by the Government by electronic funds transfer through the Treasury Fedline Payment System (FEDLINE) or the Automated Clearing House (ACH), at the option of the Government. After award, but no later than 14 days before an invoice is submitted, the recipient shall designate a financial institution for receipt of electronic funds transfer payments, and shall submit this designation to the Grant Officer or other Government official, as directed.

(b) For payment through FEDLINE, the recipient shall provide the following information:

(1) Name, address, and telegraphic abbreviation of the financial institution receiving payment.

(2) The American Bankers Association 9-digit identifying number for wire transfers of the financing institution receiving payment if the institution has access to the Federal Reserve Communication System.

(3) Payee's account number at the financial institution where funds are to be transferred.

(4) If the financial institution does not have access to the Federal Reserve Communications System, name, address, and telegraphic abbreviation of the correspondent financial institution through which the financial institution receiving payment obtains wire transfer activity. Provide the telegraphic abbreviation and American Bankers Association identifying number for the correspondent institution.

(c) For payment through ACH, the recipient shall provide the following information:

(1) Routing transit number of the financial institution receiving payment (same as American Bankers Association identifying number used for FEDLINE).

(2) Number of account to which funds are to be deposited.

(3) Type of depositor account ("C" for checking, "S" for savings).

(4) If the recipient is a new enrollee to the ACH system, a "Payment Information Form," SF 3881, must be completed before payment can be processed.

(d) In the event the recipient, during the performance of this award, elects to designate a different financial institution for the receipt of any payment made using electronic funds transfer procedures, notification of such change and the required information specified above must be received by the appropriate Government official 30 days prior to the date such change is to become effective.

(e) The documents furnishing the information required in this term and condition must be dated and contain the signature, title, and telephone number of the recipient official authorized to provide it, as well as the recipient's name and award number.

(f) Failure to properly designate a financial institution or to provide appropriate payee bank account information may delay payments of amounts otherwise properly due.

(g) The requirements set forth in this term and condition shall govern to the extent these requirements are inconsistent with the requirements in term and condition "Financial Management".

(End of Term and Condition)

1800.929   INDIRECT COSTS

Prescription—The Grant Officer shall include this term and condition in all awards with indirect costs, excluding those awards to institutions of higher education and to entities using the 10% de minimis rate.

*Indirect Costs*

Unless otherwise directed in 2 CFR part 200, if during the course of this award, the approved indirect cost rate is revised, changed or removed, that rate must be applied, as allowed, to the covered direct costs that are expended during the time frame of that rate agreement. Any corrections, either up or down, to the approved budget submitted with the awarded application must be reflected in the awardees' records of costs and should be audited as such.

(End of Term and Condition)

1800.930   ACCESS TO RESEARCH RESULTS

Prescription—The Grant Officer shall include this term and condition in all research and research-related awards.

*Access to Research Results*

(a) This award is subject to the requirements of the, "NASA Plan: Increasing Access to the Results of Scientific Research," which covers public access to digital scientific data and peer-reviewed publications. For purposes of this term and condition, the following definitions apply:

(1) Awardee: Any recipient of a NASA grant or cooperative agreement, its investigators, and subrecipient (subaward or contract as defined in 2 CFR 200.92 and 200.22, respectively) at any level.

(2) Final Peer-Reviewed Manuscript: The final text version of a peer-reviewed article disclosing the results of scientific research which is authored or co-authored by the Awardee or funded, in whole or in part, with funds from a NASA award, that includes all modifications from the publishing peer review process, and all graphics and supplemental material prepared by Awardee.

(b) The recipient shall:

(1) Comply with their approved Data Management Plan submitted with its proposal, and as modified upon agreement by the recipient and NASA from time to time during the course of the period of performance.

(2) Ensure that any Final Peer-Reviewed Manuscript is submitted to the NASA-designated repository, currently the PubMed Central system at *http://www.ncbi.nlm.nih.gov/pmc/*. NASA will provide instructions for completing the submission process under separate cover. Ensure that the Final Peer-Reviewed Manuscript is submitted to PubMed Central within one year of completion of the peer review process.

(3) Ensure that any publisher's agreements entered into by an Awardee will allow for the Awardee to comply with these requirements including submission of Final Peer-Reviewed Manuscripts to the NASA-designated repository, as listed in paragraph (b)(2) of this term and condition, with sufficient rights to permit such repository to use such Final Peer-Reviewed Manuscript in its normal course, including rights to permit users to download XML and plain text formats.

(4) Hereby represent and warrant that Awardee has secured for recipient the right to submit the Final Peer-Reviewed Manuscript to the NASA-designated repository for use as set forth herein.

(5) Include in annual and final reports a list of Final Peer-Reviewed Manuscripts covered by this term and condition.

(End of Term and Condition)

[79 FR 76063, Dec. 19, 2014, as amended by 81 FR 74659, Oct. 27, 2016]

## PARTS 1801–1879 [RESERVED]

## PART 1880—NONPROCUREMENT DEBARMENT AND SUSPENSION

Sec.
1880.10   What does this part do?
1880.20   Does this part apply to me?
1880.30   What policies and procedures must I follow?

### Subpart A—General

1880.137   Who in NASA may grant an exception to let an excluded person participate in a covered transaction?

### Subpart B—Covered Transactions

1880.220   What contracts and subcontracts, in addition to those listed in 2 CFR 180.220, are covered transactions?

### Subpart C—Responsibilities of Participants Regarding Transactions

1880.332   What methods must I use to pass requirements down to participants at lower tiers with whom I intend to do business?

### Subpart D—Responsibilities of Federal Agency Officials Regarding Transactions

1880.437   What method do I use to communicate to a participant the requirements described in the OMB guidance at 2 CFR 180.435?

### Subparts E–J [Reserved]

AUTHORITY: Sec. 2455, Pub. L. 103–355, 108 Stat. 3327; E.O. 12549, 3 CFR, 1986 Comp., p. 189; E.O. 12689, 3 CFR, 1989 Comp., p. 235; 42 U.S.C. 2473(c)(1).

SOURCE: 72 FR 19783, Apr. 20, 2007, unless otherwise noted.

### §1880.10   What does this part do?

This part adopts the Office of Management and Budget (OMB) guidance in subparts A through I of 2 CFR part 180, as supplemented by this part, as the NASA policies and procedures for nonprocurement debarment and suspension. It thereby gives regulatory effect for NASA to the OMB guidance as supplemented by this part. This part satisfies the requirements in section 3 of Executive Order 12549, "Debarment and Suspension" (3 CFR 1986 Comp., p. 189), Executive Order 12689, "Debarment and Suspension" (3 CFR 1989 Comp., p. 235) and 31 U.S.C. 6101 note (Section 2455, Public Law 103–355, 108 Stat. 3327).

## § 1880.20   Does this part apply to me?

This part and, through this part, pertinent portions of the OMB guidance in subparts A through I of 2 CFR part 180 (see table at 2 CFR 180.100(b)) apply to you if you are a—

(a) Participant or principal in a "covered transaction" (see subpart B of 2 CFR part 180 and the definition of "nonprocurement transaction" at 2 CFR 180.970);

(b) Respondent in a NASA suspension or debarment action;

(c) NASA debarment or suspension official; or

(d) NASA grants officer, agreements officer, or other official authorized to enter into any type of nonprocurement transaction that is a covered transaction.

## § 1880.30   What policies and procedures must I follow?

The NASA policies and procedures that you must follow are the policies and procedures specified in each applicable section of the OMB guidance in subparts A through I of 2 CFR part 180, as that section is supplemented by the section in this part with the same section number. The contracts that are covered transactions, for example, are specified by section 220 of the OMB guidance (*i.e.*, 2 CFR 180.220) as supplemented by section 220 in this part (*i.e.*, § 1880.220). For any section of OMB guidance in subparts A through I of 2 CFR 180 that has no corresponding section in this part, NASA policies and procedures are those in the OMB guidance.

## Subpart A—General

## § 1880.137   Who in NASA may grant an exception to let an excluded person participate in a covered transaction?

The Chief Acquisition Officer has the authority to grant an exception to let an excluded person participate in a covered transaction, as provided in the OMB guidance at 2 CFR 180.135.

## Subpart B—Covered Transactions

## § 1880.220   What contracts and subcontracts, in addition to those listed in 2 CFR 180.220, are covered transactions?

NASA extends coverage of nonprocurement suspension and debarment requirements beyond first-tier procurement contracts under a covered nonprocurement action, to all lower tier subcontracts, at all dollar values, consistent with OMB guidance at 2 CFR 180.220(c) and the figure in the appendix at 2 CFR part 180. NASA does not permit subcontracting to suspended or debarred entities at any tier, at any dollar amount.

[78 FR 13211, Feb. 27, 2013]

## Subpart C—Responsibilities of Participants Regarding Transactions

## § 1880.332   What methods must I use to pass requirements down to participants at lower tiers with whom I intend to do business?

You as a participant must include a term or condition in lower-tier transactions requiring lower-tier participants to comply with subpart C of the OMB guidance in 2 CFR part 180, as supplemented by this subpart.

## Subpart D—Responsibilities of Federal Agency Officials Regarding Transactions

## § 1880.437   What method do I use to communicate to a participant the requirements described in the OMB guidance at 2 CFR 180.435?

To communicate to a participant the requirements described in 2 CFR 180.435 of the OMB guidance, you must include a term or condition in the transaction that requires the participant's compliance with subpart C of 2 CFR part 180, as supplemented by subpart C of this part, and requires the participant to include a similar term or condition in lower-tier covered transactions.

## Subparts E–J [Reserved]

## PART 1881 [RESERVED]

## PART 1882—REQUIREMENTS FOR DRUG-FREE WORKPLACE (FINANCIAL ASSISTANCE)

Sec.
1882.5 What does this part do?

### Subpart A—Purpose and Coverage

1882.120 Are any of my Federal assistance awards exempt from this part?

### Subparts B–D [Reserved]

### Subpart E—Violations of This Part and Consequences

1882.500 How are violations of this part determined for recipients other than individuals?
1882.505 How are violations of this part determined for recipients who are individuals?
1882.515 Are there any exceptions to those actions?

### Subpart F [Reserved]

AUTHORITY: 41 U.S.C. 701 *et seq.*; 51 U.S.C. 20113(e).

SOURCE: 79 FR 56487, Sept. 22, 2014, unless otherwise noted.

### §1882.5 What does this part do?

This part adopts the Office of Management and Budget (OMB) guidance in subparts A through F of 2 CFR part 182, as supplemented by this part, as the NASA policies and procedures for implementing the portion of the Drug-Free Workplace Act of 1988 (41 U.S.C. 701–707, as amended, hereafter referred to as "the Act") that applies to grants and cooperative agreements. It thereby gives regulatory effect for NASA to the OMB guidance. Further, it supplements the OMB guidance with NASA-specific regulation.

[79 FR 56487, Sept. 22, 2014. Redesignated at 79 FR 62797, Oct. 21, 2014]

### Subpart A—Purpose and Coverage

### §1882.120 Are any of my Federal assistance awards exempt from this part?

This part does not apply to any award for which the Assistant Administrator for Procurement determines that the application of this part would be inconsistent with the international obligations of the United States or the laws or regulations of a foreign government.

### Subparts B–D [Reserved]

### Subpart E—Violations of This Part and Consequences

### §1882.500 How are violations of this part determined for recipients other than individuals?

A recipient other than an individual is in violation of the requirements of this part if the Assistant Administrator for Procurement determines, in writing, that—

(a) The recipient has violated the requirements of subpart B of this part; or

(b) The number of convictions of the recipient's employees for violating criminal drug statutes in the workplace is large enough to indicate that the recipient has failed to make a good faith effort to provide a drug-free workplace.

### §1882.505 How are violations of this part determined for recipients who are individuals?

An individual recipient is in violation of the requirements of this part if the Assistant Administrator for Procurement determines, in writing, that—

(a) The recipient has violated the requirements of subpart C of this part; or

(b) The recipient is convicted of a criminal drug offense resulting from a violation occurring during the conduct of any award activity.

### §1882.515 Are there any exceptions to those actions?

The Assistant Administrator for Procurement (AA) may waive with respect to a particular award, in writing, a suspension of payments under an award or a suspension or termination of an award. The Chief Acquisition Officer (CAO) may approve an award to a suspended or debarred entity if the CAO determines that such a waiver would be in the public interest. These exception authorities cannot be delegated to any other official.

### Subpart F [Reserved]

PARTS 1883–1899 [RESERVED]

# CHAPTER XX—UNITED STATES NUCLEAR REGULATORY COMMISSION

# PART 2000—NONPROCUREMENT DEBARMENT AND SUSPENSION

## Subpart A—General

Sec.
2000.10   What does this part do?
2000.20   Does this part apply to me?
2000.30   What policies and procedures must I follow?
2000.135  Who in the Nuclear Regulatory Commission may grant an exception to let an excluded person participate in a covered transaction?

### Subpart B—Covered Transactions

2000.220  What contracts and subcontracts, in addition to those listed in 2 CFR 180.220, are covered transactions?

### Subpart C—Responsibilities of Participants Regarding Transactions

2000.330  What method must be used to pass requirements down to participants at lower tiers?

### Subparts D–H [Reserved]

### Subpart I—Definitions

2000.930   Debarring official.
2000.1010  Suspending official.

AUTHORITY: 5 U.S.C. 301; Sec. 2455, Pub. L. 103–355, 108 Stat. 3327 (31 U.S.C. 6101 note); E.O. 12549, 51 FR 6370, 3 CFR, 1986 Comp., p. 189; E.O. 12689, 54 FR 34131, 3 CFR, 1989 Comp., p. 235.

SOURCE: 75 FR 27924, May 19, 2010, unless otherwise noted.

## Subpart A—General

### § 2000.10   What does this part do?

This part promulgates a regulation adopting the Office of Management and Budget (OMB) guidance in subparts A through I of 2 CFR part 180, establishing the United States Nuclear Regulatory Commission (NRC) policies and procedures for nonprocurement debarment and suspension. NRC thereby gives regulatory effect to the OMB guidance. It also supplements the OMB guidance by identifying NRC implementing officials and identifying how to pass these requirements through to other entities.

### § 2000.20   Does this part apply to me?

This part and, through this part, pertinent portions of the OMB guidance in subparts A through I of 2 CFR part 180 (see table at 2 CFR 180.100(b)) apply to:

(a) Participant or principal in a "covered transaction";

(b) Respondent in an NRC nonprocurement suspension or debarment action;

(c) NRC debarment or suspension official; or

(d) NRC grants officer, agreements officer, or other official authorized to enter into a covered nonprocurement transaction.

### § 2000.30   What policies and procedures must I follow?

(a) The NRC policies and procedures that you must follow are the policies and procedures specified in each applicable section of the OMB guidance in Subparts A through I of 2 CFR part 180, and those in this part. The NRC has closely tracked OMB's numbering scheme. For example, the contracts under a nonprocurement transaction that are covered transactions that are in section 220 of the OMB guidance (i.e., 2 CFR 180.220) are found in § 2000.220.

(b) For any section of OMB guidance in subparts A through I of 2 CFR part 180 that has no corresponding section in this part, NRC requirements are those in the OMB guidance at 2 CFR part 180.

### § 2000.135   Who in the Nuclear Regulatory Commission may grant an exception to let an excluded person participate in a covered transaction?

The Director, Office of Administration or another official designated by the Director, has the authority to grant a written exception to let an excluded person participate in a covered transaction, as provided in guidance at 2 CFR 180.135. The Director or other official designated by the Director shall explain the reason(s) for deviating from the governmentwide policy.

## Subpart B—Covered Transactions

### § 2000.220   What contracts and subcontracts, in addition to those listed in 2 CFR 180.220, are covered transactions?

The NRC nonprocurement suspension and debarment requirements apply

445

only to first-tier procurement contracts under a covered nonprocurement transaction.

## Subpart C—Responsibilities of Participants Regarding Transactions

### § 2000.330 What method must be used to pass requirements down to participants at lower tiers?

A participant in a covered transaction must include a term or condition in any lower-tier covered transaction to require the participant of that transaction to—

(a) Comply with subpart C of the OMB guidance in 2 CFR part 180; and

(b) Include a similar term or condition in any covered transaction into which it enters at the next lower tier.

## Subparts D–H [Reserved]

## Subpart I—Definitions

### § 2000.930 Debarring official.

The Debarring Official for the United States Nuclear Regulatory Commission is the Director, Office of Administration.

### § 2000.1010 Suspending official.

The suspending official for the United States Nuclear Regulatory Commission is the Director, Office of Administration.

## PARTS 2001–2099 [RESERVED]

# CHAPTER XXII—CORPORATION FOR NATIONAL AND COMMUNITY SERVICE

447

# PART 2200—NONPROCUREMENT DEBARMENT AND SUSPENSION

Sec.
2200.10 What does this part do?
2200.20 Does this part apply to me?
2200.30 What policies and procedures must I follow?
2200.137 Who in the Corporation for National and Community Service may grant an exception to let an excluded person participate in a covered transaction?
2200.220 What contracts and subcontracts, in addition to those listed in 2 CFR 180.220, are covered transactions?
2200.332 What methods must I use to pass requirements down to participants at lower tiers with whom I intend to do business?
2200.437 What method do I use to communicate to a participant the requirements described in the OMB guidance at 2 CFR 180.435?

AUTHORITY: Sec. 2455, Pub. L. 103–355, 108 Stat. 3327; E.O. 12549, 3 CFR, 1986 Comp., p. 189; E.O. 12689, 3 CFR, 1989 Comp., p. 235; 22 U.S.C. 2503(b).

SOURCE: 72 FR 28826, May 23, 2007, unless otherwise noted.

## § 2200.10 What does this part do?

This part adopts the Office of Management and Budget (OMB) guidance in subparts A through I of 2 CFR part 180, as supplemented by this part, as the Corporation for National and Community Service policies and procedures for nonprocurement debarment and suspension. It thereby gives regulatory effect for the Corporation for National and Community Service to the OMB guidance as supplemented by this part. This part satisfies the requirements in section 3 of Executive Order 12549, "Debarment and Suspension" (3 CFR 1986 Comp., p. 189), Executive Order 12689, "Debarment and Suspension" (3 CFR 1989 Comp., p. 235) and 31 U.S.C. 6101 note (Section 2455, Pub. L. 103–355, 108 Stat. 3327).

## § 2200.20 Does this part apply to me?

This part and, through this part, pertinent portions of the OMB guidance in subparts A through I of 2 CFR part (see table at 2 CFR 180.100(b)) apply to you if you are a—

(a) Participant or principal in a "covered transaction." (see subpart B of 2 CFR part 180 and the definition of "nonprocurement transaction" at 2 CFR 180.970.

(b) Respondent in a Corporation for National and Community Service suspension or debarment action;

(c) Corporation for National and Community Service debarment or suspension official; or

(d) Corporation for National and Community Service grants officer, agreements officer, or other official authorized to enter into any type of nonprocurement transaction that is a covered transaction.

## § 2200.30 What policies and procedures must I follow?

The Corporation for National and Community Service policies and procedures that you must follow are the policies and procedures specified in each applicable section of the OMB guidance in subparts A through I of 2 CFR part 180, as that section is supplemented by the section in this part with the same section number. The contracts that are covered transactions, for example, are specified by section 220 of the OMB guidance (i.e., 2 CFR 180.220) as supplemented by section 220 in this part (i.e., Sec. 2200.220). For any section of OMB guidance in subparts A through I of 2 CFR part 180 that has no corresponding section in this part, Corporation for National and Community Service policies and procedures are those in the OMB guidance.

## § 2200.137 Who in the Corporation for National and Community Service may grant an exception to let an excluded person participate in a covered transaction?

The Chief Executive Officer (or another official designated by the Chief Executive Officer) has the authority to grant an exception to let an excluded person participate in a covered transaction, as provided in the OMB guidance at 2 CFR 180.135.

## § 2200.220 What contracts and subcontracts, in addition to those listed in 2 CFR 180.220, are covered transactions?

Although the OMB guidance at 2 CFR 180.220(c) allows a Federal agency to do so (also see optional lower tier coverage in the figure in the appendix to 2 CFR part 180), Corporation for National

449

and Community Service does not extend coverage of nonprocurement suspension and debarment requirements beyond first-tier procurement contracts under a covered nonprocurement transaction.

### § 2200.332 What methods must I use to pass requirements down to participants at lower tiers with whom I intend to do business?

You as a participant must include a term or condition in lower-tier transactions requiring lower-tier participants to comply with Subpart C of the OMB guidance in 2 CFR part 180.

### § 2200.437 What method do I use to communicate to a participant the requirements described in the OMB guidance at 2 CFR 180.435?

To communicate to a participant the requirements described in 2 CFR 180.435 of the OMB guidance, you as an agency official must include a term or condition in the transaction that requires the participant's compliance with subpart C of 2 CFR part 180, and requires the participant to include a similar term or condition in lower-tier covered transactions.

## PART 2205—IMPLEMENTATION OF AND EXEMPTIONS TO 2 CFR

AUTHORITY: 42 U.S.C. 12571(d), 12571(e)(2)(B), 12581(l), 12581a(a), 12616(c)(2), 12651c(c), 12651d(h), 12651g(b), 12653(a), 12653(h), 12653o(a), and 12657(a); 2 CFR part 200; 45 CFR 2521.95, and 2540.110.

SOURCE: 79 FR 76076, Dec. 19, 2014, unless otherwise noted.

### § 2205.100 Adoption of 2 CFR Part 200.

Under the authority listed above, the Corporation for National and Community Service adopts the Office of Management and Budget's (OMB) Guidance in 2 CFR part 200, except as specified in this part. Thus, this part gives regulatory effect to the OMB guidance and supplements the guidance for recipients of awards from the Corporation.

### § 2205.201 Use of grant agreements (including fixed amount awards), cooperative agreements, and contracts.

(a) The Corporation will determine the appropriate instrument in accordance with its authorities under the national service laws, and in accordance with the Federal Grant and Cooperative Agreement Act (31 U.S.C. 6301–6308), as appropriate.

(b) The Corporation and pass through entities may also provide fixed amount awards in the manner and in the amounts permitted under the national service laws.

### § 2205.306 Cost sharing or matching.

(a) Shared costs or matching funds must meet the criteria of 2 CFR 200.306(b), with the exception of 2 CFR 200.306(b)(5). Federal funds from other agencies may be used as match or cost sharing as authorized by 42 U.S.C. 12571(e) under the national service laws.

### § 2205.332 Fixed amount subawards.

Fixed amount subawards may be made in the manner and in amounts determined under the national service laws, as authorized by the Corporation, without respect to the Simplified Acquisition Threshold.

### § 2205.414 Indirect (F&A) costs.

Administrative costs for programs funded under subtitles B and C of the National and Community Service Act of 1990, as amended, shall be subject to 45 CFR 2521.95 and 2540.110.

## PART 2245—REQUIREMENTS FOR DRUG-FREE WORKPLACE (FINANCIAL ASSISTANCE)

### Subpart A—Purpose and Coverage
### [Reserved]

## Subpart B—Requirements for Recipients Other Than Individuals

2245.225 Whom in the Corporation does a recipient other than an individual notify about a criminal drug conviction?

## Subpart C—Requirements for Recipients Who Are Individuals

2245.300 Whom in the Corporation does a recipient who is an individual notify about a criminal drug conviction?

## Subpart D—Responsibilities of Agency Awarding Officials

2245.400 What method do I use as an agency awarding official to obtain a recipient's agreement to comply with the OMB guidance?

## Subpart E—Violations of this Part and Consequences

2245.500 Who in the Corporation determines that a recipient other than an individual violated the requirements of this part?
2245.505 Who in the Corporation determines that a recipient who is an individual violated the requirements of this part?

## Subpart F [Reserved]

AUTHORITY: 41 U.S.C. 701–707; 42 U.S.C. 12644.

SOURCE: 75 FR 22206, Apr. 28, 2010, unless otherwise noted.

## §2245.10 What does this part do?

This part requires that the award and administration of the Corporation's grants and cooperative agreements comply with Office of Management and Budget (OMB) guidance implementing the portion of the Drug-Free Workplace Act of 1988 (41 U.S.C. 701–707, as amended, hereafter referred to as "the Act") that applies to grants. It thereby—

(a) Gives regulatory effect to the OMB guidance (Subparts A through F of 2 CFR part 182) for the Corporation's grants and cooperative agreements; and

(b) Establishes the Corporation's policies and procedures for compliance with the Act that are the same as those of other Federal agencies, in conformance with the requirement in 41 U.S.C. 705 for Government-wide implementing regulations.

## §2245.20 Does this part apply to me?

This part and, through this part, pertinent portions of the OMB guidance in Subparts A through F of 2 CFR part 182 (see table at 2 CFR 182.115(b)) apply to you if you are a—

(a) Recipient of a Corporation grant or cooperative agreement; or

(b) A Corporation awarding official.

## §2245.30 What policies and procedures must I follow?

(a) *General.* You must follow the policies and procedures specified in applicable sections of the OMB guidance in Subparts A through F of 2 CFR part 182, as implemented by this part.

(b) *Specific sections of OMB guidance that this part supplements.* In implementing the OMB guidance in 2 CFR part 182, this part supplements four sections of the guidance, as shown in the following table. For each of those sections, you must follow the policies and procedures in the OMB guidance, as supplemented by this part.

| Section of OMB guidance | Section in this part where supplemented | What the supplementation clarifies |
|---|---|---|
| (1) 2 CFR 182.225(a) | §2245.225 | Whom in the Corporation a recipient other than an individual must notify if an employee is convicted for a violation of a criminal drug statute in the workplace |
| (2) 2 CFR 182.300(b) | §2245.300 | Whom in the Corporation a recipient who is an individual must notify if he or she is convicted of a criminal drug offense resulting from a violation occurring during the conduct of any award activity. |
| (3) 2 CFR 182.500 ... | §2245.500 | Who in the Corporation is authorized to determine that a recipient other than an individual is in violation of the requirements of 2 CFR part 182, as implemented by this part. |
| (4) 2 CFR 182.505 ... | §2245.505 | Who in the Corporation is authorized to determine that a recipient who is an individual is in violation of the requirements of 2 CFR part 182, as implemented by this part. |

(c) *Sections of the OMB guidance that this part does not supplement.* For any section of OMB guidance in Subparts A through F of 2 CFR part 182 that is not listed in paragraph (b) of this section, the Corporation's policies and procedures are the same as those in the OMB guidance.

## Subpart A—Purpose and Coverage [Reserved]

## Subpart B—Requirements for Recipients Other Than Individuals

**§ 2245.225 Whom in the Corporation does a recipient other than an individual notify about a criminal drug conviction?**

A recipient other than an individual that is required under 2 CFR 182.225(a) to notify Federal agencies about an employee's conviction for a criminal drug offense must notify the Corporation's awarding official or other designee.

## Subpart C—Requirements for Recipients Who Are Individuals

**§ 2245.300 Whom in the Corporation does a recipient who is an individual notify about a criminal drug conviction?**

A recipient who is an individual and is required under 2 CFR 182.300(b) to notify Federal agencies about a conviction for a criminal drug offense must notify the Corporation's awarding official or other designee.

## Subpart D—Responsibilities of Agency Awarding Officials

**§ 2245.400 What method do I use as an agency awarding official to obtain a recipient's agreement to comply with the OMB guidance?**

To obtain a recipient's agreement to comply with applicable requirements in the OMB guidance at 2 CFR part 182, you must obtain each recipient's agreement, as a condition of the award, to comply with the requirements in subpart B (or subpart C, if the recipient is an individual) of 2245, which adopts the Government-wide implementation (2 CFR part 182) of sec. 5152–5158 of the Drug-Free Workplace Act of 1988 (Pub. L. 100–690, Title V, Subtitle D; 41 U.S.C. 701–707).

## Subpart E—Violations of this Part and Consequences

**§ 2245.500 Who in the Corporation determines that a recipient other than an individual violated the requirements of this part?**

The Corporation's Chief Executive Officer or designee is authorized to make the determination under 2 CFR 182.500.

**§ 2245.505 Who in the Corporation determines that a recipient who is an individual violated the requirements of this part?**

The Corporation's Chief Executive Officer or designee is authorized to make the determination under 2 CFR 182.500.

## Subpart F [Reserved]

## PARTS 2246–2299 [RESERVED]

# CHAPTER XXIII—SOCIAL SECURITY ADMINISTRATION

# PART 2300—UNIFORM ADMINISTRATIVE REQUIREMENTS, COST PRINCIPLES, AND AUDIT REQUIREMENTS FOR FEDERAL AWARDS

AUTHORITY: 5 U.S.C. 301; 2 CFR part 200, and as noted in specific sections.

SOURCE: 79 FR 76078, Dec. 19, 2014, unless otherwise noted.

## § 2300.10 Applicable regulations.

The Uniform Administrative Requirements, Cost Principles, and Audit Requirements for Federal Awards set forth in 2 CFR part 200 shall apply to the Social Security Administration.

## §§ 2300.11–2300.2335 [Reserved]

## PARTS 2301–2335 [RESERVED]

## PART 2336—NONPROCUREMENT DEBARMENT AND SUSPENSION

Sec.
2336.10 What does this part do?
2336.20 Does this part apply to me?
2336.30 What policies and procedures must I follow?

### Subpart A—General

2336.137 Who in the SSA may grant an exception to let an excluded person participate in a covered transaction?

### Subpart B—Covered Transactions

2336.220 What contracts and subcontracts, in addition to those listed in 2 CFR 180.220, are covered transactions?

### Subpart C—Responsibilities of Participants Regarding Transactions

2336.332 What methods must I use to pass requirements down to participants at lower tiers with whom I intend to do business?

### Subpart D—Responsibilities of Federal Agency Officials Regarding Transactions

2336.437 What method do I use to communicate to a participant the requirements described in the OMB guidance at 2 CFR 180.435?

### Subparts E–J [Reserved]

AUTHORITY: 42 U.S.C. 902(a)(5); Sec. 2455, Pub. L. 103–355, 108 Stat. 3327; E.O. 12549 (3 CFR, 1986 Comp., p. 189); E.O. 12689 (3 CFR, 1989 Comp., p. 235).

SOURCE: 72 FR 46140, Aug. 17, 2007, unless otherwise noted.

## § 2336.10 What does this part do?

This part adopts the Office of Management and Budget (OMB) guidance in subparts A through I of 2 CFR part 180, as supplemented by this part, as the SSA policies and procedures for nonprocurement debarment and suspension. This part satisfies the requirements in section 3 of Executive Order 12549, "Debarment and Suspension" (3 CFR 1986 Comp., p. 189), Executive Order 12689, "Debarment and Suspension" (3 CFR 1989 Comp., p. 235) and 31 U.S.C. 6101 note (Section 2455, Pub. L. 103–355, 108 Stat. 3327).

## § 2336.20 Does this part apply to me?

This part and, through this part, pertinent portions of the OMB guidance in subparts A through I of 2 CFR part 180 (see table at 2 CFR 180.100(b)) apply to you if you are a—

(a) Participant or principal in a "covered transaction" (see subpart B of 2 CFR part 180 and the definition of "nonprocurement transaction" at 2 CFR 180.970);

(b) Respondent in an SSA suspension or debarment action;

(c) SSA debarment or suspension official; or

(d) SSA grants officer, agreements officer, or other official authorized to enter into any type of nonprocurement transaction that is a covered transaction.

## § 2336.30 What policies and procedures must I follow?

The SSA policies and procedures that you must follow are the policies and procedures specified in each applicable section of the OMB guidance in subparts A through I of 2 CFR part 180, as supplemented by the section in this part with the same section number. The contracts that are covered transactions, for example, are specified by section 220 of the OMB guidance (i.e., 2 CFR 180.220), as supplemented by section 220 in this part (i.e., § 2336.220). For any section of OMB guidance in subparts A through I of 2 CFR 180 that has no corresponding section in this part, SSA policies and procedures are those in the OMB guidance.

## Subpart A—General

**§ 2336.137 Who in the SSA may grant an exception to let an excluded person participate in a covered transaction?**

(a) Within the Social Security Administration, the Commissioner or the designated agency debarment official may grant an exception permitting an excluded person to participate in a particular covered transaction. If the Commissioner or the designated agency debarment official grants an exception, the exception must be in writing and state the reason(s) for deviating from the OMB guidance at 2 CFR 180.135.

(b) An exception granted by one agency for an excluded person does not extend to the covered transactions of another agency.

## Subpart B—Covered Transactions

**§ 2336.220 What contracts and subcontracts, in addition to those listed in 2 CFR 180.220, are covered transactions?**

Although the OMB guidance at 2 CFR 180.220(c) allows a Federal agency to do so (also see option lower tier coverage in the figure in the appendix to 2 CFR part 180), SSA does not extend coverage of nonprocurement suspension and debarment requirements beyond first-tier procurement contracts under a covered nonprocurement transaction.

## Subpart C—Responsibilities of Participants Regarding Transactions

**§ 2336.332 What methods must I use to pass requirements down to participants at lower tiers with whom I intend to do business?**

You as a participant must include a term or condition in lower-tier transactions requiring lower-tier participants to comply with subpart C of the OMB guidance in 2 CFR part 180, as supplemented by this subpart.

## Subpart D—Responsibilities of Federal Agency Officials Regarding Transactions

**§ 2336.437 What method do I use to communicate to a participant the requirements described in the OMB guidance at 2 CFR 180.435?**

To communicate to a participant the requirements described in 2 CFR 180.435 of the OMB guidance, you must include a term or condition in the transaction that requires the participant's compliance with subpart C of 2 CFR part 180, as supplemented by subpart C of this part, and requires the participant to include a similar term or condition in lower-tier covered transactions.

## Subparts E–J [Reserved]

# PART 2339—REQUIREMENTS FOR DRUG-FREE WORKPLACE (FINANCIAL ASSISTANCE)

Sec.
2339.10  What does this part do?
2339.20  Does this part apply to me?
2339.30  What policies and procedures must I follow?

### Subpart A [Reserved]

### Subpart B—Requirements for Recipients Other Than Individuals

2339.225  Who in the Social Security Administration does a recipient other than an individual notify about a criminal drug conviction?

### Subpart C [Reserved]

### Subpart D—Responsibilities of Agency Awarding Officials

2339.400  What method do I use as an agency awarding official to obtain a recipient's agreement to comply with the OMB guidance?

### Subpart E—Violations of this Part and Consequences

2339.500  Who in the Social Security Administration determines that a recipient other than an individual violated the requirements of this part?

### Subpart F [Reserved]

AUTHORITY: 41 U.S.C. 701–707.

SOURCE: 75 FR 31274, June 3, 2010, unless otherwise noted.

### §2339.10 What does this part do?

This part requires that the award and administration of Social Security Administration (SSA) grants and cooperative agreements comply with Office of Management and Budget (OMB) guidance implementing the portion of the Drug-Free Workplace Act of 1988 (41 U.S.C. 701–707, as amended, hereafter referred to as "the Act") that applies to grants. It thereby—

(a) Gives regulatory effect to the OMB guidance (subparts A through F of 2 CFR part 182) for SSA's grants and cooperative agreements; and

(b) Establishes SSA's policies and procedures for compliance with the Act that are the same as those of other Federal agencies, in conformance with the requirement in 41 U.S.C. 705 for Government-wide implementing regulations.

### §2339.20 Does this part apply to me?

This part and, through this part, pertinent portions of the OMB guidance in subparts A through F of 2 CFR part 182 (see table at 2 CFR 182.115(b)) apply to you if you are—

(a) A recipient of an SSA grant or cooperative agreement; or

(b) An SSA awarding official.

### §2339.30 What policies and procedures must I follow?

(a) *General.* You must follow the policies and procedures specified in applicable sections of the OMB guidance in Subparts A through F of 2 CFR part 182, as implemented by this part.

(b) *Specific sections of OMB guidance that this part supplements.* In implementing the OMB guidance in 2 CFR part 182, this part supplements four sections of the guidance, as shown in the following table.

| Section of OMB guidance in 2 CFR | Section in this part where supplemented, 2 CFR | What the supplementation clarifies |
|---|---|---|
| (1) 182.225(a) | §2339.225 | Who in SSA a recipient other than an individual must notify if an employee is convicted for a violation of a criminal drug statute in the workplace. |
| (2) 182.300(b) | §2339.300 | Who in SSA a recipient who is an individual must notify if he or she is convicted of a criminal drug offense resulting from a violation occurring during the conduct of any award activity. |
| (3) 182.500 | §2339.500 | Who in SSA is authorized to determine that a recipient other than an individual is in violation of the requirements of 2 CFR part 182, as implemented by this part. |
| (4) 182.505 | §2339.505 | Who in SSA is authorized to determine that a recipient who is an individual is in violation of the requirements of 2 CFR part 182, as implemented by this part. |

(c) *Sections of the OMB guidance that this part does not supplement.* Our policies and procedures are the same as those in the OMB guidance for any section not included in the table in paragraph (b) of this section.

## Subpart A [Reserved]

## Subpart B—Requirements for Recipients Other Than Individuals

### §2339.225 Who in the Social Security Administration does a recipient other than an individual notify about a criminal drug conviction?

A recipient other than an individual that is required under 2 CFR 182.225(a) to notify Federal agencies about an employee's conviction for a criminal drug offense must notify the Commissioner of Social Security or designee.

## Subpart C [Reserved]

## Subpart D—Responsibilities of Agency Awarding Officials

**§ 2339.400  What method do I use as an agency awarding official to obtain a recipient's agreement to comply with the OMB guidance?**

You must include the following term or condition in the award:

*Drug-free workplace.* You, as the recipient, must comply with drug-free workplace requirements in Subpart B, which adopts the Government-wide implementation (2 CFR part 182) of sec. 5152–5158 of the Drug-Free Workplace Act of 1988 (Pub. L. 100–690, Title V, Subtitle D; 41 U.S.C. 701–707).

## Subpart E—Violations of this Part and Consequences

**§ 2339.500  Who in the Social Security Administration determines that a recipient other than an individual violated the requirements of this part?**

The Commissioner of Social Security or designee will make the determination.

## Subpart F [Reserved]

## PARTS 2340–2399 [RESERVED]

# CHAPTER XXIV—DEPARTMENT OF HOUSING AND URBAN DEVELOPMENT

# PART 2400—UNIFORM ADMINISTRATIVE REQUIREMENTS, COST PRINCIPLES AND AUDIT REQUIRMENTS FOR FEDERAL AWARDS

AUTHORITY: 42 U.S.C. 3535(d); 2 CFR part 200.

SOURCE: 79 FR 76078, Dec. 19, 2014, unless otherwise noted.

## § 2400.101 Applicable regulations.

Unless excepted under 24 CFR chapters I through IX, the Uniform Administrative Requirements, Cost Principles, and Audit Requirements for Federal Awards, set forth in 2 CFR part 200, shall apply to Federal Awards made by the Department of Housing and Urban Development to non-Federal entities.

## PARTS 2401–2423 [RESERVED]

## PART 2424—NONPROCUREMENT DEBARMENT AND SUSPENSION

AUTHORITY: Sec. 2455, Pub. L. 103–355, 108 Stat. 3327; E.O. 12549, 3 CFR, 1986 Comp., p. 189; E.O. 12689, 3 CFR, 1989 Comp., p. 235.

SOURCE: 72 FR 73487, Dec. 27, 2007, unless otherwise noted.

### § 2424.10  What does this part do?

In this part, HUD adopts, as HUD policies, procedures, and requirements for nonprocurement debarment and suspension, the OMB guidance in subparts A through I of 2 CFR part 180, as supplemented by this part. This adoption thereby gives regulatory effect for HUD to the OMB guidance, as supplemented by this part. This part satisfies the requirements in section 3 of Executive Order 12549, "Debarment and Suspension" (3 CFR 1986 Comp., p. 189), Executive Order 12689, "Debarment and Suspension" (3 CFR 1989 Comp., p. 235) and 31 U.S.C. 6101 note (Section 2455, Pub. L. 103–355, 108 Stat. 3327).

### § 2424.20  Does this part apply to me?

This part and, through this part, pertinent portions of subparts A through I of 2 CFR part 180 (see table at 2 CFR 180.100(b)), apply to you if you are a—

(a) Participant or principal in a "covered transaction" (see subpart B of 2 CFR part 180 and the definition of "nonprocurement transaction" at 2 CFR 180.970, as supplemented by § 2424.970 of this part);

(b) Respondent in a HUD suspension or debarment action;

(c) HUD debarment or suspension official; or

(d) HUD grants officer, agreements officer, or other official authorized to enter into any type of nonprocurement transaction that is a covered transaction.

### § 2424.30  What policies and procedures must I follow?

The HUD policies and procedures that you must follow are the policies and procedures specified in each applicable section of the OMB guidance in subparts A through I of 2 CFR part 180, as that section is supplemented by the section in this part with the same section number. The contracts that are covered transactions, for example, are specified by section 220 of the OMB guidance (i.e., 2 CFR 180.220), as supplemented by section 220 in this part (i.e., § 2424.220). For any section of OMB guidance in subparts A through I of 2 CFR 180 that has no corresponding section in this part, HUD policies and procedures are those in the OMB guidance.

## Subpart A—General

### § 2424.137  Who in HUD may grant an exception to let an excluded person participate in a covered transaction?

The Secretary or designee may grant an exception permitting an excluded person to participate in a particular covered transaction. If the Secretary or a designee grants an exception, the exception must be in writing and state the reason(s) for deviating from the governmentwide policy in Executive Order 12549.

## Subpart B—Covered Transactions

### § 2424.220  What contracts and subcontracts, in addition to those listed in 2 CFR 180.220, are covered transactions?

In addition to the contracts covered under 2 CFR 180.220(b) of the OMB guidance, this part applies to any contract, regardless of tier, that is awarded by a contractor, subcontractor, supplier, consultant, or its agent or representative in any transaction, if the contract is to be funded or provided by HUD under a covered nonprocurement transaction and the amount of the contract is expected to equal or exceed $25,000. This extends the coverage of the HUD nonprocurement suspension and debarment requirements to all lower tiers of subcontracts under covered nonprocurement transactions, as permitted under the OMB guidance at 2 CFR 180.220(c) (see optional lower-tier coverage in the figure in the appendix to 2 CFR part 180).

## Subpart C—Responsibilities of Participants Regarding Transactions

### § 2424.300  What must I do before I enter into a covered transaction with another person at the next lower tier (HUD supplement to governmentwide definition at 2 CFR 180.300)?

(a) You, as a participant, are responsible for determining whether you are entering into a covered transaction with an excluded or disqualified person. You may decide the method by which you do so.

(1) You may, but are not required to, check the Excluded Parties List System (EPLS).

(2) You may, but are not required to, collect a certification from that person.

(b) In the case of an employment contract, HUD does not require employers to check the EPLS prior to making salary payments pursuant to that contract.

**§2424.332 What methods must I use to pass requirements down to participants at lower tiers with whom I intend to do business?**

To communicate the requirements to lower-tier participants, you must include a term or condition in the transaction requiring compliance with subpart C of the OMB guidance in 2 CFR part 180, as supplemented by this subpart.

## Subpart D—Responsibilities of Federal Agency Officials Regarding Transactions

**§2424.437 What method do I use to communicate to a participant the requirements described in the OMB guidance at 2 CFR 180.435?**

To communicate to a participant the requirements described in 2 CFR 180.435 of the OMB guidance, you must include a term or condition in the transaction that requires the participant to: comply with subpart C of 2 CFR part 180, as supplemented by subpart C of this part, and include a similar term or condition in lower-tier covered transactions.

## Subparts E–F [Reserved]

## Subpart G—Suspension

**§2424.747 Who conducts fact finding for HUD suspensions?**

In all HUD suspensions, the official who shall conduct additional proceedings where disputed material facts are challenged shall be a hearing officer.

## Subpart H—Debarment

**§2424.842 Who conducts fact finding for HUD debarments?**

In all HUD debarments, the official who shall conduct additional proceedings where disputed material facts are challenged shall be a hearing officer.

## Subpart I—Definitions

**§2424.952 Hearing officer.**

*Hearing Officer* means an Administrative Law Judge or Office of Appeals Judge authorized by HUD's Secretary or by the Secretary's designee to conduct proceedings under this part.

**§2424.970 Nonprocurement transaction (HUD supplement to governmentwide definition at 2 CFR 180.970).**

In the case of employment contracts that are covered transactions, each salary payment under the contract is a separate covered transaction.

**§2424.995 Principal (HUD supplement to governmentwide definition at 2 CFR 180.995).**

A person who has a critical influence on, or substantive control over, a covered transaction, whether or not employed by the participant. Persons who have a critical influence on, or substantive control over, a covered transaction may include, but are not limited to:

(a) Loan officers;

(b) Staff appraisers and inspectors;

(c) Underwriters;

(d) Bonding companies;

(e) Borrowers under programs financed by HUD or with loans guaranteed, insured, or subsidized through HUD programs;

(f) Purchasers of properties with HUD-insured or Secretary-held mortgages;

(g) Recipients under HUD assistance agreements;

(h) Ultimate beneficiaries of HUD programs;

(i) Fee appraisers and inspectors;

(j) Real estate agents and brokers;

(k) Management and marketing agents;

(l) Accountants, consultants, investment bankers, architects, engineers, and attorneys who are in a business relationship with participants in connection with a covered transaction under a HUD program;

(m) Contractors involved in the construction or rehabilitation of properties financed by HUD, with HUD-insured loans or acquired properties, including properties held by HUD as mortgagee-in-possession;

(n) Closing agents;

(o) Turnkey developers of projects financed by or with financing insured by HUD;

(p) Title companies;

(q) Escrow agents;

(r) Project owners;

(s) Administrators of hospitals, nursing homes, and projects for the elderly financed or insured by HUD; and

(t) Developers, sellers, or owners of property financed with loans insured under Title I or Title II of the National Housing Act.

### § 2424.1017  Ultimate beneficiary.

Ultimate beneficiaries of HUD programs include, but are not limited to, subsidized tenants and subsidized mortgagors, such as those assisted under Section 8 Housing Assistance Payment contracts, by Section 236 Rental Assistance, or by Rent Supplement payments.

## Subpart J—Limited Denial of Participation

### § 2424.1100  What is a limited denial of participation?

A limited denial of participation excludes a specific person from participating in a specific program, or programs, within a HUD field office's geographic jurisdiction, for a specific period of time. A limited denial of participation is normally issued by a HUD field office, but may be issued by a Headquarters office. The decision to impose a limited denial of participation is discretionary and based on the best interests of the federal government.

### § 2424.1105  Who may issue a limited denial of participation?

The Secretary designates HUD officials who are authorized to impose a limited denial of participation, affecting any participant and/or their affiliates, except mortgagees approved by the Federal Housing Administration (FHA).

### § 2424.1110  When may a HUD official issue a limited denial of participation?

(a) An authorized HUD official may issue a limited denial of participation against a person, based upon adequate evidence of any of the following causes:

(1) Approval of an applicant for insurance would constitute an unsatisfactory risk;

(2) There are irregularities in a person's past performance in a HUD program;

(3) The person has failed to maintain the prerequisites of eligibility to participate in a HUD program;

(4) The person has failed to honor contractual obligations or to proceed in accordance with contract specifications or HUD regulations;

(5) The person has failed to satisfy, upon completion, the requirements of an assistance agreement or contract;

(6) The person has deficiencies in ongoing construction projects;

(7) The person has falsely certified in connection with any HUD program, whether or not the certification was made directly to HUD;

(8) The person has committed any act or omission that would be cause for debarment under 2 CFR 180.800;

(9) The person has violated any law, regulation, or procedure relating to the application for financial assistance, insurance, or guarantee, or to the performance of obligations incurred pursuant to a grant of financial assistance or pursuant to a conditional or final commitment to insure or guarantee;

(10) The person has made or procured to be made any false statement for the purpose of influencing in any way an action of the Department; or

(11) Imposition of a limited denial of participation by any other HUD office.

(b) Filing of a criminal Indictment or Information shall constitute adequate evidence for the purpose of limited denial of participation actions. The Indictment or Information need not be based on offenses against HUD.

(c) Imposition of a limited denial of participation by any other HUD office shall constitute adequate evidence for a concurrent limited denial of participation. Where such a concurrent limited denial of participation is imposed, participation may be restricted on the same basis without the need for an additional conference or further hearing.

(d) An affiliate or organizational element may be included in a limited denial of participation solely on the basis of its affiliation, and regardless of its knowledge of or participation in the acts providing cause for the sanction. The burden of proving that a particular affiliate or organizational element is currently responsible and not controlled by the primary sanctioned party (or by an entity that itself is controlled by the primary sanctioned party) is on the affiliate or organizational element.

### § 2424.1115 When does a limited denial of participation take effect?

A limited denial of participation is effective immediately upon issuance of the notice.

### § 2424.1120 How long may a limited denial of participation last?

A limited denial of participation may remain in effect up to 12 months.

### § 2424.1125 How does a limited denial of participation start?

A limited denial of participation is made effective by providing the person, and any specifically named affiliate, with notice:

(a) That the limited denial of participation is being imposed;

(b) Of the cause(s) under § 2424.1110 for the sanction;

(c) Of the potential effect of the sanction, including the length of the sanction and the HUD program(s) and geographic area affected by the sanction;

(d) Of the right to request, in writing, within 30 days of receipt of the notice, a conference under § 2424.1130; and

(e) Of the right to contest the limited denial of participation under § 2424.1130.

### § 2424.1130 How may I contest my limited denial of participation?

(a) Within 30 days after receiving a notice of limited denial of participation, you may request a conference with the official who issued such notice. The conference shall be held within 15 days after the Department's receipt of the request for a conference, unless you waive this time limit. The official or designee who imposed the sanction shall preside. At the conference, you may appear with a representative and may present all relevant information and materials to the official or designee. Within 20 days after the conference, or within 20 days after any agreed-upon extension of time for submission of additional materials, the official or designee shall, in writing, advise you of the decision to terminate, modify, or affirm the limited denial of participation. If all or a portion of the remaining period of exclusion is affirmed, the notice of affirmation shall advise you of the opportunity to contest the notice and to request a hearing before a Departmental Hearing Officer. You have 30 days after receipt of the notice of affirmation to request this hearing. If the official or designee does not issue a decision within the 20-day period, you may contest the sanction before a Departmental Hearing Officer. Again, you have 30 days from the expiration of the 20-day period to request this hearing. If you request a hearing before the Departmental Hearing Officer, you must submit your request to the Debarment Docket Clerk, Department of Housing and Urban Development, 451 Seventh Street, SW., B–133 Portals 200, Washington DC 20410–0500.

(b) You may skip the conference with the official and you may request a hearing before a Departmental Hearing Officer. This must also be done within 30 days after receiving a notice of limited denial of participation. If you opt to have a hearing before a Departmental Hearing Officer, you must submit your request to the Debarment Docket Clerk, Department of Housing and Urban Development, 451 Seventh Street, SW., B–133 Portals 200, Washington DC 20410–0500. The hearing before the Departmental Hearing Officer is more formal than the conference before the sanctioning official described above. The Departmental Hearing Officer will conduct the hearing in accordance with 24 CFR part 26, subpart A. The Departmental Hearing Officer will issue findings of fact and make a recommended decision. The sanctioning official will then make a final decision, as promptly as possible, after the Departmental Hearing Officer's recommended decision is issued. The sanctioning official may reject the recommended decision or any findings of fact, only after specifically determining that the decision or any of the facts are arbitrary, capricious, or clearly erroneous.

(c) In deciding whether to terminate, modify, or affirm a limited denial of participation, the Departmental official or designee may consider the factors listed at 2 CFR 180.860. The Departmental Hearing Officer may also consider the factors listed at 2 CFR 180.860 in making any recommended decision.

### § 2424.1135 Do Federal agencies coordinate limited denial of participation actions?

Federal agencies do not coordinate limited denial of participation actions. As stated in § 2424.1100, a limited denial of participation is a HUD-specific action and applies only to HUD activities.

### § 2424.1140 What is the scope of a limited denial of participation?

The scope of a limited denial of participation is as follows:

(a) A limited denial of participation generally extends only to participation in the program under which the cause arose. A limited denial of participation may, at the discretion of the authorized official, extend to other programs, initiatives, or functions within the jurisdiction of an Assistant Secretary. The authorized official, however, may determine that where the sanction is based on an indictment or conviction, the sanction shall apply to all programs throughout HUD.

(b) For purposes of this subpart, participation includes receipt of any benefit or financial assistance through grants or contractual arrangements; benefits or assistance in the form of loan guarantees or insurance; and awards of procurement contracts.

(c) The sanction may be imposed for a period not to exceed 12 months, and shall be effective within the geographic jurisdiction of the office imposing it, unless the sanction is imposed by an Assistant Secretary or Deputy Assistant Secretary, in which case the sanction may be imposed on either a nationwide or a more restricted basis.

### § 2424.1145 May HUD impute the conduct of one person to another in a limited denial of participation?

For purposes of determining a limited denial of participation, HUD may impute conduct as follows:

(a) *Conduct imputed from an individual to an organization.* HUD may impute the fraudulent, criminal, or other improper conduct of any officer, director, shareholder, partner, employee, or other individual associated with an organization, to that organization when the improper conduct occurred in connection with the individual's performance of duties for or on behalf of that organization, or with the organization's knowledge, approval, or acquiescence. The organization's acceptance of the benefits derived from the conduct is evidence of knowledge, approval, or acquiescence.

(b) *Conduct imputed from an organization to an individual or between individuals.* HUD may impute the fraudulent, criminal, or other improper conduct of any organization to an individual, or from one individual to another individual, if the individual to whom the improper conduct is imputed participated in, had knowledge of, or had reason to know of the improper conduct.

(c) *Conduct imputed from one organization to another organization.* HUD may impute the fraudulent, criminal, or other improper conduct of one organization to another organization when the improper conduct occurred in connection with a partnership, joint venture, joint application, association, or similar arrangement, or when the organization to whom the improper conduct is imputed has the power to direct, manage, control, or influence the activities of the organization responsible for the improper conduct. Acceptance of the benefits derived from the conduct is evidence of knowledge, approval, or acquiescence.

### § 2424.1150 What is the effect of a suspension or debarment on a limited denial of participation?

If you have submitted a request for a hearing pursuant to § 2424.1130 of this subpart, and you also receive, pursuant to subpart G or H of this part, a notice of proposed debarment or suspension that is based on the same transaction(s) or the same conduct as the limited denial of participation, as determined by the debarring or suspending official, the following rules shall apply:

(a) During the 30-day period after you receive a notice of proposed debarment or suspension, during which you may elect to contest the debarment under 2 CFR 180.815, or the suspension pursuant to 2 CFR 180.720, all proceedings in the limited denial of participation, including discovery, are automatically stayed.

(b) If you do not contest the proposed debarment pursuant to 2 CFR 180.815, or the suspension pursuant to 2 CFR 180.720, the final imposition of the debarment or suspension shall also constitute a final decision with respect to the limited denial of participation, to the extent that the debarment or suspension is based on the same transaction(s) or conduct as the limited denial of participation.

(c) If you contest the proposed debarment pursuant to 2 CFR 180.815, or the suspension pursuant to 2 CFR 180.720, then:

(1) Those parts of the limited denial of participation and the debarment or suspension based on the same transaction(s) or conduct, as determined by the debarring or suspending official, shall be immediately consolidated before the debarring or suspending official;

(2) Proceedings under the consolidated portions of the limited denial of participation shall be stayed before the hearing officer until the suspending or debarring official makes a determination as to whether the consolidated matters should be referred to a hearing officer. Such a determination must be made within 90 days of the date of the

issuance of the suspension or proposed debarment, unless the suspending/debarring official extends the period for good cause.

(i) If the suspending or debarring official determines that there is a genuine dispute as to material facts regarding the consolidated matter, the entire consolidated matter will be referred to the hearing officer hearing the limited denial of participation, for additional proceedings pursuant to 2 CFR 180.750 or 180.845.

(ii) If the suspending or debarring official determines that there is no dispute as to material facts regarding the consolidated matter, jurisdiction of the hearing officer under 2 CFR part 2424, subpart J, to hear those parts of the limited denial of participation based on the same transaction[s] or conduct as the debarment or suspension, as determined by the debarring or suspending official, will be transferred to the debarring or suspending official, and the hearing officer responsible for hearing the limited denial of participation shall transfer the administrative record to the debarring or suspending official.

(3) The suspending or debarring official shall hear the entire consolidated case under the procedures governing suspensions and debarments, and shall issue a final decision as to both the limited denial of participation and the suspension or debarment.

### § 2424.1155 What is the effect of a limited denial of participation on a suspension or a debarment?

The imposition of a limited denial of participation does not affect the right of the Department to suspend or debar any person under this part.

### § 2424.1160 May a limited denial of participation be terminated before the term of the limited denial of participation expires?

If the cause for the limited denial of participation is resolved before the expiration of the 12-month period, the official who imposed the sanction may terminate it.

### § 2424.1165 How is a limited denial of participation reported?

When a limited denial of participation has been made final, or the period for requesting a conference pursuant to § 2424.1130 has expired without receipt of such a request, the official imposing the limited denial of participation shall notify the Director of the Compliance Division in the Departmental Enforcement Center of the scope of the limited denial of participation.

## PART 2429—REQUIREMENTS FOR DRUG-FREE WORKPLACE (FINANCIAL ASSISTANCE)

Sec.
2429.10　What does this part do?
2429.20　Does this part apply to me?
2429.30　What policies and procedures must I follow?

### Subpart A [Reserved]

### Subpart B—Requirements for Recipients Other Than Individuals

2429.225　Whom in HUD does a recipient other than an individual notify about a criminal drug conviction?

### Subpart C—Requirements for Recipients Who Are Individuals

2429.300　Whom in HUD does a recipient who is an individual notify about a criminal drug conviction?

### Subpart D—Responsibilities of Agency Awarding Officials

2429.400　What method do I use as an agency awarding official to obtain a recipient's agreement to comply with the OMB guidance?

### Subpart E—Violations of This Part and Consequences

2429.500　Who in HUD determines that a recipient other than an individual violated the requirements of this part?
2429.505　Who in HUD determines that a recipient who is an individual violated the requirements of this part?

### Subpart F [Reserved]

AUTHORITY: 41 U.S.C. 701–707; 42 U.S.C. 3535(d).

SOURCE: 76 FR 45166, July 28, 2011, unless otherwise noted.

## § 2429.10　What does this part do?

This part requires that the award and administration of HUD grants and cooperative agreements comply with Office of Management and Budget (OMB) guidance implementing the portion of the Drug-Free Workplace Act of 1988 (41 U.S.C. 701–707) (referred to as the Act in this part) that applies to grants. This part:

(a) Gives regulatory effect to the OMB guidance (Subparts A through F of 2 CFR part 182) for HUD grants and cooperative agreements; and

(b) Establishes HUD policies and procedures for compliance with the Act that are the same as those of other Federal agencies, in conformance with the requirement in 41 U.S.C. 705 for governmentwide implementing regulations.

## § 2429.20　Does this part apply to me?

This part, and through this part, pertinent portions of the OMB guidance in subparts A through F of 2 CFR part 182 (see table at 2 CFR 182.115(b)) apply to you if you are a:

(a) Recipient of a HUD grant or cooperative agreement; or

(b) HUD awarding official.

## § 2429.30　What policies and procedures must I follow?

(a) *General.* You must follow the policies and procedures specified in applicable sections of the OMB guidance in Subparts A through F of 2 CFR part 182, as implemented by this part.

(b) *Specific sections of OMB guidance that this part supplements.* In implementing the OMB guidance in 2 CFR part 182, this part supplements four sections of the guidance, as shown in the following table. For each of those sections, you must follow the policies and procedures of the OMB guidance, as supplemented by this part.

| Section of OMB guidance | Section in this part where supplemented | What the supplementation clarifies |
|---|---|---|
| (1) 2 CFR 182.225(a) .............. | § 2429.225 | Whom in HUD must a recipient other than an individual notify if an employee is convicted for a violation of a criminal drug statute in the workplace? |

| Section of OMB guidance | Section in this part where supplemented | What the supplementation clarifies |
|---|---|---|
| (2) 2 CFR 182.300(b) .............. | §2429.300 | Whom in HUD must a recipient who is an individual notify if he or she is convicted of a criminal drug offense resulting from a violation occurring during the conduct of any award activity? |
| (3) 2 CFR 182.500 ................... | §2429.500 | Who in HUD is authorized to determine that a recipient other than an individual is in violation of the requirements of 2 CFR part 182, as implemented by this part? |
| (4) 2 CFR 182.505 ................... | §2429.505 | Who in HUD is authorized to determine that a recipient who is an individual is in violation of the requirements of 2 CFR part 182, as implemented by this part? |

(c) *Sections of the OMB guidance that this part does not supplement.* For any section of OMB guidance in Subparts A through F of 2 CFR part 182 that is not listed in paragraph (b) of this section, HUD policies and procedures are the same as those in the OMB guidance.

## Subpart A [Reserved]

## Subpart B—Requirements for Recipients Other Than Individuals

§2429.225  Whom in HUD does a recipient other than an individual notify about a criminal conviction?

A recipient other than an individual who is required under 2 CFR 182.225(a) to notify Federal agencies about an employee's conviction for a criminal drug offense must notify each HUD office with which it currently has an award.

## Subpart C—Requirements for Recipients Who Are Individuals

§2429.300  Whom in HUD does a recipient who is an individual notify about a criminal conviction?

A recipient who is an individual and is required under 2 CFR 182.300(b) to notify Federal agencies about a conviction for a criminal drug offense must notify each HUD office with which he or she currently has an award.

## Subpart D—Responsibilities of Agency Awarding Officials

§2429.400  What method do I use as an agency awarding official to obtain a recipient's agreement to comply with the OMB guidance?

To obtain a recipient's agreement to comply with applicable requirements in the OMB guidance at 2 CFR part 182, you must include the following term or condition in the award:

*Drug-free workplace.* You as the recipient must comply with drug-free workplace requirements in Subpart B (or Subpart C, if the recipient is an individual) of part 2429, which adopts the governmentwide implementation (2 CFR part 182) of sections 5152–5158 of the Drug-Free Workplace Act of 1988 (Pub. L. 100–690, Title V, Subtitle D; 41 U.S.C. 701–707).

## Subpart E—Violations of This Part and Consequences

§2429.500  Who in HUD determines that a recipient other than an individual violated the requirements of this part?

The Secretary or designee is the official authorized to make the determination under 2 CFR 182.500.

§2429.505  Who in HUD determines that a recipient who is an individual violated the requirements of this part?

The Secretary or designee is the official authorized to make the determination under 2 CFR 182.505.

## Subpart F [Reserved]

## PARTS 2430–2499 [RESERVED]

# CHAPTER XXV—NATIONAL SCIENCE FOUNDATION

# PART 2500—UNIFORM ADMINISTRATIVE REQUIREMENTS, COST PRINCIPLES, AND AUDIT REQUIREMENTS FOR FEDERAL AWARDS

AUTHORITY: 42 U.S.C. 1861, *et seq.;* 2 CFR part 200.

SOURCE: 79 FR 76079, Dec. 19, 2014, unless otherwise noted.

## § 2500.100  Adoption of 2 CFR Part 200.

Under the Authority cited above, NSF has formally adopted 2 CFR part 200, Uniform Administrative Requirements, Cost Principles, and Audit Requirements for Federal Awards ("the Uniform Guidance"). The Foundation's implementation document, the NSF Proposal & Award Policies & Procedures Guide, may be found at: *http://www.nsf.gov/publications/pub_summ.jsp?ods_key=papp.*

NSF's implementation includes the following deviation from the Uniform Guidance:

Award Cash Management System— NSF is continuing collection of award financial information through the implementation of the Award Cash Management Service (ACM$) and the Program Income Worksheet. ACM$ replaced the NSF Federal Financial Report (FFR) and the NSF FastLane Cash Request process with a single web based user interface. ACM$ is used to collect award level detail financial information at the time of each payment request submitted by the awardee institution. The Program Income Worksheet is used to collect program income financial information from awardee institutions on an annual basis. ACM$ and the Program Income Worksheet utilize approved government-wide data elements from the FFR for the collection of financial information as provided for in the Uniform Guidance paragraph 505(c) and prescribed in 2 CFR 200.327. The requirement for Federal agencies to use the FFR data elements for cash management and financial reporting was publically announced in FEDERAL REGISTER on August 13, 2008.

## PARTS 2501–2519 [RESERVED]

# PART 2520—NONPROCUREMENT DEBARMENT AND SUSPENSION

AUTHORITY: 42 U.S.C. 1870(a); Sec. 2455, Pub. L. 103–355, 108 Stat. 3327; E.O. 12549, 3 CFR, 1986 Comp., p. 189; E.O. 12689, 3 CFR, 1989 Comp., p. 235.

SOURCE: 72 FR 4944, Feb. 2, 2007, unless otherwise noted.

## § 2520.10  What does this part do?

This part adopts the Office of Management and Budget (OMB) guidance in subparts A through I of 2 CFR part 180, as supplemented by this part, as the NSF policies and procedures for nonprocurement debarment and suspension. It thereby gives regulatory effect for NSF to the OMB guidance as supplemented by this part. This part satisfies the requirements in section 3 of Executive Order 12549, "Debarment and Suspension" (3 CFR 1986 Comp., p. 189), Executive Order 12689, "Debarment and Suspension" (3 CFR 1989 Comp., p. 235) and 31 U.S.C. 6101 note (Section 2455, Public Law 103–355, 108 Stat. 3327).

## § 2520.20 Does this part apply to me?

This part and, through this part, pertinent portions of the OMB guidance in subparts A through I of 2 CFR part 180 (see table at 2 CFR 180.100(b)) apply to you if you are a—

(a) Participant or principal in a "covered transaction" (see Subpart B of 2 CFR part 180 and the definition of "nonprocurement transaction" at 2 CFR 180.970).

(b) Respondent in an NSF suspension or debarment action.

(c) NSF debarment or suspension official.

(d) NSF grants officer, agreements officer, or other official authorized to enter into any type of nonprocurement transaction that is a covered transaction.

## § 2520.30 What policies and procedures must I follow?

The NSF policies and procedures that you must follow are the policies and procedures specified in each applicable section of the OMB guidance in subparts A through I of 2 CFR part 180, as that section is supplemented by the section in this part with the same section number. The contracts that are covered transactions, for example, are specified by section 220 of the OMB guidance (i.e., 2 CFR 180.220) as supplemented by section 220 in this part (i.e., § 2520.220). For any section of OMB guidance in subparts A through I of 2 CFR 180 that has no corresponding section in this part, NSF policies and procedures are those in the OMB guidance.

## Subpart A—General

## § 2520.137 Who in NSF may grant an exception to let an excluded person participate in a covered transaction?

The NSF Director and the Deputy Director have the authority to grant an exception to let an excluded person participate in a covered transaction.

## Subpart B—Covered Transactions

## § 2520.220 What contracts and subcontracts, in addition to those listed in 2 CFR 180.220, are covered transactions?

Although the OMB guidance at 2 CFR 180.220(c) allows a Federal agency to do so (also see optional lower tier coverage in the figure in the appendix to 2 CFR part 180), NSF does not extend coverage of nonprocurement suspension and debarment requirements beyond first-tier procurement contracts under a covered nonprocurement transaction.

## Subpart C—Responsibilities of Participants Regarding Transactions

## § 2520.332 What methods must I use to pass requirements down to participants at lower tiers with whom I intend to do business?

You as a participant must include a term or condition in lower-tier transactions requiring lower-tier participants to comply with subpart C of the OMB guidance in 2 CFR part 180, as supplemented by this subpart.

## Subpart D—Responsibilities of Federal Agency Officials Regarding Transactions

## § 2520.437 What method do I use to communicate to a participant the requirements described in the OMB guidance at 2 CFR 180.435?

To communicate to a participant the requirements described in 2 CFR 180.435 of the OMB guidance, you must include a term or condition in the transaction that requires the participant's compliance with subpart C of 2 CFR part 180, as supplemented by subpart C of this part, and requires the participant to include a similar term or condition in lower-tier covered transactions.

## Subparts E–I [Reserved]

## PARTS 2521–2599 [RESERVED]

# CHAPTER XXVI—NATIONAL ARCHIVES AND RECORDS ADMINISTRATION

# PART 2600—UNIFORM ADMINISTRATIVE REQUIREMENTS, COST PRINCIPLES, AND AUDIT REQUIREMENTS FOR FEDERAL AWARDS

Sec.
2600.100 Adoption of 2 CFR part 200.
2600.101 Indirect costs exception to 2 CFR 200.414.
2600.102 Additional NARA grant administration policies.

AUTHORITY: 5 U.S.C. 301; 44 U.S.C. 2104(a); 44 U.S.C. 2501–2506; 75 FR 66317 (Oct. 28, 2010); 2 CFR 200.

SOURCE: 79 FR 76079, Dec. 19, 2014, unless otherwise noted.

## § 2600.100 Adoption of 2 CFR Part 200.

Under the authority listed above, the National Archives and Records Administration (NARA), through its National Historical Publications and Records Commission (NHPRC), adopts the Office of Management and Budget (OMB) Guidance in 2 CFR part 200, except regarding indirect costs (see § 2600.101). Thus, this part gives regulatory effect to the OMB guidance and supplements the guidance as needed for NARA and NHPRC.

## § 2600.101 Indirect costs exception to 2 CFR 200.414.

As approved by the Archivist of the United States, the National Archives does not permit grant recipients to use allocated funds from NARA or NHPRC for indirect costs. Grant recipients may use cost sharing to cover indirect costs instead. NARA's policies on indirect costs are located at *http://www.archives.gov/nhprc*, and are included in grant opportunity announcements.

(Authority: 44 U.S.C. 2103–04, 2 CFR part 200)

## § 2600.102 Additional NARA grant administration policies.

Grant recipients must also follow NARA grant administration policies and procedures set out in 36 CFR parts 1202, 1206, 1208, 1211, and 1212.

# PARTS 2601–2699 [RESERVED]

# CHAPTER XXVII—SMALL BUSINESS ADMINISTRATION

479

# PART 2700—NONPROCUREMENT DEBARMENT AND SUSPENSION

AUTHORITY: Sec. 2455, Pub. L. 103–355, 108 Stat. 3327 (31 U.S.C. 6101 note); E.O. 12549 (3 CFR, 1986 Comp., p. 189); E.O. 12689 (3 CFR, 1989, 1986 Comp., p. 235); 15 U.S.C. 634(b)(6).

SOURCE: 72 FR 39728, July 20, 2007, unless otherwise noted.

## § 2700.10  What does this part do?

This part adopts the Office of Management and Budget (OMB) guidance in subparts A through I of 2 CFR part 180, as supplemented by this part, as the SBA policies and procedures for nonprocurement debarment and suspension. It thereby gives regulatory effect for SBA to the OMB guidance as supplemented by this part. This part satisfies the requirements in section 3 of Executive Order 12549, "Debarment and Suspension" (3 CFR 1986 Comp., p. 189); Executive Order 12689, "Debarment and Suspension" (3 CFR 1989 Comp., p. 235); and section 2455 of the Federal Acquisition Streamlining Act of 1994, Pub. L. 103–355 (31 U.S.C. 6101 note).

## § 2700.20  Does this part apply to me?

This part and, through this part, pertinent portions of the OMB guidance in subparts A through I of 2 CFR part 180 (see table at 2 CFR 180.100(b)) apply to you if you are a—

(a) Participant or principal in a "covered transaction" (see subpart B of 2 CFR part 180 and the definition of "nonprocurement transaction" at 2 CFR 180.970);

(b) Respondent in an SBA suspension or debarment action;

(c) SBA debarment or suspension official; or

(d) SBA grants officer, agreements officer, or other official authorized to enter into any type of nonprocurement transaction that is a covered transaction.

## § 2700.30  What policies and procedures must I follow?

The SBA policies and procedures you must follow are the policies and procedures specified in each applicable section of the OMB guidance in subparts A through I of 2 CFR part 180, as that section is supplemented by the section in this part with the same section number. The contracts that are covered transactions, for example, are specified by section 220 of the OMB guidance (i.e., 2 CFR 180.220) as supplemented by section 220 of this part (i.e., § 2700.220). For any section of OMB guidance in subparts A through I of 2 CFR 180 that has no corresponding section in this part, SBA policies and procedures are those in the OMB guidance.

## Subpart A—General

**§ 2700.137 Who in the Small Business Administration may grant an exception to let an excluded person participate in a covered transaction?**

The Director of the Office of Credit Risk Management may grant an exception permitting an excluded person to participate in a particular covered transaction under SBA's financial assistance programs. For all other Agency programs, the Associate General Counsel for Procurement Law may grant such an exception.

[72 FR 39728, July 20, 2007, as amended at 73 FR 43348, July 25, 2008]

## Subpart B—Covered Transactions

**§ 2700.220 What contracts and subcontracts, in addition to those listed in 2 CFR 180.220, are covered transactions?**

In addition to the contracts covered under 2 CFR 180.22(b) of the OMB guidance, this part applies to any contract, regardless of tier, that is awarded by a contractor, subcontractor, supplier, consultant, or its agent or representative in any transaction, if the contract is to be funded or provided by the SBA under a covered nonprocurement transaction and the amount of the contract is expected to equal or exceed $25,000. This extends the coverage of the SBA nonprocurement suspension and debarment requirements to all lower tiers of subcontracts under covered nonprocurement transactions, as permitted under the OMB guidance at 2 CFR 180.200(c) (see optional lower tier coverage in the figure in the appendix to 2 CFR part 180)

## Subpart C—Responsibilities of Participants Regarding Transactions

**§ 2700.332 What methods must I use to pass requirements down to participants at lower tiers with whom I intend to do business?**

You, as a participant, must include a term or condition in lower-tier trans-

actions requiring lower-tier participants to comply with subpart C of the OMB guidance in 2 CFR part 180, as supplemented by this part.

## Subpart D—Responsibilities of Federal Agency Officials Regarding Transactions

**§ 2700.437 What method do I use to communicate to a participant the requirements described in the OMB guidance at 2 CFR 180.435?**

To communicate to a participant the requirements described in 2 CFR 180.435 of the OMB guidance, you must include a term or condition in the transaction that requires the participant's compliance with subpart C of 2 CFR part 180, as supplemented by subpart C of this part, and requires the participant to include a similar term or condition in lower-tier covered transactions.

## Subparts E–F [Reserved]

## Subpart G—Suspension

**§ 2700.765 How may I appeal my suspension?**

(a) If the SBA suspending official issues a decision under § 180.755 to continue your suspension after you present information in opposition to that suspension under § 180.720, you may ask for review of the suspending official's decision in two ways:

(1) You may ask the suspending official to reconsider the decision for material errors of fact or law that you believe will change the outcome of the matter; or

(2) You may request that the SBA Office of Hearings and Appeals (OHA) review the suspending official's decision to continue your suspension within 30 days of your receipt of the suspending official's decision under § 180.755 or paragraph (a)(1) of this section. However, OHA may reverse the suspending official's decision only where OHA finds that the decision is based on a clear error of material fact or law, or where OHA finds that the suspending official's decision was arbitrary, capricious, or an abuse of discretion. You may appeal the suspending official's decision without requesting reconsideration, or you may appeal the decision

of the suspending official on reconsideration. The procedures governing OHA appeals are set forth in 13 CFR part 134.

(b) A request for review under this section must be in writing; state the specific findings you believe to be in error; and include the reasons or legal bases for your position.

(c) OHA, in its discretion, may stay the suspension pending review of the suspending official's decision.

(d) The SBA suspending official and OHA must notify you of their decision under this section, in writing, using the notice procedures set forth at §§ 180.615 and 180.975.

## Subpart H—Debarment

### § 2700.890 How may I appeal my debarment?

(a) If the SBA debarring official issues a decision under § 180.870 to debar you after you present information in opposition to a proposed debarment under § 180.815, you may ask for review of the debarring official's decision in two ways:

(1) You may ask the debarring official to reconsider the decision for material errors of fact or law that you believe will change the outcome of the matter; or

(2) You may request that the SBA Office of Hearings and Appeals (OHA) review the debarring official's decision to debar you within 30 days of your receipt of the debarring official's decision under § 180.870 or paragraph (a)(1) of this section. However, OHA may reverse the debarring official's decision only where OHA finds that the decision is based on a clear error of material fact or law, or where OHA finds that the debarring official's decision was arbitrary, capricious, or an abuse of discretion. You may appeal the debarring official's decision without requesting reconsideration, or you may appeal the decision of the debarring official on reconsideration. The procedures governing OHA appeals are set forth in 13 CFR part 134.

(b) A request for review under this section must be in writing; state the specific findings you believe to be in error; and include the reasons or legal bases for your position.

(c) OHA, in its discretion, may stay the debarment pending review of the debarring official's decision.

(d) The SBA debarring official and OHA must notify you of their decision under this section, in writing, using the notice procedures set forth at §§ 180.615 and 180.975.

## Subpart I—Definitions

### § 2700.930 Debarring official (SBA supplement to government-wide definition at 2 CFR 180.930).

For SBA, the debarring official for financial assistance programs is the Director of the Office of Credit Risk Management; for all other programs, the debarring official is the Associate General Counsel for Procurement Law.

[72 FR 39728, July 20, 2007, as amended at 73 FR 43348, July 25, 2008]

### § 2700.995 Principal (SBA supplement to government-wide definition at 2 CFR 180.995).

*Principal* means—

(a) Other examples of individuals who are principals in SBA covered transactions include:

(1) Principal investigators.

(2) Securities brokers and dealers under the section 7(a) Loan, Certified Development Company (CDC) and Small Business Investment Company (SBIC) programs.

(3) Applicant representatives under the section 7(a) Loan, CDC, SBIC, Small Business Development Center (SBDC), and section 7(j) programs.

(4) Providers of professional services under the section 7(a) Loan, CDC, SBIC, SBDC, and section 7(j) programs.

(5) Individuals that certify, authenticate or authorize billings.

(b) [Reserved]

### § 2700.1010 Suspending official (SBA supplement to government-wide definition at 2 CFR 180.1010).

For SBA, the suspending official for financial assistance programs is the Director of the Office of Credit Risk Management; for all other programs, the suspending official is the Associate General Counsel for Procurement Law.

[72 FR 39728, July 20, 2007, as amended at 73 FR 43348, July 25, 2008]

## Subpart J [Reserved]

## PART 2701—UNIFORM ADMINIS-TRATIVE REQUIREMENTS, COST PRINCIPLES, AND AUDIT RE-QUIREMENTS FOR FEDERAL AWARDS

Sec.

AUTHORITY: 15 U.S.C. 634(b)(6), 2 CFR part 200.

SOURCE: 79 FR 76080, Dec. 19, 2014, unless otherwise noted.

### § 2701.1   Adoption of 2 CFR Part 200.

(a) Under the authority listed above, the U.S. Small Business Administration adopts the Office of Management and Budget (OMB) Guidance in 2 CFR part 200, except for 2 CFR 200.74, 200.92, and 200.93. Thus, this part gives regulatory effect to the OMB guidance and supplements the guidance as needed for the Administration.

### § 2701.74   Pass-through entity.

SBA will only make awards to pass-through entities where expressly authorized by statute.

### § 2701.92   Subaward.

SBA will only permit pass-through entities to make awards to subrecipients where expressly authorized by statute.

### § 2701.93   Subrecipient.

SBA will only permit non-Federal entities to receive subawards where expressly authorized by statute.

### § 2701.112   Conflict of Interest.

The following conflict of interest policies apply to all SBA awards of financial assistance:

(a) Where an employee or contractor of a non-Federal entity providing assistance under an SBA award also provides services in exchange for pay in her or his private capacity, that employee or contractor may not accept as a client for her or his private services any individual or firm she or he assists under an SBA award.

(b) No non-Federal entity providing assistance under an SBA award (nor any subrecipient, employee, or contractor of such an entity) may give preferential treatment to any client referred to it by an organization with which it has a financial, business, or other relationship.

(c) Except where otherwise provided for by law, no non-Federal entity may seek or accept an equity stake in any firm it assists under the auspices of an SBA award. Additionally, no principal, officer, employee, or contractor of such an entity (nor any of their Close or Secondary Relatives as those terms are defined by 13 CFR 108.50) may seek or accept an equity stake or paid position in any firm the entity assists under an SBA award.

### § 2701.414   Indirect (F&A) Costs.

(a) When determining whether a deviation from a negotiated indirect cost rate is justified, SBA will consider the following factors:

(1) The degree to which a non-Federal entity has been able to defray its overhead expenses via those indirect costs it has recovered under other, concurrent SBA awards;

(2) The amount of funding that must be devoted to conducting program activities in order for a project to result in meaningful outcomes; and

(3) The amount of project funds that will remain available for conducting program activities after a negotiated rate is applied.

(b) After conducting the analysis required in paragraph (a) above, the head of each SBA grant program office will determine in writing whether there is sufficient justification to deviate from a negotiated indirect cost rate.

(c) Where SBA determines that deviation from a negotiated rate is justified, it will provide a copy of that determination to OMB and will inform potential applicants of the deviation in the corresponding funding announcement.

### § 2701.503  Relation to other audit requirements.

Non-Federal entities that are not subject to the requirements of the Single Audit Act and that are performing projects under SBA awards will be required to submit copies of their audited financial statements for their most recently completed fiscal year. Costs associated with the auditing of a non-Federal entity's financial statements may be included in its negotiations for an indirect cost rate agreement in accordance with 2 CFR 200.425.

### § 2701.513  Responsibilities.

For SBA, the Single Audit Senior Accountable Official is the Deputy Chief Operating Officer. The Single Audit Liaison is the Director, Office of Grants Management.

[81 FR 1115, Jan. 11, 2016]

### § 2701.600  Other regulatory guidance.

(a) In addition to the general regulations set forth above and those contained in 2 CFR part 200, the program-specific regulations governing the operation of SBA's individual grant programs may be found in title 13 of the Code of Federal Regulations beginning at the sections noted below:

(1) New Markets Venture Capital program—13 CFR 108.2000.

(2) Program for Investment in Microentrepreneurs (PRIME)—13 CFR 119.1.

(3) Microloan program—13 CFR 120.700.

(4) 7(j) Management and Technical Assistance program—13 CFR 124.701.

(5) Small Business Development Center program—13 CFR 130.100.

(b) [Reserved]

# PARTS 2702–2799 [RESERVED]

# CHAPTER XXVIII—DEPARTMENT OF JUSTICE

# PART 2800—UNIFORM ADMINISTRATIVE REQUIREMENTS, COST PRINCIPLES, AND AUDIT REQUIREMENTS FOR FEDERAL AWARDS BY THE DEPARTMENT OF JUSTICE

Sec.
2800.101  Adoption of 2 CFR part 200.
2800.313  Equipment.
2800.314  Supplies.

AUTHORITY: 5 U.S.C. 301; 28 U.S.C. 509; 28 U.S.C. 530C(a)(4); 42 U.S.C. 3789; 2 CFR part 200.

SOURCE: 79 FR 76081, Dec. 19, 2014, unless otherwise noted.

## § 2800.101  Adoption of 2 CFR part 200.

Under the authority listed above, the Department of Justice adopts the Office of Management and Budget (OMB) Guidance in 2 CFR part 200, except as otherwise may be provided by this Part. Unless expressly provided otherwise, any reference in this part to any provision of law not in this part shall be understood to constitute a general reference and thus to include any subsequent changes to the provision.

[81 FR 61982, Sept. 8, 2016]

## § 2800.313  Equipment.

Title I of the Omnibus Crime Control and Safe Streets Act of 1968, Public Law 90–351, section 808 (42 U.S.C. 3789), creates a special rule for disposition and use of equipment and supplies purchased by funds made available under that Title, which rule, where applicable, supersedes any conflicting provisions of 2 CFR 200.313. Section 808 currently provides that such equipment and supplies shall vest in the criminal justice agency or nonprofit organization that purchased the property if such agency or nonprofit certifies to the appropriate State office (as indicated in the statute) that it will use the property for criminal justice purposes, and further provides that, if such certification is not made, title to the property shall vest in the State office, which shall seek to have the property used for criminal justice purposes elsewhere in the State prior to using it or disposing of it in any other manner.

## § 2800.314  Supplies.

Title I of the Omnibus Crime Control and Safe Streets Act of 1968, Public Law 90–351, section 808 (42 U.S.C. 3789) creates a special rule for disposition and use of equipment and supplies purchased by funds made available under that Title, which rule, where applicable, supersedes any conflicting provisions of § 200.314. Section 808 currently provides that such equipment and supplies shall vest in the criminal justice agency or nonprofit organization that purchased the property if such agency or nonprofit certifies to the appropriate State office (as indicated in the statute) that it will use the property for criminal justice purposes, and further provides that, if such certification is not made, title to the property shall vest in the State office, which shall seek to have the property used for criminal justice purposes elsewhere in the State prior to using it or disposing of it in any other manner.

# PARTS 2801–2866 [RESERVED]

# PART 2867—NONPROCUREMENT DEBARMENT AND SUSPENSION

Sec.
2867.10  What does this part do?
2867.20  To whom does this part apply?
2867.30  What policies and procedures must be followed?

### Subpart A—General

2867.137  Who in the Department of Justice may grant an exception to let an excluded person participate in a covered transaction?

### Subpart B—Covered Transactions

2867.220  What contracts and subcontracts, in addition to those listed in 2 CFR 180.220, are covered transactions?

### Subpart C—Responsibilities of Participants Regarding Transactions

2867.332  What method must a participant use to pass requirements down to participants at lower tiers with whom the participant intends to do business?

489

## Subpart D—Responsibilities of Federal Agency Officials Regarding Transactions

2867.437   What method must be used to communicate to a participant the requirements described in the OMB guidance at 2 CFR 180.435?

### Subparts E–J [Reserved]

AUTHORITY: Sec. 2455, Pub. L. 103–355, 108 Stat. 3327; E.O. 12549, 3 CFR, 1986 Comp., p. 189; E.O. 12689, 3 CFR, 1989 Comp., p. 235; 5 U.S.C. 301; 28 U.S.C. 509, 510, 515–519.

SOURCE: 72 FR 11286, Mar. 13, 2007, unless otherwise noted.

### § 2867.10   What does this part do?

This part adopts the Office of Management and Budget (OMB) guidance in subparts A through I of 2 CFR part 180, as supplemented by this part, as the Department of Justice policies and procedures for nonprocurement debarment and suspension. It thereby gives regulatory effect for the Department of Justice to the OMB guidance as supplemented by this part. This part satisfies the requirements in section 3 of Executive Order 12549, "Debarment and Suspension" (3 CFR 1986 Comp., p. 189), Executive Order 12689, "Debarment and Suspension" (3 CFR 1989 Comp., p. 235) and 31 U.S.C. 6101 note (Section 2455, Pub. L. 103–355, 108 Stat. 3327).

### § 2867.20   To whom does this part apply?

This part and, through this part, pertinent portions of the OMB guidance in subparts A through I of 2 CFR part 180 (see table at 2 CFR 180.100(b)) apply to any—

(a) Participant or principal in a "covered transaction" (sees subpart B of 2 CFR part 180 and the definition of "nonprocurement transaction" at 2 CFR 180.970 (as supplemented by subpart B of this part));

(b) Respondent in a Department of Justice suspension or debarment action;

(c) Department of Justice debarment or suspension official;

(d) Department of Justice grants officer, agreements officer, or other official authorized to enter into any type of nonprocurement transaction that is a covered transaction.

### § 2867.30   What policies and procedures must be followed?

The Department of Justice policies and procedures that must be followed are the policies and procedures specified in each applicable section of the OMB guidance in subparts A through I of 2 CFR part 180, as that section is supplemented by the section in this part with the same section number. The contracts that are covered transactions, for example, are specified by section 220 of the OMB guidance (i.e., 2 CFR 180.220) as supplemented by section 220 in this part (i.e., § 2867.220). For any section of OMB guidance in subparts A through I of 2 CFR 180 that has no corresponding section in this part, Department of Justice policies and procedures are those in the OMB guidance.

## Subpart A—General

### § 2867.137   Who in the Department of Justice may grant an exception to let an excluded person participate in a covered transaction?

Within the Department of Justice, the Attorney General or designee has the authority to grant an exception to let an excluded person participate in a covered transaction, as provided in the OMB guidance at 2 CFR 180.135.

## Subpart B—Covered Transactions

### § 2867.220   What contracts and subcontracts, in addition to those listed in 2 CFR 180.220, are covered transactions?

Although the OMB guidance at 2 CFR 180.220(c) allows a Federal agency to do so (also see optional lower tier coverage in the figure in the appendix to 2 CFR part 180), the Department of Justice does not extend coverage of nonprocurement suspension and debarment requirements beyond first-tier procurement contracts under a covered nonprocurement transaction.

## Subpart C—Responsibilities of Participants Regarding Transactions

**§ 2867.332  What method must a participant use to pass requirements down to participants at lower tiers with whom the participant intends to do business?**

A participant must include a term or condition in lower-tier transactions requiring lower-tier participants to comply with subpart C of the OMB guidance in 2 CFR part 180, as supplemented by this subpart.

## Subpart D—Responsibilities of Federal Agency Officials Regarding Transactions

**§ 2867.437  What method must be used to communicate to a participant the requirements described in the OMB guidance at 2 CFR 180.435?**

To communicate to a participant the requirements described in 2 CFR 180.435 of the OMB guidance, the communication must include a term or condition in the transaction that requires the participant's compliance with subpart C of 2 CFR part 180, as supplemented by subpart C of this part, and requires the participant to include a similar term or condition in lower-tier covered transactions.

## Subparts E–J [Reserved]

## PARTS 2868–2899 [RESERVED]

# CHAPTER XXIX—DEPARTMENT OF LABOR

# PART 2900—UNIFORM ADMINISTRATIVE REQUIREMENTS, COST PRINCIPLES, AND AUDIT REQUIREMENTS FOR FEDERAL AWARDS

AUTHORITY: 5 U.S.C. 301; 2 CFR 200.

SOURCE: 79 FR 76081, Dec. 19, 2014, unless otherwise noted.

## Subpart A—Acronyms and Definitions

### § 2900.1  Budget.

In the DOL, approval of the budget as awarded does not constitute prior approval of those items requiring prior approval, including those items the Federal Awarding agency specifies as requiring prior approval. See § 200.407 and § 2900.16 for more information about prior approval. (See 2 CFR 200.8)

[80 FR 81440, Dec. 30, 2015]

### § 2900.2  Non-Federal entity.

In the DOL, *Non-Federal entity* means a state, local government, Indian tribe, institution of higher education (IHE), for-profit entity, foreign public entity, foreign organization or nonprofit organization that carries out a Federal award as a recipient or subrecipient. (See 2 CFR 200.69)

### § 2900.3  Questioned cost.

In the DOL, in addition to the guidance contained in 2 CFR 200.84, a *Questioned cost* means a cost that is questioned by an auditor, Federal Project Officer, Grant Officer, or other authorized Awarding agency representative because of an audit or monitoring finding:

(a) Which resulted from a violation or possible violation of a statute, regulation, or the terms and conditions of a Federal award, including for funds used to match Federal funds;

(b) Where the costs, at the time of the audit, are not supported by adequate documentation; or

(c) Where the costs incurred appear unreasonable and do not reflect the actions a prudent person would take in the circumstances.

[79 FR 76081, Dec. 19, 2014, as amended at 80 FR 81440, Dec. 30, 2015]

## Subpart B—General Provisions

### § 2900.4  Adoption of 2 CFR Part 200.

Under the authority listed above, the Department of Labor adopts the Office of Management and Budget (OMB) Guidance in the Uniform Administrative Requirements, Cost Principles, and Audit Requirements for Federal

Awards to Non-Federal Entities (subparts A through F of 2 CFR 200), as supplemented by this part, as the Department of Labor policies and procedures for financial assistance administration. This part satisfies the requirements of 2 CFR 200.110(a) and gives regulatory effect to the OMB guidance as supplemented by this part. The DOL also has programmatic and administrative regulations located in 20 and 29 CFR.

## Subpart C—Pre-Federal Award Requirements and Contents of Federal Awards

### § 2900.5  Federal awarding agency review of merit of proposals.

In the DOL, audits and monitoring reports containing findings, issues of non-compliance or questioned costs are in addition to reports and findings from audits performed under Subpart F—Audit Requirements of 2 CFR 200 or the reports and findings of any other available audits. (See 2 CFR 200.205(c)(4)).

[80 FR 81440, Dec. 30, 2015]

## Subpart D—Post Federal Award Requirements

### § 2900.6  Advance Payment.

In the DOL, except as authorized under 2 CFR 200.207, specific conditions, the non-Federal entity must be paid in advance. (See 2 CFR 200.305(b)(1))

### § 2900.7  Payment.

In addition to the guidance set forth in 2 CFR 200.305(b), for Federal awards from the Department of Labor, the non-Federal entity should liquidate existing advances before it requests additional advances.

[80 FR 81440, Dec. 30, 2015]

### § 2900.8  Cost sharing or matching.

In addition to the guidance set forth in 2 CFR 200.306(b), for Federal awards from the Department of Labor, the non-Federal entity accounts for funds used for cost sharing or match within their accounting systems as the funds are expended.

### § 2900.9  Revision of budget and program plans.

In the DOL, approval of the budget as awarded does not constitute prior approval of those items requiring prior approval, including those items the Federal awarding agency specifies as requiring prior approval (see 2 CFR 200.407 and 2 CFR 200.308(a))

### § 2900.10  Prior approval requests.

In addition to the guidance set forth in 2 CFR 200.308(c), for Federal awards from the Department of Labor, the non-Federal entity must request prior approval actions at least 30 days prior to the effective date of the requested action.

### § 2900.11  Revision of budget and program plans including extension of the period of performance.

In addition to the guidance set forth in 2 CFR 200.308(c), for Federal awards from the Department of Labor, the non-Federal entity must request prior approval for an extension to the period of performance.

### § 2900.12  Revision of budget and program plans approval from Grant Officers.

In the DOL, unless otherwise noted in the Grant Agreement, prior written approval must come from the Grant Officer (See 2 CFR 200.308(d))

### § 2900.13  Intangible property.

In addition to the guidance set forth in 2 CFR 200.315(d), the Department of Labor requires intellectual property developed under a competitive Federal award process to be licensed under a Creative Commons Attribution license. This license allows subsequent users to copy, distribute, transmit and adapt the copyrighted work and requires such users to attribute the work in the manner specified by the recipient.

[80 FR 81440, Dec. 30, 2015]

### § 2900.14  Financial reporting.

In addition to the guidance set forth in 2 CFR 200.327, for Federal awards from the Department of Labor, the DOL awarding agency will prescribe whether the report will be on a cash or an accrual basis. If the DOL awarding agency requires reporting on an accrual basis and the recipient's accounting system is not on the accrual basis, the recipient will not be required to convert its accounting system, but must develop and report such accrual information through best estimates based on an analysis of the documentation on hand.

§ 2900.15   Closeout.

In addition to the guidance set forth in 2 CFR 200.343(b), for Federal awards from the Department of Labor, the non-Federal entity must liquidate all obligations and/or accrued expenditures incurred under the Federal award. For non-Federal entities reporting on an accrual basis and operating on an expenditure period, unless otherwise noted in the grant agreement, the only liquidation that can occur during closeout is the liquidation of accrued expenditures (NOT obligations) for goods and/or services received during the grant period.

[80 FR 81441, Dec. 30, 2015]

## Subpart E—Cost Principles

§ 2900.16   Prior written approval (prior approval).

In addition to the guidance set forth in 2 CFR 200.407, for Federal awards from the Department of Labor, the non-Federal entity must request prior written approval which should include the timeframe or scope of the agreement and be submitted not less than 30 days before the requested action is to occur. Unless otherwise noted in the grant agreement, the Grant Officer is the only official with the authority to provide prior written approval (prior approval). Items included in the statement of work or budget as awarded does not constitute prior approval.

[80 FR 81441, Dec. 30, 2015]

§ 2900.17   Adjustment of negotiated IDC rates.

In the DOL, in addition to the requirements under 2 CFR 200.411(a)(2), adjustments to indirect cost rates resulting from a determination of unallowable costs being included in the rate proposal may result in the reissuance of negotiated rate agreement.

§ 2900.18   Contingency provisions.

In addition to the guidance set forth in 2 CFR 200.433(c), for Federal awards from the Department of Labor, excepted citations include 2 CFR 200.333 Retention requirements for records, and 2 CFR 200.334 Requests for transfers of records.

§ 2900.19   Student activity costs.

In the Department of Labor, the provisions of 2 CFR 200.469 apply unless the activities meet a program requirement and have prior written approval from the Federal awarding agency.

## Subpart F—Audit Requirements

§ 2900.20   Federal Agency Audit Responsibilities.

In the DOL, in addition to 2 CFR 200.513, the department employs a collaborative resolution process with non-federal entities.

(a) *Department of Labor Cooperative Audit Resolution Process.* The DOL official(s) responsible for resolution shall promptly evaluate findings and recommendations reported by auditors and the corrective action plan developed by the recipient to determine proper actions in response to audit findings and recommendations. The process of audit resolution includes at a minimum an initial determination, an informal resolution period, and a final determination.

(1) *Initial determination.* After the conclusion of any comment period for audits provided the recipient/contractor, the responsible DOL official(s) shall make an initial determination on the allowability of questioned costs or activities, administrative or systemic findings, and the corrective actions outlined by the recipient. Such determination shall be based on applicable statutes, regulations, administrative directives, or terms and conditions of the grant/contract award instrument.

(2) *Informal resolution.* The recipient/contractor shall have a reasonable period of time (as determined by the DOL official(s) responsible for audit resolution) from the date of issuance of the initial determination to informally resolve those matters in which the recipient/contractor disagrees with the

decisions of the responsible DOL official(s).

(3) *Final determination.* After the conclusion of the informal resolution period, the responsible DOL official(s) shall issue a final determination that:

(i) As appropriate, indicate that efforts to informally resolve matters contained in the initial determination have either been successful or unsuccessful;

(ii) Lists those matters upon which the parties continue to disagree;

(iii) Lists any modifications to the factual findings and conclusions set forth in the initial determination;

(iv) Lists any sanctions and required corrective actions; and

(v) Sets forth any appeal rights.

(4) *Time limit.* Insofar as possible, the requirements of this section should be met within 180 days of the date the final approved audit report is received by the DOL official(s) responsible for audit resolution.

[79 FR 76081, Dec. 19, 2014, as amended at 80 FR 81441, Dec. 30, 2015]

### § 2900.21  Management decision.

In the DOL, ordinarily, a management decision is issued within six months of receipt of an audit from the audit liaison of the Office of the Inspector General and is extended an additional six months when the audit contains a finding involving a subrecipient of the pass-through entity being audited. The pass-through entity responsible for issuing a management decision must do so within twelve months of acceptance of the audit report by the FAC. The auditee must initiate and proceed with corrective action as rapidly as possible and should begin corrective action no later than upon receipt of the audit report. (See 2 CFR 200.521(d)).

[80 FR 81441, Dec. 30, 2015]

### § 2900.22  Audit Requirements—Appeal Process for Department of Labor Recipients.

In the DOL, the DOL grantor agencies shall determine which of the two appeal options set forth in paragraphs (a) and (b) of this section the recipient may use to appeal the final determination of the grant officer. All awards within the same Federal financial assistance program shall follow the same appeal procedure.

(a) Appeal to the head of the grantor agency, or his/her designee, for which the audit was conducted.

(1) *Jurisdiction.* (i) Request for hearing. Within 21 days of receipt of the grant officer's final determination, the recipient may transmit, by certified mail, return receipt requested, a request for hearing to the head of the grantor agency, or his/her designee, as noted in the final determination. A copy must also be sent to the grant officer who signed the final determination.

(ii) *Statement of issues.* The request for a hearing shall be accompanied by a copy of the final determination, if issued, and shall specifically state those portions of the final determination upon which review is requested. Those portions of the final determination not specified for review shall be considered resolved and not subject to further review.

(iii) *Failure to request review.* When no timely request for a hearing is made, the final determination shall constitute final action by the Secretary of Labor and shall not be subject to further review.

(2) *Conduct of hearings.* The grantor agency shall establish procedures for the conduct of hearings by the head of the grantor agency, or his/her designee.

(3) *Decision of the head of the grantor agency, or his/her designee.* The head of the grantor agency, or his/her designee, should render a written decision no later than 90 days after the closing of the record. This decision constitutes final action of the Secretary.

(b) *Appeal to the DOL Office of Administrative Law Judges.* (1) *Jurisdiction.* (i) *Request for hearing.* Within 21 days of receipt of the grant officer's final determination, the recipient may transmit by certified mail, return receipt requested, a request for hearing to the Chief Administrative Law Judge, United States Department of Labor, 800 K Street NW., Suite 400, Washington, DC 20001, with a copy to the grant officer who signed the final determination. The Chief Administrative Law Judge shall designate an administrative law judge to hear the appeal.

(ii) *Statement of issues.* The request for a hearing shall be accompanied by a copy of the final determination, if issued, and shall specifically state those portions of the final determination upon which review is requested. Those portions of the final determination not specified for review shall be considered resolved and not subject to further review.

(iii) *Failure to request review.* When no timely request for a hearing is made, the final determination shall constitute final action by the Secretary and shall not be subject to further review.

(2) *Conduct of hearings.* The DOL Rules of Practice and Procedure for Administrative Hearings Before the Office of Administrative Law Judges, set forth at 29 CFR part 18, shall govern the conduct of hearings under paragraph (b) of this section.

(3) *Decision of the administrative law judge.* The administrative law judge should render a written decision no later than 90 days after the closing of the record.

(4) *Filing exceptions to decision.* The decision of the administrative law judge shall constitute final action by the Secretary of Labor, unless, within 21 days after receipt of the decision of the administrative law judge, a party dissatisfied with the decision or any part thereof has filed exceptions with the Secretary, specifically identifying the procedure or finding of fact, law, or policy with which exception is taken. Any exceptions not specifically urged shall be deemed to have been waived. Thereafter, the decision of the administrative law judge shall become the decision of the Secretary, unless the Secretary, within 30 days of such filing, has notified the parties that the case has been accepted for review.

(5) *Review by the Secretary of Labor.* Any case accepted for review by the Secretary shall be decided within 180 days of such acceptance. If not so decided, the decision of the administrative law judge shall become the final decision of the Secretary.

## PARTS 2901–2997 [RESERVED]

## PART 2998—NONPROCUREMENT DEBARMENT AND SUSPENSION

AUTHORITY: 5 U.S.C. 301; E.O. 12549 (3 CFR, 1986 Comp., p.189); E.O. 12689 (3 CFR, 1989 Comp., p.235); sec 2455 Pub. L. 103–355, 108 Stat. 3327 (31 U.S.C. 6101 note).

SOURCE: 81 FR 25586, Apr. 29, 2016, unless otherwise noted.

### §2998.10   What does this part do?

This part adopts the Office of Management and Budget (OMB) guidance in subparts A through I of 2 CFR part 180, as supplemented by this part, as the Department of Labor (DOL) policies and procedures for non-procurement debarment and suspension. It thereby gives regulatory effect for DOL to the OMB guidance as supplemented by this part. This part satisfies the requirements in section 3 of Executive Order 12549, "Debarment and Suspension" (3 CFR 1986 Comp., p. 189); Executive Order 12689, "Debarment and Suspension" (3 CFR 1989 Comp., p. 235); and section 2455 of the Federal Acquisition

Streamlining Act of 1994, 103 (31 U.S.C. 6101 note).

### § 2998.20  Does this part apply to me?

This part and, through this part, pertinent portions of the OMB guidance in subparts A through I of 2 CFR part 180 (see table at 2 CFR 180.100(b)) apply to you if you are a—

(a) Participant or principal in a "covered transaction" (see subpart B of 2 CFR part 180 and the definition of "non-procurement transaction" at 2 CFR 180.970);

(b) Respondent in a Department of Labor suspension or debarment action;

(c) Department of Labor debarment or suspension official; or

(d) Department of Labor grants officer, agreements officer, or other official authorized to enter into any type of non-procurement transaction that is a covered transaction.

### § 2998.30  What policies and procedures must I follow?

(a) The Department of Labor's policies and procedures that you must follow are specified in:

(1) Each applicable section of the OMB guidance in subparts A through I of 2 CFR part 180; and

(2) The supplement to each section of the OMB guidance that is found in this part under the same section number. (The contracts that are covered transactions, for example, are specified by section 220 of the OMB guidance (*i.e.*, 2 CFR 180.220) as supplemented by section 220 in this part (*i.e.*, Sec. 2998.220)).

(b) For any section of OMB guidance in subparts A through I of 2 CFR part 180 that has no corresponding section in this part, the Department of Labor's policies and procedures are those in the OMB guidance.

## Subpart A—General

### § 2998.137  Who in DOL may grant an exception to let an excluded person participate in a covered transaction?

Within the Department of Labor, the Secretary of Labor or designee has the authority to grant an exception to let an excluded person participate in a covered transaction, as provided in the OMB guidance at 2 CFR 180.135. If any designated official grants an exception, the exception must be in writing and state the reason(s) for deviating from the government-wide policy in Executive Order 12549.

## Subpart B—Covered Transactions

### § 2998.220  What contracts and subcontracts, in addition to those listed in 2 CFR 180.220, are covered transactions?

In addition to the contracts covered under 2 CFR 180.220(b) of the OMB guidance, this part applies to any contract, regardless of tier, that is awarded by a contractor, subcontractor, supplier, consultant, or its agent or representative in any transaction, if the contract is to be funded or provided by the Department of Labor under a covered non-procurement transaction. This extends the coverage of the Department of Labor non-procurement suspension and debarment requirements to all lower tiers of subcontracts under covered non-procurement transactions, as permitted under the OMB guidance at 2 CFR 180.220(c) (see optional lower tier coverage in the figure in the appendix to 2 CFR part 180).

## Subpart C—Responsibilities of Participants Regarding Transactions

### § 2998.332  What requirements must I pass down to persons at lower tiers with whom I intend to do business?

You, as a participant, must include a term or condition in lower-tier transactions requiring lower-tier participants to comply with subpart C of the OMB guidance in 2 CFR part 180, as supplemented by this subpart.

## Subpart D—Responsibilities of Federal Agency Officials Regarding Transactions

### § 2998.437  What method do I use to communicate to a participant the requirements described in the OMB guidance at 2 CFR 180.435?

To communicate to a participant the requirements described in 2 CFR 180.435 of the OMB guidance, you must include a term or condition in the transaction that requires the participant's compliance with Subpart C of 2 CFR part 180, and supplemented by subpart C of this part, and requires the participant to include a similar term or condition in lower-tier covered transactions.

## Subparts E–J [Reserved]

## PART 2999 [RESERVED]

# CHAPTER XXX—DEPARTMENT OF HOMELAND SECURITY

# PART 3000—NONPROCUREMENT DEBARMENT AND SUSPENSION

Sec.
3000.10 What does this part do?
3000.20 Does this part apply to me?
3000.30 What policies and procedures must I follow?

## Subpart A—General

3000.137 Who in the Department of Homeland Security may grant an exception to let an excluded person participate in a covered transaction?

## Subpart B—Covered Transactions

3000.220 What contracts and subcontracts, in addition to those listed in 2 CFR 180.220, are covered transactions?

## Subpart C—Responsibilities of Participants Regarding Transactions

3000.332 What methods must I use to pass requirements down to participants at lower tiers with whom I intend to do business?

## Subpart D—Responsibilities of Department of Homeland Security Officials Regarding Transactions

3000.437 What method do I use to communicate to a participant the requirements described in the Office of Management and Budget guidance at 2 CFR 180.435?

## Subparts E-I [Reserved]

AUTHORITY: Sec. 2455, Public Law 103–355, 108 Stat. 3327; E.O. 12549, 3 CFR, 1986 Comp., p. 189; E.O. 12689, 3 CFR, 1989 Comp., p. 235; Public Law 107–296, 116 Stat. 2135.

SOURCE: 74 FR 34497, July 16, 2009, unless otherwise noted.

## § 3000.10  What does this part do?

This part adopts the Office of Management and Budget (OMB) guidance in Subparts A through I of 2 CFR part 180, as supplemented by this part, as the Department of Homeland Security policies and procedures for nonprocurement debarment and suspension. It thereby gives regulatory effect for the Department of Homeland Security to the OMB guidance as supplemented by this part. This part satisfies the requirements in section 3 of Executive Order 12549, "Debarment and Suspension" (3 CFR 1986 Comp., p. 189), Executive Order 12689, "Debarment and Suspension" (3 CFR 1989 Comp., p. 235) and 31 U.S.C. 6101 note (Section 2455, Pub. L. 103–355, 108 Stat. 3327).

## § 3000.20  Does this part apply to me?

This part and, through this part, pertinent portions of the OMB guidance in Subparts A through I of 2 CFR part 180 (see table at 2 CFR 180.100(b)) apply to you if you are a—

(a) Participant or principal in a "covered transaction" (see Subpart B of 2 CFR Part 180 and the definition of "nonprocurement transaction" at 2 CFR 180.970);

(b) Respondent in a Department of Homeland Security suspension or debarment action;

(c) Department of Homeland Security debarment or suspension official;

(d) Department of Homeland Security grants officer, agreements officer, or other official authorized to enter into any type of nonprocurement transaction that is a covered transaction.

## § 3000.30  What policies and procedures must I follow?

The Department of Homeland Security policies and procedures that you must follow are the policies and procedures specified in each applicable section of the OMB guidance in Subparts A through I of 2 CFR Part 180, as that section is supplemented by the section in this part with the same section number. The contracts that are covered transactions, for example, are specified by section 220 of the OMB guidance (i.e., 2 CFR 180.220) as supplemented by section 220 in this part (i.e., § 3000.220). For any section of OMB guidance in Subparts A through I of 2 CFR Part 180 that has no corresponding section in this part, Department of Homeland Security policies and procedures are those in the OMB guidance.

## Subpart A—General

## § 3000.137  Who in the Department of Homeland Security may grant an exception to let an excluded person participate in a covered transaction?

Within the Department of Homeland Security, the Secretary of Homeland Security has delegated the authority

505

to grant an exception to let an excluded person participate in a covered transaction to the Head of the Contracting Activity for each DHS component as provided in the OMB guidance at 2 CFR 180.135.

## Subpart B—Covered Transactions

**§ 3000.220 What contracts and subcontracts, in addition to those listed in 2 CFR 180.220, are covered transactions?**

Department of Homeland Security extends coverage of nonprocurement suspension and debarment requirements beyond first-tier procurement contracts under a covered nonprocurement transaction.

## Subpart C—Responsibilities of Participants Regarding Transactions

**§ 3000.332 What methods must I use to pass requirements down to participants at lower tiers with whom I intend to do business?**

You as a participant in a covered transaction must include a term or condition in any lower-tier covered transaction into which you enter, to require the participant of that transaction to—

(a) Comply with Subpart C of the OMB guidance in 2 CFR part 180; and

(b) Include a similar term or condition in any covered transaction into which it enters at the next lower tier.

## Subpart D—Responsibilities of Department of Homeland Security Officials Regarding Transactions

**§ 3000.437 What method do I use to communicate to a participant the requirements described in the Office of Management and Budget guidance at 2 CFR 180.435?**

You as a DHS component official must include a term or condition in each covered transaction into which you enter, to communicate to the participant the requirements to—

(a) Comply with subpart C of the OMB guidance in 2 CFR part 180; and

(b) Include a similar term or condition in any lower-tier covered trans-

actions into which the participant enters.

## Subparts E–I [Reserved]

# PART 3001—REQUIREMENTS FOR DRUG-FREE WORKPLACE (FINANCIAL ASSISTANCE)

Sec.
3001.10  What does this part do?
3001.20  Does this part apply to me?
3001.30  What policies and procedures must I follow?

### Subpart A—Purpose and Coverage [Reserved]

### Subpart B—Requirements for Recipients Other Than Individuals

3001.225  Who in DHS does a recipient other than an individual notify about a criminal drug conviction?

### Subpart C—Requirements for Recipients Who Are Individuals

3001.300  Who in DHS does a recipient who is an individual notify about a criminal drug conviction?

### Subpart D—Responsibilities of Agency Awarding Officials

3001.400  What method do I use as an agency awarding official to obtain a recipient's agreement to comply with the OMB guidance?

### Subpart E—Violations of This Part and Consequences

3001.500  Who in DHS determines that a recipient other than an individual violated the requirements of this part?
3001.505  Who in DHS determines that a recipient who is an individual violated the requirements of this part?
3001.510  What actions will the Federal Government take against a recipient determined to have violated this part?

### Subpart F—Definitions

3001.605  Award.
3001.661  Reimbursable Agreement.

AUTHORITY: 5 U.S.C. 301; 41 U.S.C. 701–707; OMB Guidance for Drug-Free Workplace Requirements, codified at 2 CFR part 182.

SOURCE: 76 FR 10207, Feb. 24, 2011, unless otherwise noted.

## §3001.10 What does this part do?

This part requires that the award and administration of Department of Homeland Security (DHS) grants and cooperative agreements comply with Office of Management and Budget (OMB) guidance implementing the portion of the Drug-Free Workplace Act of 1988 (41 U.S.C. 701–707, as amended, hereafter referred to as "the Act") that applies to grants. It thereby—

(a) Gives regulatory effect to the OMB guidance, as supplemented by this part (Subparts A through F of 2 CFR part 182) for DHS's grants and cooperative agreements; and

(b) Establishes DHS policies and procedures, as supplemented by this part, for compliance with the Act that are the same as those of other Federal agencies, in conformance with the requirement in 41 U.S.C. 705 for Government-wide implementing regulations.

## §3001.20 Does this part apply to me?

This part and, through this part, pertinent portions of the OMB guidance in Subparts A through F of 2 CFR part 182 (see table at 2 CFR 182.115(b)) apply to you if you are a—

(a) Recipient of a DHS grant or cooperative agreement; or

(b) DHS awarding official.

## §3001.30 What policies and procedures must I follow?

(a) *General.* You must follow the policies and procedures specified in applicable sections of the OMB guidance in Subparts A through F of 2 CFR part 182, as implemented by this part.

(b) *Specific sections of OMB guidance that this part supplements.* This part supplements the OMB guidance in 2 CFR part 182 as shown in the following table. For each of those sections, you must follow the policies and procedures in the OMB guidance, as supplemented by this part.

| Section of OMB guidance | Section in this part where supplemented | What the supplementation clarifies |
|---|---|---|
| 2 CFR 182.225(a) | §3001.225 | Who in DHS a recipient other than an individual must notify if an employee is convicted for a violation of a criminal drug statute in the workplace. |
| 2 CFR 182.300(b) | §3001.300 | Who in DHS a recipient who is an individual must notify if he or she is convicted of a criminal drug offense resulting from a violation occurring during the conduct of any award activity. |
| 2 CFR 182.400 | §3001.400 | What method do I use as an agency awarding official to obtain a recipient's agreement to comply with the OMB guidance. |
| 2 CFR 182.500 | §3001.500 | Who in DHS is authorized to determine that a recipient other than an individual is in violation of the requirements of 2 CFR part 182, as implemented by this part. |
| 2 CFR 182.505 | §3001.505 | Who in DHS is authorized to determine that a recipient who is an individual is in violation of the requirements of 2 CFR part 182, as implemented by this part. |
| 2 CFR 182.510 | §3001.510 | What actions the Federal Government will take against a recipient determined to have violated 2 CFR part 182, as implemented by this part. |
| 2 CFR 182.605 | §3001.605 | What types of assistance are included in the definition of "award." |
| None | §3001.661 | What types of assistance are included in the definition of "reimbursable agreement." |

(c) *Sections of the OMB guidance that this part does not supplement.* For any section of OMB guidance in Subparts A through F of 2 CFR part 182 that is not listed in paragraph (b) of this section, DHS policies and procedures are the same as those in the OMB guidance.

## Subpart A—Purpose and Coverage [Reserved]

## Subpart B—Requirements for Recipients Other Than Individuals

## §3001.225 Who in DHS does a recipient other than an individual notify about a criminal drug conviction?

A recipient other than an individual that is required under 2 CFR 182.225(a) to notify Federal agencies about an employee's conviction for a criminal drug offense must notify the DHS Office of Inspector General and each DHS office from which the recipient currently has an award.

## Subpart C—Requirements for Recipients Who Are Individuals

**§ 3001.300  Who in DHS does a recipient who is an individual notify about a criminal drug conviction?**

A recipient who is an individual and is required under 2 CFR 182.300(b) to notify Federal agencies about a conviction for a criminal drug offense must notify the DHS Office of Inspector General and each DHS office from which the recipient currently has an award.

## Subpart D—Responsibilities of Agency Awarding Officials

**§ 3001.400  What method do I use as an agency awarding official to obtain a recipient's agreement to comply with the OMB guidance?**

To obtain a recipient's agreement to comply with applicable requirements in the OMB guidance at 2 CFR part 182, you must include the following term or condition in the award:

Drug-free workplace. You as the recipient must comply with drug-free workplace requirements in Subpart B (or Subpart C, if the recipient is an individual) of 2 CFR part 3001, which adopts the Government-wide implementation (2 CFR part 182) of sec. 5152–5158 of the Drug-Free Workplace Act of 1988 (Pub. L. 100–690, Title V, Subtitle D; 41 U.S.C. 701–707).

## Subpart E—Violations of This Part and Consequences

**§ 3001.500  Who in DHS determines that a recipient other than an individual violated the requirements of this part?**

The Secretary of Homeland Security, or his or her official designee, will make the determination that a recipient other than an individual violated the requirements of this part.

**§ 3001.505  Who in DHS determines that a recipient who is an individual violated the requirements of this part?**

The Secretary of Homeland Security, or his or her official designee, will make the determination that a recipient who is an individual violated the requirements of this part.

**§ 3001.510  What actions will the Federal Government take against a recipient determined to have violated this part?**

If a recipient is determined to have violated 2 CFR part 182, as implemented by this part, the agency will take one or more of the following actions—

(a) Suspension of payments under the award;

(b) Suspension or termination of the award; and

(c) Suspension or debarment of the recipient under 2 CFR part 180 and 2 CFR part 3000, for a period not to exceed five years.

## Subpart F—Definitions

**§ 3001.605  Award.**

*Award* means an award of financial assistance by a Federal agency directly to a recipient.

(a) The term award includes:

(1) A Federal grant, cooperative agreement or reimbursable agreement, in the form of money or property in lieu of money.

(2) A block grant or a grant in an entitlement program, whether or not the grant is exempted from coverage under 2 CFR part 182 and specifies uniform administrative requirements.

(b) The term "award" does not include:

(1) Technical assistance that provides services instead of money.

(2) Loans.

(3) Loan guarantees.

(4) Interest subsidies.

(5) Insurance.

(6) Direct appropriations.

(7) Veterans' benefits to individuals (*i.e.*, any benefit to veterans, their families, or survivors by virtue of the service of a veteran in the Armed Forces of the United States).

(8) Other Transactional Authority Award.

### § 3001.661 Reimbursable Agreement.

*Reimbursable Agreement* means an award in which the recipient is reimbursed for expenditures only, and is not eligible for advance payments.

## PART 3002—UNIFORM ADMINISTRATIVE REQUIREMENTS, COST PRINCIPLES, AND AUDIT REQUIREMENTS FOR FEDERAL AWARDS

AUTHORITY: 31 U.S.C. 503, 2 CFR part 200, and as noted in specific sections.

SOURCE: 79 FR 76084, Dec. 19, 2014, unless otherwise noted.

### § 3002.10 Adoption of 2 CFR Part 200.

Under the authority listed above, the Department of Homeland Security adopts the Office of Management and Budget (OMB) Guidance in 2 CFR part 200. Thus, this part gives regulatory effect to the OMB guidance and supplements the guidance as needed for the Department.

## PARTS 3003–3099 [RESERVED]

# CHAPTER XXXI—INSTITUTE OF MUSEUM AND LIBRARY SERVICES

# PARTS 3100–3184 [RESERVED]

# PART 3185—NONPROCUREMENT DEBARMENT AND SUSPENSION

Sec.
3185.10  What does this part do?
3185.20  Does this part apply to me?
3185.30  What policies and procedures must I follow?

### Subpart A—General

3185.137  Who in IMLS may grant an exception to let an excluded person participate in a covered transaction?

### Subpart B—Covered Transactions

3185.220  What contracts and subcontracts, in addition to those listed in 2 CFR 180.220, are covered transactions?

### Subpart C—Responsibilities of Participants Regarding Transactions

3185.332  What methods must I use to pass requirements down to participants at lower tiers with whom I intend to do business?

### Subpart D—Responsibilities of Federal Agency Officials Regarding Transactions

3185.437  What method do I use to communicate to a participant the requirements described in the OMB guidance at 2 CFR 180.435?

### Subparts E–I [Reserved]

AUTHORITY: 20 U.S.C. 9103(f); Sec. 2455, Pub. L. 103–355, 108 Stat. 3327; E.O. 12549, 3 CFR, 1986 Comp., p. 189; E.O. 12689, 3 CFR, 1989 Comp., p. 235.

SOURCE: 73 FR 46529, Aug. 11, 2008, unless otherwise noted.

## § 3185.10  What does this part do?

This part adopts the Office of Management and Budget (OMB) guidance in subparts A through I of 2 CFR part 180, as supplemented by this part, as the Institute of Museum and Library Services (IMLS) policies and procedures for nonprocurement debarment and suspension. It thereby gives regulatory effect for IMLS to the OMB guidance as supplemented by this part. This part satisfies the requirements in section 3 of Executive Order 12549, "Debarment and Suspension" (3 CFR 1986 Comp., p. 189), Executive Order 12689, "Debar-

ment and Suspension" (3 CFR 1989 Comp., p. 235) and 31 U.S.C. 6101 note (Section 2455, Pub. L. 103–355, 108 Stat. 3327).

## § 3185.20  Does this part apply to me?

This part and, through this part, pertinent portions of the OMB guidance in subparts A through I of 2 CFR part 180 (see table at 2 CFR 180.100(b)) apply to you if you are a—

(a) Participant or principal in a "covered transaction" (see subpart B of 2 CFR part 180 and the definition of "nonprocurement transaction" at 2 CFR 180.970).

(b) Respondent in an IMLS suspension or debarment action.

(c) IMLS debarment or suspension official;

(d) IMLS grants officer, agreements officer, or other official authorized to enter into any type of nonprocurement transaction that is a covered transaction.

## § 3185.30  What policies and procedures must I follow?

The IMLS policies and procedures that you must follow are the policies and procedures specified in each applicable section of the OMB guidance in subparts A through I of 2 CFR part 180, as that section is supplemented by the section in this part with the same section number. The contracts that are covered transactions, for example, are specified by section 220 of the OMB guidance (i.e., 2 CFR 180.220) as supplemented by section 220 in this part (i.e., § 3185.220). For any section of OMB guidance in subparts A through I of 2 CFR 180 that has no corresponding section in this part, IMLS policies and procedures are those in the OMB guidance.

## Subpart A—General

### § 3185.137  Who in the IMLS may grant an exception to let an excluded person participate in a covered transaction?

The IMLS Director has the authority to grant an exception to let an excluded person participate in a covered transaction, as provided in the OMB guidance at 2 CFR 180.135.

513

## Subpart B—Covered Transactions

**§ 3185.220  What contracts and subcontracts, in addition to those listed in 2 CFR 180.220, are covered transactions?**

Although the OMB guidance at 2 CFR 180.220(c) allows a Federal agency to do so (also see optional lower-tier coverage in the figure in the appendix to 2 CFR part 180), IMLS does not extend coverage of nonprocurement suspension and debarment requirements beyond first-tier procurement contracts under a covered nonprocurement transaction.

## Subpart C—Responsibilities of Participants Regarding Transactions

**§ 3185.332  What methods must I use to pass requirements down to participants at lower tiers with whom I intend to do business?**

You as a participant must include a term or condition in lower-tier transactions requiring lower-tier participants to comply with subpart C of the OMB guidance in 2 CFR part 180, as supplemented by this subpart.

## Subpart D—Responsibilities of Federal Agency Officials Regarding Transactions

**§ 3185.437  What method do I use to communicate to a participant the requirements described in the OMB guidance at 2 CFR 180.435?**

To communicate to a participant the requirements described in 2 CFR 180.435 of the OMB guidance, you must include a term or condition in the transaction that requires the participant's compliance with subpart C of 2 CFR part 180, as supplemented by subpart C of this part, and requires the participant to include a similar term or condition in lower-tier covered transactions.

## Subparts E–I [Reserved]

# PART 3186—REQUIREMENTS FOR DRUG-FREE WORKPLACE (FINANCIAL ASSISTANCE)

Sec.
3186.10　What does this part do?
3186.20　Does this part apply to me?
3186.30　What policies and procedures must I follow?

### Subpart A—Purpose and Coverage [Reserved]

### Subpart B—Requirements for Recipients Other Than Individuals

3186.225　Whom in the IMLS does a recipient other than an individual notify about a criminal drug conviction?

### Subpart C—Requirements for Recipients Who Are Individuals

3186.300　Whom in the IMLS does a recipient who is an individual notify about a criminal drug conviction?

### Subpart D—Responsibilities of Agency Awarding Officials

3186.400　What method do I use as an agency awarding official to obtain a recipient's agreement to comply with the OMB guidance?

### Subpart E—Violations of this Part and Consequences

3186.500　Who in the IMLS determines that a recipient other than an individual violated the requirements of this part?
3186.505　Who in the IMLS determines that a recipient who is an individual violated the requirements of this part?

Authority: 41 U.S.C. 701–707.

Source: 75 FR 39134, July 8, 2010, unless otherwise noted.

**§ 3186.10  What does this part do?**

This part requires that the award and administration of IMLS grants and cooperative agreements comply with Office of Management and Budget (OMB) guidance implementing the portion of the Drug-Free Workplace Act of 1988 (41 U.S.C. 701–707, as amended, hereafter referred to as "the Act") that applies to grants. It thereby—

(a) Gives regulatory effect to the OMB guidance (Subparts A through F of 2 CFR part 182) for the IMLS's grants and cooperative agreements; and

(b) Establishes IMLS policies and procedures for compliance with the Act that are the same as those of other Federal agencies, in conformance with the requirement in 41 U.S.C. 705 for Governmentwide implementing regulations.

### §3186.20  Does this part apply to me?

This part and, through this part, pertinent portions of the OMB guidance in Subparts A through F of 2 CFR part 182 (see table at 2 CFR 182.115(b)) apply to you if you are a—

(a) Recipient of an IMLS grant or cooperative agreement; or

(b) IMLS awarding official.

### §3186.30  What policies and procedures must I follow?

(a) *General.* You must follow the policies and procedures specified in applicable sections of the OMB guidance in Subparts A through F of 2 CFR part 182, as implemented by this part.

(b) *Specific sections of OMB guidance that this part supplements.* In implementing the OMB guidance in 2 CFR part 182, this part supplements four sections of the guidance, as shown in the following table. For each of those sections, you must follow the policies and procedures in the OMB guidance, as supplemented by this part.

| Section of OMB guidance | Section in this part where supplemented | What the supplementation clarifies |
|---|---|---|
| (1) 2 CFR 182.225(a) ........ | §3186.225 | Whom in the IMLS a recipient other than an individual must notify if an employee is convicted for a violation of a criminal drug statute in the workplace. |
| (2) 2 CFR 182.300(b) ........ | §3186.300 | Whom in the IMLS a recipient who is an individual must notify if he or she is convicted of a criminal drug offense resulting from a violation occurring during the conduct of any award activity. |
| (3) 2 CFR 182.500 ............ | §3186.500 | Who in the IMLS is authorized to determine that a recipient other than an individual is in violation of the requirements of 2 CFR part 182, as implemented by this part. |
| (4) 2 CFR 182.505 ............ | §3186.505 | Who in the IMLS is authorized to determine that a recipient who is an individual is in violation of the requirements of 2 CFR part 182, as implemented by this part. |

(c) *Sections of the OMB guidance that this part does not supplement.* For any section of OMB guidance in Subparts A through F of 2 CFR part 182 that is not listed in paragraph (b) of this section, IMLS policies and procedures are the same as those in the OMB guidance.

## Subpart A—Purpose and Coverage [Reserved]

## Subpart B—Requirements for Recipients Other Than Individuals

### §3186.225  Whom in the IMLS does a recipient other than an individual notify about a criminal drug conviction?

A recipient other than an individual that is required under 2 CFR 182.225(a) to notify Federal agencies about an employee's conviction for a criminal drug offense must notify each IMLS office from which it currently has an award.

## Subpart C—Requirements for Recipients Who Are Individuals

### §3186.300  Whom in the IMLS does a recipient who is an individual notify about a criminal drug conviction?

A recipient who is an individual and is required under 2 CFR 182.300(b) to notify Federal agencies about a conviction for a criminal drug offense must notify each IMLS office from which it currently has an award.

## Subpart D—Responsibilities of Agency Awarding Officials

### §3186.400  What method do I use as an agency awarding official to obtain a recipient's agreement to comply with the OMB guidance?

To obtain a recipient's agreement to comply with applicable requirements in the OMB guidance at 2 CFR part 182, you must include the following term or condition in the award:

Drug-free workplace. You as the recipient must comply with drug-free workplace requirements in Subpart B (or Subpart C, if the recipient is an individual) of 2 CFR part 3186, which adopts the Governmentwide implementation (2 CFR part 182) of sec. 5152–5158 of the Drug-Free Workplace Act of 1988 (Pub. L. 100–690, Title V, Subtitle D; 41 U.S.C. 701–707).

## Subpart E—Violations of this Part and Consequences

### § 3186.500   Who in the IMLS determines that a recipient other than an individual violated the requirements of this part?

The IMLS Chief Financial Officer is the official authorized to make the determination under 2 CFR 182.500.

### § 3186.505   Who in the IMLS determines that a recipient who is an individual violated the requirements of this part?

The IMLS Chief Financial Officer is the official authorized to make the determination under 2 CFR 182.505.

## PART 3187—UNIFORM ADMINISTRATIVE REQUIREMENTS, COST PRINCIPLES, AND AUDIT REQUIREMENTS FOR FEDERAL AWARDS

Sec.
3187.1   Adoption of 2 CFR part 200.

#### Subpart A—Scope, Definitions, and Eligibility

3187.2   Applicable regulations and scope of this part.
3187.3   Definition of a museum.
3187.4   Other definitions.
3187.5   Museum eligibility and burden of proof—Who may apply.
3187.6   Related institutions.
3187.7   Basic materials which an applicant must submit to be considered for funding.

#### Subpart B—General Application, Selection and Award Procedures

APPLICATIONS

3187.8   Deadline date and method for submitting applications.

SELECTION AND AWARD PROCEDURES

3187.9   Rejection of an application.
3187.10   Rejection for technical deficiency—appeal.

#### Subpart C—General Conditions Which Must Be Met

COMPLIANCE WITH LEGAL REQUIREMENTS

3187.11   Compliance with statutes, regulations, approved application and Federal award.

NONDISCRIMINATION

3187.12   Federal statutes and regulations on nondiscrimination.

EVALUATION

3187.13   Federal evaluation—Cooperation by a non-Federal entity.

ALLOWABLE COSTS

3187.14   Subawards
3187.15   Allowable costs.

AUTHORITY: 20 U.S.C. 9101–9176, 9103(h); 20 U.S.C. 80r–5; 2 CFR part 200.

SOURCE: 79 FR 76088, Dec. 19, 2014, unless otherwise noted.

### § 3187.1   Adoption of 2 CFR Part 200.

Under the authority listed above, the Institute of Museum and Library Services (IMLS) adopts the Office of Management and Budget (OMB) Guidance in 2 CFR part 200, with the additions that are provided below. Thus, this part gives regulatory effect to the OMB guidance and supplements the guidance as needed for IMLS.

## Subpart A—Scope, Definitions, and Eligibility

### § 3187.2   Applicable regulations and scope of this part.

(a) Except as set forth in this 2 CFR part 3187, the Uniform Administrative Requirements, Cost Principles, and Audit Requirements for Federal Awards set forth in 2 CFR part 200 shall apply to awards from funds appropriated to the Institute of Museum and Library Services (the "Institute" or "IMLS").

(b) The IMLS authorizing statutes, including 20 U.S.C. 9101 *et seq.* and 20 U.S.C. 80r–5, ("IMLS Statutes") are controlling in the event of any conflict between the IMLS Statutes and the regulations in 2 CFR part 200.

## §3187.3  Definition of a museum.

For the purpose of this part:

(a) Museum means a public or private nonprofit institution which is organized on a permanent basis for essentially educational or aesthetic purposes and which, using a professional staff:

(1) Owns or uses tangible objects, either animate or inanimate;

(2) Cares for these objects; and

(3) Exhibits them to the general public on a regular basis.

(i) An institution that exhibits objects to the general public for at least 120 days a year shall be deemed to meet this requirement.

(ii) An institution that exhibits objects by appointment may meet this requirement if it can establish, in light of the facts under all the relevant circumstances, that this method of exhibition does not unreasonably restrict the accessibility of the institution's exhibits to the general public.

(b) The term "museum" in paragraph (a) of this section includes museums that have tangible and digital collections. Museums include, but are not limited to, the following types of institutions, if they otherwise satisfy the provisions of this section:

(1) Aquariums;

(2) Arboretums;

(3) Botanical gardens;

(4) Art museums;

(5) Children's museums;

(6) General museums;

(7) Historic houses and sites;

(8) History museums;

(9) Nature centers;

(10) Natural history and anthropology museums;

(11) Planetariums;

(12) Science and technology centers;

(13) Specialized museums; and

(14) Zoological parks.

(c) For the purposes of this section, an institution uses a professional staff if it employs at least one staff member, or the fulltime equivalent, whether paid or unpaid primarily engaged in the acquisition, care, or exhibition to the public of objects owned or used by the institution.

(d)(1) Except as set forth in paragraph (d)(2) of this section, an institution exhibits objects to the general public for the purposes of this section if such exhibition is a primary purpose of the institution.

(2) An institution that does not have as a primary purpose the exhibition of objects to the general public but which can demonstrate that it exhibits objects to the general public on a regular basis as a significant, separate, distinct, and continuing portion of its activities, and that it otherwise meets the requirements of this section, may be determined to be a museum under this section. In order to establish its eligibility, such an institution must provide information regarding the following:

(i) The number of staff members devoted to museum functions as described in paragraph (a) of this section.

(ii) The period of time that such museum functions have been carried out by the institution over the course of the institution's history.

(iii) Appropriate financial information for such functions presented separately from the financial information of the institution as a whole.

(iv) The percentage of the institution's total space devoted to such museum functions.

(v) Such other information as the Director requests.

(3) The Director uses the information furnished under paragraph (d)(2) of this section in making a determination regarding the eligibility of such an institution under this section.

(e) For the purpose of this section, an institution exhibits objects to the public if it exhibits the objects through facilities which it owns or operates.

## §3187.4  Other definitions.

The following other definitions apply in this part:

*Act* means The Museum and Library Services Act, Pub. L. 104–208 (20 U.S.C. 9101–9176), as amended.

*Collection* includes objects owned, used or loaned by a museum as well as those literary, archival and documentary resources specifically required for the study and interpretation of these objects.

*Director* means the Director of the Institute of Museum and Library Services.

*Institute* or *IMLS* means the Institute of Museum and Library Services established under Section 203 of the Act.

*Museum services* means services provided by a museum, primarily exhibiting objects to the general public, and including but not limited to preserving and maintaining its collections, and providing educational and other programs to the public through the use of its collections and other resources.

### § 3187.5  Museum eligibility and burden of proof—Who may apply.

(a) A museum located in any of the 50 States of the United States, the District of Columbia, the Commonwealth of Puerto Rico, the United States Virgin Islands, Guam, American Samoa, the Commonwealth of the Northern Mariana Islands, the Republic of the Marshall Islands, the Federated States of Micronesia, and the Republic of Palau may apply for a Federal award under the Act.

(b) A public or private nonprofit agency which is responsible for the operation of a museum may, if necessary, apply on behalf of the museum.

(c) A museum operated by a department or agency of the Federal Government is not eligible to apply.

(d) An applicant has the burden of establishing that it is eligible for assistance under these regulations.

### § 3187.6  Related institutions.

(a) If two or more institutions are under the common control of one agency or institution or are otherwise organizationally related and apply for assistance under the Act, the Director determines under all the relevant circumstances whether they are separate museums for the purpose of establishing eligibility for assistance under these regulations. *See* § 3187.5 (Museum eligibility and burden of proof—Who may apply).

(b) IMLS regards the following factors, among others, as showing that a related institution is a separate museum:

(1) The institution has its own governing body;

(2) The institution has budgetary autonomy; and

(3) The institution has administrative autonomy.

### § 3187.7  Basic materials which an applicant must submit to be considered for funding.

(a) *Application.* To apply for an IMLS Federal award, an applicant must submit the designated application form containing all information requested.

(b) *IRS letter.* An applicant applying as a private, nonprofit institution must submit a copy of the letter from the Internal Revenue Service indicating the applicant's eligibility for nonprofit status under the applicable provision of the Internal Revenue Code of 1954, as amended.

## Subpart B—General Application, Selection and Award Procedures

APPLICATIONS

### § 3187.8  Deadline date and method for submitting applications.

(a) The notice of funding opportunity sets the deadline date and method(s) for applications to be submitted to the Institute.

(b) If the application notice permits mailing of an application, an applicant must be prepared to show one of the following as proof of timely mailing:

(1) A legibly dated U.S. Postal Service postmark.

(2) A legible mail receipt with the date of mailing stamped by the U.S. Postal Service.

(3) A dated shipping label, invoice, or receipt from a commercial carrier.

(4) Any other dated proof of mailing acceptable to the Director.

(c) If the application notice permits mailing of an application, and the application is mailed through the U.S. Postal Service, the Director does not accept either of the following as proof of mailing:

(1) A private metered postmark.

(2) A mail receipt that is not date cancelled by the U.S. Postal Service.

SELECTION AND AWARD PROCEDURES

### § 3187.9  Rejection of an application.

(a) The Director rejects an application if:

(1) The applicant is not eligible;

(2) The applicant fails to comply with procedural rules that govern the submission of the application;

(3) The application does not contain the information required;

(4) The application cannot be funded under the authorizing statute or implementing regulations.

(b) If the Director rejects an application under this section, the Director informs the applicant and explains why the application was rejected.

§ 3187.10  Rejection for technical deficiency—appeal.

An applicant whose application is rejected because of technical deficiency may appeal such rejection in writing to the Director within 10 business days of electronic or postmarked notice of rejection, whichever is earlier.

## Subpart C—General Conditions Which Must Be Met

COMPLIANCE WITH LEGAL REQUIREMENTS

§ 3187.11  Compliance with statutes, regulations, approved application and Federal award.

(a) A recipient and subrecipient, as applicable, shall comply with the rel-evant statutes, regulations, and the approved application and Federal award, and shall use Federal funds in accordance therewith.

(b) No act or failure to act by an official, agent, or employee of the Institute can affect the authority of the Director to enforce regulations.

(c) In any circumstance for which waiver is provided, the determination of the Director shall be final.

NONDISCRIMINATION

§ 3187.12  Federal statutes and regulations on nondiscrimination.

(a) Each recipient and subrecipient, as applicable, shall comply with the relevant nondiscrimination statutes and public policy requirements including, but not limited to, the following:

| Subject | Statute |
| --- | --- |
| Discrimination on the basis of race, color or national origin ....... | Title VI of the Civil Rights Act of 1964 (42 U.S.C. 2000d through 2000d–4). |
| Discrimination on the basis of sex ............................................. | Title IX of the Education Amendments of 1972 (20 U.S.C. 1681–1683). |
| Discrimination on the basis of disability ..................................... | Section 504 of the Rehabilitation Act of 1973 (29 U.S.C. 794). |
| Discrimination on the basis of age ............................................ | The Age Discrimination Act (420 U.S.C. 8101 *et. seq*). |

(b) *Regulations under section 504 of the Rehabilitation Act of 1973.* The Institute applies the regulations in 45 CFR part 1170, issued by the National Endowment for the Humanities and relating to nondiscrimination on the basis of handicap in federally assisted programs and activities, in determining the compliance with section 504 of the Rehabilitation Act of 1973 as it applies to recipients of Federal financial assistance from the Institute. These regulations apply to each program or activity that receives such assistance. In applying these regulations, references to the *Endowment* or the *agency* shall be deemed to be references to the Institute and references to the *Chairman* shall be deemed to be references to the Director.

EVALUATION

§ 3187.13  Federal evaluation—Cooperation by a non-Federal entity.

A non-Federal entity shall cooperate in any evaluation by the Director of the particular IMLS Federal financial assistance program in which the non-Federal entity has participated.

ALLOWABLE COSTS

§ 3187.14  Subawards.

(a) A recipient may not make a subaward unless expressly authorized by the Institute. In the event the Institute authorizes a subaward, the recipient shall:

(1) Ensure that the subaward includes any clauses required by Federal law as

well as any program-related conditions imposed by the Institute;

(2) Ensure that the subrecipient is aware of the applicable legal and program requirements; and

(3) Monitor the activities of the subrecipient as necessary to ensure compliance with Federal law and program requirements.

(b) A recipient may contract for supplies, equipment, and services, subject to applicable law, including but not limited to applicable Office of Management and Budget (OMB) Uniform Administrative Requirements, Cost Principles, and Audit Requirements for Federal Awards set forth in 2 CFR part 200.

## § 3187.15  Allowable costs.

(a) Determination of costs allowable under a Federal award is made in accordance with the government-wide cost principles in the Office of Management and Budget (OMB) Uniform Administrative Requirements, Cost Principles, and Audit Requirements for Federal Awards set forth in 2 CFR part 200.

(b) No costs shall be allowed for the purchase of any object to be included in the collection of a museum, except library, literary, or archival material specifically required for a designated activity under a Federal award under the Act.

# PARTS 3188–3199 [RESERVED]

# CHAPTER XXXII—NATIONAL ENDOWMENT FOR THE ARTS

# PARTS 3200–3253 [RESERVED]

# PART 3254—NONPROCUREMENT DEBARMENT AND SUSPENSION

AUTHORITY: Sec. 2455, Pub. L. 103–355, 108 Stat. 3327; E.O. 12549, 3 CFR, 1986 Comp., p. 189; E.O. 12689, 3 CFR, 1989 Comp., p. 235.

SOURCE: 72 FR 6141, Feb. 9, 2007, unless otherwise noted.

## § 3254.10  What does this part do?

This part adopts the Office of Management and Budget (OMB) guidance in subparts A through I of 2 CFR part 180, as supplemented by this part, as the National Endowment for the Arts (NEA) policies and procedures for nonprocurement debarment and suspension. It thereby gives regulatory effect for the NEA to the OMB guidance as supplemented by this part. This part satisfies the requirements in section 3 of Executive Order 12549, "Debarment and Suspension" (3 CFR 1986 Comp., p. 189), Executive Order 12689, "Debarment and Suspension" (3 CFR 1989 Comp., p. 235) and 31 U.S.C. 6101 note (Section 2455, Public Law 103–355, 108 Stat. 3327).

## § 3254.20  Does this part apply to me?

This part and, through this part, pertinent portions of the OMB guidance in subparts A through I of 2 CFR part 180 (see table at 2 CFR 180.100(b)) apply to you if you are a—

(a) Participant or principal in a "covered transaction" (see subpart B of 2 CFR part 180 and the definition of "nonprocurement transaction" at 2 CFR 180.970.

(b) Respondent in a NEA suspension or debarment action.

(c) NEA debarment or suspension official;

(d) NEA grants officer, agreements officer, or other official authorized to enter into any type of nonprocurement transaction that is a covered transaction;

## § 3254.30  What policies and procedures must I follow?

The NEA policies and procedures that you must follow are the policies and procedures specified in each applicable section of the OMB guidance in subparts A through I of 2 CFR part 180, as that section is supplemented by the section in this part with the same section number. The contracts that are covered transactions, for example, are specified by section 220 of the OMB guidance (i.e., 2 CFR 180.220) as supplemented by section 220 in this part (i.e., § 3254.220). For any section of OMB guidance in subparts A through I of 2 CFR 180 that has no corresponding section in this part, NEA policies and procedures are those in the OMB guidance.

## Subpart A—General

## § 3254.137  Who in the NEA may grant an exception to let an excluded person participate in a covered transaction?

The NEA Chairman has the authority to grant an exception to let an excluded person participate in a covered transaction, as provided in the OMB guidance at 2 CFR 180.135.

## Subpart B—Covered Transactions

**§ 3254.220  What contracts and sub-contracts, in addition to those listed in 2 CFR 180.220, are covered transactions?**

Although the OMB guidance at 2 CFR 180.220(c) allows a Federal agency to do so (also see options lower tier coverage in the figure in the appendix to 2 CFR part 180), NEA does not extend coverage of nonprocurement suspension and debarment requirements beyond first-tier procurement contracts under a covered nonprocurement transaction.

## Subpart C—Responsibilities of Participants Regarding Transactions

**§ 3254.332  What methods must I use to pass requirements down to participants at lower tiers with whom I intend to do business?**

You as a participant must include a term or condition in lower-tier transactions requiring lower-tier participants to comply with subpart C of the OMB guidance in 2 CFR part 180, as supplemented by this subpart.

## Subpart D—Responsibilities of Federal Agency Officials Regarding Transactions

**§ 3254.437  What method do I use to communicate to a participant the requirements described in the OMB guidance at 2 CFR 180.435?**

To communicate to a participant the requirements described in 2 CFR 180.435 of the OMB guidance, you must include a term or condition in the transaction that requires the participant's compliance with subpart C of 2 CFR part 180, as supplemented by subpart C of this part, and requires the participant to include a similar term or condition in lower-tier covered transactions.

## Subparts E–I [Reserved]

# PART 3255—UNIFORM ADMINISTRATIVE REQUIREMENTS, COST PRINCIPLES, AND AUDIT REQUIREMENTS FOR FEDERAL AWARDS

AUTHORITY: 5 U.S.C. 301, 20 U.S.C. 954, 2 CFR part 200.

SOURCE: 79 FR 76090, Dec. 19, 2014, unless otherwise noted.

**§ 3255.1  Adoption of 2 CFR Part 200.**

Under the authority listed above, the National Endowment for the Arts (NEA) adopts the Office of Management and Budget (OMB) Guidance in 2 CFR part 200. Thus, this part gives regulatory effect to the OMB guidance and supplements the guidance as needed for the NEA.

# PART 3256—REQUIREMENTS FOR DRUG–FREE WORKPLACE (FINANCIAL ASSISTANCE)

Sec.
3256.100  What does this part do?
3256.105  Does this part apply to me?
3256.110  What policies and procedures must I follow?

### Subpart A [Reserved]

### Subpart B—Requirements for Recipients Other Than Individuals

3256.200  Whom in the NEA does a recipient other than an individual notify about a criminal drug conviction?

### Subpart C—Requirements for Recipients Who Are Individuals

3256.300  Whom in the NEA does a recipient who is an individual notify about a criminal drug conviction?

### Subpart D—Responsibilities of NEA Awarding Officials

3256.400  What method do I use as an agency awarding official to obtain a recipient's agreement to comply with the OMB guidance?

### Subpart E—Violations of This Part and Consequences

3256.500  Who in the NEA determines that a recipient other than an individual violated the requirements of this part?

3256.505 Who in the NEA determines that a recipient who is an individual violated the requirements of this part?

### Subpart F [Reserved]

AUTHORITY: 41 U.S.C. 701 et seq.

SOURCE: 80 FR 33156, June 11, 2015, unless otherwise noted.

### § 3256.100 What does this part do?

This part requires that the award and administration of NEA grants and cooperative agreements comply with Office of Management and Budget (OMB) guidance implementing the portion of the Drug-Free Workplace Act of 1988 (41 U.S.C. 701–707, as amended, hereafter referred to as "the Act") that applies to grants. It thereby—

(a) Gives regulatory effect to the OMB guidance (subparts A through F of 2 CFR part 182) for the NEA's grants and cooperative agreements; and

(b) Establishes NEA policies and procedures for compliance with the Act that are the same as those of other Federal agencies, in conformance with the requirement in 41 U.S.C. 705 for Governmentwide implementing regulations.

### § 3256.105 Does this part apply to me?

This part and, through this part, pertinent portions of the OMB guidance in subparts A through F of 2 CFR part 182 (see table at 2 CFR 182.115(b)) apply to you if you are a—

(a) Recipient of an NEA grant or cooperative agreement; or

(b) NEA awarding official.

### § 3256.110 What policies and procedures must I follow?

(a) *General.* You must follow the policies and procedures specified in the applicable sections of the OMB guidance in subparts A through F of 2 CFR part 182, as implemented by this part.

(b) *Specific sections of OMB guidance that this part supplements.* In implementing the guidance in 2 CFR part 182, this part supplements four sections of that guidance, as shown in the following table. For each of those sections, you must follow the policies and procedures in the OMB guidance, as supplemented by this part.

| Section of OMB guidance | Section in this part where supplemented | What the supplementation clarifies |
|---|---|---|
| (1) 2 CFR 182.225(a) | § 3256.200 | Whom in the NEA a recipient other than an individual must notify if an employee is convicted for a violation of a criminal drug statute in the workplace. |
| (2) 2 CFR 182.300(b) | § 3256.300 | Whom in the NEA a recipient who is an individual must notify if he or she is convicted of a criminal drug offense resulting from a violation occurring during the conduct of any award activity. |
| (3) 2 CFR 182.500 | § 3256.500 | Who in the NEA is authorized to determine that a recipient other than an individual is in violation of the requirements of 2 CFR part 182, as implemented by this part. |
| (4) 2 CFR 182.505 | § 3256.505 | Who in the NEA is authorized to determine that a recipient who is an individual is in violation of the requirements of 2 CFR part 182, as implemented by this part. |

(c) *Sections of the OMB guidance that this part does not supplement.* For any section of OMB guidance in subparts A through F of 2 CFR part 182 that is not listed in paragraph (b) of this section, the NEA's policies and procedures are the same as those in the OMB guidance.

### Subpart A [Reserved]

## Subpart B—Requirements for Recipients Other Than Individuals

### § 3256.200 Whom in the NEA does a recipient other than an individual notify about a criminal drug conviction?

A recipient other than an individual that is required under 2 CFR 182.225(a) to notify Federal agencies about an employee's conviction for a criminal drug offense must notify the NEA awarding official or other designee for each award that it currently has.

## Subpart C—Requirements for Recipients Who Are Individuals

**§ 3256.300  Whom in the NEA does a recipient who is an individual notify about a criminal drug conviction?**

A recipient who is an individual and is required under 2 CFR 182.300(b) to notify Federal agencies about a conviction for a criminal drug offense must notify the NEA awarding official or other designee for each award that he or she currently has.

## Subpart D—Responsibilities of NEA Awarding Officials

**§ 3256.400  What method do I use as an agency awarding official to obtain a recipient's agreement to comply with the OMB guidance?**

To obtain a recipient's agreement to comply with applicable requirements in the OMB guidance at 2 CFR part 182, you must include the following term or condition in the award: Drug-free workplace. You as the recipient must comply with drug-free workplace requirements in subpart B (or subpart C,

if the recipient is an individual) of this part, which adopts the Government-wide implementation (2 CFR part 182) of sec. 5152–5158 of the Drug-Free Workplace Act of 1988 (Pub. L. 100–690, Title V, Subtitle D; 41 U.S.C. 701–707).

## Subpart E—Violations of This Part and Consequences

**§ 3256.500  Who in the NEA determines that a recipient other than an individual violated the requirements of this part?**

The Chairman of the National Endowment for the Arts is the official authorized to make the determination under 2 CFR 182.500.

**§ 3256.505  Who in the NEA determines that a recipient who is an individual violated the requirements of this part?**

The Chairman of the National Endowment for the Arts is the official authorized to make the determination under 2 CFR 182.505.

## Subpart F [Reserved]

## PARTS 3257–3299 [RESERVED]

# CHAPTER XXXIII—NATIONAL ENDOWMENT FOR THE HUMANITIES

# PARTS 3300–3368 [RESERVED]

# PART 3369—NONPROCUREMENT DEBARMENT AND SUSPENSION

Sec.
3369.10   What does this part do?
3369.20   Does this part apply to me?
3369.30   What policies and procedures must I follow?

### Subpart A—General

3369.137   Who in the NEH may grant an exception to let an excluded person participate in a covered transaction?

### Subpart B—Covered Transactions

3369.220   What contracts and subcontracts, in addition to those listed in 2 CFR 180.220, are covered transactions?

### Subpart C—Responsibilities of Participants Regarding Transactions

3369.332   What methods must I use to pass requirements down to participants at lower tiers with whom I intend to do business?

### Subpart D—Responsibilities of Federal Agency Officials Regarding Transactions

3369.437   What method do I use to communicate to a participant the requirements described in the OMB guidance at 2 CFR 180.435?

### Subparts E–I [Reserved]

AUTHORITY: 20 U.S.C. 959(a)(1); Sec. 2455, Pub. L. 103–355, 108 Stat. 3327; E.O. 12549, 3 CFR, 1986 Comp., p. 189; E.O. 12689, 3 CFR, 1989 Comp., p. 235.

SOURCE: 72 FR 9236, Mar. 1, 2007, unless otherwise noted.

## § 3369.10   What does this part do?

This part adopts the Office of Management and Budget (OMB) guidance in subparts A through I of 2 CFR part 180, as supplemented by this part, as the National Endowment for the Humanities (NEH) policies and procedures for nonprocurement debarment and suspension. It thereby gives regulatory effect for the NEH to the OMB guidance as supplemented by this part. This part satisfies the requirements in section 3 of Executive Order 12549, "Debarment and Suspension" (3 CFR 1986 Comp., p. 189), Executive Order 12689, "Debar-

ment and Suspension" (3 CFR 1989 Comp., p. 235) and 31 U.S.C. 6101 note (Section 2455, Public Law 103–355, 108 Stat. 3327).

## § 3369.20   Does this part apply to me?

This part and, through this part, pertinent portions of the OMB guidance in subparts A through I of 2 CFR part 180 (see table at 2 CFR 180.100(b)) apply to you if you are a—
(a) Participant or principal in a "covered transaction" (see subpart B of 2 CFR part 180 and the definition of "nonprocurement transaction" at 2 CFR 180.970).
(b) Respondent in a NEH suspension or debarment action.
(c) NEH debarment or suspension official;
(d) NEH grants officer, agreements officer, or other official authorized to enter into any type of nonprocurement transaction that is a covered transaction;

## § 3369.30   What policies and procedures must I follow?

The NEH policies and procedures that you must follow are the policies and procedures specified in each applicable section of the OMB guidance in subparts A through I of 2 CFR part 180, as that section is supplemented by the section in this part with the same section number. The contracts that are covered transactions, for example, are specified by section 220 of the OMB guidance (i.e., 2 CFR 180.220) as supplemented by section 220 in this part (i.e., § 3369.220). For any section of OMB guidance in subparts A through I of 2 CFR 180 that has no corresponding section in this part, NEH policies and procedures are those in the OMB guidance.

## Subpart A—General

## § 3369.137   Who in the NEH may grant an exception to let an excluded person participate in a covered transaction?

The NEH Chairman has the authority to grant an exception to let an excluded person participate in a covered transaction, as provided in the OMB guidance at 2 CFR 180.135.

## Subpart B—Covered Transactions

**§ 3369.220 What contracts and subcontracts, in addition to those listed in 2 CFR 180.220, are covered transactions?**

Although the OMB guidance at 2 CFR 180.220(c) allows a Federal agency to do so (also see optional lower tier coverage in the figure in the appendix to 2 CFR part 180), NEH does not extend coverage of nonprocurement suspension and debarment requirements beyond first-tier procurement contracts under a covered nonprocurement transaction.

## Subpart C—Responsibilities of Participants Regarding Transactions

**§ 3369.332 What methods must I use to pass requirements down to participants at lower tiers with whom I intend to do business?**

You as a participant must include a term or condition in lower-tier transactions requiring lower-tier participants to comply with subpart C of the OMB guidance in 2 CFR part 180, as supplemented by this subpart.

## Subpart D—Responsibilities of Federal Agency Officials Regarding Transactions

**§ 3369.437 What method do I use to communicate to a participant the requirements described in the OMB guidance at 2 CFR 180.435?**

To communicate to a participant the requirements described in 2 CFR 180.435 of the OMB guidance, you must include a term or condition in the transaction that requires the participant's compliance with subpart C of 2 CFR part 180, as supplemented by subpart C of this part, and requires the participant to include a similar term or condition in lower-tier covered transactions.

## Subparts E–I [Reserved]

# PART 3373—REQUIREMENTS FOR DRUG-FREE WORKPLACE (FINANCIAL ASSISTANCE)

AUTHORITY: 41 U.S.C. 701–707.

SOURCE: 75 FR 52858, Aug. 30, 2010, unless otherwise noted.

**§ 3373.10 What does this part do?**

This part requires that the award and administration of NEH grants and cooperative agreements comply with Office of Management and Budget (OMB) guidance implementing the portion of the Drug-Free Workplace Act of 1988 (41 U.S.C. 701–707, as amended, hereafter referred to as "the Act") that applies to grants. It thereby—

(a) Gives regulatory effect to the OMB guidance (Subparts A through F of 2 CFR part 182) for the NEH's grants and cooperative agreements; and

(b) Establishes NEH policies and procedures for compliance with the Act that are the same as those of other Federal agencies, in conformance with the requirement in 41 U.S.C. 705 for Governmentwide implementing regulations.

§ 3373.20   Does this part apply to me?

This part and, through this part, pertinent portions of the OMB guidance in Subparts A through F of 2 CFR part 182 (*see* table at 2 CFR 182.115(b)) apply to you if you are a—

(a) Recipient of a NEH grant or cooperative agreement; or

(b) NEH awarding official.

§ 3373.30   What policies and procedures must I follow?

(a) *General.* You must follow the policies and procedures specified in applicable sections of the OMB guidance in Subparts A through F of 2 CFR part 182, as implemented by this part.

(b) *Specific sections of OMB guidance that this part supplements.* In implementing the OMB guidance in 2 CFR part 182, this part supplements four sections of the guidance, as shown in the following table. For each of those sections, you must follow the policies and procedures in the OMB guidance, as supplemented by this part.

| Section of OMB guidance | Section in this part where supplemented | What the supplementation clarifies |
|---|---|---|
| (1) 2 CFR 182.225(a) ................ | § 3373.225 | Whom in the NEH a recipient other than an individual must notify if an employee is convicted for a violation of a criminal drug statute in the workplace. |
| (2) 2 CFR 182.300(b) ................ | § 3373.300 | Whom in the NEH a recipient who is an individual must notify if he or she is convicted of a criminal drug offense resulting from a violation occurring during the conduct of any award activity. |
| (3) 2 CFR 182.500 .................... | § 3373.500 | Who in the NEH is authorized to determine that a recipient other than an individual is in violation of the requirements of 2 CFR part 182, as implemented by this part. |
| (4) 2 CFR 182.505 .................... | § 3373.505 | Who in the NEH is authorized to determine that a recipient who is an individual is in violation of the requirements of 2 CFR part 182, as implemented by this part. |

(c) *Sections of the OMB guidance that this part does not supplement.* For any section of the OMB guidance in Subparts A through F of 2 CFR part 182 that is not listed in paragraph (b) of this section, NEH policies and procedures are the same as those in the OMB guidance.

## Subpart A—Purpose and Coverage [Reserved]

## Subpart B—Requirements for Recipients Other Than Individuals

§ 3373.225   Whom in the NEH does a recipient other than an individual notify about a criminal drug conviction?

A recipient other than an individual that is required under 2 CFR 182.225(a) to notify Federal agencies about an employee's conviction for a criminal drug offense must notify the Director, Office of Grant Management, NEH.

## Subpart C—Requirements for Recipients Who Are Individuals

§ 3373.300   Whom in the NEH does a recipient who is an individual notify about a criminal drug conviction?

A recipient who is an individual and is required under 2 CFR 182.300(b) to notify Federal agencies about a conviction for a criminal drug offense must notify the Director, Office of Grant Management, NEH.

## Subpart D—Responsibilities of Agency Awarding Officials

§ 3373.400   What method do I use as an agency awarding official to obtain a recipient's agreement to comply with the OMB guidance?

To obtain a recipient's agreement to comply with applicable requirements in the OMB guidance at 2 CFR part 182, you must include the following term or condition in the award:

*Drug-free workplace.* You as the recipient must comply with drug-free workplace requirements in Subpart B (or Subpart C, if the recipient is an individual) of 2 CFR Part 3373, which adopts the Governmentwide implementation (2 CFR part 182) of sec. 5152–5158 of the Drug-Free Workplace Act of 1988 (Pub. L. 100–690, Title V, Subtitle D; 41 U.S.C. 701–707).

## Subpart E—Violations of This Part and Consequences

**§ 3373.500  Who in the NEH determines that a recipient other than an individual violated the requirements of this part?**

The NEH General Counsel is the agency official authorized to make the determination under 2 CFR 182.500.

**§ 3373.505  Who in the NEH determines that a recipient who is an individual violated the requirements of this part?**

The NEH General Counsel is the agency official authorized to make the determination under 2 CFR 182.505.

## Subpart F—Definitions [Reserved]

# PART 3374—UNIFORM ADMINISTRATIVE REQUIREMENTS, COST PRINCIPLES, AND AUDIT REQUIREMENTS FOR FEDERAL AWARDS

AUTHORITY: 5 U.S.C. 301, 20 U.S.C. 956, 2 CFR part 200.

SOURCE: 79 FR 76091, Dec. 19, 2014, unless otherwise noted.

**§ 3374.1  Adoption of 2 CFR Part 200.**

Under the authority listed above, the National Endowment for the Humanities (NEH) adopts the Office of Management and Budget (OMB) Guidance in 2 CFR part 200. Thus, this part gives regulatory effect to the OMB guidance and supplements the guidance as needed for NEH.

# PARTS 3375–3399 [RESERVED]

# CHAPTER XXXIV—DEPARTMENT OF EDUCATION

## PARTS 3400–3473 [RESERVED]

## PART 3474—UNIFORM ADMINIS-TRATIVE REQUIREMENTS, COST PRINCIPLES, AND AUDIT RE-QUIREMENTS FOR FEDERAL AWARDS

Sec.
3474.1  Adoption of 2 CFR part 200.
3474.5  How exceptions are made to 2 CFR part 200.
3474.10  Clarification regarding 2 CFR 200.207.
3474.15  Contracting with faith-based organizations and nondiscrimination.
3474.20  Open licensing requirement for competitive grant programs.

AUTHORITY: 20 U.S.C. 1221e–3, 3474, and 2 CFR part 200, unless otherwise noted.

SOURCE: 79 FR 76091, Dec. 19, 2014, unless otherwise noted.

### § 3474.1  Adoption of 2 CFR part 200.

(a) The Department of Education adopts the Office of Management and Budget (OMB) Guidance in 2 CFR part 200, except for 2 CFR 200.102(a) and 2 CFR 200.207(a). Thus, this part gives regulatory effect to the OMB guidance and supplements the guidance as needed for the Department.

(b) The authority for all of the provisions in 2 CFR part 200 as adopted in this part is listed as follows.

(Authority: 20 U.S.C. 1221e–3, 3474, and 2 CFR part 200.)

### § 3474.5  How exceptions are made to 2 CFR part 200.[1]

(a) With the exception of Subpart F—Audit Requirements of 2 CFR part 200, the Secretary of Education, after consultation with OMB, may allow exceptions for classes of Federal awards or non-Federal entities subject to the requirements of this part when exceptions are not prohibited by statute. However, in the interest of maximum uniformity, exceptions from the requirements of this part will be permitted only in unusual circumstances.

(b) Exceptions for classes of Federal awards or non-Federal entities will be

published on the OMB Web site at *www.whitehouse.gov/omb*.

(Authority: 20 U.S.C. 1221e–3, 3474, and 2 CFR part 200)

### § 3474.10  Clarification regarding 2 CFR 200.207.[2]

The Secretary or a pass-through entity may, in appropriate circumstances, designate the specific conditions established under 2 CFR 200.207 as "high-risk conditions" and designate a non-Federal entity subject to specific conditions established under § 200.207 as "high–risk".

(Authority: 20 U.S.C. 1221e–3, 3474, and 2 CFR part 200)

### § 3474.15  Contracting with faith-based organizations and nondiscrimination.

(a) This section establishes responsibilities that grantees and subgrantees have in selecting contractors to provide direct Federal services under a program of the Department. Paragraphs (c)(1), (d)(1), and (f) of this section establish requirements that supplement the procurement requirements in 2 CFR 200.313 through 200.326. Every contract between a grantee or subgrantee and a faith-based organization under a program of direct Federal financial assistance must include conditions to implement the requirements in paragraphs (c)(1), (d)(1), and (f) of this section.

(b)(1) A faith-based organization is eligible to contract with grantees and subgrantees, including States, on the same basis as any other private organization, with respect to contracts for which such other organizations are eligible.

(2) In selecting providers of goods and services, grantees and subgrantees, including States, must not discriminate for or against a private organization on the basis of the organization's religious character or affiliation and must ensure that the award of contracts is free from political interference, or even the appearance of such interference, and is done on the basis of merit, not on the basis of religion or religious belief, or lack thereof.

---

[1] C. Ref. 2 CFR 200.102.

[2] C. Ref. 2 CFR 200.205, 200.207.

(c)(1) The provisions of 34 CFR 75.532 and 76.532 (Use of funds for religion prohibited), 75.712 and 76.712 (Beneficiary protections: Written notice), and 75.713 and 76.713 (Beneficiary protections: Referral requirements) that apply to a faith-based organization that is a grantee or subgrantee also apply to a faith-based organization that contracts with a grantee or subgrantee, including a State.

(2) The requirements referenced under paragraph (c)(1) of this section do not apply to a faith-based organization that provides goods or services to a beneficiary under a program supported only by indirect Federal financial assistance, as defined in 34 CFR 75.52(c)(3) and 76.52(c)(3).

(d)(1) A private organization that engages in explicitly religious activities, such as religious worship, instruction, or proselytization, must offer those activities separately in time or location from any programs or services supported by a contract with a grantee or subgrantee, including a State, and attendance or participation in any such explicitly religious activities by beneficiaries of the programs and services supported by the contract must be voluntary.

(2) The limitations on explicitly religious activities under paragraph (d)(1) of this section do not apply to a faith-based organization that provides services to a beneficiary under a program supported only by indirect Federal financial assistance, as defined in 34 CFR 75.52(c)(3) and 76.52(c)(3).

(e)(1) A faith-based organization that contracts with a grantee or subgrantee, including a State, may retain its independence, autonomy, right of expression, religious character, and authority over its governance.

(2) A faith-based organization may, among other things—

(i) Retain religious terms in its name;

(ii) Continue to carry out its mission, including the definition, development, practice, and expression of its religious beliefs;

(iii) Use its facilities to provide services without removing or altering religious art, icons, scriptures, or other symbols from these facilities;

(iv) Select its board members and otherwise govern itself on a religious basis; and

(v) Include religious references in its mission statement and other chartering or governing documents.

(f) A private organization that contracts with a grantee or subgrantee, including a State, may not discriminate against a beneficiary or prospective beneficiary in the provision of program goods or services on the basis of religion or religious belief, a refusal to hold a religious belief, or refusal to attend or participate in a religious practice. However, an organization that participates in a program funded by indirect financial assistance need not modify its program activities to accommodate a beneficiary who chooses to expend the indirect aid on the organization's program.

(g) A religious organization's exemption from the Federal prohibition on employment discrimination on the basis of religion, in section 702(a) of the Civil Rights Act of 1964, 42 U.S.C. 2000e–1(a), is not forfeited when the organization contracts with a grantee or subgrantee.

(Authority: 20 U.S.C. 1221e–3 and 3474; 2 CFR Part 200, E.O. 13559)

[81 FR 19405, Apr. 4, 2016]

## § 3474.20 Open licensing requirement for competitive grant programs.

For competitive grants awarded in competitions announced after February 21, 2017:

(a) A grantee or subgrantee must openly license to the public the rights set out in paragraph (b)(1) of this section in any grant deliverable that is created wholly or in part with Department competitive grant funds, and that constitutes a new copyrightable work; provided, however, that when the deliverable consists of modifications to pre-existing works, the license shall extend only to those modifications that can be separately identified and only to the extent that open licensing is permitted under the terms of any licenses or other legal restrictions on the use of pre-existing works.

(b)(1) With respect to copyrightable work identified in paragraph (a) of this section, the grantee or subgrantee must grant to the public a worldwide, non-exclusive, royalty-free, perpetual, and irrevocable license to—

(i) Access, reproduce, publicly perform, publicly display, and distribute the copyrightable work;

(ii) Prepare derivative works and reproduce, publicly perform, publicly display and distribute those derivative works; and

(iii) Otherwise use the copyrightable work, provided that in all such instances attribution is given to the copyright holder.

(2) Grantees and subgrantees may select any open licenses that comply with the requirements of this section, including, at the grantee's or subgrantee's discretion, a license that limits use to noncommercial purposes. The open license also must contain—

(i) A symbol or device that readily communicates to users the permissions granted concerning the use of the copyrightable work;

(ii) Machine-readable code for digital resources;

(iii) Readily accessed legal terms; and

(iv) The statement of attribution and disclaimer specified in 34 CFR 75.620(b).

(c) A grantee or subgrantee that is awarded competitive grant funds must have a plan to disseminate the openly licensed copyrightable works identified in paragraph (a) of this section.

(d)(1) The requirements of paragraphs (a), (b), and (c) of this section do not apply to—

(i) Grants that provide funding for general operating expenses;

(ii) Grants that provide support to individuals (*e.g.*, scholarships, fellowships);

(iii) Grant deliverables that are jointly funded by the Department and another Federal agency if the other Federal agency does not require the open licensing of its grant deliverables for the relevant grant program;

(iv) Copyrightable works created by the grantee or subgrantee that are not created with Department grant funds;

(v) Peer-reviewed scholarly publications that arise from any scientific research funded, either fully or partially, from grants awarded by the Department;

(vi) Grantees or subgrantees under the Ready To Learn Television Program, as defined in the Elementary and Secondary Education Act of 1965, as amended, Title II, Subpart 3, Sec. 2431, 20 U.S.C. 6775;

(vii) A grantee or subgrantee that has received an exception from the Secretary under 2 CFR 3474.5 and 2 CFR 200.102 (*e.g.*, where the Secretary has determined that the grantee's dissemination plan would likely achieve meaningful dissemination equivalent to or greater than the dissemination likely to be achieved through compliance with paragraph (a) or (b) of this section, or compliance with paragraph (a) or (b) of this section would impede the grantee's ability to form the required partnerships necessary to carry out the purpose of the grant); and

(viii) Grantees or subgrantees for which compliance with these requirements would conflict with, or materially undermine the ability to protect or enforce, other intellectual property rights or obligations of the grantee or subgrantee, in existence or under development, including those provided under 15 U.S.C. 1051, *et seq.*, 18 U.S.C. 1831–1839, and 35 U.S.C. 200, *et seq.*

(2) The requirements of paragraphs (a), (b), and (c) of this section do not alter any applicable rights in the grant deliverable available under 17 U.S.C. 106A, 203 or 1202, 15 U.S.C. 1051, *et seq.*, or State law.

(e) The license set out in paragraph (b)(1) of this section shall not extend to any copyrightable work incorporated in the grant deliverable that is owned by a party other than the grantee or subgrantee, unless the grantee or subgrantee has acquired the right to provide such a license in that work.

(f) *Definition.* For purposes of this section,

(1) A *grant deliverable* is a final version of a work, including any final version of program support materials necessary to the use of the deliverable, developed to carry out the purpose of the grant, as specified in the grant announcement.

(2) A *derivative work* means a *derivative work* as defined in the Copyright Act, 17 U.S.C. 101.

[82 FR 7397, Jan. 19, 2017]

# PART 3485—NONPROCUREMENT DEBARMENT AND SUSPENSION

Authority: E.O. 12549 (3 CFR 1986 Comp., p. 189); E.O. 12689 (3 CFR 1989 Comp., p. 235); sec. 2455, Pub. L. 103–355, 108 Stat. 3327 (31 U.S.C. 6101 note); 20 U.S.C. 1082, 1094, 1221e–3, and 3474, unless otherwise noted.

Source: 77 FR 18673, Mar. 28, 2012, unless otherwise noted.

## § 3485.12   What does this part do?

(a)(1) The Department of Education (the "Department" or "ED") adopts subparts A through I of the Office of Management and Budget guidance in 2 CFR part 180. Thus, this part gives regulatory effect to the OMB guidance and supplements the guidance as needed for the Department. This part satisfies the requirements in section 3 of Executive Order 12549, "Debarment and Suspension" (3 CFR part 1986 Comp., p. 189), Executive Order 12689, "Debarment and Suspension" (3 CFR part 1989 Comp., p. 235) and 31 U.S.C. 6101 note (Section 2455, Pub. L. 103–355, 108 Stat. 3327).

(2) The table of contents for this part contains only those sections in part 3485 that include supplements to the guidance in part 180 and new sections needed to implement the guidance for the Department's programs. In those sections of the OMB guidance that are supplemented, the section in part 3485 includes both the text of the OMB guidance that is not affected by the change and any additional paragraphs that need to be added to the OMB guidance. For example, § 180.220 of this title contains only paragraphs (a) and (b). The text of § 3485.220, which supplements § 180.220 to extend lower-tier transactions to certain transactions below the primary tier, includes both the text of paragraph (a) and (b) of § 180.220 and the text of added paragraph (c).

(3) In those sections in part 180 that do not have paragraph designations and that the Department supplements, the section in this part implementing

the OMB guidance designates the undesignated paragraph from part 180 as paragraph (a) and the first supplemental paragraph as paragraph (b). For example, 2 CFR 180.330 includes an undesignated lead in paragraph and two subparagraphs designated (a) and (b). In § 3485.330, the undesignated paragraph in 2 CFR 180.330 is designated paragraph (a) and the two subparagraphs are designated paragraphs (1) and (2). The added paragraphs are designated paragraph (b) and (c).

(b) The authority for all the provisions in 2 CFR part 180 as adopted in this part is listed as follows.

AUTHORITY: E.O. 12549 (3 CFR 1986 Comp., p. 189); E.O. 12689 (3 CFR 1989 Comp., p. 235); sec. 2455, Pub. L. 103–355, 108 Stat. 3327 (31 U.S.C. 6101 note); 20 U.S.C. 1082, 1094, 1221e–3, and 3474.

(Authority: E.O. 12549 (3 CFR 1986 Comp., p. 189); E.O. 12689 (3 CFR 1989 Comp., p. 235); sec. 2455, Pub. L. 103–355, 108 Stat. 3327 (31 U.S.C. 6101 note); 20 U.S.C. 1082, 1094, 1221e–3, and 3474, unless otherwise noted.)

### § 3485.22   Does this part apply to me?

This part applies to you if you are—

(a) A participant or principal in a "covered transaction" (see subpart B of this part and the definition of "nonprocurement transaction" in § 180.970 of this title).

(b) A respondent in a suspension or debarment action of the Department.

(c) An ED deciding official; or

(d) An ED officer authorized to enter into any type of nonprocurement transaction that is a covered transaction.

(Authority: E.O. 12549 (3 CFR 1986 Comp., p. 189); E.O. 12689 (3 CFR 1989 Comp., p. 235); sec. 2455, Pub. L. 103–355, 108 Stat. 3327 (31 U.S.C. 6101 note); 20 U.S.C. 1082, 1094, 1221e–3, and 3474)

### § 3485.32   What policies and procedures must I follow?

The Department's policies and procedures that you must follow are the policies and procedures specified in this part and in Subparts A through I of 2 CFR part 180. The contracts that are covered transactions, for example, are specified in § 3485.220. Section 180.205 of this title does not require supplementation, so it is not included in the table of contents for this part

and is not separately stated in this part.

(Authority: E.O. 12549 (3 CFR 1986 Comp., p. 189); E.O. 12689 (3 CFR 1989 Comp., p. 235); sec. 2455, Pub. L. 103–355, 108 Stat. 3327 (31 U.S.C. 6101 note); 20 U.S.C. 1082, 1094, 1221e–3, and 3474)

## Subpart A—General

### § 3485.137   May the Department grant an exception to let an excluded person participate in a covered transaction?

(a) Yes, the Secretary delegates to the ED Deciding Official the authority under this section to grant an exception permitting an excluded person to participate in a particular covered transaction.

(b) If the ED Deciding Official grants an exception, the exception must be in writing and state the reason(s) for deviating from the Governmentwide policy in Executive Order 12549.

(Authority: E.O. 12549 (3 CFR 1986 Comp., p. 189); E.O. 12689 (3 CFR 1989 Comp., p. 235); sec. 2455, Pub. L. 103–355, 108 Stat. 3327 (31 U.S.C. 6101 note); 20 U.S.C. 1082, 1094, 1221e–3, and 3474)

## Subpart B—Covered Transactions

### § 3485.220   Are any procurement contracts included as covered transactions?

(a) Covered transactions under this part—

(1) Do not include any procurement contracts awarded directly by a Federal agency; but

(2) Do include some procurement contracts awarded by non-Federal participants in nonprocurement covered transactions.

(b) Specifically, a contract for goods or services is a covered transaction if any of the following applies:

(1) The contract is awarded by a participant in a nonprocurement transaction that is covered under § 180.210 of this title, and the amount of the contract is expected to equal or exceed $25,000.

(2) The contract requires the consent of an official of a Federal agency. In that case, the contract, regardless of the amount, always is a covered transaction, and it does not matter who

awarded it. For example, it could be a subcontract awarded by a contractor at a tier below a nonprocurement transaction, as shown in the Appendix to Part 3485—Covered Transactions.

(3) The contract is for Federally-required audit services.

(4) The contract is to perform services as a third party servicer in connection with a title IV, HEA program.

(c) In addition to the contracts covered under 2 CFR 180.220(b) of the OMB guidance, this part applies to any contract, regardless of tier, that is awarded by a contractor, subcontractor, supplier, consultant, or its agent or representative in any transaction, if the contract is to be funded or provided by ED under a covered nonprocurement transaction and the amount of the contract is expected to equal or exceed $25,000. This extends the coverage of the ED nonprocurement suspension and debarment requirements to all lower tiers of subcontracts under covered nonprocurement transactions, as permitted under the OMB guidance at 2 CFR 180.220(c) (see optional lower tier coverage in the figure in Appendix A to Part 3485—Covered Transactions).

(Authority: E.O. 12549 (3 CFR 1986 Comp., p. 189); E.O. 12689 (3 CFR 1989 Comp., p. 235); sec. 2455, Pub. L. 103–355, 108 Stat. 3327 (31 U.S.C. 6101 note); 20 U.S.C. 1082, 1094, 1221e–3, and 3474)

## Subpart C—Responsibilities of Participants Regarding Transactions

### § 3485.310  What must I do if a Federal agency excludes a person with whom I am already doing business in a covered transaction?

(a) You as a participant may continue covered transactions with an excluded person if the transactions were in existence when the agency excluded the person. However, you are not required to continue the transactions, and you may consider termination. You should make a decision about whether to terminate and the type of termination action, if any, only after a thorough review to ensure that the action is proper and appropriate.

(b) You may not renew or extend covered transactions (other than no-cost time extensions) with any excluded person, unless another Federal agency responsible for the transaction grants an exception under § 180.135 of this title or ED grants an exception under § 3485.137.

(c) If you are a title IV, HEA participant, you may not continue a title IV, HEA transaction with an excluded person after the effective date of the exclusion unless permitted by 34 CFR 668.26, 682.702, or 668.94, as applicable.

(Authority: E.O. 12549 (3 CFR 1986 Comp., p. 189); E.O. 12689 (3 CFR 1989 Comp., p. 235); sec. 2455, Pub. L. 103–355, 108 Stat. 3327 (31 U.S.C. 6101 note); 20 U.S.C. 1082, 1094, 1221e–3, and 3474)

### § 3485.315  May I use the services of an excluded person as a principal under a covered transaction?

(a) You as a participant may continue to use the services of an excluded person as a principal under a covered transaction if you were using the services of that person in the transaction before the person was excluded. However, you are not required to continue using that person's services as a principal. You should make a decision about whether to discontinue that person's services only after a thorough review to ensure that the action is proper and appropriate.

(b) You may not begin to use the services of an excluded person as a principal under a covered transaction unless another Federal agency responsible for the transaction grants an exception under § 180.135 of this title or, if ED took the action, an ED deciding official grants an exception under § 3485.137.

(c) If you are a title IV, HEA participant—

(1) You may not renew or extend the term of any contract or agreement for the services of an excluded person as a principal with respect to a title IV, HEA transaction; and

(2) You may not continue to use the services of that excluded person as a principal under this kind of an agreement or arrangement more than 90 days after you learn of the exclusion or after the close of the Federal fiscal

year in which the exclusion takes effect, whichever is later.

(Authority: E.O. 12549 (3 CFR 1986 Comp., p. 189); E.O. 12689 (3 CFR 1989 Comp., p. 235); sec. 2455, Pub. L. 103–355, 108 Stat. 3327 (31 U.S.C. 6101 note); 20 U.S.C. 1082, 1094, 1221e–3, and 3474)

**§3485.330 What methods must I use to pass requirements down to participants at lower tiers with whom I intend to do business?**

(a) Before entering into a covered transaction with a participant at the next lower tier, you must require that participant to—

(1) Comply with this subpart as a condition of participation in the transaction. You must do so using the method specified in paragraph (b) of this section; and

(2) Pass the requirement to comply with this subpart to each person with whom the participant enters into a covered transaction at the next lower tier.

(b) To communicate the requirements in this part to a participant, you must include a term or condition in the transaction that requires the participant's compliance with part 180, subpart C, of this title, as adopted at §3485.12, and requires the participant to include a similar term or condition in lower-tier covered transactions.

(c) The failure of a participant to include a requirement to comply with Subpart C of 2 CFR part 180 in the agreement with a lower tier participant does not affect the lower tier participant's responsibilities under this part.

(Authority: E.O. 12549 (3 CFR 1986 Comp., p. 189); E.O. 12689 (3 CFR 1989 Comp., p. 235); sec. 2455, Pub. L. 103–355, 108 Stat. 3327 (31 U.S.C. 6101 note); 20 U.S.C. 1082, 1094, 1221e–3, and 3474)

## Subpart D—Responsibilities of the Department's Officials Regarding Transactions

**§3485.415 What must I do if a Federal agency excludes the participant or a principal after I enter into a covered transaction?**

(a) You as a Federal agency official may continue covered transactions with an excluded person, or under which an excluded person is a principal, if the transactions were in existence when the person was excluded. You are not required to continue the transactions, however, and you may consider termination. You should make a decision about whether to terminate and the type of termination action, if any, only after a thorough review to ensure that the action is proper.

(b) You may not renew or extend covered transactions (other than no-cost time extensions) with any excluded person, or under which an excluded person is a principal, unless you obtain an exception under §3485.137.

(c) *Title IV, HEA transactions.* If you are a title IV, HEA participant—

(1) You may not renew or extend the term of any contract or agreement for the services of an excluded person as a principal with respect to a title IV, HEA transaction; and

(2) You may not continue to use the services of that excluded person as a principal under this kind of an agreement or arrangement more than 90 days after you learn of the exclusion or after the close of the Federal fiscal year in which the exclusion takes effect, whichever is later.

(Authority: E.O. 12549 (3 CFR 1986 Comp., p. 189); E.O. 12689 (3 CFR 1989 Comp., p. 235); sec. 2455, Pub. L. 103–355, 108 Stat. 3327 (31 U.S.C. 6101 note); 20 U.S.C. 1082, 1094, 1221e–3, and 3474)

**§3485.437 What method do I use to communicate to a participant the requirements described in §180.435 of this title?**

To communicate the requirements in this part to a participant, you must include a term or condition in the transaction that requires the participant's compliance with part 180, subpart C, of this title, as adopted at §3485.12 and requires the participant to include a similar term or condition in lower-tier covered transactions.

(Authority: E.O. 12549 (3 CFR 1986 Comp., p. 189); E.O. 12689 (3 CFR 1989 Comp., p. 235); sec. 2455, Pub. L. 103–355, 108 Stat. 3327 (31 U.S.C. 6101 note); 20 U.S.C. 1082, 1094, 1221e–3, and 3474)

## Subpart E [Reserved]

## Subpart F—General Principles Relating to Suspension and Debarment Actions

### § 3485.611 What procedures do we use for a suspension or debarment action involving a title IV, HEA transaction?

(a) If we suspend a title IV, HEA participant under Executive Order 12549, we use the following procedures to ensure that the suspension prevents participation in title IV, HEA transactions:

(1) The notification procedures in § 180.715 of this title.

(2) Instead of the procedures in §§ 180.720 through 180.760 of this title, the procedures in 34 CFR part 668, subpart G, or 34 CFR part 682, subpart D or G, as applicable.

(3) In addition to the findings and conclusions required by 34 CFR part 668, subpart G, or 34 CFR part 682, subpart D or G, the suspending official, and, on appeal, the Secretary determines whether there is sufficient cause for suspension as explained in § 180.700 of this title.

(b) If we debar a title IV, HEA participant under E.O. 12549, we use the following procedures to ensure that the debarment also precludes participation in title IV, HEA transactions:

(1) The notification procedures in §§ 180.805 and 180.870 of this title.

(2) Instead of the procedures in §§ 180.810 through 180.885 of this title, the procedures in 34 CFR part 668, subpart G, or 34 CFR part 682, subpart D or G, as applicable.

(3) On appeal from a decision debarring a title IV, HEA participant, we issue a final decision after we receive any written materials from the parties.

(4) In addition to the findings and conclusions required by 34 CFR part 668, subpart G, or 34 CFR part 682, subpart D or G, the debarring official, and, on appeal, the Secretary determines whether there is sufficient cause for debarment as explained in § 180.800 of this title.

(Authority: E.O. 12549 (3 CFR 1986 Comp., p. 189); E.O. 12689 (3 CFR 1989 Comp., p. 235); sec. 2455, Pub. L. 103–355, 108 Stat. 3327 (31 U.S.C. 6101 note); 20 U.S.C. 1082, 1094, 1221e–3, and 3474)

### § 3485.612 When does an exclusion by another agency affect the ability of the excluded person to participate in a title IV, HEA transaction?

(a) If a title IV, HEA participant is debarred by another agency under E.O. 12549, using procedures described in paragraph (d) of this section, that party is not eligible to enter into title IV, HEA transactions for the duration of the debarment.

(b)(1) If a title IV, HEA participant is suspended by another agency under E.O. 12549 or under a proposed debarment under the Federal Acquisition Regulation (FAR) (48 CFR part 9, subpart 9.4), using procedures described in paragraph (d) of this section, that party is not eligible to enter into title IV, HEA transactions for the duration of the suspension.

(2)(i) The suspension of title IV, HEA eligibility as a result of suspension by another agency lasts for at least 60 days.

(ii) If the excluded party does not object to the suspension, the 60-day period begins on the 35th day after that agency issues the notice of suspension.

(iii) If the excluded party objects to the suspension, the 60-day period begins on the date of the decision of the suspending official.

(3) The suspension of title IV, HEA eligibility does not end on the 60th day if—

(i) The excluded party agrees to an extension; or

(ii) Before the 60th day we begin a limitation or termination proceeding against the excluded party under 34 CFR part 668, subpart G, or part 682, subpart D or G.

(c)(1) If a title IV, HEA participant is debarred or suspended by another Federal agency—

(i) We notify the participant whether the debarment or suspension prohibits participation in title IV, HEA transactions; and

(ii) If participation is prohibited, we state the effective date and duration of the prohibition.

(2) If a debarment or suspension by another agency prohibits participation in title IV, HEA transactions, that prohibition takes effect 20 days after we mail notice of our action.

(3) If the Department or another Federal agency suspends a title IV, HEA participant, we determine whether grounds exist for an emergency action against the participant under 34 CFR part 668, subpart G, or part 682, subpart D or G, as applicable.

(4) We use the procedures in §3485.611 to exclude a title IV, HEA participant excluded by another Federal agency using procedures that did not meet the standards in paragraph (d) of this section.

(d) If a title IV, HEA participant is excluded by another agency, we debar, terminate, or suspend the participant— as provided under this part, 34 CFR part 668, or 34 CFR part 682, as applicable—if that agency followed procedures that gave the excluded party—

(1) Notice of the proposed action;

(2) An opportunity to submit and have considered evidence and argument to oppose the proposed action;

(3) An opportunity to present its objection at a hearing—

(i) At which the agency has the burden of persuasion by a preponderance of the evidence that there is cause for the exclusion; and

(ii) Conducted by an impartial person who does not also exercise prosecutorial or investigative responsibilities with respect to the exclusion action;

(4) An opportunity to present witness testimony, unless the hearing official finds that there is no genuine dispute about a material fact;

(5) An opportunity to have agency witnesses with personal knowledge of material facts in genuine dispute testify about those facts, if the hearing official determines their testimony to be needed, in light of other available evidence and witnesses; and

(6) A written decision stating findings of fact and conclusions of law on which the decision is rendered.

(Authority: E.O. 12549 (3 CFR 1986 Comp., p. 189); E.O. 12689 (3 CFR 1989 Comp., p. 235); sec. 2455, Pub. L. 103–355, 108 Stat. 3327 (31 U.S.C. 6101 note); 20 U.S.C. 1082, 1094, 1221e–3, and 3474)

## Subpart G—Suspension

### §3485.711 When does a suspension affect title IV, HEA transactions?

(a) A suspension under §3485.611(a) takes effect immediately if the Secretary takes an emergency action under 34 CFR part 668, subpart G, or 34 CFR part 682, subpart D or G, at the same time the Secretary issues the suspension.

(b)(1) Except as provided under paragraph (a) of this section, a suspension under §3485.611(a) takes effect 20 days after those procedures are complete.

(2) If the respondent appeals the suspension to the Secretary before the expiration of the 20 days under paragraph (b)(1) of this section, the suspension takes effect when the respondent receives the Secretary's decision.

(Authority: E.O. 12549 (3 CFR 1986 Comp., p. 189); E.O. 12689 (3 CFR 1989 Comp., p. 235); sec. 2455, Pub. L. 103–355, 108 Stat. 3327 (31 U.S.C. 6101 note); 20 U.S.C. 1082, 1094, 1221e–3, and 3474)

## Subpart H—Debarment

### §3485.811 When does a debarment affect title IV, HEA transactions?

(a) A debarment under §3485.611(b) takes effect 30 days after those procedures are complete.

(b) If the respondent appeals the debarment to the Secretary before the expiration of the 30 days under paragraph (a) of this section, the debarment takes effect when the respondent receives the Secretary's decision.

(Authority: E.O. 12549 (3 CFR 1986 Comp., p. 189); E.O. 12689 (3 CFR 1989 Comp., p. 235); sec. 2455, Pub. L. 103–355, 108 Stat. 3327 (31 U.S.C. 6101 note); 20 U.S.C. 1082, 1094, 1221e–3, and 3474)

## Subpart I—Definitions

### §3485.937 ED Deciding Official.

The ED Deciding Official is an officer of the Department who has delegated authority under the procedures of the Department of Education to decide whether to affirm a suspension or enter a debarment.

(Authority: E.O. 12549 (3 CFR 1986 Comp., p. 189); E.O. 12689 (3 CFR 1989 Comp., p. 235); sec. 2455, Pub. L. 103–355, 108 Stat. 3327 (31 U.S.C. 6101 note); 20 U.S.C. 1082, 1094, 1221e–3, and 3474)

## § 3485.952  HEA.

*HEA* means the Higher Education Act of 1965, as amended.

(Authority: E.O. 12549 (3 CFR 1986 Comp., p. 189); E.O. 12689 (3 CFR 1989 Comp., p. 235); sec. 2455, Pub. L. 103–355, 108 Stat. 3327 (31 U.S.C. 6101 note); 20 U.S.C. 1082, 1094, 1221e–3, and 3474)

## § 3485.995  Principal.

*Principal* means—

(a) An officer, director, owner, partner, principal investigator, or other person within a participant with management or supervisory responsibilities related to a covered transaction; or

(b) A consultant or other person, whether or not employed by the participant or paid with Federal funds, who—

(1) Is in a position to handle Federal funds;

(2) Is in a position to influence or control the use of those funds; or

(3) Occupies a technical or professional position capable of substantially influencing the development or outcome of an activity required to perform the covered transaction.

(c) For the purposes of Department of Education title IV, HEA transactions—

(1) A third-party servicer, as defined in 34 CFR 668.2 or 682.200; or

(2) Any person who provides services described in 34 CFR 668.2 or 682.200 to a title IV, HEA participant, whether or not that person is retained or paid directly by the title IV, HEA participant.

(Authority: E.O. 12549 (3 CFR 1986 Comp., p.189); E.O. 12689 (3 CFR 1989 Comp., p.235); sec. 2455, Pub. L. 103–355, 108 Stat. 3327 (31 U.S.C. 6101 note); 20 U.S.C. 1082, 1094, 1221e–3, and 3474)

## § 3485.1016  Title IV, HEA participant.

A title IV, HEA participant is—

(a) An institution described in 34 CFR 600.4, 600.5, or 600.6 that provides postsecondary education; or

(b) A lender, third-party servicer, or guaranty agency, as those terms are defined in 34 CFR 668.2 or 682.200.

(Authority: E.O. 12549 (3 CFR 1986 Comp., p.189); E.O. 12689 (3 CFR 1989 Comp., p.235); sec. 2455, Pub. L. 103–355, 108 Stat. 3327 (31 U.S.C. 6101 note); 20 U.S.C. 1082, 1094, 1221e–3, and 3474)

## § 3485.1017  Title IV, HEA program.

A title IV, HEA program includes any program listed in 34 CFR 668.1(c).

(Authority: E.O. 12549 (3 CFR 1986 Comp., p.189); E.O. 12689 (3 CFR 1989 Comp., p. 235); sec. 2455, Pub. L. 103–355, 108 Stat. 3327 (31 U.S.C. 6101 note); 20 U.S.C. 1082, 1094, 1221e–3, and 3474)

## § 3485.1018  Title IV, HEA transaction.

A title IV, HEA transaction includes—

(a) A disbursement or delivery of funds provided under a title IV, HEA program to a student or borrower;

(b) A certification by an educational institution of eligibility for a loan under a title IV, HEA program;

(c) Guaranteeing a loan made under a title IV, HEA program; and

(d) The acquisition or exercise of any servicing responsibility for a grant, loan, or work study assistance under a title IV, HEA program.

(Authority: E.O. 12549 (3 CFR 1986 Comp., p.189); E.O. 12689 (3 CFR 1989 Comp., p.235); sec. 2455, Pub. L. 103–355, 108 Stat. 3327 (31 U.S.C. 6101 note); 20 U.S.C. 1082, 1094, 1221e–3, and 3474)

## Subpart J [Reserved]

APPENDIX A TO PART 3485—COVERED TRANSACTIONS

Appendix A to Part 3485--Covered Transactions

```
┌─────────────────────────┐
│  Covered Transactions   │
│  for the Department of   │
│       Education          │
└─────────────────────────┘
            │
            │
    ┌───────────────────┐
    │  All Primary Tier │
    │  Nonprocurement   │
    │   Transactions    │
    └───────────────────┘
            │
            │
    ┌───────────────────┐
    │  All Lower Tier   │
    │  Nonprocurement   │
    │   Transactions    │
    └───────────────────┘
```

```
┌──────────────┐  ┌──────────────┐  ┌──────────────┐  ┌───────────────────────────┐
│  All First   │  │  All First   │  │  All Third   │  │ Any Person Who Provides   │
│    Tier      │  │    Tier      │  │    Party     │  │ the Services Described in │
│ Procurement  │  │ Procurement  │  │  Servicer    │  │  34 CFR 668.2 or 682.200  │
│  Contracts   │  │  Contracts   │  │  Contracts   │  │                           │
│  ≥ $25,000   │  │  Subject to  │  │              │  │                           │
│              │  │    Agency    │  │              │  │                           │
│              │  │   Consent    │  │              │  │                           │
└──────────────┘  └──────────────┘  └──────────────┘  └───────────────────────────┘
        │                 │
┌──────────────┐  ┌──────────────┐
│  All Lower   │  │  All Lower   │
│    Tier      │  │    Tier      │
│ Procurement  │  │ Procurement  │
│  Contracts   │  │  Contracts   │
│  ≥ $25,000   │  │  Subject to  │
│              │  │    Agency    │
│              │  │   Consent    │
└──────────────┘  └──────────────┘
```

**PARTS 3486–3499 [RESERVED]**

# CHAPTER XXXV—EXPORT-IMPORT BANK OF THE UNITED STATES

# PARTS 3500–3512 [RESERVED]

# PART 3513—NONPROCUREMENT DEBARMENT AND SUSPENSION

Sec.
3513.10  What does this part do?
3513.20  Does this part apply to me?
3513.30  What policies and procedures must I follow?

### Subpart A—General

3513.137  Who at Ex-Im Bank may grant an exception to let an excluded person participate in a covered transaction?

### Subpart B—Covered Transactions

3513.220  What contracts and subcontracts, in addition to those listed in 2 CFR 180.220, are covered transactions?

### Subpart C—Responsibilities of Participants Regarding Transactions

3513.332  What methods must I use to pass requirements down to participants at lower tiers with whom I intend to do business?

### Subpart D—Responsibilities of Federal Agency Officials Regarding Transactions

3513.437  What method do I use to communicate to a participate the requirements described in the OMB guidance at 2 CFR 180.435?

### Subparts E–J [Reserved]

AUTHORITY: Sec. 2455, Pub. L. 103–355, 108 Stat. 3327; E.O. 12549, 3 CFR, 1986 Comp., p. 189; E.O. 12689, 3 CFR, 1989 Comp., p. 235.

SOURCE: 72 FR 30244, May 31, 2007, unless otherwise noted.

## § 3513.10  What does this part do?

This part adopts the Office of Management and Budget (OMB) guidance in subparts A through I of 2 CFR part 180, as supplemented by this part, as the Export Import Bank of the United States (Ex-Im Bank) policies and procedures for nonprocurement debarment and suspension. It thereby gives regulatory effect for Ex-Im Bank to the OMB guidance as supplemented by this part. This part satisfies the requirements in section 3 of Executive Order 12549, "Debarment and Suspension" (3 CFR 1986 Comp., p. 189), Executive Order 12689, "Debarment and Suspen-

sion" (3 CFR 1989 Comp., p. 235) and 31 U.S.C. 6101 note (Section 2455, Pub. L. 103–355, 108 Stat. 3327).

## § 3513.20  Does this part apply to me?

This part and, through this part, pertinent portions of the OMB guidance in subparts A through I of 2 CFR part 180 (see table at 2 CFR 180.100(b)) apply to you if you are a—

(a) Participant or principal in a "covered transaction" (see subpart B of 2 CFR part 180 and the definition of "nonprocurement transaction" at 2 CFR 180.970, as supplemented by subpart B of this part).

(b) Respondent in an Ex-Im Bank suspension or debarment action.

(c) Ex-Im Bank debarment or suspension official;

(d) Ex-Im Bank grants officer, agreements officer, or other official authorized to enter into any type of nonprocurement transaction that is a covered transaction;

## § 3513.30  What policies and procedures must I follow?

Ex-Im Bank policies and procedures that you must follow are the policies and procedures specified in each applicable section of the OMB guidance in subparts A through I of 2 CFR part 180, as that section is supplemented by the section in this part with the same section number. The contracts that are covered transactions, for example, are specified by section 220 of the OMB guidance (i.e., 2 CFR 180.220) as supplemented by section 220 in this pat (i.e., § 3513.220). For any section of OMB guidance in subparts A through I of 2 CFR 180 that has no corresponding section in this part, Ex-Im Bank policies and procedures are those in the OMB guidance.

## Subpart A—General

### § 3513.137  Who in Ex-Im Bank may grant an exception to let an excluded person participate in a covered transaction?

(a) The Ex-Im Bank agency head or designee may grant an exception permitting an excluded person to participate in a particular covered transacting. If the Ex-Im Bank agency head or designee grants an exception,

549

the exception must be in writing and state the reason(s) for deviating from the government wide policy in Executive Order 12549.

(b) An exception granted by one agency for an excluded person does not extend to the covered transactions of another agency.

## Subpart B—Covered Transactions

**§ 3513.220 What contracts and subcontracts, in addition to those listed in 2 CFR 180.220, are covered transactions?**

Although the OMB guidance at 2 CFR 180.220(c) allows a Federal agency to do so (also see optional lower tier coverage in the figure in the appendix to 2 CFR part 180), Ex-Im Bank does not extend coverage of nonprocurement suspension and debarment requirements beyond first-tier procurement under a covered nonprocurement transaction.

## Subpart C—Responsibilities of Participants Regarding Transactions

**§ 3513.332 What methods must I use to pass requirements down to participants at lower tiers with whom I intend to do business?**

To communicate the requirements, you must include a term or condition in the transaction requiring the participants' compliance with subpart C of this part and requiring them to include a similar term or condition in lower-tiered covered transactions.

## Subpart D—Responsibilities of Federal Agency Officials Regarding Transactions

**§ 3513.437 What method do I use to communicate to a participant the requirements described in the OMB guidance at 2 CFR 180.435?**

To communicate to a participant the requirements described in 2 CFR 180.435 of the OMB guidance, you must include a term or condition in the transaction that requires the participant's compliance with subpart C of 2 CFR part 180, as supplemented by subpart C of this part, and requires the participant to include a similar term or condition in lower-tier covered transactions.

## Subparts E–J [Reserved]

## PARTS 3514–3599 [RESERVED]

# CHAPTER XXXVI—OFFICE OF NATIONAL DRUG CONTROL POLICY, EXECUTIVE OFFICE OF THE PRESIDENT

## PARTS 3600–3602 [RESERVED]

## PART 3603—UNIFORM ADMINIS-TRATIVE REQUIREMENTS, COST PRINCIPLES, AND AUDIT RE-QUIREMENTS FOR FEDERAL AWARDS

AUTHORITY: 21 U.S.C. 1706; 21 U.S.C. 1703(d), 1703(f), 21 U.S.C. 1701, 21 U.S.C. 1521–1548, 21 U.S.C. 2001–2003, Office of National Drug Control Policy Reauthorization Act of 2006, P.L 109–469 (2006), 2 CFR part 200.

SOURCE: 79 FR 76105, Dec. 19, 2014, unless otherwise noted.

### § 3603.1  Adoption of 2 CFR Part 200.

Under the authority listed above, the Executive Office of the President, Office of National Drug Control Policy (ONDCP) adopts the Office of Management and Budget (OMB) Guidance in 2 CFR part 200. Thus, this part gives regulatory effect to the OMB guidance and supplements the guidance as needed for ONDCP.

## PARTS 3604–3699 [RESERVED]

# CHAPTER XXXVII—PEACE CORPS

# PART 3700—NONPROCUREMENT DEBARMENT AND SUSPENSION

Sec.
3700.10  What does this part do?
3700.20  Does this part apply to me?
3700.30  What policies and procedures must I follow?
3700.137  Who in the Peace Corps may grant an exception to let an excluded person participate in a covered transaction?
3700.220  What contracts and subcontracts, in addition to those listed in 2 CFR 180.220, are covered transactions?
3700.332  What methods must I use to pass requirements down to participants at lower tiers with whom I intend to do business?
3700.437  What method do I use to communicate to a participant the requirements described in the OMB guidance at 2 CFR 180.435?

AUTHORITY: Sec. 2455, Pub. L. 103–355, 108 Stat. 3327; E.O. 12549, 3 CFR, 1986 Comp., p. 189; E.O. 12689, 3 CFR, 1989 Comp., p. 235; 22 U.S.C. 2503(b).

SOURCE: 71 FR 64731, Nov. 22, 2006, unless otherwise noted.

## § 3700.10  What does this part do?

This part adopts the Office of Management and Budget (OMB) guidance in subparts A through I of 2 CFR part 180, as supplemented by this part, as the Peace Corps policies and procedures for nonprocurement debarment and suspension. It thereby gives regulatory effect for the Peace Corps to the OMB guidance as supplemented by this part. This part satisfies the requirements in section 3 of Executive Order 12549, "Debarment and Suspension" (3 CFR 1986 Comp., p. 189), Executive Order 12689, "Debarment and Suspension" (3 CFR 1989 Comp., p. 235) and 31 U.S.C. 6101 note (Section 2455, Pub. L. 103–355, 108 Stat. 3327).

## § 3700.20  Does this part apply to me?

This part and, through this part, pertinent portions of the OMB guidance in subparts A through I of 2 CFR part (see table at 2 CFR 180.100(b)) apply to you if you are a—

(a) Participant or principal in a "covered transaction" (see subpart B of 2 CFR part 180 and the definition of "nonprocurement transaction" at 2 CFR 180.970);

(b) Respondent in a Peace Corps suspension or debarment action;

(c) Peace Corps debarment or suspension official; or

(d) Peace Corps grants officer, agreements officer, or other official authorized to enter into any type of nonprocurement transaction that is a covered transaction.

## § 3700.30  What policies and procedures must I follow?

The Peace Corps policies and procedures that you must follow are the policies and procedures specified in each applicable section of the OMB guidance in subparts A through I of 2 CFR part 180, as that section is supplemented by the section in this part with the same section number. The contracts that are covered transactions, for example, are specified by section 220 of the OMB guidance (i.e., 2 CFR 180.220) as supplemented by section 220 in this part (i.e., § 3700.220). For any section of OMB guidance in subparts A through I of 2 CFR 180 that has no corresponding section in this part, Peace Corps policies and procedures are those in the OMB guidance.

## § 3700.137  Who in the Peace Corps may grant an exception to let an excluded person participate in a covered transaction?

The Director of the Peace Corps has the authority to grant an exception to let an excluded person participate in a covered transaction, as provided in the OMB guidance at 2 CFR 180.135.

## § 3700.220  What contracts and subcontracts, in addition to those listed in 2 CFR 180.220, are covered transactions?

Although the OMB guidance at 2 CFR 180.220(c) allows a Federal agency to do so (also see optional lower tier coverage in the figure in the appendix to 2 CFR part 180), Peace Corps does not extend coverage of nonprocurement suspension and debarment requirements beyond first-tier procurement contracts under a covered nonprocurement transaction.

557

**§ 3700.332 What methods must I use to pass requirements down to participants at lower tiers with whom I intend to do business?**

You as a participant must include a term or condition in lower-tier transactions requiring lower-tier participants to comply with subpart C of the OMB guidance in 2 CFR part 180.

**§ 3700.437 What method do I use to communicate to a participant the requirements described in the OMB guidance at 2 CFR 180.435?**

To communicate to a participant the requirements described in 2 CFR 180.435

of the OMB guidance, you as an agency official must include a term or condition in the transaction that requires the participant's compliance with subpart C of 2 CFR part 180, and requires the participant to include a similar term or condition in lower-tier covered transactions.

## PARTS 3701–3799 [RESERVED]

# CHAPTER LVIII—ELECTION ASSISTANCE COMMISSION

---

# PART 5800—NONPROCUREMENT DEBARMENT AND SUSPENSION

AUTHORITY: Sec. 2455, Pub. L. 103–355, 108; Stat. 3327 (31 U.S.C. 6101 note); E.O. 12549; (3 CFR, 1986 Comp., p. 189); E.O. 12689 (3); CFR, 1989 Comp., p. 235).

SOURCE: 75 FR 41692, July 19, 2010, unless otherwise noted.

## § 5800.10   What does this part do?

This part adopts the Office of Management and Budget (OMB) guidance in Subparts A through I of 2 CFR part 180, as supplemented by this part, as the U.S. Election Assistance Commission ("the Commission" or "EAC") policies and procedures for nonprocurement debarment and suspension. It thereby gives regulatory effect for the Commission to the OMB guidance as supplemented by this part. This part satisfies the requirements in section 3 of Executive Order 12549, "Debarment and Suspension" and 31 U.S.C. 6101 note.

## § 5800.20   Does this part apply to me?

This part and, through this part, pertinent portions of the OMB guidance in subparts A through I of 2 CFR part (see table at 2 CFR 180.100(b)) apply to you if you are a—

(a) Participant or principal in a "covered transaction" (see subpart B of 2 CFR part 180 and the definition of "nonprocurement transaction" at 2 CFR 180.970);

(b) Respondent in a Commission suspension or debarment action;

(c) Commission debarment or suspension official; or

(d) Commission grants officer, agreements officer, or other official authorized to enter into any type of nonprocurement transaction that is a covered transaction.

## § 5800.30   What policies and procedures must I follow?

The Commission policies and procedures that you must follow are the policies and procedures specified in each applicable section of the OMB guidance in Subparts A through I of 2 CFR part 180, as that section is supplemented by the section in this part with the same section number. The contracts that are covered transactions, for example, are specified by section 220 of the OMB guidance (i.e., 2 CFR 180.220) as supplemented by section 220 in this part (i.e., § _____.220). For any section of OMB guidance in Subparts A through I of 2 CFR 180 that has no corresponding section in this part, Commission policies and procedures are those in the OMB guidance.

## Subpart A—General

### § 5800.137 Who at the Commission may grant an exception to let an excluded person participate in a covered transaction?

The Commission's Contracting Officer has the authority to grant an exception to let an excluded person participate in a covered transaction, as provided in the OMB guidance at 2 CFR 180.135.

## Subpart B—Covered Transactions

### § 5800.220 What contracts and subcontracts, in addition to those listed in 2 CFR 180.220, are covered transactions?

Pursuant to 2 CFR 180.220(c), the Commission extends coverage of nonprocurement suspension and debarment requirements beyond first-tier procurement contracts to include any subcontract to be funded by the Commission, the value of which is expected to equal to or exceed $25,000 or 30 percent of the value of first-tier transaction, whichever is lesser.

## Subpart C—Responsibilities of Participants Regarding Transactions

### § 5800.332 What methods must I use to pass requirements down to participants at lower tiers with whom I intend to do business?

If a lower-tier transaction is covered pursuant to § 5800.220, you as a participant must include a term or condition in lower-tier transactions requiring lower-tier participants to comply with Subpart C of the OMB guidance in 2 CFR part 180.

## Subpart D—Responsibilities of Federal Agency Officials Regarding Transactions

### § 5800.437 What method do I use to communicate to a participant the requirements described in the OMB guidance at 2 CFR 180.435?

To communicate to a participant the requirements described in 2 CFR 180.435 of the OMB guidance, you as an agency official must include a term or condition in the transaction that requires the participant's compliance with subpart C of 2 CFR part 180, and requires the participant to include a similar term or condition in lower-tier covered transactions.

### § 5800.765 May I ask the suspending official to reconsider a decision to suspend me?

Yes. Within 30 days of receiving a final notice of suspension, you may make a written request for the suspending official to reconsider your suspension.

### § 5800.875 May I ask the debarring official to reconsider a decision to debar me?

Yes. Within 30 days of receiving a final notice of debarment, you may make a written request for the debarring official to reconsider your debarment pursuant to § 5800.880. The disposition of your request for reconsideration; or the result of your appeal; shall be considered a final agency action.

### § 5800.880 What factors may influence the debarring official during reconsideration?

The debarring official may reduce or terminate your debarment based on:

(a) Newly discovered material evidence;

(b) A reversal of the conviction or civil judgment upon which your debarment was based;

(c) A bona fide change in ownership or management;

(d) Elimination of other causes for which the debarment was imposed; or

(e) Other reasons the debarring official finds appropriate.

### § 5800.890 How may I appeal my debarment?

(a) If the Commission debarring official issues a decision under 2 CFR 180.870 to debar you after you present information in opposition to a proposed debarment under § 180.815, you may ask for review of the debarring official's decision in two ways:

(1) You may ask the debarring official under § 875 to reconsider the decision for material errors of fact or law that you believe will change the outcome of the matter; or

(2) You may request a review by the EAC's debarment appeals body (DAP), which is composed of the Executive Director, Chief Financial Officer, and Chief Operating Officer. The DAP will review your appeal and make a determination on whether to sustain or reverse the decision of the debarring official. The DAP will then make a recommendation to the EAC Commissioners who will vote by circulation on whether to accept or reject the recommendation of the DAP. A request to review the debarring official's decision to debar you must be made within 30 days of your receipt of the debarring official's decision under § 180.870 or paragraph (a)(1) of this section. However, the DAP may recommend to the EAC Commissioners that the debarring official's decision be reversed, based on a majority vote of the DAP, only where the DAP finds that the decision is based on a clear error of material fact or law, or where DAP finds that the debarring official's decision was arbitrary, capricious, or an abuse of discretion. You may appeal the debarring official's decision without requesting reconsideration, or you may appeal the decision of the debarring official on reconsideration.

(b) A request for review under this section must be in writing; prominently state on the envelope or other cover and at the top of the first page "Debarment Appeal;" state the specific findings you believe to be in error; and include the reasons or legal bases for your position. The appeal request should be delivered or addressed to the U.S. Election Assistance Commission, 1201 New York Avenue, NW., Suite 300, Washington, DC 20005.

(c) After the circulation vote of the EAC Commissioners has been certified, either the Commission debarring official or the DAP must notify you of their decision under this section, in writing, using the notice procedures set forth at §§ 180.615 and 180.975.

(d) [Reserved]

(e) Nothing in this part prohibits the EAC from delegating the appeal review process to another Federal agency through a memorandum of understanding or interagency agreement.

## Subparts E–H [Reserved]

## Subpart I—Definitions

### § 5800.930   Debarring official.

For the Commission, the debarring official for all nonprocurement transactions is the Commission's Contracting Officer. In the case of a vacancy in the position of the Contracting Officer, the alternate debarring official is the Chief Financial Officer.

### § 5800.970   Nonprocurement transaction.

While the Commission treats all payments made to states under 42 U.S.C. 15301, 15302 and 15401 as grants, this part does not apply to grants made to states and political subdivisions therein.

### § 5800.1010   Suspending official.

For the Commission, the debarring official for all nonprocurement transactions is the Commission's Contracting Officer. In the case of a vacancy in the position of the Contracting Officer, the alternate debarring official is the Chief Financial Officer.

## Subpart J [Reserved]

## PARTS 5801–5899 [RESERVED]

# CHAPTER LIX—GULF COAST ECOSYSTEM RESTORATION COUNCIL

# PART 5900—UNIFORM ADMINISTRATIVE REQUIREMENTS, COST PRINCIPLES, AND AUDIT REQUIREMENTS FOR FEDERAL AWARDS

AUTHORITY: 5 U.S.C. 301; 33 U.S.C. 1321(t)(2); 38 U.S.C. 501; 2 CFR part 200.

SOURCE: 79 FR 76106, Dec. 19, 2014, unless otherwise noted.

## § 5900.101   Adoption of 2 CFR Part 200.

Under the authority listed above, the Gulf Coast Ecosystem Restoration Council adopts the Office of Management and Budget (OMB) Guidance in 2 CFR part 200. Thus, this part gives regulatory effect to the OMB guidance and supplements the guidance as needed for the Council.

# PARTS 5901–5999 [RESERVED]

# FINDING AIDS

A list of CFR titles, subtitles, chapters, subchapters and parts and an alphabetical list of agencies publishing in the CFR are included in the CFR Index and Finding Aids volume to the Code of Federal Regulations which is published separately and revised annually.

Table of CFR Titles and Chapters
Alphabetical List of Agencies Appearing in the CFR
List of CFR Sections Affected

# Table of CFR Titles and Chapters

**(Revised as of January 1, 2018)**

## Title 1—General Provisions

## Title 2—Grants and Agreements

## Title 2—Grants and Agreements—Continued

## Title 3—The President

## Title 4—Accounts

## Title 5—Administrative Personnel

## Title 5—Administrative Personnel—Continued

## Title 6—Domestic Security

## Title 7—Agriculture

# Title 12—Banks and Banking—Continued

# Title 13—Business Credit and Assistance

# Title 14—Aeronautics and Space

# Title 15—Commerce and Foreign Trade

## Title 15—Commerce and Foreign Trade—Continued

## Title 16—Commercial Practices

## Title 17—Commodity and Securities Exchanges

## Title 18—Conservation of Power and Water Resources

## Title 19—Customs Duties

## Title 20—Employees' Benefits

579

# Title 23—Highways—Continued

# Title 24—Housing and Urban Development

# Title 29—Labor

# Title 30—Mineral Resources

# Title 31—Money and Finance: Treasury

# Title 31—Money and Finance: Treasury—Continued

VI    Bureau of Engraving and Printing, Department of the Treasury (Parts 600—699)

VII   Federal Law Enforcement Training Center, Department of the Treasury (Parts 700—799)

VIII  Office of Investment Security, Department of the Treasury (Parts 800—899)

IX    Federal Claims Collection Standards (Department of the Treasury—Department of Justice) (Parts 900—999)

X     Financial Crimes Enforcement Network, Department of the Treasury (Parts 1000—1099)

## Title 32—National Defense

SUBTITLE A—DEPARTMENT OF DEFENSE

I     Office of the Secretary of Defense (Parts 1—399)

V     Department of the Army (Parts 400—699)

VI    Department of the Navy (Parts 700—799)

VII   Department of the Air Force (Parts 800—1099)

SUBTITLE B—OTHER REGULATIONS RELATING TO NATIONAL DEFENSE

XII   Defense Logistics Agency (Parts 1200—1299)

XVI   Selective Service System (Parts 1600—1699)

XVII  Office of the Director of National Intelligence (Parts 1700—1799)

XVIII National Counterintelligence Center (Parts 1800—1899)

XIX   Central Intelligence Agency (Parts 1900—1999)

XX    Information Security Oversight Office, National Archives and Records Administration (Parts 2000—2099)

XXI   National Security Council (Parts 2100—2199)

XXIV  Office of Science and Technology Policy (Parts 2400—2499)

XXVII Office for Micronesian Status Negotiations (Parts 2700—2799)

XXVIII Office of the Vice President of the United States (Parts 2800—2899)

## Title 33—Navigation and Navigable Waters

I     Coast Guard, Department of Homeland Security (Parts 1—199)

II    Corps of Engineers, Department of the Army, Department of Defense (Parts 200—399)

IV    Saint Lawrence Seaway Development Corporation, Department of Transportation (Parts 400—499)

## Title 34—Education

SUBTITLE A—OFFICE OF THE SECRETARY, DEPARTMENT OF EDUCATION (PARTS 1—99)

SUBTITLE B—REGULATIONS OF THE OFFICES OF THE DEPARTMENT OF EDUCATION

I     Office for Civil Rights, Department of Education (Parts 100—199)

# Title 34—Education—Continued

# Title 35 [Reserved]

# Title 36—Parks, Forests, and Public Property

# Title 37—Patents, Trademarks, and Copyrights

# Title 38—Pensions, Bonuses, and Veterans' Relief

# Title 39—Postal Service

# Title 40—Protection of Environment

# Title 41—Public Contracts and Property Management

# Title 41—Public Contracts and Property Management—Continued

## Title 42—Public Health

## Title 43—Public Lands: Interior

## Title 44—Emergency Management and Assistance

## Title 45—Public Welfare

# Title 48—Federal Acquisition Regulations System—Continued

Chap.

54   Defense Logistics Agency, Department of Defense (Parts 5400—5499)

57   African Development Foundation (Parts 5700—5799)

61   Civilian Board of Contract Appeals, General Services Administration (Parts 6100—6199)

99   Cost Accounting Standards Board, Office of Federal Procurement Policy, Office of Management and Budget (Parts 9900—9999)

## Title 49—Transportation

SUBTITLE A—OFFICE OF THE SECRETARY OF TRANSPORTATION (PARTS 1—99)

SUBTITLE B—OTHER REGULATIONS RELATING TO TRANSPORTATION

I   Pipeline and Hazardous Materials Safety Administration, Department of Transportation (Parts 100—199)

II   Federal Railroad Administration, Department of Transportation (Parts 200—299)

III   Federal Motor Carrier Safety Administration, Department of Transportation (Parts 300—399)

IV   Coast Guard, Department of Homeland Security (Parts 400—499)

V   National Highway Traffic Safety Administration, Department of Transportation (Parts 500—599)

VI   Federal Transit Administration, Department of Transportation (Parts 600—699)

VII   National Railroad Passenger Corporation (AMTRAK) (Parts 700—799)

VIII   National Transportation Safety Board (Parts 800—999)

X   Surface Transportation Board (Parts 1000—1399)

XI   Research and Innovative Technology Administration, Department of Transportation (Parts 1400—1499) [Reserved]

XII   Transportation Security Administration, Department of Homeland Security (Parts 1500—1699)

## Title 50—Wildlife and Fisheries

I   United States Fish and Wildlife Service, Department of the Interior (Parts 1—199)

II   National Marine Fisheries Service, National Oceanic and Atmospheric Administration, Department of Commerce (Parts 200—299)

III   International Fishing and Related Activities (Parts 300—399)

IV   Joint Regulations (United States Fish and Wildlife Service, Department of the Interior and National Marine Fisheries Service, National Oceanic and Atmospheric Administration, Department of Commerce); Endangered Species Committee Regulations (Parts 400—499)

V   Marine Mammal Commission (Parts 500—599)

## Title 50—Wildlife and Fisheries—Continued

# Alphabetical List of Agencies Appearing in the CFR

(Revised as of January 1, 2018)

| Agency | CFR Title, Subtitle or Chapter |
|---|---|
| Administrative Committee of the Federal Register | 1, I |
| Administrative Conference of the United States | 1, III |
| Advisory Council on Historic Preservation | 36, VIII |
| Advocacy and Outreach, Office of | 7, XXV |
| Afghanistan Reconstruction, Special Inspector General for | 5, LXXXIII |
| African Development Foundation | 22, XV |
| Federal Acquisition Regulation | 48, 57 |
| Agency for International Development | 2, VII; 22, II |
| Federal Acquisition Regulation | 48, 7 |
| Agricultural Marketing Service | 7, I, IX, X, XI |
| Agricultural Research Service | 7, V |
| Agriculture Department | 2, IV; 5, LXXIII |
| Advocacy and Outreach, Office of | 7, XXV |
| Agricultural Marketing Service | 7, I, IX, X, XI |
| Agricultural Research Service | 7, V |
| Animal and Plant Health Inspection Service | 7, III; 9, I |
| Chief Financial Officer, Office of | 7, XXX |
| Commodity Credit Corporation | 7, XIV |
| Economic Research Service | 7, XXXVII |
| Energy Policy and New Uses, Office of | 2, IX; 7, XXIX |
| Environmental Quality, Office of | 7, XXXI |
| Farm Service Agency | 7, VII, XVIII |
| Federal Acquisition Regulation | 48, 4 |
| Federal Crop Insurance Corporation | 7, IV |
| Food and Nutrition Service | 7, II |
| Food Safety and Inspection Service | 9, III |
| Foreign Agricultural Service | 7, XV |
| Forest Service | 36, II |
| Grain Inspection, Packers and Stockyards Administration | 7, VIII; 9, II |
| Information Resources Management, Office of | 7, XXVII |
| Inspector General, Office of | 7, XXVI |
| National Agricultural Library | 7, XLI |
| National Agricultural Statistics Service | 7, XXXVI |
| National Institute of Food and Agriculture | 7, XXXIV |
| Natural Resources Conservation Service | 7, VI |
| Operations, Office of | 7, XXVIII |
| Procurement and Property Management, Office of | 7, XXXII |
| Rural Business-Cooperative Service | 7, XVIII, XLII |
| Rural Development Administration | 7, XLII |
| Rural Housing Service | 7, XVIII, XXXV |
| Rural Telephone Bank | 7, XVI |
| Rural Utilities Service | 7, XVII, XVIII, XLII |
| Secretary of Agriculture, Office of | 7, Subtitle A |
| Transportation, Office of | 7, XXXIII |
| World Agricultural Outlook Board | 7, XXXVIII |
| Air Force Department | 32, VII |
| Federal Acquisition Regulation Supplement | 48, 53 |
| Air Transportation Stabilization Board | 14, VI |
| Alcohol and Tobacco Tax and Trade Bureau | 27, I |
| Alcohol, Tobacco, Firearms, and Explosives, Bureau of | 27, II |
| AMTRAK | 49, VII |
| American Battle Monuments Commission | 36, IV |
| American Indians, Office of the Special Trustee | 25, VII |

591

593

594

597

| Agency | CFR Title, Subtitle or Chapter |
|---|---|
| Workers' Compensation Programs, Office of | 20, I, VII |
| World Agricultural Outlook Board | 7, XXXVIII |

# List of CFR Sections Affected

All changes in this volume of the Code of Federal Regulations (CFR) that were made by documents published in the FEDERAL REGISTER since January 1, 2013 are enumerated in the following list. Entries indicate the nature of the changes effected. Page numbers refer to FEDERAL REGISTER pages. The user should consult the entries for chapters, parts and subparts as well as sections for revisions.

For changes to this volume of the CFR prior to this listing, consult the annual edition of the monthly List of CFR Sections Affected (LSA). The LSA is available at *www.fdsys.gov*. For changes to this volume of the CFR prior to 2001, see the "List of CFR Sections Affected, 1949–1963, 1964–1972, 1973–1985, and 1986–2000" published in 11 separate volumes. The "List of CFR Sections Affected 1986–2000" is available at *www.fdsys.gov*.

# 2 CFR—Continued

○